D0735951

Down to Earth Sociology

Introductory Readings
NINTH EDITION

JAMES M. HENSLIN, Editor

THE FREE PRESS
New York London Toronto Sydney Singapore

THE FREE PRESS
A Division of Simon & Schuster Inc.
1230 Avenue of the Americas
New York, NY 10020

Manufactured in the United States of America

10 9 8 7 6 5 4 3 2 1

Library of Congress Cataloging–in–Publication Data

Down to earth sociology : introductory readings / James M. Henslin,
    editor. — 9th ed.
        p.   cm.
    Includes bibliographical references and index.
    ISBN 0–684–82926–6
    1. Sociology.   2. United States—Social conditions.   I. Henslin,
James M.
HM51.D68   1996
301—dc20   96–40986
                                                              CIP

Credits
and Acknowledgments

Grateful acknowledgment is made to the authors and publishers who have granted permission to reprint these selections:

ARTICLE
NUMBER
1   Excerpts from *Invitation to Sociology* by Peter L. Berger. Copyright © 1963 by Peter L. Berger. Reprinted by permission of Doubleday Publishing, a division of Bantam Doubleday Dell Publishing Group, Inc.
2   Copyright © 1995 by James M. Henslin.
3   From *The Sociological Imagination* by C. Wright Mills. Copyright © 1959 by Oxford University Press, Inc.: renewed 1987 by Yaraslava Mills. Reprinted by permission of Oxford University Press, Inc.
4   Copyright © 1995 by James M. Henslin.
5   Copyright © 1985 by the Society for the Study of Social Problems. Reprinted from *Social Problems,* Vol. 32, No. 3, February 1985, pp. 251–263, by permission.
6   Reprinted by permission of the author and publisher from *Street Corner Society,* University of Chicago Press. Copyright © 1981, 1993. All rights reserved.
7   Reproduced by permission of the American Anthropological Association from *American Anthropologist,* 58:3, June 1956. Not for further reproduction.
8   With permission from *Natural History,* December 1972. Copyright the American Museum of Natural History 1972.
9   Excerpts from *The Yąnomamö: The Fierce People,* 2nd Edition, by

In Memory of Erving Goffman
1922–1982
Whose Example Is Our Legacy

Contents

Ou 6 - China dinner

Preface to the Ninth Edition

IT IS WITH PLEASURE that I introduce the ninth edition of *Down to Earth Sociology,* a pleasure akin to seeing a dear friend reach another cheerful milestone in his or her life. Adopters of earlier editions will find themselves at home, I believe, in this latest edition. They will see many selections they have already successfully used in the classroom, and I trust they will welcome the many newcomers.

Following the suggestions of those who have used earlier editions of *Down to Earth Sociology,* I have strived to continue to present down-to-earth articles in order to make the student's introduction to sociology enjoyable as well as meaningful. These selections reflect the experiences of people who have "been there" and who, with a minimum of jargon and quantification, insightfully share those experiences with the reader.

Focusing on social interaction in everyday activities and situations, these selections share some of the fascination of sociology. They reflect both the individualistic and the structural emphases of our discipline. Social structure is not simply an abstract fact of life; rather, it vitally affects our lives. The decisions of the rich, the politically powerful, and the bureaucrats provide social constraints that augment those dictated by birth, social class, and other circumstances. By social structure our vision of life is lifted or limited, our chances of success closed or opened. Social structure brings tears and laughter, hopes and despair.

Yet so much of sociology goes about its business as though data were unconnected to people, as though the world consisted of abstract social facts. From my own experiences, I know that these suppositions are far from the truth—divorced from real life—and so I have sought authors who are able to share the realities that people directly experience. At least as I see it, sociology is the most fascinating of the social sciences, and it is this fascination that these selections are designed to convey.

It is my hope that I have succeeded in accomplishing this goal, because I believe sociology is able to open new windows of perception that can touch every aspect of the individual's world. If these readings even come close to this goal, I owe a great debt to the many adopters of earlier editions, whose reactions and suggestions have helped give shape to this one.

I wish to acknowledge the help provided by the following sociologists: Peter Adler, Richard Ambler, Paula Barfield, Frederic J. Bednarek, Philip Berg, Ralph Bishop, Norman E. Budow, John Carchedi, Theresa Chandler, Paul L. Crook, Rene M. Descartes, Diane D. Everett, Larry A. Fask, Irene Fiala, Susan Frantz, R. Scott Frey, Bryan T. Froehle, Charles P. Gallmeier, Frank Glamser, Susan F. Greenwood, Alem Habtu, Bram A. Hamovitch, Wendel J. Hunigan, Jennifer Karas, Paul L. Leslie, Diane Levy, Tina Martinez, Tom McIntyre, Kristy McNamara, Elizabeth Mitchell, Jim Pass, Dan Peterson, Livia Pohlman, Pam Rosenberg, Nancy E. Sacks, Allen Scarboro, John K. Schorr, Ronald L. Schultz, Eldon Snyder, Thomas Soltis, Edward A. Thibault, Jeffrey S. Victor, Clovis L. White, Tony Williams, and Fred Zampa. Suggestions from these instructors, who shared with me their experiences with the eighth edition, proved invaluable in shaping this present version. It is to them, as well as to other colleagues who shared their counsel, that I owe a debt of gratitude. I also wish to thank my students for their candid comments, which also proved helpful.

One of the more interesting tasks in preparing this edition was to gather information on the contributors' backgrounds. In addition to biographical data concerning the authors' education, teaching, and publishing, this section also contains their statements telling us why they like sociology or became sociologists. Assigning that section with the articles helps to personalize the readings and increase the student's awareness of biographical factors that go into the choice to become a sociologist.

The selections continue to be organized to make them compatible with most introductory textbooks. Through subjects inherently interesting, we cover the major substantive areas of sociology. Part I is an introduction to the sociological perspective; it invites students to view the world in a new way by participating in the exciting enterprise we call sociology. Part II is designed to answer the basic question of how sociologists do research. Part III examines the cultural underpinnings of social life, those taken-for-granted assumptions and contexts that provide the contours of our everyday lives. In Part IV that essential component of our beings—sexuality and gender—is the focus. There we look at both the process by which we assume the social identity of male or female and how those identities provide the basis for interaction among adults.

Part V examines social groups and social structure, looking behind the scenes to see how people's assumptions, their location on social hierarchies, and the features of social settings establish both constraints and freedoms on human relationships and expressions of the self. The process of becoming deviant, the social context that shapes deviance, and social control are the subjects of Part VI. We examine social stratification in Part VII, beginning with the micro level of physical appearance and then looking at poverty, power, wealth, gender, occupation, education, and race as dimensions of social inequality. In part VIII, we analyze the social institutions of education, marriage and family, religion, sports, medicine, law, and the military, as well as the ever–increasingly intertwined economic and political interests. We conclude the book with a look at social change, the focus of Part IX. After catching a glimpse of "the way it used to be," we then examine resistance to social change, the animal rights movement, the rationalization of everyday life, and changes in racial-ethnic relations.

These selections bring the reader face-to-face with the dual emphases of contemporary sociological research: the focus on the individual's experiences, and the analysis of social structure. Uncovering the basic expectations that underlie routine social interactions, these articles emphasize the ways in which social institutions are interrelated. It is to their authors' credit that we lose sight of neither the people who are interacting nor the structural base that so directly influences the form and content of their interactions.

About the Contributors

Elijah Anderson (article 17) received his Ph.D. in Sociology at Northwestern University and is the Charles and William Day Professor of Social Sciences at the University of Pennsylvania. He is the author of *A Place on the Corner: Identity and Rank Among Black Streetcorner Men* and *Streetwise: Race, Class, and Change in an Urban Community,* the book from which his selection is taken.

Anderson says, "I have always been interested in how individuals relate to society and how society relates to the individual. My interest in the social conditions that people experience—especially the marginality that so many blacks feel and how they relate to the wider social system—motivated me to go into sociology to look for some of the answers. I also had good teachers who inspired me. Later I found myself wanting to contribute in a meaningful way to correcting what I saw to be misrepresentations of reality in the academic literature about people who live in ghettos."

Judy Root Aulette (article 22), who earned her Ph.D. in sociology at Michigan State University, is Associate Professor of Sociology at the University of North Carolina, Charlotte. She has published *Changing Families.*

Aulette was a social activist before she became a sociologist. As a secretary for a health insurance company, she was told to write letters to Congress to oppose nationalized health insurance—even though her own health benefits were inadequate. She and other secretaries recruited Legal Aid to fight this requirement. When an attorney was able to get the local newspaper to support their struggle, she realized how professional credentials can enhance one's ability to organize people, and she enrolled in graduate school. She now combines scholarship and social activism.

Joseph Bensman (article 43) received his Ph.D. from Columbia University. Now deceased, he wrote *Dollars and Sense: Ideology, Ethics, and the Meaning of Work in Profit and Non-Profit Organizations, Between Public and Private: Lost Boundaries of the Self,* and the book from which his selection is taken, *Small Town in Mass Society: Class, Politics, and Religion in a Rural Community* (with Arthur Vidich).

Peter L. Berger (article 1) received his Ph.D. in Sociology from the New School for Social Research. He is Professor of Sociology at Boston University and the author of numerous books, including *The Capitalist Revolution, A Far Glory: The Quest for Faith in an Age of Credulity,* and *Invitation to Sociology,* from which his selection in this book is taken.

Berger says, "I was born in Austria and came to the United States with my parents after the war. You might say that I became a sociologist by accident. I took some courses in sociology and liked them. I have always been curious about what makes people tick, and that is what sociology is all about."

Mae A. Biggs (article 20) earned her M.A. in Sociology at Southern Illinois University Edwardsville and is an associate of the Masters-Johnson Institute (Biological Research Institute) in St. Louis, Missouri.

Napoleon A. Chagnon (article 9) earned his Ph.D. in Anthropology at the University of Michigan. He is Professor of Anthropology at the University of California at Santa Barbara and the author of *Yqnomamö: The Last Days of Eden, Yqnomamö Warfare, Social Organization and Marriage Alliances,* and the book from which his selection is taken, *Yqnomamö: The Fierce People.*

William J. Chambliss (article 24) received his Ph.D in Sociology at Indiana University and is Professor of Sociology at George Washington University. His books include *On the Take: From Petty Crooks to Presidents, Law, Order and Power,* and *Exploring Criminology.* Professor Chambliss is a past President of the American Society of Criminology (1987–88) and a past President of the Society for the Study of Social Problems (1992–93).

Chambliss says, "I became a sociologist out of an interest in doing something about crime. I remained a sociologist because it became clear to me that until we have a greater understanding of the political and economic conditions that lead some societies to have excessive amounts of crime we will never be able to do anything about the problem. Sociology is a beautiful discipline that affords an opportunity to investigate just about anything connected with human behavior and still claim an identity with a discipline. This is its strength, its promise, and why I find it thoroughly engaging, enjoyable, and fulfilling."

John R. Coleman (article 18) was the President of Haverford College from 1967 to 1977 and then President of the Edna McConnell Clark Foundation in

New York City. He has decided to try his hand at business and now runs "The Inn at Long Last" in Chester, Vermont.

Kingsley Davis (article 12) received his Ph.D. in Sociology at Harvard University and is Distinguished Professor of Sociology at the University of Southern California and Senior Research Fellow at the Hoover Institution on War, Revolution and Peace at Stanford University. His books include *Human Society, The Population of India and Pakistan,* and *Contemporary Marriage.*

Davis, who often travels to remote places on the globe, likes sociology because "first, sociology deals with all aspects of society, not just economic behavior or political matters; second, in regard to social change, sociology takes a longer view than most other social science fields. I became a sociologist because I wanted to write and decided that I had better learn something to write, so I elected to learn sociology. Also, I wanted to know how the social system works. We were in the Great Depression at the time, so a social science should be able to analyze and explain that terrible catastrophe."

Marion V. Dearman (article 38) received his Ph.D. in Sociology from the University of Oregon. He is Professor of Sociology at California State University at Los Angeles. He publishes in the sociology of knowledge, belief, and religion.

Dearman says, "I became a sociologist because I wanted to find out why people think and believe the way they do. There is no belief too far out for human beings to share. Focusing on this in sociology has been fun. The most interesting thing about me is that I never finished high school. After working as a printer for twenty-five years, I went to college, got my B.A. when I was forty-one, the M.A. at forty-three, and the Ph.D. at forty-five. In most of may classes, I was older than my professors."

G. William Domhoff (article 33) earned his Ph.D. in Sociology at the University of Miami. He is Professor of Psychology and Sociology at the University of California, Santa Cruz. Among his books are *Blacks in the White Establishment: A Study of Race and Class in America, The Power Elite and the State: How Policy Is Made in America,* and the book from which his selection is taken, *The Bohemian Grove and Other Retreats: A Study in Ruling-Class Cohesiveness.*

Domhoff says, "I feel an attraction to sociology because I like anything that has to do with people and what makes them tick. I especially would like to understand how to bring about greater equality and freedom in all societies." He counts sports and his work among his hobbies.

Barbara Ehrenreich (article 35) is a freelance writer and political satirist who has published widely. Her books include *Debating P.C.: The Controversy over Political Correctness on College Campuses, The Snarling Citizen,* and *Fear of Falling: The Inner Life of the Middle Class.*

Douglas E. Foley (article 39) received his Ph.D. in Anthropology of Education at Stanford University and is Professor of Anthropology at the University of Texas. He is the author of *From Peones to Politicos: Class and Ethnicity in a South Texas Town, 1900–1987* and *Learning Capitalist Culture: Deep in the Heart of Tejas.*

Foley says that he likes to write cultural critiques of American society, with the hope of changing it, of helping to make it more egalitarian and humane.

Herbert J. Gans (article 30) received his Ph.D. in City Planning and Sociology from the University of Pennsylvania. He is Robert S. Lynd Professor of Sociology at Columbia University and has written such books as *The Urban Villagers, Middle American Individualism: The Future of Liberal Democracy,* and *People, Plans, and Policies: Essays on Poverty, Racism, and Other National Urban Problems.* Professor Gans is a past President of the American Sociological Association (1987–88).

Gans "finds sociology more interesting than hobbies." He says: "When I was in high school, I thought I would become a journalist, but then when I got to college I discovered that the articles I enjoyed writing most were sociology. From then on I was pretty sure I would become a sociologist." He adds, "The deeper reason I became a sociologist is because I am a refugee from Nazi Germany, and ever since I came to the United States as a teenager in 1940, I have been trying to understand the country which took me in." Whenever possible—and his family agrees—Gans rents an apartment for a month in a European city or medieval town and "explores it, living in it fully."

Erving Goffman (article 11) earned his Ph.D. in Sociology at the University of Chicago and at the time of his death in 1982 was Director of the Center for Urban Ethnography at the University of Pennsylvania. His many books include *Stigma, Behavior in Public Places,* and the book from which his selection is taken, *The Presentation of Self in Everyday Life.*

Harry L. Gracey (article 36) received his Ph.D. in Sociology at the New School for Social Research. He is in private practice in organizational development in Cambridge, Massachusetts, and has published *Curriculum or Craftsmanship?: The Dilemma of the Teacher in the Bureaucratic System* and *Readings in Introductory Sociology* (with Dennis H. Wrong).

Gracey says, "What led me to study sociology was a curiosity about how things work, which in my case got focused on the world of social life, rather than on the physical or biological world. Sociology, uniquely among the social sciences, I think, 'lifts the veil of ideology' on the working of society to see what is really going on—and who is doing it and how it is being done."

Edward T. Hall (article 10) was awarded his Ph.D. at Columbia University. He is Emeritus Professor of Anthropology at Northwestern University. His books include *The Silent Language, The Hidden Dimension,* and *An Anthropology of Everyday Life: An Autobiography.*

Mildred R. Hall (article 10) received her B.A. from Barnard College and (with Edward T. Hall) has written *The Fourth Dimension in Architecture, Hidden Differences: Studies in International Communication,* and *Understanding Cultural Differences.*

V. Lee Hamilton (article 42), who received her Ph.D. in Social Psychology in the Department of Social Relations at Harvard University, is Professor of Sociology at the University of Maryland. She has published *Crimes of Obedience* (with Herbert Kelman) and *Everyday Justice* (with Joseph Sanders).

Hamilton says: "My undergraduate degree was in psychology, but my graduate program was interdisciplinary. After I completed the Ph.D., I could have gone into psychology or sociology, and I chose sociology because of its structural emphasis. I like sociology because it is a perspective—the way a person thinks—and I tend to think that way." Some of Hamilton's favorite activities are hiking and travel.

James M. Henslin (articles 2, 4, 13, 20, and 23) earned his Ph.D. in Sociology at Washington University in St. Louis. He is Professor Emeritus of Sociology at Southern Illinois University Edwardsville. His books include *Marriage and Family in a Changing Society, Social Problems,* and *Sociology: A Down-to-Earth Approach.*

Henslin says, "My early childhood was marked by poverty. I was born in a rented room in a minister's parsonage. Then my parents made a leap in their economic status—we moved into our own home, a converted garage, with no running water or indoor plumbing! My parents continued their climb in status, and when I was thirteen they built one of the nicest houses in town. These experiences helped make me keenly aware of the significance of 'place' and opportunity in social life." He adds, "I like sociology because of its tremendous breadth—from social class and international stratification to the self and internal conflicts. No matter how diverse your curiosities, you can follow them and they are still part of sociology. Everything that is part of the landscape of human behavior comes under the lens of sociology."

Arlie Hochschild (article 37) received her Ph.D. in Sociology from the University of California, Berkeley, where she is now Professor of Sociology. She has published *The Managed Heart: Communication of Human Feeling, The Unexpected Community: Portrait of an Old Age Subculture,* and *The Second Shift: Inside the Two-Job Marriage,* the book from which her selection is taken.

Hochschild says, "I majored in international relations at Swarthmore College (a combination of history, economics, and political science) in the early sixties when my college had no sociology department. By chance I discovered David Riesman's *The Lonely Crowd,* his *Individualism Reconsidered,* and C. Wright Mills' *People, Politics and Power.* It was between the covers of these exciting books that I decided that there was a powerful lens through which to see the world—and I wanted to get on the other side of it."

Lawrence K. Hong (article 38) earned his Ph.D. in Sociology at the University of Notre Dame. He is Professor of Sociology at California State University at Los Angeles and has written articles on sex, religion, family, popular culture, computer applications, and Asian Americans.

Hong says, "I became a sociologist because I'm curious about the flux, the diversity, and the complexity of social phenomena. They keep me intellectually stimulated."

Robert A. Hummer (article 34), who received his Ph.D. from Florida State University, is Assistant Professor in the Department of Sociology at the University of Texas, Austin. He has published in several professional journals, including *Demography, Social Forces,* and *Sociological Quarterly.*

Hummer says he became a sociologist because "sociology provides me a better way of understanding the complex world in which I live." He enjoys traveling with his wife and daughter, fishing, and watching the Detroit Tigers.

Jennifer Hunt (article 41) received her Ph.D. in Sociology from the City University of New York and is Associate Professor of Sociology at Montclair State College. She is also a research candidate in the clinical training program at the Psychoanalytic Institute at the New York University Medical Center.

Hunt has written *Psychoanalytic Aspects of Fieldwork.* She likes sociology because "it provides an unusual opportunity to explore other cultural worlds by doing in-depth field work."

James M. Jasper (article 45) received his Ph.D. in sociology from the University of California at Berkeley. His books include *Nuclear Politics: Energy and the State in the United States, Sweden, and France, The Art of Moral Protest,* and the book from which his selection is taken, *The Animal Rights Crusade: The Growth of Moral Protest* (with Dorothy Nelkin).

Jasper lives and writes in New York City, and has taught at Berkeley, Columbia, Princeton, and New York University. He says he "became a sociologist because of its dazzling power to explain so many things that puzzled me when I was young. The same things still puzzle me, but I have better answers to most of them." His main area of interest is political action.

Sidney Katz (article 29), who earned a Bachelor in Social Sciences from Carleton University and a Master of Social Work at the University of Toronto, is a professional writer. He has published hundreds of articles and two books and has done considerable radio and TV broadcasting. He has been a columnist, a feature writer, and an editor at the *Toronto Star* and at *Maclean's Magazine.* He says, "I have retired several times, but it hasn't stuck."

Herbert Kelman (article 42), who received his Ph.D. in psychology from Yale University, is Richard Clarke Cabot Professor of Social Ethics at Harvard University. His books include *International Behavior: A Social-Psychological Analysis, A Time to Speak: On Human Values and Social Research,* and the book from which his selection is taken, *Crimes of Obedience: Toward a Social Psychology of Authority and Responsibility* (with V. Lee Hamilton).

Kelman says, "I was trained in psychology, but I was a social activist before I became a scholar. I like sociology because of the perspective it brings to issues in peace, justice, and social change. Outside of my work in civil rights, peace, and human rights, I like folk dancing. I also enjoy listening to ethnic music and music from the Middle Ages."

Sherryl Kleinman (article 40), who received her Ph.D. from the University of Minnesota, is Professor of Sociology at the University of North Carolina, Chapel Hill. Her books include *Equals before God, Emotions and Fieldwork,* and *Opposing Ambitions: Gender and Identity in an Alternative Organization.*

Kleinman, whose primary interest outside of academia is writing creative nonfiction, says she became a sociologist because "sociology enables me to understand how social inequalities are reproduced in everyday life, as well as at the cultural and institutional levels."

Jonathan Kozol (article 31) received a B.A. at Harvard University. After teaching in the public schools for several years, he became a professional author. His books include *Death at an Early Age, Rachel and Her Children,* and *Savage Inequalities,* the book from which his selection is adapted.

He says that he is interested in exposing the injustices that affect children.

Elliot Liebow (article 32) earned his Ph.D. in Sociology at the Catholic University of America. Until his retirement in 1985, he was a social anthropologist with the National Institute of Mental Health. He is the author of *Tally's Corner,* the book from which his selection is taken.

Zella Luria (article 14) received her Ph.D. in Psychology at Indiana University and is Professor of Psychology at Tufts University. She is the author of *The Psychology of Human Sexuality* (with Mitchel D. Rose) and *Human Sexuality* (with S. Friedman and Mitchel D. Rose).

Luria says, "What I appreciate about sociology is its exquisite attention to the group context for explanations of behavior."

Anne Machung (article 37), who works as an editor for a publishing firm, also does free-lance writing.

Arturo Madrid (article 47), who earned a Ph.D. in Spanish at the University of California at Los Angeles, is Murchison Distinguished Professor of the Humanities at Trinity University in San Antonio, Texas. He writes on issues affecting minorities and women in U.S. society and is the founding president of The Tomás Rivera Center, a national institute for policy studies on Latino issues.

Joseph Marolla (article 5) earned his Ph.D. in Sociology at the University of Denver. He is Associate Professor of Sociology at Virginia Commonwealth University. He has published articles in social psychology, criminology, sociology of education, symbolic interaction, and self-esteem.

Marolla says, "I suppose, as much as anything else, I became a sociologist because my draft lottery number was 315 in the winter of 1969—which meant that I would not be going to Vietnam. At the time, I had given very little thought to life beyond the war. Once handed the option, school seemed the reasonable thing to do since I had been doing it for a while. I was an English major, and I moved to sociology because I thought it would broaden my creative writing. . . . What I most like about sociology is that it provides a broad picture and helps us see through the facade of life as we live it. This was appealing to me, and still is. Our research on rape is an example. Psychologists are convinced that rape is due to psychological dysfunction. We have demonstrated that rape is dramatically embedded in the culture."

Patricia Yancey Martin (article 34), who received her Ph.D. from Florida State University, is Professor of Sociology at Florida State University. Her books include *Feminist Organizations* (with Myra M. Ferree) and *The Social Environment* (with Gerald O'Connor).

Martin, whose favorite activity outside of teaching, gardening, and the arts, is traveling to Europe, says that she majored in English literature, but didn't like it enough to pursue it after the bachelor's degree. She thought she might be interested in sociology, and tried graduate school. "After I was in sociology a few years," she says, "I came to see the power of the sociological perspective." She adds, "I love trying to observe and explain the social world around me."

Philip Meyer (article 16) earned an M.A. in Political Science at the University of North Carolina, where he is now Professor of Journalism. His books include *The New Precision Journalism* and *Ethical Journalism*.

Raymond Michalowski (article 22), who earned his Ph.D. at Ohio State University, is Professor in the Department of Criminal Justice at Northern Arizona University. He has published *Order, Law, and Crime* and *Radikale Kriminologie.*

Michalowski says, "I became a sociologist because I was interested in understanding how I escaped prosecution for my years of juvenile delinquency. I was also deeply curious about why my working-class background differed so much from the middle-class students I went to college with." He adds, "I have combined my academic interests with my life as a biker and am now studying biker culture. I also like to pick up my guitar and make music with my friends and hike in the wilderness of northern Arizona."

C. Wright Mills (article 3) received his Ph.D. in Sociology from the University of Wisconsin. His scathing criticisms of American society in such books as *White Collar, The Causes of World War III,* as well as the book from which his article is taken, *The Sociological Imagination,* made him one of the most controversial sociologists in the United States. At the time of his death in 1962, he was Professor of Sociology at Columbia University.

Horace Miner (article 7) earned his Ph.D. in Social Anthropology at the University of Chicago. He is Professor Emeritus of Anthropology at the University of Michigan. His books include *The Primitive City in Timbuctoo, St. Denis: A French Canadian Parish,* and *The City in Modern Africa.*

Miner says, "It was by accident that I became a sociologist. Having received my degree in social anthropology, it was easy to teach sociology when I received an offer. My courses were listed in both anthropology and sociology."

Dorothy Nelkin (article 45), who received her Bachelor's degree from Cornell University, is University Professor in Sociology and the School of Law. Her books include *The DNA Mystique: The Gene as a Cultural Icon* (with Susan Lindee), *Selling Science,* and the book from which her selection is taken, *The Animal Rights Crusade: The Growth of a Moral Protest* (with James Jasper).

George Ritzer (article 46), who received his Ph.D. from Cornell University, is Professor of Sociology at the University of Maryland. His books include *Consuming Society, Expressing America: A Critique of the Global Credit Card Society,* and *The McDonaldization of Society,* the book from which his selection is taken.

Ritzer says: "I became a sociologist because sociology offers me a variety of intellectual tools that allows me to better understand the wonderful complexity of social life." He especially enjoys the beach and long walks almost anywhere. Like many sociologists, his academic and personal lives blend into one another, making it difficult to know where one ends and the other begins.

David L. Rosenhan (article 28) received his Ph.D. in Psychology from Columbia University. His books include *Foundations of Abnormal Psychology* (with P. London), *Theory and Research in Abnormal Psychology,* and *Abnormal Psychology* (with Martin E. P. Seligman). He is Professor of Psychology and Law at Stanford University.

Jerry Savells (article 44) received his Ph.D. in Sociology at Louisiana State University. He is Professor of Sociology at Wright State University. He has edited *The Changing Family: Making Way for Tomorrow* and *Marriage and the Family in a Changing Society* (both with Larry Cross).

Savells, whose favorite activity outside of teaching and doing sociology is fishing, earned his bachelor's degree in chemistry and biology at Murray State University. He says, "After working for a few years, I found the chemistry laboratory too confining. I decided that I wanted to move into an area where I could have more impact on people, and I returned to graduate school and studied sociology. I also served as an officer in the army, where I did some teaching, and thought that I would like to teach in an academic setting. I am fascinated with human behavior, with how people get together in social groups, and I have focused on families, especially on how families respond to social change."

Diana Scully (article 5) earned her Ph.D. in Sociology at the University of Illinois. She is Associate Professor of Sociology and Coordinator of Women's Studies at Virginia Commonwealth University. She has written *Understanding Sexual Violence: A Study of Convicted Rapists* and *Men Who Control Women's Health: The Miseducation of Obstetrician Gynecologists.*

Scully says, "I changed my undergraduate major to sociology on the day that Martin Luther King was assassinated. I felt then and continue to believe that because of its focus on social structure sociology has a greater potential than other disciplines for understanding complex problems, such as racism and sexism, and therefore can be used as a tool for accomplishing change that is meaningful collectively and individually."

Allen C. Smith, III (article 40) received his Ph.D. from the University of North Carolina, Chapel Hill, where he is now Assistant Professor in the Department of Family Medicine at the School of Medicine.

Smith says, "Although I was trained in organizational development and counseling and my specialty is medical education, I learned that sociology opens a different level of understanding of medical life. It brings depth and strength to my work." Outside of academia, Smith enjoys carpentry, golf, his family, and working with Habitat for Humanity.

Deborah Tannen (article 15) earned a Ph.D. in English literature at the University of California at Berkeley. After teaching English at several universities in the U.S. and Greece, she joined the Linguistics Department at Georgetown University, where she is University Professor. Her books include *Gender and Discourse, Talking from 9 to 5,* and *You Just Don't Understand: Women and Men in Conversation.*

William E. Thompson (article 19) earned his Ph.D. in Sociology at Oklahoma State University and is Professor of Sociology at Emporia State

University and Chair of the Division of Sociology, Family Sciences, and Anthropology. He has written *Juvenile Delinquency: A Sociological Approach* (with Jack E. Bynum) and *Society in Focus* (with Joseph V. Hickey).

Coming from a working class background, Thompson is the first in his immediate family to graduate from high school. He says that he is attracted to sociology because "sociology makes the entire world your laboratory."

Arthur Vidich (article 43), who received his Ph.D. from Harvard University, is Senior Lecturer and Professor Emeritus of Sociology and Anthropology at the Graduate Faculty of the New School for Social Research. His books include *American Society: The Welfare State and Beyond* (with Joseph Bensman), *American Sociology: Worldly Rejections of Religion and Their Directions* (with Stanford Lyman), and the book from which his selection is taken, *Small Town in Mass Society: Class, Politics, and Religion in a Rural Community* (with Joseph Bensman).

Rose Weitz (article 25) received her Ph.D. from Yale University. She is Professor of Sociology at Arizona State University. She has published *Life With AIDS* and *Labor Pains: Modern Midwives and Home Birth* (with Deborah A. Sullivan).

Weitz says, "I became interested in sociology when I was sitting in psychology classes and listening to professors talk about the individual basis of mental illness. One abnormal psychology professor described a patient as paranoid when indeed she was being investigated by her employer who was keeping a file on her, and I thought, 'What is wrong with this picture?' Then in my sociology class, my professor said that classifying people as mentally ill can be a form of social control, of keeping people in power. *That* made sense to me. I think that the sociological perspective—looking at social factors, rather than individual personalities or personal problems, is often a much more useful way of looking at life. I became a sociologist because this made so much sense to me."

William Foote Whyte (article 6), after earning his Ph.D. in sociology at the University of Chicago, taught at Cornell University, where he now is Professor Emeritus of Industrial and Labor Relations. He has published widely, with *Participant Observer: An Autobiography* being his latest book. He is best known for *Street Corner Society,* the book from which his selection is taken.

Whyte says, "Sociology interested me as a way to advance my understanding of groups, organizations, and interorganization relations—and to see if I could find ways to contribute to social and economic development. Sociology has given me wide opportunities to engage in social exploration at home, in Canada, Latin America, and Spain. I have traveled extensively through Mexico and Central America, as well as brief visits to England, Switzerland, Italy, Israel, Japan, and China. I have spent two sabbatical years in Venezuela and Peru." Whyte adds, "My favorite hobby up to age 29 was playing tennis. An attack of polio ruled that out, but I have continued to travel until recently. Now, at age 79, my work and my hobby are the same: writing."

Philip G. Zimbardo (article 27) earned his Ph.D. in Social Psychology at Yale University and is Professor of Social Psychology at Stanford University. His books include *Psychology and Life, Shyness,* and (with Michael R. Leippe) *The Psychology of Attitude Change.*

Zimbardo, who has taught in Italy and enjoys collecting and studying the arts and crafts of the Native Americans of the Northwest and Southwest, says that he likes sociology because of "the scope of the significant questions it raises about human behavior."

The Sociological Perspective

I WOULD LIKE TO BEGIN this first introduction on a personal note. Since my early school days, I have immensely enjoyed reading. I used to read almost anything I could lay my hands on and was especially fascinated by books that helped me understand people better—books that described people's life situations, thoughts, relationships, hopes and dreams, challenges and obstacles. Without knowing it, I was gaining an appreciation for understanding the context in which people live out their lives—for seeing how important that context is in determining what people are like.

When I went to college, I discovered that there was a name for my interests: *sociology.* What an exciting revelation: I had found an entire academic discipline centered on understanding the general context in which people live and analyzing how their lives are influenced by it! I could not help wanting to read sociology, to take more courses, to immerse myself in it. I was hooked.

The intention of this book is threefold: to share some of the excitement and fascination of sociology, to make more visible the context of social life that affects us all—and to whet the appetite for more sociology. You will find herein an invitation to look behind the scenes—a passport, as it were, to a different way of viewing life.

As Peter L. Berger says in the opening selection, the discovery of sociology can change your life. It can help you to understand better the social forces you confront, the forces that constrain and free. This understanding has a liberating potential: By examining these forces you can stand somewhat apart from at least some aspects of society, and thereby exert more creative control over your own life.

But just what *is* sociology? In my teaching I have found that, initially, introductory students sometimes find this a vexing question. To provide a better

1

grasp of what sociology is, then, in the second selection I compare sociology with the other social sciences, showing how sociology casts an intellectual net that provides an unparalleled approach to understanding social life.

In the third article, C. Wright Mills focuses on the liberating potential offered by sociology. As he points out, this capacity centers on understanding three main issues: (1) the structure of society—that is, how the essential components of society are interrelated; (2) where one's society stands in human history and what changes are occurring in it; and (3) what types of people prevail in one's society, how they are selected for prevalence, and what types are coming to prevail.

Thinking of life in these terms, says Mills, is a quality of mind worth striving for. It is this "sociological imagination," to use his term for sociological perspective, that allows us to see beyond our immediate confines, to seek out and understand the broader social and historical forces at work in our lives. One of the rewarding consequences of this perspective, he says, is that it enables us to see ourselves in a different light.

It is the goal of this first Part, then, to let you dip your feet in the sociological waters to challenge you to venture into sociology and, while venturing, to stimulate your sociological imagination.

1   Invitation to Sociology

PETER L. BERGER

Motivated by an intense desire to know what is "really happening," what goes on "behind the scenes," sociologists study almost every aspect of life in society. As Berger indicates, nothing is too sacred or too profane to be spared the sociologist's scrutiny. But when you penetrate the surface and peer behind the masks that individuals and organizations wear, you find a reality quite unlike the one that is so carefully devised and, just as carefully, put forward for public consumption.

This changed angle of vision, however, is dangerous, for once you have peered behind the scenes and viewed life in a new light, it is nearly impossible to revert to complacent assumptions. The old, familiar, and so very comfortable ways of looking at life become upset when your angle of vision changes. This potential of sociology, of course, is also part of its attraction.

THE SOCIOLOGIST (that is, the one we would really like to invite to our game) is a person intensively, endlessly, shamelessly interested in the doings of men. His* natural habitat is all the human gathering places of the world, wherever men come together. The sociologist may be interested in many other things. But his consuming interest remains in the world of men, their institutions, their history, their passions. And since he is interested in men, nothing that men do can be altogether tedious for him. He will naturally be interested in the events that engage men's ultimate beliefs, their moments of tragedy and grandeur and ecstasy. But he will also be fascinated by the commonplace, the everyday. He will know reverence, but this reverence will not prevent him from wanting to see and to understand. He may sometimes feel revulsion or contempt. But this also will not deter him from wanting to have his questions answered. The sociologist, in his quest for understanding, moves through the world of men without respect for the usual lines of demarcation. Nobility and degradation, power and obscurity, intelligence and folly—these are equally *interesting* to him, however unequal they may be in his personal values or tastes. Thus his questions may lead him to all possible levels of soci-

*In this and a couple of other selections written before stylistic changes occurred in our language, "he," "his," and "him," "himself," "man," "world of men," and so on, are generic, referring to both males and females. Although the style is outdated, the ideas are not.—Ed.

ety, the best and the least known places, the most respected and the most despised. And, if he is a good sociologist, he will find himself in all these places because his own questions have so taken possession of him that he has little choice but to seek for answers.

It would be possible to say the same things in a lower key. We could say that the sociologist, but for the grace of his academic title, is the man who must listen to gossip despite himself, who is tempted to look through keyholes, to read other people's mail, to open cabinets. Before some otherwise unoccupied psychologist sets out now to construct an aptitude test for sociologists on the basis of sublimated voyeurism, let us quickly say that we are speaking merely by way of analogy. Perhaps some little boys consumed with curiosity to watch their maiden aunts in the bathroom later become inveterate sociologists. This is quite uninteresting. What interests us is the curiosity that grips any sociologist in front of a closed door behind which there are human voices. If he is a good sociologist he will want to open that door, to understand these voices. Behind each closed door he will anticipate some new facet of human life not yet perceived and understood.

The sociologist will occupy himself with matters that others regard as too sacred or as too distasteful for dispassionate investigation. He will find rewarding the company of priests or of prostitutes, depending not on his personal preferences but on the questions he happens to be asking at the moment. He will also concern himself with matters that others may find much too boring. He will be interested in the human interaction that goes with warfare or with great intellectual discoveries, but also in the relations between people employed in a restaurant or between a group of little girls playing with their dolls. His main focus of attention is not the ultimate significance of what men do, but the action in itself, as another example of the infinite richness of human conduct.

In these journeys through the world of men the sociologist will inevitably encounter other professional Peeping Toms. Sometimes these will resent his presence, feeling that he is poaching on their preserves. In some places the sociologist will meet up with the economist, in others with the political scientist, in yet others with the psychologist or the ethnologist. Yet chances are that the questions that have brought him to these places are different from the ones that propelled his fellow-trespassers. The sociologist's questions always remain essentially the same: "What are people doing with each other here?" "What are their relationships to each other?" "How are these relationships organized in institutions?" "What are the collective ideas that move men and institutions?" In trying to answer these questions in specific instances, the sociologist will, of course, have to deal with economic or political matters, but he will do so in a way rather different from that of the economist or the political scientist. The scene that he contemplates is the same human scene that these other scientists concern themselves with. But the sociologist's angle of vision is different. When this is understood, it becomes clear that it makes little sense to try to stake out a special enclave within which the sociologist will carry on business in his own right. Like Wesley the sociologist will have to confess that his parish is the world. But unlike some latter-day Wesleyans he will gladly share this parish with others. There is, however, one traveler whose path the sociologist will cross more often than anyone else's on his journeys. This is the historian. Indeed, as soon as the sociologist turns from the present to the past, his preoccupations are very hard indeed to distinguish from those of the historian. [T]he sociological journey will be much impoverished unless it is punctuated frequently by conversation with that other particular traveler.

Any intellectual activity derives excitement from the moment it becomes a trail of discovery. . . . The excitement of sociology is [not always to penetrate] into worlds that had previously been quite unknown . . . for instance, the world of crime, or the world of some bizarre religious sect, or the world fashioned by the exclusive concerns of some group such as medical specialists or military leaders or advertising executives. [M]uch of the time the sociologist moves in sectors of experience that are familiar to him and to most people in his society. He investigates communities, institutions, and activities that one can read about every day in the newspapers. Yet there is another excitement of discovery beckoning in his investigations. It is not the excitement of finding the familiar becoming transformed in its meaning. The fascination of sociology lies in the fact that its perspective makes us see in a new light the very world in which we have lived all of our lives. This also constitutes a transformation of consciousness. Moreover, this transformation is more relevant existentially than that of many other intellectual disciplines, because it is more difficult to segregate in some special compartment of the mind. The astronomer does not live in the remote galaxies, and the nuclear physicist can, outside his laboratory, eat and laugh and marry and vote without thinking about the insides of the atom. The geologist looks at rocks only at appropriate times, and the linguist speaks English with his wife. The sociologist lives in society, on the job and off it. His own life, inevitably, is part of his subject matter. Men being what they are, sociologists too manage to segregate their professional insights from their everyday affairs. But it is a rather difficult feat to perform in good faith.

The sociologist moves in the common world of men, close to what most of them would call real. The categories he employs in his analyses are only refinements of the categories by which other men live—power, class, status, race, ethnicity. As a result, there is a deceptive simplicity and obviousness about some sociological investigations. One reads them, nods at the familiar scene, remarks that one has heard all this before and don't people have better things to do than to waste their time on truisms—until one is suddenly brought up against an insight that radically questions everything one had previously assumed about this familiar scene. This is the point at which one begins to sense the excitement of sociology.

Let us take a specific example. Imagine a sociology class in a Southern college where almost all the students are white Southerners. Imagine a lecture on the subject of the racial system of the South. The lecturer is talking here of matters that have been familiar to his students from the time of their infancy. Indeed, it may be that they are much more familiar with the minutiae of this system than he is. They are quite bored as a result. It seems to them that he is only using more pretentious words to describe what they already know. Thus he may use the term "caste," one commonly used now by American sociologists to describe the Southern racial system. But in explaining the term he shifts to traditional Hindu society, to make it clearer. He then goes on to analyze the magical beliefs inherent in caste tabus, the social dynamics of commensalism and connubium, the economic interests concealed within the system, the way in which religious beliefs relate to the tabus, the effects of the caste system upon the industrial development of the society and vice versa—all in India. But suddenly India is not very far away at all. The lecture then goes back to its Southern theme. The familiar now seems not quite so familiar any more. Questions are raised that are new, perhaps raised angrily, but raised all the same. And at least some of the students have begun to understand that there are functions involved in this business of race that they have not read about in the newspapers (at least not those in their hometowns) and that their parents have not told them—partly, at least, because neither the newspapers nor the parents knew about them.

It can be said that the first wisdom of sociology is this—things are not what they seem. This too is a deceptively simple statement. It ceases to be simple after a while. Social reality turns out to have many layers of meaning. The discovery of each new layer changes the perception of the whole.

Anthropologists use the term "culture shock" to describe the impact of a totally new culture upon a newcomer. In an extreme instance such shock will be experienced by the Western explorer who is told, halfway through dinner, that he is eating the nice old lady he had been chatting with the previous day—a shock with predictable physiological if not moral consequences. Most explorers no longer encounter cannibalism in their travels today. However, the first encounters with polygamy or with puberty rites or even with the way some nations drive their automobiles can be quite a shock to an American visitor. With the shock may go not only disapproval or disgust but a sense of excitement that things can *really* be that different from what they are at home. To some extent, at least, this is the excitement of any first travel abroad. The experience of sociological discovery could be described as "culture shock" minus geographical displacement. In other words, the sociologist travels at home—with shocking results. He is unlikely to find that he is eating a nice old lady for dinner. But the discovery, for instance, that his own church has considerable money invested in the missile industry or that a few blocks from his home there are people who engage in cultic orgies may not be drastically different in emotional impact. Yet we would not want to imply that sociological discoveries are always or even usually outrageous to moral sentiment. Not at all. What they have in common with exploration in distant lands, however, is the sudden illumination of new and unsuspected facets of human existence in society. . . .

People who like to avoid shocking discoveries, who prefer to believe that society is just what they were taught in Sunday School, who like the safety of the rules and the maxims of what Alfred Schutz has called the "world-taken-for-granted," should stay away from sociology. People who feel no temptation before closed doors, who have no curiosity about human beings, who are content to admire scenery without wondering about the people who live in those houses on the other side of that river, should probably stay away from sociology. They will find it unpleasant or, at any rate, unrewarding. People who are interested in human beings only if they can change, convert, or reform them should also be warned, for they will find sociology much less useful than they hoped. And people whose interest is mainly in their own conceptual constructions will do just as well to turn to the study of little white mice. Sociology will be satisfying, in the long run, only to those who can think of nothing more entrancing than to watch men and to understand things human.

It may now be clear that we have, albeit deliberately, understated the case in the title of this chapter. [The chapter title from which this selection is taken is "Sociology as an Individual Pastime."] To be sure, sociology is an individual pastime in the sense that it interests some men and bores others. Some like to observe human beings, others to experiment with mice. The world is big enough to hold all kinds and there is no logical priority for one interest as against another. But the word "pastime" is weak in describing what we mean. Sociology is more like a passion. The sociological perspective is more like a demon that possesses one, that drives one compellingly, again and again, to the questions that are its own. An introduction to sociology is, therefore, an invitation to a very special kind of passion.

2 Sociology and the Social Sciences

JAMES M. HENSLIN

Introductory students often wrestle with the question of what sociology is. If you continue your sociological studies, however, that vagueness of definition—"Sociology is the study of society" or "Sociology is the study of social groups"—that frequently so bothers introductory students will come to be appreciated as one of sociology's strengths and one of its essential attractions. That sociology encompasses almost all human behavior is, indeed, precisely the appeal that draws many to sociology.

To help make clearer at the outset what sociology is, however, Henslin compares and contrasts sociology with the other social sciences. After examining similarities and differences in their approaches to understanding human behavior, he looks at how social scientists from these related academic disciplines would approach the study of juvenile delinquency.

Science and the Human Desire for Explanation

HUMAN BEINGS ARE FASCINATED with the world in which they live. And they aspire to develop ways to explain their experiences. People appear to have always felt this fascination—along with the intense desire to unravel the world's mysteries—for people in ancient times also attempted to explain their worlds. Despite the severe limitations that confronted them, the ancients explored the natural or physical world, constructing explanations that satisfied them. They also developed an understanding of their social world, the world of people with all their activities and myriad ways of dealing with one another. The explanations of the ancients, however, mixed magic and superstition with their naturalistic observations.

We contemporary people are no less fascinated with the world within which we live out our lives. We also continuously investigate both the mundane and the esoteric. We cast a quizzical eye at the common rocks we find embedded in the earth, as well as at some rare variety of insect found only in an almost inaccessible region of remote Tibet. We subject our contemporary world to the constant probings of the instruments and machines we have developed to extend our senses. In our attempts to decipher our observations, we no longer are satisfied with traditional explanations of origins or of relationships. No longer do we unquestioningly accept explanations that earlier generations took for granted. Utilizing observations derived through such technical aids as electronic microscopes and the latest generation of computers and software, we derive testable conclusions concerning the nature of our world.

As the ancients could only wish to do, we have been able to expand our objective study of the world beyond the confines of this planet. In our relentless pursuit after knowledge, we no longer are limited to speculation concerning the nature of the stars and planets. In the last couple of centuries the telescope has enabled us to make detailed and repetitive observations of the planets and other heavenly bodies. From these observations we have been able to reach conclusions startlingly different from those which people traditionally drew concerning the relative place of the earth in our galaxy and the universe. In just the past few years, by means of space technology, we have been able to extend our senses, as it were, beyond anything we had before dreamed possible. We are now able to reach out by means of our spaceships, observational satellites, and space platforms to record data from distant planets and—by means of computer-enhanced graphics—to gain a changing vision of our physical world. We have also been able to dig up and return to the earth samplings of soil from the surface of the moon as well as to send spaceships to the radiation and magnetic belts of Jupiter, over a distance so great (or, we could say, with our technology still so limited) that they must travel eighteen months before they can send reports back to earth.

A generation or so ago such feats existed only in the minds of "mad" scientists, who at that time seemed irrelevant to the public but whose ideas today are producing fascinating and frequently fearful consequences for our life on earth. Some of those scientists are now giving serious thought to plans for colonizing space, opening still another area of exciting exploration, but one whose consequences probably will be only inadequately anticipated. Others are drawing plans for real space wars, with potential outcomes so terrifying we can barely imagine them. For good and evil, science directly impinges on our contemporary life in society, leaving none of us unaffected.

The Natural and the Social Sciences

In satisfying our basic curiosities about the world, we have developed two parallel sets of sciences, each identified by its distinct subject matter. The first is called the *natural sciences,* the intellectual-academic endeavors designed to comprehend, explain, and predict the events in our *natural environment.* The endeavors of the natural scientists are divided into specialized fields of research and are given names on the basis of their particular subject matter—

such as biology, geology, chemistry, and physics. These fields of knowledge are further subdivided into even more highly specialized areas, each with a further narrowing of content—biology into botany and zoology, geology into mineralogy and geomorphology, chemistry into its organic and inorganic branches, and physics into biophysics and quantum mechanics. Each of these divisions, in turn, is subdivided into further specialized areas. Each specialized area of investigation examines a particular "slice" of the natural world.

In their pursuit of a more adequate understanding of their world, people have not limited themselves to investigating nature. They also have developed a second primary area of science that focuses on the social world. These, the *social sciences,* examine human relationships. Just as the natural sciences are an attempt to understand objectively the world of nature, so the social sciences are an attempt to understand objectively the social world. Just as the world of nature contains ordered (or lawful) relationships that are not obvious but must be abstracted from nature through controlled observations, so the ordered relationships of the human or social world also are not obvious but must be abstracted by means of controlled and repeated observations.

Like the natural sciences, the social sciences also are divided into specialized fields based on their subject matter. The usual or typical divisions of the social sciences are anthropology, economics, political science, psychology, and sociology, with history sometimes included in the enumeration, depending primarily on the preference of the person drawing the list. To be inclusive, I shall count history as a social science.

Like the natural sciences, the social sciences are also divided into further specialized fields, with these branches being named on the basis of their particular focus. Anthropology is divided into cultural and physical anthropology, economics into its macro and micro specialties, history into ancient and modern, political science into theoretical and applied, psychology into clinical and experimental, while sociology has its quantitative and qualitative branches. Except for sociology, we shall not be concerned with these finer divisions.

Sociology Contrasted with the Other Social Sciences

Since our focus is sociology, we shall take a brief look at each of the social sciences and contrast each with sociology. I should point out that the differences I shall elaborate are not always so clear in actual practice, for much that social scientists do as they practice their crafts greatly blurs the distinctions I am making.

Let us begin with *history,* the social science focusing on past events. Historians attempt to unearth the facts surrounding some event that they feel is of social significance. They attempt to establish the context, or social milieu, of the event—the important persons, ideas, institutions, social movements, or preceding events that appear in some way to have influenced the outcome they desire to explain. From this context, which they reconstruct from records of the past, they abstract what they consider to be the most important elements, or *variables,* that caused the event. By means of those "causal" factors or variables, historians "explain" the past.

Political science focuses on politics or government. The political scientist studies the ways people govern themselves—the various forms of government, their structures, and their relationships to other institutions of society. The political scientist is especially interested in how people attain ruling positions in their society, how they maintain those positions once they secure them, and the consequences of the activities of rulers for those who are governed. In studying a government that has a constitutional electorate, such as ours, the political scientist is especially concerned with voting behavior.

Economics is another discipline in the social sciences that concentrates on a single social institution. Economists study the production, distribution, and allocation of the material goods and services of a society. They want to know what goods are being produced at what rate at what cost, and the variables that determine who gets what. They are also interested in the choices that underlie production—for example, why with limited resources a certain item is being produced instead of another. Some economists, but not nearly enough in my judgment, also are interested in the consequences for human life of the facts of production, distribution, and allocation of goods and services.

The traditional focus of *anthropology* has been on preliterate and peasant peoples. Although there are other emphases, the primary concern of anthropologists is to understand *culture,* the total way of life of a group of people. Culture includes (1) the artifacts people produce, such as their tools, art, and weapons; (2) the group's structure, that is, the hierarchy and other group patterns that determine people's relationships to their fellow members; (3) ideas and values, especially the belief system of a people, and their effects on the people's lives; and (4) their forms of communication, especially their language. The anthropologists' traditional focus on past societies and contemporary preliterate peoples has widened, and some anthropologists study groups in industrialized settings. Anthropologists who focus on modern societies are practically indistinguishable from sociologists.

Psychology concentrates on processes occurring within the individual, within what they call the "skin-bound organism." The psychologist is primarily concerned with what is sometimes referred to as the "mind." Although still regularly used by the public, this term is used with increasing reservation by psychologists, probably, among other reasons, because no physical entity can be located that exactly corresponds to "mind." Psychologists typically study such phenomena as perception, attitudes, and values. They are also especially interested in personality, in mental aberration (or illness), and in how individuals cope with the problems they face.

Sociology is like history in that sociologists also attempt to establish the social contexts that influence people. Sociology is also similar to political science in that sociologists, too, study how people govern one another, especially the consequences for people's lives of various forms of government. Sociology is like economics in that sociologists also are highly interested in what happens to the goods and services of a society, especially the social consequences of production and distribution. Sociology is similar to anthropology in that sociologists also study culture and are particularly interested in the social consequences of material goods, group structure, and belief systems, as well as how people communicate with one another. Sociology is like psychology in that sociologists also are very much concerned with how people adjust to the various contingencies they confront in life.

With these overall similarities, then, where are the differences? Unlike historians, sociologists are primarily concerned with events in the present. Unlike political scientists and economists, sociologists do not concentrate on only a single social institution. Unlike anthropologists, sociologists primarily focus on industrialized societies. And unlike psychologists, to determine what influences people sociologists stress variables external to the individual.

The Example of Juvenile Delinquency

Because all the social sciences study human behavior, they differ from one another not so much in the content of what each studies but, rather, in what the social scientists look for when they conduct their studies. It is basically their approaches, their orientations, or their emphases that differentiate the social sciences. Accordingly, to make clearer the differences between them, it might be helpful to look at how different social scientists might approach the same topic. We shall use juvenile delinquency as our example.

Historians interested in juvenile delinquency would examine juvenile delinquency in some particular past setting, such as New York City in the 1920s or Los Angeles in the 1950s. The historian would try to interpret the delinquency by stressing the social context (or social milieu) of the period. For example, if delinquent gangs in New York City in the 1920s were the focus, historians would especially emphasize the social disruption caused by World War I; the problems of unassimilated, recently arrived ethnic groups; competition and rivalry for social standing among those ethnic groups; intergenerational conflict; the national, state, and local political and economic situation; and so on. The historian might also document the number of gangs, as well as their ethnic makeup. He or she would then produce a history of juvenile delinquency in New York City in the 1920s.

Political scientists are less likely to be interested in juvenile delinquency. But if they were, they would want to know how the existence of juvenile gangs is related to politics. For example, are the children of people who have less access to political leaders more likely to join gangs? Or political scientists might study the power structure within one particular gang by identifying its leaders and followers. They might then compare one gang with another, perhaps even drawing analogies with the political structure of some legitimate group.

Economists also are not likely to study delinquent gangs or juvenile delinquency. But if they did, they, of course, would emphasize the economic aspects of delinquency. They might determine how material goods, such as "loot," are allocated within a gang. But they would be more inclined to focus on delinquency in general, emphasizing the relationship of gangs to economic factors in the country. Economists might wish to examine the effects of economic conditions, such as booms and busts, on the formation of gangs or on the incidence or prevalence of delinquency. They might also wish to determine the cost of juvenile delinquency to the nation in terms of property stolen and destroyed and wages paid to police and social workers.

Anthropologists are likely to be highly interested in studying juvenile delinquency and the formation of juvenile gangs. If anthropologists were to study a particular gang, they probably would examine the implements of delinquency, such as tools used in car theft or in burglary. They would focus on the social organization of the gang, perhaps looking at its power structure. They would study the belief system of the group to see how it supports the group's delinquent activities. They would also concentrate on the ways in which group members communicate with one another, especially their *argot,* or special language. Anthropologists would stress the larger cultural context in order to see what it is about a culture that leads to the formation of such groups. They would compare their findings with what anthropologists have discovered about delinquency in other cultures. In making such a *cross-cultural comparison,* they probably would note that juvenile delinquency is not a universal phenomenon but is largely a characteristic of industrialized nations. They would point out that industrialized societies extend formal education, especially for males. This postpones the age at which males are allowed to assume the role of manhood, and it is during this "in-between status," this literal "no-man's-land," that delinquency occurs. The emphasis given by anthropologists in such a study, then, would be true to their calling: That is, anthropologists would be focusing on culture.

Psychologists also exhibit high interest in juvenile delinquency. When psychologists approach the subject, however, they tend to focus on what exists *within* the delinquent. They might test the assumption (or *hypothesis*) that, compared with their followers, gang leaders have more outgoing personality traits, or greater hostility and aggressiveness. Psychologists might also compare the personality traits of adolescent males who join gangs with boys in the general population who do not become gang members. They might give a series of tests to determine whether gang members are more insecure, dominant, hostile, or aggressive than nonmembers.

Sociologists are also interested in most of the aspects emphasized by the other social scientists. Sociologists, however, ordinarily are not concerned with a particular gang from some past period, as historians might be, although they, too, try to identify the relevant social context. Sociologists focus on the power structure of gangs, as would political scientists, and they are also interested in certain aspects of property, as an economist might be. But sociologists would be more interested in the gang members' attitudes toward property, why delinquents feel it is legitimate to steal and vandalize, and how they divide up the property they steal.

Sociologists would also approach delinquency in a way quite similar to that of anthropologists and be interested in the same sorts of things. But sociologists would place strong emphasis on *social class* (which is based on occupation, income, and education). They would want to know if there is greater likelihood that a person will join a gang if his or her parents have little education, and how gang membership varies with income. If sociologists found that delinquency varies with education, age, sex, religion, income, or race, they would want to know the reasons for this. Do children of unskilled workers have a greater chance of becoming delinquent than the children of doctors and lawyers? If so, why?

The sociologists' emphases also separate them from psychologists. Sociologists are inclined to ignore the primary focus of psychologists, personality, and instead to stress the effects of social class on recruitment into delinquency. Sociologists also examine group structure and interaction. For example, both sociologists and psychologists would be interested in differences between a gang's leaders and followers. To discover these, however, sociologists are less inclined to give paper-and-pencil tests and more inclined to observe *face-to-face interaction* among gang members (what they do in each other's presence). Sociologists would want to see if leaders and followers uphold the group's values differently; who suggests their activities; and who does what when they do them—whether the activity be simply some form of recreation or a criminal act. For example, do leaders maintain their leadership by committing more acts of daring and bravery than their followers?

Compared with other social scientists, sociologists are more likely to emphasize the routine activities of the police, the courts, and changing norms. The police approach their job with preconceived ideas about who is likely to commit crimes and who is not. Their ideas are based on what they have experienced "on the streets," as well as on stereotypes nurtured within their occupation. The police typically view some people (usually lower-class males living in some particular area of the city) to be more apt to commit crimes than males from other areas of the city, males from a higher social class, or females in general. How do the police develop their ideas? How are such stereotypes supported in their occupational subculture? What effects do they have on the police and on those whom they encounter? In other words, sociologists are deeply interested in finding out how the police define people and how those definitions help to determine whom the police arrest.

Sociologists are also interested in what occurs following an arrest. Prosecutors wield much discretion. For the same act they can level a variety of charges. They can charge an individual with first degree burglary, second degree burglary, breaking and entering, or merely trespassing. Sociologists want to know how such decisions are made, as well as their effects on the lives of those charged with crimes. Sociologists also study what happens when an individual comes before a judge, especially the outcome of the trial by the type of offense and the sex, age, or race of the offender. They also focus on the effects of detention and incarceration, as well as how people adjust when they are released back into the community.

Norms, the behaviors that people expect of others, obviously change over time. What was considered proper behavior a generation ago is certainly not the same as what is considered proper today. Consequently, the law changes, and acts considered to be law violations at one time are not necessarily considered criminal at another time. Similarly, acts not now considered criminal may become law violations at a later date. For example, at one point in our history drinking alcohol in public at age sixteen was within the law in many communities, while today it would be an act of delinquency. In the same way, a person under sixteen who is on the streets after 10 P.M. unaccompanied by an adult is breaking the law in some communities. But if the law is changed or if the sixteen-year-old moves to a different community, the same act is not a violation of the law. With marijuana the case is similar. Millions of Americans break the law when they smoke grass, but for several years Alaska allowed possession of marijuana for personal use, a legal right later revoked.

Perhaps more than any of the other social scientists, the sociologist maintains a critical interest in the effects of changing legal definitions in determining what people are arrested for and charged with. In effect, sociologists are interested in what juvenile delinquency is in the first place. They take the definition of delinquency not as obvious but as problematic, something to be studied in the context of lawmaking, lawbreaking, and the workaday world of the judicial system.

By means of this example of juvenile delinquency, it is easy to see that the social sciences greatly overlap one another. Sociology, however, is an *overarching* social science, because sociologists are, for the most part, interested in the same things that other social scientists are interested in. They are, however, not as limited in their scope or focus as are the others. Except for its traditional concerns with preliterate societies, anthropology is similarly broad in its treatment of human behavior.

Types of Sociology: Structural and Interactional

As sociologists study human behavior, they focus on people's *patterned* relationships; that is, sociologists study the recurring aspects of human behavior. This leads them to focus on two principal aspects of life in society: (1) *group membership* (including the *institutions* of society, the customary arrangements by which humans attempt to solve their perennial problems, such as the need for social order or dealing with sickness and death) and (2) *face-to-face interaction,* that is, what people do when they are in one another's presence. These twin foci lead to two principal forms of sociology, the structural and the interactional.

In the first type of sociology, *structural,* the focus is placed on the *group.* Structural sociologists are interested in determining how membership in a group, such as a religion, influences people's behavior and attitudes, such as how they vote, or perhaps how education affects the stand they take on social issues. For example, are there voting differences among Roman Catholics, Lutherans, Jews, and Baptists? If so, on what issues? And within the same religion, do people's voting patterns differ according to their income and education?

Also of interest to sociologists who focus on group memberships would be how people's attitudes toward social issues (or their voting) differ according to their age, sex, occupation, race or ethnicity, or even geographical residence— both by region of the country and by urban or rural setting. As you probably have gathered, the term "group" is being used in an extended sense. People do not have to belong to an actual group to be counted; sociologists simply "group" together people who have similar characteristics, such as age, height, weight, education, or, if it is thought relevant, even those who take their vacations in the winter versus those who take them during the summer. These are known as *aggregates,* people grouped together for the purpose of social research because of characteristics they have in common.

Note that sociologists with this first orientation concentrate on how group memberships affect people's attitudes and behavior. Ordinarily they do not simply want to know the proportion of Roman Catholics who vote Democratic (or, in sociological jargon, "the correlation between religious-group membership and voting behavior") but may try to determine what difference being a Roman Catholic makes in people's dating practices, in premarital sex, in birth control, in abortion, in what they do for recreation, in how they treat their spouses, or in what their goals and dreams are and how they rear their children.

In the second type of sociology, the *interactional,* greater emphasis is placed on individuals. Some sociologists with this orientation focus on what people do when they are in the presence of one another. They directly observe their behavior, recording the interaction by taking notes or by using tape, video, or film. Other sociologists tap people's attitudes and behaviors more indirectly by interviewing them. Still others examine social records—from diaries and letters to court transcripts, even memorabilia of pop culture from *Playboy* and *Playgirl* to science fiction and comic books. They may systematically observe soap operas, children's cartoons, police dramas, and situation comedies. Sociologists who focus on interaction develop ways of classifying the *data*—what they have observed, read, recorded, or been told. From their direct and indirect observations of people, they draw conclusions about their attitudes and what significantly affects their lives.

Types of Sociology: Qualitative and Quantitative

Another important division among sociologists is based on the *methods* they use to study people. Some sociologists are statistically oriented, attempting to determine *numbers* to represent the behavioral patterns of people. They stress that proper measurement by the use of statistical techniques is necessary if one is to understand human behavior. Many refer to this emphasis as *quantitative* sociology.

A group of sociologists who strongly disagree with this position concentrate instead on the *meaning* of what is happening to people. They focus on how people construct their worlds, how they develop their ideas and attitudes, and how they communicate with one another. They attempt to determine how people's meanings (called symbols, mental constructs, ideas, and stereotypes) affect their ideas about the self and their relationships to one another. Many refer to this emphasis as *qualitative* sociology.

Conclusion

From chicken to sociology, there are many ways of dividing up anything in life. And just as those most familiar with chicken may disagree about the proper way of cutting up a chicken, so those most familiar with sociology will disagree about how to slice up sociology. From my experiences, however, the divisions I have presented here appear to reflect accurately what is taking place in sociology today. Inevitably, however, other sociologists would disagree with this classification and probably would present another way of looking at our discipline. Nonetheless, I think you will find this presentation helpful for visualizing sociology.

It is similarly the case when it comes to evaluating the divisions within sociology. These are *not* neutral matters. For example, almost all sociologists *feel strongly* about whether a qualitative or quantitative approach is the *proper* way to study humanity.

Certainly my own biases strongly favor qualitative sociology. For me, there simply is no contest. I see qualitative sociology as more accurately reflecting people's lives, as being more closely tied into the realities that people experience—how they make sense of their worlds, how they cope with their problems, and how they try to maintain some semblance of order in their lives. Because I find this approach fascinatingly worthwhile, the qualitative approach is stressed in this book. You should note, however, that many sociologists find the quantitative approach to be the most rewarding way to study social life.

Wherever and whenever people come into one another's presence, there are potential data for the sociologist. The street, the bar, the classroom, or even the bedroom—all provide material for sociologists to observe and analyze. Nothing is really taboo for them. Sociologists are probably right now raising questions about most aspects of social life. Sociologists can whet their curiosity simply by overhearing a conversation or by catching a glimpse of some unusual happening. In following that curiosity, they can simply continue to "overhear" conversations, but this time purposely, or they can conduct an elaborate study with a scientifically selected random sample backed by huge fundings from some agency. What sociologists study can be as socially significant as an urban riot or as common but personally significant as two people greeting with a handshake or parting with a kiss.

In this sense, then, the world belongs to the sociologist—for to the sociologist everything is fair game. The all-inclusiveness of sociology, indeed, is what makes sociology so intrinsically fascinating for many: Sociology offers a framework that provides a penetrating perspective on almost everything in which people are interested.

Some of you who are being introduced to sociology through this essay may find the sociological approach to understanding human life rewarding enough to take other courses in sociology and, after college, to be attracted to books of sociological interest. A few, perhaps, may even make sociology your life's vocation and thus embark on a lifelong journey that takes you to the far corners of human endeavor, as well as to the more familiar pursuits. Certainly some of us, already captivated by sociology's enchantment, have experienced an unfolding panorama of intellectual delight in the midst of an intriguing exploration of the social world. And, in this enticing process, we have the added pleasure of constantly discovering and rediscovering our changing selves.

3 The Promise

C. WRIGHT MILLS

The "sociological imagination" is seeing how the unique historical circumstances of a particular society affect people and, at the same time, seeing how people affect history. Every individual lives out his or her life in a particular society, with the historical circumstances of that society greatly influencing what that individual becomes. People thus shaped by their society contribute, in turn, to the formation of their society and to the course of its history.

It is this quality of mind (termed the "sociological imagination" by Mills and the "sociological perspective" by others) that is presented for exploration in the readings of this book. As this intersection of biography and history becomes more apparent to you, your own sociological imagination will bring you a deepened and broadened understanding of social life—and of your own place within it.

NOWADAYS, MEN* OFTEN FEEL that their private lives are a series of traps. They sense that, within their everyday worlds, they cannot overcome their troubles, and, in this feeling, they are quite correct: What ordinary men are directly aware of and what they try to do are bounded by the private orbits in which they live; their visions and their powers are limited to the close-up scenes of job, family, neighborhood; in other milieux, they move vicariously and remain spectators. And the more aware they become, however vaguely, of ambitions and of threats that transcend their immediate locales, the more trapped they seem to feel.

Underlying this sense of being trapped are seemingly impersonal changes in the very structure of continent-wide societies. The facts of contemporary history are also facts about the success and the failure of individual men and women. When a society is industrialized, a peasant becomes a worker; a feudal lord is liquidated or becomes a businessman. When classes rise or fall, a man is employed or unemployed; when the rate of investment goes up or down, a man takes new heart or goes broke. When wars happen, an insurance salesman becomes a rocket launcher; a store clerk, a radar man; a wife lives alone; a child grows up without a father. Neither the life of an individual nor the history of a society can be understood without understanding both.

Yet, men do not usually define the troubles they endure in terms of historical change and institutional contradiction. The well-being they enjoy, they

*Again, as in several articles in this book, "man" is used in its generic sense; that is, it refers to both males and females. This form of expression is outdated, but the ideas are not.

do not usually impute to the big ups and downs of the societies in which they live. Seldom aware of the intricate connection between the patterns of their own lives and the course of world history, ordinary men do not usually know what this connection means for the kinds of men they are becoming and for the kinds of history-making in which they might take part. They do not possess the quality of mind essential to grasp the interplay of man and society, of biography and history, of self and world. They cannot cope with their personal troubles in such ways as to control the structural transformations that usually lie behind them.

Surely, it is no wonder. In what period have so many men been so totally exposed at so fast a pace to such earthquakes of change? That Americans have not known such catastrophic changes as have the men and women of other societies is due to historical facts that are now quickly becoming "merely history." The history that now affects every man is world history. Within this scene and this period, in the course of a single generation, one-sixth of mankind is transformed from all that is feudal and backward into all that is modern, advanced, and fearful. Political colonies are freed; new and less visible forms of imperialism, installed. Revolutions occur; men feel the intimate grip of new kinds of authority. Totalitarian societies rise, and are smashed to bits—or succeed fabulously. After two centuries of ascendancy, capitalism is shown up as only one way to make society into an industrial apparatus. After two centuries of hope, even formal democracy is restricted to a quite small portion of mankind. Everywhere in the underdeveloped world, ancient ways of life are broken up and vague expectations become urgent demands. Everywhere in the overdeveloped world, the means of authority and of violence become total in scope and bureaucratic in form. Humanity itself now lies before us, the supernation at either pole concentrating its most coordinated and massive efforts upon the preparation of World War III.

The very shaping of history now outpaces the ability of men to orient themselves in accordance with cherished values. And which values? Even when they do not panic, men often sense that older ways of feeling and thinking have collapsed, and that newer beginnings are ambiguous to the point of moral stasis. Is it any wonder that ordinary men feel they cannot cope with the larger worlds with which they are so suddenly confronted? That they cannot understand the meaning of their epoch for their own lives? That—in defense of selfhood—they become morally insensible, trying to remain altogether private men? Is it any wonder that they come to be possessed by a sense of the trap?

It is not only information that they need—in this Age of Fact, information often dominates their attention and overwhelms their capacities to assimilate it. It is not only the skills of reason that they need—although their struggles to acquire these often exhaust their limited moral energy.

What they need, and what they feel they need, is a quality of mind that will help them to use information and to develop reason in order to achieve lucid summations of what is going on in the world and of what may be happening within themselves. It is this quality, I am going to contend, that journalists and scholars, artists and publics, scientists and editors are coming to expect of what may be called the sociological imagination.

The sociological imagination enables its possessor to understand the larger historical scene in terms of its meaning for the inner life and the external career of a variety of individuals. It enables him to take into account how individuals, in the welter of their daily experience, often become falsely conscious of their social positions. Within that welter, the framework of modern society is sought, and within that framework the psychologies of a variety of men and women are formulated. By such means, the personal uneasiness of individuals is focused upon explicit troubles, and the indifference of publics is transformed into involvement with public issues.

The first fruit of this imagination—and the first lesson of the social science that embodies it—is the idea that the individual can understand his own experience and gauge his own fate only by locating himself within his period, that he can know his own chances in life only by becoming aware of those of all individuals in his circumstances. In many ways, it is a terrible lesson; in many ways, a magnificent one. We do not know the limits of man's capacities for supreme effort or willing degradation, for agony or glee, for pleasurable brutality or the sweetness of reason. But in our time we have come to know that the limits of "human nature" are frighteningly broad. We have come to know that every individual lives, from one generation to the next, in some society; that he lives out a biography, and that he lives it out within some historical sequence. By the fact of his living he contributes, however minutely, to the shaping of this society and to the course of its history, even as he is made by society and by its historical push and shove.

The sociological imagination enables us to grasp history and biography and the relations between the two within society. That is its task and its promise. To recognize this task and this promise is the mark of the classic social analyst. It is characteristic of Herbert Spencer—turgid, polysyllabic, comprehensive; of E. A. Ross—graceful, muckraking, upright; of Auguste Comte and Emile Durkheim; of the intricate and subtle Karl Mannheim. It is the quality of all that is intellectually excellent in Karl Marx; it is the clue to Thorstein Veblen's brilliant and ironic insight, to Joseph Schumpeter's many-sided constructions of reality; it is the basis of the psychological sweep of W. E. H. Lecky no less than of the profundity and clarity of Max Weber. And it is the signal of what is best in contemporary studies of man and society.

No social study that does not come back to the problems of biography, of history, and of their intersections within a society has completed its intellectual journey. Whatever the specific problems of the classic social analysts, however limited or however broad the features of social reality they have examined, those who have been imaginatively aware of the promise of their work have consistently asked three sorts of questions:

1. What is the structure of this particular society as a whole? What are its essential components, and how are they related to one another? How does it differ from other varieties of social order? Within it, what is the meaning of any particular feature for its continuance and for its change?

2. Where does this society stand in human history? What are the mechanics by which it is changing? What is its place within, and its meaning for, the development of humanity as a whole? How does any particular feature we are examining affect, and how is it affected by, the historical period in which it moves? And this period—what are its essential features? How does it differ from other periods? What are its characteristic ways of history-making?

3. What varieties of men and women now prevail in this society and in this period? And what varieties are coming to prevail? In what ways are they selected and formed, liberated and repressed, made sensitive and blunted? What kinds of "human nature" are revealed in the conduct and character we observe in this society in this period? And what is the meaning for "human nature" of each and every feature of the society we are examining?

Whether the point of interest is a great power state or a minor literary mood, a family, a prison, a creed—these are the kinds of questions the best social analysts have asked. They are the intellectual pivots of classic studies of man in society—and they are the questions inevitably raised by any mind possessing the sociological imagination. For that imagination is the capacity to shift from one perspective to another—from the political to the psychological; from examination of a single family to comparative assessment of the national budgets of the world; from the theological school to the military establishment; from considerations of an oil industry to studies of contemporary poetry. It is the capacity to range from the most impersonal and remote transformations to the most intimate features of the human self—and to see the relations between the two. Back of its use, there is always the urge to know the social and historical meaning of the individual in the society and in the period in which he has his quality and his being.

That, in brief, is why it is by means of the sociological imagination that men now hope to grasp what is going on in the world, and to understand what is happening in themselves as minute points of the intersections of biography and history within society. In large part, contemporary man's self-conscious view of himself as at least an outsider, if not a permanent stranger, rests upon an absorbed realization of social relativity and of the transformative power of history. The sociological imagination is the most fruitful form of this self-consciousness. By its use, men whose mentalities have swept only a series of limited orbits often come to feel as if suddenly awakened in a house with which they had only supposed themselves to be familiar. Correctly or incorrectly, they often come to feel that they can now provide themselves with adequate summations, cohesive assessments, comprehensive orientations. Older decisions that once appeared sound now seem to them products of a mind unaccountably dense. Their capacity for astonishment is made lively again. They acquire a new way of thinking; they experience a transvaluation of values. In a word, by their reflection and by their sensibility, they realize the cultural meaning of the social sciences.

Perhaps the most fruitful distinction with which the sociological imagination works is between the "personal troubles of milieu" and the "public issues of social structure." This distinction is an essential tool of the sociological imagination and a feature of all classic work in social science.

Troubles occur within the character of the individual and within the range of his immediate relations with others; they have to do with his self and with those limited areas of social life of which he is directly and personally aware. Accordingly, the statement and the resolution of troubles properly lie within the individual as a biographical entity and within the scope of his immediate milieu—the social setting that is directly open to his personal experience and, to some extent, his willful activity. A trouble is a private matter: Values cherished by an individual are felt by him to be threatened.

Issues have to do with matters that transcend these local environments of the individual and the range of his inner life. They have to do with the organization of many such milieux into the institutions of a historical society as a whole, with the ways in which various milieux overlap and interpenetrate to form the larger structure of social and historical life. An issue is a public matter: Some value cherished by publics is felt to be threatened. Often, there is a debate about what that value really is and about what it is that really threatens it. This debate is often without focus, if only because it is the very nature of an issue, unlike even widespread trouble, that it cannot very well be defined in terms of the immediate and everyday environments of ordinary men. An issue, in fact, often involves a crisis in institutional arrangements, and often, too, it involves what Marxists call "contradictions" or "antagonisms."

In these terms, consider unemployment. When, in a city of 100,000, only one man is unemployed, that is his personal trouble, and for its relief we properly look to the character of the man, his skills, and his immediate opportunities. But when, in a nation of 50 million employees, 15 million men are unemployed, that is an issue, and we may not hope to find its solution within the range of opportunities open to any one individual. The very structure of opportunities has collapsed. Both the correct statement of the problem and range of possible solutions require us to consider the economic and political institutions of the society, and not merely the personal situation and character of a scatter of individuals.

Consider war. The personal problem of war, when it occurs, may be how to survive it or how to die in it with honor; how to make money out of it; how to climb into the higher safety of the military apparatus; or how to contribute to the war's termination. In short, according to one's values, to find a set of milieux and within it to survive the war or make one's death in it meaningful. But the structural issues of war have to do with its causes; with what types of men its throws up into command; with its effects upon economic and political, family and religious institutions; with the unorganized irresponsibility of a world of nation-states.

Consider marriage. Inside a marriage, a man and a woman may experience personal troubles; but, when the divorce rate during the first four years of marriage is 250 out of every 1,000 attempts, this is an indication of a structural issue having to do with the institutions of marriage and the family and other institutions that bear upon them.

Or consider the metropolis—the horrible, beautiful, ugly, magnificent sprawl of the great city. For many upper-class people, the personal solution to the problem of the city is to have an apartment with private garage under it in the heart of the city, and forty miles out, a house by Henry Hill, garden by Garrett Eckbo, on a hundred acres of private land. In these two controlled environments—with a small staff at each end and a private helicopter connection—most people could solve many of the problems of personal milieux caused by the facts of the city. But all this, however splendid, does not solve the public issues that the structural fact of the city poses. What should be done with this wonderful monstrosity? Break it all up into scattered units, combining residence and work? Refurbish it as it stands? Or, after evacuation, dynamite it and build new cities according to new plans in new places? What should those plans be? And who is to decide and to accomplish whatever choice is made? These are structural issues; to confront them and to solve them requires us to consider political and economic issues that affect innumerable milieux.

Insofar as an economy is so arranged that slumps occur, the problem of unemployment becomes incapable of personal solution. Insofar as war is inherent in the nation-state system and in the uneven industrialization of the world, the ordinary individual in his restricted milieu will be powerless—with or without psychiatric aid—to solve the troubles this system or lack of system imposes upon him. Insofar as the family as an institution turns women into darling little slaves and men into their chief providers and unweaned dependents, the problem of a satisfactory marriage remains incapable of purely private solution. Insofar as the overdeveloped megalopolis and the overdeveloped automobile are built-in features of the overdeveloped society, the issues of urban living will not be solved by personal ingenuity and private wealth.

What we experience in various and specific milieux, I have noted, is often caused by structural changes. Accordingly, to understand the changes of many personal milieux, we are required to look beyond them. And the number and variety of such structural changes increase as the institutions within which we live become more embracing and more intricately connected with one another. To be aware of the idea of social structure and to use it with sensibility is to be capable of tracing such linkages among a great variety of milieux. To be able to do that is to possess the sociological imagination.

What are the major issues for publics and the key troubles of private individuals in our time? To formulate issues and troubles, we must ask what values are cherished yet threatened, and what values are cherished and supported, by the characterizing trends of our period. In the case both of threat and of support, we must ask what salient contradictions of structure may be involved.

When people cherish some set of values and do not feel any threat to them, they experience *well-being*. When they cherish values but *do* feel them to be threatened, they experience a crisis—either as a personal trouble or as a public issue. And, if all their values seem involved, they feel the total threat of panic.

But suppose people are neither aware of any cherished values nor experience any threat? That is the experience of *indifference,* which, if it seems to involve all their values, becomes apathy. Suppose, finally, they are unaware of any cherished values, but still are very much aware of a threat? That is the experience of *uneasiness,* of anxiety, which, if it is total enough, becomes a deadly, unspecified malaise.

Ours is a time of uneasiness and indifference—not yet formulated in such ways as to permit the work of reason and the play of sensibility. Instead of troubles—defined in terms of values and threats—there is often the misery of vague uneasiness; instead of explicit issues, there is often merely the beat feeling that all is somehow not right. Neither the values threatened nor whatever threatens them has been stated; in short, they have not been carried to the point of decision. Much less have they been formulated as problems of social science.

In the 1930s, there was little doubt—except among certain deluded business circles—that there was an economic issue that was also a pack of personal troubles. In these arguments about the "crisis of capitalism," the formulations of Marx and the many unacknowledged reformulations of his work probably set the leading terms of the issue, and some men came to understand their personal troubles in these terms. The values threatened were plain to see and cherished by all; the structural contradictions that threatened them also seemed plain. Both were widely and deeply experienced. It was a political age.

But the values threatened in the era after World War II are often neither widely acknowledged as values nor widely felt to be threatened. Much private uneasiness goes unformulated; much public malaise and many decisions of enormous structural relevance never become public issues. For those who accept such inherited values as reason and freedom, it is the uneasiness itself that is the trouble; it is the indifference itself that is the issue. And it is the condition, of uneasiness and indifference, that is the signal feature of our period.

All this is so striking that it is often interpreted by observers as a shift in the very kinds of problems that need now to be formulated. We are frequently told that the problems of our decade, or even the crises of our period, have shifted from the external realm of economics and now have to do with the quality of individual life—in fact, with the question of whether there is soon going to be anything that can properly be called individual life. Not child labor but comic books, not poverty but mass leisure, are at the center of concern. Many great public issues as well as many private troubles are described in terms of "psychiatric"—often, it seems in a pathetic attempt to avoid the large issues and problems of modern society. Often, this statement seems to rest upon a provincial narrowing of interest to the Western societies, or even to the United States—thus ignoring two-thirds of mankind; often, too, it arbitrarily divorces the individual life from the larger institutions within which that life is enacted, and which on occasion bear upon it more grievously than do the intimate environments of childhood.

Problems of leisure, for example, cannot even be stated without considering problems of work. Family troubles over comic books cannot be formulated as problems without considering the plight of the contemporary family in its new relations with the newer institutions of the social structure. Neither leisure nor its debilitating uses can be understood as problems without recognition of the extent to which malaise and indifference now form the social and personal climate of contemporary American society. In this climate, no problems of the "private life" can be stated and solved without recognition of the crisis of ambition that is part of the very career of men at work in the incorporated economy.

It is true, as psychoanalysts continually point out, that people do often have the "increasing sense of being moved by obscure forces within themselves that they are unable to define." But it is *not* true, as Ernest Jones asserted, that "man's chief enemy and danger is his own unruly nature and the dark forces pent up within him." On the contrary: "Man's chief danger" today lies in the unruly forces of contemporary society itself, with its alienating methods of production, its enveloping techniques of political domination, its international anarchy—in a word, its pervasive transformations of the very "nature" of man and the conditions and aims of his life.

It is now the social scientist's foremost political and intellectual task—for here the two coincide—to make clear the elements of contemporary uneasiness and indifference. It is the central demand made upon him by other cultural workmen—by physical scientists and artists, by the intellectual community in general. It is because of this task and these demands, I believe, that the social sciences are becoming the common denominator of our cultural period, and the sociological imagination, our most needed quality of mind.

Doing Sociological Research

I<small>N THE INTRODUCTION TO PART</small> I, you learned that sociologists are fascinated with the unknown—how we constantly want to peer behind locked doors to better understand social life. This second Part will show you how sociologists open those doors. I wrote the first selection to give you an overview of the research methods that sociologists use. Diana Scully and Joseph Marolla then follow with an article on interviewing in a difficult situation, and William Foote Whyte then closes this Part with an analysis of field work.

As we begin to open some of the doors that people so carefully lock, you will be able to catch a glimpse of what goes on behind them. From Scully's and Marolla's research, for example, you will better understand why men rape. In and of itself, such an understanding is valuable, but the selections in this Part have an additional purpose—to introduce you to the two major activities of sociologists: (1) constructing a theoretical base and (2) conducting empirical research. Let us look at each of these activities.

These tasks are so joined to one another that neither is more important than the other—nor does one necessarily come before the other. When scientists do their craft, these twin tasks merge during their endeavors. For the sake of presentation, however, let us say that the *first* task of science is to conduct empirical research. *Empirical* means "based on objective observations." Sociologists cannot simply draw conclusions based on guesswork, hunches, custom, superstition, or common sense. They must conduct studies to gather information that accurately represents people's attitudes and behaviors, and they must report their observations openly, spelling out in detail how they conducted their studies so that others can test their conclusions.

Sociologists use a variety of research methods, several of which are represented by articles in this book. To mention a few: an experiment (article 16, on compliance to authority), interviewing (article 5, on motivations for rape), and documents or secondary sources (article 12, the classic report on abused children, Anna and Isabelle). There is even a method for which we have no standard name, perhaps post-event reflexivity will do, or more simply, recall and analysis (article 13, on childhood). Often, sociologists combine methods in their research. The study of jails reported in article 26, for example, comes from interviewing combined with participant observation, as does article 40, the analysis of how medical students learn to handle their emotions. Most of the articles, however, are based on one particular method, participant observation, which you will read about in the opening selection to this Part.

Because no specific reading summarizes the *second* task of science, constructing a theoretical base, I shall provide an overview at this point.

A theoretical base is necessary, for facts never interpret themselves. They must always be interpreted from within some conceptual framework. An explanation of how pertinent "facts" are related to one another is called a *theory*. By providing a framework in which to fit observations, each theory offers a unique interpretation of reality. Sociology has three dominant theories, each of which reveals a contrasting picture of social life.

The first theory is called *symbolic interaction* (or symbolic interactionism). It stresses what you already know quite well: that you live in a world filled with meaning. You are surrounded by *people* who mean something to you (from your parents to your friends), by *objects* that represent something special (your clothing, your pet, your car, your room), and by *events* that are filled with meaning (first kiss, first date, first job, birthdays, holidays, anniversaries). The term *symbol* refers to the meanings that something has for us, and symbolic interactionists focus on symbols—how we construct meanings, how we use symbols to communicate with one another, and how symbols are the foundation of our social world.

Symbolic interactionism has three major themes: (1) human beings have a self, (2) people construct meanings, and act on the basis of those meanings, and (3) people take into account the possible reactions of others. Let us look at each of these points.

1. *Human beings have a self.* This means that we have the capacity to think and to talk about ourselves. We are able to reflect on our own actions, about what we have done or what we will do, or even what we hope to do or regret having done. We are even able to tell others what was going on in our mind when we did something. That is, we can reflect on our own person (self), analyzing our actions and motives, just as we can reflect on the actions and motives of others. (This is called "making the self an object.") We are aware of things in our environment, and we consider their possible effects on us.

2. *People construct meanings, and act on the basis of those meanings.* As we interact with one another, we reflect on our situation and interpret (or give meaning to) what we experience. As we recall our experiences and discuss

them with others, we further refine those meanings. The significance of this human trait is that the meanings we give to our experiences (the objects, events, and so on) become the basis for how we act. For example, if someone makes physical contact with us, we want to know what it means. If we interpret it as an "accidental bump," it requires nothing but a mumbled apology—but if we interpret it as a "push," our reactions are quite different. As far as we are concerned, these are two entirely different acts. The basis for their being different, however, lies not in the act but in the symbols we apply—that is, in our interpretation (or definition) of the act.

To say that a bump, accidental though it may be, has a certain meaning is inadequate. The meaning—and the "appropriate" reaction to it—is much more complicated than this, for even an accidental bump has different meanings to people of different backgrounds. I am reminded of this by Kody Scott's fascinating book, *Monster,* in which an accidental bump may be an unwitting invitation to death.

3. *People take into account the possible reactions of others.* To anticipate how others might react to something we are thinking about doing, we *take the role of others;* that is, we think about how others might react if we do so and so, and we adjust our behavior accordingly. We take the role of individuals (specific others), as well as groups of people (the generalized other). For example, if we are tempted to steal, we might think, "What would my friend think if I took this?" (a specific other). A professional baseball player tempted to accept a bribe might think, "What would other players and the American public think of me if they found out?" (a generalized other).

In sum: Central to symbolic interaction is the principle that to understand people's behavior we must understand their symbolic worlds. Accordingly, sociologists study the meanings that people give things, for symbols hold the key to understanding both our attitudes and our behavior.

The second theory is called *functionalism.* Functionalists stress that society is an integrated system made up of various parts. When working properly, each part contributes to the stability of society; that is, each part fulfills a function that contributes to society's equilibrium. At times, however, a part may fail to work correctly (be dysfunctional)—which creates problems for other parts of the system. In short, functionalists stress how the parts of society are interrelated, and how change in one part of society affects its other parts.

To illustrate functionalism, let us consider why divorce is so prevalent in U.S. society. Functionalists first point out that the family performs functions for the entire society. Over the millennia, the family's traditional functions have been economic production, the distribution of property, the socialization of children, reproduction, recreation, sexual control of its members, and taking care of its sick, injured, and aged. During the past couple of hundred years (especially the last hundred), however, society industrialized—bringing about profound changes that have left no aspect of social life untouched.

The consequences for the family have been especially remarkable:

Industrialization has eroded its traditional functions. For example, medical personnel now take care of the sick and injured, many elderly are placed in homes for the aged, and almost all economic production has moved to factories. As its basic functions have been at least partially taken over by other units of society, the family has weakened. Simply put, the "ties that bind" have become fewer—and with fewer functions holding them together, husbands and wives have become more prone to break up.

The third dominant theory is *conflict theory*. From this perspective, society is viewed as a system in which the various parts are in conflict. Each part competes for a larger share of resources—and there are not enough to go around to satisfy each group. Each group seems to want more power, more wealth, more prestige, and so on. And those groups that already have more than their share are not about to willingly redistribute it. Instead, they hold on for dear life—and try to enlarge what they already have.

As a consequence, say conflict theorists, society is not like a smoothly running machine, as the functionalists picture it, with each part contributing to the well-being of the other parts, but more like a machine running wildly out of kilter and ready to break apart. The results of this inherent conflict show up as racism, with one racial group pitted against another; sexism, with males and females squared off in the struggle for dominance; the exploitation of the powerless by a ruling elite, and so on.

Due to space limitations, I can provide only this brief sketch of these theories. However, each has had numerous books written about it. Among the many examples of *symbolic interactionism* (the dominant orientation of *this* book), you might look at selections by Anderson, Foley, Henslin and Biggs, and Thorne and Luria. The readings by Gans and Savells provide examples of *functionalism,* while the ones by Gracey, Kozol, and Aulette and Michalowski are examples of *conflict theory.*

This Part of the book, then, builds upon the first Part. I hope that it will help you to better appreciate how sociologists do their research.

4 How Sociologists Do Research

JAMES M. HENSLIN

Guesswork does not go very far in helping us to understand the social world. Our guesses, hunches, and the ideas that pass for common sense may or may not be correct. Sociologists must gather data in such a way that what they report is objective—presenting information that represents what is really "out there." To do so, they must use methods that other researchers can repeat (*replicate*) to check their findings. They also must tie their findings into both theory and what other researchers have already reported. In this overview of *research methods*, Henslin outlines the procedures that sociologists use to gather data.

Renée had never felt fear before—at least not like this. It had begun as a vague feeling that something was out of place. Then she felt it creep up her spine, slowly tightening as it clawed its way upwards. Now it was like a fist pounding inside her skull.

Renée never went anywhere with strangers. Hadn't her parents hammered that into her head since she was a child? And now, at 19, she wasn't about to start breaking *that* rule.

And yet here she was, in a car with a stranger. He seemed nice enough. And it wasn't as though he were some strange guy on the side of the road or anything. She had met George at Patricia's party, and. . . .

Renée had first been attracted by his dark eyes. They seemed to light up his entire face when he smiled. And when he asked her to dance, Renée felt flattered. He was a little older, a little more sure of himself than most of the guys she knew. Renée liked that: It was a sign of maturity.

As the evening wore on and he continued to be attentive to her, it seemed natural to accept his offer to take her home.

But then they passed the turn to her dorm. She didn't understand his mumbled reply about "getting something." And as he turned off on the country road, that clawing at the back of her neck had begun.

As he looked at her, his eyes almost pierced the darkness. "It's time to pay, Babe," he said, as he clawed at her blouse.

Renée won't talk about that night. She doesn't want to recall anything that happened then.

IN THIS PAPER we examine how sociologists do research. As we look at how they gather data, we focus on this basic question: How can we gather reliable information on rape—which is to say on both rapists *and* their victims?

Sociology and Common Sense

Common sense will give us some information. From common sense (a kind of knowledge not based on formal investigation, but on ideas that we pick up from our groups, mixed with abstractions from our own experiences) we know that her rape was a significant event in Renée's life. And from common sense we know that rape has ongoing effects, that it can trigger fears and anxieties, and that it can make women distrust men.

It so happens that these ideas are true. But many other common-sense ideas, even though glaringly obvious to us, are *not* true, and so we need research to test the validity and accuracy of our ideas. For example, common sense also tells us that one reason men rape is the revealing clothing that some women wear. And common sense tells us that men who rape are sexually deprived. These common-sense ideas, however, are not on target. Researchers have found that men who rape don't care what a woman is wearing; most don't even care who the woman is. She is simply an object for their lust, drives for power and exploitation, and, sometimes, frustration and anger. Researchers have also found that rapists may or may not be sexually deprived—the same as with men who do not rape. For example, many rapists have wives or girl friends with whom they have an ongoing sexual relationship.

If it is neither provocative clothing nor sexual deprivation, then, what *does* cause rape? And what effects does rape have on victims? Phrasing the matter this way—instead of assuming that we know the answers—not only opens up our minds but also underscores the pressing need for sociological research, the need to search for empirical findings that will take us completely out of the realm of guesswork and well beyond common sense.

Let us see now how sociologists do their research. We shall look first at a research model, and then at the research methods used in sociology.

A Research Model

As shown in Figure 4.1, eight basic steps are involved in social research. As you look at each of these steps, be aware that this is an ideal model. In some research these steps are collapsed, in others their order may be rearranged, while in still others one or more steps may be omitted.

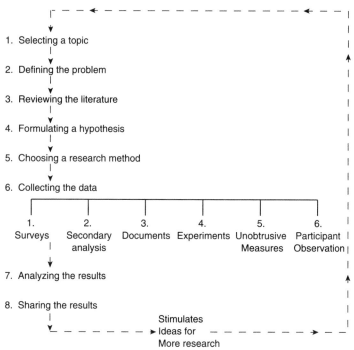

Figure 4.1 The Research Model (*Modification of Fig. 2.2 in Schaefer 1989.*)

1. SELECTING A TOPIC

The first step is to select a topic. What is it that you want to know more about? Many sociologists simply follow their curiosity, their drive to know. They become interested in a particular topic, and they pursue it. Sometimes sociologists choose a topic simply because funds are available. At other times, some social problem, such as rape, has become a pressing issue and the sociologist wants to gather data that will help people better understand—and perhaps help solve it.

2. DEFINING THE PROBLEM

The second step is to define the problem, to determine what you want to learn about the topic. To develop a researchable question, you need to focus on a specific area or problem. For example, you may want to determine the education and work experiences of rapists, or the average age of their victims.

3. REVIEWING THE LITERATURE

The third step is to review the literature. Nobody wants to rediscover the wheel. If the question has already been answered, you want to know that. In addition, a review of what has been written on the topic can stir your ideas, help sharpen your questions, and help you accomplish the next step.

4. FORMULATING A HYPOTHESIS

The fourth step is to formulate a *hypothesis,* a statement of what you expect to find according to predictions from a theory. A hypothesis predicts a relationship between or among *variables* (factors thought to be significant). For example, the statement "Men who are more socially isolated are more likely to rape than are men who are more socially integrated" is an example of a hypothesis. Hypotheses (the plural) need *operational definitions*—that is, precise ways to measure their concepts. In this example, you would need operational definitions for three concepts: social integration, social isolation, and rape.

5. CHOOSING A RESEARCH METHOD

The ways by which sociologists collect data are called *research methods.* You need to select a method that will answer the questions you have formulated. (In the next section, beginning on page 36, I go into detail concerning the six research methods used by sociologists.)

6. COLLECTING THE DATA

The next step is to gather the data. Great care needs to be taken to assure that the data are both valid and reliable. *Validity* means the extent to which the operational definitions measure what you intend to measure. In other words, do your definitions or measures of social isolation and integration *really* measure these concepts and not something else?

The concept of rape is not as simple to define (or operationalize) as it may seem. For example, there are various degrees of sexual assault. Look at Table 4.1, which depicts a variety of forced sexual activities. Deciding which of these constitute rape for the purposes of your research project is an example of the difficulties of developing operational definitions. Certainly not all of these acts are rape—and, therefore, not all of those who did them are rapists.

Reliability refers to the extent to which your measures and studies give consistent results. Inadequate operational definitions and sampling (covered later) will prevent reliability. For example, if your measure of rape is inadequate, other researchers will exclude acts that you included, and include acts that you excluded. In that case, how can you compare the results?

TABLE 4.1 Date Rape and Other Unwanted Sexual Activities Experienced by College Undergraduates

UNWANTED SEXUAL ACTIVITY	WOMEN WHO REPORTED THIS HAD HAPPENED TO THEM (%)	MEN WHO REPORTED THEY HAD DONE THIS (%)
He kissed without tongue contact	3.7	2.2
He kissed with tongue contact	12.3	0.7
He touched/kissed her breasts through her clothes	24.7	7.3
He touched/kissed her breasts under her clothes	22.6	13.1
He touched her genitals through her clothes	28.8	15.3
He touched her genitals under her clothes	28.4	13.9
He performed oral sex on her	9.9	8.8
He forced her to touch his genitals through his clothes	2.9	0.7
He forced her to touch his genitals under his clothes	5.8	2.2
He forced her to perform oral sex on him	2.5	4.4
He forced her to have sexual intercourse	20.6	15.3

These are the results of a survey of 380 women and 368 men enrolled in introductory psychology courses at Texas A&M University. Percentages add up to more than 100 because often more than one unwanted sexual activity occurred on one date.

Source: Based on Muehlenhard and Linton 1987:190.

7. ANALYZING THE RESULTS

After the data are gathered, it is time to analyze them. Sociologists have specific techniques for doing this, each of which requires special training. They range from statistical tests (of which there are many, each with its own rules for application) to *content analysis* (examining the content of something in order to identify its themes—in this case perhaps magazine articles and television reports about rape, or even diaries kept by women who have been raped). If a hypothesis has been part of the research (and not all social research has hypotheses), it is during this step that it is tested.

8. SHARING THE RESULTS

Now it is time to wrap up the research. In this step you write a report that shares your findings with the scientific community. You relate your findings to the literature, to show how they are connected to what has previously been discovered. You carefully explain your research procedures so others can *replicate* them—i.e., can repeat the study to test its findings. In this way science slowly builds, adding finding to finding.

Now let us look in greater detail at the fifth step to examine the research methods that sociologists use.

Six Research Methods

Sociologists use six *research methods* (also called research designs). These *procedures for gathering data* are surveys, secondary analysis, documents, experiments, unobtrusive measures, and participant observation.

SURVEYS

Let us suppose that you want to know how many women are raped each year. The *survey*—having people answer a series of questions—would be an appropriate method to use.

Before using this method, however, you have to decide whom you will survey. What is your *population;* that is, what is the target group that you want to learn about? Is it all females in the world? Only U.S. or Canadian females? The females in a particular state, county, or city? Only females above a certain age? Or only those on your college campus?

Let us suppose that your research interest is modest—that you want only to know the extent of rape on your campus. Ideally, you would survey all female students. But let us also suppose that your college enrollment is large, making this impractical. To get at the answer, then, you must select a smaller group, a *sample* of individuals, from whom you can generalize to the entire campus. Choosing a sample is critical, for it will affect the results of your study. For example, you will get different results if you survey only freshmen or seniors—or only women taking introductory sociology or advanced physics classes.

What kind of sample will allow you to *generalize* to the entire campus? The best is a *random* sample. This does *not* mean that you stand on some campus corner and ask questions of whomever happens to walk by. *In a random sample everyone in the population has the same chance of being included in the study.* In this case, since the population is all women taking classes at your college, all such women must have the same chance of being included in your study—whether they are freshmen, sophomores, juniors, seniors, or graduate students. It also means that such factors (*variables*) as a woman's choice of major, her grade point average, or whether she is a day or evening student cannot affect her chances of being a part of your sample.

To obtain a random sample, you would need a list of all women currently enrolled in your college. To determine which students become part of the sample, you might assign a number to each name on the list and then use random numbers to determine which particular persons become part of the sample. (Random numbers are available on tables in statistics books, and can be generated by computer.)

Because a random sample represents the population (in this case women students at your college), you can generalize your findings to all the women students on your campus, whether they were part of the sample or not.

In some surveys, *questionnaires*, a list of questions, are mailed to people. Although such *self-administered questionnaires* allow a large number of people to be sampled at a lower cost, control is lost. For example, under what conditions did people (*respondents*) fill them out? Who influenced their answers?

Other surveys use *interviews:* Respondents are asked questions directly. This is usually done on a face-to-face basis, although some interviews are conducted over the telephone. The advantage of this type of survey is that the researchers bring control to the situation. They know the conditions under which the interview took place and that each question was asked in precisely the same way. Its disadvantages include not only the more limited number of questionnaires that can be completed, and the increased cost, but also *interviewer bias*, the effects that interviewers can have on respondents that lead to biased answers. For example, although respondents may be willing to write an anonymous answer, they may not want to express their opinions to another person directly. Some even try to make their answers match what they think the interviewer wants to hear.

Sociologists sometimes use *closed-ended questions*, called *structured interviews*. Each question is followed by a list of possible answers. The advantages are that these are faster to administer, and make it easier for the answers to be *coded* (categorized) so they can be fed into a computer for analysis. If you use closed-ended questions, you will have to be careful to make sure that they represent people's opinions. For example, if you were to ask "What do you think should be done to rapists?" and the only choices you provide are to castrate or kill them, you would not be taking accurate measurements of people's opinions. Similarly, if you begin a question with, "Don't you agree that" ("rapists should be locked up for life"—or whatever you want to add), you would tilt the results toward agreement with a particular position.

Questions, then, must be carefully worded so they do not slant answers— because biased findings are worthless. It takes a great deal of training to construct questions that are free of bias, and sociologists are extremely critical of both how questions are worded and how they are administered (given).

To better tap the depth and diversity of people's experiences and attitudes, you may wish to use *open-ended questions*, called *unstructured interviews*, that allow people to answer in their own words. The primary advantage of this type of interview is that it allows people to express their full range of opinions. The major disadvantage is that it is difficult to compare people's answers. For example, how would you compare these answers to the question "What do you think causes rape?"

> "They haven't been raised right."
> "I think they must have had problems with their mother."
> "We ought to kill every one!"
> "They're all sick."
> "I don't want to talk about it."

The research topic we are considering also brings up another significant item. Let us suppose that you want to interview rape victims. Would they really give honest answers? Will a woman even admit to a stranger that she has been raped, much less talk about it? Wouldn't all your efforts be futile?

If you were to simply walk up to a stranger on the street and ask if she had ever been raped, you can guess the results—and they certainly would give little basis for placing confidence in your findings. Researchers must establish *rapport* (pronounced ruh–pour), a feeling of trust, with their respondents. When it comes to sensitive topics, areas about which people may feel embarrassment, shame, hostility, or other deep emotions, rapport is all the more important.

Once rapport is gained (often through building trust by explaining the significance of the research, assuring anonymity, and first asking nonsensitive questions), victims usually will talk about rape. For example, each year researchers conduct a national crime survey in which they interview a random sample of 49,000 households—about 90,000 Americans. They find that most rape victims will talk about their experiences. The national crime surveys show that rape is twice as high as the official statistics, and that most rape is committed by someone the victim knows (Schafran 1995).

SECONDARY ANALYSIS

In *secondary analysis,* the second research method we shall consider, the researcher analyzes data already collected by others. For example, if you were to examine the basic data gathered by the interviewers who did the national crime survey just mentioned, you would be doing secondary analysis.

Ordinarily, researchers prefer to gather their own data, but lack of resources, especially time and money, may make this preference impossible to fulfill. In addition, data already gathered may contain a wealth of information not pertinent to the purposes of those who did the original study. It simply lies there, waiting to be analyzed.

While this approach can solve problems of access, it also poses its own problems. Not having directly carried out the research, how can you be sure that the data were systematically gathered and accurately recorded, and biases avoided? That may not be an easy task, especially if the original data were gathered by numerous researchers, not all of whom were equally qualified.

DOCUMENTS

The use of *documents,* written sources, is a third research method employed by sociologists. To investigate social life, sociologists examine such diverse sources as books, newspapers, diaries, bank records, police reports, immigration records, household accounts, and records kept by various organizations. (Although they are not commonly called documents, also included here are movies, television programs, videotapes, computer disks, and CD-ROMs.)

To apply this method to the study of rape, you might examine police reports. They may reveal what proportion of all arrests are for rape; how many of the men arrested go to trial; what proportion is convicted, put on probation, sent to prison; and so forth. If these are your questions, police statistics could be valuable.

But for other questions, police records would be useless. For example, if you want to know about the adjustment of rape victims, they would tell you nothing. Other documents, however, may lend themselves to this question. If your campus has a rape crisis center, for example, it might have records that would provide key information. Or you may obtain diaries kept by victims, and search them for clues to their reactions—especially how their orientations change over time. If you couldn't find such diaries, you might contact a sample of rape victims and ask them to keep diaries. Locating that sample is extremely difficult—but, again, the rape crisis center could be the key. Their personnel might ask victims to keep the diaries. (To my knowledge, however, no sociologist has yet studied rape in this way.)

I am writing, of course, about an ideal case, as though the rape crisis center is opening its arms to you. In actual fact it may not cooperate at all, refusing to ask victims to keep diaries and not even letting you near their records. Access, then, is another problem researchers constantly face. Simply put, you can't study something unless you can gain access to it.

EXPERIMENTS

A fourth research method is the *experiment.* This is the classic method of the natural sciences. Sociologists seldom use it, however, because they are more likely to be interested in broad features of society and social behavior, or in studying a social group in a natural setting, neither of which lends itself to an experiment.

The basic purpose of an experiment is to identify cause-and-effect relationships—to find out what causes what. Ordinarily, experiments are used to test a hypothesis. Experiments involve *independent variables* (those factors that cause a change in something) and *dependent variables* (those factors that are changed). Before the experiment, you must measure the dependent variable. Then, after introducing the independent variable, you again measure the dependent variable in order to see what change has occurred.

Let us assume, for example, that you want to test the hypothesis that pornography creates attitudes that favor rape. The independent variable would be pornography, the dependent variable attitudes toward rape. You can measure a group of men's attitudes toward rape and then use random numbers to divide the men into two subgroups. To one group, the *experimental group,* you introduce the independent variable (such as violent pornographic movies). The other group, the *control group,* is not exposed to the independent variable (that is, they are not shown these movies). You then measure the dependent variable in both groups. Changes in the dependent variable (in this case attitudes toward rape) are due to what only the experimental group received, the independent variable (in this case, the pornography).

Because there is always some chance that unknown third variables have not been evenly distributed among the groups, you would need to retest your results by repeating the experiment with other groups of men.

UNOBTRUSIVE MEASURES

The fifth method we shall consider is *unobtrusive measures:* observing social behavior when people do not know they are being studied. For example, social researchers have studied the level of whiskey consumption in a "dry" town by counting empty bottles in trash cans; the degree of fear induced through telling ghost stories by measuring the shrinking diameter of a circle of seated children; and the popularity of exhibits at Chicago's Museum of Science and Industry by the wear upon tiles in front of the various displays (Webb et al. 1966).

Unobtrusive measures could also be used to study rape. For example, you could observe rapists in prison when they do not know they are being watched. You might arrange for the leader of a therapy group for rapists to be called out of the room. During his absence, you could use a one-way mirror to observe the men's interactions, and video cameras to preserve what they say and do. Such an approach would probably tell you more about their real attitudes than most other techniques.

Professional ethics, however, might disallow such a study. And I know of no research that has applied this method to the study of rape.

PARTICIPANT OBSERVATION (FIELD WORK)

Let's turn to my favorite method, one that involves the researcher in the most direct way. In *participant observation* (or field work) the researcher *participates* in a research setting while *observing* what is happening in that setting.

How is it possible to study rape by participant observation? It would seem that this method would not apply. If one considers being present during rape, it certainly does not. But there are many other questions about rape that can be answered by participant observation, answers that cannot be gained as adequately by any other method.

Let us suppose that your interest is the adjustment of rape victims. You would like to learn how the rape has affected their behavior and their orientations to the world. For example, how has their victimization affected their hopes and goals, their dating patterns, their ideas about men and intimacy? Participant observation can provide detailed answers to such questions.

Let's go back to your campus again. Assume that, like mine, your campus has a rape crisis intervention center. This setting lends itself to participant observation, for here you can observe rape victims from the time they first report the attack to their later participation in individual and group counseling. With good rapport, you can even spend time with victims outside this setting, observing how it affects other aspects of their lives.

Participant observation has the added benefit of allowing you to study whatever happens to occur while you are in the setting. In this instance, you would also be able to study the operation of the rape crisis center. As you observe counselors at work, you could also study *their* attitudes and behaviors.

As you may have noticed, in participant observation personal characteristics of the researcher become highly important. Could a male researcher, for example, conduct such research? Technically, the answer is yes. Properly introduced and with the right attitudes, male sociologists could do this research. But granted the topic, and especially the emotional states of females who have been brutally victimized by males, it may be more appropriate for female sociologists to conduct this research. Their chances of success are likely to be higher.

In conducting research, then, sociologists must be aware of such variables as the sex, age, race, personality, and even height and weight of the researcher (Henslin 1990). While important in all research methods (for example, male respondents to a survey may be more talkative to young, shapely female researchers than to obese males), these variables are especially important in participant observation (Snyder 1982).

Participant observers face a problem with generalizability. Although they look for principles of human behavior, it is difficult to know the extent to which their findings apply beyond the setting in which they occur. Consequently, most participant observation is exploratory in nature: The findings document in detail what people in a particular setting are experiencing and how they are reacting to those experiences, suggesting that other people who face similar situations will react in similar ways.

I find participant observation the most exciting of the methods. It is the type of sociology that I like to do and the type I like to read about. From these studies, I gain a depth of understanding of settings that I want to know more about but for whatever reason am not able to study, and in some cases am not even able to enter. If I were a woman, for example, I might have volunteered for work in my campus's rape crisis center—a technique often used by sociologists to solve the problem of access.

Conclusion: A Note on Choosing Research Methods

As you have seen, a critical factor in choosing a research method is the questions you wish to answer. Each method lends itself much better to answering particular interests or questions than do other methods. You also have seen that access to subjects is critical in deciding which research method to use. Two other factors are significant in this choice: the resources available to the researcher, and the researcher's background or training. For example, a researcher who prefers to conduct a survey may find that finances will not permit it, and instead turn to the study of documents. The researcher's background is similarly significant in this choice. Researchers who have been trained in *quantitative techniques* (an emphasis on precise measurement, numbers, statistics) are more likely to use surveys, while researchers who have been trained in *qualitative techniques* (generally, making direct observations of what people do and say) lean toward participant observation. The particular training that sociologists receive in graduate school, which sometimes depends on capricious events, orients them toward certain research methods. They feel comfortable with those, and tend to continue to use them throughout their careers.

References

Henslin, James M. (1990). "It's not a lovely place to visit, and I wouldn't want to live there." In Robert G. Burgess (ed.), *Studies in Qualitative Methodology II*: 51–76. Greenwich, CT: JAI Press.

Muehlenhard, Charlene L., and Melaney A. Linton (1987). "Date rape: Familiar strangers." *Journal of Counseling Psychology 34:* 186–96.

Schaefer, Richard T. (1989). *Sociology.* 3d ed. New York: McGraw-Hill.

Schafran, Lynn Hecht. "Rape Is Still Underreported." *New York Times,* August 29, 1995:19.

Snyder, Mark (1982). "Self-fulfilling stereotypes." *Psychology Today,* July: 60, 65, 67–68.

Webb, Eugene J., Donald T. Campbell, Richard D. Schwartz, and Lee Sechrest (1966). *Unobtrusive Measures: Nonreactive Research in the Social Sciences.* Chicago: Rand McNally.

5

"Riding the Bull at Gilley's": Convicted Rapists Describe the Rewards of Rape

DIANA SCULLY
JOSEPH MAROLLA

As we saw in the previous reading, sociologists can choose from a variety of research methods. Rape was used as the example to illustrate the various ways in which sociologists collect data. In this selection, you can see how two sociologists used the research method known as *unstructured interviewing* to gather data on rape. What prompted their research was a question that many people wonder about: "Just why do men rape?"

Scully and Marolla interviewed a sample of men who had been sent to prison for rape. In what was a difficult situation, they established enough *rapport* that the men felt free to talk about their motives. From this selection you should gain an understanding of the reasons why men commit this violent act. To determine how widespread (representative) these motives are, we need more studies, preferably with both convicted and unconvicted rapists. Perhaps you, now a student reading this book in the introductory course, will become a sociologist who will build on this study.

OVER THE PAST SEVERAL DECADES, rape has become a "medicalized" social problem. That is to say, the theories used to explain rape are predicated on psychopathological models. They have been generated from clinical experiences with small samples of rapists, often the therapists' own clients. Although these psychiatric explanations are most appropriately applied to the atypical rapist, they have been generalized to all men who rape and have come to inform the public's view on the topic.

Two assumptions are at the core of the psychopathological model; that

43

rape is the result of idiosyn... and... mental disorder which includes an
uncontrollable sexual imp... At odds, there is the... The
presumption of psychopath... methodological work of the male
Groth (1979). While Groth... personal nature of rape (power,
anger, sadism), he also con... Rape is also a symptom of some psychological dysfunction, either temporary or chronic, acute or persistent
(Groth, 1979:5). Thus, in the p... rapists... unless able to
control their behavior; they are... individuals... no longer a
society.

In contradiction to this model, e... research has consistently failed to
find a consistent pattern of personality ty... character disorder that clearly
discriminates rapists from other groups of men... (Fisher and Rivlin, 1971;
Hammer and Jacks, 1955; Rada, 1978). Indeed, other research has found that
fewer than 5 percent of men were psychotic when they rape...
1980).

Evidence indicates that rape is not a behavior confined to a few "sick"
men, but many men have the attitudes and beliefs necessary to commit a sexually aggressive act. In research conducted at a midwestern university, Koss and
her coworkers reported that 85 percent of men defined as highly sexually aggressive had victimized women with whom they were romantically involved
(Koss and Leonard, 1984). A survey quoted in *The Chronicle of Higher
Education* estimates that more than 20 percent of college women are the victims of rape and attempted rape (Meyer, 1984). These findings mirror research published several decades earlier which also concluded that sexual aggression was commonplace in dating relationships (Kanin, 1957, 1965, 1967,
1969; Kirkpatrick and Kanin, 1957). In their study of 53 college males,
Malamuth, Haber, and Feshback (1980) found that 51 percent indicated a
likelihood that they, themselves, would rape if assured of not being punished.

In addition, the frequency of rape in the United States makes it unlikely
that responsibility rests solely with a small lunatic fringe of psychopathic men.
Johnson (1980), calculating the lifetime risk of rape to girls and women aged
twelve and over, makes a similar observation. Using Law Enforcement
Assistance Association and Bureau of Census Crime Victimization Studies, he
calculated that, excluding sexual abuse in marriage and assuming equal risk to
all women, 20 to 30 percent of girls now 12 years old will suffer a violent sexual
attack during the remainder of their lives. Interestingly, the lack of empirical
support for the psychopathological model has not resulted in the de-medical-
ization of rape, nor does it appear to have diminished the belief that rapists are
"sick" aberrations in their own culture. This is significant because of the implications and consequences of the model.

A central assumption in the psychopathological model is that male sexual
aggression is unusual or strange. This assumption removes rape from the realm
of the everyday or "normal" world and places it in the category of "special" or
"sick" behavior. As a consequence, men who rape are cast in the role of out-

sider and a connection with normative male behavior is avoided. Since, in this view, the source of the behavior is thought to be within the psychology of the individual, attention is diverted away from culture or social structure as contributing factors. Thus, the psychopathological model ignores evidence which links sexual aggression to environmental variables and which suggests that rape, like all behavior, is learned.

Cultural Factors in Rape

Culture is a factor in rape, but the precise nature of the relationship between culture and sexual violence remains a topic of discussion. Ethnographic data from pre-industrial societies show the existence of rape-free cultures (Broude and Green, 1976; Sanday, 1979), although explanations for the phenomenon differ. Sanday (1979) relates sexual violence to contempt for female qualities and suggests that rape is part of a culture of violence and an expression of male dominance. In contrast, Blumberg (1979) argues that in pre-industrial societies women are more likely to lack important life options and to be physically and politically oppressed where they lack economic power relative to men. That is, in pre-industrial societies relative economic power enables women to win some immunity from men's use of force against them.

Among modern societies, the frequency of rape varies dramatically, and the United States is among the most rape-prone of all. In 1980, for example, the rate of reported rape and attempted rape for the United States was eighteen times higher than the corresponding rate for England and Wales (West, 1983). Spurred by the Women's Movement, feminists have generated an impressive body of theory regarding the cultural etiology of rape in the United States. Representative of the feminist view, Griffin (1971) called rape "The All American Crime."

The feminist perspective views rape as an act of violence and social control which functions to "keep women in their place" (Brownmiller, 1975; Kasinsky, 1975; Russell, 1975). Feminists see rape as an extension of normative male behavior, the result of conformity or overconformity to the values and prerogatives which define the traditional male sex role. That is, traditional socialization encourages males to associate power, dominance, strength, virility, and superiority with masculinity, and submissiveness, passivity, weakness, and inferiority with femininity. Furthermore, males are taught to have expectations about their level of sexual needs and expectations for corresponding female accessibility which function to justify forcing sexual access. The justification for forced sexual access is buttressed by legal, social, and religious definitions of women as male property and sex as an exchange of goods (Bart, 1979). Socialization prepares women to be "legitimate" victims and men to be potential offenders (Weis and Borges, 1973). Herman (1984) concludes that the United States is a rape culture because both genders are socialized to regard male aggression as a natural and normal part of sexual intercourse.

Feminists view pornography as an important element in a larger system of sexual violence; they see pornography as an expression of a rape-prone culture where women are seen as objects available for use by men (Morgan, 1980; Wheeler, 1985). Based on his content analysis of 428 "adults only" books, Smith (1976) makes a similar observation. He notes that, not only is rape presented as part of normal male/female sexual relations, but the woman, despite her terror, is always depicted as sexually aroused to the point of cooperation. In the end, she is ashamed but physically gratified. The message—women desire and enjoy rape—has more potential for damage than the image of the violence *per se.*

The fusion of these themes—sex as an impersonal act, the victim's uncontrollable orgasm, and the violent infliction of pain—is commonplace in the actual accounts of rapists. Scully and Marolla (1984) demonstrated that many convicted rapists denied their crime and attempted to justify their rapes by arguing that their victim enjoyed herself despite the use of a weapon and the infliction of serious injuries, or even death. In fact, many argued, they had been instrumental in making *her* fantasy come true.

The images projected in pornography contribute to a vocabulary of motive which trivializes and neutralizes rape and which might lessen the internal controls that otherwise would prevent sexually aggressive behavior. Men who rape use this culturally acquired vocabulary to justify their sexual violence.

Another consequence of the application of psychopathology to rape is that it leads one to view sexual violence as a special type of crime in which the motivations are subconscious and uncontrollable rather than overt and deliberate as with other criminal behavior. Black (1983) offers an approach to the analysis of criminal and/or violent behavior which, when applied to rape, avoids this bias. Black suggests that it is theoretically useful to ignore that crime is criminal in order to discover what such behavior has in common with other kinds of conduct. From his perspective, much of the crime in modern societies, as in pre-industrial societies, can be interpreted as a form of "self help" in which the actor is expressing a grievance through aggression and violence. From the actor's perspective, the victim is deviant and his own behavior is a form of social control in which the objective may be conflict management, punishment, or revenge. For example, in societies where women are considered the property of men, rape is sometimes used as a means of avenging the victim's husband or father (Black, 1983). In some cultures rape is used as a form of punishment. Such was the tradition among the puritanical, patriarchal Cheyenne, where men were valued for their ability as warriors. It was Cheyenne custom that a wife suspected of being unfaithful could be "put on the prairie" by her husband. Military confreres then were invited to "feast" on the prairie (Hoebel, 1954; Llewellyn and Hoebel, 1941). The ensuing mass rape was a husband's method of punishing his wife.

Black's (1983) approach is helpful in understanding rape because it forces one to examine the goals that some men have learned to achieve through sexually violent means. Thus, one approach to understanding why some men rape is to shift attention from individual psychopathology to the important question of what rapists gain from sexual aggression and violence in a culture seemingly prone to rape. In this paper, we address this question using data from interviews conducted with 114 convicted, incarcerated rapists.

Methods

SAMPLE

During 1980 and 1981 we interviewed 114 convicted rapists. All of the men had been convicted of the rape or attempted rape of an adult woman and subsequently incarcerated in a Virginia prison. Men convicted of other types of sexual offense were omitted from the sample.

In addition to their convictions for rape, 39 percent of the men also had convictions for burglary or robbery, 29 percent for abduction, 25 percent for sodomy, 11 percent for first or second degree murder, and 12 percent had been convicted of more than one rape. The majority of the men had previous criminal histories, but only 23 percent had a record of past sex offenses and only 26 percent had a history of emotional problems. Their sentences for rape and accompanying crimes ranged from ten years to seven life sentences plus 380 years for one man. Twenty-two percent of the rapists were serving at least one life sentence. Forty-six percent of the rapists were white, 54 percent black. In age, they ranged from 18 to 60 years, but the majority were between 18 and 35 years. Based on a statistical profile of felons in all Virginia prisons prepared by the Virginia Department of Corrections, it appears that this sample of rapists was disproportionately white and, at the time of the research, somewhat better educated and younger than the average inmate.

All participants in this research were volunteers. In constructing the sample, age, education, race, severity of current offense, and past criminal record were balanced within the limitations imposed by the characteristics of the volunteer pool. Obviously the sample was not random and thus may not be typical of all rapists, imprisoned or otherwise.

How Offenders View the Rewards of Rape

REVENGE AND PUNISHMENT

As noted earlier, Black's (1983) perspective suggests that a rapist might see his act as a legitimized form of revenge or punishment. Additionally, he asserts that the idea of "collective liability" accounts for much seemingly random violence. "Collective liability" suggests that all people in a particular category are held accountable for the conduct of each of their counterparts. Thus, the victim of a violent act may merely represent the category of individual being punished.

These factors—revenge, punishment, and the collective liability of women—can be used to explain a number of rapes in our research. Several cases will illustrate ways in which these factors combined in various types of rape. Revenge-rapes were among the most brutal and often included beatings, serious injuries, and even murder.

Typically, revenge-rapes included the element of collective liability. That is, from the rapist's perspective, the victim was a substitute for the woman on whom he wanted revenge. As explained elsewhere (Scully and Marolla, 1984), an upsetting event, involving a woman, preceded a significant number of rapes. When they raped, these men were angry because of a perceived indiscretion, typically related to a rigid, moralistic standard of sexual conduct, which they required from "their woman" but, in most cases, did not abide by themselves. Over and over these rapists talked about using rape "to get even" with their wives or some other significant woman. Typical is a young man who, prior to the rape, had a violent argument with his wife over what eventually proved to be her misdiagnosed case of venereal disease. She assumed the disease had been contracted through him, an accusation that infuriated him. After fighting with his wife, he explained that he drove around "thinking about hurting someone." He encountered his victim, a stranger, on the road where her car had broken down. It appears she accepted his offered ride because her car was out of commission. When she realized that rape was pending, she called him "a son of a bitch," and attempted to resist. He reported flying into a rage and beating her, and he confided,

> I have never felt that much anger before. If she had resisted, I would have killed her. . . . The rape was for revenge. I didn't have an orgasm. She was there to get my hostile feelings off on.

Although not the most common form of revenge-rape, sexual assault continues to be used in retaliation against the victim's male partner. In one such case, the offender, angry because the victim's husband owed him money, went to the victim's home to collect. He confided, "I was going to get it one way or another." Finding the victim alone, he explained, they started to argue about the money and,

> I grabbed her and started beating the hell out of her. Then I committed the act. I knew what I was doing. I was mad. I could have stopped, but I didn't. I did it to get even with her and her husband.

Griffin (1971) points out that when women are viewed as commodities, "In raping another man's woman, a man may aggrandize his own manhood and concurrently reduce that of the other man" (p. 33).

Revenge-rapes often contained an element of punishment. In some cases, while the victim was not the initial object of the revenge, the intent was to punish her because of something that transpired after the decision to rape had been made or during the course of the rape itself. This was the case with a young man whose wife had recently left him. Although they were in the process of reconciliation, he remained angry and upset over the separation. The night of the rape, he met the victim and her friend in a bar where he had gone to watch a fight on TV. The two women apparently accepted a ride from him, but after taking her friend home, he drove the victim to his apartment. At his apartment, he found a note from his wife indicating she had stopped by to watch the fight with him. This increased his anger because he preferred his wife's company. Inside his apartment, the victim allegedly remarked that she was sexually interested in his dog, which, he reported, put him in a rage. In the ensuing attack, he raped and pistol-whipped the victim. Then he forced a vacuum cleaner hose, switched on suction, into her vagina and bit her breast, severing the nipple. He stated:

> I hated at the time, but I don't know if it was her (the victim). (Who could it have been?) My wife? Even though we were getting back together. I still didn't trust her.

During his interview, it became clear that this offender, like many of the men, believed men have the right to discipline and punish women. In fact, he argued that most of the men he knew would also have beaten the victim because "that kind of thing (referring to the dog) is not acceptable among my friends."

Finally, in some rapes, both revenge and punishment were directed at victims because they represented women whom these offenders perceived as collectively responsible and liable for their problems. Rape was used "to put women in their place" and as a method of proving their "manhood" by displaying dominance over a female. For example, one multiple rapist believed his actions were related to the feeling that women thought they were better than he was.

> Rape was a feeling of total dominance. Before the rapes, I would always get a feeling of power and anger. I would degrade women so I could feel there was a person of less worth than me.

Another, especially brutal, case involved a young man from an upper middle class background, who spilled out his story in a seven-hour interview conducted in his solitary confinement cell. He described himself as tremendously angry, at the time, with his girlfriend, who he believed was involved with him in a "storybook romance," and from whom he expected complete fidelity. When she went away to college and became involved with another man, his revenge lasted eighteen months and involved the rape and murder of five women, all strangers who lived in his community. Explaining his rape-murders, he stated:

> I wanted to take my anger and frustration out on a stranger, to be in control, to do what I wanted to do. I wanted to use and abuse someone as I felt used and abused. I was killing my girl friend. During the rapes and murders, I would think

about my girl friend. I hated the victims because they probably messed men over. I hated women because they were deceitful and I was getting revenge for what happened to me.

AN ADDED BONUS

Burglary and robbery commonly accompany rape. Among our sample, 39 percent of the rapists had also been convicted of one or the other of these crimes committed in connection with rape. In some cases, the original intent was rape, and robbery was an afterthought. However, a number of men indicated that the reverse was true in their situation. That is, the decision to rape was made subsequent to their original intent, which was burglary or robbery.

This was the case with a young offender who stated that he originally intended only to rob the store in which the victim happened to be working. He explained that when he found the victim alone,

> I decided to rape her to prove I had guts. She was just there. It could have been anybody.

Similarly, another offender indicated that he initially broke into his victim's home to burglarize it. When he discovered the victim asleep, he decided to seize the opportunity "to satisfy an urge to go to bed with a white woman, to see if it was different." Indeed a number of men indicated that the decision to rape had been made after they realized they were in control of the situation. This was also true of an unemployed offender who confided that his practice was to steal whenever he needed money. On the day of the rape, he drove to a local supermarket and paced the parking lot, "staking out the situation." His pregnant victim was the first person to come along alone and "she was an easy target." Threatening her with a knife, he reported the victim as saying she would do anything if he didn't harm her. At that point, he decided to force her to drive to a deserted area, where he raped her. He explained:

> I wasn't thinking about sex. But when she said she would do anything not to get hurt, probably because she was pregnant, I thought, "why not?"

The attitude of these men toward rape was similar to their attitude toward burglary and robbery. Quite simply, if the situation is right, "why not?" From the perspective of these rapists, rape was just another part of the crime—an added bonus.

SEXUAL ACCESS

In an effort to change public attitudes that are damaging to the victims of rape and to reform laws seemingly premised on the assumption that women both ask for and enjoy rape, many writers emphasize the violent and aggressive character of rape. Often such arguments appear to discount the part that sex plays in the crime. The data clearly indicate that from the rapists' point of view, rape is in part sexually motivated. Indeed, it is the sexual aspect of rape that distinguishes it from other forms of assault.

Rape as a means of sexual access also shows the deliberate nature of this crime. When a woman is unwilling or seems unavailable for sex, the rapist can seize what isn't volunteered. In discussing his decision to rape, one man made this clear.

> . . . a real fox, beautiful shape. She was a beautiful woman and I wanted to see what she had.

The attitude that sex is a male entitlement suggests that when a woman says "no," rape is a suitable method of conquering the "offending" object. If, for example, a woman is picked up at a party or in a bar or while hitchhiking (behavior which a number of the rapists saw as a signal of sexual availability), and the woman later resists sexual advances, rape is presumed to be justified. The same justification operates in what is popularly called "date rape." The belief that sex was their just compensation compelled a number of rapists to insist they had not raped. Such was the case of an offender who raped and seriously beat his victim when, on their second date, she refused his sexual advances.

> I think I was really pissed off at her because it didn't go as planned. I could have been with someone else. She led me on but wouldn't deliver. . . . . I have a male ego that must be fed.

The purpose of such rapes was conquest, to seize what was not offered.

Despite the cultural belief that young women are the most sexually desirable, several rapes involved the deliberate choice of a victim relatively older than the assailant. Since the rapists were themselves rather young (26 to 30 years of age on the average), they were expressing a preference for sexually experienced, rather than elderly, women. Men who chose victims older than themselves often said they did so because they believed that sexually experienced women were more desirable partners. They raped because they also believed that these women would not be sexually attracted to them.

Finally, sexual access emerged as a factor in the accounts of black men who consciously chose to rape white women. The majority of rapes in the United States are intraracial. However, for the past 20 years, according to national data based on reported rapes as well as victimization studies, which include unreported rapes, the rate of black on white (B/W) rape has significantly exceeded the rate of white on black (W/B) rape (La Free, 1982). Indeed, we may be experiencing a historical anomaly, since, as Brownmiller (1975) has documented, white men have freely raped women of color in the past. The current structure of interracial rape, however, reflects contemporary racism and race relations in several ways.

First, the status of black women in the United States today is relatively lower than the status of white women. Further, prejudice, segregation, and other factors continue to militate against interracial coupling. Thus, the desire for sexual access to higher status, unavailable women, an important function in B/W rape, does not motivate white men to rape black women. Equally important, demographic and geographic barriers interact to lower the incidence of W/B rape. Segregation as well as the poverty expected in black neighborhoods undoubtedly discourages many whites from choosing such areas as a target for housebreaking or robbery. Thus, the number of rapes that would occur in conjunction with these crimes is reduced.

Reflecting in part the standards of sexual desirability set by the dominant white society, a number of black rapists indicated they had been curious about white women. Blocked by racial barriers from legitimate sexual relations with white women, they raped to gain access to them. They described raping white women as "the ultimate experience" and "high status among my friends. It gave me a feeling of status, power, macho." For another man, raping a white woman had a special appeal because it violated a "known taboo," making it more dangerous, and thus more exciting to him, than raping a black woman.

IMPERSONAL SEX AND POWER

The idea that rape is an impersonal rather than an intimate or mutual experience appealed to a number of rapists, some of whom suggested it was their preferred form of sex. The fact that rape allowed them to control rather than care encouraged some to act on this preference. For example, one man explained,

> Rape gave me the power to do what I wanted to do without feeling I had to please a partner or respond to a partner. I felt in control, dominant. Rape was the ability to have sex without caring about the woman's response. I was totally dominant.

Another rapist commented:

> Seeing them laying there helpless gave me the confidence that I could do it. . . . With rape, I felt totally in charge. I'm bashful, timid. When a woman wanted to give in normal sex, I was intimidated. In the rapes, I was totally in command, she totally submissive.

During his interview, another rapist confided that he had been fantasizing about rape for several weeks before committing his offense. His belief was that it would be "an exciting experience—a new high." Most appealing to him was the idea that he could make his victim "do it all for him" and that he would be in control. He fantasized that she "would submit totally and that I could have anything I wanted." Eventually, he decided to act because his older brother told him, "forced sex is great, I wouldn't get caught and, besides, women love it." Though now he admits to his crime, he continues to believe his victim "enjoyed it." Perhaps we should note here that the appeal of impersonal sex is not limited to convicted rapists. The amount of male sexual activity that occurs in homosexual meeting places as well as the widespread use of prostitutes suggests that avoidance of intimacy appeals to a large segment of the male population. Through rape men can experience power and avoid the emotions related to intimacy and tenderness. Further, the popularity of violent pornography suggests that a wide variety of men in this culture have learned to be aroused by sex fused with violence (Smith, 1976). Consistent with this observation, experimental research conducted by Malamuth et al. (1980) demonstrates that men are aroused by images that depict women as orgasmic under conditions of violence and pain. They found that, for female students, arousal was high when the victim experienced an orgasm and *no* pain, whereas male students were highly aroused when the victim experienced an orgasm *and* pain. On the basis of their results, Malamuth et al. suggest that forcing a woman to climax despite her pain and abhorrence of the assailant makes the rapist feel powerful; he has gained control over the only source of power historically associated with women, their bodies. In the final analysis, dominance was the objective of most rapists.

RECREATION AND ADVENTURE

Among gang rapists, most of whom were in their late teens or early twenties when convicted, rape represented recreation and adventure, another form of delinquent activity. Part of rape's appeal was the sense of male camaraderie engendered by participating collectively in a dangerous activity. To prove one's self capable of "performing" under these circumstances was a substantial challenge and also a source of reward. One gang rapist articulated this feeling very clearly.

> We felt powerful; we were in control. I wanted sex, and there was peer pressure. She wasn't like a person, no personality, just domination on my part. Just to show I could do it—you know, macho.

Our research revealed several forms of gang rape. A common pattern was hitchhike-abduction for the purpose of having sex. Though the intent was rape, a number of men did not view it as such because they were convinced that women hitchhiked primarily to signal sexual availability and only secondarily as a form of transportation. In these cases, the unsuspecting victim was driven to a deserted area, raped, and in the majority of cases physically injured. Sometimes, the victim was not hitchhiking; she was abducted at knife or gun point from the street, usually at night. Some of these men did not view this type of attack as rape either, because they believed a woman walking alone at night to be a prostitute. In addition, they were often convinced "she enjoyed it."

"Gang date" rape was another popular variation. In this pattern, one member of the gang would make a date with the victim. Then, without her knowledge or consent, she would be driven to a predetermined location and forcibly raped by each member of the group. One young man revealed this practice was so much a part of his group's recreational routine, they had rented a house for the purpose. From his perspective, the rape was justified because "usually the girl had a bad reputation, or we knew it was what she liked."

During his interview, another offender confessed to participating in twenty or thirty such "gang date" rapes because his driver's license had been revoked, making it difficult for him to "get girls." Sixty percent of the time, he claimed, "they were girls known to do this kind of thing," but "frequently, the girls didn't want to have sex with all of us." In such cases, he said, "It might start out as rape, but, then, they (the women) would quiet down and none ever reported it to the police." He was convicted for a gang rape, which he described as "the ultimate thing I ever did," because unlike his other rapes, the victim, in this case, was a stranger whom the group abducted as she walked home from the library. He felt the group's past experience with "gang date" rape had prepared them for this crime in which the victim was blindfolded and driven to the mountains where, though it was winter, she was forced to remove her clothing. Lying on the snow, she was raped by each of the four men several times before being abandoned near a farm house. This young man continued to believe that if he had spent the night with her, rather than abandoning her, she would not have reported it to the police.

Solitary rapists also used terms like "exciting," "a challenge," "an adventure" to describe their feelings about rape. Like the gang rapists, these men found the element of danger made rape all the more exciting. Typifying this attitude was one man who described his rape as intentional. He reported:

> It was exciting to get away with it (rape), just being able to beat the system, not women. It was like doing something illegal and getting away with it.

Another rapist confided that for him "rape was just more exciting and compelling" than a normal sexual encounter because it involved forcing a stranger. A multiple rapist asserted, "It was the excitement and fear and the drama that made rape a big kick."

FEELING GOOD

When the men were asked to recall their feelings immediately following the rape, only eight percent indicated that guilt or feeling bad was part of their emotional response. The majority said they felt good, relieved, or simply nothing at all. Some indicated they had been afraid of being caught or felt sorry for themselves. Only two men out of 114 expressed any concern or feeling for the victim. Feeling good or nothing at all about raping women is not an aberration limited to men in prison. Smithyman (1978), in his study of "undetected rapists"—rapists outside of prison—found that raping women had no impact on their lives, nor did it have a negative effect on their self-image.

Significantly, a number of men volunteered the information that raping had a positive impact on their feelings. For some, the satisfaction was in revenge. For example, the man who had raped and murdered five women:

> It seems like so much bitterness and tension had built up, and this released it. I felt like I had just climbed a mountain and now I could look back.

Another offender characterized rape as habit forming: "Rape is like smoking. You can't stop once you start." Finally, one man expressed the sentiments of many rapists when he stated,

> After rape, I always felt like I had just conquered something, like I had just ridden the bull at Gilley's.

Conclusions

This paper has explored rape from the perspective of a group of convicted, incarcerated rapists. The purpose was to discover how these men viewed sexual violence and what they gained from their behavior.

We found that rape was frequently a means of revenge and punishment. Implicit in revenge-rapes was the notion that women were collectively liable for the rapists' problems. In some cases, victims were substitutes for significant women on whom the men desired to take revenge. In other cases, victims were thought to represent all women, and rape was used to punish, humiliate, and "put them in their place." In both cases women were seen as a class, a category, not as individuals. For some men, rape was almost an afterthought, a bonus added to burglary or robbery. Other men gained access to sexually unavailable or unwilling women through rape. For this group of men, rape was a fantasy come true, a particularly exciting form of impersonal sex which enabled them to dominate and control women, by exercising a singularly male form of power. These rapists talked of the pleasures of raping—how for them it was a challenge, an adventure, a dangerous and "ultimate" experience. Rape made them feel good and, in some cases, even elevated their self-image.

The pleasure these men derived from raping reveals the extreme to which they objectified women. Women were seen as sexual commodities to be used or conquered rather than as human beings with rights and feelings. One young man expressed the extreme of the contemptful view of women when he confided to the female researcher.

> Rape is a man's right. If a woman doesn't want to give it, the man should take it. Women have no right to say no. Women are made to have sex. It's all they are good for. Some women would rather take a beating, but they always give in; it's what they are for.

This man murdered his victim because she wouldn't "give in."

Undoubtedly, some rapes, like some of all crimes, are idiopathic.

However, it is not necessary to resort to pathological motives to account for all rape or other acts of sexual violence. Indeed, we find that men who rape have something to teach us about the cultural roots of sexual aggression. They force us to acknowledge that rape is more than an idiosyncratic act committed by a few "sick" men. Rather, rape can be viewed as the end point in a continuum of sexually aggressive behaviors that reward men and victimize women. In the way that motives for committing any criminal act can be rationally determined, reasons for rape can also be determined. Our data demonstrate that some men rape because they have learned that in this culture, sexual violence is rewarding. Significantly, the overwhelming majority of these rapists indicated they never thought they would go to prison for what they did. Some did not fear imprisonment because they did not define their behavior as rape. Others knew that women frequently do not report rape and of those cases that are reported, conviction rates are low, and therefore they felt secure. These men perceived rape as a rewarding, low-risk act. Understanding that otherwise normal men can and do rape is critical to the development of strategies for prevention.

We are left with the fact that all men do not rape. In view of the apparent rewards and cultural supports for rape, it is important to ask why some men do not rape. Hirschi (1969) makes a similar observation about delinquency. He argues that the key question is not "Why do they do it?" but rather "Why don't we do it?" (p. 34). Likewise, we may be seeking an answer to the wrong question about sexual assault of women. Instead of asking men who rape "Why?" perhaps we should be asking men who don't "Why not?"

References

Abel, G., J. Becker, and L. Skinner (1980). "Aggressive behavior and sex." *Psychiatric Clinics of North America 3:* 133–51.

Bart, P. (1979). "Rape as a paradigm of sexism in society—victimization and its discontents." *Women's Studies International Quarterly 2:* 347–57.

Black, D. (1983). "Crime as social control." *American Sociological Review 48:* 34–45.

Blumberg, R. L. (1979). "A paradigm for predicting the position of women: Policy implications and problems." Pp. 113–42 in J. Lipman-Blumen and J. Bernard (eds.), *Sex Roles and Social Policy.* London: Sage Studies in International Sociology.

Broude, G., and S. Green (1976). "Cross-cultural codes on twenty sexual attitudes and practices." *Ethnology 15:* 409–28.

Brownmiller, S. (1975). *Against Our Will.* New York: Simon & Schuster.

Fisher, G., and E. Rivlin (1971). "Psychological needs of rapists." *British Journal of Criminology 11:* 182–85.

Griffin, S. (1971, September). "Rape: The all American crime." *Ramparts 10:* 26–35.

Groth, N. (1979). *Men Who Rape.* New York: Plenum Press.

Hammer, E., and I. Jacks (1955). "A study of Rorschach flexnor and extensor human movements." *Journal of Clinical Psychology 11:* 63–67.

Herman, D. (1984). "The rape culture." Pp. 20–39 in J. Freeman (ed.), *Women: A Feminist Perspective.* Palo Alto, CA: Mayfield.

Hirschi, T. (1969). *Causes of Delinquency.* Berkeley: University of California Press.

Hoebel, E. A. (1954). *The Law of Primitive Man.* Boston: Harvard University Press.

Johnson, A. G. (1980). "On the prevalence of rape in the United States." *Signs* 6: 136–46.

Kanin, E. (1957). "Male aggression in dating-courtship relations." *American Journal of Sociology 63:* 197–204.

___ (1965). "Male sex aggression and three psychiatric hypotheses." *Journal of Sex Research 1:* 227–29.

___ (1967). "Reference groups and sex conduct norm violation." *Sociological Quarterly* 8: 495–504.

___ (1969). "Selected dyadic aspects of male sex aggression." *Journal of Sex Research 5:* 12–28.

Kasinsky, R. (1975, September). "Rape: A normal act?" *Canadian Forum,* pp. 18–22.

Kirkpatrick, C., and E. Kanin (1957). "Male sex aggression on a university campus." *American Sociological Review 22:* 52–58.

Koss, M. P., and K. E. Leonard (1984). "Sexually aggressive men: Empirical findings and theoretical implications." Pp. 213–32 in N. M. Malamuth and E. Donnerstein (eds.), *Pornography and Sexual Aggression.* New York: Academic Press.

LaFree, G. (1980). "The effect of sexual stratification by race on official reactions to rape." *American Sociological Review 45:* 824–54.

___ (1982). "Male power and female victimization: Towards a theory of interracial rape." *American Journal of Sociology 88:* 311–28.

Llewellyn, K. N., and E. A. Hoebel (1941). *The Cheyenne Way: Conflict and Case Law in Primitive Jurisprudence.* Norman: University of Oklahoma Press.

Malamuth, N., S. Haber, and S. Feshback (1980). "Testing hypotheses regarding rape: Exposure to sexual violence, sex difference, and the 'normality' of rapists." *Journal of Research in Personality 14:* 121–37.

Malamuth, N., M. Heim, and S. Feshback (1980). "Sexual responsiveness of college students to rape depictions: Inhibitory and disinhibitory effects." *Social Psychology 38:* 399–408.

Meyer, T. J. (1984, December 5). "'Date rape': A serious problem that few talk about." *Chronicle of Higher Education.*

Morgan, R. (1980). "Theory and practice: Pornography and rape." Pp. 134–40 in L. Lederer (ed.), *Take Back the Night: Women on Pornography.* New York: William Morrow.

Rada, R. (1978). *Clinical Aspects of Rape.* New York: Grune & Stratton.

Russell, D. (1975). *The Politics of Rape.* New York: Stein & Day.

Sanday, P. R. (1979). *The Socio-Cultural Context of Rape.* Washington, D.C.:U.S. Dept. of Commerce, National Technical Information Service.

Scully, D., and J. Marolla (1984). "Convicted rapists' vocabulary of motive: Excuses and justifications." *Social Problems 31:* 530–44.

___ (1985). "Rape and psychiatric vocabulary of motive: Alternative perspectives." Pp. 294–312 in A. W. Burgess (ed.), *Rape and Sexual Assault: A Research Handbook.* New York: Garland Publishing.

Smith, D. (1976). "The social context of pornography." *Journal of Communications 26:* 16–24.

Smithyman, S. (1978). *The Undetected Rapist.* Unpublished dissertation. Claremont Graduate School.

West, D. J. (1983). "Sex offenses and offending." Pp. 1–30 in M. Tonry and N. Morris (eds.), *Crime and Justice: An Annual Review of Research.* Chicago: University of Chicago Press.

Weis, K., and S. Borges (1973). "Victimology and rape: The case of the legitimate victim." *Issues in Criminology* 8: 71–115.

Wheeler, H. (1985). "Pornography and rape: A feminist perspective." Pp. 374–91 in A. W. Burgess (ed.), *Rape and Sexual Assault: A Research Handbook.* New York: Garland Publishing.

6   Street Corner Society

WILLIAM FOOTE WHYTE

Field work is fascinating both to do and to read about, as it unites the researcher with the data in a way that no other sociological method allows. It is the closeness of the researcher to the people being studied, the first-hand observations and even participation in the subjects' lives, that allows the reader to gain a sense of "being there."

So it is with this selection from one of the most well-known books in sociology. In this classic work, Whyte lays bare some of the essentials of doing field work. Here you can see him struggling for an acceptable role in an unfamiliar setting. He lets you look over his shoulder as he tries to discover a vantage point from which he can participate, and yet remain somewhat aloof in order to be analytical. In remarkable candor, Whyte even lets you see some of the mistakes he made in this struggle. As you join him, you may sense the excitement of discovery that has hooked many of us on sociology.

First Efforts

WHEN I BEGAN MY WORK, I had had no training in sociology or anthropology. I thought of myself as an economist and naturally looked first toward the matters that we had taken up in economics courses, such as economics of slum housing. At the time I was sitting in on a course in slums and housing in the Sociology Department at Harvard. As a term project I took on a study of one block in Cornerville. To legitimize this effort, I got in touch with a private agency that concerned itself in housing matters and offered to turn over to them the results of my survey. With that backing, I began knocking on doors, looking into flats, and talking to the tenants about the living conditions. This brought me into contact with Cornerville people, but it would be hard now to devise a more inappropriate way of beginning a study such as I was eventually to make. I felt ill at ease at this intrusion, and I am sure so did the people. I wound up the block study as rapidly as I could and wrote it off as a total loss as far as gaining a real entry into the district.

Shortly thereafter I made another false start—if so tentative an effort may even be called a start. At that time I was completely baffled at the problem of finding my way into the district. Cornerville was right before me and yet so far away. I could walk freely up and down its streets, and I had even made my way into some of the flats, and yet I was still a stranger in a world completely unknown to me.

At this time I met a young economics instructor at Harvard who impressed me with his self-assurance and his knowledge of Eastern City. He had once been attached to a settlement house, and he talked glibly about his associations with the tough young men and women of the district. He also described how he would occasionally drop in on some drinking place in the area and strike up an acquaintance with a girl, buy her a drink, and then encourage her to tell him her life-story. He claimed that the women so encountered were appreciative of this opportunity and that it involved no further obligation.

This approach seemed at least as plausible as anything I had been able to think of. I resolved to try it out. I picked on the Regal Hotel, which was on the edge of Cornerville. With some trepidation I climbed the stairs to the bar and entertainment area and looked around. There I encountered a situation for which my adviser had not prepared me. There were women present all right, but none of them was alone. Some were there in couples, and there were two or three pairs of women together. I pondered this situation briefly. I had little confidence in my skill at picking up one female, and it seemed inadvisable to tackle two at the same time. Still, I was determined not to admit defeat without a struggle. I looked around me again and now noticed a threesome: one man and two women. It occurred to me that here was a maldistribution of females which I might be able to rectify. I approached the group and opened with something like this: "Pardon me. Would you mind if I joined you?" There was a moment of silence while the man stared at me. He then offered to throw me downstairs. I assured him that this would not be necessary and demonstrated as much by walking right out of there without any assistance.

I subsequently learned that hardly anyone from Cornerville ever went into the Regal Hotel. If my efforts there had been crowned with success, they would no doubt have led somewhere but certainly not to Cornerville.

For my next effort I sought out the local settlement houses. They were open to the public, . . . [and they] proved the right place for me at this time, for it was here that I met Doc. I had talked to a number of the social workers about my plans and hopes to get acquainted with the people and study the district. [T]he head of girls' work in the Norton Street House understood what I needed. She began describing Doc to me. He was, she said, a very intelligent and talented person who had at one time been fairly active in the house but had dropped out, so that he hardly ever came in any more. Perhaps he could understand what I wanted, and he must have the contacts that I needed. . . .

In a sense, my study began on the evening of February 3, 1937, when the social worker called me in to meet Doc. She showed us into her office and then left so that we could talk. . . .

As I remember it, I said that I had been interested in congested city districts in my college study but had felt very remote from them. I hoped to study the problems in such a district. I felt I could do very little as an outsider. Only if I could get to know the people and learn their problems first hand would I be able to gain the understanding I needed.

Doc heard me out without any change of expression, so that I had no way of predicting his reaction. When I was finished, he asked: "Do you want to see the high life or the low life?"

"I want to see all that I can. I want to get as complete a picture of the community as possible."

"Well, any nights you want to see anything, I'll take you around. I can take you to the joints—gambling joints—I can take you around to the street corners. Just remember that you're my friend. That's all they need to know. I know these places, and, if I tell them that you're my friend, nobody will bother you. You just tell me what you want to see, and we'll arrange it."

The proposal was so perfect that I was at a loss for a moment as to how to respond to it. We talked a while longer, as I sought to get some pointers as to how I should behave in his company. He warned me that I might have to take the risk of getting arrested in a raid on a gambling joint but added that this was not serious. I only had to give a false name and then would get bailed out by the man that ran the place, paying only a five-dollar fine. I agreed to take this chance. I asked him whether I should gamble with the others in the gambling joints. He said it was unnecessary and, for a greenhorn like myself, very inadvisable.

At last I was able to express my appreciation. "You know, the first steps of getting to know a community are the hardest. I could see things going with you that I wouldn't see for years otherwise."

"That's right. You tell me what you want to see, and we'll arrange it. When you want some information, I'll ask for it, and you listen. When you want to find out their philosophy of life, I'll start an argument and get it for you. If there's something else you want to get, I'll stage an act for you. Not a scrap, you know, but just tell me what you want, and I'll get it for you."

"That's swell. I couldn't ask for anything better. Now I'm going to try to fit in all right, but, if at any time you see I'm getting off on the wrong foot, I want you to tell me about it."

"Now we're being too dramatic. You won't have any trouble. You come in as my friend. When you come in like that, at first everybody will treat you with respect. You can take a lot of liberties, and nobody will kick. After a while when they get to know you they will treat you like anybody else—you know, they say familiarity breeds contempt. But you'll never have any trouble. There's just one thing to watch out for. Don't spring [treat] people. Don't be too free with your money."

"You mean they'll think I'm a sucker?"

"Yes, and you don't want to buy your way in."

That was our beginning. At the time I found it hard to believe that I could move in as easily as Doc had said with his sponsorship. But that indeed was the way it turned out. . . .

Beginning with Doc

I can still remember my first outing with Doc. We met one evening at the Norton Street House and set out from there to a gambling place a couple of blocks away. I followed Doc anxiously down the long, dark hallway at the back of a tenement building. I was not worried about the possibility of a police raid. I was thinking about how I would fit in and be accepted. The door opened into a small kitchen almost bare of furnishings and with the paint peeling off the walls. As soon as we went in the door, I took off my hat and began looking around for a place to hang it. There was no place. I looked around, and here I learned my first lesson in participant observation in Cornerville: Don't take off your hat in the house—at least not when you are among men. It may be permissible, but certainly not required, to take your hat off when women are around.

Doc introduced me as "my friend Bill" to Chichi, who ran the place, and to Chichi's friends and customers. I stayed there with Doc part of the time in the kitchen, where several men would sit around and talk, and part of the time in the other room watching the crap game.

There was talk about gambling, horse races, sex, and other matters. Mostly I just listened and tried to act friendly and interested. We had wine and coffee with anisette in it, with the fellows chipping in to pay for the refreshments. (Doc would not let me pay my share on this first occasion.) As Doc had predicted, no one asked me about myself, but he told me later that, when I went to the toilet, there was an excited burst of conversation in Italian and that he had to assure them that I was not a G-man. He said he told them flatly that I was a friend of his, and they agreed to let it go at that.

We went several more times together to Chichi's gambling joint, and then the time came when I dared to go in alone. When I was greeted in a natural and friendly manner, I felt that I was now beginning to find a place for myself in Cornerville.

When Doc did not go off to the gambling joint, he spent his time hanging around Norton Street, and I began hanging with him. At first, Norton Street meant only a place to wait until I could go somewhere else. Gradually, as I got to know the men better, I found myself becoming one of the Norton Street gang.

Then the Italian Community Club was formed in the Norton Street Settlement, and Doc was invited to be a member. Doc maneuvered to get me into the club, and I was glad to join, as I could see that it represented something distinctly different from the corner gangs I was meeting.

As I began to meet the men of Cornerville, I also met a few of the girls. One girl I took to a church dance. The next morning the fellows on the street corner were asking me: "How your steady girl?" This brought me up short. I learned that going to the girl's house was something that you just did not do unless you hoped to marry her. Fortunately, the girl and her family knew that I did not know the local customs, so they did not assume that I was thus committed. However, this was a useful warning. After this time, even though I found some Cornerville girls exceedingly attractive, I never went out with them except on a group basis, and I did not make any more home visits either.

As I went along, I found that life in Cornerville was not nearly so interesting and pleasant for the girls as it was for the men. A young man had complete freedom to wander and hang around. The girls could not hang on street corners. They had to divide their time between their own homes, the homes of girl friends and relatives, and a job, if they had one. Many of them had a dream that went like this: some young man, from outside of Cornerville, with a little money, a good job, and a good education would come and woo them and take them out of the district. I could hardly afford to fill this role.

Training in Participant Observation

. . . As I began hanging about Cornerville. I found that I needed an explanation for myself and for my study. As long as I was with Doc and vouched for by him, no one asked me who I was or what I was doing. When I circulated in other groups or even among the Nortons without him, it was obvious that they were curious about me. . . . I soon found that people were developing their own explanation about me: I was writing a book about Cornerville. This might seem entirely too vague an explanation, and yet it sufficed. I found that my acceptance in the district depended on the personal relationships I developed far more than upon any explanations I might give. Whether it was a good thing to write a book about Cornerville depended entirely on people's opinions of me personally. If I was all right, then my project was all right; if I was no good, then no amount of explanation could convince them that the book was a good idea. . . .

I learned early in my Cornerville period the crucial importance of having the support of the key individuals in any groups or organizations I was studying. Instead of trying to explain myself to everyone, I found I was providing far more information about myself and my study to leaders such as Doc than I volunteered to the average corner boy. I always tried to give the impression that I was willing and eager to tell just as much about my study as anyone wished to know, but it was only with group leaders that I made a particular effort to provide really full information.

My relationship with Doc changed rapidly in this early Cornerville period. At first he was simply a key informant—and also my sponsor. As we spent more time together, I ceased to treat him as a passive informant. I discussed with him quite frankly what I was trying to do, what problems were puzzling me, and so on. Much of our time was spent in this discussion of ideas and observations, so that Doc became, in a very real sense, a collaborator in the research.

This full awareness of the nature of my study stimulated Doc to look for and point out to me the sorts of observations that I was interested in. Often when I picked him up at the flat where he lived with his sister and brother-in-law, he said to me: "Bill, you should have been around last night. You would have been interested in this." And then he would go on to tell me what had happened. Such accounts were always interesting and relevant to my study. . . .

In my interviewing methods I had been instructed not to argue with people or pass moral judgments upon them. This fell in with my own inclinations. I was glad to accept the people and to be accepted by them. However, this attitude did not come out so much in interviewing, for I did little formal interviewing. I sought to show this interested acceptance of the people and the community in my everyday participation.

I learned to take part in the street corner discussions on baseball and sex. This required no special training, since the topics seemed to be matters of almost universal interest. I was not able to participate so actively in discussions of horse-racing. I did begin to follow the races in a rather general and amateur way. I am sure it would have paid me to devote more study to the *Morning Telegraph* and other racing sheets, but my knowledge of baseball at least insured that I would not be left out of the street corner conversations.

While I avoided expressing opinions on sensitive topics, I found that arguing on some matters was simply part of the social pattern and that one could hardly participate without joining in the argument. I often found myself involved in heated but good-natured arguments about the relative merits of certain major-league ball players and managers. Whenever a girl or a group of girls would walk down the street, the fellows on the corner would make mental notes and later would discuss their evaluations of the females. These evaluations would run largely in terms of shape, and here I was glad to argue that Mary had a better "build" than Anna, or vice versa. Of course, if any of the men on the corner happened to be personally attached to Mary or Anna, no searching comments would be made, and I, too, would avoid this topic.

Sometimes I wondered whether just hanging on the street corner was an active enough process to be dignified by the term "research." Perhaps I should be asking these men questions. However, one has to learn when to question and when not to question as well as what questions to ask.

I learned this lesson one night in the early months when I was with Doc in Chichi's gambling joint. A man from another part of the city was regaling us with a tale of the organization of gambling activity. I had been told that he had once been a very big gambling operator, and he talked knowingly about many interesting matters. He did most of the talking, but the others asked questions and threw in comments, so at length I began to feel that I must say something in order to be part of the group. I said: "I suppose the cops were all paid off?"

The gambler's jaw dropped. He glared at me. Then he denied vehemently that any policemen had been paid off and immediately switched the conversation to another subject. For the rest of that evening I felt very uncomfortable.

The next day Doc explained the lesson of the previous evening. "Go easy on that 'who,' 'what,' 'why,' 'when,' 'where' stuff, Bill. You ask those questions, and people will clam up on you. If people accept you, you can just hang around, and you'll learn the answers in the long run without even having to ask the questions."

I found that this was true. As I sat and listened, I learned the answers to questions that I would not even have had the sense to ask if I had been getting my information solely on an interviewing basis. I did not abandon questioning altogether, of course. I simply learned to judge the sensitiveness of the question and my relationship to the people so that I only asked a question in a sensitive area when I was sure that my relationship to the people involved was very solid.

When I had established my position on the street corner, the data simply came to me without very active efforts on my part. It was only now and then, when I was concerned with a particular problem and felt I needed more information from a certain individual, that I would seek an opportunity to get the man alone and carry on a more formal interview.

At first I concentrated upon fitting into Cornerville, but a little later I had to face the question of how far I was to immerse myself in the life of the district. I bumped into that problem one evening as I was walking down the street with the Nortons. Trying to enter into the spirit of the small talk, I cut loose with a string of obscenities and profanity. The walk came to a momentary halt as they all stopped to look at me in surprise. Doc shook his head and said: "Bill, you're not supposed to talk like that. That doesn't sound like you."

I tried to explain that I was only using terms that were common on the street corner. Doc insisted, however, that I was different and that they wanted me to be that way.

This lesson went far beyond the use of obscenity and profanity. I learned that people did not expect me to be just like them; in fact, they were interested and pleased to find me different, just so long as I took a friendly interest in them. Therefore, I abandoned my efforts at complete immersion. My behavior was nevertheless affected by street corner life. When John Howard first came down from Harvard to join me in the Cornerville study, he noticed at once that I talked in Cornerville in a manner far different from that which I used at Harvard. This was not a matter of the use of profanity or obscenity, nor did I affect the use of ungrammatical expressions. I talked in the way that seemed natural to me, but what was natural in Cornerville was different from what was natural at Harvard. In Cornerville, I found myself putting much more animation into my speech, dropping terminal *g*'s, and using gestures much more actively. (There was also, of course, the difference in the vocabulary that I used. When I was most deeply involved in Cornerville, I found myself rather tongue-tied in my visits to Harvard. I simply could not keep up with the discussions of international relations, of the nature of science, and so on, in which I had once been more or less at home.) . . .

My first spring in Cornerville served to establish for me a firm position in the life of the district. I had only been there several weeks when Doc said to me: "You're just as much of a fixture around this street corner as that lamppost." Perhaps the greatest event signalizing my acceptance on Norton Street was the baseball game that Mike Giovanni organized against the group of Norton Street boys in their late teens. It was the old men who had won glorious victories in the past against the rising youngsters. Mike assigned me to a regular position on a team, not a key position perhaps (I was stationed in right field), but at least I was there. When it was my turn to bat in the last half of the ninth inning, the score was tied, there were two outs, and the bases were loaded. As I reached down to pick up my bat, I heard some of the fellows suggesting to Mike that he ought to put in a pinch-hitter. Mike answered them in a loud voice that must have been meant for me: "No, I've got confidence in Bill Whyte. He'll come through in the clutch." So, with Mike's confidence to buck me up, I went up there, missed two swings, and then banged a hard grounder through the hole between second and short. At least that is where they told me it went. I was so busy getting down to first base that I did not know afterward whether I had reached there on an error or a base hit.

That night, when we went down for coffee, Danny presented me with a ring for being a regular fellow and a pretty good ball player. I was particularly impressed by the ring, for it had been made by hand. Danny had started with a clear amber die discarded from his crap game and over long hours had used his lighted cigarette to burn a hole through it and to round the corners so that it came out a heart shape on top. I assured the fellows that I would always treasure the ring.

Perhaps I should add that my game-winning base hit made the score 18–17, so it is evident that I was not the only one who had been hitting the ball. Still, it was a wonderful feeling to come through when they were counting on me, and it made me feel still more that I belonged on Norton Street. . . .

Reflections on Field Research

. . . *Street Corner Society* is about particular people and situations and events. I wanted to write about Cornerville. I found that I could not write about Cornerville in general without discarding most of the data I had upon individuals and groups. It was a long time before I realized that I could explain Cornerville better through telling the stories of those individuals and groups than I could in any other way.

Instead of studying the general characteristics of classes of people, I was looking at Doc, Chick, Tony Cataldo, George Ravello, and others. Instead of getting a cross-sectional picture of the community at a particular point in time, I was dealing with a time sequence of interpersonal events.

Although I could not cover all Cornerville, I was building up the structure and functioning of the community through intensive examination of some of its parts—*in action.* I was relating the parts together through observing events between groups and between group leaders and the members of the larger institutional structures (of politics and the rackets). I was seeking to build a sociology based upon observed interpersonal events. That, to me, is the chief methodological and theoretical meaning of *Street Corner Society*.

The Cultural
Context of
Social Life

WHAT IS CULTURE? The concept is easier to grasp by description than by definition. For example, when we meet someone from a different culture, that person's culture is immediately evident to us. We see it in his or her clothing, jewelry, and gestures. We hear it if that person speaks a different language, or, if speaking our language, when the individual uses unfamiliar expressions, or even when he or she expresses opinions unlike ours. We may even smell it in different perfumes and body lotions. These characteristics, especially when they contrast sharply with our own, alert us to broad differences in the way the person was reared—to that person's culture.

Culture consists of *material* things, such as art, weapons, utensils, machines, clothing, and jewelry. Culture is also *nonmaterial,* consisting of the beliefs and patterns of behavior common to a group of people. Nonmaterial (or symbolic) culture is of primary interest to sociologists, for it provides the broad framework that people use to interpret life. Culture is the lens through which we see the world, the basis on which we construct reality and make our decisions.

Understanding how culture affects people's lives is essential to attaining a sociological imagination. But while we may become aware of culture's pervasive influence when we meet someone from a different culture, our perception of our *own* culture is quite another matter. We usually take *our* speech, *our* body language, *our* beliefs, and *our* ways of doing things for granted. We assume they are normal or natural, and almost without exception we perform them without question. As Ralph Linton said, "The last thing a fish would ever notice would be water." So it is with us: Except for unusual circumstances, the effects of our own culture generally remain imperceptible to us.

Yet culture's significance is profound—not only for our behavior, but also

69

for our orientations to life, and, ultimately, for our very being. Hardly an aspect of who and what we are is untouched by culture. We came into this life without a language, without values, with no ideas about religion, education, war, money, jobs, friendship, love, humor, family relationships, and so on. At birth, we possessed none of these fundamental orientations—so essential in determining the type of people we are. Yet now we take them for granted. This, we might say, is culture *within* us.

These learned and shared ways of believing and of doing things (another way to define culture) penetrate our beings at an early age, becoming part of our basic assumptions of what normal is. They become the screen through which we perceive and evaluate our world. Seldom do we question these assumptions, for as part of our framework for viewing life they themselves remain beyond our ordinary perception.

On occasion, however, an event may challenge these assumptions, making them visible and making us aware of how arbitrary they are. For example, when several Americans converge at a ticket booth they usually line up on the basis of time of arrival. The ticket seller, sharing the same culture, also assumes the normalcy of this behavior and expects to sell tickets on a "first come, first served" basis. To us, this seems the natural way of doing things, and we engage in this behavior routinely.

But in northern Africa, where people's ideas of how to use space sharply contrast with ours, when several people want a ticket each pushes his or her way toward the ticket booth. With no conception similar to our "first come, first served" notion, the ticket seller first dispenses tickets to the noisiest, the pushiest, and (not incidentally) those with the longest arms.

When I traveled in northern Africa, I found this part of their culture most upsetting. It violated my basic expectations of how people *ought* to act—expectations that I did not even know I held until they were so abruptly challenged. At that point I experienced *culture shock*, the sudden inability to depend on the basic orientations to everyday life learned in childhood. That I was several inches taller than most Africans, however, and was able to outreach almost everyone else, helped me to adjust (partially) to this different way of doing things. I never did get used to the idea that pushing ahead of others was "right," though, and always felt guilty about using the accident of my size to receive preferential treatment.

It is to sensitize us to this aspect of life in society—to how cultural factors so fundamentally influence our lives—that the selections in this third Part are directed. Each reading introduces us to aspects of our social lives that ordinarily go unquestioned and unnoticed. Horace Miner helps make visible our basic assumptions about taking care of the body; Neil Thompson spotlights our concern with material possessions; Napoleon Chagnon exposes our taken-for-granted assumptions about sharing, making requests, and how to treat strangers and guests; Edward and Mildred Hall illustrate how culture influences our posture, gestures, eye contact, and use of space in face-to-face communication; and Erving Goffman helps us to see how our nonverbal communications are intricate ways by which we attempt to manipulate people's opinions of us. These analyses of culture can serve as starting points from which we can begin to analyze other assumptions of reality that we hold unquestioningly, and thus gain a startlingly different perspective of social life—and of our own roles in it.

7 Body Ritual Among the Nacirema

HORACE MINER

As part of their culture, all peoples develop ideas about proper ways to care for their bodies. The Nacirema, however, have advanced these ideas to an extraordinary degree, and they spend a good deal of their time, energy, and income following the rituals prescribed by their culture. Taking care of the body in the prescribed manner is so important to these people that even a good part of their childrearing revolves around instructing their children in the precise manner of fulfilling their cultural rituals. With intense and prolonged training, accompanied by punishing children who fail to conform while shunning non-conforming adults, it is no wonder that almost all members of the Nacirema culture unquestioningly conform to their prescribed body rituals and dutifully pass them on to their own children.

A better understanding of the Nacirema culture might possibly shed some light on our own way of life.

THE ANTHROPOLOGIST HAS BECOME so familiar with the diversity of ways in which different peoples behave in similar situations that he is not apt to be surprised by even the most exotic customs. In fact, if all of the logically possible combinations of behavior have not been found somewhere in the world, he is apt to suspect that they must be present in some yet undescribed tribe. This point has, in fact, been expressed with respect to clan organization by Murdock. In this light, the magical beliefs and practices of the Nacirema present such unusual aspects that it seems desirable to describe them as an example of the extremes to which human behavior can go.

Professor Linton first brought the ritual of the Nacirema to the attention of anthropologists twenty years ago, but the culture of this people is still very poorly understood. They are a North American group living in the territory between the Canadian Cree, the Yaqui and Tarahumare of Mexico, and the Carib and Arawak of the Antilles. Little is known of their origin, although tradition states that they came from the east.

Nacirema culture is characterized by a highly developed market economy which has evolved in a rich natural habitat. While much of the people's time is devoted to economic pursuits, a large part of the fruits of these labors and a considerable portion of the day are spent in ritual activity. The focus of this activity is the human body, the appearance and health of which loom as a dominant concern in the ethos of the people. While such a concern is certainly not unusual, its ceremonial aspects and associated philosophy are unique.

The fundamental belief underlying the whole system appears to be that the human body is ugly and that its natural tendency is to debility and disease. Incarcerated in such a body, man's only hope is to avert these characteristics through the use of the powerful influences of ritual and ceremony. Every household has one or more shrines devoted to this purpose. The more powerful individuals in the society have several shrines in their houses and, in fact, the opulence of a house is often referred to in terms of the number of such ritual centers it possesses. Most houses are of wattle and daub construction, but the shrine rooms of the more wealthy are walled with stone. Poorer families imitate the rich by applying pottery plaques to their shrine walls.

While each family has at least one such shrine, the rituals associated with it are not family ceremonies but are private and secret. The rites are normally only discussed with children, and then only during the period when they are being initiated into these mysteries. I was able, however, to establish sufficient rapport with the natives to examine these shrines and to have the rituals described to me.

The focal point of the shrine is a box or chest which is built into the wall. In this chest are kept the many charms and magical potions without which no native believes he could live. These preparations are secured from a variety of specialized practitioners. The most powerful of these are the medicine men, whose assistance must be rewarded with substantial gifts. However, the medicine men do not provide the curative potions for their clients, but decide what the ingredients should be and then write them down in an ancient and secret language. This writing is understood only by the medicine men and by the herbalists who, for another gift, provide the required charm.

The charm is not disposed of after it has served its purpose, but is placed in the charm-box of the household shrine. As these magical materials are specific for certain ills, and the real or imagined maladies of the people are many, the charm-box is usually full to overflowing. The magical packets are so numerous that people forget what their purposes were and fear to use them again. While the natives are very vague on this point, we can only assume that the idea in retaining all the old magical materials is that their presence in the charm-box, before which the body rituals are conducted, will in some way protect the worshipper.

Beneath the charm-box is a small font. Each day every member of the family, in succession, enters the shrine room, bows his head before the charm-box, mingles different sorts of holy water in the font, and proceeds with a brief rite of ablution. The holy waters are secured from the Water Temple of the community, where the priests conduct elaborate ceremonies to make the liquid ritually pure.

In the hierarchy of magical practitioners, and below the medicine men in prestige, are specialists whose designation is best translated "holy-mouth-men." The Nacirema have an almost pathological horror of and fascination with the mouth, the condition of which is believed to have a supernatural influence on all social relationships. Were it not for the rituals of the mouth, they believe that their teeth would fall out, their gums bleed, their jaws shrink, their friends desert them, and their lovers reject them. They also believe that a strong relationship exists between oral and moral characteristics. For example, there is a ritual ablution of the mouth for children which is supposed to improve their moral fiber.

The daily body ritual performed by everyone includes a mouth-rite. Despite the fact that these people are so punctilious about care of the mouth, this rite involves a practice which strikes the uninitiated stranger as revolting. It was reported to me that the ritual consists of inserting a small bundle of hog hairs into the mouth, along with certain magical powders, and then moving the bundle in a highly formalized series of gestures.

In addition to the private mouth-rite, the people seek out a holy-mouth-man once or twice a year. These practitioners have an impressive set of paraphernalia, consisting of a variety of augers, awls, probes, and prods. The use of these objects in the exorcism of the evils of the mouth involves almost unbelievable ritual torture of the client. The holy-mouth-man opens the client's mouth and, using the above mentioned tools, enlarges any holes which decay may have created in the teeth. Magical materials are put into these holes. If there are no naturally occurring holes in the teeth, large sections of one or more teeth are gouged out so that the supernatural substance can be applied. In the client's view, the purpose of these ministrations is to arrest decay and draw friends. The extremely sacred and traditional character of the rite is evident in the fact that the natives return to the holy-mouth-men year after year, despite the fact that their teeth continue to decay.

It is to be hoped that, when a thorough study of the Nacirema is made, there will be careful inquiry into the personality structure of these people. One has but to watch the gleam in the eye of a holy-mouth-man, as he jabs an awl into an exposed nerve, to suspect that a certain amount of sadism is involved. If this can be established, a very interesting pattern emerges, for most of the population shows definite masochistic tendencies. It was to these that Professor Linton referred in discussing a distinctive part of the daily body ritual which is performed only by men. This part of the rite involves scraping and lacerating the surface of the face with a sharp instrument. Special women's rites are performed only four times during each lunar month, but what they lack in frequency is made up in barbarity. As part of this ceremony, women bake their heads in small ovens for about an hour. The theoretically interesting point is that what seems to be a preponderantly masochistic people have developed sadistic specialists.

The medicine men have an imposing temple, or *latipso,* in every community of any size. The more elaborate ceremonies required to treat very sick patients can only be performed at this temple. These ceremonies involve not only the thaumaturge but a permanent group of vestal maidens who move sedately about the temple chambers in distinctive costume and headdress.

The *latipso* ceremonies are so harsh that it is phenomenal that a fair proportion of the really sick natives who enter the temple ever recover. Small children whose indoctrination is still incomplete have been known to resist attempts to take them to the temple because "that is where you go to die." Despite this fact, sick adults are not only willing but eager to undergo the protracted ritual purification, if they can afford to do so. No matter how ill the supplicant or how grave the emergency, the guardians of many temples will not admit a client if he cannot give a rich gift to the custodian. Even after one has gained admission and survived the ceremonies, the guardians will not permit the neophyte to leave until he makes still another gift.

The supplicant entering the temple is first stripped of all his or her clothes. In everyday life the Nacirema avoids exposure of his body and its natural functions. Bathing and excretory acts are performed only in the secrecy of the household shrine, where they are ritualized as part of the body-rites. Psychological shock results from the fact that body secrecy is suddenly lost upon entry into the *latipso*. A man whose own wife has never seen him in an excretory act, suddenly finds himself naked and assisted by a vestal maiden while he performs his natural functions into a sacred vessel. This sort of ceremonial treatment is necessitated by the fact that the excreta are used by a diviner to ascertain the course and nature of the client's sickness. Female clients, on the other hand, find their naked bodies are subjected to the scrutiny, manipulation, and prodding of the medicine men.

Few supplicants in the temple are well enough to do anything but lie on their hard beds. The daily ceremonies, like the rites of the holy-mouth-men, involve discomfort and torture. With ritual precision, the vestals awaken their miserable charges each dawn and roll them about on their beds of pain while performing ablutions, in the formal movements of which the maidens are highly trained. At other times they insert magic wands in the supplicant's mouth or force him to eat substances which are supposed to be healing. From time to time the medicine men come to their clients and jab magically treated needles into their flesh. The fact that these temple ceremonies may not cure, and may even kill the neophyte, in no way decreases the people's faith in the medicine men.

There remains one other kind of practitioner, known as a "listener." This witchdoctor has the power to exorcise the devils that lodge in the heads of people who have been bewitched. The Nacirema believe that parents bewitch their own children. Mothers are particularly suspected of putting a curse on children while teaching them the secret body rituals. The counter-magic of the witchdoctor is unusual in its lack of ritual. The patient simply tells the "listener" all his troubles and fears, beginning with the earliest difficulties he can remember. The memory displayed by the Nacirema in these exorcism sessions is truly remarkable. It is not uncommon for the patient to bemoan the rejection he felt upon being weaned as a babe, and a few individuals even see their troubles going back to the traumatic effects of their own birth.

In conclusion, mention must be made of certain practices which have their base in native esthetics but which depend upon the pervasive aversion to the natural body and its functions. There are ritual fasts to make fat people thin and ceremonial feasts to make thin people fat. Still other rites are used to make women's breasts larger if they are small, and smaller if they are large. General dissatisfaction with breast shape is symbolized in the fact that the ideal form is virtually outside the range of human variation. A few women afflicted with almost inhuman hyper-mammary development are so idolized that they make a handsome living by simply going from village to village and permitting the natives to stare at them for a fee.

Reference has already been made to the fact that excretory functions are ritualized, routinized, and relegated to secrecy. Natural reproductive functions are similarly distorted. Intercourse is taboo as a topic and scheduled as an act. Efforts are made to avoid pregnancy by the use of magical materials or by limiting intercourse to certain phases of the moon. Conception is actually very infrequent. When pregnant, women dress so as to hide their condition. Parturition takes place in secret, without friends or relatives to assist, and the majority of women do not nurse their infants.

Our review of the ritual life of the Nacirema has certainly shown them to be a magic-ridden people. It is hard to understand how they have managed to exist so long under the burdens which they have imposed upon themselves. But even such exotic customs as these take on real meaning when they are viewed with the insight provided by Malinowski when he wrote:

> Looking from far and above, from our high places of safety in the developed civilization, it is easy to see all the crudity and irrelevance of magic. But without its power and guidance early man could not have mastered his practical difficulties as he has done, nor could man have advanced to the higher stages of civilization.

8   The Mysterious Fall of the Nacirema

NEIL B. THOMPSON

As you saw in the immediately preceding selection, the Nacirema expended vast resources of money and time on the care of their bodies. An additional central characteristic of the Nacirema was their concern with material things. Almost more than any other human group, the Nacirema prized themselves on the number of their possessions, even ruining their health working years at tedious, boring jobs they detested in order to possess more things they didn't need. Fiercely proud of what they owned, they also engaged in *conspicuous consumption;* that is, they flaunted their wealth by buying and publicly consuming things they didn't need. In some strange way, such public displays made the possessor better than the nonpossessor.

In this article, Thompson focuses on a Nacirema possession considered so important that it played a central role in their lives. (If I were a psychologist, I would say the Nacirema had become obsessed with this object.) Unfortunately, due to the Nacirema's shortsightedness, this object, though so highly valued, also destroyed their environment—bringing the Nacirema down with it.

THE REVIVAL OF CONCERN in the recently extinct culture of the Nacirema is, to say the least, most interesting, and perhaps reflects an increasing state of concern for our own society. . . .

Though exploratory digs by our archeological expeditions, we are able to say with some confidence that the Nacirema were the dominant group in the complex of North American cultures. Although the Nacirema left a large number of documents, our linguists have been unable to decipher any more than a few scattered fragments of the Nacirema language. Eventually, with the complete translation of these documents, we will undoubtedly learn a great deal about the reasons for the sudden disappearance of what, from the physical evidence, must have been an explosive and expansive culture. For the present, however, we must rely upon the physical evidence we have uncovered and analyzed in order to draw any conclusions concerning its extinction. . . .

Early research has disclosed the importance of ritualistic observance among the Nacirema. In support of these observations, we should note the presence of the quasi-religious Elibomotua Cult. This pervasive cult was devoted to the creation of an artistic symbol for a man-made environmental system.

The high esteem of the cult is demonstrated by the fact that near every population center, when not disturbed by the accumulation of debris, archaeologists have found large and orderly collections of the Elibomotua Cult symbol. The vast number of these collections has given us the opportunity to reconstruct with considerable confidence the principal ideas of the cult. The newest symbols seem to have nearly approached the ultimate of the Nacirema's cultural ideal. Their colors, material, and size suggest an enclosed mobile device that corresponds to no color or shape found in nature, although some authorities suggest that, at some early time in the development, the egg may have been the model. The device was provided with its own climate control system as well as a system that screened out many of the shorter rays of the light spectrum.

The object was designed to eliminate most sounds from the outside and to fill the interior with a hypnotic humming sound when the machine was in operation. This noise could be altered in pitch and intensity by the manipulation, through simple mechanical controls, of an ingenious mechanism located outside the operator's compartment. This mechanism also produced a gaseous substance that, in a small area, could change the appearance of the air.

In the early stages of the symbol's development, this was probably only a ritualistic performance since the production plant was small and was fueled by a small tank. This function, however, may have been the primary reason for the cult's symbol: to provide each family with its own device for altering the environment by giving it a private microuniverse with a system of producing this change in the air.

The complete machined piece was somewhat fragile. Our tests of the suspension system indicate that it was virtually immobile on unimproved terrain; by all of our physical evidence, its movement was restricted to the surfaced steerts that the Nacirema had built to geometricize the landscape.

We are relatively certain that a specially endowed and highly skilled group of educators was employed to keep the importance of these enclosed mobile devices constantly in the public eye. Working in an as yet unlocated area that they referred to as Euneva Nosidam, these specialists printed periodical matter and transmitted electronic-impulse images to boxlike apparatus in all homes.

While some of the information was aimed at describing the appearance and performance characteristics of the various kinds of machines, the greatest portion of the material was seemingly aimed at something other than these factors. A distinguished group of linguists, social psychologists, and theologians, who presented the principal symposium at our most recent anthropological conference, offered the hypothesis that the elibomotua symbols, also known as racs, replaced the processes of natural selection in the courtship and mating rituals of the Nacirema. Through unconscious suggestion, which de-

rived from Euneva Nosidam's "mcnahulesque" materials, the female was un-
controllably driven to select her mate by the kind of elibomotua he occupied.
The males of the culture were persuaded to believe that any handicap to masculine dominance could be overcome by selecting the proper cult symbol. In
this way, the future of the race, as represented by Nacirema culture, was determined by unnatural man-made techniques.

The symposium was careful to point out that we have not yet uncovered
any hard evidence to show whether or not this cultural trait actually had any
effect on the race or its population growth. We have found, however, one
strange sculpture from the Pop Loohcs depicting a male and female mating in
an elibomotua's rear compartment, indicating a direct relationship. The hypothesis has the virtue of corresponding to the standard anthropological interpretations of the Nacirema culture—that it was ritual-ridden and devoted to
the goal of control of the environment. . . .

Evidence indicates that a sizable portion of the work force and enormous amounts of space must have been devoted to the manufacture, distribution, and ceremonial care of the devices. Some of the biggest production units
of the economy were assigned this function; extensive design laboratories were
given over to the manipulation of styles and appearances, and assembly lines
turned out the pieces in serial fashion. They were given a variety of names, although all of those made in the same time period look remarkably alike.

Every family assumed the responsibility for one of the machined pieces
and venerated it for a period of two to four solar cycles. Some families who
lived in areas where a high quality of life was maintained took from two to four
pieces into their care. During the time a family held a piece, they ritually
cleansed it, housed it from the elements, and took it to special shrines where
priests gave it a variety of injections.

The Nacirema spent much of their time inside their elibomotuas moving
about on the steerts. Pictures show that almost everyone engaged, once in the
morning and once in the evening, in what must have been an important mass
ritual, which we have been unable to decipher with any surety. During these
periods of the day, people of both sexes and all ages, except the very young
and the very old, left their quarters to move about on the steerts in their racs.
Films of these periods of the day show scenes analogous to the dance one can
occasionally see in a swarm of honeybees. In large population centers this
"dance of the racs" lasted for two or three hours. . . . The ardent involvement
of the whole population from ages 6 to 65 indicates that it was one of the
strongest mores of the culture, perhaps approaching an instinctual behavior
pattern.

It should also be mentioned that, when inside their racs, people were not
restricted to their ottehgs, but were free to go anywhere they chose so long as
they remained on the steerts. Apparently, when they were confined inside a
rac, the Nacirema attained a state of equality, which eliminated the danger of
any caste contamination.

These, then, to the best of our present state of knowledge, were the principal familial uses of the Elibomotua Cult symbols. After a family had cared for a piece long enough to burnish it with a certain patina, it was routinely replaced by another, and the used rac was assigned to a gallery keeper, who placed it on permanent display in an outdoor gallery, sometimes surrounded by trees or a fence, but usually not concealed in any way. During their free time, many persons, especially those from the ottehgs of the lesser sorts, came to study the various symbols on display and sometimes carried away small parts to be used for an unknown purpose.

There seems to be little doubt that the Cult of the Elibomotua was so fervently embraced by the general population, and that the daily rituals of the rac's care and use were so faithfully performed, that the minute quantities of reagent thus distributed may have had a decisive effect on the chemical characteristics of the air. The elibomotua, therefore, may have contributed in a major way toward the prized objective of a totally man–made environment.

In summary, our evaluation of both the Nacirema's man-made environmental alterations and the artifacts found in their territories lead us to advance the hypothesis that they may have been responsible for their own extinction. The Nacirema culture may have been so successful in achieving its objectives that the inherited physiological mechanisms of its people were unable to cope with its manufactured environment.

9 Doing Fieldwork Among the Yąnomamö

NAPOLEON A. CHAGNON

As stated in the second reading, the primary difference between sociology and anthropology is the choice of research setting. That is, sociologists usually study people living in industrialized societies, while anthropologists usually focus on preliterate and peasant groups. The distinction does not always hold, however, as some anthropologists do research in urban settings, and occasionally a sociologist wanders into peasant society or even preliterate territory. Consequently, it makes little difference that the fieldwork reported here was done by an anthropologist, for if a sociologist had done participant observation among the Yąnomamö, he or she would have written a similar account of those experiences. (Sociologists, however, are considerably less interested in kinship and genealogy.)

Note how the culture of the Yąnomamö sets the stage for their behaviors. Although from our perspective their behaviors are strange, this is the way of life that the Yąnomamö have learned. What they experience is as natural for them as our way of life is for us. But for someone from our culture to experience Yąnomamö life is to encounter an alien world, as Chagnon discovered firsthand. Chagnon experienced *culture shock*—that is, the fundamentals of life that he had learned no longer applied, and he was most uncomfortable with what he confronted. How would you have felt in his place?

THE YĄNOMAMÖ INDIANS live in southern Venezuela and the adjacent portions of northern Brazil. Some 125 widely scattered villages have populations ranging from 40 to 250 inhabitants, with 75 to 80 people the most usual number. In total numbers their population probably approaches 10,000 people, but this is merely a guess. Many of the villages have not yet been contacted by outsiders, and nobody knows for sure exactly how many uncontacted villages there are, or how many people live in them. By comparison to African or Melanesian tribes, the Yąnomamö population is small. Still, they are one of the largest unacculturated tribes left in all of South America.

But they have a significance apart from tribal size and cultural purity: The Yąnomamö are still actively conducting warfare. It is in the nature of man to fight, according to one of their myths, because the blood of "Moon" spilled on this layer of the cosmos, causing men to become fierce. I describe the Yąno-mamö as "the fierce people" because that is the most accurate single phrase that describes them. That is how they conceive themselves to be, and that is how they would like others to think of them.

I spent nineteen months with the Yąnomamö, during which time I ac-quired some proficiency in their language and, up to a point, submerged my-self in their culture and way of life. The thing that impressed me most was the importance of aggression in their culture. I had the opportunity to witness a good many incidents that expressed individual vindictiveness on the one hand and collective bellicosity on the other. These ranged in seriousness from the ordinary incidents of wife beating and chest pounding to dueling and orga-nized raiding by parties that set out with the intention of ambushing and killing men from enemy villages. One of the villages was raided approximately twenty-five times while I conducted the fieldwork, six times by the group I lived among. . . .

This is not to state that primitive man everywhere is unpleasant. By way of contrast, I have also done limited fieldwork among the Yąnomamö's north-ern neighbors, the Carib-speaking Makiritare Indians. This group was very pleasant and charming, all of them anxious to help me and honor bound to show any visitor the numerous courtesies of their system of etiquette. In short, they approached the image of primitive man that I had conjured up, and it was sheer pleasure to work with them. . . .

My first day in the field illustrated to me what my teachers meant when they spoke of "culture shock." I had traveled in a small, aluminum rowboat propelled by a large outboard motor for two and a half days. This took me from the Territorial capital, a small town on the Orinoco River, deep into Yąnomamö country. On the morning of the third day we reached a small mis-sion settlement, the field "headquarters" of a group of Americans who were working in two Yąnomamö villages. The missionaries had come out of these villages to hold their annual conference on the progress of their mission work, and were conducting their meetings when I arrived. We picked up a passenger at the mission station, James P. Barker, the first non-Yąnomamö to make a sus-tained, permanent contact with the tribe (in 1950). He had just returned from a year's furlough in the United States, where I had earlier visited him before leaving for Venezuela. He agreed to accompany me to the village I had se-lected for my base of operations to introduce me to the Indians. This village was also his own home base, but he had not been there for over a year and did not plan to join me for another three months. Mr. Barker had been living with this particular group about five years.

We arrived at the village, Bisaasi-teri, about 2:00 P.M. and docked the boat along the muddy bank at the terminus of the path used by the Indians to fetch their drinking water. It was hot and muggy, and my clothing was soaked with perspiration. It clung uncomfortably to my body, as it did thereafter for the remainder of the work. The small, biting gnats were out in astronomical numbers, for it was the beginning of the dry season. My face and hands were swollen from the venom of their numerous stings. In just a few moments I was to meet my first Yąnomamö, my first primitive man. What would it be like? I had visions of entering the village and seeing 125 social facts running about calling each other kinship terms and sharing food, each waiting and anxious to have me collect his genealogy. I would wear them out in turn. Would they like me? This was important to me; I wanted them to be so fond of me that they would adopt me into their kinship system and way of life, because I had heard that successful anthropologists always get adopted by their people. I had learned during my seven years of anthropological training at the University of Michigan that kinship was equivalent to society in primitive tribes and that it was a moral way of life, "moral" being something "good" and "desirable." I was determined to work my way into their moral system of kinship and become a member of their society.

My heart began to pound as we approached the village and heard the buzz of activity within the circular compound. Mr. Barker commented that he was anxious to see if any changes had taken place while he was away and wondered how many of them had died during his absence. I felt into my back pocket to make sure that my notebook was there and felt personally more secure when I touched it. Otherwise, I would not have known what to do with my hands.

I looked up and gasped when I saw a dozen burly, naked, filthy, hideous men staring at us down the shafts of their drawn arrows! Immense wads of green tobacco were stuck between their lower teeth and lips making them look even more hideous, and strands of dark-green slime dripped or hung from their noses. We arrived at the village while the men were blowing a hallucinogenic drug up their noses. One of the side effects of the drug is a runny nose. The mucus is always saturated with the green powder and the Indians usually let it run freely from their nostrils. My next discovery was that there were a dozen or so vicious, underfed dogs snapping at my legs, circling me as if I were going to be their next meal. I just stood there holding my notebook, helpless and pathetic. Then the stench of the decaying vegetation and filth struck me and I almost got sick. I was horrified. What sort of a welcome was this for the person who came here to live with you and learn your way of life, to become friends with you? They put their weapons down when they recognized Barker and returned to their chanting, keeping a nervous eye on the village entrances.

We had arrived just after a serious fight. Seven women had been abducted the day before by a neighboring group, and the local men and their guests had just that morning recovered five of them in a brutal club fight that nearly ended in a shooting war. The abductors, angry because they lost five of the seven captives, vowed to raid the Bisaasi-teri. When we arrived and entered the village unexpectedly, the Indians feared that we were the raiders. On several occasions during the next two hours the men in the village jumped to their feet, armed themselves, and waited nervously for the noise outside the village to be identified. My enthusiasm for collecting ethnographic curiosities diminished in proportion to the number of times such an alarm was raised. In fact, I was relieved when Mr. Barker suggested that we sleep across the river for the evening. It would be safer over there.

As we walked down the path to the boat, I pondered the wisdom of having decided to spend a year and a half with this tribe before I had even seen what they were like. I am not ashamed to admit, either, that had there been a diplomatic way out, I would have ended my fieldwork then and there. I did not look forward to the next day when I would be left alone with the Indians; I did not speak a word of their language, and they were decidedly different from what I had imagined them to be. The whole situation was depressing, and I wondered why I ever decided to switch from civil engineering to anthropology in the first place. I had not eaten all day, I was soaking wet from perspiration, the gnats were biting me, and I was covered with red pigment, the result of a dozen or so complete examinations I had been given by as many burly Indians. These examinations capped an otherwise grim day. The Indians would blow their noses into their hands, flick as much of the mucus off that would separate in a snap of the wrist, wipe the residue into their hair, and then carefully examine my face, arms, legs, hair, and the contents of my pockets. I asked Mr. Barker how to say "Your hands are dirty"; my comments were met by the Indians in the following way: They would "clean" their hands by spitting a quantity of slimy tobacco juice into them, rub them together, and then proceed with the examination.

Mr. Barker and I crossed the river and slung our hammocks. When he pulled his hammock out of a rubber bag, a heavy, disagreeable odor of mildewed cotton came with it. "Even the missionaries are filthy," I thought to myself. Within two weeks everything I owned smelled the same way, and I lived with the odor for the remainder of the fieldwork. My own habits of personal cleanliness reached such levels that I didn't even mind being examined by the Indians, as I was not much cleaner than they were after I had adjusted to the circumstances.

So much for my discovery that primitive man is not the picture of nobility and sanitation I had conceived him to be. I soon discovered that it was an enormously time-consuming task to maintain my own body in the manner to which it had grown accustomed in the relatively antiseptic environment of the northern United States. Either I could be relatively well fed and relatively comfortable in a fresh change of clothes and do very little fieldwork, or, I could do considerably more fieldwork and be less well fed and less comfortable.

It is appalling how complicated it can be to make oatmeal in the jungle. First, I had to make two trips to the river to haul the water. Next, I had to prime my kerosene stove with alcohol and get it burning, a tricky procedure when you are trying to mix powdered milk and fill a coffee pot at the same time: the alcohol prime always burned out before I could turn the kerosene on, and I would have to start all over. Or, I would turn the kerosene on, hoping that the element was still hot enough to vaporize the fuel, and not start a small fire in my palm-thatched hut as the liquid kerosene squirted all over the table and walls and ignited. It was safer to start over with the alcohol. Then I had to boil the oatmeal and pick the bugs out of it. All my supplies, of course, were carefully stored in Indian-proof, ratproof, moisture-proof, and insect-proof containers, not one of which ever served its purpose adequately. Just taking things out of the multiplicity of containers and repacking them afterward was a minor project in itself. By the time I had hauled the water to cook with, unpacked my food, prepared the oatmeal, milk, and coffee, heated water for dishes, washed and dried the dishes, repacked the food in the containers, stored the containers in locked trunks and cleaned up my mess, the ceremony of preparing breakfast had brought me almost up to lunch time.

Eating three meals a day was out of the question. I solved the problem by eating a single meal that could be prepared in a single container, or, at most, in two containers, washed my dishes only when there were no clean ones left, using cold river water, and wore each change of clothing at least a week to cut down on my laundry problem, a courageous undertaking in the tropics. I was also less concerned about sharing my provisions with the rats, insects, Indians, and the elements, thereby eliminating the need for my complicated storage process. I was able to last most of the day on *café con leche,* heavily sugared espresso coffee diluted about five to one with hot milk. I would prepare this in the evening and store it in a thermos. Frequently, my single meal was no more complicated than a can of sardines and a package of crackers. But at least two or three times a week I would do something sophisticated, like make oatmeal or boil rice and add a can of tuna fish or tomato paste to it. I even saved time by devising a water system that obviated the trips to the river. I had a few sheets of zinc roofing brought in and made a rain-water trap. I caught the water on the zinc surface, funneled it into an empty gasoline drum, and then ran a plastic hose from the drum to my hut. When the drum was exhausted in the dry season, I hired the Indians to fill it with water from the river.

I ate much less when I traveled with the Indians to visit other villages. Most of the time my travel diet consisted of roasted or boiled green plantains that I obtained from the Indians, but I always carried a few cans of sardines with me in case I got lost or stayed away longer than I had planned. I found peanut butter and crackers a very nourishing food, and a simple one to prepare on trips. It was nutritious and portable, and only one tool was required to prepare the meal, a hunting knife that could be cleaned by wiping the blade on a leaf. More importantly, it was one of the few foods the Indians would let me eat in relative peace. It looked too much like animal feces to them to excite their appetites.

I once referred to the peanut butter as the dung of cattle. They found this quite repugnant. They did not know what "cattle" were, but were generally aware that I ate several canned products of such an animal. I perpetrated this myth, if for no other reason than to have some peace of mind while I ate. Fieldworkers develop strange defense mechanisms, and this was one of my own forms of adaptation. On another occasion I was eating a can of frankfurters and growing very weary of the demands of one of my guests for a share in my meal. When he asked me what I was eating, I replied: "Beef." He then asked, "What part of the animal are you eating?" to which I replied, "Guess!" He stopped asking for a share.

Meals were a problem in another way. Food sharing is important to the Yąnomamö in the context of displaying friendship. "I am hungry," is almost a form of greeting with them. I could not possibly have brought enough food with me to feed the entire village, yet they seemed not to understand this. All they could see was that I did not share my food with them at each and every meal. Nor could I enter into their system of reciprocities with respect to food; every time one of them gave me something "freely," he would dog me for months to pay him back, not with food, but with steel tools. Thus, if I accepted a plantain from someone in a different village while I was on a visit, he would most likely visit me in the future and demand a machete as payment for the time that he "fed" me. I usually reacted to these kinds of demands by giving a banana, the customary reciprocity in their culture—food for food—but this would be a disappointment for the individual who had visions of that single plantain growing into a machete over time.

Despite the fact that most of them knew I would not share my food with them at their request, some of them always showed up at my hut during mealtime. I gradually became accustomed to this and learned to ignore their persistent demands while I ate. Some of them would get angry because I failed to give in, but most of them accepted it as just a peculiarity of the subhuman foreigner. When I did give in, my hut quickly filled with Indians, each demanding a sample of the food that I had given one of them. If I did not give all a share, I was that much more despicable in their eyes.

A few of them went out of their way to make my meals unpleasant, to spite me for not sharing; for example, one man arrived and watched me eat a cracker with honey on it. He immediately recognized the honey, a particularly esteemed Yąnomamö food. He knew that I would not share my tiny bottle and that it would be futile to ask. Instead, he glared at me and queried icily, "Shaki![1] What kind of animal semen are you eating on that cracker?" His question had the desired effect, and my meal ended.

Finally, there was the problem of being lonely and separated from your own kind, especially your family. I tried to overcome this by seeking personal friendships among the Indians. This only complicated the matter because all my friends simply used my confidence to gain privileged access to my cache of steel tools and trade goods, and looted me. I would be bitterly disappointed that my "friend" thought no more of me than to finesse our relationship exclusively with the intention of getting at any locked up possessions, and my depression would hit new lows every time I discovered this. The loss of the possession bothered me much less than the shock that I was, as far as most of them were concerned, nothing more than a source of desirable items; no holds were barred in relieving me of these, since I was considered something subhuman, a non-Yąnomamö.

The thing that bothered me most was the incessant, passioned, and aggressive demands the Indians made. It would become so unbearable that I would have to lock myself in my mud hut every once in a while just to escape from it: Privacy is one of Western culture's greatest achievements. But I did not want privacy for its own sake; rather, I simply had to get away from the begging. Day and night for the entire time I lived with the Yąnomamö I was plagued by such demands as: "Give me a knife, I am poor!"; "If you don't take me with you on your next trip to Widokaiya-teri, I'll chop a hole in your canoe!"; "Don't point your camera at me or I'll hit you!"; "Share your food with me!"; "Take me across the river in your canoe and be quick about it!"; "Give me a cooking pot!"; "Loan me your flashlight so I can go hunting tonight!"; "Give me medicine . . . I itch all over!"; "Take us on a week-long hunting trip with your shotgun!"; and "Give me an axe, or I'll break into your hut when you are away visiting and steal one!" And so I was bombarded by such demands day after day, months on end, until I could not bear to see an Indian.

It was not as difficult to become calloused to the incessant begging as it was to ignore the sense of urgency, the impassioned tone of voice, or the intimidation and aggression with which the demands were made. It was likewise difficult to adjust to the fact that the Yąnomamö refused to accept "no" for an answer until or unless it seethed with passion and intimidation—which it did after six months. Giving in to a demand always established a new threshold; the next demand would be for a bigger item or favor, and the anger of the Indians even greater if the demand was not met. I soon learned that I had to become very much like the Yąnomamö to be able to get along with them on their terms: sly, aggressive, and intimidating.

Had I failed to adjust in this fashion I would have lost six months of supplies to them in a single day or would have spent most of my time ferrying them around in my canoe or hunting for them. As it was, I did spend a considerable amount of time doing these things and did succumb to their outrageous demands for axes and machetes, at least at first. More importantly, had I failed to demonstrate that I could not be pushed around beyond a certain point, I would have been the subject of far more ridicule, theft, and practical jokes than was the actual case. In short, I had to acquire a certain proficiency in their kind of interpersonal politics and to learn how to imply subtly that certain potentially undesirable consequences might follow if they did such and such to me. They do this to each other in order to establish precisely the point at which they cannot goad an individual any further without precipitating retaliation. As soon as I caught on to this and realized that much of their aggression was stimulated by their desire to discover my flash point, I got along much better with them and regained some lost ground. It was sort of like a political game that everyone played, but one in which each individual sooner or later had to display some sign that his bluffs and implied threats could be backed up. I suspect that the frequency of wife beating is a component of this syndrome, since men can display their ferocity and show others that they are capable of violence. Beating a wife with a club is considered to be an acceptable way of displaying ferocity and one that does not expose the male to much danger. The important thing is that the man has displayed his potential for violence and the implication is that other men better treat him with respect and caution.

After six months, the level of demand was tolerable in the village I used for my headquarters. The Indians and I adjusted to each other and knew what to expect with regard to demands on their part for goods, favors, and services. Had I confined my fieldwork to just that village alone, the field experience would have been far more enjoyable. But, as I was interested in the demographic pattern and social organization of a much larger area, I made regular trips to some dozen different villages in order to collect genealogies or to recheck those I already had. Hence, the intensity of begging and intimidation was fairly constant for the duration of the fieldwork. I had to establish my position in some sort of pecking order of ferocity at each and every village.

For the most part, my own "fierceness" took the form of shouting back at the Yąnomamö as loudly and as passionately as they shouted at me, especially at first, when I did not know much of their language. As I became more proficient in their language and learned more about their political tactics, I became more sophisticated in the art of bluffing. For example, I paid one young man a machete to cut palm trees and make boards from the wood. I used these to fashion a platform in the bottom of my dugout canoe to keep my possessions dry when I traveled by river. That afternoon I was doing informant work in the village; the long-awaited mission supply boat arrived, and most of the Indians ran out of the village to beg goods from the crew. I continued to work in the village for another hour or so and went down to the river to say "hello" to the men on the supply boat. I was angry when I discovered that the Indians had chopped up all my palm boards and used them to paddle their own canoes across the river. I knew that if I overlooked this incident I would have invited them to take even greater liberties with my goods in the future. I crossed the river, docked amidst their dugouts, and shouted for the Indians to come out and see me. A few of the culprits appeared, mischievous grins on their faces. I gave a spirited lecture about how hard I had worked to put those boards in my canoe, how I had paid a machete for the wood, and how angry I was that they destroyed my work in their haste to cross the river. I then pulled out my hunting knife and, while their grins disappeared, cut each of their canoes loose, set them into the current, and let them float away. I left without further ado and without looking back.

They managed to borrow another canoe and, after some effort, recovered their dugouts. The headman of the village later told me with an approving chuckle that I had done the correct thing. Everyone in the village, except, of course, the culprits, supported and defended my action. This raised my status.

Whenever I took such action and defended my rights, I got along much better with the Yąnomamö. A good deal of their behavior toward me was directed with the forethought of establishing the point at which I would react defensively. Many of them later reminisced about the early days of my work when I was "timid" and a little afraid of them, and they could bully me into giving goods away.

Theft was the most persistent situation that required me to take some sort of defensive action. I simply could not keep everything I owned locked in trunks, and the Indians came into my hut and left at will. I developed a very effective means for recovering almost all the stolen items. I would simply ask a child who took the item and then take that person's hammock when he was not around, giving a spirited lecture to the others as I marched away in a faked rage with the thief's hammock. Nobody ever attempted to stop me from doing this, and almost all of them told me that my technique for recovering my possessions was admirable. By nightfall the thief would either appear with the stolen object or send it along with someone else to make an exchange. The others would heckle him for getting caught and being forced to return the item.

With respect to collecting the data I sought, there was a very frustrating problem. Primitive social organization is kinship organization, and to understand the Yąnomamö way of life I had to collect extensive genealogies. I could not have deliberately picked a more difficult group to work with in this regard: They have very stringent name taboos. They attempt to name people in such a way that when the person dies and they can no longer use his name, the loss of the word in the language is not inconvenient. Hence, they name people for specific and minute parts of things, such as "toenail of some rodent," thereby being able to retain the words "toenail" and "(specific) rodent," but not being able to refer directly to the toenail of that rodent. The taboo is maintained even for the living: One mark of prestige is the courtesy others show you by not using your name. The sanctions behind the taboo seem to be an unusual combination of fear and respect.

I tried to use kinship terms to collect genealogies at first, but the kinship terms were so ambiguous that I ultimately had to resort to names. They were quick to grasp that I was bound to learn everybody's name and reacted, without my knowing it, by inventing false names for everybody in the village. After having spent several months collecting names and learning them, this came as a disappointment to me: I could not cross-check the genealogies with other informants from distant villages.

They enjoyed watching me learn these names. I assumed, wrongly, that I would get the truth to each question and that I would get the best information by working in public. This set the stage for converting a serious project into a farce. Each informant tried to outdo his peers by inventing a name even more ridiculous than what I had been given earlier, or by asserting that the individual about whom I inquired was married to his mother or daughter, and the like. I would have the informant whisper the name of the individual in my ear, noting that he was the father of such and such a child. Everybody would then insist that I repeat the name aloud, roaring in hysterics as I clumsily pronounced the name. I assumed that the laughter was in response to the violation of the name taboo or to my pronunciation. This was a reasonable interpretation, since the individual whose name I said aloud invariably became angry. After I learned what some of the names meant, I began to understand what the laughter was all about. A few of the more colorful examples are: "hairy vagina," "long penis," "feces of the harpy eagle," and "dirty rectum." No wonder the victims were angry.

I was forced to do my genealogy work in private because of the horseplay and nonsense. Once I did so, my informants began to agree with each other and I managed to learn a few new names, real names. I could then test any new informant by collecting a genealogy from him that I knew to be accurate. I was able to weed out the more mischievous informants this way. Little by little I extended the genealogies and learned the real names. Still, I was unable to get the names of the dead and extend the genealogies back in time, and even my best informants continued to deceive me about their own close relatives. Most of them gave me the name of a living man as the father of some individual in order to avoid mentioning that the actual father was dead.

The quality of a genealogy depends in part on the number of generations it embraces, and the name taboo prevented me from getting any substantial information about deceased ancestors. Without this information, I could not detect marriage patterns through time. I had to rely on older informants for this information, but these were the most reluctant of all. As I became more proficient in the language and more skilled at detecting lies, my informants became better at lying. One of them in particular was so cunning and persuasive that I was shocked to discover that he had been inventing his information. He specialized in making a ceremony out of telling me false names. He would look around to make sure nobody was listening outside my hut, enjoin me to never mention the name again, act very nervous and spooky, and then grab me by the head to whisper the name very softly into my ear. I was always elated after an informant session with him, because I had several generations of dead ancestors for the living people. The others refused to give me this information. To show my gratitude, I paid him quadruple the rate I had given the others. When word got around that I had increased the pay, volunteers began pouring in to give me genealogies.

I discovered that the old man was lying quite by accident. A club fight broke out in the village one day, the result of a dispute over the possession of a woman. She had been promised to Rerebawa, a particularly aggressive young man who had married into the village. Rerebawa had already been given her older sister and was enraged when the younger girl began having an affair with another man in the village, making no attempt to conceal it from him. He challenged the young man to a club fight, but was so abusive in his challenge that the opponent's father took offense and entered the village circle with his son, wielding a long club. Rerebawa swaggered out to the duel and hurled insults at both of them, trying to goad them into striking him on the head with their clubs. This would have given him the opportunity to strike them on the head. His opponents refused to hit him, and the fight ended. Rerebawa had won a moral victory because his opponents were afraid to hit him. Thereafter, he swaggered around and insulted the two men behind their backs. He was genuinely angry with them, to the point of calling the older man by the name of his dead father. I quickly seized on this as an opportunity to collect an accurate genealogy and pumped him about his adversary's ancestors. Rerebawa had been particularly nasty to me up to this point, but we became staunch allies: We were both outsiders in the local village. I then asked about other dead ancestors and got immediate replies. He was angry with the whole group and not afraid to tell me the names of the dead. When I compared his version of the genealogies to that of the old man, it was obvious that one of them was lying. I challenged his information, and he explained that everybody knew that the old man was deceiving me and bragging about it in the village. The names the old man had given me were the dead ancestors of the members of a village so far away that he thought I would never have occasion to inquire about them. As it turned out, Rerebawa knew most of the people in that village and recognized the names.

I then went over the complete genealogical records with Rerebawa, genealogies I had presumed to be in final form. I had to revise them all because of the numerous lies and falsifications they contained. Thus, after five months of almost constant work on the genealogies of just one group, I had to begin almost from scratch!

Discouraging as it was to start over, it was still the first real turning point in my fieldwork. Thereafter, I began taking advantage of local arguments and animosities in selecting my informants, and used more extensively individuals who had married into the group. I began traveling to other villages to check the genealogies, picking villages that were on strained terms with the people about whom I wanted information. I would then return to my base camp and check with local informants the accuracy of the new information. If the informants became angry when I mentioned the new names I acquired from the unfriendly group, I was almost certain that the information was accurate. For this kind of checking I had to use informants whose genealogies I knew rather well: They had to be distantly enough related to the dead person that they would not go into a rage when I mentioned the name, but not so remotely related that they would be uncertain of the accuracy of the information. Thus, I had to make a list of names that I dared not use in the presence of each and every informant. Despite the precautions, I occasionally hit a name that put the informant into a rage, such as that of a dead brother or sister that other informants had not reported. This always terminated the day's work with that informant, for he would be too touchy to continue any further, and I would be reluctant to take a chance on accidentally discovering another dead kinsman so soon after the first.

These were always unpleasant experiences, and occasionally dangerous ones, depending on the temperament of the informant. On one occasion I was planning to visit a village that had been raided about a week earlier. A woman whose name I had on my list had been killed by the raiders. I planned to check each individual on the list one by one to estimate ages, and I wanted to remove her name so that I would not say it aloud in the village. I knew that I would be in considerable difficulty if I said this name aloud so soon after her death. I called on my original informant and asked him to tell me the name of the woman who had been killed. He refused, explaining that she was a close relative of his. I then asked him if he would become angry if I read off all the names on the list. This way he did not have to say her name and could merely nod when I mentioned the right one. He was a fairly good friend of mine, and I thought I could predict his reaction. He assured me that this would be a good way of doing it. We were alone in my hut so that nobody could overhear us. I read the names softly, continuing to the next when he gave a negative reply. When I finally spoke the name of the dead woman he flew out of his chair, raised his arm to strike me, and shouted: "You son-of-a-bitch![2] If you ever say that name again, I'll kill you!" He was shaking with rage, but left my hut quietly. I shudder to think what might have happened if I had said the name unknowingly in the woman's village. I had other, similar experiences in different villages, but luckily the dead person had been dead for some time and was not closely related to the individual into whose ear I whispered the name. I was merely cautioned to desist from saying any more names, lest I get people angry with me.

I had been working on the genealogies for nearly a year when another individual came to my aid. It was Kaobawa, the headman of Upper Bisaasi-teri, the group in which I spent most of my time. He visited me one day after the others had left the hut and volunteered to help me on the genealogies. He was poor, he explained, and needed a machete. He would work only on the condition that I did not ask him about his own parents and other very close kinsmen who were dead. He also added that he would not lie to me as the others had done in the past. This was perhaps the most important single event in my fieldwork, for out of this meeting evolved a very warm friendship and a very profitable informant-fieldworker relationship.

Kaobawa's familiarity with his group's history and his candidness were remarkable. His knowledge of details was almost encyclopedic. More than that, he was enthusiastic and encouraged me to learn details that I might otherwise have ignored. If there were things he did not know intimately, he would advise me to wait until he could check things out with someone in the village. This he would do clandestinely, giving me a report the next day. As I was constrained by my part of the bargain to avoid discussing his close dead kinsmen, I had to rely on Rerebawa for this information. I got Rerebawa's genealogy from Kaobawa.

Once again I went over the genealogies with Kaobawa to recheck them, a considerable task by this time: they included about two thousand names, representing several generations of individuals from four different villages. Rerebawa's information was very accurate, and Kaobawa's contribution enabled me to trace the genealogies further back in time. Thus, after nearly a year of constant work on genealogies, Yąnomamö demography and social organization began to fall into a pattern. Only then could I see how kin groups formed and exchanged women with each other over time, and only then did the fissioning of larger villages into smaller ones show a distinct pattern. At this point I was able to begin formulating more intelligent questions because there was now some sort of pattern to work with. Without the help of Rerebawa and Kaobawa, I could not have made very much sense of the plethora of details I had collected from dozens of other informants.

Kaobawa is about 40 years old. I say "about" because the Yąnomamö numeration system has only three numbers: one, two, and more-than-two. He is the headman of Upper Bisaasi-teri. He has had five or six wives so far and temporary affairs with as many more women, one of which resulted in a child. At the present time he has just two wives, Bahimi and Koamashima. He has had a daughter and a son by Bahimi, his eldest and favorite wife. Koamashima, about 20 years old, recently had her first child, a boy. Kaobawa may give Koamashima to his youngest brother. Even now the brother shares in her sexual services. Kaobawa recently gave his third wife to another of his brothers because she was beshi: "horny." In fact, this girl had been married to two other men, both of whom discarded her because of her infidelity. Kaobawa had one daughter by her; she is being raised by his brother.

Kaobawa's eldest wife, Bahimi, is about thirty-five years old. She is his first cross-cousin. Bahimi was pregnant when I began my fieldwork, but she killed the new baby, a boy, at birth, explaining tearfully that it would have competed with Ariwari, her nursing son, for milk. Rather than expose Ariwari to the dangers and uncertainty of an early weaning, she killed the new child instead. By Yąnomamö standards, she and Kaobawa have a very tranquil household. He only beats her once in a while, and never very hard. She never has affairs with other men.

Kaobawa is quiet, intense, wise, and unobtrusive. He leads more by example than by threats and coercion. He can afford to be this way as he established his reputation for being fierce long ago, and other men respect him. He also has five mature brothers who support him, and he has given a number of his sisters to other men in the village, thereby putting them under some obligation to him. In short, his "natural" following (kinsmen) is large, and he does not have to constantly display his ferocity. People already respect him and take his suggestions seriously.

Rerebawa is much younger, only about twenty-two years old. He has just one wife by whom he has had three children. He is from Karohi-teri, one of the villages to which Kaobawa's is allied. Rerebawa left his village to seek a wife in Kaobawa's group because there were no eligible women there for him to marry.

Rerebawa is perhaps more typical than Kaobawa in the sense that he is concerned about his reputation for ferocity and goes out of his way to act tough. He is, however, much braver than the other men his age and backs up his threats with action. Moreover, he is concerned about politics and knows the details of intervillage relationships over a large area. In this respect he shows all the attributes of a headman, although he is still too young and has too many competent older brothers in his own village to expect to move easily into the position of leadership there.

He does not intend to stay in Kaobawa's group and has not made a garden. He feels that he has adequately discharged his obligations to his wife's parents by providing them with fresh game for three years. They should let him take the wife and return to his own village with her, but they refuse and try to entice him to remain permanently in Bisaasi-teri to provide them with game when they are old. They have even promised to give him their second daughter if he will stay permanently.

Although he has displayed his ferocity in many ways, one incident in particular shows what his character is like. Before he left his own village to seek a wife, he had an affair with the wife of an older brother. When he was discovered, his brother attacked him with a club. Rerebawa was infuriated so he grabbed an axe and drove his brother out of the village after soundly beating him with the flat of the blade. The brother was so afraid that he did not return to the village for several days. I recently visited his village with him. He made a point to introduce me to this brother. Rerebawa dragged him out of his hammock by the arm and told me, "This is the brother whose wife I had an affair with," a deadly insult. His brother did nothing and slunk back into his hammock, shamed, but relieved to have Rerebawa release the vise-grip on his arm.

Despite the fact that he admires Kaobawa, he has a low opinion of the others in Bisaasi-teri. He admitted confidentially that he thought Bisaasi-teri was an abominable group: "This is a terrible neighborhood! All the young men are lazy and cowards and everybody is committing incest! I'll be glad to get back home." He also admired Kaobawa's brother, the headman of Monou-teri. This man was killed by raiders while I was doing my fieldwork. Rerebawa was disgusted that the others did not chase the raiders when they discovered the shooting: "He was the only fierce one in the whole group; he was my close friend. The cowardly Monou-teri hid like women in the jungle and didn't even chase the raiders!"

Even though Rerebawa is fierce and capable of being quite nasty, he has a good side as well. He has a very biting sense of humor and can entertain the group for hours on end with jokes and witty comments. And, he is one of few

Yąnomamö that I feel I can trust. When I returned to Bisaasi-teri after having been away for a year, Rerebawa was in his own village visiting his kinsmen. Word reached him that I had returned, and he immediately came to see me. He greeted me with an immense bear hug and exclaimed, "Shaki! Why did you stay away so long? Did you know that my will was so cold while you were gone that at times I could not eat for want of seeing you?" I had to admit that I missed him, too.

Of all the Yąnomamö I know, he is the most genuine and the most devoted to his culture's ways and values. I admire him for that, although I can't say that I subscribe to or endorse these same values. By contrast, Kaobawa is older and wiser. He sees his own culture in a different light and criticizes aspects of it he does not like. While many of his peers accept some of the superstitions and explanatory myths as truth and as the way things ought to be, Kaobawa questions them and privately pokes fun at some of them. Probably, more of the Yąnomamö are like Rerebawa, or at least try to be.

Notes

1. "Shaki," or, rather, "Shakiwa," is the name they gave me because they could not pronounce "Chagnon." They like to name people for some distinctive feature when possible. *Shaki* is the name of a species of noisome bees; they accumulate in large numbers around ripening bananas and make pests of themselves by eating into the fruit, showering the people below with the debris. They probably adopted this name for me because I was also a nuisance, continuously prying into their business, taking pictures of them, and, in general, being where they did not want me.

2. This is the closest English translation of his actual statement, the literal translation of which would be nonsensical in our language.

10 The Sounds of Silence

EDWARD T. HALL
MILDRED R. HALL

When we refer to communication, we generally think about words. People who are talking, however, use much more than words to communicate with one another. *How* they say things is just as important— sometimes more so—than *what* they say. Their inflections, tones, pauses, cadence, and loudness also convey meanings. If people are speaking face-to-face, their gestures, expressions, mannerisms, and use of space also contain significant messages.

Nonverbal communication is especially significant in conveying feelings and attitudes. Through ways so subtle that they lie beyond even our own perception—and ways so obvious that no one can miss the message—we communicate feelings of comfort and discomfort, trust and distrust, pleasure or tension, suspicions, uncertainties, desires, and a host of other feelings and concerns.

Yet we seldom think about our nonverbal communications. Our body language, for example, usually seems to be "just doing what is natural." Researchers, however, have found little that is "natural" about it. Like our speech, our body language and other forms of nonverbal communication are acquired. Thus, the specific ways by which people communicate these messages vary from one group to another, as the Halls make evident in this selection.

BOB LEAVES HIS APARTMENT at 8:15 A.M. and stops at the corner drugstore for breakfast. Before he can speak, the counterman says, "The usual?" Bob nods yes. While he savors his Danish, a fat man pushes onto the adjoining stool and overflows into his space. Bob scowls, and the man pulls himself in as much as he can. Bob has sent two messages without speaking a syllable.

Henry has an appointment to meet Arthur at 11:00 A.M.; he arrives at 11:30. Their conversation is friendly, but Arthur retains a lingering hostility. Henry has unconsciously communicated that he doesn't think the appointment is very important or that Arthur is a person who needs to be treated with respect.

George is talking to Charley's wife at a party. Their conversation is entirely trivial, yet Charley glares at them suspiciously. Their physical proximity

97

and the movements of their eyes reveal that they are powerfully attracted to each other.

José Ybarra and Sir Edmund Jones are at the same party, and it is important for them to establish a cordial relationship for business reasons. Each is trying to be warm and friendly, yet they will part with mutual distrust, and their business transaction will probably fall through. José, in Latin fashion, moves closer and closer to Sir Edmund as they speak, and this movement is being miscommunicated as pushiness to Sir Edmund, who keeps backing away from this intimacy, which in turn is being miscommunicated to José as coldness. The silent languages of Latin and English cultures are more difficult to learn than their spoken languages.

In each of these cases, we see the subtle power of nonverbal communication. The only language used throughout most of the history of humanity (in evolutionary terms, vocal communication is relatively recent), it is the first form of communication you learn. You use this preverbal language, consciously and unconsciously, every day to tell other people how you feel about yourself and them. This language includes your posture, gestures, facial expressions, costume, the way you walk, even your treatment of time and space and material things. All people communicate on several different levels at the same time but are usually aware of only the verbal dialogue and don't realize that they respond to nonverbal messages. But when a person says one thing and really believes something else, the discrepancy between the two can usually be sensed. Nonverbal communication systems are much less subject to the conscious deception that often occurs in verbal systems. When we find ourselves thinking, "I don't know what it is about him, but he doesn't seem sincere," it's usually this lack of congruity between a person's words and his behavior that makes us anxious and uncomfortable.

Few of us realize how much we all depend on body movement in our conversation or are aware of the hidden rules that govern listening behavior. But we know instantly whether or not the person we're talking to is "tuned in," and we're very sensitive to any breach in listening etiquette. In white middle-class American culture, when someone wants to show he is listening to someone else, he looks either at the other person's face or, specifically, at his eyes, shifting his gaze from one eye to the other.

If you observe a person conversing, you'll notice that he indicates he's listening by nodding his head. He also makes little "Hmm" noises. If he agrees with what's being said, he may give a vigorous nod. To show pleasure or affirmation, he smiles; if he has some reservations, he looks skeptical by raising an eyebrow or pulling down the corners of his mouth. If a participant wants to terminate the conversation, he may start shifting his body position, stretching his legs, crossing or uncrossing them, bobbing his foot, or diverting his gaze from the speaker. The more he fidgets, the more the speaker becomes aware that he has lost his audience. As a last measure, the listener may look at his watch to indicate the imminent end of the conversation.

Talking and listening are so intricately intertwined that a person cannot do one without the other. Even when one is alone and talking to oneself, there is part of the brain that speaks while another part listens. In all conversations, the listener is positively or negatively reinforcing the speaker all the time. He may even guide the conversation without knowing it, by laughing or frowning or dismissing the argument with a wave of his hand.

The language of the eyes—another age-old way of exchanging feelings—is both subtle and complex. Not only do men and women use their eyes differently, but there are class, generational, regional, ethnic, and national cultural differences. Americans often complain about the way foreigners stare at people or hold a glance too long. Most Americans look away from someone who is using his eyes in an unfamiliar way because it makes them self-conscious. If a man looks at another man's wife in a certain way, he's asking for trouble, as indicated earlier. But he might not be ill-mannered or seeking to challenge the husband. He might be a European in this country who hasn't learned our visual mores. Many American women visiting France or Italy are acutely embarrassed because, for the first time in their lives, men really look at them—their eyes, hair, nose, lips, breasts, hips, legs, thighs, knees, ankles, feet, clothes, hairdo, even their walk. These same women, once they have become used to being looked at, often return to the United States and are overcome with the feeling that "No one ever really looks at me anymore."

Analyzing the mass of data on the eyes, it is possible to sort out at least three ways in which the eyes are used to communicate: dominance vs. submission, involvement vs. detachment, and positive vs. negative attitude. In addition, there are three levels of consciousness and control, which can be categorized as follows: (1) conscious use of the eyes to communicate, such as the flirting blink and the intimate nosewrinkling squint; (2) the very extensive category of unconscious but learned behavior governing where the eyes are directed and when (this unwritten set of rules dictates how and under what circumstances the sexes, as well as people of all status categories, look at each other); and (3) the response of the eye itself, which is completely outside both awareness and control—changes in the cast (sparkle) of the eye and the pupillary reflex.

The eye is unlike any other organ of the body, for it is an extension of the brain. The unconscious pupillary reflex and the cast of the eye have been known by people of Middle Eastern origin for years—although most are unaware of their knowledge. Depending on the context, Arabs and others look directly at the eyes or deeply *into* the eyes of their interlocutor. We became aware of this in the Middle East several years ago while looking at jewelry. The merchant suddenly started to push a particular bracelet at a customer and said, "You buy this one." What interested us was that the bracelet was not the one that had been consciously selected by the purchaser. But the merchant, watching the pupils of the eyes, knew what the purchaser really wanted to buy. Whether he specifically knew *how* he knew is debatable.

A psychologist at the University of Chicago, Eckhard Hess, was the first to conduct systematic studies of the pupillary reflex. His wife remarked one evening, while watching him reading in bed, that he must be very interested in the text because his pupils were dilated. Following up on this, Hess slipped some pictures of nudes into a stack of photographs that he gave to his male assistant. Not looking at the photographs but watching his assistant's pupils, Hess was able to tell precisely when the assistant came to the nudes. In further experiments, Hess retouched the eyes in a photograph of a woman. In one print, he made the pupils small, in another, large; nothing else was changed. Subjects who were given the photographs found the woman with the dilated pupils much more attractive. Any man who has had the experience of seeing a woman look at him as her pupils widen with reflex speed knows that she's flashing him a message.

The eye-sparkle phenomenon frequently turns up in our interviews of couples in love. It's apparently one of the first reliable clues in the other person that love is genuine. To date, there is no scientific data to explain eye sparkle; no investigation of the pupil, the cornea, or even the white sclera of the eye shows how the sparkle originates. Yet we all know it when we see it.

One common situation for most people involves the use of the eyes in the street and in public. Although eye behavior follows a definite set of rules, the rules vary according to the place, the needs and feelings of the people, and their ethnic background. For urban whites, once they're within definite recognition distance (sixteen to thirty-two feet for people with average eyesight), there is mutual avoidance of eye contact—unless they want something specific: a pickup, a handout, or information of some kind. In the West and in small towns generally, however, people are much more likely to look and greet one another, even if they're strangers.

It's permissible to look at people if they're beyond recognition distance, but once inside this sacred zone, you can only steal a glance at strangers. You *must* greet friends, however; to fail to do so is insulting. Yet, to stare too fixedly even at them is considered rude and hostile. Of course, all of these rules are variable.

A great many blacks, for example, greet each other in public even if they don't know each other. To blacks, most eye behavior of whites has the effect of giving the impression that they aren't there, but this is due to white avoidance of eye contact with *anyone* in the street.

Another very basic difference between people of different ethnic backgrounds is their sense of territoriality and how they handle space. This is the silent communication, or miscommunication, that caused friction between Mr. Ybarra and Sir Edmund Jones in our earlier example. We know from the research that everyone has around himself an invisible bubble of space that contracts and expands depending on several factors: his emotional state, the activity he's performing at the time, and his cultural background. This bubble is a kind of mobile territory that he will defend against intrusion. If he is accustomed to close personal distance between himself and others, his bubble will be smaller than that of someone who's accustomed to greater personal distance. People of northern European heritage—English, Scandinavian, Swiss, and German—tend to avoid contact. Those whose heritage is Italian, French, Spanish, Russian, Latin American, or Middle Eastern like close personal contact.

People are very sensitive to any intrusion into their spatial bubble. If someone stands too close to you, your first instinct is to back up. If that's not possible, you lean away and pull yourself in, tensing your muscles. If the intruder doesn't respond to these body signals, you may then try to protect yourself, using a briefcase, umbrella, or raincoat. Women—especially when traveling alone—often plant their pocketbooks in such a way that no one can get very close to them. As a last resort, you may move to another spot and position yourself behind a desk or a chair that provides screening. Everyone tries to adjust the space around himself in a way that's comfortable for him; most often, he does this unconsciously.

Emotions also have a direct effect on the size of a person's territory. When you're angry or under stress, your bubble expands and you require more space. New York psychiatrist Augustus Kinzel found a difference in what he calls body-buffer zones between violent and nonviolent prison inmates. Dr. Kinzel conducted experiments in which each prisoner was placed in the center of a small room, and then Dr. Kinzel slowly walked toward him. Nonviolent prisoners allowed him to come quite close, while prisoners with a history of violent behavior couldn't tolerate his proximity and reacted with some vehemence.

Apparently, people under stress experience other people as looming larger and closer than they actually are. Studies of schizophrenic patients have indicated that they sometimes have a distorted perception of space, and several psychiatrists have reported patients who experience their body boundaries as filling up an entire room. For these patients, anyone who comes into the room is actually inside their body, and such an intrusion may trigger a violent outburst.

Unfortunately, there is little detailed information about normal people who live in highly congested urban areas. We do know, of course, that the noise, pollution, dirt, crowding, and confusion of our cities induce feelings of stress in most of us, and stress leads to a need for greater space. The man who's packed into a subway, jostled in the street, crowded into an elevator, and forced to work all day in a bull pen or in a small office without auditory or visual privacy is going to be very stressed at the end of his day. He needs places that provide relief from constant overstimulation of his nervous system. Stress from overcrowding is cumulative, and people can tolerate more crowding early in the day than later; note the increased bad temper during the evening rush hour as compared with the morning melee. Certainly one factor in people's desire to commute by car is the need for privacy and relief from crowding (except, often, from other cars); it may be the only time of the day when nobody can intrude.

In crowded public places, we tense our muscles and hold ourselves stiff, and thereby communicate to others our desire not to intrude on their space and, above all, not to touch them. We also avoid eye contact, and the total effect is that of someone who has "tuned out." Walking along the street, our bubble expands slightly as we move in a stream of strangers, taking care not to bump into them. In the office, at meetings, in restaurants, our bubble keeps changing as it adjusts to the activity at hand.

Most white middle-class Americans use four main distances in their business and social relations: intimate, personal, social, and public. Each of these distances has a near and a far phase and is accompanied by changes in the volume of the voice. Intimate distance varies from direct physical contact with another person to a distance of six to eighteen inches and is used for our most private activities—caressing another person or making love. At this distance, you are overwhelmed by sensory inputs from the skin, the fragrance of perfume, even the sound of breathing—all of which literally envelop you. Even at the far phase, you're still within easy touching distance. In general, the use of intimate distance in public between adults is frowned on. It's also much too close for strangers, except under conditions of extreme crowding.

In the second zone—personal distance—the close phase is one and a half to two and a half feet: it's at this distance that wives usually stand from their husbands in public. If another woman moves into this zone, the wife will most likely be disturbed. The far phase—two and a half to four feet—is the distance used to "keep someone at arm's length" and is the most common spacing used by people in conversation.

The third zone—social distance—is employed during business transactions or exchanges with a clerk or repairman. People who work together tend to use close social distance—four to seven feet. This is also the distance for conversation at social gatherings. To stand at this distance from someone who is seated has a dominating effect (e.g., teacher to pupil, boss to secretary). The far phase of the third zone—seven to twelve feet—is where people stand when someone says, "Stand back so I can look at you." This distance lends a formal tone to business or social discourse. In an executive office, the desk serves to keep people at this distance.

The fourth zone—public distance—is used by teachers in classrooms or speakers at public gatherings. At its farthest phase—twenty-five feet and beyond—it is used for important public figures. Violations of this distance can lead to serious complications. During his 1970 U.S. visit, the president of France, Georges Pompidou, was harassed by pickets in Chicago, who were permitted to get within touching distance. Since pickets in France are kept behind barricades a block or more away, the president was outraged by this insult to his person, and President Nixon was obliged to communicate his concern as well as offer his personal apologies.

It is interesting to note how American pitchmen and panhandlers exploit the unwritten, unspoken conventions of eye and distance. Both take advantage of the fact that once explicit eye contact is established, it is rude to look away, because to do so means to brusquely dismiss the other person and his needs. Once having caught the eye of his mark, the panhandler then locks on, not letting go until he moves through the public zone, the social zone, the personal zone and, finally, into the intimate sphere, where people are most vulnerable.

Touch also is an important part of the constant stream of communication that takes place between people. A light touch, a firm touch, a blow, a caress are all communications. In an effort to break down barriers among people, there's been a recent upsurge in group-encounter activities, in which strangers are encouraged to touch one another. In special situations such as these, the rules for not touching are broken with group approval, and people gradually lose some of their inhibitions.

Although most people don't realize it, space is perceived and distances are set not by vision alone but with all the senses. Auditory space is perceived with the ears, thermal space with the skin, kinesthetic space with muscles of the body, and olfactory space with the nose. And, once again, it's one's culture that determines how his senses are programmed—which sensory information ranks highest and lowest. The important thing to remember is that culture is very persistent. In this country, we've noted the existence of culture patterns that determine distance between people in the third and fourth generations of some families, despite their prolonged contact with people of very different cultural heritages.

Whenever there is great cultural distance between two people, there are bound to be problems arising from differences in behavior and expectations. An example is the American couple who consulted a psychiatrist about their marital problems. The husband was from New England and had been brought up by reserved parents who taught him to control his emotions and to respect the need for privacy. His wife was from an Italian family and had been brought up in close contact with all the members of her large family, who were extremely warm, volatile, and demonstrative.

When the husband came home after a hard day at the office, dragging his feet and longing for peace and quiet, his wife would rush to him and smother him. Clasping his hands, rubbing his brow, crooning over his weary head, she never left him alone. But when the wife was upset or anxious about her day, the husband's response was to withdraw completely and leave her alone. No comforting, no affectionate embrace, no attention—just solitude. The woman became convinced her husband didn't love her, and in desperation she consulted a psychiatrist. Their problem wasn't basically psychological but cultural.

Why has man developed all these different ways of communicating messages without words? One reason is that people don't like to spell out certain kinds of messages. We prefer to find other ways of showing our feelings. This is especially true in relationships as sensitive as courtship. Men don't like to be rejected, and most women don't want to turn a man down bluntly. Instead, we work out subtle ways of encouraging or discouraging each other that save face and avoid confrontations.

How a person handles space in dating others is an obvious and very sensitive indicator of how he or she feels about the other person. On a first date, if a woman sits or stands so close to a man that he is acutely conscious of her physical presence—inside the intimate-distance zone—the man usually construes it to mean that she is encouraging him. However, before the man starts moving in on the woman, he should be sure what message she's really sending; otherwise, he risks bruising his ego. What is close to someone of northern European background may be neutral or distant to someone of Italian heritage. Also, women sometimes use space as a way of misleading a man, and there are few things that put men off more than women who communicate contradictory messages, such as women who cuddle up and then act insulted when a man takes the next step.

How does a woman communicate interest in a man? In addition to such familiar gambits as smiling at him, she may glance shyly at him, blush, and then look away. Or she may give him a real come-on look and move in very close when he approaches. She may touch his arm and ask for a light. As she leans forward to light her cigarette, she may brush him lightly, enveloping him in her perfume. She'll probably continue to smile at him, and she may use what ethologists call preening gestures—touching the back of her hair, thrusting her breasts forward, tilting her hips at she stands, or crossing her legs if she's seated, perhaps even exposing one thigh or putting a hand on her thigh and stroking it. She may also stroke her wrists as she converses or show the palm of her hand as a way of gaining his attention. Her skin may be unusually flushed or quite pale, her eyes brighter, the pupils larger.

If a man sees a woman whom he wants to attract, he tries to present himself by his posture and stance as someone who is self-assured. He moves briskly and confidently. When he catches the eye of the woman, he may hold her glance a little longer than normal. If he gets an encouraging smile, he'll move in close and engage her in small talk. As they converse, his glance shifts over her face and body. He too, may make preening gestures—straightening his tie, smoothing his hair, or shooting his cuffs.

How do people learn body language? The same way they learn spoken language—by observing and imitating people around them as they're growing up. Little girls imitate their mothers or an older female. Little boys imitate their fathers or a respected uncle or a character on television. In this way, they learn the gender signals appropriate for their sex. Regional, class, and ethnic patterns of body behavior are also learned in childhood and persist throughout life. . . .

Nonverbal communications signal to members of your own group what kind of person you are, how you feel about others, how you'll fit into and work in a group, whether you're assured or anxious, the degree to which you feel comfortable with the standards of your own culture, as well as deeply significant feelings about the self, including the state of your own psyche. For most of us, it's difficult to accept the reality of another's behavioral system. And, of course, none of us will ever become fully knowledgeable of the importance of every nonverbal signal. But as long as each of us realizes the power of these signals, the society's diversity can be a source of great strength rather than a further—and subtly powerful—source of division.

11 The Presentation of Self in Everyday Life

ERVING GOFFMAN

All the world's a stage
And all the men and women merely players.
They have their exits and their entrances;
And one man in his time plays many parts. . . .
William Shakespeare
As You Like It, Act 2, Scene 7

This quotation from Shakespeare could well serve as the keynote for the following selection. Taking Shakespeare's statement seriously, Goffman presents a dramaturgical model of human life and uses it as the conceptual framework for understanding life-in-society. In this view, people in everyday life are actors on stage, the audience consists of those persons who observe what others are doing, the parts are the roles that people play (whether occupational, familial, friendship roles, or whatever), the dialogue consists of ritualized conversational exchanges ("Hi. How ya doin'?"; "Hey, bro', wha's hapnin'?"; "How's it goin'?"; the hellos, the goodbyes, and the in-betweens), while the costuming consists of whatever clothing happens to be in style.

Goffman's insightful analysis provides a framework from which we can gain a remarkably different perspective of what we do in life—at home, at school, with friends, while on a date, or while shopping. When understood properly, however, you may find this approach to understanding human behavior disturbing. For example, if we are all actors playing roles on the stage of life, where is the "real me"? Is all of life merely a "put-on," a masquerade of some sort? Does not this framework for understanding human interaction constitute an essentially cynical and manipulative approach to life, a sort of everyday Machiavellianism?

WHEN AN INDIVIDUAL ENTERS the presence of others, they commonly seek to acquire information about him or to bring into play information about him already possessed. They will be interested in his general socio-economic status, his conception of self, his attitude toward them, his competence, his trustworthiness, etc. Although some of this information seems to be sought almost as an end in itself, there are usually quite practical reasons for acquiring it. Information about the individual helps to define the situation, enabling others to know in advance what he will expect of them and what they may expect of him. Informed in these ways, the others will know how best to act in order to call forth a desired response from him.

For those present, many sources of information become accessible and many carriers (or "sign-vehicles") become available for conveying this information. If unacquainted with the individual, observers can glean clues from his conduct and appearance which allow them to apply their previous experience with individuals roughly similar to the one before them or, more important, to apply untested stereotypes to him. They can also assume from past experience that only individuals of a particular kind are likely to be found in a given social setting. They can rely on what the individual says about himself or on documentary evidence he provides as to who and what he is. If they know, or know of, the individual by virtue of experience prior to the interaction, they can rely on assumptions as to the persistence and generality of psychological traits as a means of predicting his present and future behavior.

However, during the period in which the individual is in the immediate presence of the others, few events may occur which directly provide the others with the conclusive information they will need if they are to direct wisely their own activity. Many crucial facts lie beyond the time and place of interaction or lie concealed within it. For example, the "true" or "real" attitudes, beliefs, and emotions of the individual can be ascertained only indirectly, through his avowals or through what appears to be involuntary expressive behavior. Similarly, if the individual offers the others a product or service, they will often find that during the interaction there will be no time and place immediately available for eating the pudding that the proof can be found in. They will be forced to accept some events as conventional or natural signs of something not directly available to the senses. In Ichheiser's terms,[1] the individual will have to act so that he intentionally or unintentionally *expresses* himself, and the others will in turn have to be *impressed* in some way by him.

The expressiveness of the individual (and therefore his capacity to give impressions) appears to involve two radically different kinds of sign activity: the expression that he *gives*, and the expression that he *gives off*. The first involves verbal symbols or their substitutes which he uses admittedly and solely to convey the information that he and the others are known to attach to these symbols. This is communication in the traditional and narrow sense. The second involves a wide range of action that others can treat as symptomatic of the actor, the expectation being that the action was performed for reasons other than the information conveyed in this way. As we shall have to see, this distinction has an only initial validity. The individual does of course intentionally convey misinformation by means of both of these types of communication, the first involving deceit, the second feigning.

Taking communication in both its narrow and broad sense, one finds that when the individual is in the immediate presence of others, his activity will have a promissory character. The others are likely to find that they must accept the individual on faith, offering him a just return while he is present before them in exchange for something whose true value will not be established until after he has left their presence. (Of course, the others also live by inference in their dealings with the physical world, but it is only in the world of social interaction that the objects about which they make inferences will purposely facilitate and hinder this inferential process.) The security that they justifiably feel in making inferences about the individual will vary, of course, depending on such factors as the amount of information they already possess about him, but no amount of such past evidence can entirely obviate the necessity of acting on the basis of inferences. As William I. Thomas suggested:

> It is also highly important for us to realize that we do not as a matter of fact lead our lives, make our decisions, and reach our goals into everyday life either statistically or scientifically. We live by inference. I am, let us say, your guest. You do not know, you cannot determine scientifically, that I will not steal your money or your spoons. But inferentially I will not, and inferentially you have me as a guest.[2]

Let us now turn from the others to the point of view of the individual who presents himself before them. He may wish them to think highly of him, or to think that he thinks highly of them, or to perceive how in fact he feels toward them, or to obtain no clearcut impression; he may wish to ensure sufficient harmony so that the interaction can be sustained, or to defraud, get rid of, confuse, mislead, antagonize, or insult them. Regardless of the particular objective which the individual has in mind and of his motive for having this objective, it will be in his interests to control the conduct of the others, especially their responsive treatment of him.[3] This control is achieved largely by influencing the definition of the situation which the others come to formulate, and he can influence this definition by expressing himself in such a way as to give them the kind of impression that will lead them to act voluntarily in accordance with his own plan. Thus, when an individual appears in the presence of others, there will usually be some reason for him to mobilize his activity so that it will convey an impression to others which it is in his interests to convey. Since a girl's dormitory mates will glean evidence of her popularity from the calls she receives on the phone, we can suspect that some girls will arrange for calls to be made, and Willard Waller's finding can be anticipated.

> It has been reported by many observers that a girl who is called to the telephone in the dormitories will often allow herself to be called several times, in order to give all the other girls ample opportunity to hear her paged.[4]

Of the two kinds of communication—expressions given and expressions given off—this report will be primarily concerned with the latter, with the more theatrical and contextual kind, the non-verbal, presumably unintentional kind, whether this communication be purposely engineered or not. As an example of what we must try to examine, I would like to cite at length a novelistic incident in which Preedy, a vacationing Englishman, makes his first appearance on the beach of his summer hotel in Spain:

> But in any case he took care to avoid catching anyone's eye. First of all, he had to make it clear to those potential companions of his holiday that they were of no concern to him whatsoever. He stared through them, round them, over them—eyes lost in space. The beach might have been empty. If by chance a ball was thrown his way, he looked surprised; then let a smile of amusement lighten his face (Kindly Preedy), looked round dazed to see that there *were* people on the beach, tossed it back with a smile to himself and not a smile *at* the people, and then resumed carelessly his nonchalant survey of space.
>
> But it was time to institute a little parade, the parade of the Ideal Preedy. By devious handlings he gave any one who wanted to look a chance to see the title of the book—a Spanish translation of Homer, classic thus, but not daring, cosmopolitan too—and then gathered together his beachwrap and bag into a neat sand-resistant pile (Methodical and Sensible Preedy), rose slowly to stretch at ease his huge frame (Big-Cat Preedy), and tossed aside his sandals (Carefree Preedy, after all).
>
> The marriage of Preedy and the sea! There was alternate rituals. The first involved the stroll that turns into a run and a dive straight into the water, thereafter smoothing into a strong splashless crawl towards the horizon. But of course not really to the horizon. Quite suddenly he would turn on to his back and thrash great white splashes with his legs, somehow thus showing that he could have swum further had he wanted to, and then would stand up a quarter out of water for all to see who it was.
>
> The alternative course was simpler; it avoided the cold-water shock, and it avoided the risk of appearing too high-spirited. The point was to appear to be so used to the sea, the Mediterranean, and this particular beach, that one might as well be in the sea as out of it. It involved a slow stroll down and into the edge of the water—not even noticing his toes were wet, land and water all the same to *him!*—with his eyes up at the sky gravely surveying portents, invisible to others, of the weather (Local Fisherman Preedy).[5]

The novelist means us to see that Preedy is improperly concerned with the extensive impressions he feels his sheer bodily action is giving off to those around him. We can malign Preedy further by assuming that he has acted merely in order to give a particular impression, that this is a false impression, and that the others present receive either no impression at all, or worse still, the impression that Preedy is affectedly trying to cause them to receive. But the important point for us here is that the kind of impression Preedy thinks he is making is in fact the kind of impression that others correctly and incorrectly glean from someone in their midst.

I have said that when an individual appears before others his actions will influence the definition of the situation which they come to have. Sometimes the individual will act in a thoroughly calculating manner, expressing himself in a given way solely in order to give the kind of impression to others that is likely to evoke from them a specific response he is concerned to obtain. Sometimes the individual will be calculating in his activity but be relatively unaware that this is the case. Sometimes he will intentionally and consciously express himself in a particular way, but chiefly because the traditions of his group or social status require this kind of expression and not because of any particular response (other than vague acceptance or approval) that is likely to be evoked from those impressed by the expression. Sometimes the traditions of an individual's role will lead him to give a well-designed impression of a particular kind and yet he may be neither consciously nor unconsciously disposed to create such an impression. The others, in their turn, may be suitably impressed by the individual's efforts to convey something, or may misunderstand the situation and come to conclusions that are warranted neither by the individual's intent nor by the facts. In any case, in so far as the others act *as if* the individual had conveyed a particular impression, we may take a functional or pragmatic view and say that the individual has "effectively" projected a given definition of the situation and "effectively" fostered the understanding that a given state of affairs obtains.

There is one aspect of the others' response that bears special comment here. Knowing that the individual is likely to present himself in a light that is favorable to him, the others may divide what they witness into two parts: a part that is relatively easy for the individual to manipulate at will, being chiefly his verbal assertions, and a part in regard to which he seems to have little concern or control, being chiefly derived from the expressions he gives off. The others may then use what are considered to be the ungovernable aspects of his expressive behavior as a check upon the validity of what is conveyed by the governable aspects. In this a fundamental asymmetry is demonstrated in the communication process, the individual presumably being aware of only one stream of his communication, the witness of this stream and one other. For example, in Shetland Isle one crofter's wife, in serving native dishes to a visitor from the mainland of Britain, would listen with a polite smile to his polite claims of liking what he was eating; at the same time she would take note of the rapidity with which the visitor lifted his fork or spoon to his mouth, the eagerness with which he passed food into his mouth, and the gusto expressed in chewing the food, using these signs as a check on the stated feelings of the eater. The same woman, in order to discover what one acquaintance (A) "actually" thought of another acquaintance (B), would wait until B was in the presence of A but engaged in conversation with still another person (C). She would then covertly examine the facial expressions of A as he regarded B in conversation with C. Not being in conversation with B, and not being directly observed by him, A would sometimes relax usual constraints and tactful deceptions, and freely express what he was "actually" feeling about B. This Shetlander, in short, would observe the unobserved observer.

Now given the fact that others are likely to check up on the more controllable aspects of behavior by means of the less controllable, one can expect that sometimes the individual will try to exploit this very possibility, guiding the impression he makes through behavior felt to be reliably informing.[6] For example, in gaining admission to a tight social circle, the participant observer may not only wear an accepting look while listening to an informant, but may also be careful to wear the same look when observing the informant talking to others; observers of the observer will then not as easily discover where he actually stands. A specific illustration may be cited from Shetland Isle. When a neighbor dropped in to have a cup of tea, he would ordinarily wear at least a hint of an expectant warm smile as he passed through the door into the cottage. Since lack of physical obstructions outside the cottage and lack of light within it usually made it possible to observe the visitor unobserved as he approached the house, islanders sometimes took pleasure in watching the visitor drop whatever expression he was manifesting and replace it with a sociable one just before reaching the door. However, some visitors, in appreciating that this examination was occurring, would blindly adopt a social face a long distance from the house, thus ensuring the projection of a constant image.

This kind of control upon the part of the individual reinstates the symmetry of the communication process, and sets the stage for a kind of information game—a potentially infinite cycle of concealment, discovery, false revelation, and rediscovery. It should be added that since the others are likely to be relatively unsuspicious of the presumably unguided aspect of the individual's conduct, he can gain much by controlling it. The others of course may sense that the individual is manipulating the presumably spontaneous aspects of his behavior, and seek in this very act of manipulation some shading of conduct that the individual has not managed to control. This again provides a check upon the individual's behavior, this time his presumably uncalculated behavior, thus re-establishing the asymmetry of the communication process. Here I would like only to add the suggestion that the arts of piercing an individual's effort at calculated unintentionality seem better developed than our capacity to manipulate our own behavior, so that regardless of how many steps have occurred in the information game, the witness is likely to have the advantage over the actor, and the initial asymmetry of the communication process is likely to be retained.

When we allow that the individual projects a definition of the situation when he appears before others, we must also see that the others, however passive their role may seem to be, will themselves effectively project a definition of the situation by virtue of their response to the individual and by virtue of any lines of action they initiate to him. Ordinarily the definitions of the situation projected by the several different participants are sufficiently attuned to one another so that open contradiction will not occur. I do not mean that there will be the kind of consensus that arises when each individual present candidly expresses what he really feels and honestly agrees with the expressed feelings of the others present. This kind of harmony is an optimistic ideal and in any case not necessary for the smooth working of society. Rather, each participant is expected to suppress his immediate heartfelt feelings, conveying a view of the situation which he feels the others will be able to find at least temporarily acceptable. The maintenance of this surface of agreement, this veneer of consensus, is facilitated by each participant concealing his own wants behind statements which assert values to which everyone present feels obliged to give lip service. Further, there is usually a kind of division of definitional labor. Each participant is allowed to establish the tentative official ruling regarding matters which are vital to him but not immediately important to others, e.g., the rationalizations and justifications by which he accounts for his past activity. In exchange for this courtesy he remains silent or noncommittal on matters important to others but not immediately important to him. We have then a kind of interactional *modus vivendi.* Together, the participants contribute to a single over-all definition of the situation which involves not so much a real agreement as to what exists but rather a real agreement as to whose claims concerning what issues will be temporarily honored. Real agreement will also exist concerning the desirability of avoiding an open conflict of definitions of the situation.[7] I will refer to this level of agreement as a "working consensus." It is to be understood that the working consensus established in one interaction setting will be quite different in content from the working consensus established in a different type of setting. Thus, between two friends at lunch, a reciprocal show of affection, respect, and concern for the other is maintained. In service occupations, on the other hand, the specialist often maintains an image of disinterested involvement in the problem of the client, while the client responds with a show of respect for the competence and integrity of the specialist. Regardless of such differences in content, however, the general form of these working arrangements is the same.

In noting the tendency for a participant to accept the definitional claims made by the others present, we can appreciate the crucial importance of the information that the individual *initially* possesses or acquires concerning his fellow participants, for it is on the basis of this initial information that the individual starts to define the situation and starts to build up lines of responsive action. The individual's initial projection commits him to what he is proposing to be and requires him to drop all pretenses of being other things. As the interaction among the participants progresses, additions and modifications in this initial informational state will of course occur, but it is essential that these later developments be related without contradiction to, and even built up from, the initial positions taken by the several participants. It would seem that an individual can more easily make a choice as to what line of treatment to demand from and extend to the others present at the beginning of an encounter than he can alter the line of treatment that is being pursued once the interaction is under way.

In everyday life, of course, there is a clear understanding that first impressions are important. Thus, the work adjustment of those in service occupations will often hinge upon a capacity to seize and hold the initiative in the service relation, a capacity that will require subtle aggressiveness on the part of the server when he is of lower socio-economic status than his client. W. F. Whyte suggests the waitress as an example:

> The first point that stands out is that the waitress who bears up under pressure does not simply respond to her customers. She acts with some skill to control their behavior. The first question to ask when we look at the customer relationship is, "Does the waitress get the jump on the customer, or does the customer get the jump on the waitress?" The skilled waitress realizes the crucial nature of this question. . . .
>
> The skilled waitress tackles the customer with confidence and without hesitation. For example, she may find that a new customer has seated himself before she could clear off the dirty dishes and change the cloth. He is now leaning on the table studying the menu. She greets him, says, "May I change the cover, please?" and, without waiting for an answer, takes his menu away from him so that he moves back from the table, and she goes about her work. The relationship is handled politely but firmly, and there is never any question as to who is in charge.[8]

When the interaction that is initiated by "first impressions" is itself merely the initial interaction in an extended series of interactions involving the same participants, we speak of "getting off on the right foot" and feel that it is crucial that we do so. Thus, one learns that some teachers take the following view:

> You can't ever let them get the upper hand on you or you're through. So I start out tough. The first day I get a new class in, I let them know who's boss. . . . You've got to start off tough; then you can ease up as you go along. If you start out easy-going, when you try to be tough, they'll just look at you and laugh.[9]

Similarly, attendants in mental institutions may feel that if the new patient is sharply put in his place the first day on the ward and made to see who is boss, much future difficulty will be prevented.[10]

Given the fact that the individual effectively projects a definition of the situation when he enters the presence of others, we can assume that events may occur within the interaction which contradict, discredit, or otherwise throw doubt upon this projection. When these disruptive events occur, the interaction itself may come to a confused and embarrassed halt. Some of the assumptions upon which the responses of the participants had been predicted become untenable, and the participants find themselves lodged in an interaction for which the situation has been wrongly defined and is now no longer defined. At such moments the individual whose presentation has been discredited may feel ashamed while the others present may feel hostile, and all the participants may come to feel ill at ease, nonplussed, out of countenance, embarrassed, experiencing the kind of anomy that is generated when the minute social system of face-to-face interaction breaks down.

In stressing the fact that the initial definition of the situation projected by an individual tends to provide a plan for the cooperative activity that follows— in stressing this action point of view—we must not overlook the crucial fact that any projected definition of the situation also has a distinctive moral character. It is this moral character of projections that will chiefly concern us in this report. Society is organized on the principle that any individual who possesses certain social characteristics has a moral right to expect that others will value and treat him in an appropriate way. Connected with this principle is a second, namely that an individual who implicitly or explicitly signifies that he has certain social characteristics ought in fact to be what he claims he is. In consequence, when an individual projects a definition of the situation and thereby makes an implicit or explicit claim to be a person of a particular kind, he automatically exerts a moral demand upon the others, obliging them to value and treat him in the manner that persons of his kind have a right to expect. He also implicitly forgoes all claims to be things he does not appear to be[11] and hence forgoes the treatment that would be appropriate for such individuals. The others find, then, that the individual has informed them as to what is and as to what they *ought* to see as the "is."

One cannot judge the importance of definitional disruptions by the frequency with which they occur, for apparently they would occur more frequently were not constant precautions taken. We find that preventive practices are constantly employed to avoid these embarrassments and that corrective practices are constantly employed to compensate for discrediting occurrences that have not been successfully avoided. When the individual employs these strategies and tactics to protect his own projections, we may refer to them as "defensive practices"; when a participant employs them to save the definition of the situation projected by another, we speak of "protective practices" or "tact." Together, defensive and protective practices comprise the techniques employed to safeguard the impression fostered by an individual during his presence before others. It should be added that while we may be ready to see that no fostered impression would survive if defensive practices were not employed, we are less ready perhaps to see that few impressions could survive if those who received the impression did not exert tact in their reception of it.

In addition to the fact that precautions are taken to prevent disruption of projected definitions, we may also note that an intense interest in these disruptions comes to play a significant role in the social life of the group. Practical jokes and social games are played in which embarrassments which are to be taken unseriously are purposely engineered.[12] Fantasies are created in which devastating exposures occur. Anecdotes from the past—real, embroidered, or fictitious—are told and retold, detailing disruptions which occurred, almost occurred, or occurred and were admirably resolved. There seems to be no grouping which does not have a ready supply of these games, reveries, and cautionary tales, to be used as a source of humor, a catharsis for anxieties, and a sanction for inducing individuals to be modest in their claims and reasonable in their projected expectations. The individual may tell himself through dreams of getting into impossible positions. Families tell of the time a guest got his dates mixed and arrived when neither the house nor anyone in it was ready for him. Journalists tell of times when an all-too-meaningful misprint occurred, and the paper's assumption of objectivity or decorum was humorously discredited. Public servants tell of times a client ridiculously misunderstood form instructions, giving answers which implied an unanticipated and bizarre definition of the situation.[13] Seamen, whose home away from home is rigorously he-man, tell stories of coming back home and inadvertently asking mother to "pass the fucking butter."[14] Diplomats tell of the time a nearsighted queen asked a republican ambassador about the health of his king.[15]

To summarize, then, I assume that when an individual appears before others he will have many motives for trying to control the impression they receive of the situation.

Notes

1. Gustav Ichheiser, "Misunderstandings in Human Relations," Supplement to *The American Journal of Sociology,* 55 (September, 1949):6–7.

2. Quoted in E. H. Volkart, editor, *Social Behavior and Personality,* Contributions of W. I. Thomas to Theory and Social Research (New York: Social Science Research Council, 1951), p. 5.

3. Here I owe much to an unpublished paper by Tom Burns of the University of Edinburgh. He presents the argument that in all interaction a basic underlying theme is the desire of each participant to guide and control the responses made by the others present. A similar argument has been advanced by Jay Haley in a recent unpublished paper, but in regard to a special kind of control, that having to do with defining the nature of the relationship of those involved in the interaction.

4. Willard Waller, "The Rating and Dating Complex," *American Sociological Review,* 2:730.

5. William Sansom, *A Contest of Ladies* (London: Hogarth, 1956), pp. 230–32.

6. The widely read and rather sound writings of Stephen Potter are concerned in part with signs that can be engineered to give a shrewd observer the apparently incidental cues he needs to discover concealed virtues the gamesman does not in fact possess.

7. An interaction can be purposely set up as a time and place for voicing differences in opinion, but in such cases participants must be careful to agree not to disagree on the proper tone of voice, vocabulary, and degree of seriousness in which all arguments are to be phrased, and upon the mutual respect which disagreeing participants must carefully continue to express toward one another. This debaters' or academic definition of the situation may also be invoked suddenly and judiciously as a way of translating a serious conflict of views into one that can be handled within a framework acceptable to all present.

8. W. F. Whyte, "When Workers and Customers Meet," Chap. VII, *Industry and Society,* ed. W. F. Whyte (New York: McGraw-Hill, 1946), pp. 132–33.

9. Teacher interview quoted by Howard S. Becker, "Social Class Variations in the Teacher-Pupil Relationship," *Journal of Educational Sociology,* 25:459.

10. Harold Taxel, "Authority Structure in a Mental Hospital Ward" (unpublished Master's thesis, Department of Sociology, University of Chicago, 1953).

11. This role of the witness in limiting what it is the individual can be has been stressed by Existentialists, who see it as a basic threat to individual freedom. See Jean-Paul Sartre, *Being and Nothingness,* trans. by Hazel E. Barnes (New York: Philosophical Library, 1956), pp. 365 ff.

12. Erving Goffman, "Communication Conduct in an Island Community" (unpublished Ph.D. dissertation, Department of Sociology, University of Chicago, 1953), pp. 319–27.

13. Peter Blau, *Dynamics of Bureaucracy: A Study of Interpersonal Relationships in Two Government Agencies,* 2nd ed. (Chicago: University of Chicago Press, 1963).

14. Walter M. Beattie, Jr., "The Merchant Seaman" (unpublished M. A. Report, Department of Sociology, University of Chicago, 1950), p. 35.

15. Sir Frederick Ponsonby, *Recollections of Three Reigns* (New York: Dutton, 1952), p. 46.

PART IV Socialization and Gender

Essential to our survival following birth is *socialization*—learning to become full-fledged members of a human group. As we saw in Part III, this learning involves such fundamental, taken-for-granted aspects of group life as ideas of health and morality, and the many nuances of nonverbal communication. We saw that socialization involves learning rules (what we should and should not do under different circumstances) and values (what is considered good or bad, desirable or undesirable), as well as expectations about how we should present the self in different social settings.

The agents of socialization include our parents, brothers and sisters and other relatives, friends and neighbors, as well as clergy and school teachers. They also include people we do not know and never will know, such as clerks and shoppers who, by their very presence—and the expectations we know they have of us—help to bring our behavior under control in public settings and thereby shape it for similar situations in the future. Through this process of socialization each of us develops a *personality,* the tendency to behave in particular ways, which distinguishes us from others.

Essential to our forming an identity is socialization into gender—that is, our learning how to be masculine or feminine. (The term *sex* refers to biological characteristics, while the term *gender* refers to social expectations based on those characteristics. We inherit our sex, but we learn our gender. Sex is male or female, while gender is masculinity or femininity.)

Although we come into the world with the biological equipment of a male or female, these physical organs do not determine what we shall be like as a male or a female. Whether or not we defer to members of the opposite sex, for example, is not an automatic result of our particular sexual equipment but is due to what we learn is proper for us because of the particular biological

117

equipment we possess. This learning process is called *gender* or *sex role social-ization.*

Our gender extends into almost every area of our lives, even into situa-tions for which it may be quite irrelevant. For example, if we are grocery clerks, by means of our clothing, language, and gestures we communicate to others that we are *male* or *female* clerks. Because gender cuts across most as-pects of social life, it sometimes is referred to as a *master trait.*

Challenged for generations (the Women's Movement was active before our grandparents were born), the traditional expectations attached to the sexes have undergone substantial modification in recent years. One can no longer safely assume particular behavior on the part of another simply because of that person's sex. In spite of such changes, however, most Americans appear to fol-low rather traditional lines as they socialize their children. The changes take place slowly, and male dominance remains a fact of social life.

What would we humans be like if we were untouched by culture? Although there is much speculation, no one knows the answer to this question, for any behavior or attitude that we examine is embedded within cultural learning. The closest we can come is to look at children who have received the least introduction to a culture—as Kingsley Davis does in the opening selec-tion. Even isolated children, such as Anna and Isabelle, however, have still been exposed to a culture, although minimally. One really cannot think of hu-manity apart from culture, then, for culture shapes humanity.

In the past, an occasional naked, wild-looking child was discovered living alone in the wilderness, walking and crawling on all fours, pouncing on small animals and eating them raw. Such *feral* ("wild") *children* were thought to have been raised by animals and to be untouched by human culture. Although documented cases of feral children exist—one boy discovered in 1798 was even studied intensely by scientists—the presumption today is that feral chil-dren had been abandoned by their parents because they were mentally handi-capped. Consequently, the study of feral children does not answer the ques-tion of what humans would be like if they were untouched by culture. If it did, the answer would not be encouraging—granted the lack of language, pouncing on and devouring small animals, and so on.

It is through our association with other humans, then, that we learn what it means to be human. Essential to this process is gender socialization, the pri-mary focus in Part IV. We want to explore the question of how males and fe-males learn gender, the sex roles they are socially destined to play. Memories of childhood may surface while reading my analysis of some of the processes by which males are socialized into social dominance. Focusing on childhood, I examine experiences that direct males into a world distinct from the female world, that often lead boys and men to think of themselves as superior, and that later make it difficult for men to communicate in depth with women and to maintain "significant relationships" with the opposite sex. Barrie Thorne and Zella Luria then place the sociological spotlight on the world of children, examining how school children separate their activities and friendships on the basis of sex, and engage in forms of play that help to maintain male dominance in society. Following this analysis, Deborah Tannen analyzes how men and women express themselves, highlighting differences that not only hamper communication but which also may reflect underlying differences in orientations to social life.

Taken together, these articles help us to better understand how gender pervades our lives. They ought to provide considerable insight into your own socialization into gender—how you became masculine or feminine—and, once propelled into that role, how social constraints continue to influence your attitudes and behaviors.

12 Extreme Isolation

KINGSLEY DAVIS

What could the editor possibly mean by this article's heading in the table of contents: "Learning to be human"? Isn't it obvious that we humans are born human? Certainly that is true concerning our *biological* characteristics, that is, our possession of arms, legs, head, and torso, as well as our internal organs.

But to act like other people, to think the way others think—and perhaps even the ability to think—are *learned* characteristics. These are the result of years of exposure to people living in groups, especially the acquisition of language.

Just how much does biology contribute to what we are, and how much is due to social life? (Or, in Davis's terms, what are the relative contributions of the biogenic and the sociogenic factors?) Although this question has intrigued many, no one has yet been able to unravel its mystery. According to Davis's observations, however, the contributions of the social group reach much farther and are of greater fundamental consequence than most of us imagine. Our speech, for example, helps shape our basic attitudes and orientations to life. As indicated in this article, however, the social group may even contribute such ordinarily presumed biological characteristics as our ability to walk. Although this selection will not present any "final answers" to this age-old question, it should stir up your sociological imagination.

EARLY IN 1940 THERE APPEARED . . . an account of a girl called Anna.[1] She had been deprived of normal contact and had received a minimum of human care for almost the whole of her first six years of life. At this time observations were not complete and the report had a tentative character. Now, however, the girl is dead, and with more information available,[2] it is possible to give a fuller and more definitive description of the case from a sociological point of view.

Anna's death, caused by hemorrhagic jaundice, occurred on August 6, 1942. Having been born on March 1 or 6,[3] 1932, she was approximately ten and a half years of age when she died. The previous report covered her development up to the age of almost eight years; the present one recapitulates the earlier period on the basis of new evidence and then covers the last two and a half years of her life.

Early History

The first few days and weeks of Anna's life were complicated by frequent changes of domicile. It will be recalled that she was an illegitimate child, the second such child born to her mother, and that her grandfather, a widowed farmer in whose house her mother lived, strongly disapproved of this new evidence of the mother's indiscretion. This fact led to the baby's being shifted about.

Two weeks after being born in a nurse's private home, Anna was brought to the family farm, but the grandfather's antagonism was so great that she was shortly taken to the house of one of her mother's friends. At this time a local minister became interested in her and took her to his house with an idea of possible adoption. He decided against adoption, however, when he discovered that she had vaginitis. The infant was then taken to a children's home in the nearest large city. This agency found that at the age of only three weeks she was already in a miserable condition, being "terribly galled and otherwise in very bad shape." It did not regard her as a likely subject for adoption but took her in for a while anyway, hoping to benefit her. After Anna had spent nearly eight weeks in this place, the agency notified her mother to come and get her. The mother responded by sending a man and his wife to the children's home with a view to their adopting Anna, but they made such a poor impression on the agency that permission was refused. Later the mother came herself and took the child out of the home and then gave her to this couple. It was in the home of this pair that a social worker found the girl a short time thereafter. The social worker went to the mother's home and pleaded with Anna's grandfather to allow the mother to bring the child home. In spite of threats, he refused. The child, by then more than four months old, was next taken to another children's home in a near-by town. A medical examination at this time revealed that she had impetigo, vaginitis, umbilical hernia, and a skin rash.

Anna remained in this second children's home for nearly three weeks, at the end of which time she was transferred to a private foster-home. Since, however, the grandfather would not, and the mother could not, pay for the child's care, she was finally taken back as a last resort to the grandfather's house (at the age of five and a half months). There she remained, kept on the second floor in an attic-like room because her mother hesitated to incur the grandfather's wrath by bringing her downstairs.

The mother, a sturdy woman weighing about 180 pounds, did a man's work on the farm. She engaged in heavy work such as milking cows and tending hogs and had little time for her children. Sometimes she went out at night, in which case Anna was left entirely without attention. Ordinarily, it seems, Anna received only enough care to keep her barely alive. She appears to have been seldom moved from one position to another. Her clothing and bedding were filthy. She apparently had no instruction, no friendly attention.

It is little wonder that, when finally found and removed from the room in the grandfather's house at the age of nearly six years, the child could not talk, walk, or do anything that showed intelligence. She was in an extremely emaciated and undernourished condition, with skeletonlike legs and a bloated abdomen. She had been fed on virtually nothing except cow's milk during the years under her mother's care.

Anna's condition when found, and her subsequent improvement, have been described in the previous report. It now remains to say what happened to her after that.

Later History

In 1939, nearly two years after being discovered, Anna had progressed, as previously reported, to the point where she could walk, understand simple commands, feed herself, achieve some neatness, remember people, etc. But she still did not speak, and, though she was much more like a normal infant of something over one year of age in mentality, she was far from normal for her age.

On August 30, 1939, she was taken to a private home for retarded children, leaving the county home where she had been for more than a year and a half. In her new setting she made some further progress, but not a great deal. In a report of an examination made November 6 of the same year, the head of the institution pictured the child as follows:

> Anna walks about aimlessly, makes periodic rhythmic motions of her hands, and, at intervals, makes guttural and sucking noises. She regards her hands as if she had seen them for the first time. It was impossible to hold her attention for more than a few seconds at a time—not because of distraction due to external stimuli but because of her inability to concentrate. She ignored the task in hand to gaze vacantly about the room. Speech is entirely lacking. Numerous unsuccessful attempts have been made with her in the hope of developing initial sounds. I do not believe that this failure is due to negativism or deafness but that she is not sufficiently developed to accept speech at this time. . . . The prognosis is not favorable. . . .

More than five months later, on April 25, 1940, a clinical psychologist, the late Professor Francis N. Maxfield, examined Anna and reported the following: large for her age; hearing "entirely normal"; vision apparently normal; able to climb stairs; speech in the "babbling stage" and "promise for developing intelligible speech later seems to be good." He said further that "on the Merrill–Palmer scale she made a mental score of 19 months. On the Vineland social maturity scale she made a score of 23 months.[4]

Professor Maxfield very sensibly pointed out that prognosis is difficult in such cases of isolation. "It is very difficult to take scores on tests standardized under average conditions of environment and experience," he wrote, "and interpret them in a case where environment and experience have been so unusual." With this warning he gave it as his opinion at that time that Anna would eventually "attain an adult mental level of six or seven years."[5]

The school for retarded children, on July 1, 1941, reported that Anna had reached 46 inches in height and weighed 60 pounds. She could bounce and catch a ball and was said to conform to group socialization, though as a follower rather than a leader. Toilet habits were firmly established. Food habits were normal, except that she still used a spoon as her sole implement. She could dress herself except for fastening her clothes. Most remarkable of all, she had finally begun to develop speech. She was characterized as being at about the two-year level in this regard. She could call attendants by name and bring in one when she was asked to. She had a few complete sentences to express her wants. The report concluded that there was nothing peculiar about her, except that she was feebleminded—"probably congenital in type."[6]

A final report from the school made on June 22, 1942, and evidently the last report before the girl's death, pictured only a slight advance over that given above. It said that Anna could follow directions, string beads, identify a few colors, build with blocks, and differentiate between attractive and unattractive pictures. She had a good sense of rhythm and loved a doll. She talked mainly in phrases but would repeat words and try to carry on a conversation. She was clean about clothing. She habitually washed her hands and brushed her teeth. She would try to help other children. She walked well and could run fairly well, though clumsily. Although easily excited, she had a pleasant disposition.

Interpretation

Such was Anna's condition just before her death. It may seem as if she had not made much progress, but one must remember the condition in which she had been found. One must recall that she had no glimmering of speech, absolutely no ability to walk, no sense of gesture, not the least capacity to feed herself even when the food was put in front of her, and no comprehension of cleanliness. She was so apathetic that it was hard to tell whether or not she could hear. And all this at the age of nearly six years. Compared with this condition, her capacities at the time of her death seem striking indeed, though they do not amount to much more than a two-and-a-half-year mental level. One conclusion therefore seems safe, namely, that her isolation prevented a considerable amount of mental development that was undoubtedly part of her capacity. Just what her original capacity was, of course, is hard to say; but her development after her period of confinement (including the ability to walk and run, to play, dress, fit into a social situation, and, above all, to speak) shows that she had at least this capacity—capacity that never could have been realized in her original condition of isolation.

A further question is this: What would she have been like if she had received a normal upbringing from the moment of birth? A definitive answer would have been impossible in any case, but even an approximate answer is made difficult by her early death. If one assumes, as was tentatively surmised in the previous report, that it is "almost impossible for any child to learn to speak, think, and act like a normal person after a long period of early isolation," it seems likely that Anna might have had a normal or near-normal capacity, genetically speaking. On the other hand, it was pointed out that Anna represented "a marginal case, [because] she was discovered before she had reached six years of age," an age "young enough to allow for some plasticity."[7] While admitting, then, that Anna's isolation *may* have been the major cause (and was certainly a minor cause) of her lack of rapid mental progress during the four and a half years following her rescue from neglect, it is necessary to entertain the hypothesis that she was congenitally deficient.

In connection with this hypothesis, one suggestive though by no means conclusive circumstance needs consideration, namely, the mentality of Anna's forebears. Information on this subject is easier to obtain, as one might guess, on the mother's than on the father's side. Anna's maternal grandmother, for example, is said to have been college educated and wished to have her children receive a good education, but her husband, Anna's stern grandfather, apparently a shrewd, hard-driving, calculating farmowner, was so penurious that her ambitions in this direction were thwarted. Under the circumstances her daughter (Anna's mother) managed, despite having to do hard work on the farm, to complete the eighth grade in a country school. Even so, however, the daughter was evidently not very smart. "A schoolmate of [Anna's mother] stated that she was retarded in school work; was very gullible at this age; and that her morals even at this time were discussed by other students." Two tests administered to her on March 4, 1938, when she was thirty-two years of age, showed that she was mentally deficient. On the Standard Revision of the Binet–Simon Scale her performance was equivalent to that of a child of eight years, giving her an I.Q. of 50 and indicating mental deficiency of "middle-grade moron type."[8]

As to the identity of Anna's father, the most persistent theory holds that he was an old man about seventy-four years of age at the time of the girl's birth. If he was the one, there is no indication of mental or other biological deficiency, whatever one may think of his morals. However, someone else may actually have been the father.

To sum up: Anna's heredity is the kind that *might* have given rise to innate mental deficiency, though not necessarily.

Comparison with Another Case

Perhaps more to the point than speculations about Anna's ancestry would be a case for comparison. If a child could be discovered who had been isolated about the same length of time as Anna but had achieved a much quicker recovery and a greater mental development, it would be a stronger indication that Anna was deficient to start with.

Such a case does exist. It is the case of a girl found at about the same time as Anna and under strikingly similar circumstances. A full description of the details of this case has not been published, but in addition to newspaper reports, an excellent preliminary account by a speech specialist, Dr. Marie K. Mason, who played an important role in the handling of the child, has appeared.[9] Also the late Dr. Francis N. Maxfield, clinical psychologist at Ohio State University, as was Dr. Mason, has written an as yet unpublished but penetrating analysis of the case.[10] Some of his observations have been included in Professor Zingg's book on feral man.[11] The following discussion is drawn mainly from these enlightening materials. The writer, through the kindness of Professors Mason and Maxfield, did have a chance to observe the girl in April, 1940, and to discuss the features of her case with them.

Born apparently one month later than Anna, the girl in question, who has been given the pseudonym Isabelle, was discovered in November, 1938, nine months after the discovery of Anna. At the time she was found she was approximately six and a half years of age. Like Anna, she was an illegitimate child and had been kept in seclusion for that reason. Her mother was a deaf-mute, having become so at the age of two, and it appears that she and Isabelle had spent most of their time together in a dark room shut off from the rest of the mother's family. As a result Isabelle had no chance to develop speech; when she communicated with her mother, it was by means of gestures. Lack of sunshine and inadequacy of diet had caused Isabelle to become rachitic. Her legs in particular were affected; they "were so bowed that as she stood erect the soles of her shoes came nearly flat together, and she got about with a skittering gait."[12] Her behavior toward strangers, especially men, was almost that of a wild animal, manifesting much fear and hostility. In lieu of speech she made only a strong croaking sound. In many ways she acted like an infant. "She was apparently utterly unaware of relationships of any kind. When presented with a ball for the first time, she held it in the palm of her hand, then reached out and stroked my face with it. Such behavior is comparable to that of a child of six months."[13] At first it was even hard to tell whether or not she could hear, so unused were her senses. Many of her actions resembled those of deaf children.

It is small wonder that, once it was established that she could hear, specialists working with her believed her to be feeble-minded. Even on nonverbal tests her performance was so low as to promise little for the future. Her first score on the Stanford–Binet was 19 months, practically at the zero point of the scale. On the Vineland social maturity scale her first score was 39, representing an age level of two and a half years.[14] "The general impression was that she was wholly uneducable and that any attempt to teach her to speak, after so long a period of silence, would meet with failure."[15]

In spite of this interpretation, the individuals in charge of Isabelle launched a systematic and skillful program of training. It seemed hopeless at first. The approach had to be through pantomime and dramatization, suitable to an infant. It required one week of intensive effort before she even made her first attempt at vocalization. Gradually she began to respond, however, and, after the first hurdles had at last been overcome, a curious thing happened. She went through the usual stages of learning characteristic of the years from one to six not only in proper succession but far more rapidly than normal. In a little over two months after her first vocalization she was putting sentences together. Nine months after that she could identify words and sentences on the printed page, could write well, could add to ten, and could retell a story after hearing it. Seven months beyond this point she had a vocabulary of 1,500–2,000 words and was asking complicated questions. Starting from an educational level of between one and three years (depending on what aspect one considers), she had reached a normal level by the time she was eight and a half years old. In short, she covered in two years the stages of learning that ordinarily require six.[16] Or, to put it another way, her I.Q. trebled in a year and a half.[17] The speed with which she reached the normal level of mental development seems analogous to the recovery of body weight in a growing child after an illness, the recovery being achieved by an extra fast rate of growth for a period after the illness until normal weight for the given age is again attained.

When the writer saw Isabelle a year and a half after her discovery, she gave him the impression of being a very bright, cheerful, energetic little girl. She spoke well, walked and ran without trouble, and sang with gusto and accuracy. Today she is over fourteen years old and has passed the sixth grade in a public school. Her teachers say that she participates in all school activities as normally as other children. Though older than her classmates, she has fortunately not physically matured too far beyond their level.[18]

Clearly the history of Isabelle's development is different from that of Anna's. In both cases there was exceedingly low, or rather blank, intellectual level to begin with. In both cases it seemed that the girl might be congenitally feeble-minded. In both a considerably higher level was reached later on. But the Ohio girl achieved a normal mentality within two years, whereas Anna was still markedly inadequate at the end of four and half years. This difference in achievement may suggest that Anna had less initial capacity. But an alternative hypothesis is possible.

One should remember that Anna never received the prolonged and expert attention that Isabelle received. The result of such attention, in the case of the Ohio girl, was to give her speech at an early stage, and her subsequent rapid development seems to have been a consequence of that. "Until Isabelle's speech and language development, she had all the characteristics of a feeble-minded child." Had Anna, who, from the standpoint of psychometric tests and early history, closely resembled this girl at the start, been given a mastery of speech at an earlier point by intensive training, her subsequent development might have been much more rapid.[19]

The hypothesis that Anna began with a sharply inferior mental capacity is therefore not established. Even if she were deficient to start with, we have no way of knowing how much so. Under ordinary conditions she might have been a dull normal or, like her mother, a moron. Even after the blight of her isolation, if she had lived to maturity, she might have finally reached virtually the full level of her capacity, whatever it may have been. That her isolation did have a profound effect upon her mentality, there can be no doubt. This is proved by the substantial degree of change during the four and a half years following her rescue.

Consideration of Isabelle's case serves to show, as Anna's case does not clearly show, that isolation up to the age of six, with failure to acquire any form of speech and hence failure to grasp nearly the whole world of cultural meaning, does not preclude the subsequent acquisition of these. Indeed, there seems to be a process of accelerated recovery in which the child goes through the mental stages at a more rapid rate than would be the case in normal development. Just what would be the maximum age at which a person could remain isolated and still retain the capacity for full cultural acquisition is hard to say. Almost certainly it would not be as high as age fifteen; it might possibly be as low as age ten. Undoubtedly various individuals would differ considerably as to the exact age.

Anna's is not an ideal case for showing the effects of extreme isolation, partly because she was possibly deficient to begin with, partly because she did not receive the best training available, and partly because she did not live long enough. Nevertheless, her case is instructive when placed in the record with numerous other cases of extreme isolation. This and the previous article about her are meant to place her in the record. It is to be hoped that other cases will be described in the scientific literature as they are discovered (as unfortunately they will be), for only in these rare cases of extreme isolation is it possible "to observe *concretely separated* two factors in the development of human personality which are always otherwise only analytically separated, the biogenic and the sociogenic factors."[20]

Notes

1. Kingsley Davis, "Extreme Social Isolation of a Child," *American Journal of Sociology,* XLV (January, 1940), 554–65.

2. Sincere appreciation is due to the officials in the Department of Welfare, Commonwealth of Pennsylvania, for the kind cooperation in making available the records concerning Anna and discussing the case frankly with the writer. Helen C. Hubbell, Florentine Hackbusch, and Eleanor Mecklenburg were particularly helpful, as was Fanny L. Matchette. Without their aid neither of the reports on Anna could have been written.

3. The records are not clear as to which day.

4. Letter to one of the state officials in charge of the case.

5. *Ibid.*

6. Progress report of the school.

7. Davis, *op. cit.,* p. 564.

8. The facts set forth here as to Anna's ancestry are taken chiefly from a report of mental tests administered to Anna's mother by psychologists at a state hospital where she was taken for this purpose after the discovery of Anna's seclusion. This excellent report was not available to the writer when the previous paper on Anna was published.

9. Marie K. Mason, "Learning to Speak after Six and One-Half Years of Silence," *Journal of Speech Disorders,* VII (1942), 295–304.

10. Francis N. Maxfield, "What Happens When the Social Environment of a Child Approaches Zero." The writer is greatly indebted to Mrs. Maxfield and to Professor Horace B. English, a colleague of Professor Maxfield, for the privilege of seeing this manuscript and other materials collected on isolated and feral individuals.

11. J. A. L. Singh and Robert M. Zingg, *Wolf-Children and Feral Man* (New York: Harper & Bros., 1941), pp. 248–51.

12. Maxfield, unpublished manuscript cited above.

13. Mason, *op. cit.,* p. 299.

14. Maxfield, unpublished manuscript.

15. Mason, *op. cit.,* p. 299.

16. *Ibid.,* pp. 300–304.

17. Maxfield, unpublished manuscript.

18. Based on a personal letter from Dr. Mason to the writer, May 13, 1946.

19. This point is suggested in a personal letter from Dr. Mason to the writer, October 22, 1946.

20. Singh and Zingg, *op. cit.,* pp. xxi–xxii, in a foreword by the writer.

13 On Becoming Male: Reflections of a Sociologist on Childhood and Early Socialization

JAMES M. HENSLIN

Although relations between men and women are enveloped in social change, men still dominate the social institutions of the Western world: law, politics, business, religion, education, the military, medicine, science, sports, and in many ways, even the family. In spite of far-reaching social change, women often find themselves in the more backstage, nurturing, and supportive roles—and those roles are generally supportive of the more dominant roles men play.

Why? Is this a consequence of genetic heritage—males and females being born with different predispositions? Or is it due to culture, because males are socialized into dominance? While there is considerable debate among academics on this matter, sociologists side almost unanimously with the proponents of socialization. In this article, Henslin analyzes some of the socialization experiences that place males in a distinctive social world and prepare them for dominance. This selection is an attempt to penetrate the taken-for-granted, behind-the-scenes aspects of socialization into masculine sexuality. Whether male or female, you might find it useful to contrast your experiences in growing up with those the author describes.

ACCORDING TO THE PREVAILING sociological perspective, our masculinity or femininity is not biologically determined. Although our biological or genetic inheritance gives each of us the sex organs of a male or female, how our "maleness" or "femaleness" is expressed depends on what we learn. Our masculinity or femininity, that is, what we are like as sexual beings—our orientations and how we behave as a male or a female—does not depend on biology but on social learning. It can be said that while our gender is part of our biological inheritance, our sexuality (or masculinity or femininity) is part of our social inheritance.

If this sociological position is correct—that culture, not anatomy, is our destiny—how do we become the "way we are"?[1] What factors shape or influence us into becoming masculine or feminine? If our characteristic behaviors do not come from our biology, how do we end up having those that we do have? What is the *process* by which we come to possess behaviors typically associated with our gender? If they *are* learned, how do our behaviors, attitudes, and other basic orientations come to be felt by us as natural and essential to our identity? (And they are indeed essential to our identity.) In what ways is the process of "becoming" related to the social structure of society?

Not only would it take volumes to answer these questions fully, but it would also be impossible, since the answers are only now slowly being unraveled by researchers. In this short and rather informal article, I will be able only to indicate some of the basics underlying this foundational learning. I will focus exclusively on being socialized into masculinity, and will do this by reflecting on (1) my own experience in "becoming"; (2) my observations as a sociologist of the experiences of others; and (3) what others have shared with me concerning their own experiences. The reader should keep in mind that this article is meant to be neither definitive nor exhaustive, but is designed to depict general areas of male socialization and thereby to provide insight into the acquisition of masculinity in our culture.

In the Beginning . . .

Except for a few rare instances,[2] each of us arrives in this world with a clearly definable physical characteristic that sets us apart from about half the rest of the world. This characteristic makes a literal world of difference. Our parents become excited about whether we have been born with a penis or a vagina. They are usually either happy or disappointed about which organ we possess, seldom feeling neutral about the matter. They announce it to friends, relatives, and sometimes to complete strangers ("It's a boy!" "It's a girl!"). Regardless of how they feel about it, on the basis of our possessing a particular physical organ they purposely, but both consciously and subconsciously, separate us into two worlds. Wittingly and unwittingly, they thereby launch us onto a career that will encompass almost every aspect of our lives—and will remain with us until death.

Colors, Clothing, and Toys

While it is not inherently more masculine or feminine than red, yellow, purple, orange, white, or black, the color blue has become arbitrarily associated with *infantile masculinity*. After what is usually a proud realization that the neonate possesses a penis (which marks him as a member of the overlords of the universe), the inheritor of dominance is wrapped in blue. This color is merely an arbitrary choice, as originally any other would have done as well. But now that the association is made, no other will do. The announcing colors maintain their meaning for only a fairly short period, gradually becoming sexually neutralized.[3] Pink, however, retains at least part of its meaning of sexuality, for even as adults males tend to shy away from it.

Our parents gently and sometimes not so gently push us onto a predetermined course. First they provide clothing designated appropriate to our masculine status. Even as infants our clothing displays sexual significance, and our parents are extremely careful that we never are clothed in either dresses or ruffles. For example, while our plastic panties are designed to keep mothers, fathers, and their furniture and friends dry, our parents make absolutely certain that ours are never pink with white ruffles. Even if our Mom had run out of all other plastic panties, she would rather stay home than take us out in public wearing ruffled pinkies. Mom would probably feel a twinge of guilt over such cross-dressing even in private.[4]

So both Mom and Dad are extremely cautious about our clothing. Generally plain, often simple, and usually sturdy, our clothing is designed to take the greater "rough and tumble" that they know boys are going to give it. They also choose clothing that will help groom us into future adult roles; depending on the style of the period, they dress us in little sailor suits, miniature jogging togs, or two-piece suits with matching ties. Although at this early age we could care less about such things, and their significance appears irrelevant to us, our parents' concern is always present. If during a supermarket expedition even a stranger mistakes our sexual identity, this agitates our parents, challenging their sacred responsibility to maintain the reality-ordering structure of the sex worlds. Such mistaken identification forces them to rethink their activities in proper sex typing, their deep obligation to make certain that their offspring is receiving the right start in life. They will either ascribe the mistake to the stupidity of the stranger or immediately forswear some particular piece of clothing.

Our parents' "gentle nudging" into masculinity does not overlook our toys. These represent both current activities thought sexually appropriate and those symbolic of our future masculinity of courage, competition, and daring. We are given trucks, tanks, and guns. Although our mother might caution us about breaking them, it is readily apparent by her tone and facial expressions that she does not mean what she says. We can continue to bang them together roughly, and she merely looks at us—sometimes quite uncomprehendingly, and occasionally muttering something to the effect that boys will be boys. We somehow perceive her sense of confirmation and we bang them all the more, laughing gleefully at the approval we know it is bringing.

Play and the Sexual Boundaries of Tolerance

We can make all sorts of expressive sounds as we play. We can shout, grunt, and groan on the kitchen floor or roll around in the sandbox. As she shoves us out the door, Mom always cautions us not to get dirty, but when we come in filthy her verbal and gestural disapproval is only mild. From holistic perception, of which by now we have become young masters, we have learned that no matter what Mom's words say, they do not represent the entirety of her feelings.

When we are "all dressed up" before going somewhere, or before company comes, Mom acts differently. We learn that at those times she means what she says about not getting dirty. If we do not want "fire in our pants," we'd better remain clean—at least for a while, for we also learn that after company has come and has had a glimpse of the neat and clean little boy (or, as they say, "the nice little gentleman" or the "fine young man"), we can go about our rough and tumble ways. Pushing, shouting, running, climbing, and other expressions of competition, glee, and freedom then become permissible. We learn that the appearance required at the beginning of a visit is quite unlike that which is passable at the end of the visit.

Our more boisterous and rougher play continues to help us learn the bounds of our parents' tolerance limits. As we continuously test those limits, somewhat to our dismay we occasionally find ourselves having crossed beyond them. Through what is at times painful trial and error, we learn both the limits and how they vary with changed circumstance. We eventually learn those edges extremely well and know, for example, precisely how much more we can "get away with" when company comes than when only the immediate family is present, when Mom and Dad are tired or when they are arguing.

As highly rational beings, who are seldom adequately credited by adults for our keen cunning, we learn to calculate those boundaries exceedingly carefully. We eventually come to the point where we know precisely where the brink is—that one more word of back talk, one more quarrel with our brother, sister, or friend, even a small one, or even one more whine will move our parents from words to deeds, and their wrath will fall abruptly upon us with full force. Depending on our parents' orientation to childrearing (or often simply upon their predilection of the moment, for at these times theory tends to fly out the window), this will result in either excruciating humiliation in front of our friends accompanied by horrible (though momentary) physical pain, or excruciating humiliation in front of our friends accompanied by the horrifying (and longer) deprivation of a privilege (which of course we know is really a "right" and is being unjustifiably withheld from us).

On Freedom and Being

As we calculate those boundaries of tolerance (or in the vernacular used by our parents and well understood by us, find out how much they can "stand"), we also learn something about our world vis-à-vis that of those strange female creatures who coinhabit our space. We learn that we can get dirtier, play rougher, speak louder, act more crudely, wander farther from home, stay away longer, and talk back more.

We see that girls live in a world foreign to ours. Theirs is quieter, neater, daintier, and in general more subdued. Sometimes our worlds touch, but then only momentarily. We learn, for example, that while little sisters might be all right to spend an occasional hour with on a rainy afternoon, they are, after all, "only girls." They cannot really enter our world, and we certainly do not want to become part of theirs, with its greater restrictions and fewer challenges. Occasionally, we even find ourselves delighting in this distinction as we taunt them about not being able to do something because it is "not for girls."

If we sometimes wonder about the reason for the differences between our worlds, our curiosity quickly runs its course, for we know deep down that these distinctions are proper. They are *girls,* and, as our parents have told us repeatedly, we are NOT girls. We have internalized the appropriateness of our worlds; some things are right for us, others for them. Seldom are we sorry for the tighter reins placed on girls. We are just glad that we are not one of "them." We stick with "our own kind" and immensely enjoy our greater freedom. Rather than lose ourselves in philosophical reflections about the inequalities of this world (greatly beyond our mental capacities at this point anyway), we lose ourselves in exultation over our greater freedom and the good fortune that made us boys instead of girls.

That greater freedom becomes the most prized aspect of our existence. Before we are old enough to go to school (and later, during summer or weekends and any other nonschool days), when we awaken in the morning we can hardly wait to get our clothes on. Awaiting us is a world of adventure. If we are up before Mom, we can go outside and play in the yard. Before venturing beyond voice distance, however, we have to eat our "wholesome" breakfast, one that somehow is always in the process of "making a man" out of us. After this man-producing breakfast, which might well consist of little more than cereal, we are free to roam, to discover, to experience. There are no dishes to do, no dusting, sweeping, or cleaning. Those things are for sisters, mothers, and other females.

Certainly we have spatial and associational restrictions placed on us, but they are much more generous than those imposed on girls of our age. We know how many blocks we can wander and whom we are allowed to see. But just as significant, we know how to go beyond that distance without getting caught and how to play with the "bad boys" and the "too big boys" without

Mom ever being the wiser. So long as we are home within a certain time limit, in spite of verbal restrictions we really are free to come and go.

We do learn to accept limited responsibility in order to guard our free-dom, and we are always pestering other mothers for the time or, when we are able, arranging for them to tell us when it is "just about noon" so we can make our brief appearance for lunch—and then quickly move back into the exciting world of boy activities. But we also learn to lie a lot, finding out that it is better to say anything plausible rather than to admit that we violated the boundaries and be "grounded," practically the worst form of punishment a boy can re-ceive. Consequently, we learn to deny, to avoid, to deceive, to tell half-truths, and to involve ourselves in other sorts of subterfuge rather than to admit viola-tions that might restrict our freedom of movement.

Our freedom is infinitely precious to us, for whether it is cops and rob-bers or space bandits, the Lone Ranger or Darth Vader, ours is an imaginary world filled with daring and danger. Whether it is six-shooters with bullets or space missiles with laser disintegrators, we are always shooting or getting shot. There are always the good guys and the bad guys. Always there is a moral vic-tory to be won. We are continuously running, shouting, hiding, and discover-ing. The world is filled with danger, with the inopportune and unexpected lurking just around the corner. As the enemy stalks us, the potential of sudden discovery and the sweet joys of being undetected are unsurpassable. Nothing in adulthood, in spite of its great allure, its challenges and victories yet to be experienced, will ever be greater than this intense bliss of innocence—and part of the joy of this period lies in being entirely unaware of that savage fact of life.

. . . And the Twain Shall Never Meet

Seldom do we think about being masculine. Usually we are just being. The radical social differences that separate us from girls have not gone unnoticed, of course. Rather, these essential differences in life-orientations not only have penetrated our consciousness but have saturated our very beings. Our initial indifference to things male and female has turned to violent taste and distaste. We have learned our lessons so well that we sometimes end up teaching our own mothers lessons in sexuality. For example, we would rather be caught dead than to wear sissy clothing, and our tantrums will not cease until our mothers come to their senses and relent concerning putting something on us that we consider sissified.

We know there are two worlds, and we are grateful for the one we are in. Ours is superior. The evidence continually surrounds us, and we exult in mas-culine privilege. We also protect our sexual boundaries from encroachment and erosion. The encroachment comes from tomboys who strive to become part of our world. We tolerate them—up to a point. But by excluding them from some activities, we let them know that there are irrevocable differences that forever separate us.

The erosion comes from sissies. Although we are not yet aware that we are reacting to a threat to our developing masculine identity, we do know that sissies make us uncomfortable. We come to dislike them intensely. To be a sissy is to be a traitor to one's very being. It is to be "like a girl," that which we are not—and that which we definitely never will be.

Sissies are to be either pitied or hated. While they are not girls, neither are they real boys. They look like us, but they bring shame on us because they do not represent anything we are. We are everything they are not. Consequently, we separate ourselves from them in the most direct manner possible. While we may be brutal, this breach is necessary, for we must define clearly the boundaries of our own existence—and one way that we know who we are is by knowing what we are not.

So we shame sissies. We make fun of anyone who is not the way he "ought" to be. If he hangs around the teacher or girls during recess instead of playing our rough and tumble games, if he will not play sports because he is afraid of getting dirty or being hurt, if he backs off from a fight, if he cries or whines, or even if he gets too many A's, we humiliate and ridicule him. We gather around him in a circle. We call him a sissy. We say, "Shame! Shame!" We call him gay, fag, and queer. We tell him he is a girl and not fit for us.

And as far as we are concerned, he never will be fit for us. He belongs to some strange status, not quite a girl and not quite a boy. Whatever he is, he certainly is not one of us. WE don't cry when we are punished or hurt. WE don't hang around girls. WE are proud of our average grades. WE play rough games. WE are not afraid of getting hurt. (Or if we are, we would never let it show.) WE are not afraid of sassing the teacher—or at least of calling the teacher names when his or her back is turned. We know who we are. We are boys.

The Puberty Shock

We never know, of course, how precarious our sexual identity is. From birth we have been set apart from females, and during childhood we have severely separated ourselves both from females and from those who do not match our standards of masculinity. Our existence is well defined, our world solid. By the end of grade school the pecking order is clear. For good or ill, each of us has been locked into a system of well-honed, peer-determined distinctions, our destiny determined by a heavily defended social order. Our masculine world seems secure, with distinct boundaries that clearly define "us" from "them." We know who we are, and we are cocky about it.

But then comes puberty, and overnight the world undergoes radical metamorphosis. Girls suddenly change. Right before our eyes the flat chests we have always taken for granted begin to protrude. Two little bumps magically appear, and while we are off playing our games, once in a while we cast quizzical glances in the direction of the girls. Witnessing a confusing, haunting change, we shrug off the dilemma and go back to our games.

Then the change hits us. We feel something happening within our own bodies. At first the feeling is vague, undefined. There is no form to it. We just know that something is different. Then we begin to feel strange stirrings within us. These stirrings come on abruptly, and that abruptness begins to shake everything loose in our secure world. Until this time our penis has never given us any particular trouble. It has just "been there," appended like a finger or toenail. It has been a fact of life, something that "we" had and "they" didn't. But now it literally springs to life, taking on an existence of its own and doing things that we once could not even imagine would ever take place. This sometimes creates embarrassment, and there are even times when, called to the blackboard to work out some problem, we must play dumb because of the bulge that we never willed.

It is a new game. The girls in our class are different. We are different. And we never will be the same.

We are forced into new concepts of masculinity. We find this upsetting, but fortunately we do not have to begin from scratch. We can build on our experiences, for mostly the change involves just one area of our lives, girls, and we are able to keep the rest intact. We can still swagger, curse, sweat, get dirty, and bloody ourselves in our games. While the girls still watch us admiringly from the sidelines as we "do our manly thing," we also now watch them more closely as they "do their womanly thing" and strut before us in tight sweaters.

While the girls still admire our toughness, a change is now demanded. At times we must show gentleness. We must be cleaner and watch our language more than before. We must even show consideration. Those shifting requirements are not easy to master, but we have the older, more experienced boys to count on—and they are more than willing to initiate us into this new world and, while doing so, to demonstrate their (always) greater knowledge and skills in traversing the social world.

The Transition into Artificiality

It is with difficulty that we make the transition. A new sexuality is really required, and such radical change could be easy for no one. We already have been fundamentally formed, and what we really learn at this point is to be more adept role-players. We behave one way when we are with the guys. This is the "natural" way, the way we feel. It is relaxed and easy. And we learn to act a different way while we are around girls. This form of presentation we find more contrived and artificial, for it requires greater politeness, consideration, and gentleness. In other words, it is contrary to all that we have previously learned, to all that we have become.

Consequently we hone our acting skills, the ability to put on expected performances. We always have been actors; it is just that we learned our earlier role at a more formative period, and, *having formed us,* this role now provides greater fit. And acting differently while we are around females is nothing new. We have been practicing that since we were at our mother's knee. But now the female expectations are more pressing as our worlds more frequently intersect. Although we become fairly skilled at meeting these expectations, they never become part of our being. Always they consist of superficial behaviors added onto what is truly and, by this time, "naturally" us.

This lesson in artificiality reinforces our many exercises in manipulation. We learn that to get what we want, whether that be an approving smile, a caress, a kiss, or more, we must meet the expectations of the one from whom we desire something. We are no strangers to this foundational fact of life, of course, but the masks we must wear in these more novel situations, our uncomfortable gestures and the requisite phrasing, make us awkward strangers to ourselves. We wonder why we are forced into situations that require such constant posing and posturing.

But awkward or not (and as we become more proficient in the game, much of the initial discomfort leaves), we always come back for more. By now sports and games with the fellows are no longer enough. Females seemingly hold the key to our happiness. They can withhold or grant as they see fit. And for favors to be granted, this demanding intersexual game must be played.

The Continuing Masculine World—and Marriage

Eventually we become highly adept players in this intersexual game. We even come to savor our maturing manipulative abilities as the game offers highly stimulating physical payoffs. Our growing skills let us determine if a particular encounter will result in conquest, and thus calculate if it is worth the pursuit. To meet the challenge successfully provides yet another boost to our masculinity.

The hypocrisies and deceits the game requires sometimes disturb us. We really want to be more honest than the game allows. But we do not know how to bring that about—and still succeed at the game *and* our masculinity.

Discomforts arising from the game, especially the intimate presence of the female world, must be relieved. Manly activities provide us refuge from this irritant, endeavors in which we men can truly understand one another, where we share a world of aspiration, conflict, and competition. Here we can laugh at the same things and talk the way we really feel with much less concern about the words we choose. We know that among men our interests, activities, and desires form an essential part of a shared, self-encapsulating world.

To continue to receive the rewards offered by females, on occasion we must leave our secure world of manliness momentarily to penetrate the conjoint world occupied by our feminine counterparts. But such leave-takings remain temporary, never a "real" part of us. Always waiting for us are the "real" conversations that reflect the "real" world, that exciting realm whose challenging creativity, competition, and conflict help make life worth living.

And we are fortunate in having at our fingertips a socially constructed semi-imaginary masculine world, one we can summon at will to retreat into its beckoning confines. This world of televised football, baseball, basketball, wrestling, boxing, hockey, soccer, and car racing is part of the domain of men. At least here is a world, manly and comfortable, that offers us refuge from that threatening feminine world, allowing us to withdraw from its suffocating demands of sharing and intimacy. This semi-imaginary world offers continual appeal because it summons up subconscious feelings from our childhood, adolescence, and, eventually as we grow older, early manhood.

Many of us would not deny that the characteristics we males learn or, if you prefer, the persons we tend to become, fail to provide an adequate basis for developing fulfilling intersexual relationships. But those characteristics, while underlying what is often the shallowness of our relationships with females, are indeed us. They are the logical consequence of our years of learning our culture. We have become what we have been painstakingly shaped to become. Although willing participants in our social destiny, we are heirs of a cultural inheritance that preceded our arrival on the social scene.

Some of us, only with great difficulty, have overcome our masculine socialization into intersexual superficiality and have developed relationships with wives and girlfriends that transcend the confines of those cultural dictates. But such relearning, painfully difficult, comes at a price, leaving in its wake much hurt and brokenness.

Hardly any of this process of becoming a man in our society augurs well for marriage. The separateness of the world that we males join at birth signals our journey into an intricate process whereby we become a specifically differentiated type of being. Our world diverges in almost all respects from the world of females. Not only do we look different, not only do we talk differently and act differently, but our fundamental thinking and orientations to life sharply contrast with theirs. This basic divergence is difficult for females to grasp and, when grasped, is often accompanied by a shudder of disbelief and distaste at the revelatory insight into such dissimilar reality. Yet we are expected to unite permanently with someone from this contradispositional world and, in spite of our essential differences, not only to share a life space but also to join our goals, hopes, dreams, and aspirations.

Is it any wonder, then, that in the typical case men remain strangers to women, women to men, with marriage a crucible of struggle?

Notes

1. The diversity of opinion among sociologists regarding the nature/nurture causes of behavioral differences of males and females is illustrated in *Society* magazine (September/October 1986:4–39). The connection between ideology and theoretical interpretation of data is especially apparent in this heated exchange.

2. Of about one in every 30,000 births, the sex of a baby is unclear. A genetic disorder called congenital adrenal hyperplasia results in the newborn having parts of both male and female genitals (*St. Louis Globe-Democrat,* March 10–11, 1979, p. 3D).

3. When people (almost exclusively women) are invited to a baby shower and the expectant mother has not yet given birth (or if they wish to take advantage of a sale and buy a gift in advance of the delivery), they find themselves in a quandary. The standard solution to this problem of not knowing the sex of the child (at least in the Midwest) is to purchase either clothing of yellow color or a "sex neutral" item.

4. Duly noted, of course, are the historical arbitrariness and relativity of the gender designation of clothing, with the meaning of ruffles and other stylistic variations depending on the historical period.

14 Sexuality and Gender in Children's Daily Worlds

BARRIE THORNE
ZELLA LURIA

In this selection, two sociologists take children's play seriously and examine its implications for relations between males and females. Their observations are likely to bring back many memories of your childhood. You also will become aware that children's play is not simply play, but has serious sociological meaning—in this instance the fierce maintenance of social boundaries between males and females.

To gather their data, Thorne and Luria studied fourth- and fifthgraders in four schools within three states. They found that the children usually are very careful to separate their friendships and activities on the basis of sex. Girls of this age are more concerned about "being nice," while the interests of boys center on sports and testing the limits of rules. The larger groups into which they band provide each boy a degree of protection and anonymity. The sociological significance of children's play is that both boys and girls are helping to socialize one another into primary adult gender roles, females being more concerned with intimacy, emotionality, and romance, and boys with independence and sexuality. They are writing the "scripts" that they will follow as adults.

THE AMBIGUITIES OF "SEX"—a word used to refer to biological sex, to cultural gender, and also to sexuality—contain a series of complicated questions. Although our cultural understandings often merge these three domains, they can be separated analytically; their interrelationships lie at the core of the social organization of sex and gender. In this paper we focus on the domains of gender and sexuality as they are organized and experienced among elementary school children, especially nine- to eleven-year-olds. This analysis helps illuminate age-based variations and transitions in the organization of sexuality and gender.

We use "gender" to refer to cultural and social phenomena—divisions of labor, activity, and identity which are associated with but not fully determined

141

by biological sex. The core of sexuality, as we use it here, is desire and arousal. Desire and arousal are shaped by and associated with socially learned activities and meanings which Gagnon and Simon (1973) call "sexual scripts." Sexual scripts—defining who does what, with whom, when, how, and what it means—are related to the adult society's view of gender (Miller and Simon, 1981). Nine- to eleven-year-old children are beginning the transition from the gender system of childhood to that of adolescence. They are largely defined (and define themselves) as children, but they are on the verge of sexual maturity, cultural adolescence, and a gender system organized around the institution of heterosexuality. Their experiences help illuminate complex and shifting relationships between sexuality and gender.

First we explore the segregated gender arrangements of middle childhood as contexts for learning adolescent and adult sexual scripts. We then turn from their separate worlds to relations *between* boys and girls, and examine how fourth- and fifth-grade children use sexual idioms to mark gender boundaries. Separate gender groups and ritualized, asymmetric relations between girls and boys lay the groundwork for the more overtly sexual scripts of adolescence.

The Daily Separation of Girls and Boys

Gender segregation—the separation of girls and boys in friendships and casual encounters—is central to daily life in elementary schools. A series of snapshots taken in varied school settings would reveal extensive spatial separation between girls and boys. When they choose seats, select companions for work or play, or arrange themselves in line, elementary school children frequently cluster into same-sex groups. At lunchtime, boys and girls often sit separately and talk matter-of-factly about "girls' tables" and "boys' tables." Playgrounds have gendered spaces: boys control some areas and activities, such as large playing fields and basketball courts; and girls control smaller enclaves like jungle-gym areas and concrete spaces for hopscotch or jump-rope. Extensive gender segregation in everyday encounters and in friendships has been found in many other studies of elementary- and middle-school children. Gender segregation in elementary and middle schools has been found to account for more segregation than race (Schofield, 1982).

Gender segregation is not total. Snapshots of school settings would also reveal some groups with a fairly even mix of boys and girls, especially in games like kickball, dodgeball, and handball, and in classroom and playground activities organized by adults. Some girls frequently play with boys, integrating their groups in a token way, and a few boys, especially in the lower grades, play with groups of girls. In general, there is more gender segregation when children are freer to construct their own activities.

Most of the research on gender and children's social relations emphasizes patterns of separation, contrasting the social organization and cultures of girls' groups with those of boys. In brief summary: Boys tend to interact in larger and more publicly visible groups; they more often play outdoors, and their activities take up more space than those of girls. Boys engage in more physically aggressive play and fighting; their social relations tend to be overtly hierarchical and competitive. Organized sports are both a central activity and a major metaphor among boys; they use a language of "teams" and "captains" even when not engaged in sports.

Girls more often interact in smaller groups or friendship pairs, organized in shifting alliances. Compared with boys, they more often engage in turn-taking activities like jump-rope and doing tricks on the bars, and they less often play organized sports. While boys use a rhetoric of contests and teams, girls describe their relations using language which stresses cooperation and "being nice." But the rhetorics of either group should not be taken for the full reality. Girls *do* engage in conflict, although it tends to take more indirect forms than the direct insults and challenges more often found in interactions among boys, and between girls and boys.

Interaction Among Boys

In daily patterns of talk and play, boys in all-male groups often build towards heightened and intense moments, moments one can describe in terms of group arousal with excited emotions. This especially happens when boys violate rules.

Dirty words are a focus of rules, and rule breaking, in elementary schools. Both girls and boys know dirty words, but flaunting of the words and risking punishment for their use was more frequent in boys' than in girls' groups in all the schools we studied. In the middle-class Massachusetts public school, both male and female teachers punished ballplayers for [their dirty words]. But teachers were not present after lunch and before school, when most group-directed play took place. A female paraprofessional, who alone managed almost 150 children on the playground, never intervened to stop bad language in play; the male gym teacher who occasionally appeared on the field at after-lunch recess always did. Boys resumed dirty talk immediately after he passed them. Dirty talk is a staple part of the repertoire of the boys' groups (also see Fine, 1980). Such talk defines their groups as, at least in part, outside the reach of the school's discipline.

Some of the dirty talk may be explicitly sexual, as it was in the Massachusetts public school when a group of five fifth-grade boys played a game called "Mad Lib" (also described in Luria, 1983). The game consisted of a paragraph (in this case, a section of a textbook discussing the U.S. Constitution) with key words deleted, to be filled in by the players. Making the paragraph absurd and violating rules to create excitement seemed to be the goal of the game. The boys clearly knew that their intentions were "dirty": They requested the field observer not to watch the game.

Sports, dirty words, and testing the limits are part of what boys teach boys how to do. The assumption seems to be: Dirty words, sports interest and knowledge, and transgression of politeness are closely connected.

RULE TRANSGRESSION: COMPARING GIRLS' AND BOYS' GROUPS

Rule transgression in *public* is exciting to boys in their groups. Boys' groups are attentive to potential consequences of transgression, but, compared with girls, groups of boys appear to be greater risk-takers. Adults tending and teaching children do not often undertake discipline of an entire boys' group; the adults might lose out and they cannot risk that. Girls are more likely to affirm the reasonableness of rules, and, when it occurs, rule-breaking by girls is smaller scale. This may be related to the smaller size of girls' groups and to adults' readiness to use rules on girls who seem to believe in them. It is dubious if an isolated pair of boys (a pair is the model size of girls' groups) could get away with the rule-breaking that characterizes the larger male group. A boy may not have power, but a boys' *group* does. Teachers avoid disciplining whole groups of boys, partly for fear of seeming unfair. Boys rarely identify those who proposed direct transgressions and, when confronted, they claim (singly), "I didn't start it; why should I be punished?"

Boys are visibly excited when they break rules together—they are flushed as they play, they wipe their hands on their jeans, some of them look guilty. The Mad Lib game described above not only violates rules, it also evokes sexual meanings within an all-male group. Arousal is not purely individual; in this case, it is shared by the group. . . . The audience for the excitement is the gender-segregated peer group, where each boy increases the excitement by adding still a "worse" word. All of this takes place in a game ("rules") context, and hence with anonymity despite the close-up contact of the game.

While we never observed girls playing a Mad Lib game of this sort, some of our female students recall playing the game in grade school but giving it up after being caught by teachers, or out of fear of being caught. Both boys and girls may acquire knowledge of the game, but boys repeatedly perform it because their gender groups give support for transgression.

These instances all suggest that boys experience a shared, arousing context for transgression, with sustained gender group support for rule-breaking. Girls' groups may engage in rule-breaking, but the gender group's support for repeated public transgression is far less certain. The smaller size of girls' gender groupings in comparison with those of boys, and girls' greater susceptibility to rules and social control by teachers, make girls' groups easier to control. Boys' larger groups give each transgressor a degree of anonymity. Anonymity—which means less probability of detection and punishment—enhances the contagious excitement of rule-breaking.

The higher rates of contagious excitement, transgression, and limit-testing in boys' groups means that when they are excited, boys are often "playing" to male audiences. The public nature of such excitement forges bonds among boys. This kind of bonding is also evident when boys play team sports, and when they act aggressively toward marginal or isolated boys. Such aggression is both physical and verbal (taunts like "sissy," "fag," or "mental"). Sharing a target of aggression may be another source of arousal for groups of boys.

THE TIE TO SEXUALITY IN MALES

When Gagnon and Simon (1973) argued that there are gender-differentiated sexual scripts in adolescence, they implied what our observations suggest: the gender arrangements and subcultures of middle childhood prepare the way for the sexual scripts of adolescence. Fifth- and sixth-grade boys share pornography, in the form of soft-core magazines like *Playboy* and *Penthouse,* with great care to avoid confiscation. Like the Mad Lib games with their forbidden content, soft-core magazines are also shared in all-male contexts, providing explicit knowledge about what is considered sexually arousing and about attitudes and fantasies. Since pornography is typically forbidden for children in both schools and families, this secret sharing occurs in a context of rule-breaking.

While many theorists since Freud have stressed the importance of boys loosening ties and identification with females (as mother surrogates), few theorists have questioned why "communally aroused" males do not uniformly bond sexually to other males. If the male groups of fifth and sixth grade are the forerunners of the "frankly" heterosexual gender groups of the junior and high school years, what keeps these early groups from open homosexual expression? Scripting in same-gender peer groups may, in fact, be more about gender than about sexual orientation. Boys, who will later view themselves as having homosexual or heterosexual preferences, are learning patterns of masculinity. The answer may also lie in the teaching of homophobia.

By the fourth grade, children, especially boys, have begun to use homophobic labels—"fag," "faggot," "queer"—as terms of insult, especially for marginal boys. They draw upon sexual allusions (often not fully understood, except for their negative and contaminating import) to reaffirm male hierarchies and patterns of exclusion. As "fag" talk increases, relaxed and cuddling patterns of touch decrease among boys. Kindergarten and first-grade boys touch one another frequently and with ease, with arms around shoulders, hugs, and holding hands. By fifth grade, touch among boys becomes more constrained, gradually shifting to mock violence and the use of poking, shoving, and ritual gestures like "give five" (flat hand slaps) to express bonding. The tough surface of boys' friendships is no longer like the gentle touching of girls in friendship.

Interaction Among Girls

In contrast with the larger, hierarchical organization of groups of boys, fourth- and fifth-grade girls more often organize themselves in pairs of "best friends" linked in shifting coalitions. These pairs are not "marriages"; the pattern is more one of dyads moving into triads, since girls often participate in two or more pairs at one time. This may result in quite complex social networks. Girls often talk about who is friends with or "likes" whom; they continually negotiate the parameters of friendships.

For example, in the California school, Chris, a fifth-grade girl, frequently said that Kathryn was her "best friend." Kathryn didn't proclaim the friendship as often; she also played and talked a lot with Judy. After watching Kathryn talk to Judy during a transition period in the classroom, Chris went over, took Kathryn aside, and said with an accusing tone, "You talk to Judy more than me." Kathryn responded defensively, "I talk to you as much as I talk to Judy."

In talking about their relationships with one another, girls use a language of "friends," "nice," and "mean." They talk about who is most and least "liked," which anticipates the concern about "popularity" found among junior high and high school girls (Eder, 1985). Since relationships sometimes break off, girls hedge bets by structuring networks of potential friends. The activity of constructing and breaking dyads is often carried out through talk with third parties. Some of these processes are evident in a sequence recorded in a Massachusetts school:

> The fifth-grade girls, Flo and Pauline, spoke of themselves as "best friends," while Flo said she was "sort of friends" with Doris. When a lengthy illness kept Pauline out of school, Flo spent more time with Doris. One day Doris abruptly broke off her friendship with Flo and began criticizing her to other girls. Flo, who felt very badly, went around asking others in their network, "What did I do? Why is Doris being so mean? Why is she telling everyone not to play with me?"

On school playgrounds girls are less likely than boys to organize themselves into team sports. They more often engage in small-scale, turn-taking kinds of play. When they jump rope or play on the bars, they take turns performing and watching others perform in stylized movements which may involve considerable skill. Sometimes girls work out group choreographies, counting and jumping rope in unison, or swinging around the bars. In other synchronized body rituals, clusters of fifth- and sixth-grade girls practice cheerleading routines or dance steps. In interactions with one another, girls often use relaxed gestures of physical intimacy, moving bodies in harmony, coming close in space, and reciprocating cuddly touches. We should add that girls also poke and grab, pin one another from behind, and use hand-slap rituals like "giving five," although less frequently than boys.

In other gestures of intimacy, which one rarely sees among boys, girls stroke or comb their friends' hair. They notice and comment on one another's physical appearance such as haircuts or clothes. Best friends monitor one another's emotions. They share secrets and become mutually vulnerable through self-disclosure, with an implicit demand that the expression of one's inadequacy will induce the friend to disclose a related inadequacy. In contrast, disclosure of weakness among boys is far more likely to be exposed to others through joking or horsing around.

IMPLICATIONS FOR SEXUALITY

Compared with boys, girls are more focused on constructing intimacy and talking about one-to-one relationships. Their smaller and more personal groups provide less protective anonymity than the larger groups of boys. Bonding through mutual self-disclosure, especially through disclosure of vulnerability, and breaking off friendships by "acting mean," teach the creation, sustaining, and ending of emotionally intimate relations. Girls' preoccupation with who is friends with whom, and their monitoring of cues of "nice" and "mean," liking and disliking, teach them strategies for forming and leaving personal relationships. In their interactions girls show knowledge of motivational rules for dyads and insight into both outer and inner realities of social relationships. Occasionally, girls indicate that they see boys as lacking such "obvious" knowledge.

Girls' greater interest in verbally sorting out relationships was evident during an incident in the Massachusetts public school. The fifth-grade boys often insulted John, a socially isolated boy who was not good at sports. On one such occasion during gym class, Bill, a high status boy, angrily yelled "creep" and "mental" when John fumbled the ball. The teacher stopped the game and asked the class to discuss the incident. Both boys and girls vigorously talked about "words that kill," with Bill saying he was sorry for what he said, that he had lost control in the excitement of the game. The girls kept asking, "How could anyone do that?" The boys kept returning to, "When you get excited, you do things you don't mean." Both girls and boys understood and verbalized the dilemma, but after the group discussion the boys dropped the topic. The girls continued to converse, with one repeatedly asking, "How could Bill be so stupid? Didn't he know how he'd make John feel?"

When talking with one another, girls use dirty words much less often than boys do. The shared arousal and bonding among boys which we think occurs around public rule-breaking has as its counterpart the far less frequent giggling sessions of girls, usually in groups larger than three. The giggling often centers on carefully guarded topics, sometimes, although not always, about boys.

The sexually related discourse of girls focuses less on dirty words than on themes of romance. In the Michigan school, first- and second-grade girls often jumped rope to rhymes about romance. A favorite was, "Down in the Valley Where the Green Grass Grows," a saga of heterosexual romance which, with the name of the jumper and a boy of her choice filled in, concludes: " . . . along came Jason, and kissed her on the cheek . . . first comes love, then comes marriage, then along comes Cindy with a baby carriage." In the Michigan and California schools, fourth- and fifth-grade girls talked privately about crushes and about which boys were "cute," as shown in the following incident recorded in the lunchroom of the Michigan school:

> The girls and boys from one of the fourth-grade classes sat at separate tables. Three of the girls talked as they peered at a nearby table of fifth-grade boys, "Look behind you," one said. "Ooh," said the other two. "That boy's named Todd." "I know where my favorite guy is . . . there," another gestured with her head while her friends looked.

In the Massachusetts private school, fifth-grade girls plotted about how to get particular boy–girl pairs together.

As Gagnon and Simon (1973) have suggested, two strands of sexuality are differently emphasized among adolescent girls and boys. Girls emphasize and learn about the emotional and romantic before the explicitly sexual. The sequence for boys is the reverse; commitment to sexual acts precedes commitment to emotion-laden, intimate relationships and the rhetoric of romantic love. Dating and courtship, Gagnon suggests, are processes in which each sex teaches the other what each wants and expects. The exchange, as they point out, does not always go smoothly. Indeed, in heterosexual relationships among older adults, tension often persists between the scripts (and felt needs) of women and of men.

Children's Sexual Meanings and the Construction of Gender Arrangements

Girls and boys, who spend considerable time in gender-separate groups, learn different patterns of interaction which, we have argued, lay the groundwork for the sexual scripts of adolescence and adulthood. However, sexuality is not simply delayed until adolescence. Children engage in sexual practices—kissing, erotic forms of touch, masturbation, and sometimes intercourse. As school-based observers, we saw only a few overt sexual activities among children, mostly incidents of public, cross-gender kissing, surrounded by teasing, chasing, and laughter.

HETEROSEXUAL TEASING AND THE IMPORTANCE OF THIRD PARTIES

The special loading of sexual words and gestures makes them useful for accomplishing non-sexual purposes. Sexual idioms provide a major resource which children draw upon as they construct and maintain gender segregation. Through the years of elementary school, children use with increasing frequency heterosexual idioms—claims that a particular girl or boy "likes," "has a crush on," or is "goin' with" someone from the other gender group.

Children's language for heterosexual relationships consists of a very few, often repeated, and sticky words. In a context of teasing, the charge that a particular boy "likes" a particular girl (or vice versa) may be hurled like an insult. The difficulty children have in countering such accusations was evident in a conversation between the observer and a group of third-grade girls in the lunchroom at the Michigan school:

> Susan asked me what I was doing, and I said I was observing the things children do and play. Nicole volunteered, "I like running when boys chase all the girls. See Tim over there? Judy chases him all around the school. She likes him." Judy, sitting across the table, quickly responded, "I hate him. I like him for a friend." "Tim loves Judy," Nicole said in a loud, sing-song voice.

Sexual and romantic teasing marks social hierarchies. The most popular children and the pariahs—the lowest status, excluded children—are most frequently mentioned as targets of "liking." Linking someone with a pariah suggests shared contamination and is an especially vicious tease.

When a girl or boy publicly says that she or he "likes" someone or has a boyfriend or girlfriend, that person defines the romantic situation and is less susceptible to teasing than those targeted by someone else. Crushes may be secretly revealed to friends, a mark of intimacy, especially among girls. The entrusted may then go public with the secret ("Wendy likes John"), which may be experienced as betrayal, but which also may be a way of testing the romantic waters. Such leaks, like those of government officials, can be denied or acted upon by the original source of information.

Third parties—witnesses and kibbitzers—are central to the structure of heterosexual teasing. The teasing constructs dyads (very few of them actively "couples"), but within the control of larger gender groups. Several of the white fifth graders in the Michigan and California schools and some of the black students in the Massachusetts schools occasionally went on dates, which were much discussed around the schools. Same-gender groups provide launching pads, staging grounds, and retreats for heterosexual couples, both real and imagined. Messengers and emissaries go between groups, indicating who likes whom and checking out romantic interest. By the time "couples" actually get together (if they do at all), the groups and their messengers have provided a network of constructed meanings, a kind of agenda for the pair. As we have argued, gender-divided peer groups sustain different meanings of the sexual. They also regulate heterosexual behavior by helping to define the emerging sexual scripts of adolescence (who "likes" whom, who might "go with" whom, what it means to be a couple).

HETEROSEXUALLY CHARGED RITUALS

Boundaries between boys and girls are also emphasized and maintained by heterosexually charged rituals like cross-sex chasing. Formal games of tag and informal episodes of chasing punctuate life on playgrounds. The informal episodes usually open with a provocation—taunts like "You can't get me!" or

"Slobber monster!"; bodily pokes; or the grabbing of possessions like a hat or scarf. The person who is provoked may ignore the taunt or poke, handle it verbally ("Leave me alone!"), or respond by chasing. After a chasing sequence, which may end after a short run or a pummeling, the chaser and chased may switch roles.

Chasing has a gendered structure. When boys chase one another, they often end up wrestling or in mock fights. When girls chase girls, they less often wrestle one another to the ground. Unless organized as a formal game like "freeze tag," same-gender chasing goes unnamed and usually undiscussed. But children set apart cross-gender chasing with special names—"girls chase the boys," "boys chase the girls"; "the chase"; "chasers"; "chase and kiss"; "kiss-chase"; "kissers and chasers"; "kiss or kill"—and with animated talk about the activity. The names vary by region and school, but inevitably contain both gender and sexual meanings.

When boys and girls chase one another, they become, by definition, separate teams. Gender terms override individual identities, especially for the other team: "Help, a girl's chasin' me!"; "C'mon Sarah, let's get that boy"; "Tony, help save me from the girls." Individuals may call for help from, or offer help to, others of their gender. In acts of treason they may also grab someone of their gender and turn them over to the opposing team, as when, in the Michigan school, Ryan grabbed Billy from behind, wrestled him to the ground, and then called, "Hey girls, get 'im."

Names like "chase and kiss" mark the sexual meanings of cross-gender chasing. The threat of kissing—most often girls threatening to kiss boys—is a ritualized form of provocation. Teachers and aides are often amused by this form of play among children in the lower grades. They are more perturbed by cross-gender chasing among fifth- and sixth-graders, perhaps because at those ages some girls "have their development" (breasts make sexual meanings seem more consequential), and because of the more elaborate patterns of touch and touch avoidance in chasing rituals among older children. The principal of one Michigan school forbade the sixth-graders from playing "pom-pom," a complicated chasing game, because it entailed "inappropriate touch."

Cross-gender chasing is sometimes structured around rituals of pollution, such as "cooties," where individuals or groups are treated as contaminating or "carrying germs." Children have rituals for transferring cooties (usually touching someone else and shouting "You've got cooties!"), for immunization (e.g., writing "CV" for "cootie vaccination" on their arms), and for eliminating cooties (e.g., saying "no gives" or using "cootie catchers" made of folded paper). Boys may transmit cooties, but cooties usually originate with girls. One version of cooties played in Michigan is called "girl stain." Although cooties is framed as play, the import may be serious. Female pariahs—the ultimate school untouchables by virtue of gender and some added stigma such as being overweight or from a very poor family—are sometimes called "cootie queens" or "cootie girls." Conversely, we have never heard or read about "cootie kings" or "cootie boys."

In these cross-gender rituals girls are defined as sexual. Boys sometimes threaten to kiss girls, but it is girls' kisses and touch which are deemed especially contaminating. Girls more often use the threat of kissing to tease boys and to make them run away, as in this example recorded among fourth-graders on the playground of the California school:

> Smiling and laughing, Lisa and Jill pulled a fourth-grade boy along by his hands, while a group of girls sitting on the jungle-gym called out, "Kiss him, kiss him." Grabbing at his hair, Lisa said to Jill, "Wanna kiss Jonathan?" Jonathan got away, and the girls chased after him. "Jill's gonna kiss your hair," Lisa yelled.

The use of kisses as a threat is double-edged, since the power comes from the threat of pollution. A girl who frequently uses this threat may be stigmatized as a "kisser."

Gender-marked rituals of teasing, chasing, and pollution heighten the boundaries between boys and girls. They also convey assumptions which get worked into later sexual scripts: (1) that girls and boys are members of distinctive, opposing, and sometimes antagonistic groups; (2) that cross-gender contact is potentially sexual and contaminating, fraught with both pleasure and danger; and (3) that girls are more sexually defined (and polluting) than boys.

Conclusion

Social scientists have often viewed the heterosexual dating rituals of adolescence—when girls and boys "finally" get together—as the concluding stage after the separate, presumably non-sexual, boys' and girls' groups that are so prevalent in childhood. We urge a closer look at the organization of sexuality and of gender in middle and late childhood. The gender-divided social worlds of children are not totally asexual. And same-gender groups have continuing import in the more overtly sexual scripts of adolescence and adulthood.

From an early age "the sexual" is prescriptively heterosexual and male homophobic. Children draw on sexual meanings to maintain gender segregation—to make cross-gender interaction risky and to mark and ritualize boundaries between "the boys" and "the girls." In their separate gender groups, girls and boys learn somewhat different patterns of bonding—boys sharing the arousal of group rule-breaking; girls emphasizing the construction of intimacy, and themes of romance. Coming to adolescent sexual intimacy from different and asymmetric gender subcultures, girls and boys bring somewhat different needs, capacities, and types of knowledge.

References

Eder, Dona (1985). "The cycle of popularity: interpersonal relations among female adolescents." *Sociology of Education* 58: 154–65.

Fine, Gary Alan (1980). "The natural history of preadolescent male friendship groups." Pp. 293–320 in Hugh C. Foot, Antony J. Chapman, and Jean R. Smith (eds.), *Friendship and Social Relations in Children*. New York: Wiley.

Gagnon, John H., and William Simon (1973). *Sexual Conduct*. Chicago: Aldine.

Luria, Zella (1983). "Sexual fantasy and pornography: two cases of girls brought up with pornography." *Archives of Sexual Behavior* 11: 395–404.

Miller, Patricia Y., and William Simon (1981). "The development of sexuality in adolescence." Pp. 383–407 in Joseph Adelson (ed.), *Handbook of Adolescent Psychology*. New York: Wiley.

Schofield, Janet (1982). *Black and White in School*. New York: Praeger.

15 But What Do You Mean? Women and Men in Conversation

DEBORAH TANNEN

We seldom realize how precarious social interaction is between men and women. For the most part, we manage to get our ideas across to one another with little difficulty. Sometimes, however, communication across gender lines leaves us headshakingly confused that "the other" could have said that, thought that, done that, giving us a glimmer that our worlds really are different. Sociologically, men and women represent separate worlds of socialization—with all the differences this implies, from ideas about sex and love to the best ways to get ahead in life.

Are there really major differences in male/female communications? Or are these statements exaggerations? You be the judge, as you read Tannen's summary of how women and men communicate. See how her analysis compares with your own experiences. You might also consider the implications of this analysis for problems experienced by couples "going together," as well as for difficulties between husbands and wives.

CONVERSATION IS A RITUAL. We say things that seem obviously the thing to say, without thinking of the literal meaning of our words, any more than we expect the question "How are you?" to call forth a detailed account of aches and pains.

Unfortunately, women and men often have different ideas about what's appropriate, different ways of speaking. Many of the conversational rituals common among women are designed to take the other person's feelings into account, while many of the conversational rituals common among men are designed to maintain the one-up position, or at least avoid appearing one-down. As a result, when men and women interact—especially at work—it's often women who are at the disadvantage. Because women are not trying to avoid the one-down position, that is unfortunately where they may end up.

Here, the biggest areas of miscommunication.

1. Apologies

Women are often told they apologize too much. The reason they're told to stop doing it is that, to many men, apologizing seems synonymous with putting oneself down. But there are many times when "I'm sorry" isn't self-deprecating, or even an apology; it's an automatic way of keeping both speakers on an equal footing. For example, a well-known columnist once interviewed me and gave me her phone number in case I needed to call her back. I misplaced the number and had to go through the newspaper's main switchboard. When our conversation was winding down and we'd both made ending-type remarks, I added "Oh, I almost forgot—I lost your direct number, can I get it again?" "Oh, I'm sorry," she came back instantly, even though she had done nothing wrong and *I* was the one who'd lost the number. But I understood she wasn't really apologizing; she was just automatically reassuring me she had no intention of denying me her number.

Even when "I'm sorry" *is* an apology, women often assume it will be the first step in a two-step ritual: I say "I'm sorry" and take half the blame, then you take the other half. At work, it might go something like this:

A. When you typed this letter, you missed this phrase I inserted.
B. Oh, I'm sorry. I'll fix it.
A. Well, I wrote it so small it was easy to miss.

When both parties share blame, it's a mutual face-saving device. But if one person, usually the woman, utters frequent apologies and the other doesn't, she ends up looking as if she's taking the blame for mishaps that aren't her fault. When she's only partially to blame, she looks entirely in the wrong.

I recently sat in on a meeting at an insurance company where the sole woman, Helen, said "I'm sorry" or "I apologize" repeatedly. At one point she said, "I'm thinking out loud. I apologize." Yet the meeting was intended to be an informal brain-storming session, and *everyone* was thinking out loud.

The reason Helen's apologies stood out was that she was the only person in the room making so many. And the reason I was concerned was that Helen felt the annual bonus she had received was unfair. When I interviewed her colleagues, they said that Helen was one of the best and most productive workers—yet she got one of the smallest bonuses. Although the problem might have been outright sexism, I suspect her speech style, which differs from that of her male colleagues, masks her competence.

Unfortunately, not apologizing can have its price too. Since so many women use ritual apologies, those who don't may be seen as hard-edged. What's important is to be aware of how often you say you're sorry (and why), and to monitor your speech based on the reaction you get.

2. Criticism

A woman who cowrote a report with a male colleague was hurt when she read a rough draft to him and he leapt into a critical response—"Oh, that's too dry! You have to make it snappier!" She herself would have been more likely to say, "That's a really good start. Of course, you'll want to make it a little snappier when you revise."

Whether criticism is given straight or softened is a matter of convention. In general, women use more softeners. I noticed this difference when talking to an editor about an essay I'd written. While going over changes she wanted to make, she said, "There's one more thing. I know you may not agree with me. The reason I noticed the problem is that your other points are so lucid and elegant." She went on hedging for several more sentences until I put her out of her misery: "Do you want to cut that part?" I asked—and of course she did. But I appreciated her tentativeness. In contrast, another editor (a man) I once called summarily rejected my idea for an article by barking, "Call me when you have something new to say."

Those who are used to ways of talking that soften the impact of criticism may find it hard to deal with the right-between-the-eyes style. It has its own logic, however, and neither style is intrinsically better. People who prefer criticism given straight are operating on an assumption that feelings aren't involved. "Here's the dope. I know you're good; you can take it."

3. Thank-Yous

A woman manager I know starts meetings by thanking everyone for coming, even though it's clearly their job to do so. Her "thank-you" is simply a ritual.

A novelist received a fax from an assistant in her publisher's office; it contained suggested catalogue copy for her book. She immediately faxed him her suggested changes and said, "Thanks for running this by me," even though her contract gave her the right to approve all copy. When she thanked the assistant, she fully expected him to reciprocate: "Thanks for giving me such a quick response." Instead, he said, "You're welcome." Suddenly, rather than an equal exchange of pleasantries, she found herself positioned as the recipient of a favor. This made her feel like responding, "Thanks for nothing!"

Many women use "thanks" as an automatic conversation starter and closer; there's nothing literally to thank you for. Like many rituals typical of women's conversation, it depends on the goodwill of the other to restore the balance. When the other speaker doesn't reciprocate, a woman may feel like someone on a seesaw whose partner abandoned his end. Instead of balancing in the air, she has plopped to the ground, wondering how she got there.

4. Fighting

Many men expect the discussion of ideas to be a ritual fight—explored through verbal opposition. They state their ideas in the strongest possible terms, thinking that if there are weaknesses someone will point them out, and by trying to argue against those objections, they will see how well their ideas hold up.

Those who expect their own ideas to be challenged will respond to another's ideas by trying to poke holes and find weak links—as a way of *helping*. The logic is that when you are challenged you will rise to the occasion: Adrenaline makes your mind sharper, you get ideas and insights you would not have thought of without the spur of battle.

But many women take this approach as a personal attack. Worse, they find it impossible to do their best work in such a contentious environment. If you're not used to ritual fighting, you begin to hear criticism of your ideas as soon as they are formed. Rather than making you think more clearly, it makes you doubt what you know. When you state your ideas, you hedge in order to fend off potential attacks. Ironically, this is more likely to *invite* attack because it makes you look weak.

Although you may never enjoy verbal sparring, some women find it helpful to learn how to do it. An engineer who was the only woman among four men in a small company found that as soon as she learned to argue, she was accepted and taken seriously. A doctor attending a hospital staff meeting made a similar discovery. She was becoming more and more angry with a male colleague who'd loudly disagreed with a point she'd made. Her better judgment told her to hold her tongue, to avoid making an enemy of this powerful senior colleague. But finally she couldn't hold it any longer, and she rose to her feet and delivered an impassioned attack on his position. She sat down in a panic, certain she had permanently damaged her relationship with him. To her amazement, he came up to her afterward and said, "That was a great rebuttal. I'm really impressed. Let's go out for a beer after work and hash out our approaches to this problem."

5. Praise

A manager I'll call Lester had been on his new job six months when he heard that the women reporting to him were deeply dissatisfied. When he talked to them about it, their feelings erupted; two said they were on the verge of quitting because he didn't appreciate their work, and they didn't want to wait to be fired. Lester was dumbfounded: He believed they were doing a fine job. Surely, he thought, he had said nothing to give them the impression he didn't like their work. And indeed he hadn't. That was the problem. He had said *nothing*—and the women assumed he was following the adage "If you can't say something nice, don't say anything." He thought he was showing confidence in them by leaving them alone.

Men and women have different habits in regard to giving praise. For example, Deidre and her colleague William both gave presentations at a conference. Afterward, Deidre told William, "That was a great talk." He thanked her. Then she asked, "What did you think of mine?" and he gave her a lengthy and detailed critique. She found it uncomfortable to listen to his comments. But she assured herself that he meant well, and that his honesty was a signal that she, too, should be honest when he asked for a critique of his performance. As a matter of fact, she had noticed quite a few ways in which he could have improved his presentation. But she never got a chance to tell him because he never asked—and she felt put down. The worst part was that it seemed she had only herself to blame, since she *had* asked what he thought of her talk.

But had she really asked for his critique? The truth is, when she asked for his opinion, she was expecting a compliment, which she felt was more or less required following anyone's talk. When he responded with criticism, she figured, Oh, he's playing 'Let's critique each other'—not a game she'd initiated, but one which she was willing to play. Had she realized he was going to criticize her and not ask her to reciprocate, she would never have asked in the first place.

It would be easy to assume that Deidre was insecure, whether she was fishing for a compliment or soliciting a critique. But she was simply talking automatically, performing one of the many conversational rituals that allow us to get through the day. William may have sincerely misunderstood Deidre's intention—or may have been unable to pass up a chance to one-up her when given the opportunity.

6. Complaints

"Troubles talk" can be a way to establish rapport with a colleague. You complain about a problem (which shows that you are just folks) and the other person responds with a similar problem (which puts you on equal footing). But while such commiserating is common among women, men are likely to hear it as a request to *solve* the problem.

One woman told me she would frequently initiate what she thought would be pleasant complaint-airing sessions at work. She'd just talk about situations that bothered her just to talk about them, maybe to understand them better. But her male office mate would quickly tell her how she could improve the situation. This left her feeling condescended to and frustrated. She was delighted to see this very impasse in a section in my book *You Just Don't Understand,* and showed it to him. "Oh," he said, "I see the problem. How can we solve it?" Then they both laughed, because it had happened again: He short-circuited the detailed discussion she'd hoped for and cut to the chase of finding a solution.

Sometimes the consequences of complaining are more serious: A man might take a woman's lighthearted griping literally, and she can get a reputation as a chronic malcontent. Furthermore, she may be seen as not up to solving the problems that arise on the job.

7. Jokes

I heard a man call in to a talk show and say, "I've worked for two women and neither one had a sense of humor. You know, when you work with men, there's a lot of joking and teasing." The show's host and the guest (both women) took his comment at face value and assumed the women this man worked for were humorless. The guest said, "Isn't it sad that women don't feel comfortable enough with authority to see the humor?" The host said, "Maybe when more women are in authority roles, they'll be more comfortable with power." But although the women this man worked for *may* have taken themselves too seriously, it's just as likely that they each had a terrific sense of humor, but maybe the humor wasn't the type he was used to. They may have been like the woman who wrote to me: "When I'm with men, my wit or cleverness seems inappropriate (or lost!) so I don't bother. When I'm with my women friends, however, there's no hold on puns or cracks and my humor is fully appreciated."

The types of humor women and men tend to prefer differ. Research has shown that the most common form of humor among men is razzing, teasing, and mock-hostile attacks, while among women it's self-mocking. Women often mistake men's teasing as genuinely hostile. Men often mistake women's mock self-deprecation as truly putting themselves down.

Women have told me they were taken more seriously when they learned to joke the way the guys did. For example, a teacher who went to a national conference with seven other teachers (mostly women) and a group of administrators (mostly men) was annoyed that the administrators always found reasons to leave boring seminars, while the teachers felt they had to stay and take notes. One evening, when the group met at a bar in the hotel, the principal asked her how one such seminar had turned out. She retorted, "As soon as you left, it got much better." He laughed out loud at her response. The playful insult appealed to the men—but there was a trade-off. The women seemed to back off from her after this. (Perhaps they were put off by her using joking to align herself with the bosses.)

There is no "right" way to talk. When problems arise, the culprit may be style differences—and *all* styles will at times fail with others who don't share or understand them, just as English won't do you much good if you try to speak to someone who knows only French. If you want to get your message across, it's not a question of being "right"; it's a question of using language that's shared—or at least understood.

PART V

Social Groups and Social Structure

No one is only a member of humanity in general; each of us is also a member of particular social groups. We live in a certain country and in a particular neighborhood. We belong to a family and are members of a gender and ethnic group. Most of us work at a job and have friends, and many of us go to school and belong to churches, clubs, and other social organizations. The articles in this Part are meant to sensitize us to how social groups and social structure have far-reaching effects on our lives. Let us see what some of those effects are.

No fact of social life is more important than group membership. *To belong to a group is to yield to others the right to make certain decisions about our behavior, while assuming obligations to act according to the expectations of those others.* This is illustrated by a parent saying to a teenage daughter or son: "As long as you are living under my roof, you had better be home by midnight." In this instance, the parents are saying that as long as the daughter or son wants to remain a member of the social group known as the household, her or his behavior must conform to their expectations. So it is with *all* the groups to which we belong: by our membership and participation in them we relinquish to others at least some control over our own lives.

Those groups that provide little option to belong or not are called *involuntary memberships* or *associations*. These include our family and the sexual, ethnic, and racial groups into which we are born. In contrast, those groups which we choose to join are called *voluntary memberships* or *associations*. The Boy and Girl Scouts, professional associations, church groups, clubs, friendship cliques, and work groups are examples. In certain instances we willingly, sometimes even gladly, conform to their rules and expectations in order to be-

159

come members. In all, we must modify some of our behaviors in order to belong to them and to remain members in good standing.

Not all memberships in voluntary associations involve the same degree of willingness to yield to others a measure of control over our lives. There even are groups, as with some jobs, where we can hardly bear to remain a member but feel that, under the circumstances, we cannot quit. Sociologists still use the term voluntary association to refer to this situation. *Both* voluntary and involuntary memberships vitally affect our lives, for, whether it is willing or unwilling, our participation in a group shapes not only our behaviors but also our ideas about life.

It is easy to see that social groups have far-reaching influence on our lives—for, as stressed in Part IV, we would not even be "human" without group membership. But what about the second term that heads the title of this Part? What does *social structure* mean? By this term, sociologists mean that the various social groups that make up our lives are not simply a random collection of components; rather, they are interrelated and form a significant unit that surrounds us.

I know that if any term in sociology sounds vague and irrelevant, it is "social structure." This term, however, also refers to highly significant matters—for *the social organization that underlies your life determines your relationships with others.* To better see what this term means, we can note that "social structure" encompasses five "levels." As I summarize them, I shall go from the broadest to the smallest level.

The first two levels are *intersocietal;* that is, they refer to international relationships. *First,* on the broadest level, social structure refers to relationships among blocs (or groups) of nations. Examples are the West's dependence on the Mideast for much of its oil, and the domination of the poor, least industrialized nations by the wealthy, most industrialized nations. The *second* level, the next broadest, refers to relationships between particular nations, such as the extensive role that the United States plays in the Canadian economy, and regional trading treaties such as NAFTA (North American Free Trade Agreement) and GATT (General Agreement on Tariffs and Trade). These first two levels—the international dimensions of social structure—sensitize us to relationships based on historical events as well as current balances of power and resources.

The next three levels are *intra*societal; that is, they refer to relationships within a society. The *first* level is quite broad. It refers to how the social institutions *within* a society are related to one another. This level sensitizes us to how political decisions affect the military, how economic booms and busts affect families, and the like. The *second,* a smaller level, refers to patterns between social groups, such as the relationship between McDonald's and other firms in the fast-food business. The *third,* the smallest level, deals with such matters as how people are organized *within* a particular group—such as an individual's role as leader or follower, or the parents' authority over their young children that empowers them to determine what the children will eat, where they will live, what schools they attend, and how they are to be disciplined.

Part V, which focuses on the influences of social groups and social structure on our lives, opens with a provocative question. Just how much control do groups have over people? Because of them, will people even willingly participate in extreme acts that go against their conscience? As Philip Meyer recounts the classic experiments of Stanley Milgram, you will see that groups do have such coercive power.

The next two selections focus on city life. Elijah Anderson examines the uneasy coexistence of the inner-city poor and middle-class gentrifiers (those who are rehabbing and thereby reclaiming an area of the city from the poor). Their interactions, often tense, are marked by social class and racial-ethnic distinctions. This provocative analysis is followed by John Coleman's focus on the urban homeless, which pinpoints the debilitating isolation that sometimes exists in the city.

The next two articles examine interaction in smaller settings. William Thompson turns our attention to interaction at work, looking at how workers struggle with the assembly line in the meat-packing industry. Then Mae Biggs and I use Goffman's dramaturgical model to uncover the means by which non-sexuality is sustained during vaginal examinations. Amy Waldman then turns our focus onto the isolated and lonely, people who crave the satisfying social interactions that most of us take for granted. Judy Root Aulette's and Raymond Michalowski's exposure of how social structure was manipulated to the harm of defenseless workers closes this Part.

A Digression on Research Methods

Because most of the articles in this Part—and in the book itself—are based on participant observation, it is useful to take a closer look at this research method. For many years, Anderson lived in the neighborhood he describes. Coleman wandered the city streets and slept in shelters for the homeless. Thompson worked in a meat-packing plant, and Biggs as a gynecological nurse. As these researchers *participated* in the lives of the people they were studying, they systematically *observed* what was happening; hence the label "participant observation."

To gather their data, participant observers sometimes place greater emphasis on observing people, at other times on participating in their lives. Whyte moved into a particular urban neighborhood in order to analyze it, while Anderson moved into an urban neighborhood to live there, found the experiences interesting, and began to analyze them. Because she didn't become a sociologist until after her many years of work as a gynecological nurse, Biggs's emphasis was almost solely on participation. Regardless of whether participation or observation receives the greater emphasis, when a researcher reports on observations of a social setting, the term "participant observation" is used to describe this method of studying social life. (The terms "field research," "field work," "ethnographic research," and "qualitative research" are also used to refer to this technique of studying people.) This research method allows authors to provide rich, detailed descriptions that, by retaining some of the "flavor" of the settings, bring the reader close to the events that occurred.

Thus, in the article on the homeless you can sense the crushing despair of living on the streets, while in the article on jails, if you put yourself in the shoes of a prisoner or deputy, you should feel some of their frustrations. Although participant observation lends itself to such rich descriptions, it is not the method, of course, but the author, who does the communicating. We depend on an author's skills for learning what life is like in other settings, even for gaining a sense of being there. Consequently, in an article that is far from participant observation, one that summarizes an experiment, you will feel the dilemma faced by the experimenter's victims.

As I stressed in my article on research methods in Part II, a chief concern of sociologists is that they gather accurate information about the people they study. To do this, sociologists try to be objective, to leave their biases behind both when they gather data and as they interpret those data for books, articles, and other reports they write. A primary distinction between research methods is whether they are *quantitative* or *qualitative.* Participant observation is an example of a qualitative method, and is more exploratory or descriptive. Quantitative methods place the emphasis on measuring precise differences between individuals and groups.

Through their training and experience, sociologists come to prefer some particular method of gathering data. They also associate with one another on the basis of the subject matter they are interested in *and* on the basis of the research methods they employ. Consequently, the qualitative and quantitative approaches to social research have become major identifiers among sociologists. Although sociologists have their preferences, and sometimes feel strongly that one approach is vastly superior, both qualitative and quantitative methods are valid means with which to gather data about social life.

In this book, the emphasis is on studies based on the qualitative approach, selections that impart the meanings and experiences of the groups being studied, even the "flavor" of being a member of these groups. As I see it (and as probably does your instructor), this approach best imparts the excitement of sociological discovery.

16 If Hitler Asked You to Electrocute a Stranger, Would You? Probably

PHILIP MEYER

Let's take the title of this selection seriously for a moment. Suppose that Hitler did ask you to electrocute a stranger, would you? "Of course, I wouldn't" is our immediate response. "*I* wouldn't even *hurt* a stranger just because someone asked me, much less electrocute the person."

Such an answer certainly seems reasonable, but unfortunately it may not be true. Consider two aspects of the power of groups over our lives. First, we all do things that we prefer not to—from going to work and taking tests when we really want to stay in bed to mowing the grass or doing the dishes when we want to watch television. Our roles and relationships require that we do them, and our own preferences become less important than fulfilling the expectations of others. Second, at least on occasion, most of us feel social pressures so strongly that we do things that conflict with our morals. Both these types of behavior are fascinating to sociologists, for they indicate how social structure—the way society is organized—shapes our lives.

But electrocute someone? Isn't that carrying the point a little too far? One would certainly think so. The experiments described by Meyer, however, indicate that people's positions in groups are so significant that even "nice, ordinary" people will harm strangers upon request. You may find the implications of authority and roles arising from these experiments disturbing. Many of us do.

IN THE BEGINNING, Stanley Milgram was worried about the Nazi problem. He doesn't worry much about the Nazis anymore. He worries about you and me, and perhaps himself a little bit too.

Stanley Milgram is a social psychologist, and when he began his career at Yale University in 1960 he had a plan to prove, scientifically, that Germans are different. The Germans-are-different hypothesis had been used by historians, such as William L. Shirer, to explain the systematic destruction of the Jews by the Third Reich. One madman could decide to destroy the Jews and even create a master plan for getting it done. But to implement it on the scale that

163

Hitler did meant that thousands of other people had to go along with the scheme and help to do the work. The Shirer thesis, which Milgram set out to test, is that Germans have a basic character flaw which explains the whole thing, and this flaw is a readiness to obey authority without question, no matter what outrageous acts the authority commands.

The appealing thing about this theory is that it makes those of us who are not Germans feel better about the whole business. Obviously, you and I are not Hitler, and it seems equally obvious that we would never do Hitler's dirty work for him. But now, because of Stanley Milgram, we are compelled to wonder. Milgram developed a laboratory experiment which provided a systematic way to measure obedience. His plan was to try it out in New Haven on Americans and then go to Germany and try it out on Germans. He was strongly motivated by scientific curiosity, but there was also some moral content in his decision to pursue this line of research, which was in turn colored by his own Jewish background. If he could show that Germans are more obedient than Americans, he could then vary the conditions of the experiment and try to find out just what it is that makes some people more obedient than others. With this understanding, the world might, conceivably, be just a little bit better.

But he never took his experiment to Germany. He never took it any farther than Bridgeport. The first finding, also the most unexpected and disturbing finding, was that we Americans are an obedient people: not blindly obedient, and not blissfully obedient, just obedient. "I found so much obedience," says Milgram softly, a little sadly, "I hardly saw the need for taking the experiment to Germany."

There is something of the theater director in Milgram, and his technique, which he learned from one of the old masters in experimental psychology, Solomon Asch, is to stage a play with every line rehearsed, every prop carefully selected, and everybody an actor except one person. That one person is the subject of the experiment. The subject, of course, does not know he is in a play. He thinks he is in real life. The value of this technique is that the experimenter, as though he were God, can change a prop here, vary a line there, and see how the subject responds. Milgram eventually had to change a lot of the script just to get people to stop obeying. They were obeying so much, the experiment wasn't working—it was like trying to measure oven temperature with a freezer thermometer.

The experiment worked like this: If you were an innocent subject in Milgram's melodrama, you read an ad in the newspaper or received one in the mail asking for volunteers for an educational experiment. The job would take about an hour and pay $4.50. So you make an appointment and go to an old Romanesque stone structure on High Street with the imposing name of The Yale Interaction Laboratory. It looks something like a broadcasting studio. Inside, you meet a young, crew-cut man in a laboratory coat who says he is Jack Williams, the experimenter. There is another citizen, fiftyish, Irish face, an accountant, a little overweight, and very mild and harmless looking. This other citizen seems nervous and plays with his hat while the two of you sit in chairs side by side and are told that the $4.50 checks are yours no matter what happens. Then you listen to Jack Williams explain the experiment.

It is about learning, says Jack Williams in a quiet, knowledgeable way. Science does not know much about the conditions under which people learn and this experiment is to find out about negative reinforcement. Negative re-inforcement is getting punished when you do something wrong, as opposed to positive reinforcement which is getting rewarded when you do something right. The negative reinforcement in this case is electric shock. You notice a book on the table, titled, *The Teaching-Learning Process,* and you assume that this has something to do with the experiment.

Then Jack Williams takes two pieces of paper, puts them in a hat, and shakes them up. One piece of paper is supposed to say, "Teacher," and the other, "Learner." Draw one and you will see which you will be. The mild-look-ing accountant draws one, holds it close to his vest like a poker player, looks at it, and says, "Learner." You look at yours. It says, "Teacher." You do not know that the drawing is rigged, and both slips say "Teacher." The experimenter beckons to the mild-mannered "learner."

"Want to step right in here and have a seat, please?" he says. "You can leave your coat on the back of that chair . . . roll up your right sleeve, please. Now what I want to do is strap down your arms to avoid excessive movement on your part during the experiment. This electrode is connected to the shock generator in the next room.

"And this electrode paste," he says, squeezing some stuff out of a plastic bottle and putting it on the man's arm, "is to provide a good contact and to avoid a blister or burn. Are there any questions now before we go into the next room?"

You don't have any, but the strapped-in "learner" does.

"I do think I should say this," says the learner. "About two years ago, I was in the veterans' hospital . . . they detected a heart condition. Nothing seri-ous, but as long as I'm having these shocks, how strong are they—how danger-ous are they?"

Williams, the experimenter, shakes his head casually. "Oh, no," he says. "Although they may be painful, they're not dangerous. Anything else?"

Nothing else. And so you play the game. The game is for you to read a se-ries of word pairs: for example, blue-girl, nice-day, fat-neck. When you finish the list, you read just the first word in each pair and then a multiple-choice list of four other words, including the second word of the pair. The learner, from his remote, strapped-in position, pushes one of four switches to indicate which of the four answers he thinks is the right one. If he gets it right, nothing hap-pens and you go on to the next one. If he gets it wrong, you push a switch that buzzes and gives him an electric shock. And then you go on to the next word. You start with 15 volts and increase the number of volts by 15 for each wrong answer. The control board goes from 15 volts on one end to 450 volts on the other. So that you know what you are doing, you get a test-shock yourself, at 45 volts. It hurts. To further keep you aware of what you are doing to that man in there, the board has verbal descriptions of the shock levels, ranging from "Slight Shock" at the left-hand side, through "Intense Shock" in the middle, to "Danger: Severe Shock" toward the far right. Finally, at the very end, under 435- and 450-volt switches, there are three ambiguous X's. If, at any point, you hesitate, Mr. Williams calmly tells you to go on. If you still hesitate, he tells you again.

Except for some terrifying details, which will be explained in a moment, this is the experiment. The object is to find the shock level at which you disobey the experimenter and refuse to pull the switch.

When Stanley Milgram first wrote this script, he took it to 14 Yale psychology majors and asked them what they thought would happen. He put it this way: Out of one hundred persons in the teacher's predicament, how would their break-off points be distributed along the 15- to 450-volt scale? They thought a few would break off very early, most would quit someplace in the middle, and a few would go all the way to the end. The highest estimate of the number out of 100 who would go all the way to the end was three. Milgram then informally polled some of his fellow scholars in the psychology department. They agreed that very few would go to the end. Milgram thought so too.

"I'll tell you quite frankly," he says, "before I began this experiment, before any shock generator was built, I thought that most people would break off at 'Strong Shock' or 'Very Strong Shock.' You would get only a very, very small proportion of people going out to the end of the shock generator, and they would constitute a pathological fringe."

In his pilot experiments, Milgram used Yale students as subjects. Each of them pushed the shock switches, one by one, all the way to the end of the board.

So he rewrote the script to include some protests from the learner. At first, they were mild, gentlemanly, Yalie protests, but "it didn't seem to have as much effect as I thought it would or should," Milgram recalls. "So we had more violent protestation on the part of the person getting the shock. All of the time, of course, what we were trying to do was not to create a macabre situation, but simply to generate disobedience. And that was one of the first findings. This was not only a technical deficiency of the experiment, that we didn't get disobedience. It really was the first finding: that obedience would be much greater than we had assumed it would be and disobedience would be much more difficult than we had assumed."

As it turned out, the situation did become rather macabre. The only meaningful way to generate disobedience was to have the victim protest with great anguish, noise, and vehemence. The protests were tape-recorded so that all the teachers ordinarily would hear the same sounds and nuances, and they started with a grunt at 75 volts, proceeded through a "Hey, that really hurts," at 125 volts, got desperate with, "I can't stand the pain—don't do that," at 180 volts, reached complaints of heart trouble at 195, an agonized scream at 285, a refusal to answer at 315, and only heartrending, ominous silence after that.

Still, 65 percent of the subjects, 20- to 50-year-old American males, everyday, ordinary people, like you and me, obediently kept pushing those levers in the belief that they were shocking the mild-mannered learner, whose name was Mr. Wallace, and who was chosen for the role because of his innocent appearance, all the way up to 450 volts.

Milgram was not getting enough disobedience so that he had something he could measure. The next step was to vary the circumstances to see what would encourage or discourage obedience. There seemed very little left in the way of discouragement. The victim was already screaming at the top of his lungs and feigning a heart attack. So whatever new impediment to obedience reached the brain of the subject had to travel by some route other than the ear. Milgram thought of one.

He put the learner in the same room with the teacher. He stopped strapping the learner's hand down. He rewrote the script so that at 150 volts the learner took his hand off the shock plate and declared that he wanted out of experiment. He rewrote the script some more so that the experimenter then told the teacher to grasp the learner's hand and physically force it down on the plate to give Mr. Wallace his unwanted electric shock.

"I had the feeling that very few people would go on at that point, if any," Milgram says. "I thought that would be the limit of obedience that you would find in the laboratory."

It wasn't.

Although [years have] gone by, Milgram still remembers the first person to walk into the laboratory in the newly rewritten script. He was a construction worker, a very short man. "He was so small," says Milgram, "that when he sat on the chair in front of the shock generator, his feet didn't reach the floor. When the experimenter told him to push the victim's hand down and give the shock, he turned to the experimenter, and he turned to the victim, his elbow went up, he fell down on the hand of the victim, his feet kind of tugged to one side, and he said, 'Like this, boss?' Zzumph!"

The experiment was played out to its bitter end. Milgram tried it with 40 different subjects. And 30 percent of them obeyed the experimenter and kept on obeying.

"The protests of the victim were strong and vehement, he was screaming his guts out, he refused to participate, and you had to physically struggle with him in order to get his hand down on the shock generator," Milgram remembers. But 12 out of 40 did it.

Milgram took his experiment out of New Haven. Not to Germany, just 20 miles down the road to Bridgeport. Maybe, he reasoned, the people obeyed because of the prestigious setting of Yale University. If they couldn't trust a learning center that had been there for two centuries, whom could they trust? So he moved the experiment to an untrustworthy setting.

The new setting was a suite of three rooms in a run-down office building in Bridgeport. The only identification was a sign with a fictitious name: "Research Associates of Bridgeport." Questions about professional connections got only vague answers about "research for industry."

Obedience was less in Bridgeport. Forty-eight percent of the subjects stayed for the maximum shock, compared to 65 percent at Yale. But this was enough to prove that far more than Yale's prestige was behind the obedient behavior.

[Since the experiments] Stanley Milgram has been trying to figure out what makes ordinary American citizens so obedient. The most obvious answer—that people are mean, nasty, brutish, and sadistic—won't do. The subjects who gave the shocks to Mr. Wallace to the end of the board did not enjoy it. They groaned, protested, fidgeted, argued, and in some cases, were seized by fits of nervous, agitated giggling.

"They even try to get out of it," says Milgram, "but they are somehow engaged in something from which they cannot liberate themselves. They are locked into a structure, and they do not have the skills or inner resources to disengage themselves. . . ."

"The results, as seen and felt in the laboratory," he has written, "are disturbing. They raise the possibility that human nature, or more specifically the kind of character produced in American democratic society, cannot be counted on to insulate its citizens from brutality and inhumane treatment at the direction of malevolent authority. A substantial proportion of people do what they are told to do, irrespective of the content of the act and without limitation of conscience, so long as they perceive that the command comes from a legitimate authority. If, in this study, an anonymous experimenter can successfully command adults to subdue a 50-year-old man and force on him painful electric shocks against his protest, one can only wonder what government, with its vastly greater authority and prestige, can command of its subjects. . . ."

Stanley Milgram has his problems, too. He believes that in the laboratory situation, he would not have shocked Mr. Wallace. His professional critics reply that in his real-life situation he has done the equivalent. He has placed innocent and naive subjects under great emotional strain and pressure in selfish obedience to his quest for knowledge. When you raise this issue with Milgram, he has an answer ready. There is, he explains patiently, a critical difference between his naive subjects and the man in the electric chair. The man in the electric chair (in the mind of the naive subject) is helpless, strapped in. But the naive subject is free to go at any time.

Immediately after he offers this distinction, Milgram anticipates the objection.

"It's quite true," he says. "that this is almost a philosophic position, because we have learned that some people are psychologically incapable of disengaging themselves. But that doesn't relieve them of the moral responsibility."

The parallel is exquisite. "The tension problem was unexpected," says Milgram in his defense. But he went on anyway. The naive subjects didn't expect the screaming protests from the strapped-in learner. But they went on.

"I had to make a judgment," says Milgram. "I had to ask myself, was this harming the person or not? My judgment is that it was not. Even in the extreme cases, I wouldn't say that permanent damage results."

Sound familiar? "The shocks may be painful," the experimenter kept saying, "but they're not dangerous."

After the series of experiments was completed, Milgram sent a report of the results to his subjects and a questionnaire, asking whether they were glad or sorry to have been in the experiment. Eighty-three and seven-tenths percent said they were glad and only 1.3 percent were sorry; 15 percent were neither sorry nor glad. However, Milgram could not be sure at the time of the experiment that only 1.3 percent would be sorry.

Kurt Vonnegut, Jr., put one paragraph in the preface to *Mother Night,* in 1966, which pretty much says it for the people with their fingers on the shock-generator switches, for you and me, and maybe even for Milgram. "If I'd been born in Germany," Vonnegut said, "I suppose I would have *been* a Nazi, bopping Jews and gypsies and Poles around, leaving boots sticking out of snowbanks, warming myself with my sweetly virtuous insides. So it goes."

Just so. One thing that happened to Milgram back in New Haven during the days of the experiment was that he kept running into people he'd watched from behind the one-way glass. It gave him a funny feeling, seeing those people going about their everyday business in New Haven and knowing what they would do to Mr. Wallace if ordered to. Now that his research results are in and you've thought about it, you can get this funny feeling too. You don't need one-way glass. A glance in your own mirror may serve just as well.

17 Streetwise

ELIJAH ANDERSON

Master statuses are those characteristics that cut across our other statuses. As noted in the introduction to Part IV, gender is an example of a
master status. A woman may be a professor, physician, or laborer, but
she is perceived as a *female* professor, a *female* physician, or a *female*
laborer. Similarly, ex-con, convicted rapist, multimillionaire, paraplegic,
and elderly are master statuses. No matter what else these individuals
may do in life, their activities are perceived through the screen of these
statuses. In this article, Anderson, who did participant observation in a
changing neighborhood for 14 years, analyzes how the master status of
"young black male" affects interaction.

   Anderson lives in the Philadelphia neighborhood he refers to as
the Village-Northton. The Village has undergone *gentrification,* a
process by which the relatively affluent move into an urban area inhabited by the poor and renovate the buildings. Gentrification increases
property values, and the neighborhood becomes too expensive for the
poor to remain. Next to the Village is a ghetto, whose high crime rate
spills over into the Village. Consequently, for the relatively affluent
African Americans and whites who live in the Village, the presence of
strangers makes even walking down the street a problem, and the middle class interacts uneasily with the poor. This selection examines public interaction when distrust and the threat of violence enshroud people's relationships.

AN OVERWHELMING NUMBER OF young black males in the
Village are committed to civility and law-abiding behavior. They often have a
hard time convincing others of this, however, because of the stigma attached
to their skin color, age, gender, appearance, and general style of self-presenta-
tion. Moreover, most residents ascribe criminality, incivility, toughness, and
street smartness to the anonymous black male, who must work hard to make
others trust his common decency.

   This state of affairs is worth exploring [because] . . . the situation of young
black men as a group encapsulates the stigmatizing effect of "negative" status-
determining characteristics, in this case gender and race. Because public encounters between strangers on the streets of urban America are by nature
brief, the participants must draw conclusions about each other quickly, and

they generally rely on a small number of cues. This process is universal, and it unavoidably involves some prejudging—prejudice—but its working out is especially prominent in the public spaces of the Village-Northton. . . .

The residents of the area, including black men themselves, are likely to defer to unknown black males, who move convincingly through the area as though they "run it," exuding a sense of ownership. They are easily perceived as symbolically inserting themselves into any available social space, pressing against those who might challenge them. The young black males, the "big winners" of these little competitions, seem to feel very comfortable as they swagger confidently along. Their looks, their easy smiles, and their spontaneous laughter, singing, cursing, and talk about the intimate details of their lives, which can be followed from across the street, all convey the impression of little concern for other pedestrians. The other pedestrians, however, are very concerned about them. . . .

People, black or white, who are more familiar with the black street culture are less troubled by sharing the streets with young black males. Older black men, for instance, frequently adopt a refined set of criteria. In negotiating the streets, they watch out particularly for a certain *kind* of young black male: "jitterbugs" or those who might belong to "wolf packs," small bands of black teenage boys believed to travel about the urban areas accosting and robbing people.

Many members of the Village community, however, both black and white, lack these more sophisticated insights. Incapable of making distinctions between law-abiding black males and others, they rely for protection on broad stereotypes based on color and gender, if not outright racism. They are likely to misread many of the signs displayed by law-abiding black men, thus becoming apprehensive of almost any black male they spot in public. . . . The "master status-determining characteristic" of race (Hughes 1945) is at work in the most casual street encounter. Becker's application of Hughes's conception of the contradictions and dilemmas of status has special relevance:

> Some statuses, in our society as in others, override all other statuses and have a certain priority. Race is one of these. Membership in the Negro race, as socially defined, will override most other status considerations in most situations; the fact that one is a physician or middle class or female will not protect one from being treated as a Negro first and any of these other things second. The status of deviant (depending on the kind of deviance) is this kind of master status. One receives the status as a result of breaking a rule, and the identification proves to be more important than most others. One will be identified as a deviant first, before other identifications are made. The question raised: "What kind of person would break such an important rule?" And the answer given: "One who is different from the rest of us, who cannot or will not act as a moral human being and therefore might break other important rules." The deviant identification becomes the controlling one.
>
> Treating a person as though he were generally rather than specifically deviant produces a self-fulfilling prophecy. It sets in motion several mechanisms

which conspire to shape the person in the image people have of him. (Becker
1963: 33, 34)

In the minds of many Village residents, black and white, the master status of the
young black male is determined by his youth, his blackness, his maleness, and
what these attributes have come to stand for in the shadow of the ghetto. . . .

Because public interactions generally matter for only a few crucial seconds, people are conditioned to rapid scrutiny of the looks, speech, public behavior, gender, and color of those sharing the environment. . . . The central
strategy in maintaining safety on the streets is to avoid strange black males.
The public awareness is color-coded: white skin denotes civility, law-abiding-
ness, and trustworthiness, while black skin is strongly associated with poverty,
crime, incivility, and distrust. Thus an unknown young black male is readily
deferred to. If he asks for anything, he must be handled quickly and summarily. If he is persistent, help must be summoned.

This simplistic racial interpretation of crime creates a "we/they" di-
chotomy between whites and blacks. Yet here again the underlying issue is
class. . . . Middle-income blacks in the Village, who also are among the
"haves," often share a victim mentality with middle-income whites and appear
just as distrustful of black strangers. Believing they are immune to the charge
of racism, Village blacks make some of the same remarks as whites do, sometimes voicing even more incisive observations concerning "street blacks" and
black criminality. . . .

Street Etiquette

A set of informal rules has emerged among residents and other users of the
public spaces of the Village. These rules allow members of diverse groups orderly passage with the promise of security, or at least a minimum of trouble
and conflict. . . . The process begins something like this. One person sees another walking down the street alone, with another person, or perhaps with a
few others. Those seen might be getting out of an unusual car, riding a ten-
speed bicycle, walking a dog, strolling on the grounds of a dwelling in the
neighborhood, or simply crossing the street at the light or leaving a store carrying groceries. The sight of people engaging in such everyday activities helps
to convey what may be interpreted as the usual picture of public life—what
residents take for granted.

Skin color, gender, age, dress, and comportment are important markers
that characterize and define the area. Depending on the observer's biases,
such specific markers can become the most important characteristics determining the status of those being watched, superseding other meaningful attributes. However, the most important aspect of the situation is simply that
the observer takes mental note of the other person: a significant social contact,

though usually not a reciprocal one, is made. The person seen, and the category he or she is believed to represent, comes to be considered an ordinary part of the environment.

Although the initial observation is important, it is not the crucial element in "knowing about" others and feeling comfortable. Rather, it helps determine the social context for any other meaningful interactions, whether unilateral or bilateral. It gives users of the streets a sense of whom to expect where and when, and it allows them to adjust their plans accordingly.

The significance of the initial encounter is contingent upon subsequent meetings and interactions. If the person is never seen again, the encounter gradually loses significance. But if the observer sees the person again or meets others who are similar, the initial impression may become stronger and might develop into a theory about the category of people, a working conception of a social type. The strength of such impressions—nurtured and supported through repeated encounters, observations, and talk with other residents—gradually builds.

Background information and knowledge may provide a basis for social connection. A stranger may be seen in one context, then in another, then in a third. In time the observer might say to himself, "I know that person." Certainly he does know the person, if only by sight. He has noticed him many times in various neighborhood contexts, and with each successive encounter he has become increasingly familiar with him and the class he has come to represent. Probably the two are not yet speaking, though they may have exchanged looks that establish the minimal basis for trust. If asked directly, the observer might say, "Yeah, I've seen him around." In this way strangers may know each other and obtain a degree of territorial communion without ever speaking a word. It is quite possible that they will never reach speaking terms.

But there are circumstances where the social gap between visual and verbal interaction in public is pressed and the relationship between incomplete strangers is required to go further. People sometimes feel silly continually passing others they know well by sight without speaking to them. They may resolve their discomfort by greeting them or by contrived avoidance. If they choose to speak, they may commit themselves to a series of obligatory greetings.

Introductions may also occur when two people who have seen each other in the neighborhood for some time happen to meet in a different part of town; there, despite some awkwardness, they may feel constrained to greet each other like long-lost friends. Perhaps they had not yet reached the point of speaking but had only warily acknowledged one another with knowing looks, or even with the customary offensive/defensive scowl used on the street for keeping strangers at a distance. After this meeting, previously distant villagers may begin to speak regularly on the neighborhood streets. In this way trust can be established between strangers, who may then come to know each other in limited ways or very well.

Just the fact of their regular presence offers a sense of security, or at least continuity, to their neighbors. Thus, many people walk the streets with a confidence that belies their serious concerns. They use those they "know" as buffers against danger. Although they may still be strangers, they feel they can call on each other as allies when neighborhood crises emerge, when they would otherwise be seriously short of help, or when they must protect themselves or their loved ones. For example, during emergencies such as house fires, street crimes in which someone clearly needs help, or some other event where partial strangers have an opportunity to gather and compare notes with neighbors who seemed out of reach before, they may first provide help and only then reach out a hand and introduce themselves, saying, "Hello, my name is. . . . "

EYE WORK

Many blacks perceive whites as tense or hostile to them in public. They pay attention to the amount of eye contact given. In general, black males get far less time in this regard than do white males. Whites tend not to "hold" the eyes of a black person. It is more common for black and white strangers to meet each other's eyes for only a few seconds, and then to avert their gaze abruptly. Such behavior seems to say, "I am aware of your presence," and no more. Women especially feel that eye contact invites unwanted advances, but some white men feel the same and want to be clear about what they intend. This eye work is a way to maintain distance, mainly for safety and social purposes. . . .

Many people, particularly those who see themselves as more economically privileged than others in the community, are careful not to let their eyes stray, in order to avoid an uncomfortable situation. As they walk down the street they pretend not to see other pedestrians, or they look right at them without speaking, a behavior many blacks find offensive.

Moreover, whites of the Village often scowl to keep young blacks at a social and physical distance. As they venture out on the streets of the Village and, to a lesser extent, of Northton, they may plant this look on their faces to ward off others who might mean them harm. Scowling by whites may be compared to gritting by blacks as a coping strategy. At times members of either group make such faces with little regard for circumstances, as if they were dressing for inclement weather. But on the Village streets it does not always storm, and such overcoats repel the sunshine as well as the rain, frustrating many attempts at spontaneous human communication.

MONEY

Naturally, given two adjacent neighborhoods representing "haves" and "have-nots," there is tremendous anxiety about money: how much to carry, how to hold it, how to use it safely in public. As in other aspects of Village life, shared anecdotes and group discussions help newcomers recognize the underlying rules of comportment.

Perhaps the most important point of etiquette with regard to money in public places is to be discreet. For example, at the checkout counter one looks into one's wallet or purse and takes out only enough to cover the charge, being careful that the remaining contents are not on display. Further, one attempts to use only small bills so as not to suggest that one has large ones.

When walking on the streets at night, it is wise to keep some money in a wallet or purse and hide the rest in other parts of one's clothing—some in a jacket pocket, some in the back pocket of one's jeans, maybe even some in a sock. In this way one would not lose everything in a mugging, yet the mugger would get something to appease him.

A final rule, perhaps the most critical, is that in a potentially violent situation it is better to lose one's money than one's life. Thus the person who plans to travel at dangerous times or in dangerous areas should have some money on hand in case of an assault:

> It was 9:00 P.M., and the Christmas party had ended. I was among the last to leave. John [a forty-five-year-old professional], the host, had to run an errand and asked if I wanted to go with him. I agreed. While I was waiting, Marsha, John's wife, said in a perfectly serious voice, "Now, John, before you go, do you have $10 just in case you get mugged?" "No, I don't have it, do you?"
>
> Marsha fetched $10 and gave it to John as what was in effect protection money, a kind of consolation prize designed to cool out a prospective mugger. As we walked the three blocks or so on the errand, John said, "We've come two blocks, and it's not so bad." His tone was that of a nervous joke, as though he really half expected to encounter muggers.

The reality of the Village is that residents can make their lives safer by "expecting" certain problems and making plans to cope with them. The mental preparation involved—imagining a bad situation and coming up with the best possible solution, acting it out in one's mind—may well be a valuable tool in learning to behave safely on the streets. . . .

OTHER SAFETY RULES AND STRATEGIES

Dress is an important consideration when walking the Village streets, day or night. Women wear clothing that negates stereotypical "female frailty" and symbolizes aggressiveness. Unisex jackets, blue jeans, and sneakers are all part of the urban female costume. "Sexy" dresses are worn only when women are in a group, accompanied by a man, or traveling by car.

Village men also stick to practical, nonshowy clothing. Most times this means blue jeans or a sweat suit. More expensive clothing is relegated to daytime work hours or, as for females, travel by car.

The safety of cars and things in them is a major worry. Newcomers learn to park on the east-west streets to avoid nighttime vandalism and theft. They buy "crime locks" and hood locks for their cars. They learn, sometimes through painful error, to remove attractive items like tape decks and expensive briefcases, or anything that looks valuable, before they lock up and leave.

Their homes may be similarly barricaded. They sometimes have chains for their bicycles, bars for their first-floor windows, and dead bolts for their back doors. Some install elaborate and expensive burglar alarms or keep dogs for the same purpose. They may build high fences to supplement the quaint waist-high wrought-iron fences from the early 1900s when the wealthy still claimed hegemony in the area.

Watching from the car as companions go into their houses is a standard precaution for city dwellers. The driver idles the motor out front and keeps an eye on the street until the resident has unlocked the door and is safely inside. This common practice has become ritualized in many instances, perhaps more important as a sign of a caring bond between people than as a deterrent of assault. It helps to make people feel secure, and residents understand it as a polite and intelligent action.

But some people are given to overreaction and to overelaboration of "mug-proofing" behaviors and are likely to see a potential mugger in almost anyone with certain attributes, most noticeably black skin, maleness, and youth. A middle-aged white woman told me this story:

> I had a white taxi driver drive me home once, and he was horrified at the neighborhood I lived in. It was night, and he told me what a horrible neighborhood I lived in, speaking of how dangerous it was here. He said, "This neighborhood is full of blacks. You'll get raped; you'll get murdered, or robbed." I replied, "I've lived here for a long time. I really like this neighborhood." He let me out on the opposite side of Thirty-fourth Street. He said, "OK, you go straight in your door, and I'll cover you." And he pulled out a gun. I said, "Please put it away." But he wouldn't. I was scared to death he was going to shoot me or something as I walked toward the house. It was so offensive to me that this man [did this], whom I trusted less than I trusted any of my neighbors, even those I knew only by sight. I felt sick for days.

The woman surmised that the taxi driver "must have been from a white ethnic and working-class background." It is commonly assumed among local blacks that such men feel especially threatened by blacks. But some middle- and upper-middle-class whites within the Village are susceptible to similar situational behavior.

Street Wisdom

. . . Street wisdom and street etiquette are comparable to a scalpel and a hatchet. One is capable of cutting extremely fine lines between vitally different organs; the other can only make broader, more brutal strokes. . . .

The streetwise individual thus becomes interested in a host of signs, emblems, and symbols that others exhibit in everyday life. Besides learning the "safety signals" a person might display—conservative clothing, a tie, books, a newspaper—he also absorbs the vocabulary and expressions of the street. If he is white, he may learn for the first time to make distinctions among different kinds of black people. He may learn the meaning of certain styles of hats, sweaters, jackets, shoes, and other emblems of the subculture, thus rendering the local environment "safer" and more manageable. . . .

A primary motivation for acquiring street wisdom is the desire to have the upper hand. It is generally believed that this will ensure safe passage, allowing one to outwit a potential assailant. In this regard a social game may be discerned. Yet it is a serious game, for failing could mean loss of property, injury, or even death. To prevail means simply to get safely to one's destination, and the ones who are most successful are those who are "streetwise." Street wisdom is really street etiquette wisely enacted. . . .

Typically, those generally regarded as streetwise are veterans of the public spaces. They know how to get along with strangers, and they understand how to negotiate the streets. They know whom to trust, whom not to trust, what to say through body language or words. They have learned how to behave effectively in public. Probably the most important consideration is the experience they have gained through encounters with "every kind of stranger." Although one may know about situations through the reports of friends or relatives, this pales in comparison with actual experience. It is often sheer proximity to the dangerous streets that allows a person to gain street wisdom and formulate some effective theory of the public spaces. As one navigates there is a certain edge to one's demeanor, for the streetwise person is both wary of others and sensitive to the subtleties that could salvage safety out of danger.

The longer people live in this locale, having to confront problems on the streets and public spaces every day, the greater chance they have to develop a sense of what to do without seriously compromising themselves. Further, the longer they are in the area, the more likely they are to develop contacts who might come to their aid, allowing them to move boldly.

This self-consciousness makes people likely to be alert and sensitive to the nuances of the environment. More important, they will project their ease and self-assurance to those they meet, giving them the chance to affect the interaction positively. For example, the person who is "streetdumb," relying for guidance on the most superficial signs, may pay too much attention to skin color and become needlessly tense just because the person approaching is black. A streetwise white who meets a black person will probably just go about his or her business. In both cases the black person will pick up the "vibe" being projected—in the first instance fear and hostility, in the second case comfort and a sense of commonality. There are obviously times when the "vibe" itself could tip the balance in creating the subsequent interaction.

CRISIS AND ADAPTATION

Sometimes the balance tips severely, and the whole neighborhood reacts with shock and alarm. A wave of fear surges through the community when violent crimes are reported by the media or are spread by word of mouth through the usually peaceful Village. One February a young woman, a new mother, was stabbed and left for dead in her home on one of the well-traveled north-south streets. Her month-old baby was unharmed, but it was weeks before the mother, recuperating in the hospital, remembered she had recently given birth. Word of how the stabbing occurred spread up and down the blocks of the Village. Neighbors said the woman often went out her back door to take out the garbage or call in the dog. But to uninitiated newcomers, the brick streets and large yards seem deceptively peaceful. Crises like these leave in their wake a deeper understanding of the "openness" that characterizes this quaint area of the city.

They also separate those who survive by brittle etiquette from those who—despite increased temporary precautions—can continue to see strangers as individuals. Less than half a block away from the scene of the attack, in a building facing an east-west street, a friend of the young mother was overcome with fear. Her husband was scheduled to go out of town the week after the vicious attack on her friend. She was so frightened that he had to arrange for a neighbor to "baby-sit" with his wife and children at night while he was away.

Security all over the Village was tightened for a time. People who used to go in and out, feeding the birds, shoveling walks, visiting their neighbors and friends, no longer came and went so carelessly. As the news traveled, fear rippled out from the young victim's immediate neighbors to affect behavior in other parts of the Village. One young black man reported that after the attack he was greeted with suspicious stares on his way to Mr. Chow's. "Everyone's looking over their shoulder suddenly," he said. "All black people are suspects."

"It makes you stop and wonder about living here," said one young mother shortly after the stabbing became the main item of conversation. "I've never lived in such a dangerous neighborhood. I run upstairs and leave my back door open sometimes. Like today, I got both kids and took them upstairs, and all of a sudden I said, "Oh, no! I left the door unlocked!" and I just stopped what I was doing and ran downstairs to lock it." This kind of fear-induced behavior occurs as neighbors work out their group perspective on what is possible, if not probable, in the aftermath of such a crime.

Violence causes residents to tense up and begin taking defensive action again. They may feel uncomfortable around strangers on the streets, particularly after dark. They become especially suspicious of black males. An interview with a young black man from the area sheds some light on how residents react to neighborhood blacks shortly after a violent incident:

> People come out of the door and they're scared. So when they see blacks on the streets they try to get away. Even ones who live right next door. All of a sudden

they change attitudes toward each other. They're very suspicious. The guy that killed that lady and her husband down on Thirty-fourth in the Village, he from the Empire [gang]. He tried to rape the lady right in front of the husband—he stabbed the husband and killed him. He'll get the electric chair now; they gave him the death penalty. They caught him comin' out. Wouldn't been so bad, the cops got another call to next door to where he did it at. She was screamin' and the cops heard and came around to the door.

After that happened, you could feel the vibes from the whites. When things like that happen, things get very tense between blacks and whites. And you can feel it in the way they look at you, 'cause they think you might be the one who might do the crime. Every time they see a black they don't trust 'em. Should stay in their own neighborhood.

That's the Village. They paranoid.

In time the fear recedes. Through successive documentations and neighborhood gossip, Villagers slowly return to some level of complacency, an acceptance of the risks of living in the city. Familiar people on the streets are "mapped" and associated with their old places, much as veteran Villagers have mapped them before. Streets, parks, and playgrounds are again made theirs. When these mental notations remain reliable and undisturbed for a time, a kind of "peace" returns. More and more can be taken for granted. Night excursions become more common. Children may be given a longer tether. Villagers gather and talk about the more pleasant aspects of neighborhood life. But they know, and are often reminded, that the peace is precarious. . . .

References

Becker, Howard S. 1963. *Outsiders: Studies in the sociology of deviance.* New York: Macmillan.

Hughes, Everett C. 1945. Dilemmas and contradictions of status. *American Journal of Sociology* 50:353–59.

18 Diary of a Homeless Man

JOHN R. COLEMAN

Can you imagine yourself being without a home? Think of what it must be like not to have a house or apartment, not to have your own room or even one you must share with a sibling. No living room with television, no kitchen with a refrigerator you can "raid" whenever you want. Night falls, and you don't know where you'll sleep. Day breaks, and you still have no place to go, nothing to do—and no one who cares.

Such is life for some people in our society—the discards of the advanced technological society, those who have been left behind in our culturally mandated frantic pursuit after material wealth. Like others, Coleman, a college president, had seen these strange people on the streets of the city. Like others, he wondered what their life was like. but unlike most others, he decided to find out first hand—by directly experiencing their world. He left his comfortable, middle-class home and joined the street people. This is his engrossing account of that experience.

Wednesday, 1/19

Somehow, 12 degrees at 6 A.M. was colder than I had counted on. I think of myself as relatively immune to cold, but standing on a deserted sidewalk outside Penn Station with the thought of ten days ahead of me as a homeless man, the immunity vanished. When I pulled my collar closer and my watch cap lower, it wasn't to look the part of a street person; it was to keep the wind out.

My wardrobe wasn't much help. I had bought my "new" clothes—flannel shirt, baggy sweater, torn trousers, the cap and the coat—the day before on Houston Street for $19. "You don't need to buy shoes," the shop-keeper had said. "The ones you have on will pass for a bum's." I was hurt; they were shoes I often wore to the office.

Having changed out of my normal clothes in the Penn Station men's room and stowed them in a locker, I was ready for the street. Or thought so.

Was I imagining it, or were people looking at me in a completely different way? I felt that men, especially the successful-looking ones in their forties and over, saw me and wondered. For the rest, I wasn't there.

At Seventh Avenue and 35th Street, I went into a coffee shop. The counterman looked me over carefully. When I ordered the breakfast special—99 cents plus tax—he told me I'd have to pay in advance. I did (I'd brought $40 to see me through the ten days), but I noticed that the other customers were given checks, and paid only when they left.

By 9:30, I had read a copy of the *Times* retrieved from a trash basket; I had walked most of the streets around the station; I had watched the construction at the new convention center. There was little else to do.

Later, I sat and watched the drug sales going on in Union Square. Then I went into the Income Maintenance Center on 14th Street and watched the people moving through the welfare lines. I counted the trucks on Houston Street.

I vaguely remembered a quote to the effect that "idleness is only enjoyable when you have a lot to do." It would help to be warm, too.

There was ample time and incentive to stare at the other homeless folk on the street. For the most part, they weren't more interesting than the typical faces on Wall Street or upper Madison Avenue. But the extreme cases caught and held the eye. On Ninth Avenue, there was a man on the sidewalk directing an imaginary (to me) flow of traffic. And another, two blocks away, tracing the flight of planes or birds—or spirits—in the winter sky. And there was a woman with gloves tied to her otherwise bare feet.

Standing outside the Port Authority Bus Terminal was a man named Howard. He was perhaps my age, but the seasons had left deeper marks on his face. "Come summertime, it's all going to be different," he told me. "I'm going to have a car to go to the beach. And I'm going to get six lemons and make me a jug of ice-cold lemonade to go with the car.

"This whole country's gone too far with the idea of one person being at the top. It starts with birthday parties. Who gets to blow out the candle? One person. And it takes off from there. If we're ever going to make things better, we gotta start with those candles."

Was there any chance of people like us finding work?

"Jobs are still out there for the young guys who want them," Howard said. "But there's nothing for us. Never again. No, I stopped dreaming about jobs a long time ago. Now I dream about cars. And lemonade."

Drugs and alcohol are common among the homeless. The damage done by them was evident in almost every street person I saw. But which was cause, and which was effect? Does it matter, once this much harm has been done?

My wanderings were all aimless. There was no plan, no goal, no reason to be anywhere at any time. Only hours into this role, I felt a useless part of the city streets. I wasn't even sure why I was doing this. . . .

A weathered drifter told me about a hideaway down in the bowels of the station, where it was warm and quiet. I found my way there and lay down on some old newspapers to sleep.

How long did I sleep? It didn't seem long at all. I was awakened by a flashlight shining in my eyes, and a voice, not an unkind one, saying, "You can't sleep here. Sorry, but you have to go outside."

I hadn't expected to hear that word "sorry." It was touching.

I left and walked up to 47th Street, between Fifth and Madison Avenues, where I knew there was a warm grate in the sidewalk. (I've been passing it every morning for over five years on my way to work.) One man was asleep there already. But there was room for two, and he moved over.

Thursday, 1/20

When you're spending the night on the street, you learn to know morning is coming by the kinds of trucks that roll by. As soon as there are other than garbage trucks—say, milk or bread trucks—you know the night will soon be over.

I went back to Penn Station to clean up in the washroom. The care with which some of the other men with me bathed themselves at the basins would have impressed any public-health officer. And I couldn't guess from the appearance of their clothes who would be the most fastidious.

I bought coffee and settled back to enjoy it out of the main traffic paths in the station. No luck. A cop found me and told me to take it to the street.

After breakfast ($1.31 at Blimpie), I walked around to keep warm until the public library opened. I saw in a salvaged copy of the *Times* that we had just had our coldest night of the year, well below zero with the windchill factor, and that a record 4,635 people had sought shelter in the city's hostels.

The library was a joy. The people there treated me the same as they might have had I been wearing my business suit. To pass the time, I got out the city's welfare reports for 50 years ago. In the winter of 1933, the city had 4,524 beds available for the homeless, and all were said to be filled every night. The parallel to 1983 was uncanny. But, according to the reports, the man in charge of the homeless program in 1933, one Joseph A. Manning, wasn't worried about the future. True, the country was in the midst of a depression. But there had been a slight downturn in the numbers served in the shelters in the two months immediately preceding his report. This meant, wrote Manning, that "the depression, in the parlance of the ring, is K.O.'d."

Already, I notice changes in me. I walk much more slowly. I no longer see a need to beat a traffic light or to be the first through a revolving door. Force of habit still makes me look at my wrist every once in a while. But there's no watch there, and it wouldn't make any difference if there were. The thermometer has become much more important to me now than any timepiece could be. . . .

The temperature rose during the day. Just as the newspaper headlines seem to change more slowly when you're on the streets all day long, so the temperature seems to change more rapidly and tellingly.

At about 9 P.M., I went back to the heated grate on 47th Street. The man who had been there last night was already in place. He made it clear that there was again room for me.

I asked him how long he had been on the streets.

"Eleven years, going on twelve," he said.

"This is only my second night."

"You may not stick it out. This isn't for every man."

"Do you ever go into the shelters?"

"I couldn't take that. I prefer this anytime."

Friday, 1/21

When I left my grate mate—long before dawn—he wished me a good day. I returned the gesture. He meant his, and I meant mine.

In Manhattan's earliest hours, you get the feeling that the manufacture and removal of garbage is the city's main industry. So far, I haven't been lucky or observant enough to rescue much of use from the mounds of trash waiting for the trucks and crews. The best find was a canvas bag that will fit nicely over my feet at night.

I'm slipping into a routine: Washing up at the station. Coffee on the street. Breakfast at Blimpie. A search for the *Times* in the trash baskets. And then a leisurely stretch of reading in the park.

Some days bring more luck than others. Today I found 20 cents in a pay-phone slot and heard a young flutist playing the music of C.P.E. Bach on Sixth Avenue between 9th and 10th streets. A lot of people ignored her, even stepped over her flute case as if it were litter on the sidewalk. More often than not, those who put money in the case looked embarrassed. They seemed to be saying, "Don't let anyone see me being appreciative."

By nightfall, the streets were cruelly cold once again. . . .

I headed for the 47th Street grate again but found my mate gone. There was no heat coming up through it. Do they turn it off on Friday nights? Don't we homeless have any rights?

On the northwest corner of Eighth Avenue and 33rd Street, there was a blocked-off subway entrance undergoing repair. I curled up against the wall there under some cardboard sheets. Rain began to fall, but I stayed reasonably dry and was able to get to sleep.

At some point, I was awakened by a man who had pulled back the upper piece of cardboard.

"You see my partner here. You need to give us some money."

I was still half-asleep. "I don't have any."

"You must have something, man."

"Would I be sleeping here in the rain if I did?"

His partner intervened. "C'mon. Leave the old bastard alone. He's not worth it."

"He's got something. Get up and give it to us."

I climbed to my feet and began fumbling in my pocket. Both men were on my left side. That was my chance. Suddenly I took off and ran along 33rd Street toward Ninth Avenue. They gave no chase. And a good thing, too, because I was too stiff with cold to run a good race.

Saturday, 1/22

A man I squatted next to in a doorway on 29th Street said it all: "The onliest thing is to have a warm place to sleep. That and having somebody care about you. That'd be even onlier."

He had what appeared to be rolls of paper toweling wrapped around one leg and tied with red ribbon. But the paper, wet with rain by now, didn't seem to serve any purpose.

I slept little. The forecast was for more rain tomorrow, so why wish the night away?

The morning paper carried news of Mayor Koch's increased concern about the homeless.

But what can he do? He must worry that the more New York does to help, the greater the numbers will grow. At the moment he's berating the synagogues for not doing anything to take street people in.

Watching people come and go at the Volvo tennis tournament at Madison Square Garden, I sensed how uncomfortable they were at the presence of the homeless. Easy to love in the abstract, not so easy face to face.

It's no wonder that the railway police are under orders to chase us out of sight.

Perhaps a saving factor is that we're not individuals. We're not people anybody knows. So far I've had eye contact with only three people who know me in my other life. None showed a hint of recognition. One was the senior auditor at Arthur Andersen & Company, the accounting firm that handles the Clark Foundation, my employer. One was a fellow lieutenant in the Auxiliary Police Force, a man with whom I had trained for many weeks. And one was an owner in the cooperative apartment where I live. . . .

Early in the evening I fell asleep on the Seventh Avenue steps outside the Garden. Three Amtrak cops shook me awake to ask if two rather good-looking suitcases on the steps were mine. I said that I had never seen them.

One cop insisted that I was lying, but then a black man appeared and said they belonged to a friend of his. The rapid-fire questioning from two of the cops soon made that alibi rather unlikely. The third cop was going through the cases and spreading a few of the joints he found inside on the ground.

As suddenly as it had begun, the incident was over. The cops walked away, and the man retrieved the bags. I fell back to sleep. Some hours later when I woke up again, the black man was still there, selling.

Sunday, 1/23

A new discovery of a warm and dry, even scenic, place to sit on a rainy day: the Staten Island Ferry.

For one 25-cent fare, I had four crossings of the harbor, read all I wanted of the copy of the Sunday *Times* I'd found, and finished the crossword puzzle.

When I got back to the Garden, where the tennis tournament was in its last hours, I found the police were being extra diligent in clearing us away from the departing crowds. One older woman was particularly incensed at being moved. "You're ruining my sex life," she shouted. "That's what you're doing. My sex life. Do you hear?"

A younger woman approached me to ask if I was looking for love. "No, ma'am. I'm just trying to stay out of the rain." . . .

So, back to the unused subway entrance, because there was still no heat across town on the 47th Street grate.

The night was very cold. Parts of me ached as I tried to sleep. Turning over was a chore, not only because the partially wet cardboard had to be re-arranged with such care, but also because the stiffer parts of my body seemed to belong to someone else. Whatever magic there was in those lights cutting down through the fog was gone by now. All I wanted was to be warm and dry once more. Magic could wait.

Monday, 1/24

Early this morning I went to the warren of employment agencies on 14th Street to see if I could get a day's work. There was very little action at most of these last-ditch offices, where minimum wages and sub-minimum conditions are the rule.

But I did get one interview and thought I had a dishwashing job lined up. I'd forgotten one thing. I had no identification with me. No identification, no job.

There was an ageless, shaggy woman in Bryant Park this morning who delivered one of the more interesting monologues I've heard. For a full ten minutes, with no interruption from me beyond an occasional "Uh huh," she analyzed society's ills without missing a beat.

Beginning with a complaint about the women's and men's toilets in the park being locked ("What's a poor body to do?"), she launched into the strengths of the Irish, who, though strong, still need toilets more than others, and the weaknesses of the English and the Jews, the advantages of raising turkeys over other fowl, and the wickedness of Eleanor Roosevelt in letting the now Queen Mother and that stuttering king of hers rave so much about the hot dogs served at Hyde Park that we had no alternative but to enter World War II on their side. The faulty Russian satellite that fell into the Indian Ocean this morning was another example of shenanigans, she said. It turns out the Russian and Lady Diana, "that so-called Princess of Wales," are in cahoots to keep us so alarmed about such things far away from home that we don't get anything done about prayer in schools or the rest of it. But after all, what would those poor Protestant ministers do for a living if the children got some real religion in school, like the kind we got from the nuns, God bless them?

That at least was the gist of what she said. I know I've missed some of the finer points.

At 3:30 P.M., with more cold ahead, I sought out the Men's Shelter at 8 East 3rd Street. This is the principal entry point for men seeking the city's help. It provides meals for 1,300 or so people every day and beds for some few of those. I had been told that while there was no likelihood of getting a bed in this building I'd be given a meal here and a bed in some other shelter.

I've seen plenty of drawings of London's workhouses and asylums in the times of Charles Dickens. Now I've seen the real thing, in the last years of the twentieth century in the world's greatest city.

The lobby and the adjacent "sitting room" were jammed with men standing, sitting, or stretched out in various positions on the floor. It was as lost a collection of souls as I could have imagined. Old and young, scarred and smooth, stinking and clean, crippled and hale, drunk and sober, ranting and still, parts of another world and parts of this one. The city promises to take in anyone who asks. Those rejected everywhere else find their way to East 3rd Street.

The air was heavy with the odors of Thunderbird wine, urine, sweat, and, above all, nicotine and marijuana. Three or four Human Resources Administration police officers seemed to be keeping the violence down to tolerable levels, but barely so.

After a long delay, I got a meal ticket for dinner and was told to come back later for a lodging ticket.

It was time to get in line to eat. This meant crowding into what I can only compare to a cattle chute in a stockyard. It ran along two walls of the sitting room and was already jammed. A man with a bullhorn kept yelling at us to stand up and stay in line. One very old and decrepit (or drunk?) man couldn't stay on his feet. He was helped to a chair, from which he promptly fell onto the floor. The bullhorn man had some choice obscenities for him, but they didn't seem to have any effect. The old man just lay there; and we turned our thoughts back to the evening meal.

I made a quick, and probably grossly unfair, assessment of the hundreds of men I could see in the room. Judging them solely by appearance, alertness, and body movements, I decided that one-quarter of them were perfectly able to work; they, more likely than not, were among the warriors who helped us win the battle against inflation by the selfless act of joining the jobless ranks. Another quarter might be brought back in time into job-readiness by some counseling and some caring for them as individuals. But the other half seemed so ravaged by illness, addiction, and sheer neglect that I couldn't imagine them being anything but society's wards from here on out to—one hopes—a peaceful end.

At the appointed hour, we were released in groups of twenty or thirty to descend the dark, filthy steps to the basement eating area. The man with the bullhorn was there again, clearly in charge and clearly relishing the extra power given to his voice by electric amplification. He insulted us collectively and separately without pause, but because his vocabulary was limited it tended to be the same four-letter words over and over.

His loudest attack on me came when I didn't move fast enough to pick up my meal from the counter. His analysis of certain flaws in my white ancestry wasn't hard to follow, even for a man in as much of a daze as I was.

The shouting and the obscenities didn't stop once we had our food. Again and again we were told to finish and get out. Eating took perhaps six minutes, but those minutes removed any shred of dignity a man might have brought in with him from the street.

Back upstairs, the people in charge were organizing the people who were to go to a shelter in Brooklyn. Few had volunteered, so there was more haranguing.

In the line next to the one where I was waiting for my lodging ticket a fight suddenly broke out. One man pulled a long knife from his overcoat pocket. The other man ran for cover, and a police officer soon appeared to remove the man with the knife from the scene. The issue, it seems, was one of proper places in the line.

There still weren't enough Brooklyn volunteers to suit the management, so they brought in their big gun: Mr. Bullhorn. "Now, listen up," he barked. "There aren't any buses going to Ft. Washington [another shelter] until 11:30, so if you want to get some sleep, go to Brooklyn. Don't ask me any questions. Just shut up and listen. It's because you don't listen up that you end up in a place like this."

I decided to ask a question anyway, about whether there would still be a chance for me to go to Brooklyn once I got my lodging ticket. He turned on me and let me have the full force of the horn: "Don't ask questions, I said. You're not nobody."

The delays at the ticket-issuing window went on and on. Three staff members there seemed reasonably polite and even efficient. The fourth and heaviest one—I have no idea whether it was a man or woman—could not have moved more slowly without coming to a dead halt. The voice of someone who was apparently a supervisor came over the public-address system from time to time to apologize for the delay in going to the Ft. Washington shelter, which was in an armory, but any good he did from behind the scenes was undone by the staff out front and a "see-no-work, hear-no-work, do-no-work" attendant in the office.

As 11:30 approached, we crowded back into the sitting room to get ready to board the buses. A new martinet had appeared on the scene. He got as much attention through his voice, cane, and heavy body as Mr. Bullhorn had with his amplifying equipment. But this new man was more openly vile and excitable; he loved the power that went with bunching us all up close together and then ordering us to stretch out again in a thinner line. We practiced that routine several times. . . .

Long after the scheduled departure, the lines moved. We sped by school buses to the armory at Ft. Washington Avenue and 168th Street. There we were met, just before 2:30 A.M., by military police, social workers, and private guards. They marched us into showers (very welcome), gave us clean underwear, and sent us upstairs to comfortable cots arranged in long rows in a room as big as a football field.

There were 530 of us there for the night, and we were soon quiet.

Tuesday, 1/25

We were awakened at 6 A.M. by whistles and shouting, and ordered to get back onto the buses for the return trip to lower Manhattan as soon as possible.

Back at 8 East 3rd Street, the worst of the martinets were off duty. So I thought breakfast might be a bit quieter than dinner had been. Still, by eight, I had seen three incidents a bit out of the ordinary for me.

A man waiting for breakfast immediately ahead of me in the cattle chute suddenly grabbed a chair from the adjoining area and prepared to break it over his neighbor's head. In my haste to get out of the way, I fell over an older man sleeping against the wall. After some shouts about turf, things cooled off between the fighters, and the old man forgave me.

In the stairwell leading down to the eating area, a young man made a sexual advance to me. When I withdrew from him and stupidly reached for my coat pocket, he thought I was going for a weapon. He at once pinned me against the wall and searched my pockets; there was nothing there.

As I came out of the building onto East 3rd Street, two black Human Resources Administration policemen were bringing two young blacks into the building. One officer had his man by the neck. The other officer had his man's hands cuffed behind his back and repeatedly kicked him hard in the buttocks.

My wanderings were still more aimless today. I couldn't get East 3rd Street out of my mind. What could possibly justify some of that conduct? If I were a staff member there, would I become part of the worst in that pattern? Or would I simply do as little, and think as little, as possible?

At day's end I can't recall much of where I went or why I went there.

Only isolated moments remain with me. Like . . . staring at the elegant crystal and silver in the shops just north of Madison Square Park and wondering what these windows say to the people I'd spent the night with.

Much too soon it was time to go back to the shelter for dinner and another night. At first I thought I didn't have the guts to do it again. Does one have to do *this* to learn who the needy are? I wanted to say, "Enough! There's only so much I need to see."

But I went back to the shelter anyway, probably because it took more guts to quit than it did to go ahead.

A man beside me in the tense dinner line drove one truth of this place home to me. "I never knew hell came in this color," he said.

I was luckier in my assignment for the night. I drew the Keener Building, on Wards Island, a facility with a capacity of 416 men. The building was old and neglected, and the atmosphere of a mental hospital, which it once was, still hung over it. But the staff was polite, the rooms weren't too crowded (there were only twelve beds in Room 326), the single sheet on each bed was clean, and there was toilet paper in the bathroom.

There were limits and guards and deprivations, but there was also an orderliness about the place. Here, at least, I didn't feel I had surrendered all of my dignity at the door.

Wednesday, 1/26

. . . Back to the shelter on East 3rd Street for dinner.

There is simply no other situation I've seen that is so devoid of any graces at all, so tense at every moment, or so empty of hope. The food isn't bad, and the building is heated; that's all it has going for it.

The only cutlery provided is a frail plastic spoon. With practice you can spread hard oleo onto your bread with the back of one. If there's liver or ham, you don't have to cut it; just put it between the two pieces of bread that go with each meal. Everything else—peas, collard greens, apple pudding, plums—can be managed with the spoon. And talk over dinner or sipping, rather than gulping, coffee isn't all that important.

What is hardest to accept is the inevitable jungle scene during the hour you stand in line waiting to eat. Every minute seems to be one that invites an explosion. You know instinctively that men can't come this often to the brink without someone going over. One person too many is going to try to jump ahead in line. One particular set of toes is going to be stepped on by mistake. And the lid is going to blow.

The most frightening people here are the many young, intensely angry blacks. Hatred pours out in all of their speech and some of their actions. I could spend a lot of time imagining how and why they became so completely angry—but if I were the major, the counselor, or the man with the bullhorn, I wouldn't know how to divert them from that anger any more. Hundreds and hundreds of men here have been destroyed by alcohol or drugs. A smaller, but for me more poignant, number are being destroyed by hate.

Their loudest message—and because their voices are so strong it is very loud indeed—is "Respect me, man." The constant theme is that someone or some group is putting them down, stepping on them, asking them to conform to a code they don't accept, getting in their way, writing them off.

So most of the fights begin over turf. A place in line. A corner to control. The have-nots scrapping with the have-nots. . . .

Tonight, I chose the Brooklyn shelter because I thought the buses going there would leave soonest. The shelter, a converted school, is on Williams Avenue and has about 400 beds.

We left in fairly good time but learned when we got to the shelter that no new beds would be assigned until after 11 P.M. We were to sit in the auditorium until then.

At about ten, a man herded as many of us newcomers as would listen to him into a corner of the auditorium. There he delivered an abusive diatribe outlining the horror that lay ahead for our possessions and our bodies during the night to come. It made the ranting at East 3rd Street seem tame.

It's illustrative of what the experience of homelessness and helplessness does to people that all of us—regardless of age, race, background, or health—listened so passively.

Only at midnight, when some other officials arrived, did we learn that this man had no standing whatsoever. He was just an underling who strutted for his time on the stage before any audience cowed enough to take what he dished out. . . .

Thursday, 1/27

Back on the street this morning, I became conscious of how little time I had left to live this way. There seemed so much still to do, and so little time in which to do it.

One part of me tells me I have been fully a part of this. I know I walk with slower steps and bent shoulders. . . . I know I worry a lot more about keeping clean.

But then I recall how foolish that is, I'm acting. This will end tomorrow night. I can quit any time I want to. And unlike my mate from 47th Street, I haven't the slightest idea of what eleven years of sleeping on a grate amount to.

Early this afternoon, I went again to the Pavilion restaurant, where I had eaten five times before. I didn't recognize the man at the cash register.

"Get out," he said.

"But I have money."

"You heard me. Get out." His voice was stronger.

"That man knows me," I said, looking toward the owner in the back of the restaurant.

The owner nodded, and the man at the register said, "Okay, but sit in the back."

If this life in the streets had been real, I'd have gone out the door at the first "Get out." And the assessment of me as not worthy would have been self-fulfilling; I'd have lost so much respect for myself that I wouldn't have been worthy of being served the next time. The downward spiral would have begun.

Until now I haven't understood the extent of nicotine addiction. Dependencies on drugs and alcohol have been around me for a long time, but I thought before that smoking was a bad habit rather easy to overcome.

How many times have I, a nonsmoker, been begged for a cigarette in these days? Surely hundreds. Cigarettes are central. A few folks give them away, a small number sell them for up to 8 cents apiece, and almost all give that last pathetic end of a butt to the first man who asks for what little bit is left. I know addiction now as I didn't before.

Tonight, after a repeat of the totally degrading dinner-line scene at East 3rd Street, I signed up for Keener once again. No more Brooklyn for me.

Sitting upstairs with the other Keener-bound men, I carelessly put my left foot on the rung of the chair in front of me, occupied by a young black.

"Get your foot off, yo."

("Yo" means "Hey, there," "Watch yourself," "Move along," and much more.)

I took it off. "Sorry," I said.

But it was too late. I had broken a cardinal rule. I had violated the man's turf. As we stood in the stairwell waiting for the buses, he told a much bigger, much louder, much angrier friend what I had done.

That man turned on me.

"Wait till we get you tonight, whitey. You stink. Bad. The worst I've ever smelled. And when you put your foot on that chair, you spread your stink around. You better get yourself a shower as soon as we get there, but it won't save you later on. . . . And don't sit near me or him on the bus. You hear, whitey?"

I didn't reply.

The bombardment went on as we mounted the bus. No one spoke up in my defense. Three people waved me away when I tried to sit next to them. The next person, black and close to my age, made no objection when I sat beside him.

The big man continued to tirade for a while, but he soon got interested in finding out from the driver how to go about getting a bus-driver's license. Perhaps he had come down from a high.

I admit I was scared. I wrote my name, address, and office telephone number on a piece of paper and slipped it into my pocket. At least someone would know where to call if the threats were real. I knew I couldn't and wouldn't defend myself in this setting.

While we stood in line on Wards Island waiting for our bed assignments, there were plenty of gripes about the man who was after me. But no one said anything directly to him. Somehow it didn't seem that this was the night when the meek would inherit the earth.

I slept fitfully. I don't like lying with the sheet hiding my face.

Friday, 1/28

I was up and out of Keener as early as possible. That meant using some of my little remaining money for a city-bus ride back to Manhattan, but it was worth it to get out of there.

After breakfast on East 3rd Street, I was finished with the public shelters. That was an easy break for me to make, because I had choices and could run.

The day was cold and, for the early hours, clear. I washed the memory of the big man at 3rd Street out of my mind by wandering through the Fulton Fish Market. I walked across the Brooklyn Bridge and even sang as I realized how free I was to relax and enjoy its beauty.

With a cup of coffee and the *Times,* I sat on a cinder block by the river and read. In time, I wandered through the Wall Street district and almost learned the lay of some of the streets.

I walked up to the Quaker Meeting House at Rutherford Place and 15th Street. Standing on the porch outside, I tried hard to think how the doctrine that "there is that of God in every person" applied to that man last night and to some of the others I had encountered in these ten days. I still think it applies, but it isn't always easy to see how. . . .

Darkness came. I got kicked out of both the bus terminal and Grand Central. I got my normal clothes out of the locker at Penn Station, changed in the men's room, and rode the AA train home.

My apartment was warm, and the bed was clean.

That's the onliest thing.

19 Hanging Tongues: A Sociological Encounter with the Assembly Line

WILLIAM E. THOMPSON

Few of us are born so wealthy—or so deprived—that we do not have to work for a living. Some jobs seem to be of little importance, as with those we take during high school and college. We simply accept what is available and look at it as a temporary activity to help us get by for the time being. When its time is up, we discard it as we would worn-out clothing. In contrast, the jobs we take after we have completed our education—those full-time, more or less permanent endeavors at which we labor so long and hard—in these we invest much of ourselves. In turn, as our schedules come to revolve around their demands, we become aware of how central these jobs are to our lives.

All jobs, however, whether full-time and permanent or temporary, expedient, and discarded, are significant for our lives. Each contributes in its own way to our thinking and attitudes, becoming a part of the general stockpile of experiences that culminates in our basic orientation to life. Because of the significance of work for our lives, then, sociologists pay a great deal of attention to the work setting. They focus on interaction in that setting, as well as the social organization of work (how tasks are performed and how one job is related to another).

Of all jobs, one of the most demanding, demeaning, and demoralizing is that of the assembly line. Those of us who have worked on an assembly line have shared a work experience unlike any other, and for many of us education was the way by which we escaped from this form of modern slavery. As Thompson examines the assembly line in the meat-packing industry, he makes evident how this job affects all aspects of the workers' lives. His analysis provides a good framework for you to use in reflecting on your own work experiences.

THIS QUALITATIVE SOCIOLOGICAL STUDY analyzes the experience of working on a modern assembly line in a large beef plant. It explores and examines a special type of assembly line work which involves the slaugh-

193

tering and processing of cattle into a variety of products intended for human consumption and other uses.

Working in the beef plant is "dirty work," not only in the literal sense of being drenched with perspiration and beef blood, but also in the figurative sense of performing a low-status, routine, and demeaning job. Although the work is honest and necessary in a society which consumes beef, slaughtering and butchering cattle is generally viewed as an undesirable and repugnant job. In that sense, workers at the beef plant share some of the same experiences as other workers in similarly regarded occupations (for example, ditch-diggers, garbage collectors, and other types of assembly line workers). . . .

The Setting

The setting for the field work was a major beef processing plant in the Midwest. At the time of the study, the plant was the third largest branch of a corporation which operated ten such plants in the United States. . . .

The beef plant was organizationally separated into two divisions: Slaughter and Processing. This study focused on the Slaughter division in the area of the plant known as the *kill floor*. A dominant feature of the kill floor was the machinery of the assembly line itself. The line was composed of an overhead stainless steel rail which began at the slaughter chute and curved its way around every work station in the plant. Every work station contained specialized machinery for the job performed at that place on the line. Dangling from the rail were hundreds of stainless steel hooks pulled by a motorized chain. Virtually every part of the line and all of the implements (tubs, racks, knives, etc.) were made of stainless steel. The walls were covered with a ceramic tile and the floor was made of sealed cement. There were floor drains located at every work station, so that at the end of each work segment (at breaks, lunch, and shift's end) the entire kill floor could be hosed down and cleaned for the next work period.

Another dominant feature of the kill floor was the smell. Extremely difficult to describe, yet impossible to forget, this smell combined the smells of live cattle, manure, fresh beef blood, and internal organs and their contents. This smell not only permeated the interior of the plant, but was combined on the outside with the smell of smoke from various waste products being burned and could be smelled throughout much of the community. This smell contributed greatly to the general negative feelings about work at the beef plant, as it served as the most distinguishable symbol of the beef plant to the rest of the community. The single most often asked question of me during the research by those outside the beef plant was, "How do you stand the smell?" In typical line workers' fashion, I always responded, "What smell? All I smell at the beef plant is money." . . .

Method

The method of this study was nine weeks of full-time participant observation as outlined by Schatzman and Strauss (1973) and Spradley (1979; 1980). To enter the setting, the researcher went through the standard application process for a summer job. No mention of the research intent was made, though it was made clear that I was a university sociology professor. After initial screening, a thorough physical examination, and a helpful reference from a former student and part-time employee of the plant, the author was hired to work on the *Offal* crew in the Slaughter division of the plant. . . .

The Work

. . . The line speed on the kill floor was 187. That means that 187 head of cattle were slaughtered per hour. At any particular work station, each worker was required to work at that speed. Thus, at my work station, in the period of one hour, 187 beef tongues were mechanically pulled from their hooks; dropped into a large tub filled with water; had to be taken from the tub and hung on a large stainless steel rack full of hooks; branded with a "hot brand" indicating they had been inspected by a USDA inspector; and then covered with a small plastic bag. The rack was taken to the cooler, replaced with an empty one, and the process began again.

It would be logical to assume that if a person worked at a steady, continuous pace of handling 187 tongues per hour, everything would go smoothly; not so. In addition to hanging, branding, and bagging tongues, the worker at that particular station also cleaned the racks and cleaned out a variety of empty stainless steel tubs used to hold hearts, kidneys, and other beef organs. Thus, in order to be free to clean the tubs when necessary, the "tongue-hanger" had to work at a slightly faster pace than the line moved. Then, upon returning from cleaning the tubs, the worker would be behind the line (*in a hole*) and had to work much faster to catch up with the line. Further, one fifteen-minute break and a thirty-minute lunch break were scheduled for an eight-hour shift. Before the "tongue-hanger" could leave his post for one of these, all tongues were required to be properly disposed of, all tubs washed and stored, and the work area cleaned.

My first two nights on the job, I discovered the consequences of working at the line speed (hanging, branding, and bagging each tongue as it fell in the tub). At the end of the work period when everybody else was leaving the work floor for break or lunch, I was furiously trying to wash all the tubs and clean the work area. Consequently, I missed the entire fifteen minute break and had only about ten minutes for lunch. By observing other workers, I soon caught on to the system. Rather than attempting to work at a steady pace consistent with the line speed, the norm was to work sporadically at a very frenzied pace, actually running ahead of the line and plucking tongues from the hooks before they got to the station. With practice, I learned to hang two or three tongues at a time, perform all the required tasks, and then take an unscheduled two or three minute break until the line caught up with me. Near break and lunch everybody worked at a frantic pace, got ahead of the line, cleaned the work areas, and even managed to add a couple of minutes to the scheduled break or lunch.

Working ahead of the line seems to have served as more than merely a way of gaining a few minutes of extra break time. It also seemed to take on a symbolic meaning. The company controlled the speed of the line. Seemingly, that took all element of control over the work process away from the workers. . . . However, when the workers refused to work at line speed and actually worked faster than the line, they not only added a few minutes of relaxation from the work while the line caught up, but they symbolically regained an element of control over the pace of their own work. . . .

Coping

One of the difficulties of work at the beef plant was coping with three aspects of the work: monotony, danger, and dehumanization. While individual workers undoubtedly coped in a variety of ways, some distinguishable patterns emerged.

MONOTONY

The monotony of the line was almost unbearable. At my work station, a worker would hang, brand, and bag between 1,350 and 1,500 beef tongues in an eight-hour shift. With the exception of the scheduled fifteen-minute break and a thirty-minute lunch period (and sporadic brief gaps in the line), the work was mundane, routine, and continuous. As in most assembly line work, one inevitably drifted into daydreams (e.g., Garson, 1975; King, 1978; Linhart, 1981). It was not unusual to look up or down the line and see workers at various stations singing to themselves, tapping their feet to imaginary music, or carrying on conversations with themselves. I found that I could work with virtually no attention paid to the job, with my hands and arms automatically performing their tasks. In the meantime, my mind was free to wander over a variety of topics, including taking mental notes. In visiting with other workers, I found that daydreaming was the norm. Some would think about their families, while others fantasized about sexual escapades, fishing, or anything unrelated to the job. One individual who was rebuilding an antique car at home in his spare time would meticulously mentally rehearse the procedures he was going to perform on the car the next day.

Daydreaming was not inconsequential, however. During these periods, items were most likely to be dropped, jobs improperly performed, and accidents incurred. Inattention to detail around moving equipment, stainless steel hooks, and sharp knives invariably leads to dangerous consequences. Although I heard rumors of drug use to help fight the monotony, I never saw any workers take any drugs nor saw any drugs in any worker's possession. It is certainly conceivable that some workers might have taken something to help them escape the reality of the line, but the nature of the work demanded enough attention that such a practice could be ominous.

DANGER

The danger of working in the beef plant was well known. Safety was top priority (at least in theory) and management took pride in the fact that only three employee on-the-job deaths had occurred in twelve years. Although deaths were uncommon, serious injuries were not. The beef plant employed over 1,800 people. Approximately three-fourths of those employed had jobs which demanded the use of a knife honed to razor-sharpness. Despite the use of wire-mesh aprons and gloves, serious cuts were almost a daily occurrence. Since workers constantly handled beef blood, danger of infection was ever present. As one walked along the assembly line, a wide assortment of bandages on fingers, hands, arms, necks, and faces could always be seen.

In addition to the problem of cuts, workers who cut meat continuously sometimes suffered muscle and ligament damage to their fingers and hands. In one severe case, I was told of a woman who worked in processing for several years who had to wear splints on her fingers while away from the job to hold them straight. Otherwise, the muscles in her hand would constrict her fingers into the grip position, as if holding a knife. . . .

When I spoke with fellow workers about the dangers of working in the plant, I noticed interesting defense mechanisms. . . . After a serious accident, or when telling about an accident or death which occurred in years past, the workers would almost immediately dissociate themselves from the event and its victim. Workers tended to view those who suffered major accidents or death on the job in much the same way that nonvictims of crime often view crime victims as either partially responsible for the event, or at least as very different from themselves (Barlow, 1981). "Only a part-timer," "stupid," "careless" or something similar was used, seemingly to reassure the worker describing the accident that it could not happen to him. The reality of the situation was that virtually all the jobs on the kill floor were dangerous, and any worker could have experienced a serious injury at any time. . . .

DEHUMANIZATION

Perhaps the most devastating aspect of working at the beef plant (worse than the monotony and the danger) was the dehumanizing and demeaning elements of the job. In a sense, the assembly line worker became a part of the assembly line. The assembly line is not a tool used by the worker, but a machine which controls him/her. A tool can only be productive in the hands of somebody skilled in its use, and hence becomes an extension of the person using it. A machine, on the other hand, performs specific tasks; thus its operator becomes an extension of it in the production process. . . . When workers are viewed as mere extensions of the machines with which they work, their human needs become secondary in importance to the smooth mechanical functioning of the production process. In a bureaucratic structure, when "human needs collide with systems needs, the individual suffers" (Hummel, 1977:65).

Workers on the assembly line are seen as interchangeable as the parts of the product on the line itself. An example of one worker's perception of this phenomenon at the beef plant was demonstrated the day after a fatal accident occurred. I asked the men in our crew what the company did in the case of an employee death (I wondered if there was a fund for flowers, or if the shift was given time off to go to the funeral, etc.). One worker's response was: "They drag off the body, take the hard hat and boots and check 'em out to some other poor sucker, and throw him in the guy's place." While employee death on the job was not viewed quite that coldly by the company, the statement fairly accurately summarized the overall result of a fatal accident, and importance of any individual worker to the overall operation of the production process. It accurately summarized the workers' perceptions about management's attitudes toward them. . . .

Sabotage

It is fairly common knowledge that assembly line work situations often led to employee sabotage or destruction of the product or equipment used in the production process (Garson, 1975; Balzer, 1976; Shostak, 1980). This is the classic experience of alienation as described by Marx (1964a,b). . . . At the beef plant I quickly learned that there was an art to effective sabotage. Subtlety appeared to be the key. "The art lies in sabotaging in a way that is not immediately discovered," as a Ford worker put it (King, 1978:202). This seemed to hold true at the beef plant as well. . . .

The greatest factor influencing the handling of beef plant products was its status as a food product intended for human consumption. . . . Though not an explicitly altruistic group, the workers realized that the product would be consumed by people (even family, relatives, and friends), so consequently, they rarely did anything to actually contaminate the product.

Despite formal norms against sabotage, some did occur. It was not uncommon for workers to deliberately cut chunks out of pieces of meat for no reason (or for throwing at other employees). While regulations required that anything that touched the floor had to be put in tubs marked "inedible," the informal procedural norms were otherwise. When something was dropped, one usually looked around to see if an inspector or foreman noticed. If not, the item was quickly picked up and put back on the line.

Several explanations might be offered for this type of occurrence. First, since the company utilized a profit-sharing plan, when workers damaged the product, or had to throw edible pieces into inedible tubs (which sold for pet food at much lower prices), profits were decreased. A decrease in profits to the company ultimately led to decreased dividend checks to employees. Consequently, workers were fairly careful not to actually ruin anything. Second, when something was dropped or mishandled and had to be rerouted to "inedible," it was more time-consuming than if the product had been handled properly and kept on the regular line. In other words, if no inspector noticed, it was easier to let it go through on the line. There was a third, and seemingly more meaningful, explanation for this behavior, however. It was against the rules to do it, it was a challenge to do it, and thus it was fun to do it.

The workers practically made a game out of doing forbidden things simply to see if they could get away with it. . . . New workers were routinely socialized into the subtle art of rulebreaking as approved by the line workers. At my particular work station, it was a fairly common practice for other workers who were covered with beef blood to come over to the tub of swirling water designed to clean the tongues, and as soon as the inspector looked away, wash their hands, arms, and knives in the tub. This procedure was strictly forbidden by the rules. If witnessed by a foreman or inspector, the tub had to be emptied, cleaned, and refilled, and all the tongues in the tub at the time had to be put in the "inedible" tub. All of that would be a time-consuming and costly procedure, yet the workers seemed to absolutely delight in successfully pulling off the act. As Balzer (1976:90) indicates:

> Since a worker often feels that much if not all of what he does is done in places designated by the company, under company control, finding ways to express personal freedom from this institutional regimentation is important.

Thus, artful sabotage served as a symbolic way in which the workers could express a sense of individuality, and hence, self-worth.

The Financial Trap

Given the preceding description and analysis of work at the beef plant, why did people work at such jobs? Obviously, there are a multitude of plausible answers to that question. Without doubt, however, the key is money. The current economic situation, the lack of steady employment opportunities (especially for the untrained and poorly educated), combined with the fact that the beef plant's starting wage exceeded the minimum wage by approximately $5.50 per hour emerge as the most important reasons people went to work there.

Despite the high hourly wage and fringe benefits, however, the monotony, danger, and hard physical work drove many workers away in less than a week. During my study, I observed much worker turnover. Those who stayed displayed an interesting pattern which helps explain why they did not leave. Every member of my work crew answered similarly my questions about why they stayed at the beef plant. Each of them took the job directly after high school, because it was the highest-paying job available. Each of them had intended to work through the summer and then look for a better job in the fall. During that first summer on the job they fell victim to what I label the "financial trap."

The "financial trap" was a spending pattern which demanded the constant weekly income provided by the beef plant job. This scenario was first told to me by an employee who had worked at the plant for over nine years. He began the week after his high school graduation, intending only to work that summer in order to earn enough money to attend college in the fall. After about four weeks' work he purchased a new car. He figured he could pay off the car that summer and still save enough money for tuition. Shortly after the car purchase, he added a new stereo sound system to his debt; next came a motorcycle; then the decision to postpone school for one year in order to continue working at the beef plant and pay off his debts. A few months later he married; within a year purchased a house; had a child; and bought another new car. Nine years later, he was still working at the beef plant, hated every minute of it, but in his own words "could not afford to quit." His case was not unique. Over and over again, I heard stories about the same process of falling into the "financial trap." The youngest and newest of our crew had just graduated from high school and took the job for the summer in order to earn enough money to attend welding school the following fall. During my brief tenure at the beef plant, he purchased a new motorcycle, a new stereo, and a house trailer. When I left, he told me he had decided to postpone welding school for one year in order "to get everything paid for." I saw the financial trap closing in on him fast; he did, too. . . .

Summary and Conclusions

There are at least three interwoven phenomena in this study which deserve further comment and research.

First is the subtle sense of unity which existed among the line workers. . . . The line both symbolically and literally linked every job, and consequently every worker, to each other. . . . A system of "uncooperative teamwork" seemed to combine simultaneously a feeling of "one-for-all, all-for-one, and every man for himself." Once a line worker made it past the first three or four days on the job which "weeded out" many new workers, his status as a *beefer* was assured and the sense of unity was felt as much by the worker of nine weeks as it was by the veteran of nine years. Because the workers maintained largely secondary relationships, this feeling of unification is not the same as the unity typically found on athletic teams, in fraternities, or among various primary groups. Yet it was a significant social force which bound the workers together and provided a sense of meaning and worth. Although their occupation might not be highly respected by outsiders, they derived mutual self-respect from their sense of belonging.

A second important phenomenon was the various coping methods . . . the beef plant line workers developed and practiced . . . for retaining their humanness. Daydreaming, horseplay, and occasional sabotage protected their sense of self. Further, the prevailing attitude among workers that it was "us" against "them" served as a reminder that, while the nature of the job might demand subjugation to bosses, machines, and even beef parts, they were still human beings. . . .

A third significant finding was that consumer spending patterns among the beefers seemed to "seal their fate" and make leaving the beef plant almost impossible. A reasonable interpretation of the spending patterns of the beefers is that having a high-income/low-status job encourages a person to consume conspicuously. The prevailing attitude seemed to be "I may not have a nice job, but I have a nice home, a nice car, etc." This conspicuous consumption enabled workers to take indirect pride in their occupations. One of the ways of overcoming drudgery and humiliation on the job was to surround oneself with as many desirable material things as possible off the job. These items (cars, boats, motorcycles, etc.) became tangible rewards for the sacrifices endured at work.

The problem, of course, is that the possession of these expensive items required the continual income of a substantial paycheck which most of these men could only obtain by staying at the beef plant. These spending patterns were further complicated by the fact that they were seemingly "contagious." Workers talked to each other on breaks about recent purchases, thus reinforcing the norm of immediate gratification. A common activity of a group of workers on break or lunch was to run to the parking lot to see a fellow worker's new truck, van, car, or motorcycle. Even the seemingly more financially conservative were usually caught up in this activity and often could not wait to display their own latest acquisitions. Ironically, as the workers cursed their jobs, these expensive possessions virtually destroyed any chance of leaving them.

Working at the beef plant was indeed "dirty work." It was monotonous, difficult, dangerous, and demeaning. Despite this, the workers at the beef plant worked hard to fulfill employer expectations in order to obtain financial rewards. Through a variety of symbolic techniques, they managed to overcome the many negative aspects of their work and maintain a sense of self-respect about how they earned their living.

References

Balzer, Richard (1976). *Clockwork: Life In and Outside an American Factory.* Garden City, NY: Doubleday.

Barlow, Hugh (1981). *Introduction to Criminology.* 2d ed. Boston: Little, Brown.

Garson, Barbara (1975). *All the Livelong Day: The Meaning and Demeaning of Routine work.* Garden City, NY: Doubleday.

Hummel, Ralph P. (1977). *The Bureaucratic Experience.* New York: St. Martin's Press.

King, Rick (1978). "In the sanding booth at Ford," Pp. 199–205 in John and Erna Perry (eds.), *Social Problems in Today's World.* Boston: Little, Brown.

Linhart, Robert (translated by Margaret Crosland) (1981). *The Assembly Line.* Amherst: University of Massachusetts Press.

Marx, Karl (1964a). *Economic and Philosophical Manuscripts of 1844.* New York: International Publishing (1844).

——— (1964b). *The Communist Manifesto.* New York: Washington Square Press (1848).

Schatzman, Leonard, and Anselm L. Strauss (1973). *Field Research.* Englewood Cliffs, NJ: Prentice-Hall.

Shostak, Arthur (1980). *Blue Collar Stress.* Reading, MA: Addison-Wesley.

Spradley, James P. (1979). *The Ethnographic Interview.* New York: Holt, Rinehart & Winston.

——— (1980). *Participant Observation.* New York: Holt, Rinehart & Winston.

20 Behavior in Pubic Places: The Sociology of the Vaginal Examination

JAMES M. HENSLIN
MAE A. BIGGS

All of us depend on others for the successful completion of the roles we play. In many ways, this makes cooperation the essence of social life (with due apologies to my conflict-theorist friends). Without teamwork, performances fall apart, people become disillusioned, jobs don't get done—and, ultimately, society is threatened. Accordingly, much of our socialization centers on learning to be good team players.

The work setting lends itself well to examining cooperative interaction and to seeing how people develop ways of handling differences—"working arrangements" that defuse threats to fragile social patterns. For example, instructors often accept from students excuses that they know do not match reality. For their part, students often publicly accept what instructors teach, even though they privately disagree with those interpretations. Confrontation not only is unpleasant, and therefore preferable to avoid, but also is a threat to the continuity of interaction. Thus both instructors and students generally allow one another enough leeway to "get on with business" (which some might say is education, while others—more cynical—might say is the one earning a living and the other a degree).

One can gain much insight into the nature of society by trying to identify the implicit understandings that guide our interactions in everyday life. In this selection, Henslin and Biggs draw heavily on Goffman's dramaturgical framework as they focus on the vaginal examination. Note how much teamwork is required to make the definition stick that nothing sexual is occurring.

GENITAL BEHAVIOR IS PROBLEMATIC in U.S. society. Americans are socialized at a very early age into society's dictates concerning the situations, circumstances, and purposes of allowable and unallowable genital exposure.

Our thanks to Erving Goffman for commenting on this paper while it was in manuscript form and for suggesting the title, a play on his book, "Behavior in Public Places." Because the physicians in this study are men, the pronoun he is used.

203

After a U.S. female has been socialized into her society's expectations regarding the covering and privacy of specified areas of her body, especially her vagina, exposure of her pubic area becomes something that is extremely problematic for her. Even for a woman who has overcome feelings of modesty and perhaps of shame at genital exposure in the presence of her sexual partner, the problem frequently recurs during the vaginal examination. Although her exposure is supposed to be nonsexual, the vaginal examination can be so threatening that for many women it not only punctures their feelings of modesty but it also threatens their self, their feelings of who they are.

Because emotions become associated with the genital area through the learning of meanings and taboos, the vaginal examination is an especially interesting process; it is an elaborately ritualized form of social interaction designed to desexualize the sexual organs. From a sociological point of view, what happens during such interaction? Since a (if not *the*) primary concern of the persons involved is that all the interaction be defined as nonsexual, with even the hint of sexuality being avoided, what structural restraints on behavior operate? How does the patient cooperate in maintaining this definition of nonsexuality? In what ways are the roles of doctor, nurse, and patient performed such that each contributes to this definition?

This analysis is based on a sample of 12,000 to 14,000 vaginal examinations. The female author served as an obstetrical nurse in hospital settings and as an office nurse for general practitioners for fourteen years, giving us access to this area of human behavior which ordinarily is not sociologically accessible. Based on these observations, we have divided the interaction of the vaginal examination into five major scenes. We shall now examine what occurs as each of these scenes unfolds.

The setting for the vaginal examination may be divided into two areas (see Figure 20.1). Although there are no physical boundaries that demarcate the two areas, highly specific and ritualized interaction occurs in each. Area 1, where Scenes I and V are played, includes that portion of the "office-examination" room which is furnished with a desk and three chairs. Area 2, where Scenes II, III, and IV take place, contains an examination table, a swivel stool, a gooseneck lamp, a table for instruments, and a sink with a mirror above it.

Scene I: The Personalized Stage: The Patient as Person

The interaction flow of Scene I is as follows: (a) the doctor enters the "office-examination" room; (b) greets the patient; (c) sits down; (d) asks the patient why she is there; (e) questions her on specifics; (f) decides on a course of action, specifically whether a pelvic examination is needed or not; (g) if he thinks a pelvic is needed, he signals the nurse on the intercom and says, "I want a pelvic in room (X)"; (h) he gets up, and (i) leaves the room.

During this scene, the patient is treated as a full person; that is, the cour-

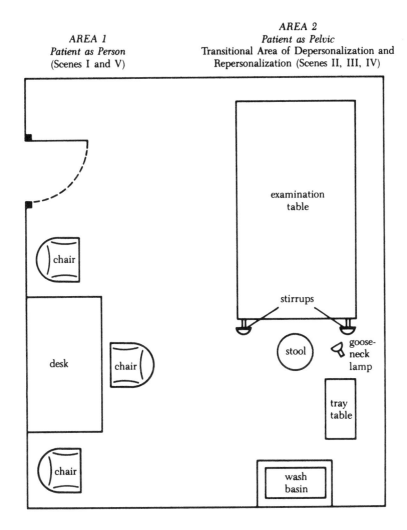

AREA 1
Patient as Person
(Scenes I and V)

AREA 2
Patient as Pelvic
Transitional Area of Depersonalization and
Repersonalization (Scenes II, III, IV)

examination
table

stirrups

chair

desk

chair

goose-
neck
lamp

stool

tray
table

chair

wash
basin

Figure 20.1 The Doctor's Office—Examination Room

tesies of middle-class talk are followed, and, in addition to gathering medical information, if the doctor knows the patient well he may intersperse his medical queries with questions about her personal life. The following interaction that occurred during Scene I demonstrates the doctor's treatment of his patient as a full person:

> DOCTOR (upon entering the room): Hello, Joyce, I hear you're going to Southern Illinois University.
> PATIENT: Yes, I am. I've been accepted, and I have to have my health record completed.

The doctor then seated himself at his desk and began filling out the health record that the patient gave him. He interspersed his questions concerning the record form with questions about the patient's teaching, about the area of study she was pursuing, about her children, their health and their schooling. He then said, "Well, we have to do this right. We'll do a pelvic on you." He then announced via the intercom, "I want to do a pelvic on Joyce in room 1." At that point he left the room.

This interaction sequence is typical of the interaction that occurs in Scene I between a doctor and a patient he knows well. When the doctor does not know the patient well, he does not include his patient's name, either her first or last name, in his announcement to the nurse that she should come into the room. In such a case, he simply says, "I want to do a pelvic in room 1," or, "Pelvic in room 1." The doctor then leaves the room, marking the end of the scene.

Scene II: The Depersonalized Stage: Transition from Person to Pelvic

When at the close of Scene I the doctor says, "Pelvic in room (X)," he is in effect announcing the transition of the person to a pelvic. It is a sort of advance announcement, however, of a coming event, because the transition has not yet been effected. The doctor's signal for the nurse to come in is, in fact, a signal that the nurse should now help the patient make the transition from a person to a pelvic. Additionally, it also serves as an announcement to the patient that she is about to undergo this metamorphosis.

The interaction flow which accomplishes the transition from person to pelvic is as follows: Upon entering the room, the nurse, without preliminaries, tells the patient, "The doctor wants to do a vaginal examination on you. Will you please remove your panties?" While the patient is undressing, the nurse prepares the props. She positions the stirrups of the examination table and arranges the glove, the lubricant, and the speculum (the instrument which, when inserted into the vagina, allows visual examination of the vaginal tract). She then removes the drape sheet from a drawer and directs the patient onto the table, covers the patient with the drape sheet, assists her in placing her feet into the stirrups, and positions her hips, putting her into the lithotomy position (lying on her back with knees flexed and out).

MEANING OF THE DOCTOR'S ABSENCE

The doctor's exiting just before this scene means that the patient will be undressing in his absence. This is not accidental. In many cases, the doctor may leave because another patient is waiting, but even if there are no waiting patients, the doctor always exits at the end of Scene I. His leaving means that he will not witness the patient undressing, thereby successfully removing any suggestion whatsoever that a striptease is being performed, or that he is acting as a voyeur. From the patient's point of view, the problem of undressing is lessened since a strange male is not present. Thus sexuality is removed from the undressing room, and when the doctor returns, only a particularized portion of her body will be exposed for the ensuing interaction. As we shall see, at that point the doctor is no longer dealing with a person, but he is, rather, confronted by a "pelvic."

THE PROBLEM OF UNDERCLOTHING

Undressing and nudity are problematic for the patient since she has been socialized into not undressing before strangers.[1] Almost without exception, when the woman undresses in Scene II, she turns away from the nurse and the door, even though the door is closed. She removes only her panties in the typical case, but a small number of patients also remove their shoes.

After the patient has removed her panties and/or girdle, she faces the problem of what to do with them. Panties and girdles do not have the same meaning as other items of clothing, such as a sweater, that can be casually draped around the body or strewn on furniture. Clothing is considered to be an extension of the self (Gross and Stone 1964), and in some cases the clothing comes to represent the particular part of the body that it covers. In this case, this means that panties represent to women their "private area." Comments made by patients that illustrate the problematics of panty exposure include: "The doctor doesn't want to look at these," "I want to get rid of these before he comes in," and, "I don't want the doctor to see these old things."

Some patients seem to be at a loss in solving this problem and turn to the nurse for guidance, asking her directly what they should do with their underclothing. Most patients, however, do not ask for directions, but hide their panties in some way. The favorite hiding or covering seems to be in or under the purse.[2] Other women put their panties in the pocket of their coat or in the folds of a coat or sweater, some cover them with a magazine, and some cover them with their own body on the examination table. It is rare that a woman leaves her panties exposed somewhere in the room.

THE DRAPE SHEET

Another problematic area in the vaginal examination is what being undressed can signify. Disrobing for others frequently indicates preparation for sexual relations. Since sexuality is the very thing that this scene is oriented toward removing, a mechanism is put into effect to eliminate sexuality—the drape sheet. After the patient is seated on the table, the nurse places a drape sheet from just below her breasts (she still has her blouse on) to over her legs. Although the patient is draped by the sheet, when she is positioned on the table with her legs in the stirrups, her pubic region is exposed. Usually it is not necessary for the doctor even to raise a fold in the sheet in order to examine her genitals.

Since the drape sheet does not cover the genital area, but, rather, leaves it exposed, what is its purpose? The drape sheet depersonalizes the patient. It sets the pubic area apart, letting the doctor view the pubic area in isolation, separating the pubic area from the person. The pubic area or female genitalia becomes an object isolated from the rest of the body. Because of the drape sheet, the doctor, in his position on the low stool, does not see the patient's face. He no longer sees or needs to deal with a person, just the exposed genitalia marked off by the drape sheet. Yet, from the patient's point of view in her supine position, her genitals are covered! When she looks down at her body, she does not see exposed genitalia. The drape sheet effectively hides her pubic area *from herself* while exposing it to the doctor.

THIGH BEHAVIOR

American girls are given early and continued socialization in "limb discipline," being taught at a very early age to keep their legs close together while they are sitting or while they are retrieving articles from the ground. They receive such instructions from their mothers as, "Keep your dress down," "Put your legs together," and "Nice girls don't let their panties show." Evidence of socialization into "acceptable" thigh behavior shows up in the vaginal examination while the women are positioned on the examination table and waiting for the doctor to arrive. They do not let their thighs fall outwards in a relaxed position, but they try to hold their upper or mid-thighs together until the doctor arrives. They do this even in cases where it is very difficult for them to do so, such as when the patient is in her late months of pregnancy.

Although the scene has been carefully orchestrated to desexualize the ensuing interaction, and although the patient is being depersonalized such that when the doctor returns he primarily has a pelvic to deal with and not a person, at this point in the interaction sequence the patient's "proper" thigh behavior shows that she is still holding onto her sexuality and "personality." Only later, when the doctor reenters the scene, will she fully consent to the desexualized and depersonalized role and let her thighs fall outwards.

After the props are ready and the patient is positioned, the nurse announces to the doctor via intercom that the stage is set for the third scene, saying, "We're ready in room (X)."

Scene III: The Depersonalized Stage: The Person as Pelvic

FACE-TO-PUBIC INTERACTION

The interaction to this point, as well as the use of props, has been structured to project a singular definition of the situation—that of legitimate doctor–

patient interaction and, specifically, the nonsexual examination of a woman's vaginal region by a male. To support this definition, a team performance is now given in this scene (Goffman 1959: 104). Although the previous interaction has been part of an ongoing team performance, it has been sequential, leading to the peak of the performance, the vaginal examination itself. At this time, the team goes into a tandem cooperative act, utilizing its resources to maintain and continue the legitimation of the examination, and by its combined performance reinforcing the act of each team member. The doctor, while standing, places a plastic glove on his right hand, again symbolizing the depersonalized nature of the action: By using the glove, he is saying that he will not himself be actually touching the "private area," that the glove will serve as an insulator.[3] It is at this point that he directs related questions to the patient regarding such things as her bowels or bladder. Then, while he is still in this standing position, the nurse in synchronization actively joins the performance by squeezing a lubricant onto his outstretched gloved fingers, and the doctor inserts the index and middle fingers of his right hand into the patient's vagina while externally palpating (feeling) the uterus. He then withdraws his fingers from the vagina, seats himself on the stool, inserts a speculum, and while the nurse positions the gooseneck lamp behind him, he visually examines the cervix.

Prior to this third scene, the interaction has been dyadic only, consisting of nurse and patient in Scene II and doctor and patient in Scene I. In this scene, however, the interaction becomes triadic in the sense that the doctor, nurse, and patient are simultaneously involved in the performance. The term triadic, however, does not even come close to accurately describing the role-playing of this scene. Since the patient has essentially undergone a metamorphosis from a person to an object—having been objectified or depersonalized, the focus of the interaction is now on a specific part of her body. The positioning of her legs, the use of the drape sheet, the shining of the light, and the doctor's location on the stool have effectively made the patient's pubic region the interaction focus. This location of actors and arrangement and use of props also blocks out the "talklines" between the doctor and patient, physically obstructing their exchange of glances (Goffman 1963: 161). Interaction between the doctor and the patient is no longer "face-to-face," being perhaps now more accurately described as "face-to-pubic" interaction.

BREASTS AS NONSEXUAL OBJECTS

To project and maintain the definition of nonsexuality in the vaginal examination also requires the desexualization of other parts of the body that are attributed to have sexual meaning in our culture, specifically the breasts. When the breasts are to be examined in conjunction with a vaginal examination, a rather interesting ritual is employed. The goal of this ritual—like that of the vaginal ritual—is to objectify the breasts by isolating them from the rest of the body, permitting the doctor to see the breasts apart from the person. In this ritual, after the patient has removed her upper clothing, a towel is placed across her breasts, and the drape sheet is then placed on top of the towel. Since the towel in and of itself more than sufficiently covers the breasts, we can only conclude that the purpose of the drape sheet is to enhance the definition of nonsexual interaction. Additionally, the doctor first removes the sheet from the breasts and exposes the towel. He then lifts the towel from *one* breast, makes his examination, and *replaces* the towel over that breast. He then examines the other breast in exactly the same way, again replacing the towel after the examination.

THE NURSE AS CHAPERONE

That interaction in Scene III is triadic is not accidental, nor is it instrumentally necessary. It is, rather, purposely designed to help desexualize the vaginal examination. Instrumentally, the nurse functions merely to lubricate the doctor's fingers and to hand him the speculum. These acts obviously could be handled quite well without the nurse's presence. It becomes apparent, then, that these acts are not the purpose of the nurse's presence, that she plays an entirely different role in this scene. That role is chaperone, the person assigned to be present when an unmarried male and female come together in order to give assurance to interested persons that no forbidden sexual acts take place. Although the patient has been depersonalized, or at least this is the definition that the team has been attempting to maintain, the possibility exists that the vaginal examination can erupt into a sexual scene. Because of this possibility (or the potential accusation that sexual behavior has taken place), the nurse is always present.[4] Interestingly, with contemporary sexual mores so vastly different from those of a century ago, this medical setting is one of the few remaining examples of the chaperone in our society. It is a significant role, for it helps the performance to be initiated and to continue smoothly to its logical conclusion.

THE PATIENT AS A NONPERSON TEAM MEMBER

With this definition of objectification and desexualization, the patient represents a vagina disassociated from a person. She has been dramaturgically transformed for the duration of this scene into a nonperson (Goffman 1959:152).[5] This means that while he is seated and performing the vaginal examination, the doctor need not interact with the patient as a person, being, for example, constrained neither to carry on a conversation nor to maintain eye contact with her. Furthermore, this means that he now is permitted to carry on a "side conversation" with the person with whom he does maintain eye contact, his nurse. For example, during one examination the doctor looked up at the nurse and said: "Hank and I really caught some good-sized fish while we were on vacation. He really enjoyed himself." He then looked at his "work" and announced, "Cervix looks good; no inflammation—everything appears fine down here." Ordinarily, for middle-class interactions such ignoring of the presence of a third person would constitute a breach of etiquette, but *in this case there really isn't a third person present.* The patient has been "depersonalized," to such an extent that the rules of conversation have changed, and no breach of etiquette has taken place.[6]

Although she has been defined as an object, the patient is actually the third member of the team. Her assignment is to "play the role of an object"; that is, she contributes to the flow of the interaction by acting as an object and not as a person. She contributes to the definition of herself as an object through studied alienation from the interaction, demonstrating what is known as dramaturgical discipline (Goffman 1959:216–18). She studiously gazes at the ceiling or wall, only occasionally allowing herself the luxury (or is it the danger?) of fleeting eye contact with the nurse. Eye contact with the doctor, of course, is prevented by the position of her legs and the drape sheet.

After the doctor tells the patient to get dressed, he leaves the room, and the fourth scene is ready to unfold.

Scene IV: The Repersonalizing Stage: The Transition from Pelvic to Person

During this stage of the interaction the patient undergoes a demetamorphosis, dramaturgically changing from vaginal object to person. Immediately after the doctor leaves, the nurse assists the patient into a sitting position, and she gets off the table. The nurse then asks the patient if she would like to use a towel to cleanse her genital area, and about 80 percent of the patients accept the offer. In this scene, it is not uncommon for patients to make some statement concerning their relief that the examination is over. Statements such as "I'm glad that's over with" seem to indicate the patient's overt recognition of the changing scene, to acknowledge that she is now entering a different phase of the drama.

During this repersonalizing stage, the patient is concerned with regrooming and recostuming. Patients frequently ask if they look all right, and the common question "My dress isn't too wrinkled, is it?" appears to indicate the patient's awareness of and desire to be ready for the resumption of roles other than vaginal object. Her dress isn't too wrinkled for what? It must be that she is asking whether it is too wrinkled for (1) her resumption of the role of (patient as) person and (2) her resumption of nonpatient roles.

Modesty continues to operate during this scene, and it is interesting that patients who have just had their genital area thoroughly examined both visually and tactually by the doctor are concerned that this same man will see their underclothing. ("He won't be in before I get my underwear on, will he?") They are now desiring and preparing for the return to the feminine role. They apparently fear that the doctor will reenter the room as they literally have one foot in and one foot out of their panties. They want to have their personal front reestablished to their own satisfaction before the return of this male and the onset of the next scene. For this, they strive for the poise and composure that they deem fitting the person role for which they are now preparing, frequently using either their own pocket-mirror or the mirror above the sink to check their personal front.

During this transitional role, patients indicate by their comments to the nurse that they are to again be treated as persons. While they are dressing, they frequently speak about their medical problems, their aches and pains, their fight against gaining weight, or feelings about their pregnancy. In such ways they are reasserting the self and are indicating that they are again entering "personhood."

The patient who best illustrates awareness that she had undergone a process of repersonalization is the woman who, after putting on her panties, said, "There! Just like new again." She had indeed moved out of her temporary and uncomfortable role as object, and her reappearance as person matched her self-concept.

After the patient has recostumed and regroomed, the nurse directs the patient to the chair alongside the doctor's desk, and she then announces via intercom to the doctor, "The patient is dressed," or, "The patient is waiting." It is significant that at this point the woman is referred to as "patient" in the announcement to the doctor and not as "pelvic" as she was at the end of the second scene. Sometimes the patient is also referred to by name in this announcement. The patient has completed her demetamorphosis at this point, and the nurse, by the way she refers to her, is officially acknowledging the transition.

The nurse then leaves the room, and her interaction with the patient ceases.

Scene V: The Repersonalized Stage: The Patient as Person Once Again

When the doctor makes his third entrance, the patient has again resumed the role of person and is interacted with on this basis. She is both spoken to and receives replies from the doctor, with her whole personal front being visible during the interaction. During this fifth scene the doctor informs the patient of the results of her examination, he may prescribe medications, and, wherever indicated, he suggests further care. He also tells the patient whether or not she need see him again.

For us, the significance of the interaction of Scene V is that the patient is again allowed to interact *as a person within the role of patient*. The doctor allows room for questions that the patient might have about the results of the examination, and he also gives her the opportunity to ask about other medical problems that she might be experiencing.

Interaction between the doctor and patient terminates as the doctor gets up from his chair and moves toward the door.

Conclusion: Desexualization of the Sacred

In concluding this analysis, we shall briefly indicate that conceptualizing the vagina as a sacred object yields a perspective that appears to be of value in analyzing the vaginal examination. Sacred objects are surrounded by rules protecting the object from being profaned, rules governing who may approach the "sacred," under what circumstances it may be approached, and what may and may not be done during such an approach (Durkheim 1965:51–59). If these rules are followed, the "sacred" will lose none of its "sacredness," but if they are violated, the sacred will be profaned.

Apart from the husband (with contemporary changes duly noted),[7] except in a medical setting and by the actors about whom we are speaking, no one else may approach the vagina other than the self and still have it retain its sacred character.[8] Because of this, the medical profession has taken great pains to establish a dramaturgical ritual that will ensure the continued sacredness of the vaginas of its female patients, one that will avoid even the imputation of taboo violation. Accordingly, as we have herein analyzed, by dramaturgically desexualizing the vagina by dissociating it from the person, and by elaborately defining it as just another organ of the body, this ritual of the vaginal examination allows the doctor to approach the sacred without profaning it or violating taboos. Thus, the vaginal examination is a fascinating example of how reality is socially constructed, in this instance of how physicians are able to handle a woman's vagina and yet maintain a definition of nonsexuality.

Notes

1. With a society that is as clothing conscious and bodily conscious as is ours, undressing and nudity are problematic for many, but perhaps more for females than for males since males are more likely to experience structured situations in which they undress and are nude before others, such as showering after high school physical education classes, while females in the same situation are often afforded a greater degree of privacy with, for example, private shower stalls in place of the mass showers of the males. This is not always the case, however, and Theresa France (private communication) reports that in her classes the females also had communal showers.

2. From a psychiatric orientation this association of the panties with the purse is fascinating, given the Freudian interpretation that the purse signifies the female genitalia.

In some examination rooms, the problem of where to put the undergarments is solved by the provision of a special drawer for them located beneath the examination table.

3. It is true, of course, that the glove also serves instrumental purposes, such as protecting the physician from diseases that might be transmitted by means of digital–vaginal contact—and patients from diseases the physician might transmit from one patient to another.

4. It is interesting to note that even the corpse of a female is defined as being in need of such chaperonage. Erving Goffman, on reading this paper in manuscript form, commented that hospital etiquette dictates that "when a male attendant moves a female stiff from the room to the morgue he be accompanied by a female nurse."

5. Compare what Goffman (1959:104) has to say about secrets shared by team members. Remember that the patient in this interaction is not simply a member of the audience. She is a team member, being also vitally interested in projecting and maintaining the definition of nonsexuality. Another reader of this paper, who wishes to remain anonymous, reports that during one of her pregnancies she had a handsome, young, and unmarried Hungarian doctor and that during vaginal examinations with him she would "concentrate on the instruments being used and the uncomfortableness of the situation" so as not to become sexually aroused.

6. In this situation a patient is "playing the role" of an object, but she is still able to hear verbal exchange, and she could enter the interaction if she so desired. As such, side comments between doctor and nurse must be limited. In certain other doctor-patient situations, however, the patient completely leaves the "person role," such as when the patient is anesthetized, which allows much freer banter among medical personnel. In delivery rooms of hospitals, for example, it is not uncommon for the obstetrician to comment while stitching the episiotomy, "She's like a new bride now," or, when putting in the final stitch, to say, "This is for the old man." Additionally, while medical students are stitching their first episiotomy, instructing doctors have been known to say, "It's not tight enough. Put one more in for the husband."

7. While consensual approaches by boyfriends certainly run less risk of violating the sacred than at earlier periods in our history, this depends a good deal on the individual's religion, education, age, and social class membership.

8. It is perhaps for this reason that prostitutes ordinarily lack respect: They have profaned the sacred. And in doing so, not only have they failed to limit vaginal access to culturally prescribed individuals, but they have added further violation by allowing vaginal access on a monetary basis. They have, in effect, sold the sacred.

References

Durkheim, Emile (1965). *The Elementary Forms of the Religious Life*. New York: The Free Press (1915 copyright by George Allen & Unwin Ltd.).

Goffman, Erving (1959). *The Presentation of Self in Everyday Life*. Garden City, NY: Doubleday Anchor Books.

Goffman, Erving (1963). *Behavior in Public Places: Notes on the Social Organization of Gatherings*. New York: The Free Press.

Gross, Edward, and Gregory Stone (1964). "Embarrassment and the Analysis of Role Requirements," *American Journal of Sociology* 70: 1–15.

21 Lonely Hearts, Classy Dreams, Empty Wallets

AMY WALDMAN

Who we are—our goals, hopes, feelings about the self—originates with others. They—this larger social group—provide us a language and set us within relationships from which we learn our place in life. From them, we learn our attitudes, how to express ourselves, even our dreams of what can be in life. None of us came into this world with any of these vital aspects of personal identity, this unique sense of who we are.

With the rare exception of a hermit or two, we all need companionship, for associating with others validates our identity, our socially rooted sense of being. Consequently, we find loneliness a bitter thing. Yet, at times we do find ourselves cut off from others. For most of us, this is but an occasional, fleeting sense of differences, a gap we perceive between ourselves and significant people around us. The feeling soon passes, and, with relief, we again welcome the sense of belonging. For some, however, the experience is not fleeting. They are cut off from others, sometimes physically, perhaps housebound with few visitors, certainly socially. Their isolation makes them vulnerable and easily exploited, as is apparent in Waldman's analysis of a newly developed pseudo community.

AFTER A MAN DIED several months ago at the Virginian Retirement Community in Fairfax, his family went to collect his worldly goods. They found more than they bargained for: His home was crammed, floor to ceiling, with possessions they never knew he had. There were kitchen gadgets, costume jewelry, bed linens, and cleansers, all by the dozens.

He had bought it all from the world's most accessible stores: the home shopping networks that came through his television into his living room twenty-four hours a day, seven days a week. This man, whose name the retirement home withheld for privacy, ordered a package from QVC or Home Shopping Network (HSN), the two leading home shopping channels, almost every day. Some of what came he gave away. Most of it simply piled up, unused.

What had brought him to line his walls with the fruits of home shopping? In a word, companionship. Home shopping hosts didn't just sell to him—they spoke to him. An employee at the Virginian recalls that the man spent a lot of time by himself. He did not make friends easily and he spoke of being lonely. But when he bought, he said he could keep operators chatting to him for half an hour. He had found a way to fill his days and sleepless nights.

He was not alone in his discovery. As the hours cycle past on home shopping channels, the disembodied voices of buyers, calling in to offer "testimonials" on their purchases, float above the sparkling descriptions of cubic zirconium jewelry. Most are female—Dorothy from Daytona, Betty from Fresno, Helen from Mexico City, Indiana. Many of the voices are beginning to crack with age. And their extraordinary enthusiasm for the products—and the hosts, and the show itself—masks something else: a deep, abiding need for human contact. "I live alone," says a woman named Erma who calls in on a Monday morning. "All I've got to do is watch QVC."

To Erma, the man from Virginia, and many others like them, home shopping channels sold more than $3 billion of goods last year. QVC, which stands for Quality Value Control, alone sold $1.4 billion worth of goods, logging 55 million phone calls. The channel is the world's largest purveyor of gold jewelry. It once sold $1.4 million worth of Kodak products in 70 minutes and $1.9 million of Mighty Morphin Power Rangers paraphernalia in two hours. In a record day, it took $18 million in orders. The second-place Home Shopping Network, or "Club" (as it's known on the air), nearly matches that pace.

That the two channels, and a host of smaller rivals, could do so well runs counter to conventional wisdom, for in an age of ironic, sophisticated advertising, the home shopping pitch seems amateurish. The camera zooms in on an item, which rocks back and forth, back and forth on a pedestal; the hosts, in living-room sets, praise each bauble in a frenzy of superlatives. A clock counts down to whip up a sense of urgency as the number sold mounts on the screen. The suggested retail price hovers above the low, low home shopping price.

Many of the goods—imitation jewelry, collectibles, gadgets, polyester pantsuits—are junk, often selling at more-than-junk prices. And while "convenience" is a favorite home shopping buzzword, the description could not be less apt: It might take hours, even days, of home shopping viewing to come upon something you need.

Spend some time in front of the television, though, and you sense that while the pitch is predictable, it is anything but amateurish. As low-tech as they are, the home shopping networks understand that the real work of advertising is not to publicize bargains—it is to appeal to deeper needs. They turn their constant, mesmerizing presence and viewer participation into a mock community, a "universe," as QVC calls it, that seems to break the isolation television perpetuates. And even for those who are not lonely, home shopping promises something else: the lives of the rich, the famous, the glamorous—on the cheap, and just a phone call away.

Someplace Very Special

Home shopping is just one more chapter in the evolution of marketing to a consumer culture—a process that began in earnest in the twenties and accelerated with the post–World War II economic expansion that established America's middle class as a potent consumer force. In response, advertisers went to work creating what one General Motors executive called the "organized culture of dissatisfaction"—bringing out the new, "better" models each year so previous models seemed inadequate, or offering consumers a choice of, say, fifteen shoe colors so one no longer seemed enough.

Advertisers were so successful in unleashing desire that a traditionally frugal nation began to redefine "need" as whatever ads told them they had to have. It was the creation and fulfillment of these needs that John Kenneth Galbraith probed in his 1958 classic, *The Affluent Society.* Ad men, he wrote, "are effective only with those who do not know what they want. In this state alone, men are open to persuasion."

In such a culture, home shopping, with its introduction of newer, better items every ten minutes, finds fertile ground. The channels target the credit-card-carrying working- and middle-class consumers who may have enough but can be persuaded they need more. "It's things you need, but you don't realize you need," one regular home shopper tells me. "But then you see it and it looks so good."

Between midnight and 1 A.M. one night, QVC sells 8,400 terrycloth robes ($24.95 apiece—the day's "special value"), an item the host also pushes as "a beach cover-up." Nancy calls from Middletown, Ohio. "What did you like about the robe?" the host asks. "Well, I thought it would make a nice beach cover-up," Nancy says. "Do you live near a beach?" asks the host. "No," admits Nancy, "no, I don't."

In their effort to cultivate such needs, the effervescent female home shopping hosts and their unctuous male counterparts know their audience well: more than 80 percent female, mainly middle-aged or older. Occasionally, they fall back on the tactics glossy women's magazines have used for decades to target younger women in the prime of their insecurity. "Summer's coming up," says the no-nonsense marketer of a nail buffing kit. "That means beach weather, that means sandals, ladies. Do you want to show your toenails the way they look right now? . . . If you're not picking up our kit today, you're a loser."

But most often, the hosts head straight for the class-anxiety jugular. They play to a modern-day version of Gustave Flaubert's Emma Bovary, the woman who drives her family into debt because of her conviction that material things will bring some sort of transcendence from her bourgeois existence. "In Rouen she saw ladies with charms dangling from their watch fobs; she bought some charms. . . . Though she had no one to write to, she had bought herself a blotter, a writing case, a pen, and envelopes."

In America after the twenties, the rich held their edge over the Bovarys not by the gaudiness of their wealth but by their elite tastes—knowing the right vintages or the right vacation spots, which meant shunning Cancun once the Smiths from Des Moines could afford it.

In the eighties, arguably for the first time since the twenties, conspicuous consumption came back into style. Television programs like *Dallas* and *Dynasty* ogled the lifestyles of the rich and famous, and the media elevated moneymakers like Donald Trump to celebrity status. Taste was suddenly very, very expensive. For those on the outside looking in, the problem was, as home shopping hosts put it, how to get gemstones at costume jewelry prices.

Into this anxious void rushed HSN, which went on the air in 1985, and QVC, which followed a year later. Both began offering truckloads of low-quality "luxury" items, most of it costume jewelry and imitation gemstones—merchandise that caters to the need to look like you have more than you do.

Home shopping pretends to offer the requisite knowledge to establish good taste. For several hundred dollars, the host sells a rug and the conversation to go with it: "Well, it's an Aubusson rug, it goes back to the time of Louis XV, Marie Antoinette, and so on. . . . It's made from long-haired sheep in Northern China. They have long hair because it gets very cold up near Siberia and Mongolia. . . ."

"This bracelet says money, money, money, money," QVC's Gwen Owen gushes over a fake diamond bracelet, which sells for $80. The home shopping hosts are marketing the pearly gates of upper-class heaven. They just happen to be *faux* pearl.

That this market is a gold mine is apparent in the cadre of celebrities— from Pete Rose to Joan Rivers to John Tesh—who now peddle on home shopping channels. Since home shopping is about making excess affordable, it's no surprise that among the most popular celebrity-salespeople are the icons of the eighties. A decade ago, on *Dallas,* Victoria Principal embodied everything out of reach. Today, on QVC, dressed down, with minimal makeup, she's in middle-America's living room, eager to talk and take calls. Her presence seems to represent a leveling, an accessibility unprecedented in American culture.

The idea is tantalizing, but deceptive. The celebrities foment status anxiety as successfully from a living room like yours and mine as they did from the pages of glossy magazines a decade ago. HSN showcases Vanna White, the *Wheel of Fortune* letter-turner who rocketed to fame in the eighties by wearing a different designer dress every night, and who now, stripped of her gowns, sells her own label clothes and shoes on Home Shopping Club. A woman calls in to tell Vanna she has twenty pairs of Vanna White shoes, and begins listing the colors: red, white, gold, silver. . . . "I'm so happy to hear that," White interrupts, "but do you have this one?" She is holding up a shoe described as "halfway between gold and silver."

And then there is Ivana Trump, perhaps the ultimate emblem of eighties excess-as-success, a woman, her co-host Bobbi reminds us, "who knows what it is to roll down Rodeo Drive and go shopping." In her pink silk "House of Ivana" outfit, girlish blond curls, and what looks like tens of thousands of dollars of plastic surgery, she comes to HSN to share her designs and her secrets (and plug her new book). She is holding out a hand from the Beautiful People to the Little People.

"You have the opportunity to have in your wardrobe items that Ivana has in her collection," co-host Bobbi observes, "and that takes you someplace very special." You can, Ivana explains, wear an outfit "to drop your kids off in the morning, go to the doctor, go shopping, put some earrings on and go to a lovely lunch. It's perfect for a cruise."

That women are unnervingly grateful for these nuggets from Park Avenue, Palm Beach, and Hollywood lives is a poignant reminder of just how central an issue class continues to be in American life. "You can afford anything, Ivana," one caller says, "and due to you, people like me—I'm a nurse—can, too. We live vicariously through you."

But even as Ivana seems to forsake her class advantage, she leverages it. Her perfume must be good because "I could purchase any perfume in the world," she boasts. "Silver is in this year," she proclaims. "I already knew that last year, because I go to parties . . . I'm always dead ahead." And then comes the tease: "But now everyone's going to catch up to me."

Truth is, Ivana has no intention of letting everyone catch up to her. "I have a suggestion," a caller named Anne says to Ivana. "Everyone is crazy about your engagement ring. You should do it in imitation stones and put it in the collection." Ivana giggles: "I have to discuss it with my fiancé. I don't think he will like it. He'll say, 'I spent millions on it and now you share it with the ladies?'"

In the end, home shopping channels peddle only the illusion that you can fake your way into the upper class, that snobbery can come cheap. They are less interested in democratizing status than preserving the status quo. Like all home shopping hosts, HSN's Alan Skanz regularly plugs cubic zirconium by asking: Why pay for diamonds when you can get Como Diamante (as they call the imitation gems) for so much less? "You are going to walk into a room," he says, "and people are going to think you spent $15,000 for these earrings." So it seems a cruel joke when one afternoon he sells a diamond ring by mocking its cheap cousin: "Enjoy your cubic zirconium," he says sarcastically. "I have a *real* diamond."

24 Hours of Sunshine

In their possession of an audience's hopes and fears, home shopping hosts are like no one so much as the fictional advice columnist in Nathanael West's 1933 novella *Miss Lonelyhearts*. A young reporter takes the job as a joke, but then realizes that the letters to him are genuine expressions of suffering. Even worse, their writers take him seriously.

"Dear Miss Lonelyhearts . . ." begin the letters from "Desperate," Disillusioned-with-tubercular-husband," "Sick-of-it-All." "On most days," West wrote, "he received more than 30 letters, all of them alike, stamped from the dough of human suffering with a heart-shaped cookie knife."

The pain in his correspondents' lives, and his own powerlessness to help them, eats away at Miss Lonelyhearts. For each letter, he searches for a sincere reply, and always, he comes up empty. Finally, unable to bear the pathos of human existence, he is driven to self-destruction.

Today, the lonely and desperate turn to home shopping hosts who seem to have no such interest in acknowledging the limits of their powers. They appear perfectly comfortable marketing miracles. "It's raining," says one caller with a hint of sadness. "We'll keep the sunshine going," Bobbi replies.

Another host reads a written testimonial from Bethlehem, Pennsylvania. The letter begins like any to Miss Lonelyhearts could: "I was really at a low point. I needed something." But then comes a distinctly un-Westian salvation: "Then someone turned me on to Destiny Perfume. It seems so good that it has really given me strength to go on for me and my family."

When real pain and loneliness do seep through, the home shopping solution is to studiously ignore it. Alan and Wendi are plugging a diamond ring. Edna from Ohio calls in. "If you think your life is going pretty good right now, wait until you buy this ring," says Alan. "Well actually," Edna responds, "It's going pretty bad." Her words vanish, unacknowledged, beneath the chatter of the hosts.

Sally from Chicago has bought some perfume, and she calls in to talk about it: "I'm lying in bed, this is my day off, I'm being a princess." Her voice is raspy with age and cigarettes. She works in a store, and says men tell her how good she smells. "That's wonderful," the host asks, and then asks, suggestively, "Did you put some on before you went to bed last night?" "No," says Sally. "I'm a widow."

When women describe their bouts with cancer or their hospital stays, as many do, the testimonials become farcical struggles between hosts trying to truncate the calls or push them toward the product-driven point, and callers hanging on for dear life, trying to prolong the conversation.

The question is why anyone would turn for comfort to talking heads out to make a sale. The answer lies partly in the same post–World War II social transformation that gave more Americans spending power. With increased income, Americans moved into dispersed suburbs. As women moved into the work force, neighborhood networks and social clubs shrank, isolating the women left behind. Driven to spend more, men and women worked more. Families broke more easily, and even those that held together felt the pressures of work and mobility. And television pulled us off streets and front porches and into living rooms.

As political scientist Robert Putnam writes in "Bowling Alone, Revisited," affiliation to organized religion, parental involvement in schools, participation in voluntary associations have all declined over the past two decades. Our community participation now takes the form of writing checks to organizations. . . .

To belong to the home shopping "club," you have to buy. If you don't, you can't go on-air to talk to your friends, and you can't win their approval. And that is how home shopping channels prey on the lonely, the alienated: by offering a haven, then charging admission.

Despite the cynical sell, it's not hard to understand the appeal of home shopping's soothing, ever-positive hosts, who respond to their devoted customers with matching enthusiasm: "Thank you so, so, so much for calling in today. . . . We took a risk and brought some new items. You responded with an outpouring of support—and we love you for it."

The format plays on our nostalgia for a simpler, friendlier time. The cheery home shopping pitch—"Get some coffee and OJ and come right back!"—is a far cry from the bleak, unsmiling Calvin Klein ads that characterize the cutting edge of advertising today. The home shopping hosts exclaim "Nice to meet you!" and "Thanks for stopping by tonight!"—as if the caller had ambled into the corner store in a small town for an evening's gossip.

In its evocation of Tupperware parties, the kaffeeklatsch, Mary Kay cosmetics saleswomen stopping by your home—all traditions that have fallen, or are falling, by the wayside—home shopping hearkens back to the past in another way: It speaks to women as they were before women's liberation. Callers are "honey" and "dear." "That executive look" is just another fashion statement. Women lunch, they shop, they entertain, they go on cruises, they have craft parties. Femininity sells. Dolls, cooed over by hosts as if they were children, are very popular.

Watching this throwback to another era, it's easy to forget that for many women, the underbelly of that era was a gnawing sense of dissatisfaction. But that's the idea: to banish both the dark side of history and the bright side of real life from living rooms. For a woman like Dorothy from North Carolina, who says, "I watch home shopping from the time I get up until my husband comes home from work," home shopping channels affirm, indeed encourage, her choice to wile away her days with them. "I hope you're going to stay with us for the whole show," hosts implore callers.

The community that home shopping offers is made even more enticing by something no real community can offer: anonymity—the freedom to dream without being judged. The flip side of that, though, is the absence of any of the complex, enriching interactions, images, or conversations of daily life. There is no such thing as neighborliness or charity or civic virtue in this universe, no relationship that extends beyond the purchase.

Telefriend

In fact, home shopping is the latest advancement in business's quest to make spending money as painless as possible, an effort that picked up steam with layaways and installment plans in the twenties and made a quantum leap with credit cards in the fifties. Academics have proven what common sense suggests: We spend more with credit cards because it feels like we're spending nothing. That's one reason that debt, once a social embarrassment, has become socially acceptable, and why consumer debt in the United States today is close to $1 trillion.

Before, advertisers had to make their message powerful enough to motivate shoppers to go to a store. Now it just has to be good enough to get you to pick up the phone. After your first purchase, your credit card number is in the computer. You can punch your "membership" number and the item number into an automated voice system, or feed it to a friendly operator. That's not what spending money feels like.

And so women call to confess they have "maxed out" on their credit cards, or to offer thanks for "flex" and "easy pay" plans that enable them to keep buying while putting off the paymaster. "I've got about two-thirds of your things," Vada Sue from Winston-Salem, North Carolina, tells Home Shopping Club when she calls in to make yet another purchase, "and you all have about two-thirds of my money."

The marriage of technology and commerce will make consuming ever more convenient: Our homes can become retail outlets, we can visit virtual shopping malls from our couches, shop for new homes on CD-ROM. We will, in other words, never have to leave home to fill the needs that marketing creates.

The potential is enormous, but so are the implications. One virtue of the postwar consumer binge in America was the number of jobs it created in manufacturing and retail. But over the last decade, automation of industry eliminated many manufacturing jobs, and now retailing is automating too.

"We don't need bricks and mortar," QVC president Douglas Briggs boasted to *USA Today*. "We can cover the whole nation with twenty salespeople." QVC racked up $1.4 billion in sales last year with a mere 6,100 employees, and that's only the beginning. Shopping services are going on-line; stores are experimenting with robots in place of human salespeople. Since 1989, more than 411,000 retail jobs have been eliminated. The reduction of labor, and costs, is great news for corporations like QVC; it's lousy news for Americans who at least could count on a consumer culture to provide jobs.

And then there is the human cost, the deepening of isolation, the erosion of live—in the human, not television, sense—communities. If the success of home shopping portends the future, marketing will turn to ever more sophisticated attempts to play on our nostalgia for what we've lost, to peddle connections to other people via commerce. Take First National Bank in Chicago, which now charges $3 for the use of a human teller rather than an automated one: Getting some warmth requires cold cash.*

Home shopping foreshadows what's so insidious about that prospect: Even as QVC and HSN try to mimic the feeling of community, they draw us, as television always has, even further away from the real thing. At 6 A.M., a woman named Doris phones HSN to purchase a portable copier for $229. "How are you?" the host asks. "Fair," Doris replies, her voice shaking slightly. She explains that she orders things from home shopping and mail-order catalogues, forgets what she orders, and then orders them again. She wants the copier to keep track of her purchases.

"Good idea," the host says, smothering her pathos with his enthusiasm. "And running down to the corner copier is *so* inconvenient." Doris will have her copier. And she will be yoked even more tightly to an isolation that only her television—and another purchase—can penetrate.

---

*After public protest and national publicity, the bank rescinded this charge.

22 Fire in Hamlet: A Case Study of State-Corporate Crime

JUDY ROOT AULETTE
RAYMOND MICHALOWSKI

All of us have fears, some of us of drowning, others of small places, of rats, snakes, or spiders, or of urban violence, of being raped or murdered. To be caught in a crowded room with flames licking at us and unable to find an escape no matter how frantically we pursue it is also a fear that haunts some of us. Such a situation is rare, of course, but it is just that rare moment that is detailed here. Trapped and panic stricken, 25 workers died this horrifying death.

This article is not so much about fires, however, as it is about its causes. Like other fires that take lives, this one, too, should never have happened. What Aulette and Michalowski discovered as they probed this event is that the safeguards set up to prevent such a catastrophe had broken down. The social structure on which we depend for our survival had been tampered with—and, sad to say, the motive was raw profit.

ON SEPTEMBER 3, 1991, an explosion and fire at the Imperial Food Products chicken-processing plant in Hamlet, North Carolina, killed 25 workers and injured another 56. This human disaster, which devastated the small working-class community of Hamlet, immediately became the subject of both controversy and investigation. Shortly after the fire there was speculation that Imperial might face felony manslaughter charges in the deaths because fire doors that would have led the workers to safety were deliberately kept locked. According to a number of workers at the plant, fire doors were "routinely locked to keep employees from stealing chicken nuggets." Subsequent inquiry indicated that not only did the company lock the fire doors, one of which displayed the bloody footprints of workers who tried to batter it open before they died, but also that an interwoven pattern of regulatory failure on the part of several state and federal agencies played a significant role in creating the conditions that led to the tragedy. . . .

The fire at the Imperial Food Processing plant and the regulatory environment that made it possible underscore the importance of the interplay between corporations and government in the production of life-threatening criminal conduct by businesses. The *technical cause* of the Imperial plant fire was the rupture of a hydraulic line near a deep fryer. This resulted in an explosion and a fireball that not only destroyed the plant and the lives of 25 workers, but also shattered the social makeup of an entire town. Those who died or were injured in the Hamlet fire, however, were the victims of much more than a simple mechanical breakdown. They were the victims of a series of *social decisions* made by a broad array of institutions. These include Imperial Food Products, the U.S. Occupational Safety and Health Administration, the U.S. Food and Drug Administration, the legislature and governor of the State of North Carolina, the North Carolina Occupational Safety and Health Administration, and, finally, local agencies responsible for building inspection and fire protection. These organizational units pursued a pattern of actions and relations that made it possible and routine that workers in the Imperial chicken-processing plant would be denied adequate escape routes in case of fire. This pattern does not represent an aberrant moment in North Carolina labor history. . . .

State-Corporate Crime in Context

In his 1939 Presidential Address to the American Sociological Society, Edwin Sutherland introduced the concept of *white-collar crime,* which later served as the basis for his pioneering book by the same title. Although Sutherland was primarily concerned with the social-class positions of "white-collar" offenders as *individuals,* the data he actually analyzed consisted of violations charged against corporations and businesses as *organizations.* This contradiction in Sutherland's work ultimately led to the study of what has become known as "corporate crime." The study of corporate crime focuses on deviant organizational patterns rather than on the deviance of individuals. This approach has resulted in an important insight and an important oversight. The *insight* is that corporate crime is a form of organizational deviance. Insofar as corporations are formal organizations, the study of corporate crime can and should incorporate the theoretical and substantive insights of organizational research. The *oversight* is the failure to recognize that since the modern corporation emerged as the basic unit of economic activity within private-production systems in the late nineteenth century, corporations and governments have been functionally interdependent. The modern corporation in the United States could not have developed, nor could it currently function, without the legal, economic, and political infrastructure provided by government. . . .

Our argument here is that many injurious events, such as the killing fire at the Imperial chicken-processing factory, are generated at the interstices of corporations and governments. . . .

The relationship between the overarching government policies and the specific goals of business and industry is well illustrated by North Carolina's labor history. Since the late nineteenth century the political leadership of North Carolina has pursued a policy of industrial development through, among other things, limiting unionization and blocking the power of regulatory agencies. By contrast, the Imperial Food Processing company, like most industries, had a very specific goal of profit maximization through (among other things) worker discipline. This goal and the methods used to attain it, however, dovetailed nicely with the state's general concern with industrial development through (among other things) creating a climate within which businesses were not burdened with either unions or extensive safety regulation. . . .

Blocking Worker Organization

The most consistent specific vehicle by which unions have been undercut in North Carolina is the state's right-to-work law. This law hinders the ability of unions to organize, and legally limits the strength of unions by outlawing union shops. Under the right-to-work law, which is more appropriately named a "right-not-to-unionize law," if a union wins the right to represent a plant, only those workers who wish to join the union, pay union dues, and abide by union decisions, such as a strike vote, do so. In states without such laws, when a union wins recognition, all of the workers in the plant must join the union, pay dues, and abide by union decisions.

Because it is a right-to-work state, even a unionized plant in North Carolina may have up to 49 percent of its work force who are not union members. Consequently, the economic strength of the union is diminished because not all workers pay dues, and its bargaining strength is substantially weakened because employers know that even if there is a strike vote, only the union members will walk out. Thus, while strikes may be an inconvenience, in many plants they do not threaten a total shutdown of operations. . . .

Blocking Worker Safety: The Case of NC-OSHA

In the case of workplace safety, a relatively strong Federal law has been in place since 1970 in the form of the Occupational Safety and Health Act. The Act's stated goal is "to assure as far as possible every working man and woman in the Nation safe and healthful working conditions." The Act requires that each employer furnish each employee "a place of employment which is free from recognized hazards that are causing or likely to cause death or serious physical harm" to employees.

The law gives impressive rights to American workers. First it obliges companies to reduce the risks in the workplace. While other labor laws limit businesses from preventing efforts by workers to make improvements in the safety of their workplace, the OSH Act not only allows workers to fight for safety and health, it places the burden of responsibility on the employer, demanding that the company take action to improve the workplace in ways that benefit the worker. The second way in which the Act is impressive is in its breadth of coverage compared to other protective legislation. Public-sector employees are the only group of workers who are not protected by the Act. The OSH Act also differs from all previous worker health and safety legislation because it gives employees the right to participate in agency inspections. . . .

Unheeded Warnings

In order for workers to be protected from dangerous work environments, at least in any work environment where they are not empowered to alter their own work conditions, someone must recognize the problems and make them known to those who *do have* the power to alter the hazardous conditions. There is evidence that the workers at the Hamlet plant were aware of safety problems and that they attempted to make their voices heard.

At the hearings on the fire, Mr. Bobby Quick, an employee at the plant, was asked if any fellow employee had made a complaint about the locked doors. Mr. Quick said his immediate co-workers knew about the problem although they had not gone to management.

> The maintenance [workers] talked about it amongst ourselves. We never took it to the office. We said amongst ourselves we hope a fire doesn't break out.

Among other departments in the plant, however, people did complain to management, although their efforts apparently did not lead to any changes in the hazardous conditions. Quick testified that:

> A lot of people talked about it catching on fire and killing people. I recall one day Brad [plant supervisor and the son of its owner Emmett Roe] was there. I think it was a white lady who told him, it was the day that it smoked up. She said, "This thing is going to kill somebody." Brad did not pay her no attention. He was always rushing the maintenance men to fix something so they would not lose money and product. All they cared about was the product, getting it out.

At the Congressional hearings, representatives asked why more people did not question the safety of the plant, or why they were not more persistent in their complaints. Mr. Quick was asked if people were fearful of making a complaint. He answered by saying:

> If you try to make a statement to Brad he did not want to hear it. What you said did not matter. He was running the show. If you keep making a stink, he will fire you, you know. . . .

The Failure of OSHA

Had the concerned workers at Imperial chosen to contact OSHA instead of bringing their complaints directly to the plant's management, they, like many other workers in North Carolina, would not likely have met with success. First of all, they would have been informed by a poster in the plant to call an 800 number. Three-fourths of the 160,000 workplace posters publicizing the phone number for safety complaints, including the posters at Imperial, listed a number that had been disconnected with no forwarding number. Thus, the basic requirement of being able to contact the safety agency could not be met. Certainly, a highly motivated worker, familiar with the process of hunting through a bureaucratic tangle of phone numbers and disconnected lines, might have reached OSHA. But the more likely response of the average worker who called the NC-OSHA number only to be told it was disconnected would be to conclude that the office was no longer in operation. At the very least, the incorrect posters, and the failure to replace them with correct ones, constituted a serious limitation on the accessibility of OSHA to the workers at Imperial and elsewhere in North Carolina.

The incorrect posters and other problems faced by NC-OSHA reflect in part the organization's inadequate level of funding. . . .

In 1980 North Carolina had 1.9 million workers and 47 OSHA safety inspectors. Ten years later, when North Carolina's work force had grown by 37 percent, to a total of 2.6 million, the number of OSHA inspectors had declined by 12 percent, to 42 inspectors. . . .

In addition to the inadequate numbers of inspectors, Brooks reported to the Congressional committee that until late in 1991 the inspectors NC-OSHA did have were able to work in the field only four days a week because the department lacked sufficient travel funds. Since then they have been able to work in the field only three days a week because of further cuts in NC-OSHA funding. . . .

The Imperial Fire

The accumulated evidence in the Hamlet fire indicates that the single most important factor leading to the 25 deaths was the lack of readily accessible routes to safety. All but one of the 25 deaths resulted from smoke inhalation. Only one person died of extensive burns. The fire itself and the heat it produced were not large enough within the 30,000-square-foot building Imperial occupied to kill the number of people it did. Rather, people died because they could not escape the smoke the fire produced. Particularly telling is the fact that a number of the dead were found in a large freezer where they had retreated to escape the fire. Once inside the freezer they were protected from the heat and fire, but unfortunately they were unable to close the door tightly enough to keep out the toxic smoke. Considering that these workers had suffi-cient time to reach the freezer, in all likelihood they would also have had suffi-cient time to escape the building, *if* there had been adequate pathways to safety. This point is underscored by the example of one woman who survived because, although she could not get out of a blocked door, she was able to put her face out of the door where a friend who was outside fanned away the smoke with his baseball cap. . . .

Approximately a dozen current and former plant workers told news re-porters that doors were routinely locked to keep employees from stealing chicken nuggets. Police records show the company reported employee thefts three times in recent years. "Hamlet police records show Imperial employees stole chicken valued at between $24 and $245." If the theft of chicken was, in fact, the reason for locking the doors, it suggests that Imperial management operated according to a frightening calculus wherein preventing the theft of several hundred dollars worth of chicken parts justified risking human lives by cutting off what would be escape routes in case of fire, and doing so in viola-tion of the law. It is also disturbing that in all of the discussion and reportage about the locking of the doors, there appears little evidence that the simple so-lution of installing fire doors with alarms that sound whenever the door is opened, a commonplace installation in many buildings and a solution that would have both insured safe exits *and* minimized the use of these doors for il-licit commerce, was ever seriously considered.

In addition to locked doors, exits were unmarked and employees were not made aware of where exits were and whether they were locked or not. There had never been a fire drill in the plant nor any fire safety instruction of employees.

The fire itself started because of the unsafe practice of repairing hoses carrying hydraulic fuel while continuing to maintain cooking temperatures with gas flames under large vats of oil. To minimize down-time, Imperial Food Products routinely left its gas-fired chicken fryer on while repairing adjacent hoses carrying flammable hydraulic fuel, a maintenance worker testified. On the day of the fire, repairs were being made on hoses carrying hydraulic fuel to the cooking vats. The cooking was not stopped as the repairs were made. The insurance department of the State of North Carolina filed a report describing how the fire started.

> The cause of the fire was determined to be the ignition of hydraulic oil from a ruptured line only a few feet from a natural-gas-fueled cooker used in preparation of the chicken. Investigators determined that during a repair operation, the in-coming hydraulic line separated from its coupling at a point approximately 60 inches above the concrete floor and began to discharge the fluid at high pressure. This high pressure and subsequent flow resulted in the hydraulic fluid being sprayed against the floor and onto the nearby cooker. Ignition of the fuel was im-mediate; likely from the nearby gas burners. . . . The intense fire also impinged upon a natural gas regulator (located directly above the ruptured hydraulic line)

on the supply line to the burners which soon failed and added to the fuels being consumed.

To make matters worse, there were no automatic cutoffs on the hydraulic or gas lines, there was only one fire extinguisher in the plant, and there were no working telephones to call the fire department when the fire broke out. An employee had to drive several blocks to the fire station to inform them that there was a serious fire at the plant.

Omission by the Federal Government

Two Federal agencies failed the workers at Hamlet in important ways. The first of these is OSHA. OSHA was statutorily responsible for insuring the quality of services provided by state-run NC-OSHA. While Federal OSHA had known for quite some time about the inadequacy and ineffectiveness of the North Carolina agency's operations, no effective effort was taken to remedy the situation, except to file a report.

The second agency that could have acted, but did not, to prevent the disaster in Hamlet came as a surprise to most people—the United States Department of Agriculture (USDA). Because Imperial Foods in Hamlet is a meat-processing plant, a USDA agent visited the plant *daily* in order to make sure that the meat was being handled properly.

Kenneth Booker, the regular inspector for the USDA, told a Congressional panel that he knew about the locked doors because workers had complained to him, and that he had talked with plant managers about the problem. He did not do anything further because he believed he lacked authority, and because Imperial management told him the door could be quickly unlocked in an emergency. . . .

The summer before the fire, on June 19, 1991, Grady Hussey, a USDA inspector who sometimes substituted for the regular inspector, Booker, cited Imperial Foods for allowing flies to enter the plant and for leaving two doors open to a trash bin. An Imperial official, Joseph Kelly, responded to the citation, writing on it that he had solved the problem and stating, "Inside door closed and outside door closed and locked. Outside door to this area will be locked at all times unless for an emergency." Hussey signed his name on the citation noting that "corrective action has taken place."

The USDA claimed that it had no responsibility in the case. Carol Foreman, former assistant U.S. Agriculture secretary who supervised meat and poultry inspections from 1977 to 1981, disagreed, stating, "Every USDA inspector is a law enforcement officer, they carry a badge and they are sworn to uphold all laws of the United States." She said the inspector should have noticed locked doors. "This inspector had time to pick up a telephone and call the N.C. Department of Labor and say there's a serious hazard here. If the inspector saw somebody get raped or murdered in that plant, would he say that wasn't his responsibility too?" . . .

Local Government

The operations of local government agencies also played their part in contributing to the Hamlet fire. Hamlet is located in Richmond County, which is responsible for regularly conducting inspections to identify unsafe or unlawful buildings in the county. According to the North Carolina Insurance Department, the Hamlet plant was in violation of building codes because it did not have a sprinkler system, did not have enough doors, workers had to walk more than the allowable 150 feet to exit the building, one door opened to the inside, four doors were locked, and there were no exit signs. Some of these violations were a result of Imperial management having made changes in the building without requesting inspections and without obtaining building permits. . . .

The other local government agency that played a role in the deaths of the 25 workers, although perhaps a minor one, was the Hamlet Fire Department. Here the story takes a racial twist. The town of Hamlet is predominately white, and its fire department is all white. Although Hamlet is a small town, it has a suburb—the town of Dobbins—which, as a reflection of the continuing patterns of residential racial segregation in North Carolina, is predominately black and has a black fire department. When the fire at the plant started, the Dobbins Fire Department arrived at the scene. They were not, however, allowed to assist in the rescue and were asked to leave. Members of the Dobbins Fire Department claim they were asked to leave for racial reasons. Specifically, they contend that members of the Hamlet Fire Department believe that because the members of the Dobbins Fire Department are black, they are not qualified firefighters. It will never be known for sure whether or not the added aid of the Dobbins Fire Department might have saved additional lives, but the simple fact that they were not allowed to assist in the rescue raises serious questions about the relative priorities that guided the Hamlet Fire Department in attempting to assist the workers trapped inside the Hamlet plant.

Conclusion

The fire in Hamlet was caused by an array of actors, actions, omissions, and social circumstances that surrounded the workers in concentric circles from the closest supervisors and owners to local, state, and Federal agencies, and finally to the organization of both the North Carolina and the U.S. political economy itself. Like a noose, these concentric circles closed around Hamlet and interacted in a way that brought about the death of 25 workers. When the list of factors arrayed against worker safety in North Carolina is tallied, it is surprising that there are not more workplace disasters such as the one at Imperial. It also suggests that many other industrial employees in North Carolina work on the fine edge of potential disaster. The Hamlet fire was not an aberration. It was almost predictable. In fact, it had been predicted by some workers.

In the final analysis, what is particularly disturbing and particularly telling is that *so many* components of the system designed to protect the health and safety of workers, from Federal OSHA, to NC-OSHA, to local inspectors *had to fail* in order for this killing fire to have occurred. The deaths in Hamlet are clear evidence that laws alone are not sufficient to protect worker safety. They require political will for their effective enforcement. Without this will, they become more symbolic than real. The Hamlet fire constitutes a clear instance of state-corporate crime precisely because it was the absence of this *political will* and the omissions on the part of *politically constituted agencies* that enabled the management of Imperial to continue violating basic safety requirements at the plant in its pursuit of private profit.

PART VI

Deviance and Social Control

For SOCIETY TO EXIST, people must be able to know what to expect of others. If they couldn't do this, the world would be in chaos. Because the behavior of humans is not controlled by instincts, people develop *norms* (rules and expectations) to provide regularity, or patterns, to social life. Norms provide a high degree of certainty in what would be a hopelessly disoriented world if everyone followed his or her own inclinations and no one knew what to expect of others.

The confidence we can place in others is only relative, however, because not everyone follows all the rules all the time. In fact, *deviance*, the violation of rules and expectations, is universal. All members of society violate some of the expectations that others have of them. In this sense, all of us are deviants.

The norms that people develop to control one another cover a fascinating variety of human behavior. They include rules and expectations concerning our appearance, manner, and conduct.

1. *Appearance* (what we look like): the norms concerning clothing, make-up, hairstyle, and other such presentational aspects of our body, including its cleanliness and odors. These rules also cover the *social extensions of the person,* those objects thought to represent the individual in some way, such as one's home, car, or, in some instances, even one's pet.

2. *Manner* (our style of doing things): people's expectations about how we will express ourselves, such as our facial expressions, gestures, and other body language. Manner includes *personal style* (gruff, direct-to-the-point, pleasant, charming), expectations others have of us because of how we acted in the past. Manner also includes *group style,* expectations attached to us because of our membership in a social group (race, ethnic, gender, occupation, age, and so on—"the way they are").

3. *Conduct* (what we say, what we do): rules covering the rest of human behavior, specifying what we can and cannot do or say. These rules are so specific that they vary with changing circumstances. Among others, they include rules of *authority* (who has the right to give which order to whom), rules of *obligation* (who has the responsibility to do what for whom), and rules of *account giving* (what we are expected to say when asked for an explanation). Account-giving rules even specify the degree to which we are expected to be honest, to go into detail, or to avoid implicating others.

These everyday rules of appearance, manner, and conduct are sliced very fine. They specify the circumstances under which we can or cannot do or say something, how we must phrase what we say, such as with varying degrees of respect or informality, even our facial expressions when we do or say it. In other words, hardly a single aspect of our lives goes untouched by rules made by others. We all are immersed in pervasive expectations, most of which were set up by people long ago dead. None of us is a free agent, able to do as we please. Rather, *social control* is a basic fact of social life.

Norms follow social status. They differ according to people's social identities (age, gender, occupation, social class, and so on). That is, they vary according to the groups to which people are thought to belong. For example, the rules of conduct, appearance, and manner differ for convicts, CEOs, students, children, old people, men and women—that is, these expectations depend on reputation, prestige, wealth, occupation, age, and gender. In some instances, they also vary according to race-ethnicity.

The rules also change as we switch audiences. For example, as teenagers know so well, their parents' expectations differ markedly from their friends' expectations. Similarly, we are expected to act one way when we are with members of our own age, gender, or racial-ethnic group, but differently when we are with others. Our everyday norms even dictate distinct clothing for different occasions—for a college classroom, for a formal dance, for the beach, and so on. In short, to change physical locations is to transform stages and audiences, bringing distinct expectations of how we are to present the self.

These complex expectations define *in* and define *out:* Those who conform to the norms are accorded the status of members in good standing, while those who deviate usually are defined as outsiders of some sort. Viewed with suspicion, deviants are reacted to in a number of ways. They may be given more attention in order to bring them back into line, or they may be ostracized or kicked out of the group. For mild deviations, they may simply be stared at. People also may gossip about them, joke about them, divorce them, strike their names from guest lists, or demote or fire them. In more extreme cases, they may be shunned or physically attacked. In the most extreme cases, they are tried and imprisoned—or even put to death.

This list of some of the social reactions to deviance indicates that people are extremely concerned with rule-following and rule-breaking behaviors. Challenging fundamental expectations about how social life is run, deviants often are seen as a threat to people's welfare. With such a stake in the conformity of others, then, people react to deviants—sharply and negatively if they consider the deviance threatening, but tolerantly and perhaps even with amusement if they believe it to be mild.

As the word is used in sociology, deviance is not a term of negative judgment, as it usually is when used by nonsociologists. To sociologists, the term is meant simply to describe activities that violate the expectations of others, passing judgment neither on the merit of the rules nor on those who violate them.

In this Part, in which we focus on deviant acts and statuses and on responses to them, we look especially at processes of social control. In the opening selection, I tell the story of an airplane crash in the Andes—looking at how social control operated among the survivors who ate their deceased friends and relatives. William Chambliss then examines how different community reactions to lower-class and middle-class delinquents had far-reaching effects on their adult lives. Rose Weitz follows with an analysis of techniques that victims of AIDS use to reduce the stigma attached to their disease. In his analysis of jails, John Irwin examines how social control itself can be a problem. Philip Zimbardo continues this topic with a description of his intriguing experiment in which he uncovered organizational bases for the hostile relationships between prisoners and prison guards. David Rosenhan then closes this Part by asking an intriguing question: Can we tell the sane from the insane?

23 The Survivors of the F-227

JAMES M. HENSLIN

As has been stressed in previous readings, each culture provides guidelines for how to view the world, and for determining right and wrong. The perspective we learn envelops us much as a fish is immersed in water. Almost all the world's cultures uphold the idea that it is wrong to eat human flesh. (Some exceptions do apply, such as warriors who used to eat the heart or kidneys of slain enemies in an attempt to acquire the source of their strength or courage.) Thus it is safe to say that nowhere in the world is there a culture whose members regularly consume people as food. Yet, in the unusual situation recounted here, that is precisely what these people did.

Note how, even in the midst of reluctantly committing acts they themselves found extremely repugnant—and ones they fully knew that the world condemns—this group developed norms to govern their behavior. This was crucial for these survivors, because group support, along with its attendant norms, is critical in maintaining a sense of a "good" self. At the conclusion of the article, Henslin shows how this event is more than simply an interesting story—that it represents the essence of social life.

LOCATED BETWEEN BRAZIL AND ARGENTINA, near Buenos Aires, is tiny Uruguay. On October 12, 1972, a propeller-driven Fairchild F-227 left Uruguay's capital, Montevideo, bound for Santiago, Chile—a distance of about 900 miles. On board were 15 members of an amateur rugby team from Uruguay, along with 25 of their relatives and friends. The pilots, from the Uruguayan Air Force, soon became concerned about turbulence over the Andes Mountains. Winds blowing in from the Pacific were colliding with air currents coming from the opposite direction, creating a turbulence that could toss a plane around like a scrap of paper in a wind storm.

Since the threat was so great, the pilots decided to land in Mendoza, Argentina, where everyone spent the night. The next day, with the weather only slightly improved, the crew debated about turning back. Several of the rugby players taunted them, saying they were cowards. When the captain of a plane which had just flown over the Andes reported that the F-227 should be

237

able to fly over the turbulence, the Fairchild's pilots decided to continue the trip. Once again airborne, the young passengers laughed about its being Friday the 13th as some threw a rugby ball around and others played cards. Many of them still in their teens, and all of them from Uruguay's upper class (two were nephews of the president of Uruguay), they were in high spirits.

Over the Andes the plane flew into a thick cloud, and the pilots had to fly by instrument. Amid the turbulence they hit an "air pocket," and the plane suddenly plunged 3,000 feet. When the passengers abruptly found themselves below the cloud, one young man turned to another and said, "Is it normal to fly so close?" He was referring to the mountainside just 10 feet off the right wing.

With a deafening roar, the right wing sheared off as it hit the side of the mountain. The wing whipped over the plane and knocked off the tail. The steward, the navigator, and three of the rugby players still strapped in their seats were blown out of the gaping hole. Then the left wing broke off and, like a toboggan going 200 miles an hour, the fuselage slid on its belly into a steep, snow-covered valley.

As night fell, the survivors huddled in the wreckage. At 12,000 feet the cold, especially at night, was brutal. There was little fuel, because not much wood is used in the construction of airplanes. They had almost no food—basically some chocolate that the passengers had bought on their overnight stay in Mendoza. There were a few bottles of wine, and the many cartons of cigarettes they had purchased at a duty-free shop.

The twenty-seven who survived the crash expected to be rescued quickly. At most, they thought, they would have to spend the night on the mountain top. Seventy days later, only sixteen remained alive.

The chocolate and wine didn't go very far, and provided little nourishment. The plane, off course by a hundred miles or so and painted white, was not only difficult to track, but virtually invisible against the valley's deep layer of snow: Search planes were unable to locate the wreckage.

As the days went by, the survivors' spirits seemed to be sucked into a hopeless pit. Hunger and starvation began to bear down on them. They felt cold all the time. They became weaker and had difficulty keeping their balance. Their skin became wrinkled, like that of old people. Although no one mentioned it, several of the young men began to realize that their only chance to survive was to eat the bodies of those who died in the crash. The corpses lay strewn in the snow around the plane, perfectly preserved by the bitter cold.

The thought of cutting into the flesh of their friends was too ghastly a prospect to put into words. Finally, however, Canessa, a medical student, brought up the matter with his friends. He asserted that the bodies were no longer people. The soul was gone, he said, and the body was simply meat— and essential to their survival. They were growing weaker, and they could not survive without food. And what food was there besides the corpses? "They are no more human beings than the dead flesh of the cattle we eat at home," he said.

Days later, the topic moved from furtive discussion in a small group to open deliberation among all the survivors. Inside the plane, arguing the matter, Canessa reiterated his position. His three closest friends supported him, adding, "We have a duty to survive. If we don't eat the bodies, it is a sin. We must do this not just for our own sakes but also for our families. In fact," they continued, "God wants us to survive, and He has provided these bodies so we can live." Some, however, just shook their heads, the thought too disturbing to even contemplate.

Serbino pushed the point. He said, "If I die, I want you to eat my body. I want you to use it." Some nodded in agreement. In an attempt to bring a little humor to the black discussion, he added, "If you don't, I'll come back and give you a swift kick in the butt." Some said that while they did not think it would be wrong to eat the bodies, they themselves could never do it. The arguments continued for hours.

Four of the young men went outside. Near the plane, the buttocks of a body protruded from the snow. No one spoke as they stared at it. Wordlessly, Canessa knelt and began to cut with the only instrument he had found, a piece of broken glass. The flesh was frozen solid, and he could cut only slivers the size of matchsticks. Canessa laid the pieces on the roof of the plane, and the young men went back inside. They said that the meat was drying in the sun. The others looked mutely at one another. No one made a move to leave the plane.

Canessa decided that he would have to be the first to act. Going outside, he picked up a sliver of meat. Staring at it, almost transfixed, he became as though paralyzed. He simply couldn't make his hand move to his mouth. Summoning every ounce of courage, he forced his hand upwards. While his stomach recoiled, he pushed the meat inside his mouth and forced himself to swallow. Later, Serbino took a piece. He tried to swallow, but the sliver hung halfway down his throat. Quickly grabbing some snow, he managed to wash it down. Canessa and Serbino were joined by others, who also ate.

The next morning, on the transistor radio they had struggled so hard to get working, their hearts plunged when they heard that the air force had called off the search. The survivors knew that this announcement almost sealed their fate. The only way out, if there was one, was on their own. They held a meeting and decided that the fittest should try to seek help—even though no one knew where to seek it. But none was strong enough to try. With the snow's crust breaking under every step, even to walk was exhausting. There was only one way to regain strength, and, without giving the thought words, everyone knew what it was.

Canessa and Strauch went outside. The corpse was in the same position as before. They took a deep breath and began to hack meat off the bone. They laid the strips on the plane to thaw in the sun. The knowledge that no rescuers were looking for them encouraged others to join in eating the human flesh. They forced themselves to swallow—their consciences, seconded by their stomachs, accusing them of extreme wrongdoing. Still, they forced the flesh down, telling themselves over and over that there was no other way to survive.

Some, however, could not. Javier and Liliana Methol, husband and wife, though they longed to return to their children, could not eat human flesh. They said that the others could do as they liked, but perhaps God wanted them to choose to die.

The survivors began to organize. Canessa took charge of cutting up the bodies, while a group of the younger ones had the job of preventing the corpses from rotting by keeping them covered with snow. Another group had the task of seeing that the plane was kept in order. Even the weakest had a job to do: They were able to hold pieces of aluminum in the sun to melt snow for drinking water.

The first corpses they ate were those of the crew, strangers to them.

One day, when it was too cold to melt snow, they burned wooden Coca-Cola crates that they had found in the luggage compartment. After they had water, they roasted some meat over the embers. There was only enough heat to brown the pieces, but they found the flavor better—tasting, as they said, like beef, but softer. Canessa said they should never do this again, for heat destroys proteins. "You have to eat it raw to get its full value," he argued. Rejecting his advice, the survivors cooked the meat when they had the chance, about once or twice a week. Daily, the recurring question was, "Are we cooking today?"

Liliana told Javier that after they got back home she wanted to have another baby. He agreed. As they looked at one another, though, they saw eyes sunken into their sockets and bones protruding from their cheeks. They knew there was no hope, unless. . . . Liliana and Javier shuddered as they picked up a piece of meat.

Some never could eat. Although the others argued with them, even trying to force them to eat, they never could overcome their feelings of revulsion. They continued to refuse, and so day by day grew weaker. Others, however, grew accustomed to what they were doing. They became able to cut meat from a body before everyone's eyes. They could even eat larger pieces, which they had to chew and taste.

As time went on, they developed a set of rules. They would not eat the women's bodies. No one *had* to eat. The meat would be rationed, and no one could eat more than his or her share. The three who were going to leave in search of help could eat more than the others. One corpse would always be finished before another would be started. (It was overlooked when those who had the disagreeable job of cutting the corpses ate a little as they cut.)

They refused to eat certain parts of the body—the lungs, the skin, the head, and the genitals.

There were some things they never could get used to, such as cutting up a close friend. When they dug a corpse out of the snow, it was preserved just as it had been at the moment of death. If the eyes had been open when the friend died, they were still open, now staring back at them. Everyone understood that no one had to eat a friend or relative.

Survival work became more organized. Those who could stomach it would cut large chunks from a body and pass them to another team, who would slice them with razor blades into smaller pieces. This was not as disagreeable a task, for, separated from the body, the meat was easier to deal with.

The sheets of fat from a body lay outside the rules. They were dried in the sun until a crust formed. Anyone could eat as much as they wished. But the fat wasn't as popular as the meat.

Also outside the rationing system were the pieces of the first carcasses they had cut up, before they developed the rules. Those pieces lay about the snow, and anyone who wanted could scavenge them. Some could never stomach the liver, others the heart or kidneys, and many could not eat the intestines of the dead. Three young men refused the red meat of the muscles.

The dead became part of their lives. One night, Inciarte reached up to get something from the hat rack and was startled when an icy hand brushed against his cheek. Apparently someone had sneaked it in as a late snack.

Constipation was an unexpected complication of their diet. As day after day went by without defecation, they began to worry that their insides would burst. Eventually they developed a sort of contest, wondering who would be the last hold-out. After 28 days, only two had not defecated. At 32, only one. Finally, on the 34th day, Bobby François joined the others.

The three who had been selected to go in search of rescuers had to solve the problem of preventing their feet from freezing. The skin of the dead provided the solution. By cutting an arm just above and below the elbow, and slowly pulling, the skin came away with its subcutaneous layers of fat. Sewing up the lower end made an insulated pair of socks.

Their bland diet became boring. As their bodies and minds cried out for variety, they began to seek new tastes. After eating the meat from a bone, they would crack it open and scoop out the marrow. Everyone liked the marrow. Some sought out the blood clots from around the heart. Others even ate parts of bodies that had started to rot. Many were revolted by this, but, as time went on, more of the survivors did the same.

Canessa, Parrado, and Vizintin were selected to go in search of help. Before they left, Parrado took aside a couple of friends and said that they might run short of food before help could arrive. "I prefer you don't," he whispered, "but I'll understand if you eat my mother and sister."

Ten days after the expeditionaries set out, they stumbled into a shepherd's hut. The news of their survival, long after they had been given up for dead, came as a shock to their friends and relatives. Those still waiting on the mountain were rescued by helicopter—just four days before Christmas.

Although the survivors felt a compulsive need to talk about what they had done, at first physicians and government officials kept the cannibalism a secret. When the news leaked out, however, it made headlines around the world. One survivor explained, "It was like a heart transplant. The dead sustained the living." Another said, "It was like holy communion. God gives us the body and blood of Christ in holy communion. God gave us these bodies and blood to eat."

All were Roman Catholics, and they asked forgiveness. The priests replied that they did not need forgiveness, for they had done nothing wrong. There was no soul in the bodies, the priests explained, and in extreme conditions, if there is no other way to survive, it is permissible to eat the dead. After consultation with relatives, it was decided to bury what was left of the dead at the crash site.

The young men, rejoining their families, became celebrities. They shunned the spotlight, however, banded together, and thought of themselves as special people. As persons who had survived the impossible, they felt that they had a unique purpose in life.

The world's reaction to the events in the Andes was shock and horror—mixed with fascination. As one Chilean paper asked in its headlines, "What would *you* have done?"

The Social Construction of Reality

I was going to let the story stop here, but I was told by a person very influential in my life that I really ought to make the sociology explicit. So let's see what sociological lessons we can derive from this tragedy in the Andes.

First, the main lesson, one from which the other points follow, comes from the symbolic interactionists, who stress that *our world is socially constructed.* By this, they mean that nothing contains built-in meanings. In other words, whatever meaning something has is arbitrary: We humans have given it a particular meaning, but we could just as well have given it a different meaning. *Second,* it is through a social process that we determine meanings; that is, people jointly decide on the meanings to assign events and objects. *Third,* because meanings (or what things symbolize to people) are arbitrary, people can change them. I am aware that these statements may sound extremely vague, but they should become clear as we look at how these survivors constructed their reality.

We might begin by asking what the meaning of a human body is. As with other aspects of life, a group can assign to a body any meaning that it wishes, for, by itself, a body has no meaning. These survivors did not begin to develop their definitions from scratch, however, for they brought to the Andes meanings that they had learned in their culture—basically that a body, while not a person, is still human, and must be treated with respect. A related meaning they had learned is that a human body is "not food." Such an understanding may seem natural to us because it matches our own cultural definitions—which obscures the arbitrary nature of the definition.

Fourth, when circumstances change, definitions can become outmoded—even definitions about fundamental aspects of life. *Fifth,* even though definitions no longer "work," changes in basic orientations do not come easily. *Sixth,* anyone who suggests such changes is likely to be seen as a threatening deviant. Shock, horror, or ridicule may be the reactions, and—for persons who persist on a disorienting course—shunning, ostracism, and violence may result. *Seventh,* the source of radical new ideas is extremely significant in determining whether or not they gain acceptance. *Eighth,* if an individual can drum up group support, then there exists a *social* basis for the new, competing definition. *Ninth,* if the group that offers the new definition can get enough others to accept it, then the common definition of reality will change. *Tenth,* changed circumstances make people more open to accepting new definitions of reality.

In this case, Canessa did not want to appear as a deviant, so he furtively proposed a new definition—entrusting it at first to only a few close friends. Even there, however, since it violated basic definitions acquired in early socialization, it was initially met with resistance. But the friends had high respect for Canessa, who had completed a year of medical school, and they were won over. This small group then proposed their new definition of human bodies to the larger group. Eventually, in the growing realization that death was imminent, this definition won out.

Eleventh, behavior follows definitions. That is, definitions of reality are not just abstract ideas; they also indicate the boundaries of what is allowable. We tend to do what our definitions allow. In this case, when the definition of human bodies changed, so did the survivors' behavior: The changed definition allowed them to eat human corpses.

Twelfth, definitions also follow behavior. That is, as people engage in an activity, they tend to develop ideas that lend support to what they are doing. In this instance, the eating of human flesh—especially since it was a group activity—reinforced the initial definition that had been only tentatively held, that the flesh was no longer human. Eventually, at least for many, the flesh indeed became meat—so much so that some people were even able to take a human hand to bed for a late-night snack.

Thirteenth, for their very survival, all groups must have norms. By allowing people to know what to expect in a given situation, norms provide a basic structure for people's relationships with one another. Without norms, anarchy and chaos would reign.

This principle also applies to groups that make deviance part of their activities. Although a superficial view from the outside may make such groups appear disorganized and without rules, they are in fact very normative. Groups of outlaw motorcyclists, for example, share an elaborate set of rules about what they expect from one another, most of which, like those of other groups, are not in written form. In short, norms cover even deviant activities, for, without them, how can group members know what to expect of one another?

The Andes survivors developed a basic set of norms to provide order to their deviant activity. Some of those norms were:

1. No one had to violate his or her conscience. If someone did not wish to eat human flesh, no one would force them.
2. Some bodies were "off limits."
3. Meat was rationed, with a specified amount for each person:
   a. Fat was outside the rationing system, and
   b. Leftover parts from the first bodies were outside the rationing system.
4. Meat was distributed according to an orderly system, namely:
   a. Everyone who wished to could eat, and
   b. Designated parts of the body could be "wasted."

Fourteenth, human groups tend to stratify, that is, to sort themselves out on a basis of inequality, with some getting more of a group's resources, some less. A norm concerning eating human flesh that I did not mention above illustrates this principle: Those persons deemed most valuable to the group were allowed to eat more. These were persons who were going in search of rescue and those who performed the disagreeable task of cutting up the bodies. This unequal division of resources represents the formation of a basic system of social stratification.

Fifteenth, human groups tend to organize themselves. In this instance, the survivors did not just randomly cut away at the bodies, but specific tasks were assigned. Teamwork developed to coordinate tasks, with some individuals performing specialized jobs in making the meat edible. Even the weakest had a part to play. The incipient social stratification just mentioned is another example of organization, one that sociologists call the division of labor. *Sixteenth,* an essential part of the human tendency to organize is the emergence of leadership—to direct and coordinate the activities of others. In this case, Canessa stands out.

Seventeenth, people attempt to maintain a respectable sense of self. These survivors were highly conforming individuals in that they had accepted the norms of their society and were striving for a respectable place within it. They wanted to continue to think of themselves as good people. Yet, they had to make a decision about doing an activity that went beyond the bounds of what they looked at as normal—one they even knew that "everyone" defined as wrong.

Eighteenth, it is possible to maintain a "good" self-image and still engage in deviant activities. Because the essence of human society is the social construction of reality, so the key to the self also lies in how reality is defined. If you can redefine an activity to make it "not deviant," then it does not threaten your sense of a "good" self. In this present instance, the Andes survivors looked on eating human flesh as part of their "duty to survive." To do a duty is a good thing, and, accordingly, the acts required by it cannot be "bad." In fact, they must be "good." (The most infamous example of the use of this basic principle was Hitler's SS, who looked on killing Jews as necessary for the survival of the "Aryan" race and culture. They even termed the slaughter a "good" act and their participation in it as patriotic and self-sacrificing.)

This principle helps many people get through what otherwise would be excruciatingly painful nights—for they would toss sleeplessly owing to a gnawing conscience. Redefinition, by keeping one's sense of self intact, allows people to participate in a variety of acts condemned by society—even those disapproved by the self. For most people, redefinition involves much less dramatic acts than eating human flesh, such as a college student cheating on a test or a boss firing a worker.

Nineteenth, some people participate in deviant acts even though they remain unconvinced about such redefinitions. (Some do not even attempt to redefine them.) They may do so from a variety of motives—from what they consider "sheer necessity" to the desire to reach a future goal. Liliana and Javier, who decided that they wanted a baby, are an example. Such persons have greater difficulty adjusting to their acts than those who redefine them as "good." (Even the latter may have difficulty, for redefinitions may be only partial, especially in the face of competing definitions.)

Twentieth, people feel they must justify their actions to others. This process of justifying the self involves clothing definitions of reality in forms thought to be acceptable to others. In order for definitions to be accepted, they must be made to fit into the others' already-existing definitional framework. In this case, the survivors—speaking to a Roman Catholic audience—used the analogy of holy communion to try to justify their act.

Twenty-first, to gain institutional support is to secure a broad, solid base for one's definitions of reality. Then one no longer stands alone, which is to invite insanity, nor is one a member of a small group, which is to invite ridicule and may require cutting off oneself from the larger group. In this case, institutional support was provided by the Roman Catholic Church, which, while not accepting the survivors' analogy of cannibalism as communion, allowed them to avoid the label of sin by defining their actions as allowable under the circumstances.

Finally, note that these principles are fundamental to human life. They do not simply apply to the Andes survivors—or to deviants in general—but they underlie human society. For all of us, reality is socially constructed, and the story of the Andes survivors contains the essence of human society.

24 The Saints and the Roughnecks

WILLIAM J. CHAMBLISS

When people deviate from what is expected of them, other people react. But on what do their reactions depend? Do they depend simply on the nature of the deviance itself, or is more involved? If so, what sorts of things?

It is these fascinating questions that Chambliss examines in this study of two groups of delinquents in the same high school. He found that although both groups were involved in serious and repetitive delinquent acts, while one was perceived as a group of saints, the other was viewed as a bunch of roughnecks. After analyzing what influenced people's perceptions, and hence their reactions to the boys, Chambliss examines the far-reaching effects of those reactions. He indicates that in the case of the roughnecks, people's reactions helped lock the boys into behaviors that continued after high school, eventually leading to prison or to low-paying jobs, while social reactions to the saints set them on a life-course that not only meant staying out of prison but also entering well-paying positions of prestige.

EIGHT PROMISING YOUNG MEN—children of good, stable, white upper-middle-class families, active in school affairs, good pre-college students—were some of the most delinquent boys at Hanibal High School. While community residents knew that these boys occasionally sowed a few wild oats, they were totally unaware that sowing wild oats completely occupied the daily routine of these young men. The Saints were constantly occupied with truancy, drinking, wild driving, petty theft, and vandalism. Yet no one was officially arrested for any misdeed during the two years I observed them.

This record was particularly surprising in light of my observations during the same two years of another gang of Hanibal High School students, six lower-class white boys known as the Roughnecks. The Roughnecks were constantly in trouble with police and community even though their rate of delinquency was about equal with that of the Saints. What was the cause of this disparity? the result? The following consideration of the activities, social class, and community perceptions of both gangs may provide some answers.

The Saints from Monday to Friday

The Saints' principal daily concern was with getting out of school as early as possible. The boys managed to get out of school with minimum danger that they would be accused of playing hookey through an elaborate procedure for obtaining "legitimate" release from class. The most common procedure was for one boy to obtain the release of another by fabricating a meeting of some committee, program, or recognized club. Charles might raise his hand in his 9:00 chemistry class and ask to be excused—a euphemism for going to the bathroom. Charles would go to Ed's math class and inform the teacher that Ed was needed for a 9:30 rehearsal of the drama club play. The math teacher would recognize Ed and Charles as "good students" involved in numerous school activities and would permit Ed to leave at 9:30. Charles would return to his class, and Ed would go to Tom's English class to obtain his release. Tom would engineer Charles's escape. The strategy would continue until as many of the Saints as possible were freed. After a stealthy trip to the car (which had been parked in a strategic spot), the boys were off for a day of fun.

Over the two years I observed the Saints, this pattern was repeated nearly every day. There were variations on the theme, but in one form or another, the boys used this procedure for getting out of class and then off the school grounds. Rarely did all eight of the Saints manage to leave school at the same time. The average number avoiding school on the days I observed them was five.

Having escaped from the concrete corridors the boys usually went either to a pool hall on the other (lower-class) side of town or to a café in the suburbs. Both places were out of the way of people the boys were likely to know (family or school officials), and both provided a source of entertainment. The pool hall entertainment was the generally rough atmosphere, the occasional hustler, the sometimes drunk proprietor and, of course, the game of pool. The café's entertainment was provided by the owner. The boys would "accidentally" knock a glass on the floor or spill cola on the counter—not all the time, but enough to be sporting. They would also bend spoons, put salt in sugar bowls and generally tease whoever was working in the café. The owner had opened the café recently and was dependent on the boys' business which was, in fact, substantial since between the horsing around and the teasing they bought food and drinks.

The Saints on Weekends

On weekends the automobile was even more critical than during the week, for on weekends the Saints went to Big Town—a large city with a population of over a million 25 miles from Hanibal. Every Friday and Saturday night most of the Saints would meet between 8:00 and 8:30 and would go into Big Town. Big Town activities included drinking heavily in taverns or nightclubs, driving drunkenly through the streets, and committing acts of vandalism and playing pranks.

By midnight on Fridays and Saturdays the Saints were usually thoroughly high, and one or two of them were often so drunk they had to be carried to the cars. Then the boys drove around town, calling obscenities to women and girls; occasionally trying (unsuccessfully so far as I could tell) to pick girls up; and driving recklessly through red lights and at high speeds with their lights out. Occasionally they played "chicken." One boy would climb out the back window of the car and across the roof to the driver's side of the car while the car was moving at high speed (between 40 and 50 miles an hour); then the driver would move over and the boy who had just crawled across the car roof would take the driver's seat.

Searching for "fair game" for a prank was the boys' principal activity after they left the tavern. The boys would drive alongside a foot patrolman and ask directions to some street. If the policeman leaned on the car in the course of answering the question, the driver would speed away, causing him to lose his balance. The Saints were careful to play this prank only in an area where they were not going to spend much time and where they could quickly disappear around a corner to avoid having their license plate number taken.

Construction sites and road repair areas were the special province of the Saints' mischief. A soon-to-be-repaired hole in the road inevitably invited the Saints to remove lanterns and wooden barricades and put them in the car, leaving the hole unprotected. The boys would find a safe vantage point and wait for an unsuspecting motorist to drive into the hole. Often, though not always, the boys would go up to the motorist and commiserate with him about the dreadful way the city protected its citizenry.

Leaving the scene of the open hole and the motorist, the boys would then go searching for an appropriate place to erect the stolen barricade. An "appropriate place" was often a spot on a highway near a curve in the road where the barricade would not be seen by an oncoming motorist. The boys would wait to watch an unsuspecting motorist attempt to stop and (usually) crash into the wooden barricade. With saintly bearing the boys might offer help and understanding.

A stolen lantern might well find its way onto the back of a police car or hang from a street lamp. Once a lantern served as a prop for a reenactment of the "midnight ride of Paul Revere" until the "play," which was taking place at 2:00 A.M. in the center of a main street of Big Town, was interrupted by a police car several blocks away. The boys ran, leaving the lanterns on the street, and managed to avoid being apprehended.

Abandoned houses, especially if they were located in out-of-the-way places, were fair game for destruction and spontaneous vandalism. The boys would break windows, remove furniture to the yard and tear it apart, urinate on the walls, and scrawl obscenities inside.

Through all the pranks, drinking, and reckless driving the boys managed miraculously to avoid being stopped by police. Only twice in two years was I aware that they had been stopped by a Big Town policeman. Once was for speeding (which they did every time they drove whether they were drunk or sober), and the driver managed to convince the policeman that it was simply an error. The second time they were stopped they had just left a nightclub and were walking through an alley. Aaron stopped to urinate and the boys began making obscene remarks. A foot patrolman came into the alley, lectured the boys and sent them home. Before the boys got to the car one began talking in a loud voice again. The policeman, who had followed them down the alley, arrested this boy for disturbing the peace and took him to the police station where the other Saints gathered. After paying a $5.00 fine, and with the assurance that there would be no permanent record of the arrest, the boy was released.

The boys had a spirit of frivolity and fun about their escapades. They did not view what they were engaged in as "delinquency," though it surely was by any reasonable definition of that word. They simply viewed themselves as having a little fun and who, they would ask, was really hurt by it? The answer had to be no one, although this fact remains one of the most difficult things to explain about the gang's behavior. Unlikely though it seems, in two years of drinking, driving, carousing, and vandalism no one was seriously injured as a result of the Saints' activities.

The Saints in School

The Saints were highly successful in school. The average grade for the group was "B," with two of the boys having close to a straight "A" average. Almost all of the boys were popular and many of them held offices in the school. One of the boys was vice president of the student body one year. Six of the boys played on athletic teams.

At the end of their senior year, the student body selected ten seniors for special recognition as the "school wheels"; four of the ten were Saints. Teachers and school officials saw no problem with any of these boys and anticipated that they would all "make something of themselves."

How the boys managed to maintain this impression is surprising in view of their actual behavior in school. Their technique for covering truancy was so successful that teachers did not even realize that the boys were absent from school much of the time. Occasionally, of course, the system would backfire and then the boy was on his own. A boy who was caught would be most contrite, would plead guilty and ask for mercy. He inevitably got the mercy he sought.

Cheating on examinations was rampant, even to the point of orally communicating answers to exams as well as looking at one another's papers. Since none of the group studied, and since they were primarily dependent on one another for help, it is surprising that grades were so high. Teachers contributed to the deception in their admitted inclination to give these boys (and presumably others like them) the benefit of the doubt. When asked how the boys did in school, and when pressed on specific examinations, teachers might admit that they were disappointed in John's performance, but would quickly add that they "knew that he was capable of doing better," so John was given a higher grade than he had actually earned. How often this happened is impossible to know. During the time that I observed the group, I never saw any of the boys take homework home. Teachers may have been "understanding" very regularly.

One exception to the gang's generally good performance was Jerry, who had a "C" average in his junior year, experienced disaster the next year, and failed to graduate. Jerry had always been a little more nonchalant than the others about the liberties he took in school. Rather than wait for someone to come get him from class, he would offer his own excuse and leave. Although he probably did not miss any more class than most of the others in the group, he did not take the requisite pains to cover his absences. Jerry was the only Saint whom I ever heard talk back to a teacher. Although teachers often called him a "cut up" or a "smart kid," they never referred to him as a troublemaker or as a kid headed for trouble. It seems likely, then, that Jerry's failure his senior year and his mediocre performance his junior year were consequences of his not playing the game the proper way (possibly because he was disturbed by his parents' divorce). His teachers regarded him as "immature" and not quite ready to get out of high school.

The Police and the Saints

The local police saw the Saints as good boys who were among the leaders of the youth in the community. Rarely, the boys might be stopped in town for speeding or for running a stop sign. When this happened the boys were always polite, contrite, and pled for mercy. As in school, they received the mercy they asked for. None ever received a ticket or was taken into the precinct by the local police.

The situation in Big Town, where the boys engaged in most of their delinquency, was only slightly different. The police there did not know the boys at all, although occasionally the boys were stopped by a patrolman. Once they were caught taking a lantern from a construction site. Another time they were stopped for running a stop sign, and on several occasions they were stopped for speeding. Their behavior was as before: contrite, polite, and penitent. The urban police, like the local police, accepted their demeanor as sincere. More important, the urban police were convinced that these were good boys just out for a lark.

The Roughnecks

Hanibal townspeople never perceived the Saints' high level of delinquency. The Saints were good boys who just went in for an occasional prank. After all, they were well dressed, well mannered, and had nice cars. The Roughnecks were a different story. Although the two gangs of boys were the same age, and both groups engaged in an equal amount of wild-oat sowing, everyone agreed that the not-so-well-dressed, not-so-well-mannered, not-so-rich boys were heading for trouble. Townspeople would say, "You can see the gang members at the drugstore, night after night, leaning against the storefront (sometimes drunk) or slouching around inside buying cokes, reading magazines, and probably stealing old Mr. Wall blind. When they are outside and girls walk by, even respectable girls, these boys make suggestive remarks. Sometimes their remarks are downright lewd."

From the community's viewpoint, the real indication that these kids were in trouble was that they were constantly involved with the police. Some of them had been picked up for stealing, mostly small stuff, of course, "but still it's stealing small stuff that leads to big time crimes." "Too bad," people said. "Too bad that these boys couldn't behave like the other kids in town; stay out of trouble, be polite to adults, and look to their future."

The community's impression of the degrees to which this group of six boys (ranging in age from 16 to 19) engaged in delinquency was somewhat distorted. In some ways the gang was more delinquent than the community thought; in other ways they were less.

The fighting activities of the group were fairly readily and accurately perceived by almost everyone. At least once a month, the boys would get into some sort of fight, although most fights were scraps between members of the group or involved only one member of the group and some peripheral hanger-on. Only three times in the period of observation did the group fight together: once against a gang from across town, once against two blacks, and once against a group of boys from another school. For the first two fights the group went out "looking for trouble"—and they found it both times. The third fight followed a football game and began spontaneously with an argument on the football field between one of the Roughnecks and a member of the opposition's football team.

Jack has a particular propensity for fighting and was involved in most of the brawls. He was a prime mover of the escalation of arguments into fights.

More serious than fighting, had the community been aware of it, was theft. Although almost everyone was aware that the boys occasionally stole things, they did not realize the extent of the activity. Petty stealing was a frequent event for the Roughnecks. Sometimes they stole as a group and coordinated their efforts; other times they stole in pairs. Rarely did they steal alone.

The thefts ranged from very small things like paperback books, comics, and ballpoint pens to expensive items like watches. The nature of the thefts varied from time to time. The gang would go through a period of systematically lifting items from automobiles or school lockers. Types of thievery varied with the whim of the gang. Some forms of thievery were more profitable than others, but all thefts were for profit, not just thrills.

Roughnecks siphoned gasoline from cars as often as they had access to an automobile, which was not very often. Unlike the Saints, who owned their own cars, the Roughnecks would have to borrow their parents' cars, an event which occurred only eight or nine times a year. The boys claimed to have stolen cars for joy rides from time to time.

Ron committed the most serious of the group's offenses. With an unidentified associate the boy attempted to burglarize a gasoline station. Although this station had been robbed twice previously in the same month, Ron denied any involvement in either of the other thefts. When Ron and his accomplice approached the station, the owner was hiding in the bushes beside the station. He fired both barrels of a double-barreled shotgun at the boys. Ron was severely injured; the other boy ran away and was never caught. Though he remained in critical condition for several months, Ron finally recovered and served six months of the following year in reform school. Upon release from reform school, Ron was put back a grade in school, and began running around with a different gang of boys. The Roughnecks considered the new gang less delinquent than themselves, and during the following year Ron had no more trouble with the police.

The Roughnecks, then, engaged mainly in three types of delinquency: theft, drinking, and fighting. Although community members perceived that this gang of kids was delinquent, they mistakenly believed that their illegal activities were primarily drinking, fighting, and being a nuisance to passersby. Drinking was limited among the gang members, although it did occur, and theft was much more prevalent than anyone realized.

Drinking would doubtless have been more prevalent had the boys had ready access to liquor. Since they rarely had automobiles at their disposal, they could not travel very far, and the bars in town would not serve them. Most of the boys had little money, and this, too, inhibited their purchase of alcohol. Their major source of liquor was a local drunk who would buy them a fifth if they would give him enough extra to buy himself a pint of whiskey or a bottle of wine.

The community's perception of drinking as prevalent stemmed from the fact that it was the most obvious delinquency the boys engaged in. When one of the boys had been drinking, even a casual observer seeing him on the corner would suspect that he was high.

There was a high level of mutual distrust and dislike between the Roughnecks and the police. The boys felt very strongly that the police were unfair and corrupt. Some evidence existed that the boys were correct in their perception.

The main source of the boys' dislike for the police undoubtedly stemmed from the fact that the police would sporadically harass the group. From the standpoint of the boys, these acts of occasional enforcement of the law were whimsical and uncalled for. It made no sense to them, for example, that the police would come to the corner occasionally and threaten them with arrest for loitering when the night before the boys had been out siphoning gasoline from cars and the police had been nowhere in sight. To the boys, the police were stupid on the one hand, for not being where they should have been and catching the boys in a serious offense, and unfair on the other hand, for trumping up "loitering" charges against them.

From the viewpoint of the police, the situation was quite different. They knew, with all the confidence necessary to be a policeman, that these boys were engaged in criminal activities. They knew this partly from occasionally catching them, mostly from circumstantial evidence ("the boys were around when those tires were slashed"), and partly because the police shared the view of the community in general that this was a bad bunch of boys. The best the police could hope to do was to be sensitive to the fact that these boys were engaged in illegal acts and arrest them whenever there was some evidence that they had been involved. Whether or not the boys had in fact committed a particular act in a particular way was not especially important. The police had a broader view: their job was to stamp out these kids' crimes; the tactics were not as important as the end result.

Over the period that the group was under observation, each member was arrested at least once. Several of the boys were arrested a number of times and spent at least one night in jail. While most were never taken to court, two of the boys were sentenced to six months' incarceration in boys' schools.

The Roughnecks in School

The Roughnecks' behavior in school was not particularly disruptive. During school hours they did not all hang around together, but tended instead to spend most of their time with one or two other members of the gang who were their special buddies. Although every member of the gang attempted to avoid school as much as possible, they were not particularly successful and most of them attended school with surprising regularity. They considered school a burden—something to be gotten through with a minimum of conflict. If they were "bugged" by a particular teacher, it could lead to trouble. One of the boys, Al, once threatened to beat up a teacher and, according to the other boys, the teacher hid under a desk to escape him.

Teachers saw the boys the way the general community did, as heading for trouble, as being uninterested in making something of themselves. Some were also seen as being incapable of meeting the academic standards of the school. Most of the teachers expressed concern for this group of boys and were willing to pass them despite poor performance, in the belief that failing them would only aggravate the problem.

The group of boys had a grade point average just slightly above "C." No one in the group failed either grade, and no one had better than a "C" average. They were very consistent in their achievement or, at least, the teachers were consistent in their perception of the boys' achievement.

Two of the boys were good football players. Herb was acknowledged to be the best player in the school, and Jack was almost as good. Both boys were criticized for their failure to abide by training rules, for refusing to come to practice as often as they should, and for not playing their best during practice. What they lacked in sportsmanship they made up for in skill, apparently, and played every game no matter how poorly they had performed in practice or how many practice sessions they had missed.

Two Questions

Why did the community, the school, and the police react to the Saints as though they were good, upstanding, nondelinquent youths with bright futures but to the Roughnecks as though they were tough, young criminals who were headed for trouble? Why did the Roughnecks and the Saints in fact have quite different careers after high school—careers which, by and large, lived up to the expectations of the community?

The most obvious explanation for the differences in the community's and law enforcement agencies' reactions to the two gangs is that one group of boys was "more delinquent" than the other. Which group was more delinquent? The answer to this question will determine in part how we explain the differential responses to these groups by the members of the community and, particularly, by law enforcement and school officials.

In sheer number of illegal acts, the Saints were the more delinquent. They were truant from school for at least part of the day almost every day of the week. In addition, their drinking and vandalism occurred with surprising regularity. The Roughnecks, in contrast, engaged sporadically in delinquent episodes. While these episodes were frequent, they certainly did not occur on a daily or even a weekly basis.

The difference in frequency of offenses was probably caused by the Roughnecks' inability to obtain liquor and to manipulate legitimate excuses from school. Since the Roughnecks had less money than the Saints, and teachers carefully supervised their school activities, the Roughnecks' hearts may have been as black as the Saints', but their misdeeds were not nearly as frequent.

There are really no clear-cut criteria by which to measure qualitative differences in antisocial behavior. The most important dimension is generally referred to as the "seriousness" of the offenses.

If seriousness encompasses the relative economic costs of delinquent acts, then some assessment can be made. The Roughnecks probably stole an average of about $5.00 worth of goods a week. Some weeks the figure was considerably higher, but these times must be balanced against long periods when almost nothing was stolen.

The Saints were more continuously engaged in delinquency, but their acts were not for the most part costly to property. Only their vandalism and occasional theft of gasoline would so qualify. Perhaps once or twice a month they would siphon a tankful of gas. The other costly items were street signs, construction lanterns, and the like. All of these acts combined probably did not quite average $5.00 a week, partly because much of the stolen equipment was abandoned and presumably could be recovered. The difference in cost of stolen property between the two groups was trivial, but the Roughnecks probably had a slightly more expensive set of activities than did the Saints.

Another meaning of seriousness is the potential threat of physical harm to members of the community and to the boys themselves. The Roughnecks were more prone to physical violence; they not only welcomed an opportunity to fight; they went seeking it. In addition, they fought among themselves frequently. Although the fighting never included deadly weapons, it was still a menace, however minor, to the physical safety of those involved.

The Saints never fought. They avoided physical conflict both inside and outside the group. At the same time, though, the Saints frequently endangered their own and other people's lives. They did so almost every time they drove a car, especially if they had been drinking. Sober, their driving was risky; under the influence of alcohol it was horrendous. In addition, the Saints endangered the lives of others with their pranks. Street excavations left unmarked were a very serious hazard.

Evaluating the relative seriousness of the two gangs' activities is difficult. The community reacted as though the behavior of the Roughnecks was a problem, and they reacted as though the behavior of the Saints was not. But the members of the community were ignorant of the array of delinquent acts that characterized the Saints' behavior. Although concerned citizens were unaware of much of the Roughnecks' behavior as well, they were much better informed about the Roughnecks' involvement in delinquency than they were about the Saints'.

Visibility

Differential treatment of the two gangs resulted in part because one gang was infinitely more visible than the other. This differential visibility was a direct function of the economic standing of the families. The Saints had access to automobiles and were able to remove themselves from the sight of the community. In as routine a decision as to where to go to have a milkshake after school, the Saints stayed away from the mainstream of community life. Lacking transportation, the Roughnecks could not make it to the edge of town. The center of town was the only practical place for them to meet since their homes were scattered throughout the town and any noncentral meeting place put an undue hardship on some members. Through necessity the Roughnecks congregated in a crowded area where everyone in the community passed frequently, including teachers and law enforcement officers. They could easily see the Roughnecks hanging around the drugstore.

The Roughnecks, of course, made themselves even more visible by making remarks to passersby and by occasionally getting into fights on the corner. Meanwhile, just as regularly, the Saints were either at the café on one edge of town or in the pool hall at the other edge of town. Without any particular realization that they were making themselves inconspicuous, the Saints were able to hide their time-wasting. Not only were they removed from the mainstream of traffic, but they were almost always inside a building.

On their escapades the Saints were also relatively invisible, since they left Hanibal and traveled to Big Town. Here, too, they were mobile, roaming the city, rarely going to the same area twice.

Demeanor

To the notion of visibility must be added the difference in the responses of group members to outside intervention with their activities. If one of the Saints was confronted with an accusing policeman, even if he felt he was truly innocent of a wrongdoing, his demeanor was apologetic and penitent. A Roughneck's attitude was almost the polar opposite. When confronted with a threatening adult authority, even one who tried to be pleasant, the Roughneck's hostility and disdain were clearly observable. Sometimes he might attempt to put up a veneer of respect, but it was thin and was not accepted as sincere by the authority.

School was no different from the community at large. The Saints could manipulate the system by feigning compliance with the school norms. The availability of cars at school meant that once free from the immediate sight of the teacher, the boys could disappear rapidly. And this escape was well enough planned that no administrator or teacher was nearby when the boys left. A Roughneck who wished to escape for a few hours was in a bind. If it were possible to get free from class, downtown was still a mile away, and even if he arrived there, he was still very visible. Truancy for the Roughnecks meant almost certain detection, while the Saints enjoyed almost complete immunity from sanctions.

Bias

Community members were not aware of the transgressions of the Saints. Even if the Saints had been less discreet, their favorite delinquencies would have been perceived as less serious than those of the Roughnecks.

In the eyes of the police and school officials, a boy who drinks in an alley and stands intoxicated on the street corner is committing a more serious offense than is a boy who drinks to inebriation in a nightclub or a tavern and drives around afterwards in a car. Similar, a boy who steals a wallet from a store will be viewed as having committed a more serious offense than a boy who steals a lantern from a construction site.

Perceptual bias also operates with respect to the demeanor of the boys in the two groups when they are confronted by adults. It is not simply that adults dislike the posture affected by boys of the Roughneck ilk; more important is the conviction that the posture adopted by the Roughnecks is an indication of their devotion and commitment to deviance as a way of life. The posture becomes a cue, just as the type of the offense is a cue, to the degree to which the known transgressions are indicators of the youths' potential for other problems.

Visibility, demeanor, and bias are surface variables which explain the day-to-day operations of the police. Why do these surface variables operate as they do? Why did the police choose to disregard the Saints' delinquencies while breathing down the backs of the Roughnecks?

The answer lies in the class structure of American society and the control of legal institutions by those at the top of the class structure. Obviously, no representative of the upper class drew up the operational chart for the police which led them to look in the ghettos and on street corners—which led them to see the demeanor of lower-class youth as troublesome and that of upper-middle-class youth as tolerable. Rather, the procedures simply developed from experience—experience with irate and influential upper-middle-class parents insisting that their son's vandalism was simply a prank and his drunkenness only a momentary "sowing of wild oats"—experience with cooperative or indifferent, powerless, lower-class parents who acquiesced to the law's definition of their son's behavior.

Adult Careers of the Saints and the Roughnecks

The community's confidence in the potential of the Saints and the Roughnecks apparently was justified. If anything, the community members underestimated the degree to which these youngsters would turn out "good" or "bad."

Seven of the eight members of the Saints went on to college immediately after high school. Five of the boys graduated from college in four years. The sixth one finished college after two years in the army, and the seventh spent four years in the air force before returning to college and receiving a B.A. degree. Of these seven college graduates, three went on for advanced degrees. One finished law school and is now active in state politics, one finished medical school and is practicing near Hanibal, and one boy is now working for a

Ph.D. The other four college graduates entered submanagerial, managerial, or executive training positions with larger firms.

The only Saint who did not complete college was Jerry. Jerry had failed to graduate from high school with the other Saints. During his second senior year, after the other Saints had gone on to college, Jerry began to hang around with what several teachers described as a "rough crowd"—the gang that was heir apparent to the Roughnecks. At the end of his second senior year, when he did graduate from high school, Jerry took a job as a used-car salesman, got married, and quickly had a child. Although he made several abortive attempts to go to college by attending night school, when I last saw him (ten years after high school) Jerry was unemployed and had been living on unemployment for almost a year. His wife worked as a waitress.

Some of the Roughnecks have lived up to community expectations. A number of them were headed for trouble. A few were not.

Jack and Herb were the athletes among the Roughnecks, and their athletic prowess paid off handsomely. Both boys received unsolicited athletic scholarships to college. After Herb received his scholarship (near the end of his senior year), he apparently did an about-face. His demeanor became very similar to that of the Saints. Although he remained a member in good standing of the Roughnecks, he stopped participating in most activities and did not hang out on the corner as often.

Jack did not change. If anything, he became more prone to fighting. He even made excuses for accepting the scholarship. He told the other gang members that the school had guaranteed him a "C" average if he would come to play football—an idea that seems far-fetched, even in this day of highly competitive recruiting.

During the summer after graduation from high school, Jack attempted suicide by jumping from a tall building. The jump would certainly have killed most people trying it, but Jack survived. He entered college in the fall and played four years of football. He and Herb graduated in four years, and both are teaching and coaching in high schools. They are married and have stable families. If anything, Jack appears to have a more prestigious position in the community than does Herb, though both are well respected and secure in their positions.

Two of the boys never finished high school. Tommy left at the end of his junior year and went to another state. That summer he was arrested and placed on probation on a manslaughter charge. Three years later he was arrested for murder; he pleaded guilty to second degree murder and is serving a 30-year sentence in the state penitentiary.

Al, the other boy who did not finish high school, also left the state in his senior year. He is serving a life sentence in a state penitentiary for first degree murder.

Wes is a small-time gambler. He finished high school and "bummed around." After several years he made contact with a bookmaker who employed him as a runner. Later he acquired his own area and has been working it ever since. His position among the bookmakers is almost identical to the position he had in the gang; he is always around, but no one is really aware of him. He makes no trouble, and he does not get into any. Steady, reliable, capable of keeping his mouth closed, he plays the game by the rules, even though the game is an illegal one.

That leaves only Ron. Some of his former friends reported that they had heard he was "driving a truck up north," but no one could provide any concrete information.

Reinforcement

The community responded to the Roughnecks as boys in trouble, and the boys agreed with that perception. Their pattern of deviancy was reinforced, and breaking away from it became increasingly unlikely. Once the boys acquired an image of themselves as deviants, they selected new friends who affirmed that self-image. As that self-conception became more firmly entrenched, they also became willing to try new and more extreme deviances. With their growing alienation came freer expression of disrespect and hostility for representatives of the legitimate society. This disrespect increased the community's negativism, perpetuating the entire process of commitment to deviance. Lack of a commitment to deviance works the same way. In either case, the process will perpetuate itself unless some event (like a scholarship to college or a sudden failure) external to the established relationship intervenes. For two of the Roughnecks (Herb and Jack), receiving college athletic scholarships created new relations and culminated in a break with the established pattern of deviance. In the case of one of the Saints (Jerry), his parents' divorce and his failing to graduate from high school changed some of his other relations. Being held back in school for a year and losing his place among the Saints had sufficient impact on Jerry to alter his self-image and virtually to assure that he would not go on to college as his peers did. Although the experiments of life can rarely be reversed, it seems likely in view of the behavior of the other boys who did not enjoy this special treatment by the school that Jerry, too, would have "become something" had he graduated as anticipated. For Herb and Jack outside intervention worked to their advantage; for Jerry it was his undoing.

Selective perception and labeling—finding, processing, and punishing some kinds of criminality and not others—means that visible, poor, nonmobile, outspoken, undiplomatic "tough" kids will be noticed, whether their actions are seriously delinquent or not. Other kids, who have established a reputation for being bright (even though underachieving), disciplined, and involved in respectable activities, who are mobile and monied, will be invisible when they deviate from sanctioned activities. They'll sow their wild oats—perhaps even wider and thicker than their lower-class cohorts—but they won't be noticed. When it's time to leave adolescence most will follow the expected path, settling into the ways of the middle class, remembering fondly the delinquent but unnoticed fling of their youth. The Roughnecks and others like them may turn around, too. It is more likely that their noticeable deviance will have been so reinforced by police and community that their lives will be effectively channeled into careers consistent with their adolescent background.

25 Coping with AIDS

ROSE WEITZ

As we just saw with the Saints and the Roughnecks, labeling is one of the most significant events of our lives. If we are labeled as "basically good people," we are treated quite differently than if we are labeled as "no-goods" of some sort—with the consequences likely to carry over into many areas of our lives. As mentioned in the introduction to Part IV, *master statuses* cut across our other statuses. Some labels work in this fashion, imparting such extreme identities that they color everything else we may be or do in life. Examples include child molester and rapist on the negative side, and genius and saint on the positive side. All other characteristics of the individual are interpreted through labels like these.

Stigma, a blot or stain that can't be wiped out, is the term sociologists use to refer to negative labels that have this "horns effect," that send up a red flag and overwhelm almost all other aspects of a person's reputation. How do people who have such stains cope with their stigma? In this selection, Weitz examines how the victims of AIDS try to avoid and reduce stigma, and then how they live and die with the disease.

TO INDIVIDUALS WHO FIRST LEARN that they have HIV disease, the problems this will bring can seem overwhelming. For some men and women, these problems remain overwhelming until death overtakes them. Others, however, over time, develop strategies to make living with HIV disease more manageable despite the physical, social, and emotional problems it causes. These strategies help individuals cope with the fear and the reality of social stigma, the changes in their social relationships, the impact of illness on their bodies, and their impending deaths.

Avoiding Stigma

A central part of having HIV disease is the experience of stigma. Stigma is a concern during all phases of the illness, from before diagnosis, when individuals must evaluate the risk of discrimination if they get tested for HIV, to the

261

time when death seems inevitable and they must cope with the possibility of discrimination by funeral directors. As a result, one of the basic tasks persons with HIV disease confront is learning to avoid or reduce stigma.

A basic stratagem used by persons with HIV disease, as by those who have other stigmatized illnesses, is to hide the nature of their illness. Hiding can begin at the time of diagnosis, if individuals and their doctors decide to provide false or misleading information to government disease registries or health insurance companies, and can occur in all social relationships.

Persons with HIV disease use a variety of methods to hide their illnesses. Jeremy routinely transfers his zidovudine pills to an unmarked bottle because he fears that others might recognize the drug as one used to treat HIV disease. Those whose tongues show the telltale whitish spots of candidiasis (an infection that frequently accompanies this illness) close their mouths partially while smiling or talking. Others select clothing or use makeup to hide their emaciation or skin problems.

Most importantly, individuals learn to gauge how sick they look on any given day. Whenever possible, they try to look healthy when out in public. Kevin, for example, says, "Every time I go out [to a bar] I try to hide it. I try to act energetic and normal and I always have them put a squeeze of lime in my drinks so it's like a mixed drink." When their health makes it impossible to appear normal, they stay home. As David explains, "There are days that I really feel shitty and I look bad and I won't let anybody see me. I won't go around anybody. And then there are days I really force myself to put myself together so I will look decent and I'm not afraid to go out then."

This strategy is no help on days when individuals must go out despite visible symptoms. To protect their secret in these circumstances, individuals must devise plausible alternative explanations for their symptoms. In the early stages, they can claim that their weight loss is caused by stress or exercise, and that other symptoms are caused by minor illnesses, such as colds or influenza. In the latter stages, they can claim that they have some other serious, but less stigmatized illness, such as leukemia or cancer.

Although hiding one's illness offers some protection against rejection, it carries a high price. Relationships with friends and families suffer when persons with HIV disease feel it is unsafe to discuss their illness with these others. At the same time, individuals forfeit any emotional or practical support they might otherwise receive from those who do not know of their illness. In addition, persons with HIV disease risk losing their jobs when they can offer no acceptable reason for their reduced productivity and increased absences. As a result, they eventually must disclose the nature of their illness to at least some individuals.

Following disclosure, individuals can avoid further stigma and emotional stress by reducing contact with those who prove unsupportive. As a result, however, their social lives shrink significantly. As Kevin says, "[Before getting AIDS-related complex (ARC)], I was out all the time. I loved to be around people. I hated to be by myself. But now, I find that I don't like to be around people that much except if it's people I know are not going to reject me because I don't want the rejection. I don't want to be hurt. I'm tired of being hurt."

To cope with losing their former social ties to friends, colleagues, and relatives, individuals can join support groups or participate in other social activities organized specifically for those who share their illness. In this way, they can garner the benefits of a social life without risking rejection or social awkwardness. Jeremy explains that he mostly socializes with others who have HIV disease "mainly because I guess I'm still afraid of people's reactions" but also "because I think they [those who have this illness] can understand more what your feelings are, what is going through your head. It's a lot easier to sit around and have a conversation with someone who is also ill with this disease, and you don't have to worry about avoiding certain topics." Persons with HIV disease also benefit from participating in these activities because everyone in these groups is stigmatized. As a result, the illness loses its "shock value" and instead becomes something that can be taken for granted. Consequently, they can engage in normal social interactions rather than interactions that are strained by the constant awareness of the illness. For example, Caleb, who was abandoned by most of his friends, tells of his pleasure at attending a potluck social for persons with HIV disease. At the potluck, he learned that he "was not alone":

> I met a lot of really beautiful people, a lot of really nice friends. They took your phone number. They call you, socialize with you. You go to the show with them. You do things with them. If you need any help or whatever, they're there. . . . I went through hiding myself in my house and every time the facial sores started I would be afraid to go out and let people see me. These people don't care. You're not the only one that's had the facial sores and they don't care. You're welcome there. . . . Nobody [at the potluck] was afraid because a person with ARC or AIDS made a dish. We all rather enjoyed the food. It was like all the barriers went down when you were with these other people.

. . . Even for gay men, support groups are mixed blessings. Although socializing with persons who have HIV disease solves some problems, it creates others. . . . [W]hen they are with such others, they cannot avoid thinking about their illness. Moreover, those who become friends must cope with their friends' illnesses and dying as well as their own. As a result, the pleasure derived from support groups can turn to pain. Once this happens, individuals may decide to protect themselves emotionally by withdrawing from support groups and social networks made up of persons who share their illness.

Reducing Stigma

Although both hiding one's illness and restricting one's social circle can help persons with HIV disease avoid stigma, they will not reduce that stigma. Consequently, some individuals, like others who are stigmatized by society, consider these strategies inadequate and choose to attack the roots of that stigma directly.

The decision to come out of the closet about their illness is not an easy one. Several men and women I interviewed would like to do so, but their doctors, husbands, friends, and relatives, fearing the potential for stress and stigma, have urged them not to. These warnings are particularly effective with those who have children and who fear that their children might also be stigmatized if their diagnosis becomes known.

Nevertheless, some do choose to reveal their condition publicly. They work for community organizations that deal with HIV disease, serve as "resources" for acquaintances who have unanswered questions about the illness, or even speak to the media about their situation. Those who take these actions believe that it is the only way to truly improve their situation. For example, after his friends shunned him and his mother refused to help him obtain health insurance, Hugh decided to speak out publicly about having ARC. He explains, "The only way that I could see getting rid of that stigma is to stick up for myself and become publicly known, to say it's okay to be my friend, it's okay to hug me, it's okay to sit down on a couch with me and watch TV." Other individuals continue to conceal their own diagnoses but nonetheless try to teach those around them that persons with HIV disease should not be shunned. David, for example, describes a confrontation with a neighbor who accused him of having AIDS and asked him not to use the pool in their apartment complex. David denied that he had AIDS, but also told the neighbor that "ignorance is no excuse. You ought to read up on AIDS—you can't get it that way."

To reduce stigma, individuals . . . assert that it was simply bad luck that the first Americans affected by HIV disease were gay men or drug users. Gay men who have HIV disease seem especially likely to argue that this illness originated with heterosexuals in Africa and thus cannot be a punishment for homosexuality. As Chris says, "It didn't start out as a homosexual disease, and it's not going to finish that way."

These alternative explanations for their illnesses allow Chris and others like him to reject their rejecters as prejudiced or ignorant. Others, however, themselves believe that they deserve HIV disease. . . . Instead of offering excuses for their behavior, these men and women first accept responsibility for their drug use or, more commonly, homosexuality and affirm their belief in the social norms that label those activities immoral. Second, they claim that they have reformed and are no longer the person who engaged in these activities. On this basis, they ask their families, churches, and God to accept their apologies, forgive their former sins, and believe that the new persons they have become are their real selves.

Finally, persons with HIV disease can reduce stigma through bravado—putting on what amounts to a show to convince others of the reality of their situation, that they are, in fact, still functioning and worthwhile human beings.

David describes how he and other persons with HIV disease occasionally go to a bar to "show these people that we can live with AIDS, that we can have a good time, that we can dance, that we can socialize, that we're not people with plagues." Describing a recent visit to a local bar, he says, "I just walked in, put my arms around somebody, said 'Hi, how're you doing? Everything going ok with you?' and he said, 'Well, how are you doing?' and I said, 'Well, ARC hasn't gotten me down yet. I don't think it will.' I said, 'I'm going to beat this thing.' And I just acted like nothing was wrong."

Living with HIV Disease

As their illness progresses, both the concerns of persons with HIV disease and the resources available to them shift. Stigma becomes a less critical issue, as their interactions with others necessarily become more limited and as they develop a supportive, if narrower, circle of friends, relatives, and health care workers. With time, too, the shock individuals feel at how some of their relatives and friends have reacted lessens, and they learn to accept the distance between them and those who once were close. Calvin, who was completely rejected by his family, says:

> Like anything else, any other disappointment that you have in life, you adjust. You categorize it in a fashion that's comfortable to you and you put it on the shelf with the rest of your hurts and you get on with your life. You don't let it destroy you. There's nothing wrong with hurting as long as you don't stay in that position too long and hurt for too long of a time. I can't change AIDS and I can't change my family, so I accept and go forward. That's all I can do.

Time also can help individuals recover from their own feelings of shame. At the follow-up interview, Brent, whose diagnosis had changed since the first interview from ARC to AIDS, said:

> In the beginning I had horrible feelings of dirtiness. Just the "leprosy" [feeling] was just overpowering. I wanted to hide it from the world. As I've had time to accustom myself to having this and give myself time to think and rationalize and come to intellectual ideas rather than emotional responses, the feelings are less. . . . I've changed and become accustomed to it and I'm used to the idea.

As stigma recedes as an issue, and as the physical consequences of their illness become more overwhelming, other concerns come to the forefront. With the changes in their bodies, persons with HIV disease increasingly lose the ability to meet their own expectations for how they should perform in the roles and relationships that they retain. This loss of abilities and the resulting failed performances seriously threaten individuals' self-concepts. Psychologists have documented that, whenever possible, people will avoid recognizing any evidence that might force them to change their self-concepts, especially if that evidence might result in lowering their self-esteem. The desire to maintain a consistent self-concept and level of self-esteem leads people to assume that their own motives are pure, acknowledge only favorable evaluations from others, recall and take credit for successes but not failures, and perceive new data selectively so as to confirm their preexisting self-concepts. Given the overwhelming changes produced by HIV disease, however, these strategies cannot work for long. As a result, as their illness progresses, individuals must develop ways to maintain their self-concepts and self-esteem despite unavoidable evidence that their lives have changed. To do so, they must construct new philosophical frameworks that allow them to downgrade the importance of their losses and to value the persons they now are and the lives they now lead.

To begin with, persons with HIV disease can reevaluate the importance of physical appearances. Typically, those I interviewed report that whereas previously they had thought "if I lose my looks I'll lose everything," now they believe that "the important thing is that I'm alive." As a result, they can separate their ideas about their appearance from their ideas about their inherent self-worth.

Similarly, persons with HIV disease can reevaluate their ideas about the importance of sexual activity; this is especially relevant for gay men. As those activities diminish, they may learn to value relationships that provide friendship more than those that provide sexual gratification. In addition, as their social circles shrink due to both stigma and their diminishing physical abilities, individuals quickly learn who are their true friends. As a result, they often feel that their remaining relationships with friends and lovers are now better and more meaningful than ever before. They therefore are able to replace their former self-concepts as sexual beings with new and equally valued self-concepts as loving beings.

Persons with HIV disease also find worth in their lives and their selves by emphasizing past accomplishments or present joys rather than future losses. This strategy additionally aids individuals by restoring some of their sense of control over their lives, for they can assert far more control over how they conceptualize the past and experience the present than over what will happen in the future.

Chris's case illustrates how one can derive a sense of self-worth by focusing on the past rather than the future. A former alcoholic now diagnosed with AIDS, Chris has made peace with the thought of his death by emphasizing what he has accomplished in his life. As he says, "I used to think about it all the time, that I didn't want to die. . . . But I'm proud of my life. I've changed it. I've done something with it. . . . I've stayed sober, and I've passed along some sobriety to people. I've helped some people understand it, and that's important."

Other individuals deemphasize their diminished futures by stressing the benefits of focusing on the present and deriving pleasure from the wonders of everyday life. This is an especially important change for those whose previous focus on future goals had left them perennially dissatisfied with their lives. As a result, persons with HIV disease can experience greater happiness than ever before. Robert, who also has AIDS, says, "I think I just enjoy life so much more now. Everybody I come into contact with, it seems I notice the good things about them. You notice the flowers more. . . . You notice the sky more. You just notice all the things that are created in this world, and most all of them are beautiful. . . . I think I've gained life, actually [from having AIDS]. The beauty of it and what it really means, the caring, the sharing, the pretty flowers, the ugly flowers, the weeds or whatever, the sunshine, and the rain. I like all of it now." . . .

Political activism can also allow individuals to develop enhanced selves. This is especially true for those who can no longer contribute to the world through their work. David, who has appeared on the local news to describe his problems in obtaining social security benefits, recalls, "I didn't want everybody to know. But . . . once it was over and done with, I felt good about what I had done. Because it wasn't only for me that I was doing it. It was for a lot of other people out there that got the same problem." Similarly, others I interviewed point to their participation in this and other research studies as "legacies" that they are leaving to help others. Calvin, explaining why he agreed to do the interview, says, "It's important to me to try to do something for mankind. To create enough interest that somebody will do something." Activities such as these help individuals to supplant failed performances in old roles with successful performances in valued new roles, and thus to maintain their self-esteem.

In addition, persons with HIV disease believe that they can help others simply because their deaths will add to the toll from this illness. They believe that, as that toll rises, the government eventually will have to devote more resources to seeking a cure or vaccine. Calvin continues, "I feel that I am making a positive approach toward mankind with dying from AIDS. . . . I feel that with my dying from AIDS I am becoming part of the statistics. Once there is enough statistics, then somebody is going to do something about it, but they are not going to do anything until there is an emergency." This philosophy allows individuals both to find meaning in their suffering and to retain a sense of worth.

For gay men, having HIV disease can also improve their self-esteem by making them more comfortable with their sexuality. Several report that in the past they had experienced considerable guilt and ambivalence about their lifestyles. Although they had engaged in gay sexual activities, they had found it difficult to embrace gay identities. Their illness has enabled them to integrate their sexual activities and sexual identities into coherent sexual self-concepts in one of two ways. For some, the process of dealing with a fatal, sexually transmitted disease has caused them to reexamine their feelings toward being gay. In this process, some have found a new self-acceptance. As Dick says, "I think I'm more comfortable with myself, now that I've had to deal with it [being gay] again. It's almost like coming out again. You can come out feeling better about yourself and feeling better about being gay." . . .

For other gay men, HIV disease can eliminate dissonance between their sexual identities and sexual activities by ending those activities. Once concern about infecting others or worsening their own health forces them to abandon sexual activities, they no longer face contradictions between those activities and their sense of who they are or should be. Subsequently, both they and their families may stop considering them either deviant or sinful. As a result, they experience both more peace with themselves and improved self-esteem.

Dying with HIV Disease

. . . Although most persons with HIV disease continue to hope for a cure, eventually their frenetic search for one abates, both because they lose hope and because they learn that the constant search for a cure can be physically and emotionally damaging. Jill, for example, describes how initially she would try to "do everything":

> But you see what that means is I'd get real hyped [on] things in the newspaper, the media, you know, cures and stuff. . . . [But] I knew if I got that high I'd have to come down and get that low. Do you know what I mean? So then I'd get real high about cures or ideas. Or I'd read something, you know, "This is wonderful!" And, you know, "This is going to just—this will do it. This will save my life." And, "This will make some of the things better." And then I'd get real high about that, and I'd rush around and get real positive. And believe it or not, it wasn't real healthy because, you know, I'd either be so physically exhausted from just being so hyper about something that the next day I'd either sleep all day or I would have a depression. It's the highs and lows that get you.

Jill no longer will read stories about HIV disease in the newspapers, but instead relies on her doctor to let her know of any new drug she should try.

Robert, who has AIDS, describes a different set of dangers persons with HIV disease can face if they start believing in a cure. He had taken zidovudine for a while, but was forced to stop because of life-threatening loss of blood cells. He says:

> People with AIDS need to realize they are sick, deathly sick. I had got where I think you start feeling good which I guess it was because I was on AZT [zidovudine] too. It is the difference between black and white, night and day, or whatever. The first time I went on it I lasted six weeks. It was just marvelous. I just felt so good. Then the next time it didn't work for but a week and I got scared. I had forgotten the possibility of dying.

This experience convinced Robert that he would be happier if he accepted his fate than if he continued on an emotional roller coaster of false hopes.

Those who conclude that nothing will cure them or restore their quality of life may decide to stop trying to preserve their lives. Calvin has stopped taking all medications:

> At first, I got on the bandwagon of vitamins and getting nutrition and proper meals and eating my spinach and everything. One day I finally said: "What for?" It's not going to save me. I don't know of anybody that has not died from AIDS just because they ate spinach. . . . You can't run from AIDS. There's nowhere to go. If it's any other illness, then you have hope, you have dreams, you have treatment. With AIDS you don't. You just simply don't have an alternative to dying.

. . . Once persons with HIV disease decide that death is inevitable—and to some extent regardless of how sick they currently are—their conception of the future narrows. A striking feature of conversation with these men and women is the telescoping meaning of the future, as their long-range perspective shrinks and they move from talking about the future in terms of years from now, to months, weeks, or even hours. Sharon, for example, who has ARC, feels that her future has been "snatched away" from her. She says, "I don't feel the future exists for me any longer. [In the past] I would think about ten or twenty years down the road when I would be at a certain point in my life. Now I don't think about that. I think about each day."

In this narrowed future, death looms increasingly close. The regrets individuals feel center on the pain their death will bring to others and on their own loss of potential experiences, as they realize that they will miss seeing various future events, from their children's marriages to the price of strawberries next year. Jeremy, for example, says, "I regret that I probably will never make it to the point where I'll be one of those old men sitting in the malls drinking coffee, watching." A wistfulness, rather than bitterness, pervades most such remarks.

The meaning of death, however, is not overwhelmingly negative. For those who have firm Christian convictions, death can take on especially positive connotations of salvation and rejoining God in heaven. Religion can become a "fortress in the storm"—a source of strength in this world and hope about the next—especially if they find sympathetic clergy who will listen to their fears and sorrows and provide "unconditional love."

As their physical pain increases, death also can come to seem a blessing. Calvin emphatically states, "I'm so miserable now I pray to the Lord every night that he takes me. I cry myself to sleep just begging to die. I want to die so bad I can't hardly stand it. Not because I'm suicidal, but because I hurt. I hurt, and I want it over with."

Although death can lose its power to frighten persons with HIV disease, however, dying retains its horror. Carol echoes the sentiments of most others when she says, "I'm not afraid to die. I may be afraid of the *way* it's going to happen, but I'm not afraid to die." Similarly, Dennis, who has already suffered one agonizingly debilitating episode, says, "Death doesn't bother me. Being ill as I was terrifies me." As these quotes suggest, the greatest fears of persons with HIV disease typically center on being kept alive against their will beyond the point where pain or disability makes their lives no longer worth living.

Such feelings led Dennis, along with several others I interviewed, to make plans to commit suicide should that seem warranted so that he could maintain his sense of control over the nature of his dying. As Dennis explains, "If I'm going to die, I would rather it be my business. I guess it's a lack of control. I want to reassert as much control as I can." Others have decided to let the disease take its natural course. They have signed living wills to prohibit physicians from keeping them alive through extraordinary means, instructed relatives not to let them be placed on life-support systems, and decided to stop taking their medications once life no longer seemed worthwhile. As Calvin, who has thrown away all his medications without informing his physician, explains, "I don't want to die, but I don't have a choice. I have to—period. I mean, no question. So if I have to die, why not tackle the chore and get it over with?"

Conclusions

These coping strategies undoubtedly are also used by persons faced with other chronic and terminal illnesses. Certainly a major focus of many voluntary organizations, such as the American Diabetes Association and the Epilepsy Foundation, is to educate the public about these illnesses and to dispel the myths that lead the public to stigmatize affected individuals. And certainly many who have these illnesses, whether or not they belong to these organizations, also try in their personal lives to challenge the idea that they deserve either illness or stigma. . . .

For those who consider alcoholism an illness, the parallel is clear. One of the main (if perhaps unintended) purposes alcoholism treatment programs serve is to provide recovering alcoholics with believable "apologies," in which they both take responsibility for their past actions and request forgiveness on the basis that they have reformed.

Without question, bravado can be used by ill persons regardless of their illness. Bravado occurs whenever ill persons go beyond the introspective process of believing in the "restored" self that Charmaz describes and instead actively assert to others that their lives are essentially unchanged by their illness. Similarly, we can logically conclude that those who have other illnesses, given sufficient time, social, and emotional resources, can find sources of joy and pride in their lives and can devise ways to feel in control of their dying and to give meaning to their deaths.

26 The Jail as Degradation

JOHN IRWIN

No human group can exist without norms. The equivalent of instincts in the animal world, *norms* prevent chaos among humans by laying out avenues for us to follow in social life. Similarly, no human group can exist without *sanctions*, for norms, unenforced, cease to be norms. Consequently, humans have developed a wide variety of sanctions to help maintain social order—including smiles and prizes on the positive side, and frowns and fines on the negative. Sanctions vary from people rolling their eyes for some infraction of a rule to killing someone for breaking another. *Positive sanctions* indicate approval and encourage people to follow norms. *Negative sanctions,* indicating displeasure, are designed to punish, to ridicule, to bring offenders into line, and to warn off future offenders.

Jails (and prisons) are among our strongest negative sanctions. These places of confinement could be fairly benign, even serving purposes of rehabilitation, but, instead, almost always they are places of punishment. Most of their punishment does not consist of official acts administered as part of the law, but, rather, comes about more informally, through the jail's "usual" social interaction. This becomes apparent in Irwin's analysis.

PRISONERS RECEIVE MUCH MORE than the treatment required to introduce them to the jail and hold them there. They are impersonally and systematically degraded by every step in the criminal justice process, from arrest through detention to court appearance. They are also degraded personally by the hostility and contempt directed at them by police officers, deputies, and other criminal justice functionaries.

Process Degradation

Even when police officers act in a polite and professional manner, an arrest is degrading to all but the seasoned rabble. In making an arrest, officers occasionally invade a person's private space—a home, office, or workplace—and remove him or her from the presence of shocked acquaintances or friends. Most often, however, the police arrest persons in public places where most of the witnesses are strangers; but even this remains humiliating to all but the most hardened and frequently arrested disreputables. Arrests are unusual public events, and those who witness them often express shock, dismay, or revulsion—reactions that further humiliate and degrade the person being arrested.

When arresting officers believe that danger is involved, they often take standard precautions that increase the humiliation. When police fear that suspects may be armed, they make them stand spread-eagle against a wall or hunched over a car hood until they search them. Occasionally, they may go even further. For example, in December 1983 three members of the Harlem Globetrotters basketball team were shopping in downtown Santa Barbara. They left an ice cream store, cones in hand, and hailed a taxi. After traveling for a few blocks through the heart of the business district, their cab was stopped by policemen who ordered them out of the car and commanded them to lie on the ground, face down. A jewelry store had been robbed an hour before, and the police suspected these men—even though their only physical similarity to the robbers was that they were black. Their terrifying and humiliating ordeal, which had drawn a large crowd, lasted until the storeowner arrived and saw that they were not the robbers.[1]

Sometimes persons who are inexperienced or less experienced with arrest and anxious about their suddenly powerless position will argue, joke, or even resist the police, who then respond with tougher tactics.[2] The total subjugation and immobility that continue through arrest and transportation to jail are deeply mortifying to persons who have never experienced this condition as adults. (Those who have been in the armed services may have experienced something that resembles it in their first weeks after induction.) Erving Goffman stated it well:

> First, total institutions disrupt or defile precisely those actions that in civil society have the role of attesting to the actor and those in his presence that he has some command over his world—that he is a person with "adult" self-determination, autonomy, and freedom of action. A failure to retain this kind of adult executive competency, or at least the symbols of it, can produce in the inmate the terror of feeling radically demoted in the age-grading system.[3]

Degradation increases during the time a person is being introduced to the jail. In his study of "total institutions" (of which the jail is a type), Goffman explored at length the numerous mortifying rituals, such as searching, stripping, bathing, spraying, and the taking of personal property, that are conducted with the institutional purpose of converting newcomers into manageable inmates.[4] In the jail, since it is conceived by its operators as a short-term holding facility, no elaborate conception of a desired inmate is at work. The jail, unlike other total institutions, is not trying to cure persons or engage them in any complex enterprises, such as running a prison with convict labor. What is needed and wanted in a jail are prisoners who will wait obediently wherever they are placed (in a cell, on a bench, or against a wall), who will make no demands (or few), and who will willingly perform the few required jail procedures, such as returning to their cells, standing for a count, coming to the front when called (for a visit, release, bail, or transfer), and following the procedures required when being delivered to court. Generally the method used to convert free adults into this compliant and passive state is to give commands—either short and polite orders or shouted threats—and to back them up by applying whatever force is required to immobilize a person. This often means removing a prisoner to an isolation cell (sometimes padded) where he can engage in any behavior the surroundings permit without bothering anyone else or damaging any jail property. . . .

The routine demands for compliance, the excessive attention to security, and the general lack of concern for the welfare of the rabble, whom the jail employees understand to be the jail's major clients, result in a painfully harsh introduction to the jail. The fish (new prisoners) are herded here and there, crowded together to wait in small, bare cells for unexplained periods of time, and ignored or rebuffed when they make requests; besides being sternly ordered to do whatever is required in the entrance process, they may be commanded to strip naked and bend over with buttocks spread in front of many other fish and deputies.

The degrading experiences and conditions continue during the time prisoners spend in the tanks.[5] Their loss of self-determination becomes only slightly less painful as they learn the official limits and the informal mechanisms for bypassing them. In most jails, they discover that their managers are interested in little more than their name, charge, bail, and court date. Recently many jail systems, such as those in Los Angeles and San Francisco, have also begun to classify incoming prisoners according to a set of custody concerns. Potential troublemakers and "weak" prisoners (those seen as potential victims of exploitation, particularly sexual exploitation) are selected for special placement in tanks set aside for them. Deputies look for any serious medical conditions that might cause a problem while the prisoners are in jail. And sometimes deputies are interested in identifying new prisoners who seem likely candidates for trustee status. Beyond these managerial concerns, the deputies and jail employees have virtually no interest in the individuality of the prisoners.[6]

In addition, the jail routine makes it virtually impossible for a prisoner to maintain his normal physical appearance, which is a crucial factor in sustaining his conception of self.[7] Immediately upon entering the jail, all clothing is taken from the prisoners, and they are supplied with ill-fitting, conspicuous jail uniforms, such as the baggy, bright orange jumpsuits worn by San Francisco County jail pretrial detainees. Most of the other things they use to manage their appearance—the set of tools Goffman refers to as an "identity kit"—are taken from them, and they are allowed to keep only a few (such as a toothbrush, toothpaste, hairbrush, comb, and soap) during incarceration.[8] (In San

Francisco and Los Angeles the toothbrush and toothpaste are supplied by the jail, and the other items must be purchased from the canteen.)

It is very often difficult for prisoners to keep clean. A man who had been in several small city and county jails in California told me: "If you wanted to wash you had to wash in the toilet. The whole place was so filthy that I just stayed in my clothes. After a week I got out and took off my shoes. Whew, the smell. I had the worst case of athlete's foot you ever saw. Two toes looked like they were going to fall off." In large, relatively humane county jails, such as those in San Francisco County, prisoners are scheduled to receive a change of clothing about once a week. But to many, this provision has not been reliable or sufficient; the files of the San Francisco jail ombudsman contain complaints like these: "We have not had a clothes change in three weeks. We want a full set of clean clothes once a week." And "We should be allowed to change underwear twice a week—and have two pairs, so we will not be naked while we wash underwear." Furthermore, it is virtually impossible to be "well groomed" in jail. Shaving is difficult because prisoners are not allowed to keep razor blades, and the deputies usually supply one razor blade a day to be used by many prisoners; in San Francisco, up to twenty prisoners must use one blade for their morning shave. Prisoners have no fingernail clippers. Most jails have no barbers, and prisoners either cut one another's hair with razor blades or let their hair grow. . . .

Prisoners live in tanks containing crowds of strangers. The human density and total lack of privacy expose them to one another in ways that can occur only in total institutions. They inspect one another's genitals, scars, rashes, and deformities. They smell one another's breath, sweat, gases, and feces. They hear one another's snoring, breaking wind, and masturbating.

Most people depend upon a variety of shields, such as clothing, private rooms, and deodorants, to disguise certain aspects of themselves and to hide their publicly offensive practices. These efforts are more than attempts to "look one's best" or to conform to social standards; they help maintain basic conceptions of self, of individuality. The degradation caused by all jail processes is summed up in the relatively uniform appearance of prisoners—plain, sallow, unclean, disheveled.

Attitudinal Degradation

Many criminal justice functionaries express contempt and hostility toward suspects and defendants, and this fact compounds the degradation experienced by prisoners. This contempt is not idiosyncratic, however. It stems from values shared by police officers, deputies, prosecutors, and many judges. These values are rooted in a theory of crime and society that Herbert Packer has identified as the "crime control model." He writes: "The Crime Control Model is based on the proposition that the repression of criminal conduct is by far the most important function to be performed by the criminal process. The failure of law enforcement to bring criminal conduct under tight control is viewed as leading to the breakdown of public order and thence to the disappearance of an important condition of human freedom."[9]

The majority of police officers and deputies accept this theory, but they do not see crime control as simply or mainly a practical endeavor. In their view, what threatens the public order is not crime itself but immorality, and the major threat lies in the immorality of certain classes or types of people, most of them belonging to the rabble.

ARRESTING OFFICERS

The police, who make the initial and highly discretionary arrest decisions, tend to believe that street people or disreputables—the people they arrest most frequently—are the primary source of trouble in society. As Officer C. of the San Francisco police told me in an interview: "It's the people who are hanging around on the corner. They're unemployed and don't have anything else to do. Like the guys on Eighteenth and Mission. They don't act like other people. They don't know when to stop. They're ready to do anything. People who have jobs, live in apartments or houses, they don't cause us any trouble."

Most police officers are not dispassionate toward the rabble. Their personal class prejudices and cultural distaste (to use the mildest term) are strengthened by the irritating and time-consuming task of policing a class of people who have always posed the most visible and offensive problem of social order in big cities.[10] In the neighborhoods where there are significant contingents of the rabble, most police work is directed toward managing them. Officer C. told me: "If you don't keep on top of them, then they get out of hand. If you let too big a crowd of them form, it will get out of control. They bother people who have to pass them and the business in the area. You have to keep them moving."

Some rabble types consistently show disrespect toward the police and threaten their authority. This failure to show respect often stems from a moral contest between disreputables and police. Most disreputables (as we should expect) operate according to beliefs and values that bolster their dignity and justify their position and behavior as morally correct. These beliefs usually also define police officers as lowly and despicable human beings. So instead of passively or obsequiously submitting to an officer's commands, disreputables may engage the police in a moral contest, objecting and arguing from their own moral position. When police officers who are already hostile toward the rabble are confronted with such hostility and moral condemnation, an invidious dynamic is set in motion. Anything less than complete obedience by the rabble can be seen as a moral or physical threat that must be countered with immediate force.

The hostility of police officers is clearly expressed in the names they use to label the rabble category. Officer C. explained the epithets now in use: "Some guys use slime balls and pukes. I like dirt ball. Now kronks is popular.

Assholes is still the most common term." The hostility is also evident in the way police handle disreputable types when they arrest them and take them to jail. Approximately half the persons in our felony sample reported that the arresting officers were verbally abusive to them. For example, "They talked to me like a dog." Or "They talked to me like I was an asshole. I'm not a criminal, I wasn't even high." Seven persons in the sample reported that they were handled in a physically abusive manner. One of them, a twenty-two-year-old Nicaraguan corner boy, said: "I was playing football with my cousin in a field. This cop came up to me with his gun drawn. He pushed me down on the ground. He was shaking. I was petrified. He jerked my hands way up my back and put on the cuffs." In addition, seven others stated that they were struck or kicked by the arresting officers. For example: "They hit me in the face and the stomach when they got me in the car." And this: "He was pushing me in the car and gave me a big kick in the stomach when I was bent over getting in."[11]

DEPUTIES

Like police officers, jail deputies (employees of the sheriff who run the jail) tend to hold strongly negative attitudes toward most persons who are arrested and held in jail. These attitudes stem largely from their work with prisoners, which is in many ways more annoying than police work. They must constantly handle repulsive, difficult, and even violent prisoners, some of whom are drunk, high, enraged, belligerent, or insane. Many prisoners hate deputies, and a few openly express this hate. For example, I once heard a prisoner who was being booked loudly threaten the booking room deputies as follows: "You rotten motherfuckers, if I catch you on my turf you're in trouble." (The response from one deputy was: "You haven't got any turf, asshole.")[12]

Besides occasionally expressing such hostility, prisoners regularly try to combat their deprivation by beseeching deputies for help. Deputies who do not immediately and emphatically rebuff these entreaties are inundated with pleas. New deputies who have not yet acquired the deputies' culture and may have some sympathy for prisoners are especially vulnerable. Roger Martin, a temporary deputy, described his experience in this way:

> Earlier on the job, the inmates conned me often. I learned this is standard procedure with a new deputy. He usually begins as a relatively nice guy before the jail brutalizes him. The inmates try to take advantage of this, to ask for favors and get the deputy to do things for them. I was gullible enough to be conned at first, but I quickly learned they were taking advantage of me and laughing at me behind my back.[13]

These supplications from prisoners confront deputies with a constant moral dilemma. They must work closely with other humans (prisoners) who are in a state of deprivation and visibly suffering. (If the deputies do not notice, the prisoners will remind them.) If the deputies remain committed to a philosophy of humanity and egalitarianism, or even to a basic sense of fairness, the plight of the needy and the suffering around them will eventually take a heavy toll on their peace of mind and personality organization. To avoid this, most deputies embrace and help sustain the theory that prisoners are worthless and deserve their deprivation. For some, who have operated all their lives on similar concepts (stereotypical thinking or racial prejudice), this is relatively easy. Others, however, must consciously reject more humane and tolerant conceptions of prisoners before they can accept the cynical viewpoint. In most cases they cannot accomplish this without some strain, and this strain and their lingering ambivalence often make them *more* expressive of hate and brutality. As in other situations, the convert is very often the extremist. . . .[14]

The hostility . . . of deputies is expressed in their decisions to ignore prisoners' visible medical needs; to punish them on the spot for talking, shouting, talking back, or having a "bad attitude"; to place them in cells or tanks where they will be in danger from other prisoners; to keep them locked in cells; to withhold their mail or money sent to them through the mail; to ransack their cells in cell searches; and to subject them to humiliating and painful experiences. . . .

Sometimes special events or processes inhibit the strong tendencies of deputies to develop or express malevolent attitudes. For example, several court actions apparently have restrained deputies in Los Angeles. Many prisoners and ex-prisoners have reported to me that during the middle 1970s at the Los Angeles County jail, deputies became exceptionally abusive to prisoners. One of them said: "Man, someone should do something about that jail. I mean those cops will get on people for nothing. A guy doesn't have to get out of line to get mistreated there. I watched it many times. Young guys who didn't know what was happening, and the cops would yank them out of line and treat 'em like dogs. It made me sick. I haven't seen anything like it in all my years of being in these places." Prisoners suggested to me that a series of lawsuits and court injunctions against the jail had significantly reduced the verbal and physical abuse. As one of them put it: "Yeah, they used to be bad here, but the courts have been on them, and most of that really rough stuff has stopped."

At the Yolo County jail, the friendlier rural atmosphere and the efforts of a relatively humanitarian jail supervisor, who is able to control his small staff effectively, have apparently prevented the normal deputy culture from developing. As one prisoner put it: "This place is a piece of cake. You should look at Sacramento. There it's mean. This place is a playground. Everyone treats you like a human being." . . .

Judicial Degradation

As Malcolm Feeley has noted in his study of the New Haven court system, court proceedings are conducted as a *moral* enterprise: "Many observers of the courts have become preoccupied with procedural justice, and have consequently failed to appreciate the intensity of the normative concern which in-forms the decisions of so many officials in the criminal process."[15] More con-cretely, this means that prisoners are judged not solely or even primarily for their crimes but rather for their character and that they are often profoundly degraded during their court appearances.

Degradation is built into the court routines, which are planned and exe-cuted to dignify reputability (and condemn disreputability). Usually the judge is introduced by the bailiff, who orders those present to stand while the judge whisks in to assume his high station. From his lofty seat, which is the largest and most luxurious in the room, he directs the proceedings with virtually ab-solute official power—including the power to summarily jail anybody in the room for contempt of court. The bailiff attempts to enforce the rigid code of courtroom docorum, which goes far beyond the rules necessary to maintain order and to speed the court process (men must remove their hats, no one may read a newspaper, and so on). The attorneys, clerks, and bailiffs address the court, make requests and motions, and generally perform their roles in a practiced manner that shows respect for the judge. . . .

Besides appearing out of place, most defendants fail to perform properly and skillfully, and they often disturb or disrupt the routine. When they ap-proach the bench to take their position behind "the bar," some of them mean-der awkwardly forward with small unsteady steps, hands groping for some comfortable position, head lowered. Others stride forward in an arrogant street gait, arms swinging, body swaying, and head bobbing. Whereas the at-torneys are at ease and poised before the bench, most defendants bend and slant their bodies, shift their weight from one foot to the other, fiddle with their hands or perhaps stick them into their front or back pockets. When they sit at the defense table, they slouch and fidget in their seats, jut their legs far out in front of them, and appear to be either too ill-at-ease or too relaxed.

During the hearings many of them fail to respond to the judge's com-mands or to understand essential information. The more aggressive defendants occasionally pierce the courtroom decorum with disruptive commands, re-quests, and opinions. Thus, for example, a young man accused of grabbing a radio from another man on the street and then knocking him down—a rob-bery—loudly protested against his attorney's request to be removed from the case, which would result in a delay. "I've already been here forty-one days and I want to go out and get to work. My birthday is January 26, I sure don't want to be in jail for my birthday." And another defendant argued with the judge over his attorney's motion to have him ruled incompetent. Defendant (loudly): "Certainly I'm competent!" Judge: "Your attorney is not in agreement with you." Defendant (shouting): "How could my attorney not be in agreement with me? He's supposed to defend me. What's crazy about wanting to get out of jail!"

Such behavior by poorly dressed defendants, besides being personally of-fensive, serves to remind the judge and his court of the importance of observ-ing social proprieties and respecting society's status systems. In a sense, the court is a microcosm and a symbol of society's formal and stratified aspects. The behavior of defendants here is taken as a demonstration of their general social weaknesses and as evidence that they are truly *moral inferiors.* Thus, the court functionaries—particularly the prosecutor and the judge, but also the bailiff, the court reporter, and even the defense counsel—openly or indirectly display their contempt for most defendants, who are thereby humiliated and degraded. . . .

Loss of Commitment

One basic premise behind the practice of law enforcement as a moral enterprise is the idea that persons will respond to contempt and castigation with apology, contrition, and alteration of their character and conduct. The tenacity of this belief is peculiar in the face of so much contradictory evidence. Under some conditions, of course, some defendants bow and conform when they are degraded, condemned, and disciplined. But under other conditions, which are just as common if not more so, they squirm away from the disapprobation, avoid the punishment, and refuse to follow prescriptions for future conduct. Such conditions are not hard to imagine. The disapprobation meted out to them may be severe, contemptuous, and unmitigated by any positive attitudes. Realistically, there may be no clear paths to their "rehabilitation," that is, to their achievement of dignified social status and economic self-sufficiency. And they may have contact with all the deviant viewpoints that characterize the official deliverer of disapprobation and punishment as morally inferior and the "offender" as honorable.

When these conditions apply, many marginal persons lose or relax their commitment to conventional society. This is more understandable when we consider the tremendous effort it can take to maintain that commitment when one is poor and of low social status. It means struggling to meet all the obligations required of a conventional citizen, such as paying rent, bills, taxes, fines, fees, alimony, and child support. It means avoiding deviant habits, such as stealing or excessive drinking and drug use. And it means observing society's pervasive and subtle definitions of respectability, which define in rather narrow terms just how to comport oneself in public. To many persons, the prospect of giving up this struggle looks appealing.

Rejection of conventional values and loss of commitment to society are even more likely to occur when defendants believe that those who punish them in the name of the law are hypocritical and unfair. Due process values—such as "all persons are innocent until proven guilty" and "every person has the right to a fair and impartial trial"—are widely and proudly celebrated in conventional society and often ceremoniously repeated during the judicial process. Yet what the defendants actually experience are the practices that stem from law enforcement conceived as a moral enterprise, practices that involve systematic violations of due process values. Moreover, they believe that they are being intentionally punished during all stages of the judicial process, regardless of its eventual outcome. And in this, they are correct.[16] The great majority of persons arrested do not receive jail or prison sentences; but all of them, including many whose charges are dismissed, are subjected to some punishment. The experience of harsh and unfairly delivered punishment frequently enrages or embitters defendants and makes it easier for them to reject the values of those who have dealt with them in this way.

With their commitment to conventional values damaged or destroyed and their ties to the dominant culture shaken loose, many persons—particularly those who are already living on the margins of conventional society and having difficulty conforming—"drop out": they migrate to deviant worlds and the rabble status. The jail experience prepares them for an acceptance of the rabble life.

Notes

1. See *Los Angeles Times,* Dec. 14, 1983, pt. 1, p. 2, and Dec. 15, 1983, pt. 1, pp. 3, 17; and *People's Weekly,* Feb. 13, 1984, pp. 30–31.

2. In 1982, F. Lee Bailey, a well-known criminal attorney, was arrested in San Francisco for driving under the influence of alcohol. He pleaded not guilty, and at his trial he testified that he was trying to keep his humor during the arrest by joking in a friendly manner with the police; he said that they became verbally and then physically abusive toward him and that one officer knocked a cigarette out of his hand with a "vicious karate chop." The police officers testified that Bailey was insulting and combative. He was acquitted in a lengthy jury trial. See *San Francisco Chronicle,* April 14, 1982, p. 14, and April 16, 1982, p. 1.

3. Erving Goffman, *Asylums* (Chicago: Aldine Pub. Co., 1961), p. 43.

4. Goffman, "On the Characteristics of Total Institutions," in ibid.

5. Most of these have been recognized and analyzed by Goffman, in *Asylums.*

6. Some deputies, if they work in a jail for a long time, get to know some of the jail regulars and interact with them on a broader set of characteristics; and a few prisoners who are known to possess skills and knowledge that are useful to the jail operation may be dealt with almost as if they were real people. But most prisoners never see this sort of treatment.

7. One of Goffman's major contributions to sociology is his convincing analysis of how persons "present" themselves through behavior and how important this presentation is in their definition of self. See his *Presentation of Self in Everyday Life* (New York: Doubleday, 1959).

8. Goffman, *Asylums,* p. 20.

9. Herbert Packer, *The Limits of the Criminal Sanction* (Stanford: Stanford University Press, 1968), p. 158. Packer contrasts this model with the due process model, which is dominated by other concerns: seeing that the system does not err in convicting persons of crime, restraining the extension of government power, and ensuring equality of treatment for the defendant.

10. The police were first introduced in London as a response to the rabble, who were then spoken of as "the dangerous classes." See Alan Silver, "The Demand for Order in Civil Society," in *The Police,* David J. Bordua, ed. (New York: John Wiley, 1967).

11. I have only the prisoners' accounts of these acts and do not know what actually happened or what, if anything, had provoked the officers' actions. However, four of the seven prisoners had facial bruises. In his study of police behavior, *The Police and the Public,* Albert Reiss found that in the majority of cases in which the persons arrested were "violent or aggressive" or "disgruntled or sullen," the police used "gross force" or "firm handling, generally moving the offender about by holding him by the arm, prodding him with a nightstick, or surrounding him with several police officers" (p. 54). This suggests that the expression of hostility is interactive. Nevertheless—and this is what is important for this analysis of degradation—many arrested persons in my sample *believed* that police officers had unnecessarily abused them, physically or verbally, and this made them feel both angry and degraded.

12. Many similar verbal attacks on the deputies occurred while I was observing in the booking room. If the prisoner persisted, he was firmly warned, and if he still persisted, the deputies roughly removed him to an isolation cell. In the Los Angeles County jail such outbursts were not tolerated; they precipitated either a severe warning or instant removal to an isolation cell.

13. Roger Martin, *Pigs and Other Animals* (Myco Publishing House, 1980), p. 57. Personal observation has persuaded me that the vast majority of prisoner requests are motivated by nothing more than a desire to improve upon reduced circumstances. Martin's conclusion that prisoners intended to take advantage of him made it easier for him to turn down their requests and accept the collective cynicism.

14. I witnessed this process not only in deputies, some of whom I had known as students before they became deputies, but in myself and my fellow prisoner services caseworkers. We were constantly beseeched for more help than we could deliver, and we had to cope with feelings that we were not doing enough. (One knows he can always do more.) In compensation for these feelings, we began to develop a more cynical view of our work and a more derogatory conception of the prisoner. We used the common term *burnout* to describe this process.

15. Malcolm Feeley, *The Process Is the Punishment* (New York: Russell Sage, 1979), p. 15.

16. This is Malcolm Feeley's important thesis: the primary purpose of the court process is not to determine legal guilt through due process or, as many critics have argued, to run an efficient system through plea bargaining, but rather to punish most defendants through the court process. He suggests that the sanctioning powers are distributed among several people—the arresting officers, bail bondsmen, defense attorneys, prosecutors, and judges—and that punishment is contained in the arrest, jail experience, and court appearances; see *Process Is the Punishment,* pp. 31–32. In the samples I followed in my research, slightly less than half of the felony charges and more than 50 percent of the misdemeanor charges were dismissed. Another 18 percent of those arrested for a felony and more than 31 percent of those arrested for a misdemeanor were diverted, fined, or granted probation without jail sentences. The vast majority of misdemeanor charges were dismissed or otherwise disposed of within forty-eight hours of arrest, and half of the persons arrested for a felony were released from jail within seventy-two hours. However, the process of arrest, booking, and being jailed is ex-

tremely punitive. Moreover, some categories of people were held longer before having their cases dismissed or disposed of through diversion or probation. Thirteen of the petty hustlers (46 percent) had their cases dismissed, but they waited an average of 5.3 days to be released. Among the rabble or marginal rabble types forty-two out of the hundred arrested for a felony were held for more than three days, and four were held more than fifteen days. In some other counties, persons are held much longer before dismissal. In a "tracking sample" of 2,255 persons arrested for misdemeanors and felonies in San Mateo Country from November 1981 to October 1982, the eighty-two persons who had their cases dismissed by the court or the district attorney had remained in jail for an average of thirteen days; see Institute for Law and Police Planning, *San Mateo County Needs Assessment* (Oakland, Calif., 1983). In Miami in 1981 and 1982, over 66 percent of all felony charges were dismissed, and those who waited in jail for dismissal spent an average of fifty days there; the median stay was twenty-one days; see James Austin, Barry Krisberg, and Paul Litsky, *Supervised Pretrial Release Test Design Evaluation.*

27 The Pathology of Imprisonment

PHILIP G. ZIMBARDO

Why are our prisons such powder kegs? To most people, this is not a difficult question and the answer is obvious—because of the kind of people who are locked up in prisons: They are criminals, antisocial, and disposed to violence. If not that, then they hate the guards, the food, or the restrictions of prison life (which is what they deserved in the first place!). Similarly, people have little difficulty explaining why prison guards are brutal: It is either the type of people with whom the guards must deal ("animals") or the type of people who are attracted to being prison guards in the first place ("sadistic types"). Such reasons are commonly cited to explain prison violence, but it turns out that much more fundamental social processes are involved. As Zimbardo's remarkable experiment uncovered, the structuring of relationships within the prison lays a firm foundation for prison brutality and violence.

While reading this fascinating account, you may begin to think about how prisons could be improved in order to minimize violence. To reach such a goal, what changes would you suggest that we make in the social structure of prisons?

I was recently released from solitary confinement after being held therein for 37 months [months!]. A silent system was imposed upon me and to even whisper to the man in the next cell resulted in being beaten by guards, sprayed with chemical mace, blackjacked, stomped and thrown into a strip-cell naked to sleep on a concrete floor without bedding, covering, wash basin or even a toilet. The floor served as toilet and bed, and even there the silent system was enforced. To let a moan escape your lips because of the pain and discomfort . . . resulted in another beating. I spent not days, but months there during my 37 months in solitary. . . . I have filed every writ possible against the administrative acts of brutality. The state courts have all denied the petitions. Because of my refusal to let the things die down and forget all that happened during my 37 months in solitary . . . I am the most hated prisoner in [this] penitentiary, and called a "hard-core incorrigible."

Maybe I am an incorrigible, but if true, it's because I would rather die than to accept being treated as less than a human being. I have never complained of my prison sentence as being unjustified except through legal means of appeals. I have never put a knife on a guard's throat and demanded my release. I know that

283

thieves must be punished and I don't justify stealing, even though I am a thief myself. but now I don't think I will be a thief when I am released. No, I'm not rehabilitated. It's just that I no longer think of becoming wealthy by stealing. I now only think of killing—killing those who have beaten me and treated me as if I were a dog. I hope and pray for the sake of my own soul and future life of freedom that I am able to overcome the bitterness and hatred which eats daily at my soul, but I know to overcome it will not be easy.

THIS ELOQUENT PLEA FOR PRISON REFORM—for humane treatment of human beings, for the basic dignity that is the right of every American—came to me secretly in a letter from a prisoner who cannot be identified because he is still in a state correctional institution. He sent it to me because he read of an experiment I recently conducted at Stanford University. In an attempt to understand just what it means psychologically to be a prisoner or a prison guard, Craig Haney, Curt Banks, Dave Jaffe, and I created our own prison. We carefully screened over 70 volunteers who answered an ad in a Palo Alto city newspaper and ended up with about two dozen young men who were selected to be part of this study. They were mature, emotionally stable, normal, intelligent college students from middle-class homes throughout the United States and Canada. They appeared to represent the cream of the crop of this generation. None had any criminal record and all were relatively homogeneous on many dimensions initially.

Half were arbitrarily designated as prisoners by a flip of a coin, the others as guards. These were the roles they were to play in our simulated prison. The guards were made aware of the potential seriousness and danger of the situation and their own vulnerability. They made up their own formal rules for maintaining law, order, and respect, and were generally free to improvise new ones during their eight-hour, three-man shifts. The prisoners were expectedly picked up at their homes by a city policeman in a squad car, searched, handcuffed, fingerprinted, booked at the Palo Alto station house, and taken blindfolded to our jail. There they were stripped, deloused, put into a uniform, given a number, and put into a cell with two other prisoners where they expected to live for the next two weeks. The pay was good ($15 a day), and their motivation was to make money.

We observed and recorded on videotape the events that occurred in the prison, and we interviewed and tested the prisoners and guards at various points throughout the study. Some of the videotapes of the actual encounters between the prisoners and guards were seen on the NBC News feature "Chronolog" on November 26, 1971.

At the end of only six days we had to close down our mock prison because what we saw was frightening. It was no longer apparent to most of the subjects (or to us) where reality ended and their roles began. The majority had indeed become prisoners or guards, no longer able to clearly differentiate between role playing and self. There were dramatic changes in virtually every aspect of their behavior, thinking, and feeling. In less than a week the experience of imprisonment undid (temporarily) a lifetime of learning; human values were suspended, self-concepts were challenged, and the ugliest, most base, pathological side of human nature surfaced. We were horrified because we saw some boys (guards) treat others as if they were despicable animals, taking pleasure in cruelty, while other boys (prisoners) became servile, dehumanized robots who thought only of escape, of their own individual survival, and of their mounting hatred for the guards.

We had to release three prisoners in the first four days because they had such acute situational traumatic reactions as hysterical crying, confusion in thinking, and severe depression. Others begged to be paroled, and all but three were willing to forfeit all the money they had earned if they could be paroled. By then (the fifth day) they had been so programmed to think of themselves as prisoners that when their request for parole was denied, they returned docilely to their cells. Now, had they been thinking as college students acting in an oppressive experiment, they would have quit once they no longer wanted the $15 a day we used as our only incentive. However, the reality was not quitting an experiment but "being paroled by the parole board from the Stanford County Jail." By the last days, the earlier solidarity among the prisoners (systematically broken by the guards) dissolved into "each man for himself." Finally, when one of their fellows was put into solitary confinement (a small closet) for refusing to eat, the prisoners were given a choice by one of the guards: give up their blankets and the incorrigible prisoner would be let out, or keep their blankets and he would be kept in all night. They voted to keep their blankets and to abandon their brother.

About a third of the guards became tyrannical in their arbitrary use of power, in enjoying their control over other people. They were corrupted by the power of their roles and became quite inventive in their techniques of breaking the spirit of the prisoners and making them feel they were worthless. Some of the guards merely did their jobs as tough but fair correctional officers, and several were good guards from the prisoners' point of view since they did them small favors and were friendly. However, no good guards ever interfered with a command by any of the bad guards; they never intervened on the side of the prisoners, they never told the others to ease off because it was only an experiment, and they never even came to me as prison superintendent or experimenter in charge to complain. In part, they were good because the others were bad; they needed the others to help establish their own egos in a positive light. In a sense, the good guards perpetuated the prison more than the other guards because their own need to be liked prevented them from disobeying or violating the implicit guards' code. At the same time, the act of befriending the prisoners created a social reality which made the prisoners less likely to rebel.

By the end of the week the experiment had become a reality, as if it were a Pirandello play directed by Kafka that just keeps going after the audience has left. The consultant for our prison, Carlo Prescott, an exconvict with 16 years of imprisonment in California's jails, would get so depressed and furious each time he visited our prison, because of its psychological similarity to his experiences, that he would have to leave. A Catholic priest who was a former prison chaplain in Washington, D.C., talked to our prisoners after four days and said they were just like the other first-timers he had seen.

But in the end, I called off the experiment not because of the horror I saw out there in the prison yard, but because of the horror of realizing that *I* could have easily traded places with the most brutal guard or become the weakest prisoner full of hatred at being so powerless that I could not eat, sleep, or go to the toilet without permission of the authorities. *I* could have become Calley at My Lai, George Jackson at San Quentin, one of the men at Attica, or the prisoner quoted at the beginning of this article.

Individual behavior is largely under the control of social forces and environmental contingencies rather than personality traits, character, will power, or other empirically unvalidated constructs. Thus we create an illusion of freedom by attributing more internal control to ourselves, to the individual, than actually exists. We thus underestimate the power and pervasiveness of situational controls over behavior because: (a) they are often nonobvious and subtle, (b) we can often avoid entering situations where we might be so controlled, (c) we label as "weak" or "deviant" people in those situations who do behave differently from how we believed we would.

Each of us carries around in our heads a favorable self-image in which we are essentially just, fair, humane, and understanding. For example, we could not imagine inflicting pain on others without much provocation or hurting people who had done nothing to us, who in fact were even liked by us. However, there is a growing body of social psychological research which underscores the conclusion derived from this prison study. Many people, perhaps the majority, can be made to do almost anything when put into psychologically compelling situations—regardless of their morals, ethics, values, attitudes, beliefs, or personal convictions. My colleague, Stanley Milgram, has shown that more than 60 percent of the population will deliver what they think is a series of painful electric shocks to another person even after the victim cries for mercy, begs them to stop, and then apparently passes out. The subjects complained that they did not want to inflict more pain but blindly obeyed the command of the authority figure (the experimenter) who said that they must go on. In my own research on violence, I have seen mild-mannered co-eds repeatedly give shocks (which they thought were causing pain) to another girl, a stranger whom they had rated very favorably, simply by being made to feel anonymous and put in a situation where they were expected to engage in this activity.

Observers of these and similar experimental situations never predict their outcomes and estimate that it is unlikely that they themselves would behave similarly. They can be so confident only when they are outside the situation. However, since the majority of people in these studies do act in nonrational, nonobvious ways, it follows that the majority of observers would also succumb to the social psychological forces in the situation.

With regard to prisons, we can state that the mere act of assigning labels to people and putting them into a situation where those labels acquire validity and meaning is sufficient to elicit pathological behavior. This pathology is not predictable from any available diagnostic indicators we have in the social sciences, and is extreme enough to modify in very significant ways fundamental attitudes and behavior. The prison situation, as presently arranged, is guaranteed to generate severe enough pathological reactions in both guards and prisoners as to debase their humanity, lower their feelings of self-worth, and make it difficult for them to be part of a society outside of their prison.

For years our national leaders have been pointing to the enemies of freedom, to the fascist or communist threat to the American way of life. In so doing they have overlooked the threat of social anarchy that is building within our own country without any outside agitation. As soon as a person comes to the realization that he is being imprisoned by his society or individuals in it, then, in the best American tradition, he demands liberty and rebels, accepting death as an alternative. The third alternative, however, is to allow oneself to become a good prisoner—docile, cooperative, uncomplaining, conforming in thought, and complying in deed.

Our prison authorities now point to the militant agitators who are still vaguely referred to as part of some communist plot, as the irresponsible, incorrigible troublemakers. They imply that there would be no trouble, riots, hostages, or deaths if it weren't for this small band of bad prisoners. In other words, then, everything would return to "normal" again in the life of our nation's prisons if they could break these men.

The riots in prison are coming from within—from within every man and woman who refuses to let the system turn them into an object, a number, a thing, or a no-thing. It is not communist-inspired, but inspired by the spirit of American freedom. No man wants to be enslaved. To be powerless, to be subject to the arbitrary exercise of power, to not be recognized as a human being is to be a slave.

To be a militant prisoner is to become aware that the physical jails are but more blatant extensions of the forms of social and psychological oppression experienced daily in the nation's ghettos. They are trying to awaken the conscience of the nation to the ways in which the American ideals are being perverted, apparently in the name of justice but actually under the banner of apathy, fear, and hatred. If we do not listen to the pleas of the prisoners at Attica to be treated like human beings, then we have all become brutalized by our priorities for property rights over human rights. The consequence will not only be more prison riots but a loss of all those ideals on which this country was founded.

The public should be aware that they own the prisons and that their business is failing. The 70 percent recidivism rate and the escalation in severity of crimes committed by graduates of our prisons are evidence that current prisons fail to rehabilitate the inmates in any positive way. Rather, they are breeding grounds for hatred of the establishment, a hatred that makes every citizen a target of violent assault. Prisons are a bad investment for us taxpayers. Until now we have not cared; we have turned over to wardens and prison authorities the unpleasant job of keeping people who threaten us out of our sight. Now we are shocked to learn that their management practices have failed to improve the product and instead turn petty thieves into murderers. We must insist upon new management or improved operating procedures.

The cloak of secrecy should be removed from the prisons. Prisoners claim they are brutalized by the guards; guards say it is a lie. Where is the impartial test of the truth in such a situation? Prison officials have forgotten that they work for us, that they are only public servants whose salaries are paid by our taxes. They act as if it is their prison, like a child with a toy he won't share. Neither lawyers, judges, the legislature, nor the public is allowed into prisons to ascertain the truth unless the visit is sanctioned by authorities and until all is prepared for their visit. I was shocked to learn that my request to join a congressional investigating committee's tour of San Quentin and Soledad was refused, as was that of the news media.

There should be an ombudsman in every prison, not under the pay or control of the prison authority, and responsible only to the courts, the state legislature, and the public. Such a person could report on violations of constitutional and human rights.

Guards must be given better training than they now receive for the difficult job society imposes upon them. To be a prison guard as now constituted is to be put in a situation of constant threat from within the prison, with no social recognition from the society at large. As was shown graphically at Attica, prison guards are also prisoners of the system who can be sacrificed to the demands of the public to be punitive and the needs of politicians to preserve an image. Social scientists and business administrators should be called upon to design and help carry out this training.

The relationship between the individual (who is sentenced by the courts to a prison term) and his community must be maintained. How can a prisoner return to a dynamically changing society that most of us cannot cope with after being out of it for a number of years? There should be more community involvement in these rehabilitation centers, more ties encouraged and promoted between the trainees and family and friends, more educational opportunities to prepare them for returning to their communities as more valuable members of it than they were before they left.

Finally, the main ingredient necessary to effect any change at all in prison reform, in the rehabilitation of a single prisoner, or even in the optimal development of a child is caring. Reform must start with people—especially people with power—caring about the well-being of others. Underneath the toughest, society-hating convict, rebel, or anarchist is a human being who wants his existence to be recognized by his fellows and who wants someone else to care about whether he lives or dies and to grieve if he lives imprisoned rather than lives free.

28 On Being Sane in Insane Places

DAVID L. ROSENHAN

On the one hand, it is not uncommon for people who violate *explicit* rules written into law to find themselves enmeshed in a formal system that involves passing judgment on their fitness to remain in society. As we have just seen with the preceding selection, removing people's freedom can thrust them into a highly volatile situation. On the other hand, people who violate *implicit* rules (the assumptions about what characterizes "normal" people) also can find themselves caught up in a formal system that involves passing judgment on their fitness to remain in society. "If found guilty of insanity," they, too, are institutionalized—placed in the care of keepers who oversee almost all aspects of their lives.

The fundamental taken-for-granted assumption in institutionalizing people who violate implicit rules is that we are able to tell the sane from the insane. If we cannot do so, the practice itself would be insane! In that case, we would have to explicitly question contemporary psychiatry as a mechanism of social control. But what kind of question is this? Even most of us non-psychiatrists are certain that we can tell the difference between who is sane and who is not. However, in a fascinating experiment, Rosenhan put to the test whether or not even psychiatrists can differentiate between the sane and the insane. As detailed in this account, the results contain a few surprises.

IF SANITY AND INSANITY EXIST . . . how shall we know them? The question is neither capricious nor itself insane. However much we may be personally convinced that we can tell the normal from the abnormal, the evidence is simply not compelling. It is commonplace, for example, to read about murder trials wherein eminent psychiatrists for the defense are contradicted by equally eminent psychiatrists for the prosecution on the matter of the defendant's sanity. More generally, there are a great deal of conflicting data on the reliability, utility, and meaning of such terms as "sanity," "insanity," "mental illness," and "schizophrenia."[1] Finally, as early as 1934, Benedict suggested that normality and abnormality are not universal.[2] What is viewed as normal in one culture may be seen as quite aberrant in another. Thus, notions of normality and abnormality may not be quite as accurate as people believe they are.

To raise questions regarding normality and abnormality is in no way to question the fact that some behaviors are deviant or odd. Murder is deviant. So, too, are hallucinations. Nor does raising such questions deny the existence of the personal anguish that is often associated with "mental illness." Anxiety and depression exist. Psychological suffering exists. But normality and abnormality, sanity and insanity, and the diagnoses that flow from them may be less substantive than many believe them to be.

At its heart, the question of whether the sane can be distinguished from the insane (and whether degrees of insanity can be distinguished from each other) is a simple matter: Do the salient characteristics that lead to diagnoses reside in the patients themselves or in the environments and contexts in which observers find them? From Bleuler, through Kretschmer, through the formulators of the recently revised *Diagnostic and Statistical Manual* of the American Psychiatric Association, the belief has been strong that patients present symptoms, that those symptoms can be categorized, and, implicitly, that the sane are distinguishable from the insane. More recently, however, this belief has been questioned. Based in part on theoretical and anthropological considerations, but also on philosophical, legal, and therapeutic ones, the view has grown that psychological categorization of mental illness is useless at best and downright harmful, misleading, and pejorative at worst. Psychiatric diagnoses, in this view, are in the minds of the observers and are not valid summaries of characteristics displayed by the observed.[3,4,5]

Gains can be made in deciding which of these is more nearly accurate by getting normal people (that is, people who do not have, and have never suffered, symptoms of serious psychiatric disorders) admitted to psychiatric hospitals and then determining whether they were discovered to be sane and, if so, how. If the sanity of such pseudopatients were always detected, there would be *prima facie* evidence that a sane individual can be distinguished from the insane context in which he is found. Normality (and presumably abnormality) is distinct enough that it can be recognized wherever it occurs, for it is carried within the person. If, on the other hand, the sanity of the pseudopatients were never discovered, serious difficulties would arise for those who support traditional modes of psychiatric diagnosis. Given that the hospital staff was not incompetent, that the pseudopatient had been behaving as sanely as he had been outside of the hospital, and that it had never been previously suggested that he belonged in a psychiatric hospital, such an unlikely outcome would support the view that psychiatric diagnosis betrays little about the patient but much about the environment in which an observer finds him.

This article describes such an experiment. Eight sane people gained secret admission to twelve different hospitals.[6] Their diagnostic experiences constitute the data of the first part of this article; the remainder is devoted to a description of their experiences in psychiatric institutions. Too few psychiatrists and psychologists, even those who have worked in such hospitals, know what the experience is like. They rarely talk about it with former patients, perhaps because they distrust information coming from the previously insane. Those who have worked in psychiatric hospitals are likely to have adapted so thoroughly to the settings that they are insensitive to the impact of that experience. And while there have been occasional reports of researchers who submitted themselves to psychiatric hospitalization,[7] these researchers have commonly remained in the hospitals for short periods of time, often with the knowledge of the hospital staff. It is difficult to know the extent to which they were treated like patients or like research colleagues. Nevertheless, their reports about the inside of the psychiatric hospital have been valuable. This article extends those efforts.

Pseudopatients and Their Settings

The eight pseudopatients were a varied group. One was a psychology graduate student in his twenties. The remaining seven were older and "established." Among them were three psychologists, a pediatrician, a psychiatrist, a painter, and a housewife. Three pseudopatients were women, five were men. All of them employed pseudonyms, lest their alleged diagnoses embarrass them later. Those who were in mental health professions alleged another occupation in order to avoid the special attentions that might be accorded by staff, as a matter of courtesy or caution, to ailing colleagues.[8] With the exception of myself (I was the first pseudopatient and my presence was known to the hospital administrator and chief psychologist and, so far as I can tell, to them alone), the presence of pseudopatients and the nature of the research program were not known to the hospital staffs.[9]

The settings were similarly varied. In order to generalize the findings, admission into a variety of hospitals was sought. The twelve hospitals in the sample were located in five different states on the East and West coasts. Some were old and shabby; some were quite new. Some were research-oriented, others not. Some had good staff-patient ratios; others were quite understaffed. Only one was a strictly private hospital. All of the others were supported by state or federal funds, or in one instance, by university funds.

After calling the hospital for an appointment, the pseudopatient arrived at the admissions office complaining that he had been hearing voices. Asked what the voices said, he replied that they were often unclear, but as far as he could tell they said "empty," "hollow," and "thud." The voices were unfamiliar and were of the same sex as the pseudopatient. The choice of these symptoms was occasioned by their apparent similarity to existential symptoms. Such symptoms are alleged to arise from painful concerns about the perceived meaninglessness of one's life. It is as if the hallucinating person were saying,

"My life is empty and hollow." The choice of these symptoms was also determined by the *absence* of a single report of existential psychoses in the literature.

Beyond alleging the symptoms and falsifying name, vocation, and employment, no further alterations of person, history, or circumstances were made. The significant events of the pseudopatient's life history were presented as they had actually occurred. Relationships with parents and siblings, with spouse and children, with people at work and in school, consistent with the aforementioned exceptions, were described as they were or had been. Frustrations and upsets were described along with joys and satisfactions. These facts are important to remember. If anything, they strongly biased the subsequent results in favor of detecting sanity, since none of their histories or current behaviors were seriously pathological in any way.

Immediately upon admission to the psychiatric ward, the pseudopatient ceased simulating *any* symptoms of abnormality. In some cases, there was a brief period of mild nervousness and anxiety, since none of the pseudopatients really believed that they would be admitted so easily. Indeed, their shared fear was that they would be immediately exposed as frauds and greatly embarrassed. Moreover, many of them had never visited a psychiatric ward; even those who had, nevertheless had some genuine fears about what might happen to them. Their nervousness, then, was quite appropriate to the novelty of the hospital setting, and it abated rapidly.

Apart from that short-lived nervousness, the pseudopatient behaved on the ward as he "normally" behaved. The pseudopatient spoke to patients and staff as he might ordinarily. Because there is uncommonly little to do on a psychiatric ward, he attempted to engage others in conversation. When asked by staff how he was feeling, he indicated that he was fine, that he no longer experienced symptoms. He responded to instructions from attendants, to calls for medication (which was not swallowed), and to dining-hall instructions. Beyond such activities as were available to him on the admissions ward, he spent his time writing down his observations about the ward, its patients, and the staff. Initially these notes were written "secretly," but as it soon became clear that no one much cared, they were subsequently written on standard tablets of paper in such public places as the dayroom. No secret was made of these activities.

The pseudopatient, very much as a true psychiatric patient, entered a hospital with no foreknowledge of when he would be discharged. Each was told that he would have to get out by his own devices, essentially by convincing the staff that he was sane. The psychological stresses associated with hospitalization were considerable, and all but one of the pseudopatients desired to be discharged almost immediately after being admitted. They were, therefore, motivated not only to behave sanely, but to be paragons of cooperation. That their behavior was in no way disruptive is confirmed by nursing reports, which have been obtained on most of the patients. These reports uniformly indicate that the patients were "friendly," "cooperative," and "exhibited no abnormal indications."

The Normal Are Not Detectably Sane

Despite their public "show" of sanity, the pseudopatients were never detected. Admitted, except in one case, with a diagnosis of schizophrenia,[10] each was discharged with a diagnosis of schizophrenia "in remission." The label "in remission" should in no way be dismissed as a formality, for at no time during any hospitalization had any question been raised about any pseudopatient's simulation. Nor are there any indications in the hospital records that the pseudopatient's status was suspect. Rather, the evidence is strong that, once labeled schizophrenic, the pseudopatient was stuck with that label. If the pseudopatient was to be discharged, he must naturally be "in remission"; but he was not sane, nor, in the institution's view, had he ever been sane.

The uniform failure to recognize sanity cannot be attributed to the quality of the hospitals, for, although there were considerable variations among them, several are considered excellent. Nor can it be alleged that there was simply not enough time to observe the pseudopatients. Length of hospitalization ranged from seven to fifty-two days, with an average of nineteen days. The pseudopatients were not, in fact, carefully observed, but this failure clearly speaks more to traditions within psychiatric hospitals than to lack of opportunity.

Finally, it cannot be said that the failure to recognize the pseudopatients' sanity was due to the fact that they were not behaving sanely. While there was clearly some tension present in all of them, their daily visitors could detect no serious behavioral consequences—nor, indeed, could other patients. It was quite common for the patients to "detect" the pseudopatients' sanity. During the first three hospitalizations, when accurate counts were kept, 35 of a total of 118 patients on the admissions ward voiced their suspicions, some vigorously. "You're not crazy. You're a journalist, or a professor [referring to the continual note-taking]. You're checking up on the hospital." While most of the patients were reassured by the pseudopatient's insistence that he had been sick before he came in but was fine now, some continued to believe that the pseudopatient was sane throughout his hospitalization.[11] The fact that the patients often recognized normality when staff did not raises important questions.

Failure to detect sanity during the course of hospitalization may be due to the fact that physicians operate with a strong bias toward what statisticians call the type 2 error.[5] This is to say that physicians are more inclined to call a healthy person sick (a false positive, type 2) than a sick person healthy (a false negative, type 1). The reasons for this are not hard to find: It is clearly more dangerous to misdiagnose illness than health. Better to err on the side of caution, to suspect illness even among the healthy.

But what holds for medicine does not hold equally well for psychiatry. Medical illnesses, while unfortunate, are not commonly pejorative. Psychiatric diagnoses, on the contrary, carry with them personal, legal, and social stigmas.[12] It was therefore important to see whether the tendency toward diagnosing the sane insane could be reversed. The following experiment was arranged at a research and teaching hospital whose staff had heard these findings but doubted that such an error could occur in their hospital. The staff was informed that at some time during the following three months, one or more pseudopatients would attempt to be admitted into the psychiatric hospital. Each staff member was asked to rate each patient who presented himself at admissions or on the ward according to the likelihood that the patient was a pseudopatient. A 10-point scale was used, with a 1 and 2 reflecting high confidence that the patient was a pseudopatient.

Judgments were obtained on 193 patients who were admitted for psychiatric treatment. All staff who had had sustained contact with or primary responsibility for the patient—attendants, nurses, psychiatrists, physicians, and psychologists—were asked to make judgments. Forty-one patients were alleged, with high confidence, to be pseudopatients by at least one member of the staff. Twenty-three were considered suspect by at least one psychiatrist. Nineteen were suspected by one psychiatrist and one other staff member. Actually, no genuine pseudopatient (at least from my group) presented himself during this period.

The experiment is instructive. It indicates that the tendency to designate sane people as insane can be reversed when the stakes (in this case, prestige and diagnostic acumen) are high. But what can be said of the nineteen people who were suspected of being "sane" by one psychiatrist and another staff member? Were these people truly "sane," or was it rather the case that in the course of avoiding the type 2 error the staff tended to make more errors of the first sort—calling the crazy "sane"? There is no way of knowing. But one thing is certain: Any diagnostic process that lends itself so readily to massive errors of this sort cannot be a very reliable one.

The Stickiness of Psychodiagnostic Labels

Beyond the tendency to call the healthy sick—a tendency that accounts better for diagnostic behavior on admission than it does for such behavior after a lengthy period of exposure—the data speak to the massive role of labeling in psychiatric assessment. Having once been labeled schizophrenic, there is nothing the pseudopatient can do to overcome the tag. The tag profoundly colors others' perceptions of him and his behavior.

From one viewpoint, these data are hardly surprising, for it has long been known that elements are given meaning by the context in which they occur. Gestalt psychology made this point vigorously, and Asch[13] demonstrated that there are "central" personality traits (such as "warm" versus "cold") which are so powerful that they markedly color the meaning of other information in forming an impression of a given personality.[14] "Insane," "schizophrenic," "manic-depressive," and "crazy" are probably among the most powerful of such central traits. Once a person is designated abnormal, all of his other behaviors and characteristics are colored by that label. Indeed, that label is so powerful that many of the pseudopatients' normal behaviors were overlooked entirely or profoundly misinterpreted. Some examples may clarify this issue.

Earlier I indicated that there were no changes in the pseudopatient's personal history and current status behond those of name, employment, and, where necessary, vocation. Otherwise, a veridical description of personal history and circumstances was offered. Those circumstances were not psychotic. How were they made consonant with the diagnosis of psychosis? Or were those diagnoses modified in such a way as to bring them into accord with the circumstances of the pseudopatient's life, as described by him?

As far as I can determine, diagnoses were in no way affected by the relative health of the circumstances of a pseudopatient's life. Rather, the reverse occurred: The perception of his circumstances was shaped entirely by the diagnosis. A clear example of such translation is found in the case of a pseudopatient who had had a close relationship with his mother but was rather remote from his father during his early childhood. During adolescence and beyond, however, his father became a close friend, while his relationship with his mother cooled. His present relationship with his wife was characteristically close and warm. Apart from occasional angry exchanges, friction was minimal. The children had rarely been spanked. Surely there is nothing especially pathological about such a history. Indeed, many readers may see a similar pattern in their own experiences, with no markedly deleterious consequences. Observe, however, how such a history was translated in the psychopathological context, this from the case summary prepared after the patient was discharged.

> This white 39-year-old male . . . manifests a long history of considerable ambivalence in close relationships, which begins in early childhood. A warm relationship with his mother cools during adolescence. A distant relationship to his father is described as becoming very intense. Affective stability is absent. His attempts to control emotionality with his wife and children are punctuated by angry outbursts and, in the case of the children, spankings. And while he says that he has several good friends, one senses considerable ambivalence embedded in those relationships also. . . .

The facts of the case were unintentionally distorted by the staff to achieve consistency with a popular theory of the dynamics of schizophrenic reaction.[15] Nothing of an ambivalent nature had been described in relations with parents, spouse, or friends. To the extent that ambivalence could be inferred, it was proably not greater than is found in all human relationships. It is true the pseudopatient's relationships with his parents changed over time, but in the ordinary context that would hardly be remarkable—indeed, it might very well be expected. Clearly, the meaning ascribed to his verbalizations (that is, ambivalence, affective instability) was determined by the diagnosis: schizophrenia.

An entirely different meaning would have been ascribed if it were known that the man was "normal."

All pseudopatients took extensive notes publicly. Under ordinary circumstances, such behavior would have raised questions in the minds of observers, as, in fact, it did among patients. Indeed, it seemed so certain that the notes would elicit suspicion that elaborate precautions were taken to remove them from the ward each day. But the precautions proved needless. The closest any staff member came to questioning these notes occurred when one pseudopatient asked his physician what kind of medication he was receiving and began to write down the response. "You needn't write it," he was told gently. "If you have trouble remembering, just ask me again."

If no questions were asked of the pseudopatients, how was their writing interpreted? Nursing records for three patients indicate that the writing was seen as an aspect of their pathological behavior. "Patient engages in writing behavior" was the daily nursing comment on one of the pseudopatients who was never questioned about his writing. Given that the patient is in the hospital, he must be psychologically disturbed. And given that he is disturbed, continuous writing must be a behavioral manifestation of that disturbance, perhaps a subset of the compulsive behaviors that are sometimes correlated with schizophrenia.

One tacit characteristic of psychiatric diagnosis is that it locates the sources of aberration within the individual and only rarely within the complex of stimuli that surrounds him. Consequently, behaviors that are stimulated by the environment are commonly misattributed to the patient's disorder. For example, one kindly nurse found a pseudopatient pacing the long hospital corridors." Nervous, Mr. X?" she asked. "No, bored," he said.

The notes kept by pseudopatients are full of patient behaviors that were misinterpreted by well-intentioned staff. Often enough, a patient would go "berserk" because he had, wittingly or unwittingly, been mistreated by, say, an attendant. A nurse coming upon the scene would rarely inquire even cursorily into the environmental stimuli of the patient's behavior. Rather, she assumed that his upset derived from his pathology, not from his present interactions with other staff members. Occasionally, the staff might assume that the patient's family (especially when they had recently visited) or other patients had stimulated the outburst. But never were the staff found to assume that one of themselves or the structure of the hospital had anything to do with a patient's behavior. One psychiatrist pointed to a group of patients who were sitting outside the cafeteria entrance half an hour before lunchtime. To a group of young residents, he indicated that such behavior was characteristic of the oral-acquisitive nature of the syndrome. It seemed not to occur to him that there were very few things to anticipate in the psychiatric hospital besides eating.

A psychiatric label has a life and an influence of its own. Once the impression has been formed that the patient is schizophrenic, the expectation is that he will continue to be schizophrenic. When a sufficient amount of time has passed, during which the patient has done nothing bizarre, he is considered to be in remission and available for discharge. But the label endures beyond discharge, with the unconfirmed expectation that he will behave as a schizophrenic again. Such labels, conferred by mental health professionals, are as influential on the patient as they are on his relatives and friends, and it should not surprise anyone that the diagnosis acts on all of them as a self-fulfilling prophecy. Eventually, the patient himself accepts the diagnosis, with all of its surplus meanings and expectations, and behaves accordingly.[5]

The inferences to be made from these matters are quite simple. Much as Zigler and Phillips have demonstrated that there is enormous overlap in the symptoms presented by patients who have been variously diagnosed,[16] so there is enormous overlap in the behaviors of the sane and the insane. The sane are not "sane" all of the time. We lose our tempers "for no good reason." We are occasionally depressed or anxious, again for no good reason. And we may find it difficult to get along with one or another person—again for no reason that we can specify. Similarly, the insane are not always insane. Indeed, it was the impression of the pseudopatients while living with them that they were sane for long periods of time—that the bizarre behaviors upon which their diagnoses were allegedly predicated constituted only a small fraction of their total behavior. If it makes no sense to label ourselves permanently depressed on the basis of an occasional depression, then it takes better evidence than is presently available to label all patients insane or schizophrenic on the basis of bizarre behaviors or cognitions. It seems more useful, as Mischel[17] has pointed out, to limit our discussions to *behaviors*, the stimuli that provoke them, and their correlates.

It is not known why powerful impressions of personality traits, such as "crazy" or "insane," arise. Conceivably, when the origins of and stimuli that give rise to a behavior are remote or unknown, or when the behavior strikes us as immutable, trait labels regarding the *behavior* arise. When, on the other hand, the origins and stimuli are known and available, discourse is limited to the behavior itself. Thus, I may hallucinate because I am sleeping, or I may hallucinate because I have ingested a peculiar drug. These are termed sleep-induced hallucinations, or dreams, and drug-induced hallucinations, respectively. But when the stimuli to my hallucinations are unknown, that is called craziness, or schizophrenia—as if that inference were somehow as illuminating as the others. . . .

The Consequences of Labeling and Depersonalization

Whenever the ratio of what is known to what needs to be known approaches zero, we tend to invent "knowledge" and assume that we understand more than we actually do. We seem unable to acknowledge that we simply don't know. The needs for diagnosis and remediation of behavioral and emotional problems are enormous. But rather than acknowledge that we are just embarking on understanding, we continue to label patients "schizophrenic," "manic-depressive," and "insane," as if in those words we had captured the essence of understanding. The facts of the matter are that we have known for a long time that diagnoses are often not useful or reliable, but we have nevertheless continued to use them. We now know that we cannot distinguish insanity from sanity. It is depressing to consider how that information will be used.

Not merely depressing, but frightening. How many people, one wonders, are sane but not recognized as such in our psychiatric institutions? How many have been needlessly stripped of their privileges of citizenship, from the right to vote and drive to that of handling their own accounts? How many have feigned insanity in order to avoid the criminal consequences of their behavior, and, conversely, how many would rather stand trial than live interminably in a psychiatric hospital—but are wrongly thought to be mentally ill? How many have been stigmatized by well-intentioned, but nevertheless erroneous, diagnoses? On the last point, recall again that a "type 2 error" in psychiatric diagnosis does not have the same consequences it does in medical diagnosis. A diagnosis of cancer that has been found to be in error is cause for celebration. But psychiatric diagnoses are rarely found to be in error. The label sticks, a mark of inadequacy forever.

Notes

1. P. Ash, *J. Abnorm. Soc. Psychol. 44,* 272 (1949); A. T. Beck, *Amer. J. Psychiat. 119,* 210 (1962); A. T. Boisen, *Psychiatry 2,* 233 (1938); N. Kreitman, *J. Ment. Sci. 107,* 876 (1961); N. Kreitman, P. Sainsbury, J. Morrisey, J. Towers, J. Scrivener, *ibid.,* p. 887; H. O. Schmitt and C. P. Fonda, *J. Abnorm. Soc. Psychol. 52, 262* (1956); W. Seeman, *J. Nerv. Ment. Dis. 118,* 541 (1953). For an analysis of these artifacts and summaries of the disputes, see J. Zubin, *Annu. Rev. Psychol. 18,* 373 (1967); L. Phillips and J. G. Draguns, *ibid. 22,* 447 (1971).

2. R. Benedict. *J. Gen. Psychol. 10,* 59 (1934).

3. See in this regard H. Becker, *Outsiders: Studies in the Sociology of Deviance* (New York: Free Press, 1963); B. M. Braginsky, D. D. Braginsky, K. Ring, *Methods of Madness: The Mental Hospital as a Last Resort* (New York: Holt, Rinehart & Winston, 1969); G. M. Crocetti and P. V. Lemkau, *Amer. Sociol. Rev. 30,* 577 (1965); E. Goffman, *Behavior in Public Places* (New York: Free Press, 1964); R. D. Laing, *The Divided Self: A Study of Sanity and Madness* (Chicago: Quadrangle, 1960); D. L. Phillips, *Amer. Sociol. Rev. 28,* 963 (1963); T. R. Sarbin, *Psychol. Today 6,* 18 (1972); E. Schur, *Amer J. Sociol. 75,* 309 (1969); T. Szasz, *Law, Liberty and Psychiatry* (New York: Macmillan, 1963); *The Myth of Mental Illness: Foundations of a Theory of Mental Illness* (New York: Hoeber Harper, 1963). For a critique of some of these views, see W. R. Gove, *Amer. Sociol. Rev. 35,* 873 (1970).

4. E. Goffman. *Asylums* (Garden City, NY: Doubleday, 1961).

5. T. J. Scheff, *Being Mentally Ill: A Sociological Theory* (Chicago: Aldine, 1966).

6. Data from a ninth pseudopatient are not incorporated in this report because, although his sanity went undetected, he falsified aspects of his personal history, including his marital status and parental relationships. His experimental behaviors therefore were not identical to those of the other pseudopatients.

7. A. Barry, *Bellevue Is a State of Mind* (New York: Harcourt Brace Jovanovich, 1971); I. Belknap, *Human Problems of a State Mental Hospital* (New York: McGraw-Hill, 1956); W. Caudill, F. C. Redlich, H. R. Gilmore, E. B. Brody, *Amer. J. Orthopsychiat. 22*, 314 (1952); A. R. Goldman, R. H. Bohr, T. A. Steinberg, *Prof. Psychol. 1*, 427 (1970); unauthored, *Roche Report 1* (No. 13), 8 (1971).

8. Beyond the personal difficulties that the pseudopatient is likely to experience in the hospital, there are legal and social ones that, combined, require considerable attention before entry. For example, once admitted to a psychiatric institution, it is difficult, if not impossible, to be discharged on short notice, state law to the contrary notwithstanding. I was not sensitive to these difficulties at the outset of the project, nor to the personal and situational emergencies that can arise, but later a writ of habeas corpus was prepared for each of the entering pseudopatients and an attorney was kept "on call" during every hospitalization. I am grateful to John Kaplan and Robert Bartels for legal advice and assistance in these matters.

9. However distasteful such concealment is, it was a necessary first step to examining these questions. Without concealment, there would have been no way to know how valid these experiences were; nor was there any way of knowing whether whatever detections occurred were a tribute to the diagnostic acumen of the staff or to the hospital's rumor network. Obviously, since my concerns are general ones that cut across individual hospitals and staffs, I have respected their anonymity and have eliminated clues that might lead to their identification.

10. Interestingly, of the twelve admissions, eleven were diagnosed as schizophrenic and one, with the identical symptomatology, as manic-depressive psychosis. This diagnosis has a more favorable prognosis, and it was given by the only private hospital in our sample. On the relations between social class and psychiatric diagnosis, see A. B. Hollingshead and F. C. Redlich, *Social Class and Mental Illness: A Community Study* (New York: Wiley, 1958).

11. It is possible, of course, that patients have quite broad latitudes in diagnosis and therefore are inclined to call many people sane, even those whose behavior is patently aberrant. However, although we have no hard data on this matter, it was our distinct impression that this was not the case. In many instances, patients not only singled us out for attention, but came to imitate our behaviors and styles.

12. J. Cumming and E. Cumming, *Community Ment. Health 1*, 135 (1965); A. Farina and K. Ring. *J. Abnorm. Psychol. 70*, 47 (1965); H. E. Freeman and O. G. Simmons, *The Mental Patient Comes Home* (New York: Wiley, 1963); W. J. Johannsen, *Mental Hygiene 53*, 218 (1969); A. S. Linsky, *Soc. Psychiat. 5*, 166 (1970).

13. S. E. Asch, *J. Abnorm. Soc. Psychol. 41*, 258 (1946); *Social Psychology* (New York: Prentice-Hall, 1952).

14. See also, I. N. Mensh and J. Wishner, *J. Personality 16*, 188 (1947); J. Wishner, *Psychol. Rev. 67*, 96 (1960); J. S. Bruner and R. Tagiuri, in *Handbook of Social Psychology*, G. Lindzey, ed. (Cambridge, MA: Addison-Wesley, 1954), vol. 2, pp. 634–54; J. S. Bruner, D. Shapiro, R. Tagiuri, in *Person Perception and Interpersonal Behavior*, R. Tagiuri and L. Petrullo, eds. (Stanford, CA: Stanford Univ. Press, 1958), pp. 277–88.

15. For an example of a similar self-fulfilling prophecy, in this instance dealing with the "central" trait of intelligence, see R. Rosenthal and L. Jacobson, *Pygmalion in the Classroom* (New York: Holt, Rinehart & Winston, 1968).

16. E. Zigler and L. Phillips, *J. Abnorm. Soc. Psychol.* 63, 69 (1961). See also R. K. Freudenberg and J. P. Robertson, *A.M.A. Arch. Neurol. Psychiatr.* 76, 14 (1956).

17. W. Mischel, *Personality and Assessment* (New York: Wiley, 1968).

VII Social Inequality

IN ALL KNOWN PAST SOCIETIES and every contemporary society, the members are characterized by inequalities of some sort. Some people are stronger, learn more quickly, are swifter, shoot weapons more accurately, or have more of *whatever is considered important in that particular society*. Other inequalities, whatever form they take, may appear more contrived—such as distinctions of social rank based on wealth. But, whether based on biological characteristics, social skills, or money, no system of dividing people into different groups is inevitable. Rather, each is arbitrary. Yet all societies rank their members, and whatever arbitrary criteria they use appear quite reasonable to them.

The primary social division in small, preliterate groups is drawn along the line of gender. Sorted into highly distinctive groupings, men and women in these societies engage in separate activities—ones deemed "appropriate" for each sex. Indeed, in these small groups gender usually represents a cleavage that cuts across most of social life. These peoples also draw finer distinctions along much more individualistic lines of personality, skills, and reputation. Of all human groups, hunting and gathering societies—where most activities revolve around subsistence and there is little or no material surplus—appear to have the least stratification. These societies apparently also have the least *gender typing*, or division of activities by sex.

Perhaps the primary significance of a group's hierarchies and statuses—no matter what they may be in a particular society—is that they surround the individual with *boundaries*. Setting limits and circumscribing one's possibilities in life, these social divisions establish the framework of socialization. They launch the individual onto the social scene by presenting to him or her an already existing picture of what he or she ought to expect from life.

None of us escapes this fundamental fact of social life, which sociologists variously call *social inequality* and *social stratification.* No matter into which society we are born, then, all of us inherit some system of social stratification, whose boundaries and limits envelop almost all aspects of our lives—our relationships with others, our behaviors, beliefs, and attitudes, our goals and aspirations, even our perception of the social world and of the self.

In analyzing the social inequality of contemporary society, sociologists look at very large groupings of people. They call these groups *social classes,* which are determined by people's rankings on income, education, and occupation. The more income and education one has and the higher the prestige accorded one's work, the higher one's social class. Conversely, the lower one's income, education, and prestige of occupation, the lower one's social class.

On the basis of these three criteria, one can divide Americans into three principle social classes: upper, middle, and lower. The *upper* are the very rich (a million dollars wouldn't even begin to buy your way in); the *middle*—primarily professionals, managers, executives, and other business people—is heavily rewarded with the material goods our society has to offer; and the *lower,* to understate the matter, receives the least.

Some sociologists add an upper and a lower to each of these divisions and say there are *six* social classes in the United States: an upper-upper and lower-upper, an upper-middle and lower-middle, and an upper-lower and lower-lower.

Membership in the *upper-upper* class is the most exclusive of all, accorded not only on the basis of huge wealth but also according to how long that money has been in the family. The longer, the better. Somehow or other, it is difficult to make many millions of dollars while remaining scrupulously honest in business dealings. It appears that most people who have entered the monied classes have found it necessary to cut moral corners, at least here and there. This "taint" to the money disappears with time, however, and the later generations of Vanderbilts, Rockefellers, Mellons, DuPonts, Chryslers, Kennedys, Morgans, Nashes, and so on are considered to have "clean" money simply by virtue of the passage of time. They can be philanthropic as well as rich. They have attended the best private schools and universities, the male heirs probably have entered law, and they protect their vast fortunes and economic empires with far-flung political connections and contributions.

And the *lower-upper* class? These people have money, but it is new, and therefore suspect. They lack "breeding" and proper social background. They have not gone to the "right" schools and cannot be depended on for adequate in-group loyalty. Unable themselves to make the leap into the upper-upper class, their hope for social supremacy lies in their children: if their children go to the right schools *and* marry into the upper-upper class, what has been denied the parents will be granted the children.

The *upper-middle* class consists primarily of people who have entered the professions or higher levels of management. They are doctors, professors, lawyers, dentists, pharmacists, and clergy. They are bank presidents and other successful business people. Their education is high, their income adequate for most of their needs.

The *lower-middle* class consists largely of lower-level managers, white-collar workers in the service industries, and the more highly paid and skilled blue-collar workers. Their education and income, as well as the prestige of their work, are correspondingly lower than those of their upper-middle-class counterparts.

The *upper-lower* class is also known as the working class. (Americans find this term much more agreeable than the term "lower," as the latter brings neg-ative connotations to mind, while "working" elicits more positive images.) This class consists primarily of blue-collar workers who work regularly, not season-ally, at their jobs. Their education is limited, and little prestige is attached to what they do. With the changes in wages and life styles of recent years, how-ever, it often is difficult to distinguish this class from the lower-middle class.

At the bottom of the ladder of social inequality is the *lower-lower* class. This is the social class that gets the worst of everything society has to offer. Its members have the least education and the least income, and often their work is negatively valued, since, as with share-cropping and other menial labor, it usually requires few skills, is "dirty," and is the type of work that few people prefer. The main difference between the lower-lower and the upper-lower classes is that the upper-lower class works the year round while the lower-lower class doesn't. Members of the lower-lower class are likely to be drawing welfare, and generally are considered the ne'er-do-wells of society.

To illustrate social class membership in U.S. society, let's look at the auto-motive industry. The Ford family, for example, owns and controls an interna-tional manufacturing and financial empire whose net worth is truly staggering. Their vast accumulation of wealth, not unlike their accrued power, is now sev-eral generations old. Their children attend elite schools, know how to spend money in the "right" way, and can be trusted to make their family and class in-terests paramount in life. They are without question members of the upper-upper class.

Next in line come top Ford executives. Although they may have an in-come of several hundred thousand dollars a year (and some, with stock options and bonuses, earn several million dollars annually), they are new to wealth and power. Consequently, they remain on the rung below, and are considered members of the lower-upper class.

A husband and wife who own a successful Ford agency are members of the upper-middle class. Their income clearly sets them apart from the major-ity of Americans, and they have an enviable reputation in the community. More than likely they also exert greater-than-average influence in community affairs, but find their capacity to wield power highly limited.

The sales staff, as well as those who work in the office, are members of the lower-middle class. Their income is less, their education is likely to be less, and people assign less prestige to their work than to that of the owners of the agency.

Mechanics who repair customers' cars would ordinarily be considered members of the upper-lower class. High union wages, however, have blurred this distinction, and they might more properly be classified as members of the lower-middle class. People who "detail" used cars (making them appear newer by washing and polishing them, painting their tires and floor mats, and so on) earn only minimum wage and are members of the upper-lower class.

Window washers and janitors who are hired to clean the agency only during the busy season and then are laid off are members of the lower-lower class. (If they are year-round employees of the agency, they are members of the upper-lower class.) Their income is the least, as is their education, while the prestige accorded their work is also minimal.

It is significant to note that children are automatically assigned the social class of their parents. It is for this reason that sociologists say we are born into a social class. Sociologists call this *ascribed* membership, as compared with membership one earns on one's own, called *achieved* membership. If a child of a person who "details" used cars goes on to college, works as a salesperson in the agency part-time and during vacations, and then eventually buys the agency, he or she has upgraded his or her social class. Because of this *upward social mobility,* the new class membership is said to be achieved membership. Conversely, if a child of the agency's owner becomes an alcoholic, fails to get through college, and takes a lower-status job, he or she experiences *downward social mobility.* The resulting change in social class membership is also achieved membership. ("Achieved" does not equal "achievement.")

You should note that this division into six social classes is not the only way that sociologists look at our social class system. In fact, sociologists have arrived at no single, standard, agreed-upon overview of the U.S. class system. Like others, this outline of classes is both arbitrary and useful, but does not do justice to the nuances and complexities of our class system.

One view within sociology (called *conflict* or *Marxist*) holds that to understand social inequality we need focus only on income. What is the *source* of a person's income? Know that, and you know the person's social class. There are those with money and those without money. The monied class owns the means of production—the factories and machinery and buildings—and lives off their investments. The other class exchanges its labor to produce more money for the wealthy owners. In short, the monied class (the *capitalists,* or owners) is in the controlling sector of society, while those who sell their labor (the *workers*) are controlled by them. With society divided into the haves and the have-nots, insist conflict theorists, it is misleading to pay attention to the fine distinctions among those with or without money.

Be that as it may (and this debate continues among sociologists), society certainly is stratified. And the significance of social inequality is that it determines people's *life chances,* the probabilities as to the fate one may expect in life. It is obvious that not everyone has the same chances in life, and the single most significant factor in determining a person's life chances in our society is money. Simply put, if you have money, you can do a lot of things you can't do if you do not have it. And the more money you have, the more control over life you have, and the more likely you are to find life pleasant.

Beyond this obvious point, however, lies a connection between social inequality and life chances that is not so easily evident. It involves such things as one's chances of dying during infancy; being killed by accident, fire, or homicide; becoming a drug addict; getting arrested; ending up in prison; dropping out of school; getting divorced; becoming disabled; or, upon retirement, trying to live only on Social Security. All vary inversely with social class; that is, the lower a person's social class, the higher the chances that these things will happen to him or her. Conversely, the higher a person's social class, the smaller the risk that these events pose.

As we examine social inequality in this Part, we consider some of its major dimensions and emphasize its severe and lifelong effects. Our opening article on physical appearance may seem to hit only a light note, but Sidney Katz points to implications that, ordinarily lying beyond our perception, have deep consequences for our lives. From here, we turn to poverty. After first considering Herbert Gans's claim that poverty is so functional for society it can never be eliminated, we turn to Jonathan Kozol's analysis of how U.S. schools perpetuate poverty, and then to Elliot Liebow's analysis of lower-lower-class men who are locked into poverty. Our attention is then turned to the other end of the social class spectrum with William Domhoff's analysis of how the U.S. ruling class maintains its power and wealth. The closure of this Part, an article by Patricia Martin and Robert Hummer on fraternities and rape, at first blush may seem strikingly out of place. Its implications go far beyond the specific setting and events, however, for its focus is gender inequality, the broadest and largest-scale social inequality of all.

29 The Importance of Being Beautiful

SIDNEY KATZ

A chief characteristic of all societies is *social stratification,* a term that refers to a group's system of ranking. All of us find ourselves ranked according to a variety of dimensions, from our parents' social class when we are young to our own achievements, or lack thereof, when we grow older. Where we go to high school, if we attend college, and if so, where—make a difference in people's eyes. People rank us by our speech, by our walk, and even by things we own or display, from the car we drive to the clothing we wear.

Central to much of the ranking done on a face-to-face level is attractiveness. Because of appearance, we judge others—and are judged by them. This type of ranking is ordinarily thought to have little consequence beyond such temporary, individual matters as whether or not we can get a date this weekend—personally significant and intense, yes, but probably of little long-term consequence. Katz, however, points to a long list of significant consequences that rankings based on attractiveness have on our lives.

UNLIKE MANY PEOPLE, I was neither shocked nor surprised when the national Israeli TV network fired a competent female broadcaster because she was not beautiful. I received the news with aplomb because I had just finished extensive research into "person perception," an esoteric branch of psychology that examines the many ways in which physical attractiveness—or the lack of it—affects all aspects of your life.

Unless you're a 10—or close to it—most of you will respond to my findings with at least some feelings of frustration or perhaps disbelief. In a nutshell, you can't overestimate the importance of being beautiful. If you're beautiful, without effort you attract hordes of friends and lovers. You are given higher school grades than your smarter—but less appealing—classmates. You compete successfully for jobs against men or women who are better qualified but less alluring. Promotions and pay raises come your way more easily. You are able to go into a bank or store and cash a cheque with far less hassle than a plain Jane or John. And these are only a few of the many advantages enjoyed by those with a ravishing face and body.

"We were surprised to find that beauty had such powerful effects," confessed Karen Dion, a University of Toronto social psychologist who does person perception research. "Our findings also go against the cultural grain.

People like to think that success depends on talent, intelligence, and hard work." But the scientific evidence is undeniable.

In large part, the beautiful person can attribute his or her idyllic life to a puzzling phenomenon that social scientists have dubbed the "halo effect." It defies human reason, but if you resemble Jane Fonda or Paul Newman it's assumed that you're more generous, trustworthy, sociable, modest, sensitive, interesting, and sexually responsive than the rest of us. Conversely, if you're somewhat physically unattractive, because of the "horns effect" you're stigmatized as being mean, sneaky, dishonest, antisocial, and a poor sport to boot.

The existence of the halo/horns effect has been established by several studies. One, by Dion, looked at perceptions of misbehavior in children.

Dion provided 243 female university students with identical detailed accounts of the misbehavior of a seven-year-old school child. She described how the youngster had pelted a sleeping dog with sharp stones until its leg bled. As the animal limped away, yelping in pain, the child continued the barrage of stones. The 243 women were asked to assess the seriousness of the child's offence and to give their impression of the child's normal behavior. Clipped to half of the reports were photos of seven-year-old boys or girls who had been rated "high" in physical attractiveness; the other half contained photos of youngsters of "low" attractiveness. "We found," said Dion, "that the opinions of the adults were markedly influenced by the appearance of the children."

One evaluator described the stone thrower, who in her report happened to be an angelic-looking little girl, in these glowing terms: "She appears to be a perfectly charming little girl, well mannered and basically unselfish. She plays well with everyone, but, like everyone else, a bad day may occur. . . . Her cruelty need not be taken too seriously." For the same offence, a homely girl evoked this comment from another evaluator: "I think this child would be quite bratty and would be a problem to teachers. She'd probably try to pick a fight with other children. . . . She would be a brat at home. All in all, she would be a real problem." The tendency throughout the 243 adult responses was to judge beautiful children as ordinarily well behaved and unlikely to engage in wanton cruelty in the future; the unbeautiful were viewed as being chronically antisocial, untrustworthy, and likely to commit similar transgressions again.

Dion found the implications of this study mind boggling. Every kid who was homely would be highly vulnerable in the classroom and elsewhere. Prejudged by his or her appearance, a vicious cycle is set in motion. The teacher views the child as having negative traits and treats him accordingly; the child responds by conforming to the teacher's expectations. Dion thinks that adults must realize to what extent their opinion of a child can be biased by the child's appearance: "When there's a question of who started a classroom disturbance, who broke the vase—adults are more likely to identify the unattractive child as the culprit."

The same standards apply in judging adults. The beautiful are assumed innocent. John Jurens, a colorful private investigator, was once consulted by a small Toronto firm which employed 40 people. Ten thousand dollars' worth of merchandise had disappeared, and it was definitely an inside job. After an intensive investigation, which included the use of a lie detector, Jurens was certain he had caught the thief. She was 24 years old and gorgeous—a lithe princess with high cheekbones, green eyes and shining, long black hair. The employer dismissed Jurens's proof with the comment, "You've made a mistake. It just can't be her." Jurens commented sadly, "A lot of people refuse to believe that beautiful can be bad."

David Humphrey, a prominent Ontario criminal lawyer, observed, "If a beautiful woman is on trial, you practically have to show the judge and jury a movie of her committing the crime in order to get a conviction." Another experienced lawyer, Aubrey Golden, has found it difficult defending a man charged with assault or wife-beating if he's a brutish-looking hulk. By the same token, a rape victim who happens to be stocky is a less credible witness than a slender, good-looking woman.

The halo and horns effect often plays an important role in sentencing by courts. After spending 17 days observing cases heard in an Ontario traffic court, Joan Finegan, a graduate psychology student at the University of Western Ontario, concluded that pleasant and neat-looking defendants were fined an average of $6.31 less than those who were "messy." The same pro-beauty bias was found by a British investigator in a series of simulated court cases. Physically appealing defendants were given prison terms almost three years less than those meted out to unattractive ones for precisely the same offence.

Beauty—or the lack of it—influences a person's entire life. The halo and horns effect comes into play beginning with birth and continues throughout the various stages of life.

Early Life

The flawless, seraphlike infant is irresistible. It receives an inordinate amount of attention and love. The child is constantly picked up, cuddled, and cooed to. In contrast, the unattractive baby may suffer neglect and rejection, which can have enduring effects on its personality and mental health. "When a child is unappealing because he's been born with a visible physical defect," said Dr. Ian Munro, a specialist in reconstructive facial surgery at the Hospital for Sick Children in Toronto, "parents are sometimes reluctant to touch, fondle, or give their child the normal displays of affection."

Later, when the baby attends nursery school, the halo and horns effect is even more potent. "Nursery school teachers," observed Dr. Ellen Berscheid, a psychologist who has conducted extensive person perception research at the University of Minnesota, "often insist that all children are beautiful, yet they can, when they're asked, rank their pupils by appearance." Even more note-worthy, the children themselves, despite their tender years, "behave in accordance with the adult ranking."

One nursery school study by Berscheid and Dion revealed that unattractive kids were not as well liked by their peers as the attractive ones. They were accused of "fighting a lot," "hitting other students," and "yelling at the teacher." Furthermore, other students labeled them "fraidy cats." They needed help to complete their work. When asked to name the person in class who scared them the most, the children usually nominated an unattractive classmate.

At School

It's sad but true that grade school teachers tend to judge their pupils largely on the basis of their looks. Consider the provocative study conducted by two American psychologists, Elaine Walster and Margaret Clifford: Four hundred grade five teachers were asked to examine identical report cards. They itemized the student's grades in various subjects, his or her work habits, attendance record, and attitudes. There was only one difference. Half of the report cards had the photo of an attractive boy or girl attached to the upper right-hand corner; half, the photo of a less attractive child. The teachers were then asked a number of specific questions based on the information provided. They concluded that the beautiful children had higher IQs, were more likely to go to college, and had parents who were more interested in education.

Parents should be concerned about these results. Because of an inflated opinion of the beautiful child, the teacher can be expected to give him more than his share of friendliness, encouragement, and time. And, consequently, the beautiful one will blossom—at the expense of his not-so-beautiful classmates.

The College Years

The beautiful person reaps an even richer harvest when he or she attends college. In one test, 60 male undergraduates were handed a 700-word essay on the effects of televised violence on the behavior of children. The authors, they were told, were freshmen coeds, and the undergrads were asked to assign a grade to the essay and to give their impression of the writer's abilities. Half of the students received an essay that was excellently written; the other half were given an essay that was a mishmash of clichés, grammatical errors, and sloppy writing. One-third of the papers had attached to them the photo of the alleged author—a young woman of striking beauty. Another third contained the likeness of an unappealing woman, while the remaining third were submitted without a photograph. When the evaluations were tallied, it was found that the beautiful person was consistently awarded a higher mark for her essay than the unattractive one. The essays without photos attached were usually given average marks. The investigators, David Landy and Harold Sigall, psychologists at the University of Rochester at the time of the study, concluded, "If you are ugly, you are not discriminated against as long as your performance is impressive. However, should performance be below par, attractiveness matters: you may be able to get away with inferior work if you are beautiful."

Not surprisingly, college students also preferred beauty when grading the desirability of a date. In interviews 376 young men and 376 young women assured investigators that it was "vulgar" to judge people by their appearance. They then proceeded to list the human qualities that they really valued; intelligence, friendliness, sincerity, "soul," and warmth. Yet when these same people were interviewed after going out on a blind date that was arranged by a computer, it became apparent that they were blind to everything *but* the physical appearance of their partners. The more beautiful the partner, the more he or she was liked. Features such as exceptional personality, high intelligence, and shared interests hardly seemed to count at all. "We were surprised to find that a *man's* physical attractiveness was the largest determinant of how well he was liked by a woman," observed Elaine Walster, one of the psychologists who conducted the study.

In addition to giving top marks to their beautiful classmates as dates, college students also predict glittering futures for them. In one study by Dion, Berscheid, and Walster, the opinion was almost unanimous that the physically appealing would contract better marriages, make better husbands and wives, and lead more fulfilling social and career lives. This finding is all the more impressive, Dion explained, because "the unattractive people in our sample were by no means at the extremes of unattractiveness—they possessed only a minor flaw to their beauty."

Marriage

It's logical that a beautiful person's marriage should be idyllic. An alluring woman, say, might have a busier social life than her less appealing sisters and therefore have a better chance of meeting a compatible mate. She's also apt to be more sexually responsive. Good-looking women fall in love more often and have more sexual experiences than others. "And," observed Berscheid, "since in almost all areas of human endeavor practice makes perfect, it may well be that beautiful women are indeed sexually warmer simply because of experience."

One thing is certain: the power of beauty is such that the status of even a homely man skyrockets if he marries a dazzling woman. People discover positive qualities in him they never before noticed: self-confidence, likability, friendliness. Sigall and Landy refer to this phenomenon as "a generalized halo effect" and offer this explanation: "People viewing individuals who are romantically linked to an attractive person try to make sense of the association. In effect, they may ask themselves, 'Why is *she,* desirable as she appears to be, involved with him?' The observers may answer the question by attributing favorable qualities to him."

Careers

If you're a good-looking male over six feet tall, don't worry about succeeding at your career.

A study of university graduates by the *Wall Street Journal* revealed that well proportioned wage earners who were six-foot-two or taller earned 12 percent more than men under six feet. "For some reason," explained Ronald Burke, a York University psychologist and industrial consultant, "tall men are assumed to be dynamic, decisive, and powerful. In other words, born leaders." A Toronto consultant for Drake Personnel, one of the largest employment agencies in Canada, recalled trying to find a sales manager for an industrial firm. He sent four highly qualified candidates, only to have them all turned down. "The fifth guy I sent over was different," said the consultant. "He stood six-foot-four. He was promptly hired."

The well favored woman also has a distinct edge when it comes to getting a job she's after. "We send out three prospects to be interviewed, and it's almost always the most glamorous one that's hired," said Edith Geddes of the Personnel Centre, a Toronto agency that specializes in female placements. "We sometimes feel bad because the best qualified person is not chosen." Dr. Pam Ennis, a consultant to several large corporations, observed, "Look at the photos announcing promotions in the *Globe and Mail* business section. It's no accident that so many of the women happen to be attractive and sexy-looking." Ennis, an elegant woman herself, attributes at least part of her career success to good looks. Her photograph appears on the brochures she mails out to companies soliciting new clients. "About eight out of 10 company presidents give me an appointment," she said. "I'm sure that many of them are curious to see me in person. Beauty makes it easier to establish rapport."

In an experiment designed to test the effect of stating or not stating an intent to change the listener's point of view, it was discovered that an attractive woman was more persuasive than an unattractive woman. In one session, an attractive woman disguised her good looks. Her dress was ill-fitting, she wore no makeup on her oily skin, her hair was a tattered mess, and the trace of a moustache was etched on her upper lip. She attempted to persuade a classroom of men that a general education was superior to a specialized one. Her arguments, in large part, failed to change their points of view.

The same woman then made herself as alluring as possible. She wore chic, tight-fitting clothes and tasteful makeup, and sported a fashionable coiffeur. Using the identical argument, she had little difficulty in persuading a second group of men to share her enthusiasm for a general education.

Every ugly duckling who has transformed herself into a Cinderella knows about the persuasive powers of beauty. Eleanor Fulcher, who runs a model and charm school in Toronto, says, "A woman can make things happen by improving her appearance. I've seen it hundreds of times."

Old Age

An elderly person's attractiveness influences the way in which he or she is treated in nursing homes and hospitals. Doctors and nurses give better care to the beautiful ones.

Lena Nordholm, an Australian behavioral scientist, presented 289 doctors, nurses, social workers, speech therapists, and physiotherapists with photos of eight attractive and unattractive men and women. They were asked to speculate about what kind of patients they would be. The good-lookers were judged to be more cooperative, better motivated, and more likely to improve than their less attractive counterparts. Pam Ennis, the consultant, commented, "Because the doctor feels that beautiful patients are more likely to respond to his treatment, he'll give them more time and attention."

In the myths that shape modern civilization, beauty is equated with success. It has been that way since time began. In most of literature, the heroines are beautiful. Leo Tolstoy wrote, "It is amazing how complete is the delusion that beauty is goodness."

We like to think we have moved beyond the era when the most desirable woman was the beauty queen, but we haven't. Every day we make assumptions about the personality of the bank teller, the delivery man, or the waitress by their looks. The way in which we attribute good and bad characteristics still has very little to do with fact. People seldom look beyond a pleasing facade, a superficial attractiveness. But the professors of person perception are not discouraged by this. They want to educate us. Perhaps by arming us with the knowledge and awareness of why we discriminate against the unattractive, we'll learn how to prevent this unwitting bigotry. Just maybe, we can change human nature.

30 The Uses of Poverty: The Poor Pay All

HERBERT J. GANS

Some people think that poverty simply means having to tighten your belt, but the meaning of poverty is much more profound. Sociologists have documented that the poor confront social conditions so damaging that their marriages are more likely to break up, they are sicker than others, their children are more likely to drop out of school and get in trouble with the law, they are more likely to be victimized by crime, and, on average, they die younger than most. It is difficult to romanticize poverty when one knows what its true conditions are.

In this selection, Gans does not document the degradation of the poor (although this is intrinsically present in his analysis), nor their failing health or troubled lives. Nor is his article a plea for social reform. Rather, from the observation that the poor are always present in society he concludes that this is because they perform vital services (functions) for society. (An essential assumption of *functionalism,* one of the theoretical schools in sociology, is that conditions persist in society only if they benefit—perform functions for—society or some of its parts.) In this selection, then, Gans tries to identify those functions.

Do you think the author has overlooked any "functions" of the poor? If his analysis, which many find startling, is not correct, what alternative explanation could you propose?

SOME YEARS AGO ROBERT K. MERTON applied the notion of functional analysis to explain the continuing though maligned existence of the urban political machine: If it continued to exist, perhaps it fulfilled latent—unintended or unrecognized—positive functions. Clearly it did. Merton pointed out how the political machine provided central authority to get things done when a decentralized local government could not act, humanized the services of the impersonal bureaucracy for fearful citizens, offered concrete help (rather than abstract law or justice) to the poor, and otherwise performed services needed or demanded by many people but considered unconventional or even illegal by formal public agencies.

Today, poverty is more maligned than the political machine ever was; yet it, too, is a persistent social phenomenon. Consequently, there may be some merit in applying functional analysis to poverty, in asking whether it also has positive functions that explain its persistence.

Merton defined functions as "those observed consequences [of a phenomenon] which make for the adaptation of adjustment of a given [social] system." I shall use a slightly different definition; instead of identifying functions for an entire social system, I shall identify them for the interest groups, socio-economic classes, and other population aggregates with shared values that "inhabit" a social system. I suspect that in a modern heterogeneous society, few phenomena are functional or dysfunctional for the society as a whole, and that most result in benefits to some groups and costs to others. Nor are any phenomena indispensable; in most instances, one can suggest what Merton calls "functional alternatives" or equivalents for them, i.e., other social patterns or policies that achieve the same positive functions but avoid the dysfunction. (In the following discussion, positive functions will be abbreviated as functions and negative functions as dysfunctions. Functions and dysfunctions, in the planner's terminology, will be described as benefits and costs.)

Associating poverty with positive functions seems at first glance to be unimaginable. Of course, the slumlord and the loan shark are commonly known to profit from the existence of poverty, but they are viewed as evil men, so their activities are classified among the dysfunctions of poverty. However, what is less often recognized, at least by the conventional wisdom, is that poverty also makes possible the existence or expansion of respectable professions and occupations, for example, penology, criminology, social work, and public health. More recently, the poor have provided jobs for professional and para-professional "poverty warriors," and for journalists and social scientists, this author included, who have supplied the information demanded by the revival of public interest in poverty.

Clearly, then, poverty and the poor may well satisfy a number of positive functions for many nonpoor groups in American society. I shall describe 13 such functions—economic, social, and political—that seem to me most significant.

The Functions of Poverty

First, the existence of poverty ensures that society's "dirty work" will be done. Every society has such work: physically dirty or dangerous, temporary, dead-end and underpaid, undignified, and menial jobs. Society can fill these jobs by paying higher wages than for "clean" work, or it can force people who have no other choice to do the dirty work—and at low wages. In America, poverty functions to provide a low-wage labor pool that is willing—or, rather, unable to be *un*willing—to perform dirty work at low cost. Indeed, this function of the poor is so important that in some Southern states, welfare payments have been cut off during the summer months when the poor are needed to work in the fields. Moreover, much of the debate about the Negative Income Tax and the Family Assistance Plan has concerned their impact on the work incentive, by which is actually meant the incentive of the poor to do the needed dirty work if the wages therefrom are no larger than the income grant. Many economic activities that involve dirty work depend on the poor for their existence: restaurants, hospitals, parts of the garment industry, and "truck farming," among others, could not persist in their present form without the poor.

Second, because the poor are required to work at low wages, they subsidize a variety of economic activities that benefit the affluent. For example, domestics subsidize the upper-middle and upper classes, making life easier for their employers and freeing affluent women for a variety of professional, cultural, civic, and partying activities. Similarly, because the poor pay a higher proportion of their income in property and sales taxes, among others, they subsidize many state and local governmental services that benefit more affluent groups. In addition, the poor support innovation in medical practice as patients in teaching and research hospitals and as guinea pigs in medical experiments.

Third, poverty creates jobs for a number of occupations and professions that serve or "service" the poor, or protect the rest of society from them. As already noted, penology would be minuscule without the poor, as would the police. Other activities and groups that flourish because of the existence of poverty are the numbers game, the sale of heroin and cheap wines and liquors, pentecostal ministers, faith healers, prostitutes, pawn shops, and the peacetime army, which recruits its enlisted men mainly from among the poor.

Fourth, the poor buy goods others do not want and thus prolong the economic usefulness of such goods—day-old bread, fruit and vegetables that would otherwise have to be thrown out, secondhand clothes, and deteriorating automobiles and buildings. They also provide incomes for doctors, lawyers, teachers, and others who are too old, poorly trained, or incompetent to attract more affluent clients.

In addition to economic functions, the poor perform a number of social functions.

Fifth, the poor can be identified and punished as alleged or real deviants in order to uphold the legitimacy of conventional norms. To justify the desirability of hard work, thrift, honesty, and monogamy, for example, the defenders of these norms must be able to find people who can be accused of being lazy, spendthrift, dishonest, and promiscuous. Although there is some evidence that the poor are about as moral and law-abiding as anyone else, they are more likely than middle-class transgressors to be caught and punished when they participate in deviant acts. Moreover, they lack the political and cultural power to correct the stereotypes that other people hold of them and thus continue to be thought of as lazy, spendthrift, etc., by those who need living proof that moral deviance does not pay.

Sixth, and conversely, the poor offer vicarious participation to the rest of the population in the uninhibited sexual, alcoholic, and narcotic behavior in which they are alleged to participate and which, being freed from the constraints of affluence, they are often thought to enjoy more than the middle classes. Thus many people, some social scientists included, believe that the poor not only are more given to uninhibited behavior (which may be true, although it is often motivated by despair more than by lack of inhibition) but derive more pleasure from it than affluent people (which research by Lee Rainwater, Walter Miller, and others shows to be patently untrue). However, whether the poor actually have more sex and enjoy it more is irrelevant; so long as middle-class people believe this to be true, they can participate in it vicariously when instances are reported in factual or fictional form.

Seventh, the poor also serve a direct cultural function when culture created by or for them is adopted by the more affluent. The rich often collect artifacts from extinct folk cultures of poor people; and almost all Americans listen to the blues, Negro spirituals, and country music, which originated among the Southern poor. Recently they have enjoyed the rock styles that were born, like the Beatles, in the slums; and in the last year, poetry written by ghetto children has become popular in literary circles. The poor also serve as culture heroes, particularly, of course, to the left; but the hobo, the cowboy, the hipster, and the mythical prostitute with a heart of gold have performed this function for a variety of groups.

Eighth, poverty helps to guarantee the status of those who are not poor. In every hierarchical society someone has to be at the bottom; but in American society, in which social mobility is an important goal for many and people need to know where they stand, the poor function as a reliable and relatively permanent measuring rod for status comparisons. This is particularly true for the working class, whose politics is influenced by the need to maintain status distinctions between themselves and the poor, much as the aristocracy must find ways of distinguishing itself from the *nouveaux riches.*

Ninth, the poor also aid the upward mobility of groups just above them in the class hierarchy. Thus a goodly number of Americans have entered the middle class through the profits earned from the provision of goods and services in the slums, including illegal or nonrespectable ones that upper-class and upper-middle-class businessmen shun because of their low prestige. As a result, members of almost every immigrant group have financed their upward mobility by providing slum housing, entertainment, gambling, narcotics, etc., to later arrivals—most recently to blacks and Puerto Ricans.

Tenth, the poor help to keep the aristocracy busy, thus justifying its continued existence. "Society" uses the poor as clients of settlement houses and beneficiaries of charity affairs; indeed, the aristocracy must have the poor to demonstrate its superiority over other elites who devote themselves to earning money.

Eleventh, the poor, being powerless, can be made to absorb the costs of change and growth in American society. During the nineteenth century, they did the backbreaking work that built the cities; today, they are pushed out of their neighborhoods to make room for "progress." Urban renewal projects to hold middle-class taxpayers in the city and expressways to enable suburbanites to commute downtown have typically been located in poor neighborhoods, since no other group will allow itself to be displaced. For the same reason, universities, hospitals, and civic centers also expand into land occupied by the poor. The major costs of the industrialization of agriculture have been borne by the poor, who are pushed off the land without recompense; and they have paid a large share of the human cost of the growth of American power overseas, for they have provided many of the foot soldiers for Vietnam and other wars.

Twelfth, the poor facilitate and stabilize the American political process. Because they vote and participate in politics less than other groups, the political system is often free to ignore them. Moreover, since they can rarely support Republicans, they often provide the Democrats with a captive constituency that has no other place to go. As a result, the Democrats can count on their votes, and be more responsive to voters—for example, the white working class—who might otherwise switch to the Republicans.

Thirteenth, the role of the poor in upholding conventional norms (see the *fifth* point, above) also has a significant political function. An economy based on the ideology of laissez-faire requires a deprived population that is allegedly unwilling to work or that can be considered inferior because it must accept charity or welfare in order to survive. Not only does the alleged moral deviancy of the poor reduce the moral pressure on the present political economy to eliminate poverty, but socialist alternatives can be made to look quite unattractive if those who will benefit most from them can be described as lazy, spendthrift, dishonest, and promiscuous.

The Alternatives

I have described 13 of the more important functions poverty and the poor satisfy in American society, enough to support the functionalist thesis that poverty, like any other social phenomenon, survives in part because it is useful to society or some of its parts. This analysis is not intended to suggest that because it is often functional, poverty *should* exist, or that it *must* exist. For one thing, poverty has many more dysfunctions than functions; for another, it is possible to suggest functional alternatives.

For example, society's dirty work could be done without poverty, either by automation or by paying "dirty workers" decent wages. Nor is it necessary for the poor to subsidize the many activities they support through their low-wage jobs. This would, however, drive up the costs of these activities, which would result in higher prices to their customers and clients. Similarly, many of the professionals who flourish because of the poor could be given other roles. Social workers could provide counseling to the affluent, as they prefer to do anyway; and the police could devote themselves to traffic and organized crime. Other roles would have to be found for badly trained or incompetent professionals now relegated to serving the poor, and someone else would have to pay their salaries. Fewer penologists would be employable, however. And pentecostal religion could probably not survive without the poor—nor would parts of the second- and third-hand-goods market. And in many cities, "used" housing that no one else wants would then have to be torn down at public expense.

Alternatives for the cultural functions of the poor could be found more easily and cheaply. Indeed, entertainers, hippies, and adolescents are already serving as the deviants needed to uphold traditional morality and as devotees of orgies to "staff" the fantasies of vicarious participation.

The status functions of the poor are another matter. In a hierarchical society, some people must be defined as inferior to everyone else with respect to a variety of attributes, but they need not be poor in the absolute sense. One could conceive of a society in which the "lower class," though last in the pecking order, received 75 percent of the median income, rather than 15–40 percent, as is now the case. Needless to say, this would require considerable income redistribution.

The contribution the poor make to the upward mobility of the groups that provide them with goods and services could also be maintained without the poor's having such low incomes. However, it is true that if the poor were more affluent, they would have access to enough capital to take over the provider role, thus competing with, and perhaps rejecting, the "outsiders." (Indeed, owing in part to antipoverty programs, this is already happening in a number of ghettos, where white storeowners are being replaced by blacks.) Similarly, if the poor were more affluent, they would make less willing clients for upper-class philanthropy, although some would still use settlement houses to achieve upward mobility, as they do now. Thus "Society" could continue to run its philanthropic activities.

The political functions of the poor would be more difficult to replace. With increased affluence the poor would probably obtain more political power and be more active politically. With higher incomes and more political power, the poor would be likely to resist paying the costs of growth and change. Of course, it is possible to imagine urban renewal and highway projects that properly reimbursed the displaced people, but such projects would then become considerably more expensive, and many might never be built. This, in turn, would reduce the comfort and convenience of those who now benefit from urban renewal and expressways. Finally, hippies could serve also as more deviants to justify the existing political economy—as they already do. Presumably, however, if poverty were eliminated, there would be fewer attacks on that economy.

In sum, then, many of the functions served by the poor could be replaced if poverty were eliminated, but almost always at higher costs to others, particularly more affluent others. Consequently, a functional analysis must conclude that poverty persists not only because it fulfills a number of positive functions but also because many of the functional alternatives to poverty would be quite dysfunctional for the affluent members of society. A functional analysis thus ultimately arrives at much the same conclusion as radical sociology, except that radical thinkers treat as manifest what I describe as latent: that social phenomena that are functional for affluent or powerful groups and dysfunctional for poor or powerless ones persist; that when the elimination of such phenomena through functional alternatives would generate dysfunctions for the affluent or powerful, they will continue to persist; and that phenomena like poverty can be eliminated only when they become dysfunctional for the affluent or powerful, or when the powerless can obtain enough power to change society.

Postscript

Over the years, this article has been interpreted as either a direct attack on functionalism or a tongue-in-cheek satirical comment on it. Neither interpretation is true. I wrote the article for two reasons. First and foremost, I wanted to point out that there are, unfortunately, positive functions of poverty which have to be dealt with by antipoverty policy. Second, I was trying to show that functionalism is not the inherently conservative approach for which it has often been criticized, but that it can be employed in liberal and radical analyses.

31 Savage Inequalities

JONATHAN KOZOL

Social inequality so pervades our society that it leaves no area of life untouched. Consequently, because we are immersed in it, we usually take social inequality for granted. When social inequality does become visible to us, its *social* origins often disappear from sight. We tend to see social inequality as part of the *natural* ordering of life, often explaining it on the basis of people's individual characteristics. ("They" are lazier, dumber, less moral—or whatever—than others. That's the reason they have less than we do.) This selection, however, makes the *social* base of social inequality especially vivid.

To examine the U.S. educational system, Kozol traveled around the country and observed schools in poor, middle-class, and rich communities. Because schools are financed largely by local property taxes, wealthier communities are able to offer higher salaries, purchase newer texts and equipment, and thereby provide their children better education. The extent of the disparities, however, is much greater than most people realize. As you read about the two schools contrasted in this selection, try to project yourself into each situation and see how these communities and schools would likely affect you—not only what you learn, but also your views on life, as well as your entire future.

"EAST OF ANYWHERE," writes a reporter for the *St. Louis Post-Dispatch,* "often evokes the other side of the tracks. But, for a first-time visitor suddenly deposited on its eerily empty streets, East St. Louis might suggest another world." The city, which is 98 percent black, has no obstetric services, no regular trash collection, and few jobs. Nearly a third of its families live on less than $7,500 a year; 75 percent of its population lives on welfare of some form. The U.S. Department of Housing and Urban Development describes it as "the most distressed small city in America."

Only three of the 13 buildings on Missouri Avenue, one of the city's major thoroughfares, are occupied. A 13-story office building, tallest in the city, has been boarded up. Outside, on the sidewalk, a pile of garbage fills a ten-foot crater.

The city, which by night and day is clouded by the fumes that pour from vents and smokestacks at the Pfizer and Monsanto chemical plants, has one of the highest rates of child asthma in America.

It is, according to a teacher at Southern Illinois University, "a repository for a nonwhite population that is now regarded as expendable." The *Post-Dispatch* describes it as "America's Soweto."

Fiscal shortages have forced the layoff of 1,170 of the city's 1,400 employees in the past 12 years. The city, which is often unable to buy heating fuel or toilet paper for the city hall, recently announced that it might have to cashier all but 10 percent of the remaining work force of 230. In 1989 the mayor announced that he might need to sell the city hall and all six fire stations to raise needed cash. Last year the plan had to be scrapped after the city lost its city hall in a court judgment to a creditor. East St. Louis is mortgaged into the next century but has the highest property-tax rate in the state. . . .

The dangers of exposure to raw sewage, which backs up repeatedly into the homes of residents in East St. Louis, were first noticed, in the spring of 1989, at a public housing project, Villa Griffin. Raw sewage, says the *Post-Dispatch,* overflowed into a playground just behind the housing project, which is home to 187 children, "forming an oozing lake of . . . tainted water." . . . A St. Louis health official voices her dismay that children live with waste in their backyards. "The development of working sewage systems made cities livable a hundred years ago," she notes. "Sewage systems separate us from the Third World." . . .

The sewage, which is flowing from collapsed pipes and dysfunctional pumping stations, has also flooded basements all over the city. The city's vacuum truck, which uses water and suction to unclog the city's sewers, cannot be used because it needs $5,000 in repairs. Even when it works, it sometimes can't be used because there isn't money to hire drivers. A single engineer now does the work that 14 others did before they were laid off. By April the pool of overflow behind the Villa Griffin project has expanded into a lagoon of sewage. Two million gallons of raw sewage lie outside the children's homes. . .

. . . Sister Julia Huiskamp meets me on King Boulevard and drives me to the Griffin homes.

As we ride past blocks and blocks of skeletal structures, some of which are still inhabited, she slows the car repeatedly at railroad crossings. A seemingly endless railroad train rolls past us to the right. On the left: a blackened lot where garbage has been burning. Next to the burning garbage is a row of 12 white cabins, charred by fire. Next: a lot that holds a heap of auto tires and a mountain of tin cans. More burnt houses. More trash fires. The train moves almost imperceptibly across the flatness of the land.

Fifty years old, and wearing a blue suit, white blouse, and blue headcover, Sister Julia points to the nicest house in sight. The sign on the front reads MOTEL. "It's a whorehouse," Sister Julia says.

When she slows the car beside a group of teen-age boys, one of them steps out toward the car, then backs away as she is recognized.

The 99 units of the Villa Griffin homes—two-story structures, brick on the first floor, yellow wood above—form one border of a recessed park and playground that were filled with fecal matter last year when the sewage mains exploded. The sewage is gone now and the grass is very green and looks inviting. When nine-year-old Serena and her seven-year-old brother take me for a walk, however, I discover that our shoes sink into what is still a sewage marsh. An inch-deep residue of fouled water still remains.

Serena's brother is a handsome, joyous little boy, but troublingly thin. Three other children join us as we walk along the marsh: Smokey, who is nine years old but cannot yet tell time; Mickey, who is seven; and a tiny child with a ponytail and big brown eyes who talks a constant stream of words that I can't always understand.

"Hush, Little Sister," says Serena. I ask for her name, but "Little Sister" is the only name the children seem to know.

"There go my cousins," Smokey says, pointing to two teen-age girls above us on the hill.

The day is warm, although we're only in the second week of March; several dogs and cats are playing by the edges of the marsh. "It's a lot of squirrels here," says Smokey. "There go one!"

"This here squirrel is a friend of mine," says Little Sister.

None of the children can tell me the approximate time that school begins. One says five o'clock. One says six. Another says that school begins at noon.

When I ask what song they sing after the flag pledge, one says, "Jingle Bells."

Smokey cannot decide if he is in the second or third grade.

Seven-year-old Mickey sucks his thumb during the walk.

The children regale me with a chilling story as we stand beside the marsh. Smokey says his sister was raped and murdered and then dumped behind his school. Other children add more details: Smokey's sister was 11 years old. She was beaten with a brick until she died. The murder was committed by a man who knew her mother.

The narrative begins when, without warning, Smokey says, "My sister has got killed."

"She was my best friend," Serena says.

"They had beat her in the head and raped her," Smokey says.

"She was hollering out loud," says Little Sister.

I ask them when it happened. Smokey says, "Last year." Serena then corrects him and she says, "Last week."

"It scared me because I had to cry," says Little Sister.

"The police arrested one man but they didn't catch the other," Smokey says.

Serena says, "He was some kin to her."

But Smokey objects, "He weren't no kin to me. He was my momma's friend."

"Her face was busted," Little Sister says.

Serena describes this sequence of events: "They told her go behind the school. They'll give her a quarter if she do. Then they knock her down and told her not to tell what they had did."

I ask, "Why did they kill her?"

"They was scared that she would tell," Serena says.

"One is in jail," says Smokey. "They cain't find the other."

"Instead of raping little bitty children, they should find themselves a wife," says Little Sister.

"I hope," Serena says, "her spirit will come back and get that man."

"And *kill* that man," says Little Sister.

"Give her another chance to live," Serena says.

"My teacher came to the funeral," says Smokey.

"When a little child dies, my momma say a star go straight to Heaven," says Serena.

"My grandma was murdered," Mickey says out of the blue. "Somebody shot two bullets in her head."

I ask him, "Is she really dead?"

"She dead all right," says Mickey. "She was layin' there, just dead."

"I love my friends," Serena says. "I don't care if they no kin to me. I *care* for them. I hope his mother have another baby. Name her for my friend that's dead."

"I have a cat with three legs," Smokey says.

"Snakes hate rabbits," Mickey says, again for no apparent reason.

"Cats hate fishes," Little Sister says.

"It's a lot of hate," says Smokey.

Later, at the mission, Sister Julia tells me this: "The Jefferson School, which they attend, is a decrepit hulk. Next to it is a modern school, erected two years ago, which was to have replaced the one that they attend. But the construction was not done correctly. The roof is too heavy for the walls, and the entire structure has begun to sink. It can't be occupied. Smokey's sister was raped and murdered and dumped between the old school and the new one." . . .

The problems of the streets in urban areas, as teachers often note, frequently spill over into public schools. In the public schools of East St. Louis this is literally the case.

"Martin Luther King Junior High School," notes the *Post-Dispatch* in a story published in the early spring of 1989, "was evacuated Friday afternoon after sewage flowed into the kitchen. . . . The kitchen was closed and students were sent home." On Monday, the paper continues, "East St. Louis Senior High School was awash in sewage for the second time this year." The school had to be shut because of "fumes and backed-up toilets." Sewage flowed into the basement, through the floor, then up into the kitchen and the students' bathrooms. The backup, we read, "occurred in the food preparation areas."

School is resumed the following morning at the high school, but a few days later the overflow recurs. This time the entire system is affected, since the meals distributed to every student in the city are prepared in the two schools that have been flooded. School is called off for all 16,500 students in the district. The sewage backup, caused by the failure of two pumping stations, forces officials at the high school to shut down the furnaces.

At Martin Luther King, the parking lot and gym are also flooded. "It's a disaster," says a legislator. "The streets are under water; gaseous fumes are being emitted from the pipes under the schools," she says, "making people ill."

In the same week, the schools announce the layoff of 280 teachers, 166 cooks and cafeteria workers, 25 teacher aides, 16 custodians and 18 painters, electricians, engineers and plumbers. The president of the teachers' union says the cuts, which will bring the size of kindergarten and primary classes up to 30 students, and the size of fourth to twelfth grade classes up to 35, will have "an unimaginable impact" on the students. "If you have a high school teacher with five classes each day and between 150 and 175 students . . . , it's going to have a devastating effect." The school system, it is also noted, has been using more than 70 "permanent substitute teachers," who are paid only $10,000 yearly, as a way of saving money. . . .

East St. Louis, says the chairman of the state board, "is simply the worst possible place I can imagine to have a child brought up. . . . The community is in desperate circumstances." Sports and music, he observes, are, for many children here, "the only avenues of success." Sadly enough, no matter how it ratifies the stereotype, this is the truth; and there is a poignant aspect to the fact that, even with class size soaring and one quarter of the system's teachers being given their dismissal, the state board of education demonstrates its genuine but skewed compassion by attempting to leave sports and music untouched by the overall austerity.

Even sports facilities, however, are degrading by comparison with those found and expected at most high schools in America. The football field at East St. Louis High is missing almost everything—including goalposts. There are a couple of metal pipes—no crossbar, just the pipes. Bob Shannon, the football coach, who has to use his personal funds to purchase footballs and has had to cut and rake the football field himself, has dreams of having goalposts someday. He'd also like to let his students have new uniforms. The ones they wear are nine years old and held together somehow by a patchwork of repairs. Keeping them clean is a problem, too. The school cannot afford a washing machine. The uniforms are carted to a corner laundromat with fifteen dollars' worth of quarters. . . .

In the wing of the school that holds vocational classes, a damp, unpleasant odor fills the halls. The school has a machine shop, which cannot be used for lack of staff, and a woodworking shop. The only shop that's occupied this morning is the auto-body class. A man with long blond hair and wearing a white sweat suit swings a paddle to get children in their chairs. "What we need the most is new equipment," he reports. "I have equipment for alignment, for example, but we don't have money to install it. We also need a better form of egress. We bring the cars in through two other classes." Computerized equipment used in most repair shops, he reports, is far beyond the high school's budget. It looks like a very old gas station in an isolated rural town. . . .

The science labs at East St. Louis High are 30 to 50 years outdated. John McMillan, a soft-spoken man, teaches physics at the school. He shows me his lab. The six lab stations in the room have empty holes where pipes were once attached. "It would be great if we had water," says McMillan. . . .

Leaving the chemistry labs, I pass a double-sized classroom in which roughly 60 kids are sitting fairly still but doing nothing. "This is supervised study hall," a teacher tells me in the corridor. But when we step inside, he finds there is no teacher. "The teacher must be out today," he says.

Irl Solomon's history classes, which I visit next, have been described by journalists who cover East St. Louis as the highlight of the school. Solomon, a man of 54 whose reddish hair is turning white, has taught in urban schools for almost 30 years. A graduate of Brandeis University, he entered law school but was drawn away by a concern with civil rights. "After one semester, I decided that the law was not for me. I said, 'Go and find the toughest place there is to teach. See if you like it.' I'm still here. . . .

"I have four girls right now in my senior home room who are pregnant or have just had babies. When I ask them why this happens, I am told, 'Well, there's no reason not to have a baby. There's not much for me in public school.' The truth is, that's a pretty honest answer. A diploma from a ghetto high school doesn't count for much in the United States today. So, if this is really the last education that a person's going to get, she's probably perceptive in that statement. Ah, there's so much bitterness—unfairness—there, you know. Most of these pregnant girls are not the ones who have much self-esteem. . . .

"Very little education in the school would be considered academic in the suburbs. Maybe 10 to 15 percent of students are in truly academic programs. Of the 55 percent who graduate, 20 percent may go to four-year colleges: something like 10 percent of any entering class. Another 10 to 20 percent may get some other kind of higher education. An equal number join the military. . . .

"I don't go to physics class, because my lab has no equipment," says one student. "The typewriters in my typing class don't work. The women's toilets . . . " She makes a sour face. "I'll be honest," she says. "I just don't use the toilets. If I do, I come back into class and I feel dirty."

"I wanted to study Latin," says another student. "But we don't have Latin in this school."

"We lost our only Latin teacher," Solomon says.

A girl in a white jersey with the message DO THE RIGHT THING on the front raises her hand. "You visit other schools," she says. "Do you think the children in this school are getting what we'd get in a nice section of St. Louis?"

I note that we are in a different state and city.

"Are we citizens of East St. Louis or America?" she asks. . . .

In a seventh grade social studies class, the only book that bears some relevance to black concerns—its title is *The American Negro*—bears a publication date of 1967. The teacher invites me to ask the class some questions. Uncertain where to start, I ask the students what they've learned about the civil rights campaigns of recent decades.

A 14-year-old girl with short black curly hair says this: "Every year in February we are told to read the same old speech of Martin Luther King. We read it every year. 'I have a dream. . . . ' It does begin to seem—what is the word?" She hesitates and then she finds the word: "perfunctory."

I ask her what she means.

"We have a school in East St. Louis named for Dr. King," she says. "The school is full of sewer water and the doors are locked with chains. Every student in that school is black. It's like a terrible joke on history."

It startles me to hear her words, but I am startled even more to think how seldom any press reporter has observed the irony of naming segregated schools for Martin Luther King. Children reach the heart of these hypocrisies much quicker than the grown-ups and the experts do. . . .

• • •

The train ride from Grand Central Station to suburban Rye, New York, takes 35 to 40 minutes. The high school is a short ride from the station. Built of handsome gray stone and set in a landscaped campus, it resembles a New England prep school. On a day in early June of 1990, I enter the school and am directed by a student to the office.

The principal, a relaxed, unhurried man who, unlike many urban principals, seems gratified to have me visit in his school, takes me in to see the auditorium, which, he says, was recently restored with private charitable funds ($400,000) raised by parents. The crenellated ceiling, which is white and spotless, and the polished dark-wood paneling contrast with the collapsing structure of the auditorium at [another school I visited]. The principal strikes his fist against the balcony: "They made this place extremely solid." Through a window, one can see the spreading branches of a beech tree in the central courtyard of the school.

In a student lounge, a dozen seniors are relaxing on a carpeted floor that is constructed with a number of tiers so that, as the principal explains, "they can stretch out and be comfortable while reading."

The library is wood-paneled, like the auditorium. Students, all of whom are white, are seated at private carrels, of which there are approximately 40. Some are doing homework; others are looking through the *New York Times*. Every student that I see during my visit to the school is white or Asian, though I later learn there are a number of Hispanic students and that 1 or 2 percent of students in the school are black.

According to the principal, the school has 96 computers for 546 children. The typical student, he says, studies a foreign language for four or five years, beginning in the junior high school, and a second foreign language (Latin is available) for two years. Of 140 seniors, 92 are now enrolled in AP [advanced placement] classes. Maximum teacher salary will soon reach $70,000. Per-pupil funding is above $12,000 at the time I visit.

The students I meet include eleventh and twelfth graders. The teacher tells me that the class is reading Robert Coles, Studs Terkel, Alice Walker. He tells me I will find them more than willing to engage me in debate, and this turns out to be correct. Primed for my visit, it appears, they arrow in directly on the dual questions of equality and race.

Three general positions soon emerge and seem to be accepted widely. The first is that the fiscal inequalities "do matter very much" in shaping what a school can offer ("That is obvious," one student says) and that any loss of funds in Rye, as a potential consequence of future equalizing, would be damaging to many things the town regards as quite essential.

The second position is that racial integration—for example, by the busing of black children from the city or a nonwhite suburb to this school—would meet with strong resistance, and the reason would not simply be the fear that certain standards might decline. The reason, several students say straightfor-wardly, is "racial" or, as others say it, "out-and-out racism" on the part of adults.

The third position voiced by many students, but not all, is that equity is basically a goal to be desired and should be pursued for moral reasons, but "will probably make no major difference" since poor children "still would lack the motivation" and "would probably fail in any case because of other prob-lems."

At this point, I ask if they can truly say "it wouldn't make a difference" since it's never been attempted. Several students then seem to rethink their views and say that "it might work, but it would have to start with preschool and the elementary grades" and "it might be 20 years before we'd see a differ-ence."

At this stage in the discussion, several students speak with some real feel-ing of the present inequalities, which, they say, are "obviously unfair," and one student goes a little further and proposes that "we need to change a lot more than the schools." Another says she'd favor racial integration "by whatever means—including busing—even if the parents disapprove." But a contradic-tory opinion also is expressed with a good deal of fervor and is stated by one student in a rather biting voice: "I don't see why we should do it. How could it be of benefit to us?"

Throughout the discussion, whatever the views the children voice, there is a degree of unreality about the whole exchange. The children are lucid and their language is well chosen and their arguments well made, but there is a sense that they are dealing with an issue that does not feel very vivid, and that nothing that we say about it to each other really matters since it's "just a theo-retical discussion." To a certain degree, the skillfulness and cleverness that they display seem to derive precisely from this sense of unreality. Questions of unfairness feel more like a geometric problem than a matter of humanity or conscience. A few of the students do break through the note of unreality, but, when they do, they cease to be so agile in their use of words and speak more awkwardly. Ethical challenges seem to threaten their effectiveness. There is the sense that they were skating over ice and that the issues we addressed were safely frozen underneath. When they stop to look beneath the ice they start to stumble. The verbal competence they have acquired here may have been gained by building walls around some regions of the heart.

"I don't think that busing students from their ghetto to a different school would do much good," one student says. "You can take them out of the environment, but you can't take the environment out of *them*. If someone grows up in the South Bronx, he's not going to be prone to learn." His name is Max and he has short black hair and speaks with confidence. "Busing didn't work when it was tried," he says. I ask him how he knows this and he says he saw a television movie about Boston.

"I agree that it's unfair the way it is," another student says. "We have AP courses and they don't. Our classes are much smaller." But, she says, "putting them in schools like ours is not the answer. Why not put some AP classes into *their* school? Fix the roof and paint the halls so it will not be so depressing."

The students know the term "separate but equal," but seem unaware of its historical associations. "Keep them where they are but make it equal," says a girl in the front row.

A student named Jennifer, whose manner of speech is somewhat less refined and polished than that of the others, tells me that her parents came here from New York. "My family is originally from the Bronx. Schools are hell there. That's one reason that we moved. I don't think it's our responsibility to pay our taxes to provide for *them*. I mean, my parents used to live there and they wanted to get out. There's no point in coming to a place like this, where schools are good, and then your taxes go back to the place where you began."

I bait her a bit: "Do you mean that, now that you are not in hell, you have no feeling for the people that you left behind?"

"It has to be the people in the area who want an education. If your parents just don't care, it won't do any good to spend a lot of money. Someone else can't want a good life for you. You have got to want it for yourself." Then she adds, however, "I agree that everyone should have a chance at taking the same courses. . . . "

I ask her if she'd think it fair to pay more taxes so that this was possible.

"I don't see how that benefits me," she says.

32 Tally's Corner

ELLIOT LIEBOW

Liebow studied black streetcorner men, lower-lower-class males whose chief activities and satisfactions take place "on the street." These men are materially poor because of the convergence of income, race, and education. Focusing on the adaptations these streetcorner men have made to their deprivation, Liebow analyzes their survival strategies.

In his analysis, Liebow applies the concept of the *self-fulfilling prophecy.* An example might help clarify this term. Let us suppose that reporters begin to discuss the possibility of a coming recession. They quote economists who see indicators that a recession might occur. These economists are not predicting a recession, however, and they carefully cover themselves with a lot of "ifs, ands, and buts." Some people who read the stories skip the disclaimers of the economists, however, and focus on the recession part of their statements. More and more, as they talk about the matter, people come to believe that a recession might be soon on its way. Consequently, business people cut down on their inventories "just in case," and customers reduce their purchases. When enough people cut back, unsold goods build up, factory orders diminish, economic indexes begin to decline, and business people, more worried than ever, cut back on expansion plans—making ripples felt throughout the economy. The recession arrives, because it was predicted—and because people changed their behavior accordingly.

Although it oversimplifies economic matters, the above scenario illustrates a significant concept in social life. From this article, it becomes apparent that self-fulfilling prophecies can create vicious cycles that drastically affect people's lives. Perceptions—by the men Liebow studied as well as by others of them—both predict failure at work and help cause the predicted failure (much as those that affected the Saints and the Roughnecks in Part VI).

Can you think of other self-fulfilling prophecies? Have you personally experienced any? What effect did they have on your life? How do you think the streetcorner men's cycle of self-fulfilling prophecies could be broken?

IN SUMMARY OF OBJECTIVE JOB CONSIDERATIONS [of streetcorner men], the most important fact is that a man who is able and willing to work cannot earn enough money to support himself, his wife, and one or more

330

children. A man's chances for working regularly are good only if he is willing to work for less than he can live on, and sometimes not even then. On some jobs, the wage rate is deceptively higher than on others, but the higher the wage rate, the more difficult it is to get the job, and the less the job security. Higher-paying construction work tends to be seasonal and, during the season, the amount of work available is highly sensitive to business and weather conditions and to the changing requirements of individual projects.[1] Moreover, high-paying construction jobs are frequently beyond the physical capacity of some of the men, and some of the low-paying jobs are scaled down even lower in accordance with the self-fulfilling assumption that the man will steal part of his wages on the job.[2]

Bernard assesses the objective job situation dispassionately over a cup of coffee, sometimes poking at the coffee with his spoon, sometimes staring at it as if, like a crystal ball, it holds tomorrow's secrets. He is twenty-seven years old. He and the woman with whom he lives have a baby son, and she has another child by another man. Bernard does odd jobs—mostly painting—but here it is the end of January, and his last job was with the Post Office during the Christmas mail rush. He would like postal work as a steady job, he says. It pays well (about $2.00 an hour) but he has twice failed the Post Office examination (he graduated from a Washington high school) and has given up the idea as an impractical one. He is supposed to see a man tonight about a job as a parking attendant for a large apartment house. The man told him to bring his birth certificate and driver's license, but his license was suspended because of a backlog of unpaid traffic fines. A friend promised to lend him some money this evening. If he gets it, he will pay the fines tomorrow morning and have his license reinstated. He hopes the man with the job will wait till tomorrow night.

A "security job" is what he really wants, he said. He would like to save up money for a taxi cab. (But having twice failed the postal examination and having a bad driving record as well, it is highly doubtful that he could meet the qualifications or pass the written test.) That would be "a good life." He can always get a job in a restaurant or as a clerk in a drugstore but they don't pay enough, he said. He needs to take home at least $50 to $55 a week. He thinks he can get that much driving a truck somewhere. . . . Sometimes he wishes he had stayed in the army. . . . A security job, that's what he wants most of all, a real security job. . . .

When we look at what the men bring to the job rather than at what the job offers the men, it is essential to keep in mind that we are not looking at men who come to the job fresh, just out of school perhaps, and newly prepared to undertake the task of making a living, or from another job where they earned a living and are prepared to do the same on this job. Each man comes to the job with a long job history characterized by his not being able to support himself and his family. Each man carries this knowledge, born of his experience, with him. He comes to the job flat and stale, wearied by the sameness of it all, convinced of his own incompetence, terrified of responsibility—of being tested still again and found wanting. Possible exceptions are the younger men not yet, or just, married. They suspect all this but have yet to have it confirmed by repeated personal experience over time. But those who are or have been married know it well. It is the experience of the individual and the group; of their fathers and probably their sons. Convinced of their inadequacies, not only do they not seek out those few better-paying jobs which test their resources, but they actively avoid them, gravitating in a mass to the menial, routine jobs which offer no challenge—and therefore pose no threat—to the already diminished images they have of themselves.

Thus Richard does not follow through on the real estate agent's offer. He is afraid to do on his own—minor plastering, replacing broken windows, other minor repairs and painting—exactly what he had been doing for months on a piecework basis under someone else (and which provided him with a solid base from which to derive a cost estimate).

Richard once offered an important clue to what may have gone on in his mind when the job offer was made. We were in the Carry-out, at a time when he was looking for work. He was talking about the kind of jobs available to him.

> I graduated from high school [Baltimore] but I don't know anything. I'm dumb. Most of the time I don't even say I graduated, 'cause then somebody asks me a question and I can't answer it, and they think I was lying about graduating. . . . They graduated me but I didn't know anything. I had lousy grades but I guess they wanted to get rid of me.
>
> I was at Margaret's house the other night and her little sister asked me to help her with her homework. She showed me some fractions and I knew right away I couldn't do them. I was ashamed so I told her I had to go to the bathroom.

And so it must have been, surely, with the real estate agent's offer. Convinced that "I'm dumb. . . . I don't know anything," he "knew right away" he couldn't do it, despite the fact that he had been doing just that sort of work all along.

Thus, the man's low self-esteem generates a fear of being tested and prevents him from accepting a job with responsibilities or, once on a job, from staying with it if responsibilities are thrust on him, even if the wages are commensurately higher. Richard refuses such a job, Leroy leaves one, and another man, given more responsibility and more pay, knows he will fail and proceeds to do so, proving he was right about himself all along. The self-fulfilling prophecy is everywhere at work. In a hallway, Stanton, Tonk, and Boley are passing a bottle around. Stanton recalls the time he was in the service. Everything was fine until he attained the rank of corporal. He worried about everything he did then. Was he doing the right thing? Was he doing it well? When would they discover their mistake and take his stripes (and extra pay) away? When he finally lost his stripes, everything was all right again.

Lethargy, disinterest, and general apathy on the job, so often reported by employers, has its streetcorner counterpart. The men do not ordinarily talk about their jobs or ask one another about them.[3] Although most of the men know who is or is not working at any given time, they may or may not know what particular job an individual man has. There is no overt interest in job specifics as they relate to this or that person, in large part perhaps because the specifics are not especially relevant. To know that a man is working is to know approximately how much he makes and to know as much as one needs or wants to know about how he makes it. After all, how much difference does it make to know whether a man is pushing a mop and pulling trash in an apartment house, a restaurant, or an office building, or delivering groceries, drugs, or liquor, or, if he's a laborer, whether he's pushing a wheelbarrow, mixing mortar, or digging a hole? So much does one job look like every other that there is little to choose between them. In large part, the job market consists of a narrow range of nondescript chores calling for nondistinctive, undifferentiated, unskilled labor. "A job is a job."

A crucial factor in the streetcorner man's lack of job commitment is the overall value he places on the job. *For his part, the streetcorner man puts no lower value on the job than does the larger society around him.* He knows the social value of the job by the amount of money the employer is willing to pay him for doing it. In a real sense, every pay day, he counts in dollars and cents the value placed on the job by society at large. He is no more (and frequently less) ready to quit and look for another job than his employer is ready to fire him and look for another man. Neither the streetcorner man who performs these jobs nor the society which requires him to perform them assesses the job as one "worth doing and worth doing well." Both employee and employer are contemptuous of the job. The employee shows his contempt by his reluctance to accept it or keep it, the employer by paying less than is required to support a family.[4] Nor does the low-wage job offer prestige, respect, interesting work, opportunity for learning or advancement, or any other compensation. With few exceptions, jobs filled by the streetcorner man are at the bottom of the employment ladder in every respect, from wage level to prestige. Typically, they are hard, dirty, uninteresting, and underpaid. The rest of society (whatever its ideal values regarding the dignity of labor) holds the job of the dishwasher or janitor or unskilled laborer in low esteem if not outright contempt.[5] So does the streetcorner man. He cannot do otherwise. He cannot draw from a job those social values which other people do not put into it.[6]

Only occasionally does spontaneous conversation touch on these matters directly. Talk about jobs is usually limited to isolated statements of intention, such as "I think I'll get me another gig [job]," "I'm going to look for a construction job when the weather breaks," or "I'm going to quit. I can't take no more of this shit." Job assessments typically consist of nothing more than a noncommittal shrug and "It's O.K." or "It's a job."

One reason for the relative absence of talk about one's job is, as suggested earlier, that the sameness of job experiences does not bear reiteration. Another and more important reason is the emptiness of the job experience itself. The man sees middle-class occupations as a primary source of prestige, pride, and self-respect; his own job affords him none of these. To think about his job is to see himself as others see him, to remind him of just where he stands in this society.[7] And because society's criteria for placement are generally the same as his own, to talk about his job can trigger a flush of shame and a deep, almost physical ache to change places with someone, almost anyone, else.[8] The desire to be a person in his own right, to be noticed by the world he lives in, is shared by each of the men on the streetcorner. Whether they articulate this desire (as Tally does below) or not, one can see them position themselves to catch the attention of their fellows in much the same way as plants bend or stretch to catch the sunlight.[9]

Tally and I went in the Carry-out. It was summer, Tally's peak earning season as a cement finisher, a semiskilled job a cut or so above that of the unskilled laborer. His take-home pay during these weeks was well over a hundred dollars—"a lot of bread." But for Tally, who no longer had a family to support, bread was not enough.

"You know that boy came in last night? That Black Moozlem? That's what I ought to be doing. I ought to be in his place."

"What do you mean?"

"Dressed nice, going to [night] school, got a good job."

"He's no better off than you, Tally. You make more than he does."

"It's not the money. [Pause] It's position, I guess. He's got position. When he finish school he gonna be a supervisor. People respect him. . . . Thinking about people with position and education gives me a feeling right here [pressing his fingers into the pit of his stomach]."

"You're educated, too. You have a skill, a trade. You're a cement finisher. You can make a building, pour a sidewalk."

"That's different. Look, can anybody do what you're doing? Can anybody just come up and do your job? Well, in one week I can teach you cement finishing. You won't be as good as me 'cause you won't have the experience but you'll be a cement finisher. That's what I mean. Anybody can do what I'm doing and that's what gives me this feeling. [Long pause] Suppose I like this girl. I go over to her house and I meet her father. He starts talking about what he done today. He talks about operating on somebody and sewing them up and about surgery. I know he's a doctor 'cause of the way he talks. Then she starts talking about what she did. Maybe she's a boss or a supervisor. Maybe she's a lawyer and her father says to me, 'And what do you do, Mr. Jackson?' [Pause] You remember at the courthouse, Lonny's trial? You and the lawyer was talking in the hall? You remember? I just stood there listening. I didn't say a word. You know why? 'Cause I didn't even know what you was talking about. That's happened to me a lot."

"Hell, you're nothing special. That happens to everybody. Nobody knows everything. One man is a doctor, so he talks about surgery. Another man is a teacher, so he talks about books. But doctors and teachers don't know anything about concrete. You're a cement finisher and that's your speciality."

"Maybe so, but when was the last time you saw anybody standing about talking about concrete?"

The streetcorner man wants to be a person in his own right, to be noticed, to be taken account of, but in this respect, as well as in meeting his money needs, his job fails him. The job and the man are even. The job fails the man and the man fails the job.

Furthermore, the man does not have any reasonable expectation that, however bad it is, his job will lead to better things. Menial jobs are not, by and large, the starting point of a track system which leads to even better jobs for those who are able and willing to do them. The busboy or dishwasher in a restaurant is not on a job track which, if negotiated skillfully, leads to chef or manager of the restaurant. The busboy or dishwasher who works hard becomes, simply, a hard-working busboy or dishwasher. Neither hard work nor perseverance can conceivably carry the janitor to a sitdown job in the office building he cleans up. And it is the apprentice who becomes the journeyman electrician, plumber, steam fitter, or bricklayer, not the common unskilled Negro laborer.

Thus, the job is not a stepping stone to something better. It is a dead end. It promises to deliver no more tomorrow, next month, or next year than it does today.

Delivering little, and promising no more, the job is "no big thing." The man appears to treat the job in a cavalier fashion, working and not working as the spirit moves him, as if all that matters is the immediate satisfaction of his present appetites, the surrender to present moods, and the indulgence of whims with no thought for the cost, consequences, the future. To the middle-class observer, this behavior reflects a "present-time orientation"—an "inability to defer gratification." It is this "present-time" orientation—as against the "future orientation" of the middle-class person—that "explains" to the outsider why Leroy chooses to spend the day at the Carry-out rather than report to work; why Richard, who was paid Friday, was drunk Saturday and Sunday and penniless Monday; why Sweets quits his job today because the boss looked at him "funny" yesterday.

But from the inside looking out, what appears as a "present-time" orientation to the outside observer is, to the man experiencing it, as much a future orientation as that of his middle-class counterpart.[10] The difference between the two men lies not so much in their different orientations to time as in their different orientations to future time or, more specifically, to their different futures.[11]

The future orientation of the middle-class person presumes, among other things, a surplus of resources to be invested in the future and a belief that the future will be sufficiently stable both to justify his investment (money in a bank, time and effort in a job, investment of himself in marriage and family, etc.) and to permit the consumption of his investment at a time, place, and manner of his own choosing and to his greater satisfaction. But the streetcorner man lives in a sea of want. He does not, as a rule, have a surplus of resources, either economic or psychological. Gratification of hunger and the desire for simple creature comforts cannot be long deferred. Neither can support for one's flagging self-esteem. Living on the edge of both economic and psychological subsistence, the streetcorner man is obliged to expend all his resources on maintaining himself from moment to moment.[12]

As for the future, the young streetcorner man has a fairly good picture of it. In Richard or Sea Cat or Arthur he can see himself in his middle twenties; he can look at Tally to see himself at thirty, at Wee Tom to see himself in his middle thirties, and at Budder and Stanton to see himself in his forties. It is a future in which everything is uncertain except the ultimate destruction of his hopes and the eventual realization of his fears. The most he can reasonably look forward to is that these things do not come too soon. Thus, when Richard squanders a week's pay in two days it is not because, like an animal or a child, he is "present-time oriented," unaware of or unconcerned with his future. He does so precisely because he is aware of the future and the hopelessness of it all.

Sometimes this kind of response appears as a conscious, explicit choice. Richard had had a violent argument with his wife. He said he was going to leave her and the children, that he had had enough of everything and could not take any more, and he chased her out of the house. His chest still heaving, he leaned back against the wall in the hallway of his basement apartment.

> "I've been scuffling for five years," he said. "I've been scuffling for five years from morning till night. And my kids still don't have anything, my wife don't have anything, and I don't have anything."
>
> "There," he said, gesturing down the hall to a bed, a sofa, a couple of chairs and a television set, all shabby, some broken. "There's everything I have and I'm having trouble holding onto that."
>
> Leroy came in, presumably to petition Richard on behalf of Richard's wife, who was sitting outside on the steps, afraid to come in. Leroy started to say something but Richard cut him short.
>
> "Look, Leroy, don't give me any of that action. You and me are entirely different people. Maybe I look like a boy and maybe I act like a boy sometimes but I got a man's mind. You and me don't want the same things out of life. Maybe some of the same, but you don't care how long you have to wait for yours and I—*want—mine—right—now*."[13]

Thus apparent present-time concerns with consumption and indulgences—material and emotional—reflect a future-time orientation. "I want mine right now" is ultimately a cry of despair, a direct response to the future as he sees it.[14]

In many instances, it is precisely the streetcorner man's orientation to the future—but to a future loaded with "trouble"—which not only leads to a greater emphasis on present concerns ("I want mine right now") but also contributes importantly to the instability of employment, family and friend relationships, and to the general transient quality of daily life.

Let me give some concrete examples. One day, after Tally had gotten paid, he gave me four twenty-dollar bills and asked me to keep them for him.

Three days later he asked me for the money. I returned it and asked why he did not put his money in a bank. He said that the banks close at two o'clock. I argued that there were four or more banks within a two block radius of where he was working at the time and that he could easily get to any one of them on his lunch hour. "No, man," he said, "you don't understand. They close at two o'clock and they closed Saturday and Sunday. Suppose I get into trouble and I got to make it [leave]. Me get out of town, and everything I got in the world layin' up in that bank? No good! No good!"

In another instance, Leroy and his girl friend were discussing "trouble." Leroy was trying to decide how best to go about getting his hands on some "long green" (a lot of money), and his girl friend cautioned him about "trouble." Leroy sneered at this, saying he had had "trouble" all his life and wasn't afraid of a little more. "Anyway, he said, "I'm famous for leaving town."[15]

Thus, the constant awareness of a future loaded with "trouble" results in a constant readiness to leave, to "make it," to "get out of town," and discourages the man from sinking roots into the world he lives in.[16] Just as it discourages him from putting money in the bank, so it discourages him from committing himself to a job, especially one whose payoff lies in the promise of future rewards rather than in the present. In the same way, it discourages him from deep and lasting commitments to family and friends or to any other persons, places, or things, since such commitments could hold him hostage, limiting his freedom of movement and thereby compromising his security which lies in that freedom.

. . . The streetcorner man is under continuous assault by his job experiences and job fears. His experiences and fears feed on one another. The kind of job he can get—and frequently only after fighting for it, if then—steadily confirms his fears, depresses his self-confidence and self-esteem until finally, terrified of an opportunity even if one presents itself, he stands defeated by his experiences, his belief in his own self-worth destroyed and his fears a confirmed reality.

Notes

1. The overall result is that, in the long run, a Negro laborer's earnings are not substantially greater—and may be less—than those of the busboy, janitor, or stock clerk. Herman P. Miller, for example, reports that in 1960, 40 percent of all jobs held by Negro men were as laborers or in the service trades. The average annual wage for nonwhite nonfarm laborers was $2,400. the average earning of nonwhite service workers was $2,500. *Rich Man, Poor Man* (New York: Crowell-Collier Press, 1964), p. 90. Francis Greenfield estimates that in the Washington vicinity, the 1965 earnings of the union laborer who works whenever work is available will be about $3,200. Even this figure is high for the man on the street corner. Union men in heavy construction are the aristocrats of the laborers. Casual day labor and jobs with small firms in the building and construction trades, or with firms in other industries, pay considerably less.

2. For an excellent discussion of the self-fulfilling assumption (or prophecy) as a social force, see "The Self-Fulfilling Prophecy," Ch. XI in Robert K. Merton's *Social Theory and Social Structure,* rev. ed. (Glencoe, IL.: The Free Press, 1957).

3. This stands in dramatic contrast to the leisure-time conversation of stable, working-class men. For the coal miners (of Ashton, England), for example, "the topic [of conversation] which surpasses all others in frequency is work—the difficulties which have been encountered in the day's shift, the way in which a particular task was accomplished, and so on." Josephine Klein, *Samples from English Cultures* (London: Routledge & Kegan Paul, 1965), I:88.

4. It is important to remember that the employer is not entirely a free agent. Subject to the constraints of the larger society, he acts for the larger society as well as for himself. Child labor laws, safety and sanitation regulations, minimum wage scales in some employment areas, and other constraints are already on the books; other control mechanisms, such as a guaranteed annual wage, are to be had for the voting.

5. See, for example, the U.S. Bureau of the Census, *Methodology and Scores of Socioeconomic Status.* The assignment of the lowest SES ratings to men who hold such jobs is not peculiar to our own society. A low SES rating for "the shoeshine boy or garbage man . . . seems to be true for all [industrial] countries." Alex Inkeles, "Industrial Man," *The American Journal of Sociology 66* (1960):8.

6. That the streetcorner man downgrades manual labor should occasion no surprise. Merton points out that "the American stigmatization of manual labor . . . *has been found to hold rather uniformly in all social classes*" (emphasis in original). *Social Theory and Social Structure,* p. 145. That he finds no satisfaction in such work should also occasion no surprise: "[There is] a clear positive correlation between the over-all status of occupations and the experience of satisfaction in them." Inkeles, "Industrial Man," p. 12.

7. "[In our society] a man's work is one of the things by which he is judged, and certainly one of the more significant things by which he judges himself. . . . A man's work is one of the more important parts of his social identity, of his self; indeed, of his fate in the one life he has to live." Everett C. Hughes, *Men and Their Work* (Glencoe, IL.: The Free Press, 1958), pp. 42–43.

8. Noting that lower-class persons "are constantly exposed to evidence of their own irrelevance," Lee Rainwater spells out still another way in which the poor are poor: "The identity problems of lower class persons make the soul-searching of middle class adolescents and adults seem rather like a kind of conspicuous consumption of psychic riches." "Work and Identity in the Lower Class," paper prepared for Washington University Conference on Planning for the Quality of Urban Life, April 1956 (mimeographed), p. 3.

9. Sea Cat cuts his pants legs off at the calf and puts a fringe on the raggedy edges. Tony breaks his "shades" and continues to wear the horn-rimmed frames minus the lenses. Richard cultivates a distinctive manner of speech. Lonny gives himself a birthday party. And so on.

10. Taking a somewhat different point of view, S. M. Miller and Frank Riessman suggest that "the entire concept of deferred gratification may be inappropriate to understanding the essence of workers' lives." "The Working Class Subculture: A New View," *Social Problems 9* (1961):87.

11. This sentence is a paraphrase of a statement made by Marvin Cline at a 1965 colloquium at the Mental Health Study Center, National Institute of Mental Health.

12. And if, for the moment, he does sometimes have more money than he chooses to spend or more food than he wants to eat, he is pressed to spend the money and eat the food anyway since his friends, neighbors, kinsmen, or acquaintances will beg or borrow whatever surplus he has or, failing this, they may steal it. In one extreme case, one of the men admitted taking the last of a woman's surplus food allotment after she had explained that, with four children, she could not spare any food. The prospect that consumer soft goods not consumed by oneself will be consumed by someone else may be related to the way in which portable consumer durable goods, such as watches, radios, television sets, or phonographs, are sometimes looked at as a form of savings. When Shirley was on welfare, she regularly took her television set out of pawn when she got her monthly check. Not so much to watch it, she explained, as to have something to fall back on when her money runs out toward the end of the month. For her and others, the television set or the phonograph is her savings, and the pawn ticket is her bankbook.

13. This was no simple rationalization for irresponsibility. Richard had indeed "been scuffling for five years" trying to keep his family going. Until shortly after this episode, Richard was known and respected as one of the hardest-working men on the street. Richard had said, only a couple of months earlier, "I figure you got to get out there and try. You got to try before you can get anything." His wife Shirley confirmed that he had always tried. "If things get tough with me I'll get all worried. But Richard get worried, he don't want me to see him worried. . . . He *will* get out there. He's shoveled snow, picked beans, and he's done some of everything. . . . He's not ashamed to get out there and get us something to eat." At the time of the episode reported above, Leroy was just starting marriage and raising a family. He and Richard were not, as Richard thought, "entirely different people." Leroy had just not learned, by personal experience over time, what Richard had learned. But within two years Leroy's marriage had broken up and he was talking and acting like Richard. "He just let go completely," said one of the men on the street.

14. There is no mystically intrinsic connection between "present-time" orientation and lower-class persons. Whenever people of whatever class have been uncertain, skeptical, or downright pessimistic about the future, "I want mine right now" has been one of the characteristic responses, although it is usually couched in more delicate terms: e.g., Omar Khayyam's "Take the cash and let the credit go," or Horace's "*Carpe diem.*" In wartime, especially, all classes tend to slough off conventional restraints on sexual and other behavior (i.e., become less able or less willing to defer gratification). And when inflation threatens, darkening the fiscal future, persons who formerly husbanded their resources with commendable restraint almost stampede one another rushing to spend their money. Similarly, it seems that future-time orientation tends to collapse toward the present when persons are in pain or under stress. The point here is that the label notwithstanding, (what passes for) present-time orientation appears to be a situation-specific phenomenon rather than a part of the standard psychic equipment of Cognitive Lower-Class Man.

15. And proceeded to do just that the following year when "trouble"—in this case, a grand jury indictment, a pile of debts, and a violent separation from his wife and children—appeared again.

16. For a discussion of "trouble" as a focal concern of lower-class culture, see Walter Miller, "Lower Class Culture as a Generating Milieu of Gang Delinquency," *Journal of Social Issues 14* (1958):7,8.

33 The Bohemian Grove and Other Retreats

G. WILLIAM DOMHOFF

Social inequality is a fact of life in all societies. Some people receive more of their society's goods and services, others far less. Although these divisions are much greater in some societies than they are in others, in no society on earth are all members equal. This is the way it has been in every known society of the past, is now, and—people's hopes to the contrary notwithstanding— probably always will be.

Our own society, much as many of us would wish it different, is no exception. On the one hand, in some ways we have much equality. That is especially true when we focus on our extensive middle class. Our society, indeed, holds open so many opportunities that millions of people try to enter our country each year, regardless of the obstacles they face and regardless of the legality of their entry.

On the other hand, we also are marked by vast divisions. Of these, wealth and power are among the greatest—in extent and in their effects on people's lives. Because the poor are the most accessible, in their studies of social inequality sociologists have concentrated on the poor. Domhoff, however, one of the exceptions, presents in this selection an analysis that ought to greatly expand your awareness of power and wealth in the United States.

You might ask yourself in what ways life would be different if you had been born into one of the families on which this article focuses. Beyond the external differences of material surroundings, how do you suppose your ideas of the world and of your place in it would be different?

The Bohemian Grove

PICTURE YOURSELF COMFORTABLY SEATED in a beautiful open-air dining hall in the midst of twenty-seven hundred acres of giant California redwoods. It is early evening and the clear July air is still pleasantly warm. Dusk has descended, you have finished a sumptuous dinner, and you are sitting quietly with your drink and your cigar, listening to nostalgic welcoming speeches and enjoying the gentle light and the eerie shadows that are cast by the two-stemmed gaslights flickering softly at each of the several hundred outdoor banquet tables.

You are part of an assemblage that has been meeting in this redwood grove sixty-five miles north of San Francisco for [over] a hundred years. It is not just any assemblage, for you are a captain of industry, a well-known television star, a banker, a famous artist, or maybe a member of the President's Cabinet. You are one of fifteen hundred men gathered together from all over the country for the annual encampment of the rich and the famous at the Bohemian Grove.

["Bohemians" of the 1970s and 1980s include such personages as President Ronald Reagan; Vice President George Bush; Attorney General William French Smith; Secretary of State George P. Schultz; former President Richard Nixon; former President Gerald Ford; Supreme Court Justice Potter Stewart; Herbert Hoover, Jr.; Herbert Hoover III; newspaperman William R. Hearst, Jr.; five members of the Dean Witter family of investment bankers; entertainers Art Linkletter and Edgar Bergen; presidents and chairmen of several oil companies such as Marathon Oil and Standard Oil; the president of Rockefeller University; officers of Anheuser-Busch breweries; the president of Kaiser Industries; bank presidents from California to New York; the president and chairman of Hewlett-Packard Co.; and many other representatives of American industry, finance, government, and entertainment. When these participants arrive for the annual "campout," an elaborate ritual called the Cremation of Care welcomes them and instructs them to leave all cares behind while they join together for two weeks of lavish entertainment, fellowship, and "communion with nature."]

The Cremation of Care is the most spectacular event of the midsummer retreat that members and guests of San Francisco's Bohemian Club have taken every year since 1878. However, there are several other entertainments in store. Before the Bohemians return to the everyday world, they will be treated to plays, variety shows, song fests, shooting contests, art exhibits, swimming, boating, and nature rides.

A cast for a typical Grove play easily runs to seventy-five or one hundred people. Add in the orchestra, the stagehands, the carpenters who make the sets, and other supporting personnel, and over three hundred people are involved in creating the High Jinks each year. Preparations begin a year in advance, with rehearsals occurring two or three times a week in the month before the encampment, and nightly in the week before the play.

Costs are on the order of $20,000 to $30,000 per High Jinks, a large amount of money for a one-night production which does not have to pay a penny for salaries (the highest cost in any commercial production). "And the costs are talked about, too," reports my . . . informant. "Hey, did you hear the High Jinks will cost $25,000 this year? one of them will say to another. The expense of the play is one way they can relate to its worth."

Entertainment is not the only activity at the Bohemian Grove. For a little change of pace, there is intellectual stimulation and political enlightenment every day at 12:30 P.M. Since 1932 the meadow from which people view the Cremation of Care also has been the setting for informal talks and briefings by people as varied as Dwight David Eisenhower (before he was President), Herman Wouk (author of *The Caine Mutiny*), Bobby Kennedy (while he was Attorney General), and Neil Armstrong (after he returned from the moon).

Cabinet officers, politicians, generals, and governmental advisers are the rule rather than the exception for Lakeside Talks, especially on weekends. Equally prominent figures from the worlds of art, literature, and science are more likely to make their appearance during the weekdays of the encampment, when Grove attendance may drop to four or five hundred (many of the members only come up for one week or for the weekends because they cannot stay away from their corporations and law firms for the full two weeks).

[T]he Grove is an ideal off-the-record atmosphere for sizing up politicians. "Well, of course when a politician comes here, we all get to see him, and his stock in trade is his personality and his ideas," a prominent Bohemian told a *New York Times* reporter who was trying to cover Nelson Rockefeller's 1963 visit to the Grove for a Lakeside Talk. The journalist went on to note that the midsummer encampments "have long been a major showcase where leaders of business, industry, education, the arts, and politics can come to examine each other."[1]

For 1971, [then] President Nixon was to be the featured Lakeside speaker. However, when newspaper reporters learned that the President planned to disappear into a redwood grove for an off-the-record speech to some of the most powerful men in America, they objected loudly and vowed to make every effort to cover the event. The flap caused the club considerable embarrassment, and after much hemming and hawing back and forth, the club leaders asked the President to cancel his scheduled appearance. A White House press secretary then announced that the President had decided not to appear at the Grove rather than risk the tradition that speeches there are strictly off the public record.[2]

However, the President was not left without a final word to his fellow Bohemians. In a telegram to the president of the club, which now hangs at the entrance to the reading room in the San Francisco clubhouse, he expressed his regrets at not being able to attend. He asked the club president to continue to lead people into the woods, adding that he in turn would redouble his efforts to lead people out of the woods. He also noted that, while anyone could aspire to be President of the United States, only a few could aspire to be president of the Bohemian Club.

Not all the entertainment at the Bohemian Grove takes place under the auspices of the committee in charge of special events. The Bohemians and their guests are divided into camps which evolved slowly over the years as the number of people on the retreat grew into the hundreds and then the thousands. These camps have become a significant center of enjoyment during the encampment.

At first the camps were merely a place in the woods where a half-dozen to a dozen friends would pitch their tents. Soon they added little amenities like their own special stove or a small permanent structure. Then there developed little camp "traditions" and endearing camp names like Cliff Dwellers, Moonshiners, Silverado Squatters, Woof, Zaca, Toyland, Sundodgers, and Land of Happiness. The next steps were special emblems, a handsome little lodge or specially constructed tepees, a permanent bar, and maybe a grand piano.[3] Today there are 129 camps of varying sizes, structures, and statuses. Most have between 10 and 30 members, but there are one or two with about 125 members and several with less than 10. A majority of the camps are strewn along what is called the River Road, but some are huddled in other areas within five or ten minutes of the center of the Grove.

The entertainment at the camps is mostly informal and impromptu. Someone will decide to bring together all the jazz musicians in the Grove for a special session. Or maybe all the artists or writers will be invited to a luncheon or a dinner at a camp. Many camps have their own amateur piano players and informal musical and singing groups which perform for the rest of the members.

But the joys of the camps are not primarily in watching or listening to performances. Other pleasures are created within them. Some camps become known for their gastronomical specialties, such as a particular drink or a particular meal. The Jungle Camp features mint juleps, Halcyon has a three-foot-high martini maker constructed out of chemical glassware. At the Owl's Nest [President Reagan's club] it's the gin-fizz breakfast—about a hundred people are invited over one morning during the encampment for eggs Benedict, gin fizzes, and all the trimmings.

The men of Bohemia are drawn in large measure from the corporate leadership of the United States. They include in their numbers directors from major corporations in every sector of the American economy. An indication of this fact is that one in every five resident members and one in every three non-resident members is found in Poor's *Register of Corporations, Executives, and Directors*, a huge volume which lists the leadership of tens of thousands of companies from every major business field except investment banking, real estate, and advertising.

Even better evidence for the economic prominence of the men under consideration is that at least one officer or director from 40 of the 50 largest industrial corporations in America was present, as a member or a guest, on the lists at our disposal. Only Ford Motor Company and Western Electric were missing among the top 25! Similarly, we found that officers and directors from 20 of the top 25 commercial banks (including all of the 15 largest) were on our lists. Men from 12 of the first 25 life insurance companies were in attendance (8 of these 12 were from the top 10). Other business sectors were represented somewhat less: 10 of 25 in transportation, 8 of 25 in utilities, 7 of 25 in conglomerates, and only 5 of 25 in retailing. More generally, of the top-level businesses ranked by *Fortune* for 1969 (the top 500 industrials, the top 50 commercial banks, the top 50 life insurance companies, the top 50 transportation companies, the top 50 utilities, the top 50 retailers, and the top 47 conglomerates), *29 percent of these 797 corporations were "represented" by at least 1 officer or director.*

Other Watering Holes

[Other camps and retreats were founded by wealthy and powerful men, based on the model provided by the Bohemian Grove. One example is the Rancheros Visitadores (Visiting Ranchers) who meet each May for horseback rides through the California ranch land. These are accompanied by feasts, entertainment, and general merrymaking with a Spanish-ranch motif.]

[Among the Rancheros a] common interest in horses and horseplay provides a social setting in which men with different forms of wealth get to know each other better. *Sociologically speaking, the Rancheros Visitadores is an organization which serves the function (whether the originators planned it that way or not) of helping to integrate ranchers and businessmen from different parts of the country into a cohesive social class.*

[T]he Rancheros had to divide into camps because of a postwar increase in membership. There are seventeen camps, sporting such Spanish names as Los Amigos, Los Vigilantes, Los Tontos (bums), Los Bandidos, and Los Flojos (lazy ones). They range in size from fifteen to ninety-three, with the majority of them listing between twenty and sixty members. Most camps have members from a variety of geographical locations, although some are slightly specialized in that regard. Los Gringos, the largest camp, has the greatest number of members from out of state. Los Borrachos, Los Piscadores, and Los Chingadores, the next largest camps, have a predominance of people from the Los Angeles area. Los Vigilantes, with twenty members, began as a San Francisco group, but now includes riders from Oregon, Washington, New York, and southern California.

In 1928 the Bohemian Grove provided John J. Mitchell with the inspiration for his retreat on horseback, the Rancheros Visitadores. Since 1930 the RVs have grown to the point where they are an impressive second best to the Grove in size, entertainment, and stature. Their combination of businessmen and ranchers is as unique as the Bohemian's amalgamation of businessmen and artists. It is hardly surprising that wealthy men from Los Angeles, San Francisco, Honolulu, Spokane, and Chicago would join Mitchell in wanting to be members of both.

The riders do not carry their fine camp with them. Instead, twenty camphands are employed to move the camp in trucks to the next campsite. Thus, when the Roundup Riders arrive at their destination each evening they find fourteen large sleeping tents complete with cots, air mattresses, portable toilets, and showers. Also up and ready for service are a large green dining tent and en entertainment stage. A diesel-powered generator provides the camp with electricity.

Food service is provided by Martin Jetton of Fort Worth, Texas, a caterer advertised in the Southwest as "King of the Barbecue." Breakfasts and dinners are said to be veritable banquets. Lunch is not as elaborate, but it does arrive to the riders on the trail in a rather unusual fashion that only those of the higher circles could afford: "lunches in rugged country are often delivered by light plane or helicopter."[4] One year the men almost missed a meal because a wind came up and scattered the lunches, which were being parachuted from two Cessna 170s.

In addition to the twenty hired hands who take care of the camp, there are twenty wranglers to look after the horses. The horses on the ride—predominantly such fine breeds as Arabian, Quarter Horse, and Morgan—are estimated to be worth more that $200,000. Horses and riders compete in various contests of skill and horsemanship on a layover day in the middle of the week. Skeet shooting, trap shooting, and horseshoes also are a part of this event.

The Roundup Riders, who hold their trek at the same time the Bohemians hold their encampment, must be reckoned as a more regional organization. Although there are numerous millionaires and executives among them, the members are not of the national stature of most Bohemians and many Rancheros. They can afford to invest thousands of dollars in their horses and tack, to pay a $300 yearly ride fee, and to have their lunch brought to them by helicopter, but they cannot compete in business connections and prestige with those who assemble at the Bohemian Grove. Building from the Denver branch of the upper class, the Roundup Riders reach out primarily to Nebraska (six), Texas (five), Illinois (five), Nevada (three), California (three), and Arizona (three). There are no members from New York, Boston, Philadelphia, or other large Eastern cities.

Several other regional rides have been inspired by the Rancheros: rides such as the Desert Caballeros in Wickenburg, Arizona, and the Verde Vaqueros in Scottsdale, Arizona. These groups are similar in size and membership to the Roundup Riders of the Rockies. Like the Roundup Riders, they have a few overlapping members with the Rancheros. But none are of the status of the Rancheros Visitadores. They are minor legacies of the Bohemian Grove, unlikely even to be aware of their kinship ties to the retreat in the redwoods.

Do Bohemians, Rancheros, and Roundup Riders Rule America?

The foregoing material on upper-class retreats, which I have presented in as breezy a manner as possible, is relevant to highly emotional questions concerning the distribution of power in modern America. In the final [section] I will switch styles somewhat and discuss these charged questions in a sober, simple, and straightforward way. . . .

It is my hypothesis that there is a ruling social class in the United States. This class is made up of the owners and managers of large corporations, which means the members have many economic and political interests in common, and many conflicts with ordinary working people. Comprising at most 1 percent of the total population, members of this class own 25 to 30 percent of all privately held wealth in America, own 60 to 70 percent of the privately held corporate wealth, receive 20 to 25 percent of the yearly income, direct the large corporations and foundations, and dominate the federal government in Washington.

Most social scientists disagree with this view. Some dismiss it out of hand; others become quite vehement in disputing it. The overwhelming majority of them believe that the United States has a "pluralistic" power structure, in which a wide variety of "veto groups" (e.g., businessmen, farmers, unions, consumers) and "voluntary associations" (e.g., National Association of Manufacturers, Americans for Democratic Action, Common Cause) form shifting coalitions to influence decisions on different issues. These groups and associations are said to have differing amounts of interest and influence on various questions. Contrary to my view, pluralists assert that no one group, not even the owners and managers of large corporations, has the cohesiveness and ability to determine the outcome of a large variety of social, economic, and political issues.

As noted, I believe there is a national upper class in the United States. [T]his means that wealthy families from all over the country, and particularly from major cities like New York, San Francisco, Chicago, and Houston, are part of interlocking social circles which perceive each other as equals, belong to the same clubs, interact frequently, and freely intermarry.

Whether we call it a "social class" or a "status group," many pluralistic social scientists would deny that such a social group exists. They assert that there is no social "cohesiveness" among the various rich in different parts of the country. For them, social registers, blue books, and club membership lists are merely collections of names which imply nothing about group interaction.

There is a wealth of journalistic evidence which suggests the existence of a national upper class. It ranges from Cleveland Amory's *The Proper Bostonians* and *Who Killed Society?* to Lucy Kavaler's *The Private World of High Society* and Stephen Birmingham's *The Right People*. But what is the systematic evidence which I can present for my thesis? There is first of all the evidence that has been developed from the study of attendance at private schools. It has been shown that a few dozen prep schools bring together children of the upper class from all over the country. From this evidence it can be argued that young members of the upper class develop lifetime friendship ties with like-status age-mates in every section of the country.[5]

There is second the systematic evidence which comes from studying high-status summer resorts. Two such studies show that these resorts bring together upper-class families from several different large cities.[6] Third, there is the evidence of business interconnections. Several [studies] have demonstrated that interlocking directorships bring wealthy men from all over the country into face-to-face relationships at the board meetings of banks, insurance companies, and other corporations.[7]

And finally, there is the evidence developed from studying exclusive social clubs. Such studies have been made in the past, but the present investigation of the Bohemian Club, The Rancheros Visitadores, and the Roundup Riders of the Rockies is a more comprehensive effort. *In short, I believe the present [study] to be significant evidence for the existence of a cohesive American upper class.*

The Bohemian Grove, as well as other watering holes and social clubs, is relevant to the problem of class cohesiveness in two ways. First, the very fact that rich men from all over the country gather in such close circumstances as the Bohemian Grove is evidence for the existence of a socially cohesive upper class. It demonstrates that many of these men do know each other, that they have face-to-face communications, and that they are a social network. In this sense, we are looking at the Bohemian Grove and other social retreats as a *result* of social processes that lead to class cohesion. But such institutions also can be viewed as *facilitators* of social ties. Once formed, these groups become another avenue by which the cohesiveness of the upper class is maintained.

In claiming that clubs and retreats like the Bohemians and the Rancheros are evidence for my thesis of a national upper class, I am assuming that cohesion develops within the settings they provide. Perhaps some readers will find that assumption questionable. So let us pause to ask: Are there reasons to believe that the Bohemian Grove and its imitators lead to greater cohesion within the upper class?

For one thing, we have the testimony of members themselves. There are several accounts by leading members of these groups, past and present, which attest to the intimacy that develops among members. John J. Mitchell, El Presidente of Los Rancheros Visitadores from 1930 to 1955, wrote as follows on the twenty-fifth anniversary of the group:

All the pledges and secret oaths in the universe cannot tie men, our kind of men, together like the mutual appreciation of a beautiful horse, the moon behind a cloud, a song around the campfire or a ride down the Santa Ynez Valley. These are experiences common on our ride, but unknown to most of our daily lives. Our organization, to all appearances, is the most informal imaginable. Yet there are men here who see one another once a year, yet feel a bond closer than between those they have known all their lives.[8]

F. Burr Betts, chairman of the board of Security Life of Denver, says the following about the Roundup Riders:

> I think you find out about the Roundup Riders when you go to a Rider's funeral. Because there you'll find, no matter how many organizations the man belonged to, almost every pallbearer is a Roundup Rider. I always think of the Roundup Riders as the first affiliation. We have the closest knit fraternity in the world.[9]

A second reason for stressing the importance of retreats and clubs like the Bohemian Grove is a body of research within social psychology which deals with group cohesion. "Group dynamics" suggests the following about cohesiveness. (1) *Physical proximity is likely to lead to group solidarity.* Thus, the mere fact that these men gather together in such intimate physical settings implies that cohesiveness develops. (The same point can be made, of course, about exclusive neighborhoods, private schools, and expensive summer resorts.) (2) *The more people interact, the more they will be like each other.* This is hardly a profound discovery, but we can note that the Bohemian Grove and other watering holes maximize personal interactions. (3) *Groups seen as high in status are more cohesive.* The Bohemian Club fits the category of a high-status group. Further, its stringent membership requirements, long waiting lists, and high dues also serve to heighten its valuation in the eyes of its members. Members are likely to think of themselves as "special" people, which would heighten their attractiveness to each other and increase the likelihood of interaction and cohesiveness. (4) *The best atmosphere for increasing group cohesiveness is one that is relaxed and cooperative.* Again the Bohemian Grove, the Rancheros, and the Roundup Riders are ideal examples of this kind of climate. From a group-dynamics point of view, then, we could argue that one of the reasons for upper-class cohesiveness is the fact that the class is organized into a wide variety of small groups which encourage face-to-face interaction and ensure status and security for members.[10]

In summary, if we take these several common settings together—schools, resorts, corporation directorships, and social clubs—and assume on the basis of members' testimony and the evidence of small-group research that interaction in such settings leads to group cohesiveness, then I think we are justified in saying that wealthy families from all over the United States are linked together in a variety of ways into a national upper class.

Even if the evidence and arguments for the existence of a socially cohesive national upper class are accepted, there is still the question of whether or not this class has the means by which its members can reach policy consensus on issues of importance to them.

A five-year study based upon information obtained from confidential informants, interviews, and questionnaires has shown that social clubs such as the Bohemian Club are an important consensus-forming aspect of the upper class and big-business environment. According to sociologist Reed Powell, "the clubs are a repository of the values held by the upper-level prestige groups in the community and are a means by which these values are transferred to the business environment." Moreover, the clubs are places where problems are discussed:

> On the other hand, the clubs are places in which the beliefs, problems, and values of the industrial organization are discussed and related to other elements in the larger community. Clubs, therefore, are not only effective vehicles of informal communication, but also valuable centers where views are presented, ideas are modified, and new ideas emerge. Those in the interview sample were appreciative of this asset; in addition, they considered the club as a valuable place to combine social and business contacts.[11]

The revealing interview work of Floyd Hunter, an outstanding pioneer researcher on the American power structure, also provides evidence for the importance of social clubs as informal centers of policy making. Particularly striking for our purposes is a conversation he had with one of the several hundred top leaders that he identified in the 1950s. The person in question was a conservative industrialist who was ranked as a top-level leader by his peers:

> Hall [pseudonym] spoke very favorably of the Bohemian Grove group that met in California every year. He said that although over the entrance to the Bohemian Club there was a quotation, "Weaving spiders come not here," there was a good deal of informal policy made in this association. He said that he got to know Herbert Hoover in this connection and that he started work with Hoover in the food administration of World War I.[12]

Despite the evidence presented by Powell and Hunter that clubs are a setting for the development of policy consensus, I do not believe that such settings are the only, or even the primary, locus for developing policy on class-related issues. For policy questions, other organizations are far more important, organizations like the Council on Foreign Relations, the Committee for Economic Development, the Business Council, and the National Municipal League. These organizations, along with many others, are the "consensus-seeking" and "policy-planning" organizations of the upper class. Directed by the same men who manage the major corporations, and financed by corporation and foundation monies, these groups sponsor meetings and discussions wherein wealthy men from all over the country gather to iron out differences and formulate policies on pressing problems.

No one discussion group is *the* leadership council within the upper class. While some of the groups tend to specialize in certain issue areas, they overlap and interact to a great extent. Consensus slowly emerges from the interplay of people and the ideas within and among the groups.[13] This diversity of groups is made very clear in the following comments by Frazar B. Wilde, chairman emeritus of Connecticut General Life Insurance Company and a member of the Council on Foreign Relations and the Committee for Economic Development.

Mr. Wilde was responding to a question about the Bilderbergers, a big-business meeting group which includes Western European leaders as well as American corporation and foundation directors:

> Business has had over the years many different seminars and discussion meetings. They run all the way from large public gatherings like NAM [National Association of Manufacturers] to special sessions such as those held frequently at Arden House. Bilderberg is in many respects one of the most important, if not the most important, but this is not to deny that other strictly off-the-record meetings and discussion groups such as those held by the Council on Foreign Relations are not in the front rank.[14]

Generally speaking, then, it is in these organizations that leaders within the upper class discuss the means by which to deal with problems of major concern. Here, in off-the-record settings, these leaders try to reach consensus on general issues that have been talked about more casually in corporate boardrooms and social clubs. These organizations, aided by funds from corporations and foundations, also serve several other functions:

1. They are a training ground for new leadership within the class. It is in these organizations, and through the publications of these organizations, that younger lawyers, bankers, and businessmen become acquainted with general issues in the areas of foreign, domestic, and municipal policy.
2. They are the place where leaders within the upper class hear the ideas and findings of their hired experts.
3. They are the setting wherein upper-class leaders "look over" young experts for possible service as corporation or governmental advisers.
4. They provide the framework for expert studies on important issues. Thus, the Council on Foreign Relations undertook a $1 million study of the "China question" in the first half of the 1960s. The Committee for Economic Development created a major study of money and credit about the same time. Most of the money for the studies was provided by the Ford, Rockefeller, and Carnegie foundations.[15]
5. Through such avenues as books, journals, policy statements, discussion groups, press releases, and speakers, the policy-planning organizations greatly influence the "climate of opinion" within which major issues are considered. For example, *Foreign Affairs*, the journal of the Council on Foreign Relations, is considered the most influential journal in its field, and the periodic policy statements of the Committee for Economic Development are carefully attended to by major newspapers and local opinion leaders.

It is my belief, then, that the policy-planning groups are essential in developing policy positions which are satisfactory to the upper class as a whole.

As such, I think they are a good part of the answer to any social scientist who denies that members of the upper class have institutions by which they deal with economic and political challenges.

However, the policy-planning groups could not function if there were not some common interests within the upper class in the first place. The most obvious, and most important, of these common interests have to do with the shared desire of the members to maintain the present monopolized and subsidized business system which so generously overrewards them and makes their jet setting, fox hunting, art collecting, and other extravagances possible. But it is not only shared economic and political concerns which make consensus possible. The Bohemian Grove and other upper-class social institutions also contribute to this process: *Group-dynamics research suggests that members of socially cohesive groups are more open to the opinions of other members, and more likely to change their views to those of fellow members.*[16] Social cohesion is a factor in policy consensus because it creates a desire on the part of group members to reconcile differences with other members of the group. It is not enough to say that members of the upper class are bankers, businessmen, and lawyers with a common interest in profit maximization and tax avoidance who meet together at the Council on Foreign Relations, the Committee for Economic Development, and other policy-planning organizations. We must add that they are Bohemians, Rancheros, and Roundup Riders.

Notes

1. Wallace Turner, "Rockefeller Faces Scrutiny of Top Californians: Governor to Spend Weekend at Bohemian Grove among State's Establishment," *New York Times*, July 26, 1963, p. 30. In 1964 Senator Barry Goldwater appeared at the Grove as a guest of retired General Albert C. Wedemeyer and Herbert Hoover, Jr. For that story see Wallace Turner, "Goldwater Spending Weekend in Camp at Bohemian Grove," *New York Times*, July 31, 1964, p. 10.

2. James M. Naughton, "Nixon Drops Plan for Coast Speech," *New York Times*, July 31, 1971, p. 11.

3. There is a special moisture-proof building at the Grove to hold the dozens of expensive Steinway pianos belonging to the club and various camps.

4. Robert Pattridge, "Closer to Heaven on Horseback," *Empire Magazine*, *Denver Post*, July 9, 1972, p. 12. I am grateful to sociologist Ford Cleere for bringing this article to my attention.

5. E. Digby Baltzell, *Philadelphia Gentlemen* (New York: Free Press, 1958), chapter 12, and G. William Domhoff, *The Higher Circles* (New York: Random House, 1970), p. 78.

6. Baltzell, *Philadelphia Gentleman*, pp. 248–51, and Domhoff, *The Higher Circles*, pp. 79–82. For recent anecdotal evidence on this point, see Stephen Birmingham, *The Right People* (Boston: Little, Brown, 1968), Part 3.

7. *Interlocks in Corporate Management* (Washington: U.S. Government

Printing Office, 1965) summarizes much of this information and presents new evidence as well. See also Peter Dooley, "The Interlocking Directorate," *American Economic Review*, December, 1969.

8. Neill C. Wilson, *Los Rancheros Visitadores: Twenty-Fifth Anniversary* (Rancheros Visitadores, 1955), p. 2.

9. Pattridge, "Closer to Heaven on Horseback." p. 11.

10. Dorwin Cartwright and Alvin Zander, *Group Dynamics* (New York: Harper & Row, 1960), pp 74–82; Albert J. Lott and Bernice E. Lott, "Group Cohesiveness as Interpersonal Attraction," *Psychological Bulletin 64* (1965):259–309; Michael Argyle, *Social Interaction* (Chicago: Aldine Publishing Company, 1969), pp. 220–23. I am grateful to sociologist John Sonquist of the University of California, Santa Barbara, for making me aware of how important the small-groups literature might be for studies of the upper class. Findings on influence processes, communication patterns, and the development of informal leadership also might be applicable to problems in the area of upper-class research.

11. Reed M. Powell, *Race, Religion, and the Promotion of the American Executive*, College of Administrative Science Monograph No. AA–3, Ohio State University, 1969, p. 50.

12. Floyd Hunter, *Top Leadership, U.S.A.* (Chapel Hill: University of North Carolina Press, 1959), p. 109. Hunter also reported (p. 199) that the most favored clubs of his top leaders were the Metropolitan, Links, Century, University (New York), Bohemian, and Pacific Union. He notes (p. 223 n.) that he found clubs to be less important in policy formation on the national level than they are in communities.

13. For a detailed case study of how the process works, see David Eakins, "Business Planners and America's Postwar Expansion," in David Horowitz (ed.), *Corporations and the Cold War* (New York: Monthly Review Press, 1969). For other examples and references, see Domhoff, *The Higher Circles*, chapters 5 and 6.

14. Carl Gilbert, personal communication, June 30, 1972. Mr. Gilbert has done extensive research on the Bilderberg group, and I am grateful to him for sharing his detailed information with me. For an excellent discussion of this group, whose role has been greatly distorted and exaggerated by ultraconservatives, see Eugene Pasymowski and Carl Gilbert, "Bilderberg, Rockefeller, and the CIA," *Temple Free Press*, No. 6, September 16, 1968. The article is most conveniently located in a slightly revised form in the *Congressional Record*, September 15, 1971, E9615, under the title "Bilderberg: The Cold War Internationale."

15. The recent work of arch-pluralist Nelson Polsby is bringing him dangerously close to this formulation. Through studies of the initiation of a number of new policies, Polsby and his students have tentatively concluded that "innovators are typically professors or interest group experts." Where Polsby goes wrong is in failing to note that the professors are working on Ford Foundation grants and/or Council on Foreign Relations fellowships. If he would put his work in a sociological framework, people would not gain the false impression that professors are independent experts sitting in their ivory towers thinking up innovations for the greater good of humanity. See Nelson Polsby, "Policy Initiation in the American Political System," in Irving Louis Horowitz (ed.), *The Use and Abuse of Social Science* (New Brunswick, NJ: TransAction Books, 1971), p. 303.

16. Cartwright and Zander, *Group Dynamics*, p. 89; Lott and Lott, "Group Cohesiveness as Interpersonal Attraction," pp. 291–96.

34 Fraternities and Rape on Campus

PATRICIA YANCEY MARTIN
ROBERT A. HUMMER

College certainly is a varied experience: challenging, with its many assignments, higher academic standards, and new vocabularies; frustrating, when concepts don't seem to sink in and instructors demand too much; fulfilling, with the satisfactions that come from forming new friendships and a sense of accomplishment as courses are passed and new ideas mastered; and, at the end, threatening, when the world of work and careers looms and, by comparison, college life suddenly appears so comfortable, almost serene.

On many campuses, fraternities are part of college life, a welcome respite from onerous classroom demands. They provide friendships, fun, diversion, sometimes even a test or paper to help pass a particularly grueling course. In some cases, bonds are formed that become significant for successful careers. There is a darker side to fraternities, however, a stress on hypermasculinity and calculated exploitation that destroys people. It is this dark side of fraternities that Martin and Hummer explore.

MANY RAPES, FAR MORE THAN COME to the public's attention, occur in fraternity houses on college and university campuses. . . .

The study reported here examined dynamics associated with the social construction of fraternity life, with a focus on processes that foster the use of coercion, including rape, in fraternity men's relations with women. We make no claims that all fraternities are "bad" or that all fraternity men are rapists. Our observations indicated, however, that rape is especially probable in fraternities because of the kinds of organizations they are, the kinds of members they have, the practices their members engage in, and a virtual absence of university or community oversight. . . . We conclude that unless fraternities change in fundamental ways, little improvement can be expected.

Methodology

We developed a conceptual framework from an initial case study of an alleged gang rape at Florida State University that involved four fraternity men and an eighteen-year-old coed. The group rape took place on the third floor of a fraternity house and ended with the "dumping" of the woman in the hallway of a neighboring fraternity house. According to newspaper accounts, the victim's blood-alcohol concentration, when she was discovered, was .349 percent, more than three times the legal limit for automobile driving and an almost lethal amount. One law enforcement officer reported that sexual intercourse occurred during the time the victim was unconscious. When the victim was found, she was comatose and had suffered multiple scratches and abrasions. Crude words and a fraternity symbol had been written on her thighs. When law enforcement officials tried to investigate the case, fraternity members refused to cooperate. This led, eventually, to a five-year ban of the fraternity from campus by the university and by the fraternity's national organization.

In trying to understand how such an event could have occurred, and how a group of over 150 members (exact figures are unknown because the fraternity refused to provide a membership roster) could hold rank, deny knowledge of the event, and allegedly lie to a grand jury, we analyzed newspaper articles about the case and conducted open-ended interviews with a variety of respondents about the case and about the fraternities, rapes, alcohol use, gender relations, and sexual activities on campus. Our data included over 100 newspaper articles on the initial gang rape case; open-ended interviews with Greek (social fraternity and sorority) and non-Greek (independent) students (N = 20); university administrators (N = 8, five men, three women); and alumni advisers to Greek organizations (N = 6). Open-ended interviews were held also with judges, public and private defense attorneys, victim advocates, and state prosecutors regarding the processing of sexual assault cases. . . .

Fraternities and the Social Construction of Men and Masculinity

Our research indicated that fraternities are vitally concerned—more than with anything else—with masculinity. They work hard to create a macho image and context and try to avoid any suggestion of "wimpishness," effeminacy, and homosexuality. Valued members display, or are willing to go along with, a narrow conception of masculinity that stresses competition, athleticism, dominance, winning, conflict, wealth, material possessions, willingness to drink alcohol, and sexual prowess vis-à-vis women.

VALUED QUALITIES OF MEMBERS

When fraternity members talked about the kind of pledges they prefer, a litany of stereotypical and narrowly masculine attributes and behaviors was recited and feminine or woman-associated qualities and behaviors were expressly denounced. Fraternities seek men who are "athletic," "big guys," good in intramural competition, "who can talk college sports." Males "who are willing to drink alcohol," "who drink socially," or "who can hold their liquor" are sought. Alcohol and activities associated with the recreational use of alcohol are cornerstones of fraternity social life. Non-drinkers are viewed with skepticism and rarely selected for membership.

Fraternities try to avoid "geeks," nerds, and men said to give the fraternity a "wimpy" or "gay" reputation. Art, music, and humanities majors, majors in traditional women's fields (nursing, home economics, social work, education), men with long hair, and those whose appearance or dress violate current norms are rejected. Clean-cut, handsome men who dress well (are clean, neat, conforming, fashionable) are preferred. . . .

One fraternity man, a senior, said his fraternity recruited "some big guys, very athletic" over a two-year period to help overcome its image of wimpiness. His fraternity had won the interfraternity competition for highest grade-point average several years running but was looked down on as "wimpy, dancy, even gay." With their bigger, more athletic recruits, "our reputation improved; we're a much more recognized fraternity now." Thus a fraternity's reputation and status depend on members' possession of stereotypically masculine traits. Good grades, campus leadership, and community service are "nice" but masculinity dominance—for example, in athletic events, physical size of members, athleticism of members—counts most.

One fraternity man, a junior, said: "We watch a guy [a potential pledge] talk to women . . . we want guys who can relate to girls." Assessing a pledge's ability to talk to women is, in part, a preoccupation with homosexuality and a conscious avoidance of men who seem to have effeminate manners or qualities. If a member is suspected of being gay, he is ostracized and informally drummed out of the fraternity. A fraternity with a reputation as wimpy or tolerant of gays is ridiculed and shunned by other fraternities. . . .

THE STATUS AND NORMS OF PLEDGESHIP

A pledge (sometimes called an associate member) is a new recruit who occupies a trial membership status for a specific period of time. The pledge period (typically ranging from ten to fifteen weeks) gives fraternity brothers an opportunity to assess and socialize new recruits. Pledges evaluate the fraternity also and decide if they want to become brothers. The socialization experience is structured partly through assignment of a Big Brother to each pledge. Big Brothers are expected to teach pledges how to become a brother and to support them as they progress through the trial membership period. Some pledges are repelled by the pledging experience, which can entail physical abuse; harsh discipline; and demands to be subordinate, follow orders, and engage in demeaning routines and activities, similar to those used by the military to "make men out of boys" during boot camp.

. . . One fraternity pledge who quit the fraternity he had pledged described an experience during pledgeship as follows:

> This one guy was always picking on me. No matter what I did, I was wrong. One night after dinner, he and two other guys called me and two other pledges into the chapter room. He said, "Here, X, hold this twenty-five-pound bag of ice at arm's length 'til I tell you to stop." I did it even though my arms and hands were killing me. When I asked if I could stop, he grabbed me around the throat and lifted me off the floor. I thought he would choke me to death. He cussed me and called me all kinds of names. He took one of my fingers and twisted it until it nearly broke. . . . I stayed in the fraternity for a few more days, but then I decided to quit. I hated it. Those guys are sick. They like seeing you suffer.

Fraternities' emphasis on toughness, withstanding pain and humiliation, obedience to superiors, and using physical force to obtain compliance contributes to an interpersonal style that de-emphasizes caring and sensitivity but fosters intragroup trust and loyalty. If the least macho or most critical pledges drop out, those who remain may be more receptive to, and influenced by, masculinist values and practices that encourage the use of force in sexual relations with women and the covering up of such behavior.

NORMS AND DYNAMICS OF BROTHERHOOD

Brother is the status occupied by fraternity men to indicate their relations to each other and their membership in a particular fraternity organization or group. Brother is a male-specific status; only males can become brothers, although women can become "Little Sisters," a form of pseudomembership. "Becoming a brother" is a rite of passage that follows the consistent and often lengthy display by pledges of appropriately masculine qualities and behaviors. Brothers have a quasi-familial relationship with each other, are normatively said to share bonds of closeness and support, and are sharply set off from nonmembers. Brotherhood is a loosely defined term used to represent the bonds that develop among fraternity members and the obligations and expectations incumbent upon them. . . .

Some of our respondents talked about brotherhood in almost reverential terms, viewing it as the most valuable benefit of fraternity membership. One senior, a business-school major who had been affiliated with a fairly high-status fraternity throughout four years on campus, said:

> Brotherhood spurs friendship for life, which I consider its best aspect, although I didn't see it that way when I joined. Brotherhood bonds and unites. It instills val-

ues of caring about one another, caring about community, caring about ourselves. The values and bonds [of brotherhood] continually develop over the four years [in college] while normal friendships come and go.

Despite this idealization, most aspects of fraternity practice and conception are more mundane. Brotherhood often plays itself out as an overriding concern with masculinity and, by extension, femininity. As a consequence, fraternities comprise collectivities of highly masculinized men with attitudinal qualities and behavioral norms that predispose them to sexual coercion of women. The norms of masculinity are complemented by conceptions of women and femininity that are equally distorted and stereotyped and that may enhance the probability of women's exploitation.

PRACTICES OF BROTHERHOOD

Practices associated with fraternity brotherhood that contribute to the sexual coercion of women include a preoccupation with loyalty, group protection and secrecy, use of alcohol as a weapon, and involvement in violence and physical force. . . .

Loyalty, Group Protection, and Secrecy. Loyalty is a fraternity preoccupation. Members are reminded constantly to be loyal to the fraternity and to their brothers. Among other ways, loyalty is played out in the practices of group protection and secrecy. The fraternity must be shielded from criticism. Members are admonished to avoid getting the fraternity in trouble and to bring all problems "to the chapter" (local branch of a national social fraternity) rather than to outsiders. Fraternities try to protect themselves from close scrutiny and criticism by the Interfraternity Council (a quasi-governing body composed of representatives from all social fraternities on campus), their fraternity's national office, university officials, law enforcement, the media, and the public. Protection of the fraternity often takes precedence over what is procedurally, ethically, or legally correct. Numerous examples were related to us of fraternity brothers' lying to outsiders to "protect the fraternity."

Group protection was observed in the alleged gang rape case with which we began our study. Except for one brother, a rapist who turned state's evidence, the entire remaining fraternity membership was accused by university and criminal justice officials of lying to protect the fraternity. Members consistently failed to cooperate even though the alleged crimes were felonies, involved only four men (two of whom were not even members of the local chapter), and the victim of the crime nearly died. According to a grand jury's findings, fraternity officers repeatedly broke appointments with law enforcement officials, refused to provide police with a list of members, and refused to cooperate with police and prosecutors investigating the case.

Secrecy, a priority value and practice in fraternities . . . is a boundary-maintaining mechanism, demarcating in-group from out-group, us from them. Secret rituals, handshakes, and mottos are revealed to pledge brothers as they are initiated into full brotherhood. Since only brothers are supposed to know a fraternity's secrets, such knowledge affirms membership in the fraternity and separates a brother from others. Extending secrecy tactics from protection of private knowledge to protection of the fraternity from criticism is a predictable development. Our interviews indicated that individual members knew the difference between right and wrong, but fraternity norms that emphasize loyalty, group protection, and secrecy often overrode standards of ethical correctness.

Alcohol as Weapon.   Alcohol use by fraternity men is normative. They use it on weekdays to relax after class and on weekends to "get drunk," "get crazy," and "get laid." The use of alcohol to obtain sex from women is pervasive—in other words, it is used as a weapon against sexual reluctance. According to several fraternity men whom we interviewed, alcohol is the major tool used to gain sexual mastery over women. . . . One fraternity man, a twenty-one-year-old senior, [said:] " . . . You have to buy them drinks or find out if she's drunk enough. . . . "

A similar strategy is used collectively. A fraternity man said that at parties with Little Sisters: "We provide them with 'hunch punch' and things get wild. We get them drunk and most of the guys end up with one." "'Hunch punch'" he said, "is a girls' drink made up of overproof alcohol and powdered Kool-Aid, no water or anything, just ice. It's very strong. Two cups will do a number on a female." He had plans in the next academic term to surreptitiously give hunch punch to women in a "prim and proper" sorority because "having sex with prim and proper sorority girls is definitely a goal." These women are a challenge because they "won't openly consume alcohol and won't get openly drunk as hell." Their sororities have "standards committees" that forbid heavy drinking and easy sex.

In the gang rape case, our sources said that many fraternity men on campus believed the victim had a drinking problem and was thus an "easy make." According to newspaper accounts, she had been drinking alcohol on the evening she was raped; the lead assailant is alleged to have given her a bottle of wine after she arrived at his fraternity house. Portions of the rape occurred in a shower, and the victim was reportedly so drunk that her assailants had difficulty holding her in a standing position. While raping her, her assailants repeatedly told her they were members of another fraternity under the apparent belief that she was too drunk to know the difference. Of course, if she was too drunk to know who they were, she was too drunk to consent to sex.

One respondent told us that gang rapes are wrong and can get one expelled, but he seemed to see nothing wrong in sexual coercion one-on-one. He seemed unaware that the use of alcohol to obtain sex from a woman is grounds for a claim that a rape occurred. Few women on campus (who also may not know these grounds) report date rapes, however; so the odds of detection and punishment are slim for fraternity men who use alcohol for "seduction" purposes.

Violence and Physical Force. Fraternity men have a history of violence. Their record of hazing, fighting, property destruction, and rape has caused them problems with insurance companies. Two university officials told us that fraternities "are the third riskiest property to insure behind toxic waste dumps and amusement parks." . . .

Fraternities' Commodification of Women

In claiming that women are treated by fraternities as commodities, we mean that fraternities knowingly, and intentionally, *use* women for their benefit. Fraternities use women as bait for new members, as servers of brothers' needs, and as sexual prey.

Women as Bait. Fashionably attractive women help a fraternity attract new members. As one fraternity man, a junior, said, "They are good bait." Beautiful, sociable women are believed to impress the right kind of pledges and give the impression that the fraternity can deliver this type of woman to its members. Photographs of shapely, attractive coeds are printed in fraternity brochures and videotapes that are distributed and shown to potential pledges. The women pictured are often dressed in bikinis, at the beach, and are pictured hugging the brothers of the fraternity. One university official says such recruitment materials give the message: "Hey, they're here for you, you can have whatever you want," and, "we have the best-looking women. Join us and you can have them, too." Another commented: "Something's wrong when males join an all-male organization as the best place to meet women. It's so illogical."

Fraternities compete in promising access to beautiful women. One fraternity man, a senior, commented that "the attraction of girls [i.e., a fraternity's success in attracting women] is a big status symbol for fraternities." One university official commented that the use of women as a recruiting tool is so well entrenched that fraternities that might be willing to forgo it say they cannot afford to unless other fraternities do so as well. One fraternity man said, "Look, if we don't have Little Sisters, the fraternities that do will get all the good pledges." Another said, "We won't have as good a rush [the period during which new members are assessed and selected] if we don't have these women around."

In displaying good-looking, attractive, skimpily dressed, nubile women to potential members, fraternities implicitly, and sometimes explicitly, promise sexual access to women. One fraternity man commented that "part of what being in a fraternity is all about is the sex" and explained how his fraternity uses Little Sisters to recruit new members:

> We'll tell the sweetheart [the fraternity's term for Little Sister], "You're gorgeous; you can get him." We'll tell her to fake a scam and she'll go hang all over him during a rush party, kiss him, and he thinks he's done wonderful and wants to join. The girls think it's great too. It's flattering for them.

Women as Servers.   The use of women as servers is exemplified in the Little Sister program. Little Sisters are undergraduate women who are rushed and selected in a manner parallel to the recruitment of fraternity men. They are affiliated with the fraternity in a formal but unofficial way and are able, indeed required, to wear the fraternity's Greek letters. Little Sisters are not full-fledged fraternity members, however, and fraternity national offices and most universities do not register or regulate them. Each fraternity has an officer called Little Sister Chairman who oversees their organization and activities. The Little Sisters elect officers among themselves, pay monthly dues to the fraternity, and have well-defined roles. Their dues are used to pay for the fraternity's social events, and Little Sisters are expected to attend and hostess fraternity parties and hang around the house to make it a "nice place to be." One fraternity man, a senior, described Little Sisters this way: "They are very social girls, willing to join in, be affiliated with the group, devoted to the fraternity." Another member, a sophomore, said: "Their sole purpose is social—attend parties, attract new members, and 'take care' of the guys." . . .

Women as Sexual Prey.   Little Sisters are a sexual utility. Many Little Sisters do not belong to sororities and lack peer support for refraining from unwanted sexual relations. One fraternity man (whose fraternity has 65 members and 85 Little Sisters) told us they had recruited "wholesale" in the prior year to "get lots of new women." The structural access to women that the Little Sister program provides and the absence of normative supports for refusing fraternity members' sexual advances may make women in this program particularly susceptible to coerced sexual encounters with fraternity men.

Access to women for sexual gratification is a presumed benefit of fraternity membership, promised in recruitment materials and strategies, and through brothers' conversations with new recruits. One fraternity man said: "We always tell the guys that you get sex all the time, there's always new girls. . . . After I became a Greek, I found out I could be with females at will." A university official told us that, based on his observations, "no one [i.e., fraternity men] on this campus wants to have 'relationships.' They just want to have fun [i.e., sex]." Fraternity men plan and execute strategies aimed at obtaining sexual gratification, and this occurs at both individual and collective levels.

Individual strategies include getting a woman drunk and spending a great deal of money on her. As for collective strategies, most of our undergraduate inteviewees agreed that fraternity parties often culminate in sex and that this outcome is planned. One fraternity man said fraternity parties often involve sex and nudity and can "turn into orgies." Orgies may be planned in advance, such as the Bowery Ball party held by one fraternity. A former fraternity member said of this party:

> The entire idea behind this is sex. Both men and women come to the party wearing little or nothing. There are pornographic pinups on the walls and usually porno movies playing on the TV. The music carries sexual overtones. . . . They just get schnockered [drunk] and, in most cases, they also get laid.

When asked about the women who come to such a party, he said: "Some Little Sisters just won't go. . . . The girls who do are looking for a good time, girls who don't know what it is, things like that."

Other respondents denied that fraternity parties are orgies but said that sex is always talked about among the brothers and they all know "who each other is doing it with." One member said that most of the time, guys have sex with their girlfriends "but with socials, girlfriends aren't allowed to come and it's their [members'] big chance [to have sex with other women]." The use of alcohol to help them get women into bed is a routine strategy at fraternity parties.

Conclusion

In general, our research indicated that the organization and membership of fraternities contribute heavily to coercive and often violent sex. Fraternity houses are occupied by same-sex (all men) and same-age (late teens, early twenties) peers whose maturity and judgment are often less than ideal. Yet fraternity houses are private dwellings that are mostly off-limits to, and away from scrutiny of, university and community representatives, with the result that fraternity house events seldom come to the attention of outsiders. Practices associated with the social construction of fraternity brotherhood emphasize a macho conception of men and masculinity, a narrow, stereotyped conception of women and femininity, and the treatment of women as commodities. Other practices contributing to coercive sexual relations and the cover-up of rapes include excessive alcohol use, competitiveness, and normative support for deviance and secrecy.

Some fraternity practices exacerbate others. Brotherhood norms require "sticking together" regardless of right or wrong; thus rape episodes are unlikely to be stopped or reported to outsiders, even when witnesses disapprove. The ability to use alcohol without scrutiny by authorities and alcohol's frequent association with violence, including sexual coercion, facilitate rape in fraternity houses. Fraternity norms that emphasize the value of maleness and masculinity over femaleness and femininity and that elevate the status of men and lower the status of women in members' eyes undermine perceptions and treatment of women as persons who deserve consideration and care. . . .

Our research led us to conclude that fraternity norms and practices influence members to view the sexual coercion of women, which is a felony crime, as sport, a contest, or a game. This sport is played not between men and women but between men and men. Women are the pawns or prey in the interfraternity rivalry game; they prove that a fraternity is successful or prestigious. The use of women in this way encourages fraternity men to see women as objects and sexual coercion as sport. Today's societal norms support young women's right to engage in sex at their discretion, and coercion is unnecessary in a mutually desired encounter. However, nubile young women say they prefer to be "in a relationship" to have sex while young men say they prefer to "get laid" without a commitment. In a fraternity context, getting sex without giving emotionally demonstrates "cool" masculinity. More important, it poses no threat to the bonding and loyalty of the fraternity brotherhood.

Unless fraternities' composition, goals, structures, and practices change in fundamental ways, women on campus will continue to be sexual prey for fraternity men. As all-male enclaves dedicated to opposing faculty and administration and to cementing in-group ties (i.e., fraternity members eschew any hint of homosexuality), their version of masculinity transforms women, and men with womanly characteristics, into the out-group. "Womanly men" are ostracized; feminine women are used to demonstrate members' masculinity. A case for or against fraternities cannot be made by studying individual members. The fraternity qua group and organization is at issue. Located on campus along with many vulnerable women, embedded in a sexist society, and caught up in masculinist goals, practices, and values, fraternities' violation of women—including forcible rape—should come as no surprise.

VIII Social Institutions

At first glance, the term "social institutions" appears far removed from everyday life. But in fact this term refers to concrete and highly relevant realities that profoundly affect our lives. Parents and their children, the basic family unit, constitute a social institution. So does the church, with its sacred books, clergy, and worship; and the law, with its police, lawyers, judges, courts, and prisons. Social institutions also means politics—running the full gamut of the U.S. political process, from campaign lies told with a straight face to the official acts of Congress, the president, and his Cabinet. Too, social institutions means the economic order, with new plants opening and old ones closing, working for a living, or drawing unemployment or welfare or a pension. Schools, colleges, and universities—places where people are socialized (as sociologists phrase the matter) or where they go to learn (as most other people put it)—also are examples of a social institution. Further, social institutions refers to science, with its test tubes and experiments, interviewers and questionnaires. It means doctors and nurses and hospitals, as well as the patients they treat, and the Medicare and Blue Cross and Blue Shield that people struggle to pay for in order to keep the U.S. medical enterprise from destroying their present and future finances. And social institutions means the military, with its generals and privates and tanks and planes, and the whole war game that at times threatens to become too real. Far from being removed from life, then, social institutions means all these vital aspects of life in society—and more.

To understand social life, it is necessary to understand the institutions of a society. It is not enough to understand what people do when they are in one another's presence. This certainly is significant, but it is only part of the picture.

363

The sociological (and personal) significance of social institutions is that they *provide the structure within which we live our lives.*

The characteristics of a society's institutions, in fact, dictate much of our interaction. For example, because of the way our economic order is arranged, we normally work eight hours a day, are off 16, and repeat this pattern five days a week. There is nothing natural about this pattern. Its regularity is but an arbitrarily imposed temporal arrangement for work, leisure, and personal concerns. Yet this one aspect of a single social institution has far-reaching effects on how we deal with our family and friends, how we meet our personal needs and nonwork obligations, and indeed on how we view time, and even life itself.

Each social institution has similarly far-reaching effects on our lives and viewpoints. By shaping our society as a whole and establishing the context in which we live, these institutions give form to almost everything that is of concern to us. We can say, in fact, that if the social institutions of our society were different, we would be different people. We certainly could not be the same, for our ideas and attitudes and other orientations to the physical and social worlds would be changed.

Sociologists classify social institutions as primary and secondary. The *primary* U.S. social institutions are the economy, the political system, and the military establishment. According to conflict theory, these three social institutions dominate our society. Their top leaders make the major decisions that have the greatest impact on our society, and thereby on our own lives. With the dominant position of the United States in world affairs, these three institutions are far-reaching, not only for our society but also for the rest of the world.

The *secondary* social institutions are the others: family, education, religion, sports, medicine, and law. As the name implies, they are secondary in power, and, as conflict theorists stress, these secondary social institutions exist to serve the primary. According to conflict theory, the family produces workers (for the economy), voters and taxpayers (for the political system), and soldiers (for the military); the religious institution instills patriotism and acceptance of the current arrangement of power; sports take people's minds off social issues so they remain compliant workers; the medical institution produces wealth for capitalists and patches workers up so they can continue working; and the law keeps the poor under its yoke so they don't rebel and upset current power arrangements.

To lead off this Part, Barbara Ehrenreich and Annette Fuentes pick up the topic with which we closed the previous Part. Their analysis of gender inequality adds a global dimension to the conflict perspective. Harry Gracey continues the conflict perspective as he focuses on kindergarten, analyzing it as the means by which children learn to become conformists so they can take a "proper" place in life. Arlie Hochschild and Anne Machung then turn to the family, examining the basic struggle of husbands and wives over housework.

Lawrence K. Hong and Marion V. Dearman switch the focus to the religious institution as they use symbolic interactionism to examine the approaches, motives, views, and relationships of streetcorner preachers. In his analysis of football in a Texas high school, Douglas Foley shows how sports are related to the reproduction of gender, race, and social class. In their examination of the medical institution, Allen C. Smith and Sherryl Kleinman analyze how medical schools modify the feelings of their students. Jennifer Hunt then examines the legal institution, looking at the how and why of police violence. The military is our final topic, as we conclude with Herbert Kelman's and V. Lee Hamilton's analysis of the My Lai massacre.

35 Life on the Global Assembly Line

BARBARA EHRENREICH
ANNETTE FUENTES

One of the world's most significant changes is the *globalization of capitalism.* Capitalism has won the cold war, and socialism is vanquished (at least for the time being). Victorious, capitalism is expanding rapidly into every nook and cranny of the planet. The so-called undeveloped nations ("undeveloped" only in a chauvinistic, ethnocentric sense of Western economic dominance, for they all have fully developed, intricate cultures) are part of this process. Eyeing the material wealth of the industrialized West, and mindful of its cultural dominance, like a separated lover these nations long to embrace capitalism. For their part, the capitalist nations view them as vast sources of cheap resources and expanding consumer potential.

Downsizing, a fancy way of saying that a company is firing workers, is part of globalization. In their pursuit of the bottom line, U.S. firms, followed more reluctantly by the Europeans and the Japanese, have laid off millions of workers. From the point of view of profit— which is capitalism's bottom line—this only makes sense, for in the least industrialized nations millions of workers eagerly await the crumbs of the industrialized world. This is a capitalist's dream: workers willing to accept peanuts for wages, and glad to get them. As Ehrenreich and Fuentes point out, the most needy of these workers— and thus the most willing to work for the cheapest wages—are women.

In Ciudad Juárez, Mexico, Anna M. rises at 5 A.M. to feed her son before starting on the two-hour bus trip to the maquiladora (factory). He will spend the day along with four other children in a neighbor's one-room home. Anna's husband, frustrated by being unable to find work for himself, left for the United States six months ago. She wonders, as she carefully applies her new lip gloss, whether she ought to consider herself still married. It might be good to take a night course, become a secretary. But she seldom gets home before eight *at night, and the factory, where she stitches brassieres that will be sold in the United States through J.C. Penney, pays only $48 a week.*

In Penang, Malaysia, Julie K. is up before the three other young women with whom she shares a room, and starts heating the leftover rice from last night's supper. She looks good in the company's green-trimmed uniform, and she's proud to work in a modern, American-owned factory. Only not quite so proud as when she started working three years ago—she thinks as she squints out the door at a passing group of women. Her job involves peering all day through a microscope, bonding hair-thin gold wires to a silicon chip destined to end up inside a pocket calculator, and at twenty-one, she is afraid she can no longer see very clearly.

EVERY MORNING, BETWEEN FOUR and seven, thousands of women like Anna and Julie head out for the day shift. In Ciudad Juárez, they crowd into *ruteras* (rundown vans) for the trip from the slum neighborhoods to the industrial parks on the outskirts of the city. In Penang they squeeze, sixty or more at a time, into buses for the trip from the village to the low, modern factory buildings of the Bayan Lepas free-trade zone. In Taiwan, they walk from the dormitories—where the night shift is already asleep in the still-warm beds—through the checkpoints in the high fence surrounding the factory zone.

This is the world's new industrial proletariat: young, female, Third World. Viewed from the "first world," they are still faceless, genderless "cheap labor," signaling their existence only through a label or tiny imprint—"made in Hong Kong," or Taiwan, Korea, the Dominican Republic, Mexico, the Philippines. . . . Anyone whose image of Third World women features picturesque peasants with babies slung on their backs should be prepared to update it. Just in the last decade, Third World women have become a critical element in the global economy and a key "resource" for expanding multinational corporations.

It doesn't take more than second-grade arithmetic to understand what's happening. In many Third World countries, a woman will earn $3 to $5 a *day*. The logic of the situation is compelling: why pay someone in Massachusetts $5 an hour to do what someone in Manila will do for $2.50 a day? Or, as a corollary, why pay a male worker anywhere to do what a female worker will do for 40 to 60 percent less?

And so, almost everything that can be packed up is being moved out to the Third World, not heavy industry, but just about anything light enough to travel—garment manufacture, textiles, toys, footwear, pharmaceuticals, wigs, appliance parts, tape decks, computer components, plastic goods. . . . But what's going on is much more than a matter of runaway shops. Economists are talking about a "new international division of labor," in which the process of production is broken down and the fragments are dispersed to different parts of the world. In general, the low-skilled jobs are farmed out to the Third World, where labor costs are minuscule, while control over the overall process and technology remains safely at company headquarters in "first world" countries like the United States and Japan. . . .

So much any economist could tell you. What is less often noted is the *gender* breakdown of the emerging international division of labor. Eighty to 90 percent of the low-skilled assembly jobs that go to the Third World are performed by women—in a remarkable switch from earlier patterns of foreign-dominated industrialization. Until now, "development" under the aegis of foreign corporations has usually meant more jobs for men and—compared to traditional agricultural society—a diminished economic status for women. But multinational corporations and Third World governments alike consider assembly-line work—whether the product is Barbie dolls or missile parts—to be "women's work."

One reason is that women can, in many countries, still be legally paid less than men. But the sheer tedium of the jobs adds to the multinationals' preference for women workers—a preference made clear, for example, by this ad from a Mexican newspaper: *We need female workers, older than 17, younger than 30, single and without children: minimum education primary school, maximum education one year of preparatory school [high school]; available for all shifts.*

It's an article of faith with management that only women can do, or will do, the monotonous, painstaking work that American business is exporting to the Third World. Bill Mitchell, whose job is to attract United States businesses to the Bermudez Industrial Park in Ciudad Juárez, told us with a certain macho pride: "A man just won't stay in this tedious kind of work. He'd walk out in a couple of hours." The personnel manager of a light assembly plant in Taiwan told anthropologist Linda Gail Arrigo: "Young male workers are too restless and impatient to do monotonous work with no career value. If displeased, they sabotage the machines and even threaten the foreman. But girls? At most, they cry a little."

In fact, the American businessmen we talked to claimed that Third World women genuinely enjoy doing the very things that would drive a man to assault and sabotage. "You should watch these kids going into work," Bill Mitchell told us. "You don't have any sullenness here. They smile." A top-level management consultant who specializes in advising American companies on where to relocate their factories gave us this global generalization: "The [factory] girls genuinely enjoy themselves. They're away from their families. They have spending money. They can buy motorbikes, whatever. Of course, it's a regulated experience too—with dormitories to live in—so it's a healthful experience."

What is the real experience of the women in the emerging Third World industrial work force? The conventional Western stereotypes leap to mind: You can't really compare, the standards are so different. . . . Everything's easier in warm countries. . . . They really don't have any alternatives. . . . Commenting on the low wages his company pays its women workers in Singapore, a Hewlett-Packard vice president said: "They live much differently here than we do. . . . " But the differences are ultimately very simple. To start with, they have less money.

The great majority of women in the new Third World work force live at or near the subsistence level for one person, whether they work for a multinational corporation or a locally owned factory. In the Philippines, for example, starting wages in U.S.-owned electronics plants are between $34 and $46 a month, compared to a cost of living of $37 a month; in Indonesia the starting wages are actually about $7 a month less than the cost of living. "Living," in these cases, should be interpreted minimally: a diet of rice, dried fish, and water—a Coke might cost a half-day's wages—and lodging in a room occupied by four or more other people. Rachael Grossman, a researcher with the Southeast Asia Resource Center, found women employees of U.S. multinational firms in Malaysia and the Philippines living four to eight in a room in boardinghouses, or squeezing into tiny extensions built onto squatter huts near the factory. Where companies do provide dormitories for their employees, they are not of the "healthful," collegiate variety implied by our corporate informant. Staff from the American Friends Service Committee report that dormitory space is likely to be crowded, with bed rotation paralleling shift rotation—while one shift works, another sleeps, as many as twenty to a room. In one case in Thailand, they found the dormitory "filthy," with workers forced to find their own place to sleep among "splintered floorboards, rusting sheets of metal, and scraps of dirty cloth." . . .

But wages on a par with what an eleven-year-old American could earn on a paper route, and living conditions resembling what Engels found in nineteenth-century Manchester are only part of the story. The rest begins at the factory gate. The work that multinational corporations export to the Third World is not only the most tedious, but often the most hazardous part of the production process. The countries they go to are, for the most part, those that will guarantee no interference from health and safety inspectors, trade unions, or even freelance reformers. As a result, most Third World factory women work under conditions that already have broken or will break their health—or their nerves—within a few years, and often before they've worked long enough to earn any more than a subsistence wage.

Consider first the electronics industry, which is generally thought to be the safest and cleanest of the exported industries. The factory buildings are low and modern, like those one might find in a suburban American industrial park. Inside, rows of young women, neatly dressed in the company uniform or T-shirt, work quietly at their stations. . . . In many plants toxic chemicals and solvents sit in open containers, filling the work area with fumes that can literally knock you out. "We have been told of cases where ten to twelve women passed out at once," an AFSC field worker in northern Mexico told us, "and the newspapers report this as 'mass hysteria.'"

In one stage of the electronics assembly process, the workers have to dip the circuits into open vats of acid. According to Irene Johnson and Carol Bragg, who toured the National Semiconductor plant in Penang, Malaysia, the women who do the dipping "wear rubber gloves and boots, but these sometimes leak, and burns are common." Occasionally, whole fingers are lost. More commonly, what electronics workers lose is the 20/20 vision they are required to have when they are hired. Most electronics workers spend seven to nine hours a day peering through microscopes, straining to meet their quota.

One study in South Korea found that most electronics assembly workers developed severe eye problems after only one year of employment; 88 percent had chronic conjunctivitis; 44 percent became near-sighted; and 19 percent developed astigmatism. A manager for Hewlett-Packard's Malaysia plant, in an interview with Rachael Grossman, denied that there were any eye problems: "These girls are used to working with 'scopes.' We've found no eye problems. But it sure makes me dizzy to look through those things."

Electronics, recall, is the "cleanest" of the exported industries. Conditions in the garment and textile industry rival those of any nineteenth-century (or twentieth—see below) sweatshops. The firms, generally local subcontractors to large American chains such as J.C. Penney and Sears, as well as smaller manufacturers, are usually even more indifferent to the health of their employees than the multinationals. Some of the worst conditions have been documented in South Korea, where the garment and textile industries have helped spark that country's "economic miracle." Workers are packed into poorly lit rooms, where summer temperatures rise above 100 degrees. Textile dust, which can cause permanent lung damage, fills the air. When there are rush orders, management may require forced overtime of as much as 48 hours at a stretch, and if that seems to go beyond the limits of human endurance, pep pills and amphetamine injections are thoughtfully provided. In her diary (originally published in a magazine now banned by the South Korean government), Min Chong Suk, thirty, a sewing-maching operator, wrote of working from 7 A.M. to 11:30 P.M. in a garment factory: "When [the apprentices] shake the waste threads from the clothes, the whole room fills with dust, and it is hard to breathe. Since we've been working in such dusty air, there have been increasing numbers of people getting tuberculosis, bronchitis, and eye diseases. Since we are women, it makes us so sad when we have pale, unhealthy, wrinkled faces like dried-up spinach. . . . It seems to me that no one knows our blood dissolves into the threads and seams, with sighs and sorrow."

In all the exported industries, the most invidious, inescapable health hazard is stress. On their home ground United States corporations are not likely to sacrifice human comfort for productivity. On someone else's home ground, however, anything goes. Lunch breaks may be barely long enough for a woman to stand in line at the canteen or hawkers' stalls. Visits to the bathroom are treated as a privilege; in some cases, workers must raise their hands for permission to use the toilet, and waits up to a half hour are common. Rotating shifts—the day shift one week, the night shift the next—wreak havoc with sleep patterns. Because inaccuracies or failure to meet production quotas can mean substantial pay losses, the pressures are quickly internalized; stomach ailments and nervous problems are not unusual in the multinationals' Third World female work force. . . .

As if poor health and the stress of factory life weren't enough to drive women into early retirement, management actually encourages a high turnover in many industries. "As you know, when seniority rises, wages rise," the management consultant in U.S. multinationals told us. He explained that it's cheaper to train a fresh supply of teenagers than to pay experienced women higher wages. "Older" women, aged twenty-three or twenty-four, are likely to be laid off and not rehired.

We estimate, based on fragmentary data from several sources, that the multinational corporations may already have used up (cast off) as many as 6 million Third World workers—women who are too ill, too old (thirty is over the hill in most industries), or too exhausted to be useful any more. Few "re-tire" with any transferable skills or savings. The lucky ones find husbands.

The unlucky ones find themselves at the margins of society—as bar girls, "hostesses," or prostitutes.

At 21, Julie's greatest fear is that she will never be able to find a husband. She knows that just being a "factory girl" is enough to give anyone a bad reputation. When she first started working at the electronics company, her father refused to speak to her for three months. Now every time she leaves Penang to go back to visit her home village she has to put up with a lecture on morality from her older brother—not to mention a barrage of lewd remarks from men outside her family. If they knew that she had actually gone out on a few dates, that she had been to a discotheque, that she had once kissed a young man who said he was a student . . . Julie's stomach tightens as she imagines her family's reaction. She tries to concentrate on the kind of man she would like to marry: an engineer or technician of some sort, someone who had been to California, where the company headquarters are located and where even the grandmothers wear tight pants and lipstick—someone who had a good attitude about women. But if she ends up having to wear glasses, like her cousin who worked three years at the "scopes," she might as well forget about finding anyone to marry her.

One of the most serious occupational hazards that Julie and millions of women like her may face is the lifelong stigma of having been a "factory girl." Most of the cultures favored by multinational corporations in their search for cheap labor are patriarchal in the grand old style: any young woman who is not under the wing of a father, husband, or older brother must be "loose." High levels of unemployment among men, as in Mexico, contribute to male resentment of working women. Add to all this the fact that certain companies—American electronics firms are in the lead—actively promote Western-style sexual objectification as a means of ensuring employee loyalty: there are company-sponsored cosmetics classes, "guess whose legs these are" contests, and swimsuit-style beauty contests where the prize might be a free night *for two* in a fancy hotel. Corporate-promoted Westernization only heightens the hostility many men feel toward any independent working women—having a job is bad enough, wearing jeans and mascara to work is going too far.

Anthropologist Patricia Fernandez, who has worked in a *maquiladora* herself, believes that the stigmatization of working women serves, indirectly, to keep them in line. "You have to think of the kind of socialization that girls experience in a very Catholic—or, for that matter, Muslim—society. The fear of having a 'reputation' is enough to make a lot of women bend over backward to be 'respectable' and ladylike, which is just what management wants." She points out that in northern Mexico, the tabloids delight in playing up stories of alleged vice in the *maquiladoras*—indiscriminate sex on the job, epidemics of venereal disease, fetuses found in factory rest rooms. "I worry about this because there are those who treat you differently as soon as they know you have a job at the *maquiladora*," one woman told Fernandez. "Maybe they think that if you have to work, there is a chance you're a whore."

And there is always the chance you'll wind up as one. Probably only a small minority of Third World factory workers turn to prostitution when their working days come to an end. But it is, as for women everywhere, the employment of last resort, the only thing to do when the factories don't need you and traditional society won't—or, for economic reasons, can't—take you back. In the Philippines, the brothel business is expanding as fast as the factory system. If they can't use you one way, they can use you another.

There has been no international protest about the exploitation of Third World women by multinational corporations—no thundering denunciations from the floor of the United Nations General Assembly, no angry resolutions from the Conference of the Non-Aligned Countries. Sociologist Robert Snow, who has been tracing the multinationals on their way south and eastward for years, explained why: "The Third World governments *want* the multinationals to move in. There's cutthroat competition to attract the corporations."

The governments themselves gain little revenue from this kind of investment, though—especially since most offer tax holidays and freedom from export duties in order to attract the multinationals in the first place. Nor do the people as a whole benefit, according to a highly placed Third World woman within the UN. "The multinationals like to say they're contributing to development," she told us, "but they come into our countries for one thing—cheap labor. If the labor stops being so cheap, they can move on. So how can you call that development? It depends on the people being poor and staying poor." But there are important groups that do stand to gain when the multinationals set up shop in their countries: local entrepreneurs who subcontract to the multinationals; Harvard- or Berkeley-educated "technocrats" who become local management; and government officials who specialize in cutting red tape for an "agent's fee" or an outright bribe.

In the competition for multinational investment, local governments advertise their women shamelessly, and an investment brochure issued by the Malaysian government informs multinational executives that: "The manual dexterity of the Oriental female is famous the world over. Her hands are small, and she works fast with extreme care. Who, therefore, could be better qualified by nature and inheritance, to contribute to the efficiency of a bench-assembly production line than the Oriental girl?"

The Royal Thai Embassy sends American businesses a brochure guaranteeing that in Thailand, "the relationship between the employer and the employee is like that of a guardian and ward. It is easy to win and maintain the loyalty of workers as long as they are treated with kindness and courtesy." The facing page offers a highly selective photo-study of Thai womanhood: giggling shyly, bowing submissively, and working cheerfully on an assembly line. . . .

The governments advertise their women, sell them, and keep them in line for the multinational "johns." But there are other parties to the growing international traffic in women—such as the United Nations Industrial Development Organization (UNIDO), the World Bank, and the United States government itself.

UNIDO, for example, has been a major promoter of "free trade zones." These are enclaves within nations that offer multinational corporations a range of creature comforts, including: freedom from paying taxes and export duties; low-cost water, power, and buildings; exemption from whatever labor laws may apply in the country as a whole; and, in some cases, such security features as barbed wire, guarded checkpoints, and government-paid police.

Then there is the World Bank, which over the past decade has lent several billion dollars to finance the roads, airports, power plants, and even the first-class hotels that multinational corporations need in order to set up business in Third World countries. The Sri Lankan garment industry, which like other Third World garment industries survives by subcontracting to major Western firms, was set up on the advice of the World Bank and with a $20 million World Bank loan. This particular experiment in "development" offers young women jobs at a global low of $5 for a six-day week. Gloria Scott, the head of the World Bank's Women and Development Program, sounded distinctly uncomfortable when we asked her about the bank's role in promoting the exploitation of Third World women. "Our job is to help eliminate poverty. It is not our responsibility if the multinationals come in and offer such low wages. It's the responsibility of the governments." . . .

But the most powerful promoter of exploitative conditions for Third World women is the United States government itself. For example, the notoriously repressive Korean textile industry was developed with the help of $400 million in aid from the U.S. State Department. Malaysia became a low-wage haven for the electronics industry, thanks to technical assistance financed by AID, and to U.S. money (funneled through the Asian Development Bank) to help set up free trade zones. Taiwan's status as a "showcase for the free world" and a comfortable berth for multinationals is the result of three decades of financial transfusions from the United States. . . .

But the most obvious form of United States involvement, according to

Lenny Siegel, the director of the Pacific Studies Center, is through "our consistent record of military aid to Third World governments that are capitalist, politically repressive, and are not striving for economic independence." Ironically, says Siegel, there are "cases where the United States made a big investment to make sure that any unions that formed would be pretty tame. Then we put in even more money to support some dictator who doesn't allow unions at all." . . .

What does our government have to say for itself? It's hard to get a straight answer—the few parts of the bureaucracy that deal with women and development seem to have little connection with those that are concerned with larger foreign policy issues. A spokesman for the Department of State told us that if multinationals offer poor working conditions (which he questioned), this was not their fault: "There are just different standards in different countries." Offering further evidence of a sheltered life, he told us that "corporations today are generally more socially responsible than even ten years ago. . . . We can expect them to treat their employees in the best way they can." But he conceded in response to a barrage of unpleasant examples, "Of course, you're going to have problems wherever you have human beings doing things." Our next stop was the Women's Division within AID. Staffer Emmy Simmons was aware of the criticisms of the quality of employment multinationals offer, but cautioned that "we can get hung up in the idea that it's exploitation without really looking at the alternatives for women." AID's concern, she said, was with the fact that population is outgrowing the agricultural capacity of many Third World countries, dislocating millions of people. From her point of view, multinationals at least provide some sort of alternative: "These people have to go somewhere."

36 Learning the Student Role: Kindergarten as Academic Boot Camp

HARRY L. GRACEY

As we have seen in the preceding Parts, each society (and each group) maintains a vital interest in making its members conform to expectations. A major social institution for which conformity is a primary goal is education. Educators want to graduate people who are acceptable to the community, not only in terms of marketable skills but also in terms of their ideas, attitudes, and behaviors. Whether it be grade school, high school, or college, educational administrators want instructors to teach standard ideas and facts, to steer clear of radical politics, and to not stir up trouble in the school or community. *Then* the social institution can go about its business—and that business, when you probe beyond official utterances and uncover the *"hidden curriculum,"* is producing conformists who fit well in society.

Although Gracey's focus is kindergarten, this article was chosen to represent the educational institution because it focuses on this essential nature of education, training in conformity. The primary goal of kindergarten is to teach children to be students—so they can participate in conformity. If this is what education really is about, where are intellectual stimulation, the excitement of discovery, and creativity— long associated in the public mind with education? The answer is that they may occur so long as they are noncontroversial. In other words they, too, are expected to reflect the conformist nature of the educational institution.

Based on your own extensive experiences with education, how do you react to the idea that the essence of the educational institution is training into conformity?

EDUCATION MUST BE CONSIDERED one of the major institutions of social life today. Along with the family and organized religion, however, it is a "secondary institution," one in which people are prepared for life in society as it is presently organized. The main dimensions of modern life, that is, the nature of society as a whole, are determined principally by the "primary institutions," which today are the economy, the political system, and the military establishment. Education has been defined by sociologists, classical and contemporary, as an institution which serves society by socializing people into it through a formalized, standardized procedure. At the beginning of this century Emile Durkheim told student teachers at the University of Paris that education "consists of a methodical socialization of the younger generation." He went on to add:

> It is the influence exercised by adult generations on those that are not ready for social life. Its object is to arouse and to develop in the child a certain number of physical, intellectual, and moral states that are demanded of him by the political society as a whole and by the special milieu for which he is specifically destined. . . . To the egotistic and asocial being that has just been born, [society] must, as rapidly as possible, add another, capable of leading a moral and social life. Such is the work of education.[1]

The education process, Durkheim said, "is above all the means by which society perpetually recreates the conditions of its very existence."[2] The contemporary educational sociologist Wilbur Brookover offers a similar formulation in his recent textbook definition of education:

> Actually, therefore, in the broadest sense education is synonymous with socialization. It includes any social behavior that assists in the induction of the child into membership in the society or any behavior by which the society perpetuates itself through the next generation.[3]

The educational institution is, then, one of the ways in which society is perpetuated through the systematic socialization of the young, while the nature of the society which is being perpetuated—its organization and operation, its values, beliefs, and ways of living—are determined by the primary institutions. The educational system, like other secondary institutions, *serves* the society which is *created* by the operation of the economy, the political system, and the military establishment.

Schools, the social organizations of the educational institution, are today for the most part large bureaucracies run by specially trained and certified people. There are few places left in modern societies where formal teaching and learning are carried on in small, isolated groups, like the rural, one-room schoolhouses of the last century. Schools are large, formal organizations which tend to be parts of larger organizations, local community School Districts. These School Districts are bureaucratically organized and their operations are supervised by state and local governments. In this context, as Brookover says:

> The term education is used . . . to refer to a system of schools, in which specifically designated persons are expected to teach children and youth certain types of acceptable behavior. The school system becomes a . . . unit in the total social structure and is recognized by the members of the society as a separate social institution. Within this structure a portion of the total socialization process occurs.[4]

Education is the part of the socialization process which takes place in the schools; and these are, more and more today, bureaucracies within bureaucracies.

Kindergarten is generally conceived by educators as a year of preparation for school. It is thought of as a year in which small children, five or six years old, are prepared socially and emotionally for the academic learning which will take place over the next twelve years. It is expected that a foundation of behavior and attitudes will be laid in kindergarten on which the children can acquire the skills and knowledge they will be taught in the grades. A booklet prepared for parents by the staff of a suburban New York school system says that the kindergarten experience will stimulate the child's desire to learn and cultivate the skills he will need for learning in the rest of his school career. It claims that the child will find opportunities for physical growth, for satisfying his "need for self-expression," acquire some knowledge, and provide opportunities for creative activity. It concludes, "The most important benefit that your five-year-old will receive from kindergarten is the opportunity to live and grow happily and purposefully with others in a small society." The kindergarten teachers in one of the elementary schools in this community, one we shall call the Wilbur Wright School, said their goals were to see that the children "grew" in all ways: physically, of course, emotionally, socially, and academically. They said they wanted children to like school as a result of their kindergarten experiences and that they wanted them to learn to get along with others.

None of these goals, however, is unique to kindergarten; each of them is held to some extent by teachers in the other six grades at Wright School. And growth would occur, but differently, even if the child did not attend school. The children already know how to get along with others, in their families and their play groups. The unique job of the kindergarten in the educational division of labor seems rather to be teaching children the student role. The student role is the repertoire of behavior and attitudes regarded by educators as appropriate to children in school. Observation in the kindergartens of the Wilbur Wright School revealed a great variety of activities through which children are shown and then drilled in the behavior and attitudes defined as appropriate for school and thereby induced to learn the role of student. Observations of the kindergartens and interviews with the teachers both pointed to the teaching and learning of classroom routines as the main element of the student role. The teachers expended most of their efforts, for the first half of the year at least, in training the children to follow the routines which teachers created. The children were, in a very real sense, *drilled* in tasks and activities created by the teachers for their own purposes and beginning and ending quite arbitrarily (from the child's point of view) at the command of the teacher. One teacher remarked that she hated September, because during the first month "everything has to be done rigidly, and repeatedly, until they know exactly what they're supposed to do." However, "by January," she said, "they know exactly what to do [during the day] and I don't have to be after them all the time." Classroom routines were introduced gradually from the beginning of the year in all the kindergartens, and the children were drilled in them as long as was necessary to achieve regular compliance. By the end of the school year, the successful kindergarten teacher has a well-organized group of children. They follow classroom routines automatically, having learned all the command signals and the expected responses to them. They have, in our terms, learned the student role. The following observation shows one such classroom operating at optimum organization on an afternoon late in May. It is the class of an experienced and respected kindergarten teacher.

An Afternoon in Kindergarten

At about 12:20 in the afternoon on a day in the last week of May, Edith Kerr leaves the teachers' room where she has been having lunch and walks to her classroom at the far end of the primary wing of Wright School. A group of five- and six-year-olds peers at her through the glass doors leading from the hall cloakroom to the play area outside. Entering her room, she straightens some material in the "book corner" of the room, arranges music on the piano, takes colored paper from her closet and places it on one of the shelves under the window. Her room is divided into a number of activity areas through the arrangement of furniture and play equipment. Two easels and a paint table near the door create a kind of passageway inside the room. A wedge-shaped area just inside the front door is made into a teacher's area by the placing of "her" things there: her desk, file, and piano. To the left is the book corner, marked off from the rest of the room by a puppet stage and a movable chalkboard. In it are a display rack of picture books, a record player, and a stack of children's records. To the right of the entrance are the sink and clean-up area. Four large round tables with six chairs at each for the children are placed near the walls about halfway down the length of the room, two on each side, leaving a large open area in the center for group games, block building, and toy truck driving. Windows stretch down the length of both walls, starting about three feet from the floor and extending almost to the high ceilings. Under the windows are long shelves on which are kept all the toys, games, blocks, paper, paints, and other equipment of the kindergarten. The left rear corner of the room is a play store with shelves, merchandise, and cash register; the right rear corner is a play kitchen with stove, sink, ironing board, and bassinette with baby dolls in it. This area is partly shielded from the rest of the room by a large standing display rack for posters and children's art work. A sandbox is found against the back wall between these two areas. The room is light, brightly colored, and filled with things adults feel five- and six-year-olds will find interesting and pleasing.

At 12:25 Edith opens the outside door and admits the waiting children. They hang their sweaters on hooks outside the door and then go to the center of the room and arrange themselves in a semi-circle on the floor, facing the teacher's chair, which she has placed in the center of the floor. Edith follows them in and sits in her chair checking attendance while waiting for the bell to ring. When she has finished attendance, which she takes by sight, she asks the children what the date is, what day and month it is, how many children are enrolled in the class, how many are present, and how many are absent.

The bell rings at 12:30 and the teacher puts away her attendance book. She introduces a visitor, who is sitting against the wall taking notes, as someone who wants to learn about schools and children. She then goes to the back of the room and takes down a large chart labeled "Helping Hands." Bringing it to the center of the room, she tells the children it is time to change jobs. Each child is assigned some task on the chart by placing his name, lettered on a paper "hand," next to a picture signifying the task—e.g., a broom, a blackboard, a milk bottle, a flag, and a Bible. She asks the children who wants each of the jobs and rearranges their "hands" accordingly. Returning to her chair, Edith announces, "One person should tell us what happened to Mark." A girl raises her hand, and when called on says, "Mark fell and hit his head and had to go to the hospital." The teacher adds that Mark's mother had written saying he was in the hospital.

During this time the children have been interacting among themselves, in their semi-circle. Children have whispered to their neighbors, poked one another, made general comments to the group, waved to friends on the other side of the circle. None of this has been disruptive, and the teacher has ignored it for the most part. The children seem to know just how much of each kind of interaction is permitted—they may greet in a soft voice someone who sits next to them, for example, but may not shout greetings to a friend who sits across the circle, so they confine themselves to waving and remain well within understood limits.

At 12:35 two children arrive. Edith asks them why they are late and then sends them to join the circle on the floor. The other children vie with each other to tell the newcomers what happened to Mark. When this leads to a general disorder Edith asks, "Who has serious time?" The children become quiet and a girl raises her hand. Edith nods and the child gets a Bible and hands it to Edith. She reads the Twenty-third Psalm while the children sit quietly. Edith helps the child in charge begin reciting the Lord's Prayer; the other children follow along for the first unit of sounds, and then trail off as Edith finishes for them. Everyone stands and faces the American flag hung to the right of the door. Edith leads the pledge to the flag, with the children again following the familiar sounds as far as they remember them. Edith then asks the girl in charge what song she wants and the child replies, "My Country." Edith goes to the piano and plays "America," singing as the children follow her words.

Edith returns to her chair in the center of the room and the children sit again in the semi-circle on the floor. It is 12:40 when she tells the children, "Let's have boys' sharing time first." She calls the name of the first boy sitting on the end of the circle, and he comes up to her with a toy helicopter. He turns and holds it up for the other children to see. He says, "It's a helicopter." Edith asks, "What is it used for?" and he replies, "For the army. Carry men.

For the war." Other children join in, "For shooting submarines." "To bring back men from space when they are in the ocean." Edith sends the boy back to the circle and asks the next boy if he has something. He replies "No" and she passes on to the next. He says "Yes" and brings a bird's nest to her. He holds it for the class to see, and the teacher asks, "What kind of bird made the nest?" The boy replies, "My friend says a rain bird made it." Edith asks what the nest is made of and different children reply, "mud," "leaves," and "sticks." There is also a bit of moss woven into the nest, and Edith tries to describe it to the children. They, however, are more interested in seeing if anything is inside it, and Edith lets the boy carry it around the semi-circle showing the children its insides. Edith tells the children of some baby robins in a nest in her yard, and some of the children tell about baby birds they have seen. Some children are asking about a small object in the nest which they say looks like an egg, but all have seen the nest now and Edith calls on the next boy. A number of children say, "I know what Michael has, but I'm not telling." Michael brings a book to the teacher and then goes back to his place in the circle of children. Edith reads the last page of the book to the class. Some children tell of books which they have at home. Edith calls the next boy, and three children call out, "I know what David has." "He always has the same thing." "It's a bang-bang." David goes to his table and gets a box which he brings to Edith. He opens it and shows the teacher a scale-model of an old-fashioned dueling pistol. When David does not turn around to the class, Edith tells him, "Show it to the children" and he does. One child says, "Mr. Johnson [the principal] said no guns." Edith replies, "Yes, how many of you know that?" Most of the children in the circle raise their hands. She continues, "That you aren't supposed to bring guns to school?" She calls the next boy on the circle and he brings two large toy soldiers to her which the children enthusiastically identify as being from "Babes in Toyland." The next boy brings an American flag to Edith and shows it to the class. She asks him what the stars and stripes stand for and admonishes him to treat it carefully. "Why should you treat it carefully?" she asks the boy. "Because it's our flag," he replies. She congratulates him, saying, "That's right."

"Show and Tell" lasted twenty minutes and during the last ten one girl in particular announced that she knew what each child called upon had to show. Edith asked her to be quiet each time she spoke out, but she was not content, continuing to offer her comment at each "show." Four children from other classes had come into the room to bring something from another teacher or to ask for something from Edith. Those with requests were asked to return later if the item wasn't readily available.

Edith now asks if any of the children told their mothers about their trip to the local zoo the previous day. Many children raise their hands. As Edith calls on them, they tell what they liked in the zoo. Some children cannot wait to be called on, and they call out things to the teacher, who asks them to be quiet. After a few of the animals are mentioned, one child says, "I liked the spooky house," and the others chime in to agree with him, some pantomiming fear and horror. Edith is puzzled, and asks what this was. When half the children try to tell her at once, she raises her hand for quiet, then calls on individual children. One says, "The house with nobody in it"; another, "The dark little house." Edith asks where it was in the zoo, but the children cannot describe its location in any way which she can understand. Edith makes some jokes but they involve adult abstractions which the children cannot grasp. The children have become quite noisy now, speaking out to make both relevant and irrelevant comments, and three little girls have become particularly assertive.

Edith gets up from her seat at 1:10 and goes to the book corner, where she puts a record on the player. As it begins a story about the trip to the zoo, she returns to the circle and asks the children to go sit at the tables. She divides them among the tables in such a way as to indicate that they don't have regular seats. When the children are all seated at the four tables, five or six to a table, the teacher asks, "Who wants to be the first one?" One of the noisy girls comes to the center of the room. The voice on the record is giving directions for imitating an ostrich and the girl follows them, walking around the center of the room holding her ankles with her hands. Edith replays the record, and all the children, table by table, imitate ostriches down the center of the room and back. Edith removes her shoes and shows that she can be an ostrich too. This is apparently a familiar game, for a number of children are calling out, "Can we have the crab?" Edith asks one of the children to do a crab "so we can all remember how," and then plays the part of the record with music for imitating crabs by. The children from the first table line up across the room, hands and feet on the floor and faces pointing toward the ceiling. After they have "walked" down the room and back in this posture they sit at their table and the children of the next table play "crab." The children love this; they run from their tables, dance about on the floor waiting for their turns, and are generally exuberant. Children ask for the "inch worm," and the game is played again with the children squirming down the floor. As a conclusion Edith shows them a new animal imitation, the "lame dog." The children all hobble down the floor on three "legs," table by table to the accompaniment of the record.

At 1:30 Edith has the children line up in the center of the room: she says, "Table one, line up in front of me," and children ask, "What are we going to do?" Then she moves a few steps to the side and says, "Table two over here; line up next to table one," and more children ask, "What for?" She does this for table three and table four, and each time the children ask, "Why, what are we going to do?" When the children are lined up in four lines of five each, spaced so that they are not touching one another, Edith puts on a new record and leads the class in calisthenics, to the accompaniment of the record. The children just jump around every which way in their places instead of doing the exercises, and by the time the record is finished, Edith, the only one following it, seems exhausted. She is apparently adopting the President's new "Physical Fitness" program for her classroom.

At 1:35 Edith pulls her chair to the easels and calls the children to sit on the floor in front of her, table by table. When they are all seated she asks,

"What are you going to do for worktime today?" Different children raise their hands and tell Edith what they are going to draw. Most are going to make pictures of animals they saw in the zoo. Edith asks if they want to make pictures to send to Mark in the hospital, and the children agree to this. Edith gives drawing paper to the children, calling them to her one by one. After getting a piece of paper, the children go to the crayon box on the righthand shelves, select a number of colors, and go to the tables, where they begin drawing. Edith is again trying to quiet the perpetually talking girls. She keeps two of them standing by her so they won't disrupt the others. She asks them, "Why do you feel you have to talk all the time?" and then scolds them for not listening to her. Then she sends them to their tables to draw.

Most of the children are drawing at their tables, sitting or kneeling in their chairs. They are all working very industriously and, engrossed in their work, very quietly. Three girls have chosen to paint at the easels, and having donned their smocks, they are busily mixing colors and intently applying them to their pictures. If the children at the tables are primitives and neo-realists in their animal depictions, these girls at the easels are the class abstract-expressionists, with their broad-stroked, colorful paintings.

Edith asks of the children generally, "What color should I make the cover of Mark's book?" Brown and green are suggested by some children "because Mark likes them." The other children are puzzled as to just what is going on and ask, "What book?" or "What does she mean?" Edith explains what she thought was clear to them already, that they are all going to put their pictures together in a "book" to be sent to Mark. She goes to a small table in the play-kitchen corner and tells the children to bring her their pictures when they are finished and she will write their message for Mark on them.

By 1:50 most children have finished their pictures and given them to Edith. She talks with some of them as she ties the bundle of pictures together—answering questions, listening, carrying on conversations. The children are playing in various parts of the room with toys, games, and blocks which they have taken off the shelves. They also move from table to table examining each other's pictures, offering compliments and suggestions. Three girls at a table are cutting up colored paper for a collage. Another girl is walking about the room in a pair of high heels with a woman's purse over her arm. Three boys are playing in the center of the room with the large block set, with which they are building walk-ways and walking on them. Edith is very much concerned about their safety and comes over a number of times to fuss over them. Two or three other boys are pushing trucks around the center of the room, and mild altercations occur when they drive through the block constructions. Some boys and girls are playing at the toy store, two girls are serving "tea" in the play kitchen, and one is washing a doll baby. Two boys have elected to clean the room, and with large sponges they wash the movable blackboard, the puppet stage, and then begin on the tables. They run into resistance from the children who are working with construction toys on the tables and do not want to dismantle their structures. The class is like a room full of bees, each intent on pursuing some activity, occasionally bumping into one another, but just veering off in another direction without serious altercation. At 2:05 the custodian arrives pushing a cart loaded with half-pint milk containers. He places a tray of cartons on the counter next to the sink, then leaves. His coming and going is unnoticed in the room (as, incidentally, is the presence of the observer, who is completely ignored by the children for the entire afternoon).

At 2:15 Edith walks to the entrance of the room, switches off the lights, and sits at the piano and plays. The children begin spontaneously singing the song, which is "Clean up, clean up. Everybody clean up." Edith walks around the room supervising the clean-up. Some children put their toys, the blocks, puzzles, games, and so on back their shelves under the windows. The children making a collage keep right on working. A child from another class comes in to borrow the 45-rpm adaptor for the record player. At more urging from Edith the rest of the children shelve their toys and work. The children are sitting around their tables now, and Edith asks, "What record would you like to hear while you have your milk?" There is some confusion and no general consensus, so Edith drops the subject and begins to call the children, table by table, to come get their milk. "Table one," she says, and the five children come to the sink, wash their hands and dry them, pick up a carton of milk and a straw, and take it back to their table. Two talking girls wander about the room interfering with the children getting their milk and Edith calls out to them to "settle down." As the children sit, many of them call out to Edith the name of the record they want to hear. When all the children are seated at tables with milk, Edith plays one of these records called "Bozo and the Birds" and shows the children pictures in a book which go with the record. The record recites, and the book shows the adventures of a clown, Bozo, as he walks through a woods meeting many different kinds of birds who, of course, display the characteristics of many kinds of people or, more accurately, different stereotypes. As children finish their milk, they take blankets or pads from the shelves under the windows and lie on them in the center of the room, where Edith sits on her chair showing the pictures. By 2:30 half the class is lying on the floor on their blankets, the record is still playing, and the teacher is turning the pages of the book. The child who came in previously returns the 45-rpm adaptor, and one of the kindergartners tells Edith what the boy's name is and where he lives.

The record ends at 2:40. Edith says, "Children, down on your blankets." All the class is lying on blankets now. Edith refuses to answer the various questions individual children put to her because, she tells them, "it's rest time now." Instead she talks very softly about what they will do tomorrow. They are going to work with clay, she says. The children lie quietly and listen. One of the boys raises his hand and when called on tells Edith, "The animals in the zoo looked so hungry yesterday." Edith asks the children what they think about this and a number try to volunteer opinions, but Edith accepts only those offered in a "rest-time tone," that is, softly and quietly. After a brief discussion of animal feeding, Edith calls the names of the two children on milk detail and has them collect empty milk cartons from the tables and return them to the tray. She asks the two children on clean-up detail to clean up the room. Then she gets up from her chair and goes to the door to turn on the lights. At this signal, the children all get up from the floor and return their blankets and pads to the shelf. It is raining (the reason for no outside play this afternoon) and cars driven by mothers clog the school drive and line up along the street. One of the talkative little girls comes over to Edith and pointing out the window says, "Mrs. Kerr, see my mother in the new Cadillac?"

At 2:50 Edith sits at the piano and plays. The children sit on the floor in the center of the room and sing. They have a repertoire of songs about animals, including one in which each child sings a refrain alone. They know these by heart and sing along through the ringing of the 2:55 bell. When the song is finished, Edith gets up and coming to the group says, "Okay, rhyming words to get your coats today." The children raise their hands and as Edith calls on them, they tell her two rhyming words, after which they are allowed to go into the hall to get their coats and sweaters. They return to the room with these and sit at their tables. At 2:59 Edith says, "When you have your coats on, you may line up at the door." Half of the children go to the door and stand in a long line. When the three o'clock bell rings, Edith returns to the piano and plays. The children sing a song called "Goodbye," after which Edith sends them out.

Training for Learning and for Life

The day in kindergarten at Wright School illustrates both the content of the student role as it has been learned by these children and the processes by which the teacher has brought about this learning, or, "taught" them the student role. The children have learned to go through routines and to follow orders with unquestioning obedience, even when these make no sense to them. They have been disciplined to do as they are told by an authoritative person without significant protest. Edith has developed this discipline in the children by creating and enforcing a rigid social structure in the classroom through which she effectively controls the behavior of most of the children for most of the school day. The "living with others in a small society" which the school pamphlet tells parents is the most important thing the children will learn in kindergarten can be seen now in its operational meaning, which is learning to live by the routines imposed by the school. This learning appears to be the principal content of the student role.

Children who submit to school-imposed discipline and come to identify with it, so that being a "good student" comes to be an important part of their developing identities, *become* the good students by the school's definitions. Those who submit to the routines of the school but do not come to identify with them will be adequate students who find the more important part of their identities elsewhere, such as in the play group outside school. Children who refuse to submit to the school routines are rebels, who become known as "bad students" and often "problem children" in the school, for they do not learn the academic curriculum and their behavior is often disruptive in the classroom. Today schools engage clinical psychologists in part to help teachers deal with such children.

In looking at Edith's kindergarten at Wright School, it is interesting to ask how the children learn this role of student—come to accept school-imposed routines—and what, exactly, it involves in terms of behavior and attitudes. The most prominent features of the classroom are its physical and social structures. The room is carefully furnished and arranged in ways adults feel will interest children. The play store and play kitchen in the back of the room, for example, imply that children are interested in mimicking these activities of the adult world. The only space left for the children to create something of their own is the empty center of the room, and the materials at their disposal are the blocks, whose use causes anxiety on the part of the teacher. The room, being carefully organized physically by the adults, leaves little room for the creation of physical organization on the part of the children.

The social structure created by Edith is a far more powerful and subtle force for fitting the children to the student role. This structure is established by the very rigid and tightly controlled set of rituals and routines through which the children are put during the day. There is first the rigid "locating procedure" in which the children are asked to find themselves in terms of the month, date, day of the week, and the number of the class who are present and absent. This puts them solidly in the real world as defined by adults. The day is then divided into six periods whose activities are for the most part determined by the teacher. In Edith's kindergarten the children went through Serious Time, which opens the school day, Sharing Time, Play Time (which in clear weather would be spent outside), Work Time, Clean-up Time, after which they have their milk, and Rest Time, after which they go home. The teacher has programmed activities for each of these Times.

Occasionally the class is allowed limited discretion to choose between proffered activities, such as stories or records, but original ideas for activities are never solicited from them. Opportunity for free individual action is open only once in the day, during the part of Work Time left after the general class assignment has been completed (on the day reported the class assignment was drawing animal pictures for the absent Mark). Spontaneous interests or observations from the children are never developed by the teacher. It seems that her schedule just does not allow room for developing such unplanned events. During Sharing Time, for example, the child who brought a bird's nest told Edith, in reply to her question of what kind of bird made it, "My friend says it's a rain bird." Edith does not think to ask about this bird, probably because the answer is "childish," that is, not given in accepted adult categories of birds. The children then express great interest in an object in the nest, but the teacher ignores this interest, probably because the object is uninteresting to her. The soldiers from "Babes in Toyland" strike a responsive note in the children, but this is not used for a discussion of any kind. The soldiers are treated in the same way as objects which bring little interest from the children. Finally, at the end of Sharing Time the child-world of perception literally erupts in the class with the recollection of "the spooky house" at the zoo. Apparently this made more of an impression on the children than did any of the animals, but Edith is unable to make any sense of it for herself. The tightly imposed order of the class begins to break down as the children discover a universe of discourse of their own and begin talking excitedly with one another. The teacher is effectively excluded from this child's world of perception and for a moment she fails to dominate the classroom situation. She reasserts control, however, by taking the children to the next activity she has planned for the day. It seems never to have occurred to Edith that there might be a meaningful learning experience for the children in re-creating the "spooky house" in the classroom. It seems fair to say that this would have offered an exercise in spontaneous self-expression and an opportunity for real creativity on the part of the children. Instead, they are taken through a canned animal imitation procedure, an activity which they apparently enjoy, but which is also imposed upon them rather than created by them.

While children's perceptions of the world and opportunities for genuine spontaneity and creativity are being systematically eliminated from the kindergarten, unquestioned obedience to authority and rote learning of meaningless material are being encouraged. When the children are called to line up in the center of the room they ask "Why?" and "What for?" as they are in the very process of complying. They have learned to go smoothly through a programmed day, regardless of whether parts of the program make any sense to them or not. Here the student role involves what might be called "doing what you're told and never mind why." Activities which might "make sense" to the children are effectively ruled out, and they are forced or induced to participate in activities which may be "senseless," such as calisthenics.

At the same time the children are being taught by rote meaningless sounds in the ritual oaths and songs, such as the Lord's Prayer, the Pledge to the Flag, and "America." As they go through the grades children learn more and more of the sounds of these ritual oaths, but the fact that they have often learned meaningless sounds rather than meaningful statements is shown when they are asked to write these out in the sixth grade; they write them as groups of sounds rather than as a series of words, according to the sixth grade teachers at Wright School. Probably much learning in the elementary grades is of this character, that is, having no intrinsic meaning to the children, but rather being tasks inexplicably required of them by authoritative adults. Listening to sixth grade children read social studies reports, for example, in which they have copied material from encyclopedias about a particular country, an observer often gets the feeling that he is watching an activity which has no intrinsic meaning for the child. The child who reads, "Switzerland grows wheat and cows and grass and makes a lot of cheese" knows the dictionary meaning of each of these words but may very well have no conception at all of this "thing" called Switzerland. He is simply carrying out a task assigned by the teacher *because* it is assigned, and this may be its only "meaning" for him.

Another type of learning which takes place in kindergarten is seen in children who take advantage of the "holes" in the adult social structure to create activities of their own, during Work Time or out-of-doors during Play Time. Here the children are learning to carve out a small world of their own within the world created by adults. They very quickly learn that if they keep within permissible limits of noise and action they can play much as they please. Small groups of children formed during the year in Edith's kindergarten who played together at these times, developing semi-independent little groups in which they created their own worlds in the interstices of the adult-imposed physical and social world. These groups remind the sociological observer very much of the so-called "informal groups" which adults develop in factories and offices of large bureaucracies.[5] Here, too, within authoritatively imposed social organizations people find "holes" to create little subworlds which support informal, friendly, unofficial behavior. Forming and participating in such groups seems to be as much part of the student role as it is of the role of bureaucrat.

The kindergarten has been conceived of here as the year in which children are prepared for their schooling by learning the role of student. In the classrooms of the rest of the school grades, the children will be asked to submit to systems and routines imposed by the teachers and the curriculum. The days will be much like those of kindergarten, except that academic subjects will be substituted for the activities of the kindergarten. Once out of the school system, young adults will more than likely find themselves working in large-scale bureaucratic organizations, perhaps on the assembly line in the factory, perhaps in the paper routines of the white collar occupations, where they will be required to submit to rigid routines imposed by "the company" which may make little sense to them. Those who can operate well in this situation will be successful bureaucratic functionaries. Kindergarten, therefore, can be seen as preparing children not only for participation in the bureaucratic organization of large modern school systems, but also for the large-scale occupational bureaucracies of modern society.

Notes

1. Emile Durkheim, *Sociology and Education* (New York: The Free Press, 1956), pp. 71–72.

2. *Ibid.*, p. 123.

3. Wilbur Brookover, *The Sociology of Education* (New York: American Book Company, 1957), p. 4.

4. *Ibid.*, p. 6.

5. See, for example, Peter M. Blau, *Bureaucracy in Modern Society* (New York: Random House, 1956), Chapter 3.

37 Men Who Share "The Second Shift"

ARLIE HOCHSCHILD
ANNE MACHUNG

The fast moving currents of social change have not left the U.S. family untouched. We all are familiar with many of the consequences—later age at first marriage, smaller families, two paychecks, divorce, teenage pregnancy, unwed mothers and fathers, abortion, and cohabitation. Family violence may also be higher, but this is primarily speculation for we have no firm figures to measure the present, much less the past. Some of us come from broken homes; others of us have been divorced. Hardly any of us expects our marriage to be the way our grandparents' was, and many of us even anticipate that our approach to being a husband or wife will differ markedly from that of our own parents.

Although we can mentally project ourselves into anticipated roles, we have little idea of what we will really face. Certainly, with the rapid pace of change, many of our attitudes and ideas will be different in a few years. It seems certain, however, that increasing pressures will be brought to bear on husbands to share what Hochschild and Machung call the *second shift*, the housework and family and home duties that remain to be done after the day's work-for-pay is completed. To gather data for their study, Hochschild and her colleagues interviewed fifty families, following a dozen in depth. In these families, from different social classes and racial/ethnic groups, the wife was usually a "super-mom," working the second shift herself with very little assistance from her husband. She averaged an extra *month* of work a year on the second shift than her husband. About 20 percent of the men, however, shared the second shift, and in this selection we examine differences between the men who did and those who did not and the resulting effects on the marriage and the children.

ONE OUT OF FIVE MEN in this study was as actively involved in the home as their wives—some were like Greg Alston, working the same hours as their wives but sharing in a more "male" way, doing such things as carpentry; others, like Art Winfield, shared the cooking and being a primary parent. In my study the men who shared the second shift had a happier family life, so

I wanted to know what conditions produce such men. How do men who share *differ* from other men?

The men in this study who shared the work at home were no more likely than others to have "model" fathers who helped at home. Their parents were no more likely to have trained them to do chores when they were young. Michael Sherman and Seth Stein both had fathers who spent little time with them and did little work around the house. But Michael became extremely involved in raising his twin boys, whereas Seth said hello and goodbye to his children as he went to and from his absorbing law practice. Sharers were also as likely to have had mothers who were homemakers or who worked *and* tended the home as non-sharers. . . .

Did the men who shared the work at home love their wives more? Were they more considerate? It's true, egalitarian men had more harmonious marriages, but I would be reluctant to say that men like Peter Tanagawa or Ray Judson loved their wives less than men like Art Winfield or Michael Sherman, or were less considerate in other ways. One man who did very little at home said, "Just last week I suddenly realized that for the first time I feel like my wife's life is more valuable than mine, because my son needs her more than he needs me." Men who shared were very devoted to their wives; but, in a less helpful way, so were the men who didn't.

Two other, more external factors also did *not* distinguish men who did share from men who didn't: the number of hours they worked or how much they earned. Husbands usually work a longer "full-time" job than wives. But in the families I studied, men who worked fifty hours or more per week were just *slightly* less likely to share housework than men who worked forty-five, forty, or thirty-five hours a week. In addition, fifty-hour-a-week *women* did far *more* childcare and housework than men who worked the same hours. Other national studies also show that the number of hours a man works for pay has little to do with the number of hours he works at home.

Of all the factors that influence the relations between husbands and wives, I first assumed that money would loom the largest. The man who shared, I thought, would need his wife's salary more, would value her job more, and as a result also her time. . . .

I assumed that the man who shares would not earn more, and that the wage gap between other husbands and their wives might *cause* the leisure gap between them. Both spouses might agree that because his job came first, his leisure did, too. Leaving childcare aside (since most men would want to do some of that), I assumed that men who earned *as much or less* than their wives would do more housework. I assumed that a woman who wanted fifty-fifty in the second shift but had married a high-earning man would reconcile herself to the family's greater need for her husband's work, set aside her desires, and work the extra month a year. By the same token, a traditional man married to a high-earning woman would swallow his traditional pride and pitch in at home. I assumed that money would talk louder than ideals, and invisibly shape each partner's gender strategy.

If money is the underlying principle behind men's and women's strate-gies, that would mean that no matter how much effort a woman put into her job, its lower pay would result in less help from her husband at home. Research about on-the-job stress suggests that jobs in the low-level service sector, where women are concentrated, cause more stress than blue-and-white-collar jobs, where men are concentrated. Although working mothers don't work as long hours as working fathers, they devote as much *effort* to earning money as men, and many women earn less for work that's more stress-ful. Thus, by using his higher salary to "buy" more leisure at home, he inadver-tently makes his wife pay indirectly for an inequity in the wider economy that causes her to get paid less. If money is the key organizing principle to the rela-tions between men and women in marriage, it's a pity for men because it puts their role at home at the mercy of the blind fluctuations of the marketplace and for women because if money talks at home, it favors men. The extra month a year becomes an indirect way in which the woman pays *at home* for *economic* discrimination *outside* the home.

The Limits of Economic Logic

Money mattered in the marriages I studied, but it was not the powerful "invis-ible hand" behind the men who shared. For one thing, this is clear from the family portraits. Michael Sherman earned much more than Adrienne but his job didn't matter more, and he shared the work at home. For years Ann Myerson earned more than her husband but put her husband's job first any-way. John Livingston valued his wife's job as he did his own, but she took more responsibility at home.

A number of researchers have tried to discover a link between the *wage* gap between working parents and the *leisure* gap between them, and the re-sults have been confusing. All but one study found no significant relation be-tween the amount a man earns relative to his wife and how much housework or child care he does. Among couples in this study, these two factors were not related in a statistically significant way.

An intriguing clue appeared, however, when I divided all the men into three groups: men who earn more than their wives (most men), men who earn the same amount, and men who earn less. Of the men who earned more than their wives, 21 percent shared housework. Of the men who earned about the same, 30 percent. But among men who earned less than their wives, *none* shared.

If a logic of the pocketbook is only a logic of the *pocketbook*, it should op-erate the same whether a man earns more or a woman earns more. But this "logic of the pocketbook" didn't work that way. It only worked as long as men earned as much or more than their wives. Money frequently "worked" for men (it excused them from housework) but it didn't work for women (it didn't get them out of it).

Another principle—the principle of "balancing"—seems to be at work. According to this principle, if men lose power over women in one way, they make up for it in another way—by avoiding the second shift, for example. In this way they can maintain dominance over women. How much responsibility these men assumed at home was thus related to the deeper issue of male power. Men who earn much more than their wives already have a power over their wives in that they control a scarce and important resource. The more severely a man's financial identity is threatened—by his wife's higher salary, for example—the less he can afford to threaten it further by doing "women's work" at home.

Men who shared the second shift weren't trying to make up for losing power in other realms of their marriage; they didn't feel the need to "balance." Michael Sherman had given up the *idea* that he should have more power than Adrienne. Art Winfield talked playfully about men being "brought up to be kings."

But Peter Tanagawa felt a man *should* have more power, and felt he'd given a lot of it up when Nina's career rose so dramatically. He's adjusted himself to earning much less, but to a man of his ideas, this had been a sacrifice. By making up for his sacrifice by doing more at home, Nina engaged in "balancing." Among other couples, too, it's not only men who "balance"; women do too.

Thus, more crucial than cultural beliefs about men's and women's *spheres,* were couples' beliefs about the right degree of men's and women's *power.* Women who "balanced" felt "too powerful." Sensing when their husbands got "touchy," sensing the fragility of their husbands' "male ego," not wanting them to get discouraged or depressed, such women restored their men's lost power by waiting on them at home.

Wives did this "balancing"—this restoring power to their husbands—for different reasons. One eccentric Englishman and father of three children, aged six, four, and one, took responsibility for about a third of the chores at home. A tenured member of the English department of a small college, he taught classes, and held obligatory office hours, but had abandoned research, minimized committee work, avoided corridor conversations, and had long since given up putting in for a raise. He claimed to "share" housework and childcare, but what he meant by housework was working on a new den, and what he meant by childcare was reflected in this remark, "The children do fine while I'm working on the house; they muck about by themselves." He was touchy about his accomplishments and covertly nervous, it seemed, about what he called the "limitless" ambitions of his workaholic wife. Without asking him to do more, perhaps his wife was making up for her "limitless ambitions" by carrying the load at home. In the meantime, she described herself as "crushed with work."

I looked again at other interviews I'd done with men who worked less than full time. One architect, the fourth of four highly successful brothers in a prosperous and rising black family, had lost his job in the recession of the late 1970s, become deeply discouraged, taken occasional contracting jobs, and otherwise settled into a life of semi-unemployment. His wife explained: "Eventually we're going to have to make it on my salary. But it's awfully hard on my husband right now, being trained as an architect and not being able to get a job. I take that into account." Her husband did no housework and spent time with his son only when the spirit moved him. "I do very little around the house," he said frankly, "but Beverly doesn't complain, bless her heart." Meanwhile, they lived in near-poverty, while Beverly worked part time, cared for their baby and home, and took courses in veterinary science at night, her overload the result of their economic need added to her attempt to restore a sense of power to her discouraged husband. As she let fall at the end of the interview, "Sometimes I wonder how long I can keep going."

Other men earned less and did less at home but weren't "balancing." They were going back to get a degree, and their wives were temporarily giving them the money and the time to do this. The husband's training for a job counted as much in their moral accounting system as it would if he already had that more important job. For example, one husband was unemployed while studying for a degree in pediatric nursing. His wife, a full-time administrator, cared for their home and their nine-month-old baby. The rhythm of their household life revolved around the dates of his exams. His wife explained: "My husband used to do a lot around here. He used to puree Stevy's carrots in the blender. He used to help shop, and weed the garden. Now he studies every evening until ten. His exams come first. Getting that "A" is important to him. He plays with the baby as a study break." She said she didn't mind doing the housework and caring for the baby and got upset when he complained the house was messy. She said, "I keep myself going by reminding myself this is *temporary*, until Jay gets his degree."

I heard of no women whose husbands both worked and cared for the family while the wives studied for a degree. For a woman, getting a degree was not so honored an act. There was no tradition of "putting your wife through college" analogous to the recent tradition of "putting your husband through college." A wife could imagine being supported or being better off when her husband got his degree. Husbands usually couldn't imagine either situation. One husband *had* shared the work at home fifty-fifty when his wife worked, but came to resent it terribly and finally stopped when his wife quit her job and went back to school to get a Ph.D. A job counted as legitimate recompense, but working toward a degree did not. Feeling deprived of attention and service, one man shouted into my tape recorder—half in fun and half not: "You can't eat it. You can't talk to it. It doesn't buy a vacation or a new car. I *hate* my wife's dissertation!" Women who put their husbands through school may have resented the burden, but they didn't feel they had as much right to complain about it.

Taken as a whole, this group of men—semi-unemployed, hanging back at work, or in training—neither earned the bread nor cooked it. And of all the wives, theirs were the least happy. Yet, either because they sympathized with their husbands, or expected the situation to improve, or because they felt there was no way to change it, and because they were, I believe, unconsciously maintaining the "right" balance of power in their marriage, such women worked the extra month a year. Meanwhile, their lower-earning husbands often saw their wives as intelligent, strong, "a rock"; at the same time these men could enjoy the idea that, though not a king at work, a man still had a warm throne at home.

Some women had other ways of accumulating more power than they felt "comfortable" with. One woman I know, an M.D., not in this study, married a former patient, a musician who earned far less than she. Perhaps the feeling that her status was "too great" for their joint notion of the "right" balance, she—a feminist on every other issue—quietly did all the second shift and, as her husband put it, "She never asks." Another woman, a teacher, secretly upset the power balance by having a long-term extra-marital affair almost like another marriage. Life went on as usual at home, but she quietly made up for her secret life by being "wonderful" about all the chores at home.

In these marriages, money was not the main determinant of which men did or didn't share. Even men who earned much more than their wives didn't get out of housework *because* of it. One college professor and father of three, for example, explained why he committed himself to 50 percent of housework and childcare:

> My wife earns a third of what I earn. But as a public school teacher she's doing a job that's just as important as mine. She's an extraordinarily gifted teacher, and I happen to know she works just as hard at her teaching as I do at mine. So, when we come home, she's as tired as I am. We share the housework and childcare equally. But [in a tone of exasperation] if she were to take a job in insurance or real estate, she'd just be doing another job. She wouldn't be making the contribution she's making now. We haven't talked about it, but if that were the case, I probably wouldn't break my back like this. She would have to carry the load at home.

Ironically, had his wife earned *more* at a job he admired less—had she worked only for *money*—he would *not* have shared the second shift. . . .

That doesn't mean that money has nothing to do with sharing the second shift. In two different ways, it does. In the first place, couples do need to think about and plan around financial need. Most of the men who shared at home had wives who pretty much shared at work. The men earned some but not much more. And whatever their wives earned, working-class men like Art Winfield really needed their wives' wages to live. Second, future changes in the general economy may press more couples to do "balancing." Some experts predict that the American economy will split increasingly between an elite of highly paid, highly trained workers and an enlarging pool of poorly paid, un-skilled workers. Jobs in the middle are being squeezed out as companies lose out to foreign competition or seek cheaper labor pools in the Third World. The personnel rosters of the so-called sunrise industries, the rapidly growing, high-technology companies, already reflect this split. Companies with many jobs in the middle are in the so-called sunset industries, such as car manufac-turing. As the economist Bob Kuttner illustrates: "The fast food industry em-ploys a small number of executives and hundreds of thousands of cashiers and kitchen help who make $3.50 an hour. With some variation, key punchers, chambermaids, and retail sales personnel confront the same short job ladder." In addition, unions in the sunrise industries often face companies' threats to move their plants to cheap labor markets overseas, and so these unions press less hard for better pay.

The decline in jobs in the middle mainly hits men in blue-collar union-protected jobs. Unless they can get training that allows them to compete for a small supply of highly skilled jobs, such men will be forced to choose between unemployment and a low-paid service job.

The "declining middle" is thus in the process of creating an economic cri-sis for many men. This crisis can lead to two very different results: As eco-nomic hardship means more women have to work, their husbands may feel it is "only fair" to share the work at home. Or, there may be a countervailing ten-dency for men and women to compensate for economically induced losses in male self-esteem by engaging in "balancing." If the logic of the pocketbook af-fects the way men and women divide the second shift, I think it will affect it in this way, through its indirect effect on male self-esteem.

All in all, men who shared were similar to men who didn't in that their fa-thers were just as unlikely to have been model helpers at home, and just as un-likely to have done housework as boys themselves. But the men who shared at home seemed to have more distant ties with their fathers, and closer ones with their mothers. They were similar to non-sharing men in the hours they worked, but they tended not to earn a great deal more or less than their wives.

Sharing men seemed to be randomly distributed across the class hierar-chy. There were the Michael Shermans and the Art Winfields. In the working class, more men shared without believing it corresponded to the kind of man they wanted to be. In the middle class, more men didn't share even though they believed in it. Men who both shared the work at home and believed in it seemed to come from every social class. Everything else equal, men whose wives had advanced degrees and professional careers—who had what the soci-ologist Pierre Bourdieu calls "cultural capital"—were more likely to share than men whose wives lacked such capital. Men with career wives were more likely to share than men with wives in "jobs." All these factors were part of the social backdrop to the working man's gender strategy at home.

Added to these was also the strategy of his wife. Nearly every man who shared had a wife whose strategy was to urge—or at least welcome—his involvement at home. Such women did not emotionally hoard their children, as Nancy Holt came to do with Joey. When Evan had been about to leave to take Joey to the zoo for a father-son outing, Nancy had edged Evan out by deciding at the last minute to "help" them get along. At first awkward and unconfident with children, Michael Sherman could well have developed a "downstairs" retreat had it not been for Adrienne's showdown and continual invitation to join in the care of their twins. Often, something as simple as the way a mother holds her baby so he or she can "look at Dad" indicates her effort to share. Adrienne Sherman didn't just leave her twins with Daddy; she talked to them about what Daddy could do with them; consciously or not, she fostered a tie to him. She didn't play expert. She made room.

As a result, such men were—or became—sensitive to their children's needs. They were more realistic than other fathers about the limits of what their wives provide, and about what their children really need.

Limiting the Idea of Fatherhood

Involved fathers had a much fuller, more elaborate notion of what a father was than uninvolved fathers did. Involved fathers talked about fathering much as mothers talked about mothering. Uninvolved fathers held to a far more restricted mission—to discipline the child or to teach him about sports. For example, when asked what he thought was important about being a father, one black businessman and father of two said:

> Discipline. I don't put up with whining. It bothers me. I'm shorter tempered and my wife is longer tempered. I do a significant amount of paddling. I grew up with being paddled. When I got paddled I knew damn good and well that I deserved it. I don't whip them. One good pop on their bottom and I send them down to their room. I've scared them. I've never punched them. And I'll spank them in front of people as well as not in front of them.

To him, being a disciplinarian *was* being a father. As a result, his children gravitated to their mother. She had worked for an insurance company but, under the pressure of home and work, finally quit her job. In a strangely matter-of-fact way, she remarked that she didn't "feel comfortable" leaving the children with her husband for long periods. "If I go out to the hairdresser's on Saturday, I might come back and find he didn't fix them lunch; I don't leave them with him too much." If it wasn't a matter of discipline, he didn't think caring for children was his job.

Other fathers limited their notion of fathering mainly to teaching their children about the events in the newspaper, baseball, soccer. When I asked uninvolved fathers to define a "good mother" and "good father," they gave elaborate and detailed answers for "good mother," and short, hazy answers for "good father," sometimes with a specific mission attached to it, like "teach them about cars."

I asked one man, "What's a good mother?" and he answered: "A good mother is patient. That's the first thing. Someone who is warm, caring, who can see what the child needs, physically, who stimulates the child intellectually, and helps the child meet his emotional challenges."

"What is a good father?" I asked. "A good father is a man who spends time with his children." Another man said, "A good father is a man who is around."

It is not that men have an elaborate idea of fatherhood and then don't live up to it. Their idea of fatherhood is embryonic to being with. They often limit that idea by comparing themselves only to their own fathers and not, as more involved men did, to their mothers or sisters, or to other fathers. As a Salvadoran delivery man put it, "I give my children everything my father gave me." But Michael Sherman gave his twins what his *mother* gave him.

Curtailing the Idea of What a Child Needs

Men who were greatly involved with their children react against two cultural ideas: one idea removes the actual care of children from the definition of *manhood*, and one curtails the notion of how much care a child needs. As to the first idea, involved fathers' biggest struggle was against the doubts they felt about not "giving everything to get ahead" in their jobs. But even when they conquered this fear, another cultural idea stood in the way—the idea that their child is "already grown-up," "advanced," and doesn't need much from him. A man's individual defense against seeing his children's need for him conspires with this larger social idea.

Just as the archetype of the supermom—the woman who can do it all—minimizes the real needs of women, so too the archetype of the "superkid" minimizes the real needs of children. It makes it all right to treat a young child as if he or she were older. Often uninvolved parents remarked with pride that their small children were "self-sufficient" or "very independent."

I asked the fifth-grade teacher in a private school how she thought her students from two-job families were doing. She began by saying that they did as well as the few children she had whose mothers stayed home. But having said that, her talk ran to the problems: "The good side of kids being on their own so much is that it makes them independent really early. But I think they pay a price for it. I can see them sealing off their feelings, as if they're saying, 'That's the last time I'll be vulnerable.' I can see it in their faces, especially the sixth-grade boys."

Throughout the second half of the nineteenth century, as women were increasingly excluded from the workplace, the cultural notion of what a child "needs" at home correspondingly grew to expand the woman's role at home.

As Barbara Ehrenreich and Deirdre English point out in *For Her Own Good*, doctors and ministers argued strongly that a woman's place was at home. The child needed her there. As the economic winds have reversed, so has the idea of a woman's proper place—and the child's real needs. Nowadays, a child is increasingly imagined to need time with other children, to need "independence-training," not to need "quantity time" with a parent but only a small amount of "quality time." As one working father remarked: "Children need time to play with other children their age. It's stimulating for them. Nelson enjoyed it, I think, from when he was six months."

If in the earlier part of the century, middle-class children suffered from overattentive mothers, from being "mother's only accomplishment," today's children may suffer from an underestimation of their needs. Our idea of what a *child* needs in each case reflects what *parents* need. The child's needs are thus a cultural football in an economic and marital game.

An Orwellian "superkid" language has emerged to consolidate this sense of normality. In a September 1985 *New York Times* article entitled "New Programs Come to Aid of Latch Key Children," Janet Edder quotes a child-care professional as follows: "Like other child-care professionals, Mrs. Selgison prefers to use the phrase 'Children in Self Care' rather than 'Latch Key Children,' a term coined during the depression when many children who went home alone wore a key around their necks." "Children in Self Care" suggests that the children *are* being cared for, but by themselves, independently. Unlike the term "Latch Key Children," which suggests a child who is sad and deprived, the term "Children in Self Care" suggests a happy superkid.

Another article, in the August 1984 *Changing Times*, entitled "When You Can't Be Home, Teach Your Child What to Do," suggests that working parents do home-safety checkups so that a pipe won't burst, a circuit breaker won't blow, or an electrical fire won't start. Parents should advise children to keep house keys out of sight and to conceal from callers the fact that they're alone at home. It tells about "warm lines"—a telephone number a child can call for advice or simple comfort when he or she is alone. Earlier in the century, advice of this sort was offered to destitute widows or working wives of disabled or unemployed men while the middle class shook its head in sympathy. Now the middle class has "children in self-care" too.

The parents I talked to had younger children, none of whom were in "self-care." The children I visited seemed to me a fairly jolly and resilient lot. But parents I spoke to did not feel very supported in their parenthood; like Ann Myerson, many parents in the business world felt obligated to hide concerns that related to a child. Many female clerical workers were discouraged from making calls home. Many men felt that doing anything for family reasons—moving to another city, missing the office party, passing up a promotion—would be taken as a sign they lacked ambition or manliness. As for John Livingston's coworkers, the rule of thumb was: don't go home until your wife calls.

For all the talk about the importance of children, the cultural climate has become subtly less hospitable to parents who put children first. This is not because parents love children less, but because a "job culture" has expanded at the expense of a "family culture."

As motherhood as a "private enterprise" declines and more mothers rely on the work of lower-paid specialists, the value accorded the work of mothering (not the value of children) has declined for women, making it all the harder for men to take it up.

My Wife Is Doing It

Involved fathers are aware that their children depend on them. Every afternoon Art Winfield knew Adam was waiting for him at daycare. Michael Sherman knew that around six A.M. one of his twins could call out "Daddy." John Livingston knew that Cary relied on him to get around her mother's discipline. Such men were close enough to their children to know what they were and weren't getting from their mothers.

Uninvolved fathers were not. They *imagined* that their wives did more with the children than they did. For example, one thirty-two-year-old grocery clerk praised his wife for helping their daughter with reading on the weekends—something his wife complained he didn't make time for. But when I interviewed her, I discovered that her weekends were taken with housework, church, and visiting relatives.

Sometimes I had the feeling that fathers were passing the childcare buck to their wives while the wives passed it to the baby-sitter. Each person passing on the role wanted to feel good about it, and tended to deny the problems. Just as fathers often praised their wives as "wonderful mothers," so mothers often praised their baby-sitters as "wonderful." Even women who complain about daycare commonly end up describing the daycare worker as "great." So important to parents was the care of their child that they almost had to believe that "everything at daycare was fine." Sadly, not only was the role of caretaker transferred from parent to baby-sitter, but sometimes also the illusion that the child was "in good hands."

The reasons men gave for why their wives were wonderful—for example, that they were patient—were often reasons women gave for why the baby-sitters were wonderful. Just as uninvolved fathers who praised their wives often said they wouldn't want to trade places with their wives, so wives often said they wouldn't want to trade places with their daycare worker.

As one businesswoman and mother of a three-year-old boy commented: "Our baby-sitter is just fantastic. She's with the kids from seven o'clock in the morning until six o'clock at night. And some kids stay later. I don't know how she does it. *I* couldn't." Another working mother commented: "I couldn't be as patient as Elizabeth [the daycare worker] is. I love my child, but I'm not a baby person."

The daycare worker herself was often in a difficult spot. She depended economically on the parents, so she didn't want to say anything so offensive it might lead them to withdraw the child. On the other hand, sometimes she grew concerned about a child's behavior. Typical of many daycare workers, Katherine Wilson, who had cared for children for fifteen years, remarked:

> One out of five parents just drop their children off and run. Another three will come in and briefly talk with you. Then the last person will come in and talk to you quite a bit. Not too many call during the day. A lot of parents aren't too concerned with day-to-day activities. They just trust we know what we're doing.

Some daycare centers even established a policy of check-in sheets that required parents to come inside the daycare center and sign their child in each morning, thus preventing the hurried few who might otherwise leave their children off at the sidewalk.

Pickup time was often hectic, and not a good time to talk. As one daycare worker observed:

> It's a hell of a life the parents lead. Every time I see them they're in a rush. It's rush in the morning and rush in the evening. They barely ask me what Danny had for lunch or how he seemed. I think they might feel bad when they see him around four o'clock in the afternoon. He gets kind of restless then. He's waiting. He sees the parents of the other children come and each time the doorbell rings he hopes its his parents. But, see, they come in the last—six-thirty.

Sometimes a daycare worker becomes worried about a child. As Alicia Fernandez confided:

> I've had Emily for a year and a half now. She's never been real open with me and I don't think she is with her mother either. I think, in a way, Emily was hurt that her former sitter had to give her up. It was a hard adjustment coming in to me and in fact I don't think she has adjusted. One day she took the money out of my wallet—the money her mother had given me—and tore it up. I was so shocked. It was my pay. I slapped her across the knees. She didn't even cry. I felt bad I'd done that, but even worse that she didn't even cry. I thought, hey, something's wrong.

Had she mentioned this to Emily's mother and father? I asked. She replied quickly and quietly: "Oh no. It's hard to talk about that. I feel badly about it but on the other hand if I told her mother, she might take Emily away."

The daycare worker, who could best judge how Emily's day had gone, felt afraid to confide her concerns to Emily's parents, who badly needed to hear them. Other daycare workers also kept their opinions to themselves. As another daycare worker noted: "You can feel sorry for them. I have Tim for nine hours. I have Jessica for ten and a half—now Jessie's mother is a single mother. Like I say, at the end of the day they cry." "Do you talk to their parents about the crying?" I asked. "They don't ask, and I don't bring it up." She continued, echoing a thought other daycare workers expressed as well:

Don't get me wrong. These children are adaptable, They're pliant. As long as there's a sense of love here and as long as you feed them, they know I'm the one who satisfies their needs. That's all I am to them. The children love me and some little children, like Nelson, don't want to go home. He's three now, but I've had him since he was seven months old; Stephanie's three and I've had her since she was six weeks. But I do feel sorry for the children, I do. Because I know there are days when they probably don't feel like coming here, especially Mondays.

When daycare workers feel sorry for the children they care for something is wrong. This woman, a thirty-year-old black mother of three, was gentle and kindly, a lovely person to care for children. What seemed wrong to me was the overly long hours, the blocked channels of communication, and the fathers who imagined their wives were "handling it all."

A Father's Influence

In a time of stalled revolution—when women have gone to work, but the workplace, the culture, and most of all, the men, have not adjusted themselves to this new reality—children can be the victims. Most working mothers are already doing all they can, doing that extra month a year. It is men who can do more.

Fathers can make a difference that shows in the child. I didn't administer tests to the children in the homes I visited nor gather systematic information on child development. I did ask the baby-sitters and daycare workers for their general impressions of differences between the children of single parents, two-job families in which the father was uninvolved, and two-job families in which the father was actively involved. All of them said that the children of fathers who were actively involved seemed to them "more secure" and "less anxious." Their lives were less rushed. On Monday, they had more to report about Sunday's events: "Guess what I did with my dad. . . ."

But curiously little attention has been paid to the effect of fathers on children. Current research focuses almost exclusively on the influence on children of the working *mother*. A panel of distinguished social scientists chosen by the National Academy of Sciences to review the previous research on children of working mothers concluded in 1982 that a mother's employment has no consistent ill effects on a child's school achievement, IQ, or social and emotional development. Other summary reviews offer similar but more complex findings. For example, in charting fifty years of research on children of working mothers, Lois Hoffman, a social psychologist at the University of Michigan, has concluded that most girls of all social classes and boys from working-class families, whose mothers worked, were more self-confident and earned better grades than children whose mothers were housewives. But she also found that compared to the sons of housewives, middle-class boys raised by working mothers were less confident and did less well in school. But what about the influence of the fathers?

Apart from my study, other systematic research has documented a fact one might intuitively suspect: the more involved the father, the better developed the child intellectually and socially. Professor Norma Radin and her students at the University of Michigan have conducted a number of studies that show that, all else being equal, the children of highly involved fathers are better socially and emotionally adjusted than children of noninvolved fathers and score higher on academic tests. In Professor Radin's research, "highly involved" fathers are those who score in the top third on an index comprised of questions concerning responsibility for physical care (e.g., feeding the children), responsibility for socializing the child (e.g., setting limits), power in decision-making regarding the child, availability to the child, and an overall estimate of his involvement in raising his preschooler. In one study of fifty-nine middle-class families with children between the ages of three and six, Professor Radin found that highly involved fathers had sons who were better adjusted and more socially competent, more likely to perceive themselves as masters of their fate, and a higher mental age on verbal intelligence tests. A 1985 study by Abraham Sagi found Israeli children of highly involved fathers to be more empathetic than other children.

A 1985 comprehensive and careful study by Carolyn and Phil Cowan, two psychologists at the University of California, Berkeley, found that three-and-a-half-year-old children of involved fathers achieved higher scores on certain playroom tasks (classifying objects, putting things in a series, role-taking tasks) than other children. When fathers worked longer hours outside the home, the Cowans found in their observation sessions, the three-and-a-half-year-olds showed more anxiety. The daughters of long-hours men were, in addition, less warm and less task oriented at playroom tasks, although they had fewer behavior problems. When fathers worked long hours, mothers tended to "compensate" by establishing warm relations with their sons. But when mothers worked long hours, husbands did not "compensate" with their daughters. In spite of this, the girls did well in playroom tasks. When fathers *or* mothers worked more outside the home, the parent established a closer bond with the *boy*.

Finally, the results of active fatherhood seem to last. In one study, two psychologists asked male undergraduates at the University of Massachusetts, Amherst, to respond to such statements as "My father understood my problems and worries and helped with them, hugged or kissed me goodnight when I was small, was able to make me feel better when I was upset, gave me a lot of care and attention." They were also asked to describe his availability ("away from home for days at a time, . . . out in the evening at least two nights a week, . . . home afternoons when children came home from school," and so on). The young men who ranked their fathers highly—or even moderately— nurturant and available were far more likely to describe themselves as "trusting, friendly, loyal, and dependable, industrious and honest."

In the end, caring for children is the most important part of the second shift, and the effects of a man's care or his neglect will show up again and again through time—in the child as a child, in the child as an adult, and probably also in the child's own approach to fatherhood, and in generations of fathers to come. Active fathers are often in reaction against a passive detached father, a father like Seth Stein. But an exceptionally warmhearted man, like the step-father of Art Winfield, could light the way still better. In the last forty years, many women have made a historic shift, into the economy. Now it is time for a whole generation of men to make a second historic shift—into work at home.

38 The Streetcorner Preacher

LAWRENCE K. HONG
MARION V. DEARMAN

Religion is vital to Americans, and anyone who misses this point fails to understand U.S. society adequately. Although in previous years some professionals predicted that with the rise of science and the general secularization of U.S. culture religion would quietly fade into the background, that has not happened. Americans repeatedly go through periods of decreased religious involvement—and to some it then looks as though religion is on its way out—only to enter an inevitable subsequent period of increased religious participation. Although church and synagogue membership and attendance ebb and flow, in U.S. society there always remains a strong current of genuine religiosity based on sincere convictions.

It is no exaggeration, then, to say that religion is one of the principal social institutions in the United States. In it Americans find solace and courage, as well as the answers to many of the perplexing questions that contemporary social life poses. Those who have strong religious convictions grasp the meaning of what I am writing, while those with few or none must remain "outsiders," somewhat perplexed by all the activities of which they are not a part.

While most Americans are at least "somewhat" religious, most of us also think that religion should remain primarily a private matter. "We all believe what we believe, and it is no one else's business" is likely to be the attitude most of us take. Consequently, few of us are likely to preach on streetcorners or to accost people on the sidewalk with a religious message—or to approve those who do. Streetcorner preaching strikes most of us as somewhat humorous, somehow unseemly, "pushy," and perhaps as an invasion of our privacy.

In spite of such common negative reactions, however, some people persist in preaching on streetcorners. Focusing on just this one aspect of the fascinatingly multifaceted social institution we call religion, Hong's and Dearman's analysis helps the unfamiliar take on just a little more familiarity. From the lens of these sociologists, then, we gain greater understanding of another aspect of our social world.

Alleluia, alleluia, Lord, I glorify your name. Thank you, Jesus, Heaven come to your heart, heaven come to your heart. Amen, amen. Devil is here, but Jesus is right here. Alleluia, alleluia. Praise the Lord. Thank you, Jesus.

ON A BUSY DOWNTOWN STREET CORNER a black man in his late fifties, clapping his hands, striking his arms, striding back and forth, preaches at the top of his voice to the ceaseless streams of pedestrians. Adults avert their eyes in apparent embarrassment for the preacher; children stare at him while being jerked forward by their mothers who admonish them to pay no attention. Police walk or drive by, glance at him indifferently, and go their way. These sights and sounds are part of the permanent landscape of most major cities from New York to Los Angeles. The experienced city dweller apparently takes the streetcorner preachers for granted, along with slow traffic, stale air, sleazy movies, and monotonous neon signs. But to the novice or newcomer, they add excitement and color to the kaleidoscopic, carnival atmosphere which inner city life presents to him.

Who are these streetcorner preachers? Where do they come from? What do they try to accomplish? These and other questions have brought the authors of this paper to the streets of downtown Los Angeles. Over a period of three months, we observed and interviewed the preachers, a spokesman of the church of which many were members, different types of pedestrians, and the police in an attempt to search for the answers. . . .

One Situation, Multiple Definitions

With few exceptions, all the passers-by whom we interviewed regard the streetcorner preachers as "crazy," "insane," or "mentally disturbed." The following comment from a regular downtown shopper is typical:

> I think he is crazy. Mentally unbalanced, you know. There are many of them. They always stand over in that corner, making a lot of noise. Nobody ever listens to them. I think they are nuts.

Policemen agreed with this opinion, although a desk sergeant confided to us that "some of them [the preachers] are righteous but most of them are squirrels, nuts, kooks." Another policeman told us that "they are definitely a nuisance but, you know, free speech and all that jazz" makes it impossible to eliminate them.

The preachers, in turn, define the passers-by as sinners—heathens, drunkards, thieves, and worse; the policemen are seen as would-be prosecutors of God's spokesmen, the preachers. By thus defining themselves as the representatives of God, the creator and master of the universe, the preachers perceive themselves as the "winners" while the others become poor, pitiful "losers" who are going to Hell if they fail to heed their warnings.

Very much contrary to the definitions of the police and pedestrians, we soon discovered that these preachers are quite rational, intelligent people and sincere, dedicated Christians. Our basis for this definition will emerge in the remaining pages of this paper.

Organization of "Frenetic" Behavior

It did not take us long to discover that just beneath the surface of their seem-ingly erratic behavior was a close group of people who share many of the sys-tem characteristics—mutual obligations, common goals, status hierarchy, and territoriality—of the streetcorner society that Whyte (1943) has described. The permanent cadre, or nucleus, of the street preachers are members of a major Pentecostal denomination—the Church of God in Christ (CGC)—that claims national membership of around three million.[1] Although these preach-ers are neither licensed to preach nor ordained by their church, they are well organized and follow a schedule almost as regular as that of suburban churches in conducting their religious services. They begin their preaching around noon every day and finish around five. During this five-hour interval, three or four preachers will take turns preaching, each having a time slot of about half an hour. Other preachers may also stand by, but only a few will have a chance to preach on the same day.

The street preachers feel very close to one another, and frequently have lunch or coffee breaks together in a cafeteria in the immediate area. In the cafeteria, they will also meet with other "brothers" and "sisters" who perform other religious services in the vicinity such as passing out religious tracts and mini-bibles. Their interactions are characterized by warmth and rapport. This observation is also confirmed by an ordained minister of their church (who does not preach in the street but has a regular pastoral appointment):

> They have a way to be aware of each other's needs. They preach by turns and help one another out. They get to know each other very well. Sometimes, they even live together. Some of them share the same apartment. They are very close.

When a preacher is preaching, his voice may appear to be emotional and his utterances disjunct, but the whole presentation is delivered with a deliber-ate effort and what appears to be a carefully considered style. He fully under-stands that very few individuals will stop and listen to his preaching and, there-fore, it is not necessary to deliver a coherent, logical discourse on Christianity and salvation. . . . Hence, in contrast to other downtown religious groups such as the Skid Row Missions (Bibby and Mauss, 1974), the goal of the street preacher is not concerned with immediate conversion; his goal, rather, is to "sow the seeds" by scattering discrete words and phrases of virtue and holiness to the downtown crowds, hoping that someone will pick up a word or two here and there.[2] As one of the preachers explains their technique:

What we try to accomplish here is to sow the seeds. What we do out here is like spreading the germs. They get into the air and someone may pick them up. They may not know it now, but one of these days when he is in trouble, he may remember what he has heard here today. It may turn him to the Lord. All it takes is one word, and he may be saved.

. . . The organization of the streetcorner preachers is also manifested in their informal status hierarchy. This status differentiation is determined by the style of delivery and paraphernalia. On the top of the hierarchy is "Brother James," who is a black man in his late forties. Brother James is a recognized virtuoso of streetcorner preachers. His voice is firm and forceful. He does not rattle like many of the other preachers in the lower hierarchy. He always preaches with a high degree of confidence and considerable skill. He also has a charismatic quality which holds the attention of his listeners. Furthermore, he dresses differently than the other streetcorner preachers. His suit is well tailored and his shirt well pressed, while many of the other preachers wear old clothes which desperately need a thorough cleaning. . . .

The preaching style and dress of the other preachers are visibly inferior. Accordingly, their status in the eyes of their peers is also lower. This is evident in the magnitude of support and the size of the gathering accorded to them by their colleagues while they are preaching. Brother James has the largest gathering. When he preaches, all the other preachers gather along the opposite edge of the sidewalk and respond to his utterances enthusiastically. They repeat after him, clap their hands rhythmically, and fix their attention on him intensively:

BROTHER JAMES: Alleluia, alleluia
OTHER PREACHERS: Alleluia
BROTHER JAMES: Lord, I glorify your name
OTHER PREACHERS: I glorify your name
BROTHER JAMES: Thank you Jesus
OTHER PREACHERS: Thank you Jesus
BROTHER JAMES: Lord, give us strength through this journey
OTHER PREACHERS: Through this journey

But, when a lower-status preacher preaches, at most one or two of his colleagues give him support. The type of support is also less enthusiastic. Instead of repeating in full or partially what he actually says, they tend to use standard responses such as "Praise the Lord" and "Alleluia." Furthermore, they rarely clap their hands. Sometimes, they even suspend their support by engaging in social talks. Brother James also occupies an interstitial role between the regular Church of God in Christ and the streetcorner preachers. He is an evangelist who travels from city to city preaching the gospel to down-and-outers and street people. He represents the church and his role allows church members to feel comfortable that their group is both ministering to the lost ones on the downtown streets as well as assisting the streetcorner preachers in their humble and, at first glance, unrewarding task. . . .

Another manifestation of the organization of the street preachers is their concern over territoriality. The corners where they preach are located on certain of the busiest intersections of downtown Los Angeles. The street preachers have more or less occupied these intersections as their own; other downtown religious groups such as the Salvation Army, Jesus People, and Hare Krishna respect, perhaps reluctantly, their "right" to be there and seldom conduct their activities on those corners. . . .

We have observed only one territorial violation during the period of study. The violator was a Hare Krishna who was giving out his sect's newspapers to the passers-by in the exact location where the preachers usually conduct their activities. He took over the area while the preachers were taking their coffee break inside a cafeteria. Upon discovering their spot had been occupied by an intruder (after their coffee break), the immediate response of the preachers was motionless silence. They stood across from the Hare Krishna, stared at him in silence and remained almost motionless. But the Hare Krishna ignored their "silent treatment." After waiting for a couple of minutes in futility, the preachers tried a different technique; they flooded the area with their own people and tried to crowd the Hare Krishna out.

One of the preachers walked over to the Hare Krishna, positioned next to him, and started to preach in the highest decibel. His audio output was matched by the ferocity of his bodily movement. The Hare Krishna adjusted his distance, moving a few feet away from the preacher. The preacher readjusted his position to keep close to the Hare Krishna. Standing across from the couple, the "brothers" and "sisters" of the preacher clapped their hands and responded "alleluia" and "thank you Jesus" to the beat of the preacher's delivery. Finally, the Hare Krishna left the location and moved to a new area about a block away. Although we have observed only one episode, the spontaneity of the preachers' actions and the effortlessness of their coordination in defending their territory strongly suggest that they have employed these techniques before.

Rebirth of the Evangelist

Who are these street preachers? What are their backgrounds? These are some of the most difficult questions that we encountered in our research. As a group, the street preachers are below average in education—most of them have not finished high school. We have met only one preacher who has some college experience, a geography major who dropped out from college after the second year. In spite of their lack of education, the preachers are intelligent, knowledgeable persons who have a good grasp of themselves and happenings in society. In great contrast to the style they preach in the street, they speak conventionally and coherently when they engage in social talks.

They are gregarious and interesting to talk to. Not unlike people in other walks of life, during a typical coffee break they comment on a wide variety of subjects, ranging from politics to personal events. However, there is one topic that is almost a taboo—their past life, that is, their life before their religious conversion. In a way, the street preachers are very much like the streetcorner men in Tally's corner (Liebow, 1967): They do not like to talk about their past, and not even their best friends know about the details of their past. When asked, they speak in generality. One of the preachers speaks of his past in this way:

> Before I became a Christian, I was in sin. Drink, women, and all kinds of troubles. But, I don't do that anymore. One day, I talked to myself. I didn't want to do that anymore. Jesus came into my heart. Now, I am as happy as I can be.

Another preacher relates a similar story:

> I was born in Texas, and then I moved to Tennessee. I came out here 10 years ago. I have been to many places, seen all kinds of people. I did almost everything. I have worked all kinds of jobs. I always had troubles with the law, nothing serious, you know. Traffic tickets and things like that. Nothing big. And then the Lord spoke to me in my heart. He asked me to come out here. This is where He wants me to be. I follow Him. Jesus cannot be wrong.

To the best of our reconstruction of their past, all the street preachers have gone through an experience of "rebirth."[3] Throughout their early adulthood, they worked on low-paying jobs in various cities. They were the drifters, moving from one city to another. Like many other people in similar circumstances, they had a long history of minor infractions with the law. However, unlike many of their peers, they did not get deeper into trouble. At some moments in their middle years, they decided that they could not live like that any more and resolved to do something that they considered to be meaningful. Perhaps, through the influence of a friend, or the contact with a preacher, or the experience in a revival meeting, they concluded that ministry was their vocation.

Preaching in Church

Why don't they become regular ministers? Why don't they preach in a church? In our conversation with the street preachers, it is evident that they are interested in conducting religious service in a church. When asked, they usually become somewhat defensive; one of the preachers retorted:

> I can preach in a church. Sometimes, I do. I'm a minister of Jesus Christ just like

all other ministers. I am doing the same work. Jesus sent me here just like the others. If I want to preach in a church, I can.

However, they are also quick to point out that they see street preaching as their vocation, and they are satisfied with it. As one preacher puts it:

> Yeah, I preach in the church sometimes. I like to preach in a church. But, this is my calling, out here in the street. This is where the Lord sent me. There is no difference where you preach, in the street, on TV, or in the church. They are all the same. The Lord has many ways to reach people. This is the way He wants me to do. And I am doing as He says.

But, according to a pastor in their church, the street preachers never preach in the church. However, he did point out that it is common practice for members of his congregation to "testify" during religious service. In view of the fact that these testimonials are quite long—sometimes so long that the leader of the testimony service will discreetly terminate the "testimonial" by singing a hymn, joined by the congregation, lest the testifier intrude too far into the prerogatives of the pastor—it is unclear where they end and preaching *per se* begins. Furthermore, according to the same pastor, no street preacher has ever been appointed as a regular minister in a church, and therefore street preaching cannot be viewed as a stepping stone for advancing toward a pastoral appointment. He explains:

> The street preachers are lay preachers. They are not ordained ministers. Our church believes that every Christian has the right to witness. It is a personal thing. Many of them feel the call to witness in the street. Witnessing in the street is just as significant as witnessing in the church. They are just different forms of evangelism. There might be more effective ways to preach, but I don't discourage them because I do not want to lessen their intensity, feeling and freedom. To the best of my knowledge, no street preacher has ever become a pastor in our church.

When pressed as to why their church does not ordain at least some of the preachers, he replies:

> To be ordained, you have to have education. Most of these people have very little education. It also takes time to gather your congregation. You have to have a congregation before you can have a pastoral appointment. As I said before, what they are doing in the street is very significant. It is as significant as witnessing in the church. I do not want to discourage them.

It is obvious that there is a paradox here. The street preachers view themselves as regular ministers and want to preach in a church, but their church encourages them to preach in the street and does not accept them as ordained ministers. While their lack of education may be one of the reasons that has kept them from being ordained, other factors apparently are also involved. Possibly, another factor is their church's lack of confidence in the street preachers' ability to attract and maintain a congregation. As their pastor mentioned earlier: "You have to have a congregation before you can have a pastoral appointment." This appears to be a major factor that keeps the street preachers away from the mainstream of the ministry. . . .

Summary and Conclusion

In this paper, we have attempted to demonstrate that the seemingly frenetic streetcorner preachers are actually rational, intelligent, dedicated Christians. Furthermore, their activities on the street corner display many organizational characteristics such as goals, status hierarchy, and territoriality. Thus, in a way, our findings give support to the highly publicized observation that Whyte (1943) made more than [fifty] years ago—i.e., an ostensibly disorganized street corner may have a complex and well-established organization of its own. . . .

Notes

1. This figure, provided by a spokesman of the church, is most likely too high. A yearbook of churches (Jacquet, 1973) gives the Church of God in Christ membership as 501,000 in 1971. This figure, however, is only an estimate; the last census was taken in the late 1960s. At the time of our research, the spokesman informed us that a new census is at the planning stage. Three things are certain regarding the CGC: as with all pentecostals, it is very difficult to determine their membership precisely; they are a very large and fast-growing pentecostal group and one of the largest black pentecostal sects.

(The Church of God in Christ is one of the fastest growing religious groups in the United States. According to the 1994 *World Almanac/Book of Facts*, its membership has increased to over 5,000,000,000.—Editor).

2. It should be noted this method is somewhat similar to that used by the sophisticated advertising agencies on their billboard and spot radio and television messages.

3. "Rebirth" for pentecostals usually requires some kind of proof of genuine repentance of their sins, baptism in water as a sign of this repentance, and baptism "in the Spirit," the initial sign of which is "speaking in tongues" (glossolalia).

References

Bibby, R. W., and A. L. Mauss (1974). "Skidders and their servants: Variable goals and functions of the skid road rescue mission." *J. for the Scientific Study of Religion* 13: 421–36.

Jacquet, C. H. (1973). *Yearbook of American and Canadian Churches, 1973.* New York: Abingdon.

Liebow, E. (1967). *Tally's Corner.* Boston: Little, Brown.

Whyte, W .F. (1943). *Street Corner Society.* Chicago: University of Chicago Press.

39 The Great American Football Ritual

DOUGLAS E. FOLEY

Any visitor to the United States soon notices how important sports are to Americans. Baseball, football, basketball, hockey, softball, soccer, tennis, golf, swimming, gymnastics, track and field, auto racing, bowling, polo, horseshoes, bass fishing, skateboarding, and sky diving do not begin to exhaust the list. Some sports are taken more seriously than others, and a few have even become almost national obsessions—notably baseball, football, golf, basketball, and hockey. Although most sports are played "for fun," professional sports have become part of a mass entertainment business enterprise—yielding vast profits for players, managers, owners, and the companies that use them to sell a wide variety of products.

It would not take much of a trained sociological eye for a visitor to the United States to notice that some professional sports open with the singing of the national anthem, and to conclude from this that sports are vitally linked to patriotism. Besides this vital function of engendering national, regional, and local loyalties, sociologists have also analyzed how sports reproduce social class, gender, and race. As analyzed in this article, high school football serves as a means by which the adult generation reproduces its version of society—its status hierarchy, or customary divisions, of gender, race, and social classes. Following the "first wisdom" of sociology—that things are not what they seem, that there is a deeper layer of reality than appearances would indicate—sociologists conclude that high school football is much more than a game, that it is one of the ways of perpetuating social inequalities across the generations.

. . . THE SETTING OF THIS FIELD STUDY was "North Town," a small (8,000 population) South Texas farming/ranching community with limited industry, considerable local poverty, and a population that was 80% Mexican-American. "North Town High" had an enrollment of 600 students, and its sports teams played at the Triple-A level in a five-level state ranking system.

During the football season described here, I attended a number of practices, rode on the players' bus, and hung out with the coaches at the fieldhouse and with players during extensive classroom and lunchtime observations. I also participated in basketball and tennis practices and interviewed students extensively about student status groups, friendship, dating, and race relations. The participant observation and interviewing in the sports scene involved hundreds of hours of fieldwork over a 12-month period. . . .

The Weekly Pep Rally

Shortly after arriving in North Town I attended my first pep rally. Students, whether they liked football or not, looked forward to Friday afternoons. Regular 7th-period classes were let out early to hold a mass pep rally to support the team. Most students attended these events but a few used it to slip away from school early. During the day of this pep rally I overheard a number of students planning their trip to the game. Those in the school marching band (80) and in the pep club (50) were the most enthusiastic. . . .

The Friday afternoon pep rally was age-graded. The older, most prominent students took the center seats, thus signaling their status and loyalty. Younger first- and second-year students sat next to the leaders of the school activities if they were protégés of those leaders. In sharp contrast, knots and clusters of the more socially marginal students, the "druggers" and the "punks and greasers," usually claimed the seats nearest the exits, thus signaling their indifference to all the rah-rah speeches they had to endure. The "nobodies" or "nerds," those dutiful, conforming students who were followers, tended to sit in the back of the center regions. Irrespective of the general territory, students usually sat with friends from their age group. Teachers strategically placed themselves at the margins and down in front to assist in crowd control.

The pep rally itself was dominated by the coaches and players, who were introduced to the audience to reflect upon the coming contest. In this particular pep rally the team captains led the team onto the stage. All the Anglo players entered first, followed by all the Mexicano players. Coach Trujillo started out with the classic pep talk that introduced the team captains, who in turn stepped forward and spoke in an awkward and self-effacing manner, thus enacting the ideal of a sportsman—a man of deeds, not words. They all stuttered through several "uhs" and "ers," then quickly said, "I hope y'all come support us. Thanks." Generally students expected their jocks to be inarticulate and, as the cliché goes, strong but silent types. . . .

The Marching Band

The quality of the marching band was as carefully scrutinized as the football team by some community members. The band director, Dante Aguila, was keenly aware of maintaining an excellent winning band. Like sport teams, marching bands competed in local, district, and statewide contests and won rankings. The ultimate goal was winning a top rating at the state level. In addition, each band sent its best players of various instruments to district contests to compete for individual rankings. Individual band members could also achieve top rankings at the state level.

A certain segment of the student body began training for the high school marching band during their grade school years. Band members had a much more positive view of their participation in band than the players did. The band was filled with students who tended to have better grades and came from the more affluent families. The more marginal, deviant students perceived band members as "goodie goodies," "richies," and "brains." This characterization was not entirely true because the band boosters club did make an effort to raise money to help low-income students join the band. Not all band students were top students, but many were in the advanced or academic tracks. Band members were generally the students with school spirit who were proud to promote loyalty to the school and community. The marching band was also a major symbolic expression of the community's unity and its future generation of good citizens and leaders.

The view that band members were the cream of the crop was not widely shared by the football players. Many female band members were socially prominent and "cool," but some were also studious homebodies. On the other hand, "real men" supposedly did not sign up for the North Town band. According to the football players, the physically weaker, more effeminate males tended to be in the band. Males in the band were called "band fags." The only exceptions were "cool guys" who did drugs, or had their own rock and roll band, or came from musical families and planned to become professional musicians. . . .

The main masculinity test for "band fags" was to punch their biceps as hard as possible. If the victim returned this aggression with a defiant smile or smirk, he was a real man; if he winced and whined, he was a wimp or a fag. The other variations on punching biceps were pinching the forearm and rapping the knuckles. North Town boys generally punched and pinched each other, but this kind of male play toward those considered fags was a daily ritual degradation. These were moments when physically dominant males picked on allegedly more effeminate males and reaffirmed their place in the male pecking order. Ironically, however, the players themselves rarely picked on those they called "band fags." Males who emulated jocks and hoped to hang out with them were usually the hit men. The jocks signalled their real power and prestige by showing restraint toward obviously weaker males.

Cheerleaders and Pep Squads

As in most pep rallies, on the Friday I am describing, the cheerleaders were in front of the crowd on the gym floor doing dance and jumping routines in unison and shouting patriotic cheers to whip up enthusiasm for the team. The cheerleaders were acknowledged as some of the prettiest young women in the school and they aroused the envy of nobodies and nerds. Male students incessantly gossiped and fantasized about these young women and their reputations. . . . Students invariably had their favorites to adore and/or ridicule. Yet they told contradictory stories about the cheerleaders. When privately reflecting on their physical attributes and social status, males saw going with a cheerleader as guaranteeing their coolness and masculinity. Particularly the less attractive males plotted the seduction of these young women and reveled in the idea of having them as girlfriends. When expressing their views of these young women to other males, however, they often accused the cheerleaders of being stuck-up or sluts.

This sharp contradiction in males' discourse about cheerleaders makes perfect sense, however, when seen as males talking about females as objects to possess and dominate and through which to gain status. Conversations among males about cheerleaders were rhetorical performances that bonded males together and established their rank in the patriarchal order. In public conversations, males often expressed bravado about conquest of these "easy lays." In private conversations with intimate friends, they expressed their unabashed longing for, hence vulnerable emotional need for, these fantasized sexual objects. Hence, cheerleaders as highly prized females were dangerous, status-confirming creatures who were easier to relate to in rhetorical performances than in real life. Only those males with very high social status could actually risk relating to and being rejected by a cheerleader. The rest of the stories the young men told were simply male talk and fantasy.

Many young women were not athletic or attractive enough to be cheerleaders; nevertheless they wanted to be cheerleaders. Such young women often joined the pep squad as an alternative, and a strong esprit de corps developed among the pep squad members. They were a group of 50 young women in costume who came to the games and helped the cheerleaders arouse crowd enthusiasm. The pep squad also helped publicize and decorate the school and town with catchy team-spirit slogans such as "Smash the Seahawks" and "Spear the Javelinos." In addition, they helped organize after-the-game school dances. Their uniforms expressed loyalty to the team, and pep squad members were given a number of small status privileges in the school. They were sometimes released early for pep rallies and away games. . . .

Homecoming: A Rite of Community Solidarity and Status

Ideally, North Town graduates would return to the homecoming bonfire and dance to reaffirm their support and commitment to the school and team. They would come back to be honored and to honor the new generation presently upholding the name and tradition of the community. In reality, however, few graduates actually attended the pregame bonfire rally or postgame school dance. Typically, the game itself drew a larger crowd and the local paper played up the homecoming game more. College-bound youth were noticeably present at the informal beer party after the game. Some townspeople were also at the pregame bonfire rally, something that rarely happened during an ordinary school pep rally. . . .

Three groups of boys with pickup trucks . . . created a huge pile of scrap wood and burnable objects that had been donated. The cheerleaders, band, and pep squad members then conducted the bonfire ceremonies. Several hundred persons, approximately an equal number of Anglo and Mexicano students, showed up at the rally along with a fair sprinkling of older people and others who were not in high school. Nearly all of the leaders were Anglos and they were complaining that not enough students supported the school or them. The cheerleaders led cheers and sang the school fight song after brief inspirational speeches from the coaches and players. . . .

The huge blazing fire in the school parking lot . . . added to the festive mood, which seemed partly adolescent high jinks and partly serious communion with the town's traditions. The collective energy of the youth had broken a property law or two to stage this event. Adults laughed about the "borrowed" packing crates and were pleased that others "donated" things from their stores and houses to feed the fire. The adults expressed no elaborate rationale for having a homecoming bonfire, which they considered nice, hot, and a good way to fire up the team. Gathering around the bonfire reunited all North Towners, past and present, for the special homecoming reunion and gridiron battle. . . .

After the homecoming game, a school dance was held featuring a homecoming court complete with king and queen. The queen and her court and the king and his attendants, typically the most popular and attractive students, were elected by the student body. Ideally they represented the most attractive, popular, and successful youth. They were considered the best of a future generation of North Towners. Following tradition, the queen was crowned during halftime at midfield as the band played and the crowd cheered. According to tradition, the lovely queen and her court, dressed in formal gowns, were ceremoniously transported to the crowning in convertibles. The king and his attendants, who were often football players and dirty and sweaty at that, then came running from their halftime break to escort the young women from the convertibles and to their crowning. The king and his court lingered rather uneasily until the ceremony was over and then quickly returned to their team to rest and prepare for the second half. . . .

The Powder-Puff Football Game: Another Rite of Gender Reproduction

A powder-puff football game was traditionally held in North Town on Friday afternoon before the seniors' final game. A number of the senior football players dressed up as girls and acted as cheerleaders for the game. A number of the senior girls dressed up as football players and formed a touch football team that played the junior girls. The male football players served as coaches and referees and comprised much of the audience as well. Perhaps a quarter of the student body, mainly the active, popular, successful students, drifted in and out to have a laugh over this event. More boys than girls, both Anglo and Mexicano, attended the game.

The striking thing about this ritual was the gender difference in expressive manner. Males took the opportunity to act in silly and outrageous ways. They pranced around in high heels, smeared their faces with lipstick, and flaunted their padded breasts and posteriors in a sexually provocative manner. Everything, including the cheers they led, was done in a very playful, exaggerated, and burlesque manner.

In sharp contrast, the females donned the football jerseys and helmets of the players, sometimes those of their boyfriends, and proceeded to huff and puff soberly up and down the field under the watchful eyes of the boys. They played their part in the game as seriously as possible, blocking and shoving with considerable gusto. This farce went on for several scores, until one team was the clear winner and until the females were physically exhausted and the males were satiated with acting in a ridiculous manner.

. . . Anthropologists . . . call such serious practices "rituals of inversion," specially marked moments when people radically reverse everyday cultural roles and practices. During these events people break, or humorously play with, their own cultural rules. Such reversals are possible without suffering any sanctions or loss of face. These moments are clearly marked so that no one familiar with the culture will misread such reversals as anything more than a momentary break in daily life.

Males of North Town High used this moment of symbolic inversion to parody females in a burlesque and ridiculous manner. They took great liberties with the female role through this humorous form of expression. The power of these young males to appropriate and play with female symbols of sexuality was a statement about males' social and physical dominance. Conversely, the females took few liberties with their expression of the male role. They tried to play a serious game of football. The females tried earnestly to prove they were equal. Their lack of playfulness was a poignant testimony to their subordinate status in this small town. . . .

Prominent Citizens and Their Booster Club: Reproducing Class Privileges

North Town was the type of community in which male teachers who had athletic or coaching backgrounds were more respected than other teachers. For their part, the other teachers often told "dumb coach" jokes and expressed resentment toward the school board's view of coaches. North Town school board members, many of them farmers and ranchers—rugged men of action—generally preferred that their school leaders be ex-coaches. Consequently a disproportionate number of ex-coaches became school principals and superintendents. . . . School board members invariably emphasized an ex-coach's ability to deal with the public and to discipline the youth.

Once gridiron warriors, coaches in small towns are ultimately forced to become organization men, budget administrators, and public relations experts. . . . Ultimately they must appease local factions, school boards, administrators, booster clubs, angry parents, and rebellious teenagers. The successful North Town coaches invariably become excellent public relations men who live a "down home" rural lifestyle; they like to hunt and fish and join local coffee klatches or Saturday morning quarterback groups. They must be real men who like fraternizing with the entrepreneurs, politicians, and good ole' boys who actually run the town. This role as a local male leader creates a web of alliances and obligations that puts most coaches in the debt of the prominent citizens and their booster club.

North Town's booster club, composed mainly of local merchants, farmers, and ranchers, had the all-important function of raising supplementary funds for improving the sports program and for holding a postseason awards banquet. The club was the most direct and formal link that coaches had with the principal North Town civic leaders. North Town had a long history of booster club and school board interference in coaching the team. One coach characterized North Town as follows: "One of the toughest towns around to keep a job. Folks here take their football seriously. They are used to winning, not everything, not the state, but conference and maybe bidistrict, and someday even regional. They put a lot of pressure on you to win here." . . .

The pattern of community pressures observed in North Town was not particularly exceptional. A good deal of the public criticism and grumbling about choices of players had racial overtones. The debate over which Anglo varsity quarterback to play also reflected community class differences among Anglos. North Town students and adults often expressed their fears and suspicion that racial and class prejudices were operating. It would be an exaggeration, however, to portray the North Town football team as rife with racial conflict and disunity. Nor was it filled with class prejudice. On a day-to-day basis there was considerable harmony and unity. Mexicanos and Anglos played side by side with few incidents. A number of working-class Mexicano youths and a few low-income Anglos were also members of the football program. At least in a general way, a surface harmony and equality seemed to prevail. . . .

Local sports enthusiasts are fond of arguing that coaches select players objectively, without class or racial prejudices, because their personal interest, and that of the team, is served by winning. Unfortunately, this free-market view glosses over how sport actually functions in local communities. Small-town coaches are generally subjected to enormous pressures to play everyone's child, regardless of social class and race. Success in sport is an important symbolic representation of familial social position. Men can reaffirm their claim to leadership and prominence through the success of their offspring. A son's athletic exploits relive and display the past physical and present social dominance of the father. In displaying past and present familial prominence, the son lays claim to his future potential. Every North Town coach lived and died by his ability to win games *and* his social competence to handle the competing status claims of the parents and their children.

Socially prominent families, who want to maintain their social position, promote their interests through booster clubs. The fathers of future community leaders spend much time talking about and criticizing coaches in local coffee shops. These fathers are more likely to talk to the coaches privately. Coaches who have ambitions to be socially prominent are more likely to "network" with these sportsminded community leaders. A symbiotic relationship develops between coaches, especially native ones, and the traditional community leaders. Preferential treatment of the sons of prominent community leaders flows from the web of friendships, hunting privileges, Saturday morning joking, and other such exchanges.

The booster club that coach Trujillo had to deal with was run by a small clique of Anglos, . . . "good ole' boys and redneck types." They became outspoken early in the season against their "weak Mexican coach." They fanned the fires of criticism in the coffee-drinking sessions over which of the two freshman quarterbacks should start, the "strong-armed Mexican boy" or the "all-around, smart Anglo boy." The Anglo boy was the son of a prominent car dealer and . . . booster club activist. The Mexican boy was a son of a migrant worker and small grocery store manager. The freshman coach, Jim Ryan, chose the Anglo boy. . . . In a similar vein, conflict also surfaced over the selection of the varsity quarterback. Coach Trujillo chose the son of an Anglo businessman, an underclassman, over a senior, the son of a less prominent Anglo. The less educated Anglo faction lambasted the coach for this decision, claiming he showed his preference for the children of the more socially and politically prominent [families].

Moveover, considerable pressure to favor the sons of prominent citizens comes from within the school as well. The school and its classrooms are also a primary social stage upon which students enact their social privilege. These youths establish themselves as leaders in academic, political, and social affairs, and teachers grant them a variety of privileges. This reinforces the influence of their parents in the PTA, the sports and band booster clubs, and the school board. Both generations, in their own way, advance the interests of the family on many fronts.

The Spectators: Male Socialization Through Ex-players

Another major aspect of the football ritual is how the spectators, the men in the community, socialize each new generation of players. In North Town, groups of middle-aged males with families and businesses were influential in socializing the new generation of males. These men congregated in various restaurants for the morning coffee and conversation about business, politics, the weather, and sports. Those leading citizens particularly interested in sports could be heard praising and criticizing "the boys" in almost a fatherly way. Some hired the players for part-time or summer jobs and were inclined to give them special privileges. Athletes were more like to get well-paying jobs as road-gang workers, machine operators, and crew leaders. Most players denied that they got any favors, but they clearly had more prestige than other high school students who worked. Nonplayers complained that jocks got the good jobs. On the job site the men regaled players with stories of male conquests in sports, romance, and business.

Many players reported these conversations, and I observed several during Saturday morning quarterback sessions in a local restaurant and gas station. One Saturday morning after the all-important Harris game, two starters and their good buddies came into the Cactus Bowl Café. One local rancher-businessman shouted, "Hey, Chuck, Jimmie, get over here! I want to talk to you boys about the Harris game!" He then launched into a litany of mistakes each boy and the team had made. Others in the group chimed in and hurled jokes at the boys about "wearing skirts" and being "wimps." Meanwhile the players stood slope-shouldered and "uh-huhed" their tormentors. One thing they had learned was never to argue back too vociferously. The players ridiculed such confrontations with "old-timers" privately, but the proper response from a good kid was tongue-biting deference. . . .

Some ex-players led the romanticized life of tough, brawling, womanizing young bachelors. These young men seemed suspended in a state of adolescence while avoiding becoming responsible family men. They could openly do things that the players had to control or hide because of training rules. Many of these ex-players were also able to physically dominate the younger high school players. But ex-players no longer had a stage upon which to perform heroics for the town. Consequently they often reminded current players of their past exploits and the superiority of players and teams in their era. Current players had to "learn" from these tormentors and take their place in local sports history.

Players Talking About Their Sport: The Meaning of Football

The preceding portrayal of the community sports scene has already suggested several major reasons why young males play football. Many of them are willing to endure considerable physical pain and sacrifice to achieve social prominence in their community. Only a very small percentage are skilled enough to play college football, and only one North Towner has ever made a living playing professional football. The social rewards from playing football are therefore mainly local and cultural.

However, there are other more immediate psychological rewards for playing football. When asked why they play football and why they like it, young North Town males gave a variety of answers. A few openly admitted that football was a way for them to achieve some social status and prominence, to "become somebody in this town." Many said football was fun, or "makes a man out of you," or "helps you get a cute chick." Others parroted a chamber of commerce view that it built character and trained them to have discipline, thus helping them be successful in life. Finally, many evoked patriotic motives—to beat rival towns and to "show others that South Texas plays as good a football as East Texas."

These explicit statements do not reveal the deeper . . . lessons learned in sports combat, however. In casual conversations, players used phrases that were particularly revealing. What they talked most about was "hitting" or "sticking" or "popping" someone. These were all things that coaches exhorted the players to do in practice. After a hard game, the supreme compliment was having a particular "lick" or "hit" singled out. Folkloric immortality, endless stories about that one great hit in the big game, was what players secretly strove for. For most coaches and players, really "laying a lick on" or "knocking somebody's can off" or "taking a real lick" was that quintessential football moment. Somebody who could "take it" was someone who could bounce up off the ground as if he had hardly been hit. The supreme compliment, however, was to be called a hitter or head-hunter. A hitter made bone-crushing tackles that knocked out or hurt his opponent.

Players who consistently inflicted outstanding hits were called animals, studs, bulls, horses, or gorillas. A stud was a superior physical specimen who fearlessly dished out and took hits, who liked the physical contact, who could dominate other players physically. Other players idolized a "real stud," because he seemed fearless and indomitable on the field. Off the field a stud was also cool, or at least imagined to be cool, with girls. Most players expected and wanted strong coaches and some studs to lead them into battle. They talked endlessly about who was a real stud and whether the coach "really kicks butt."

The point of being a hitter and stud is proving that you have enough courage to inflict and take physical pain. Pain is a badge of honor. Playing with pain proves you are a man. In conventional society, pain is a warning to protect your body, but the opposite ethic rules in football. In North Town bandages and stitches and casts became medals worn proudly into battle. Players constantly told stories about overcoming injuries and "playing hurt." A truly brave man was one who could fight on; his pain and wounds were simply greater obstacles to overcome. Scars were permanent traces of past battles won, or at the very least fought well. They became stories told to girlfriends and relatives. . . .

Many players, particularly the skilled ones, described what might be called their aesthetic moments as the most rewarding thing about football. Players sitting around reviewing a game always talked about themselves or others as "making a good cut" and "running a good route," or "trapping" and "blindsiding" someone. All these specific acts involved executing a particular type of body control and skill with perfection and excellence. Running backs made quick turns or cuts that left would-be tacklers grasping for thin air. Ends "ran routes" or a clever change of direction that freed them to leap into the air and catch a pass. Guards lay in wait for big opposing linemen or aggressive linebackers to enter their territory recklessly, only to be trapped or blindsided by them. Each position had a variety of assignments or moments when players used their strength and intelligence to defeat their opponents. The way this was done was beautiful to a player who had spent years perfecting the body control and timing to execute the play. Players talked about "feeling" the game and the ball and the pressure from an opponent.

Team sports, and especially American football, generally socialize males to be warriors. The young men of North Town were being socialized to measure themsleves by their animal instincts and aggressiveness. Physicality, searching for pain, enduring pain, inflicting pain, and knowing one's pain threshold emphasize the biological, animal side of human beings. These are the instincts needed to work together and survive in military combat and, in capitalist ideology, in corporate, academic, and industrial combat. The language used—head-hunter, stick 'em, and various aggressive animal symbols—conjures up visions of Wall Street stockbrokers and real estate sharks chewing up their competition.

Other Males: Brains, Farm Kids, and Nobodies

What of those males who do not play high school football? Does this pervasive community ritual require the participation of all young males? Do all non-athletes end up in the category of effeminate "band fags"? To the contrary, several types of male students did not lose gender status for being unathletic. There were a small number of "brains" who were obviously not physically capable of being gridiron warriors. Some of them played other sports with less physical contact such as basketball, tennis, track, or baseball. In this way they still upheld the ideal of being involved in some form of sport. Others, who were slight of physique, wore thick glasses, lacked hand-eye coordination, or ran and threw poorly, sometimes ended up hanging around jocks or helping them with their schoolwork. Others were loners who were labeled nerds and weirdos.

In addition, there were many farm kids or poor kids who did not participate in sports. They were generally homebodies who did not participate in many extracurricular activities. Some of them had to work to help support their families. Others had no transportation to attend practices. In the student peer groups they were often part of the great silent majority called "the nobodies."

Resistance to the Football Ritual: The Working-Class Chicano Rebels

There were also a number of Mexicano males who formed anti-school oriented peer groups. They were into a "hip" drug-oriented lifestyle. These males, often called "vatos" (cool dudes), made it a point to be anti-sports, an activity they considered straight. Although some were quite physically capable of playing, they rarely tried out for any type of team sports. They made excuses for not playing such as needing a job to support their car or van or pickup. They considered sports "kids' stuff," and their hip lifestyle as more adult, cool, and fun.

Even for the vatos, however, sports events were important moments when they could publicly display their lifestyle and establish their reputation. A number of vatos always came to the games and even followed the team to other towns. They went to games to be tough guys and "enforcers" and to establish "reps" as fighters. The vatos also went to games to "hit on chicks from other towns." During one road game, after smoking several joints, they swaggered in with cocky smiles plastered on their faces. The idea was to attract attention from your women and hopefully provoke a fight while stealing another town's women. Unlike stealing watermelons or apples from a neighbor, stealing women was done openly and was a test of courage. A man faced this danger in front of this buddies and under the eyes of the enemy.

. . . [A]fter the game the vatos told many tales about their foray into enemy territory. With great bravado they recounted every unanswered slight and insult they hurled at those "geeks." They also gloried in their mythical conquests of local young women. . . . As the players battled on the field, the vatos battled on the sidelines. They were another kind of warrior that established North Town's community identity and territoriality through the sport of fighting over and chasing young women.

The Contradiction of Being "In Training"

In other ways, even the straight young men who played football also resisted certain aspects of the game. Young athletes were thrust into a real dilemma when their coaches sought to rationalize training techniques and forbade various pleasures of the flesh. Being in training meant no drugs, alcohol, or tobacco. It also meant eating well-balanced meals, getting at least 8 hours of sleep, and not wasting one's emotional and physical energy chasing women. These dictates were extremely difficult to follow in a culture where drugs are used regularly and where sexual conquest and/or romantic love are popular cultural ideals. Add a combination of male adolescence and the overwhelming use of sex and women's bodies to sell commodities, and you have an environment not particularly conducive to making sacrifices for the coach and the team. North Town athletes envied the young bachelors who drank, smoked pot, and chased women late into the night. If they wanted to be males, American culture dictated that they break the rigid, unnatural training rules set for them.

. . . [M]any North Town football players . . . broke their training rules. They often drank and smoked pot at private teen parties. Unlike the rebellious vatos, who publicly flaunted their drinking and drugs, jocks avoided drinking in public. By acting like all-American boys, jocks won praise from adults for their conformity. Many of them publicly pretended to be sacrificing and denying themselves pleasure. They told the old-timers stories about their "rough practices" and "commitment to conditioning." Consequently, if jocks got caught breaking training, the men tended to overlook these infractions as slips or temptations. In short, cool jocks knew how to manage their public image as conformists and hide their private nonconformity. . . .

Fathers who had experienced this training contradiction themselves . . . gave their sons and other players stern lectures about keeping in shape, *but* they were the first to chuckle at the heroic stories of playing with a hangover. They told these same stories about teammates or about themselves over a cup of coffee or a beer. As a result, unless their youth were outrageously indiscreet—for example passing out drunk on the main street or in class, getting a "trashy girl" pregnant—a "little drinking and screwing around" was overlooked. They simply wanted the school board to stop being hypocritical and acknowledge that drinking was all part of growing up to be a prominent male.

In the small sports world of North Town, a real jock actually enhances his public image of being in shape by occasionally being a "boozer" or "doper." Indeed, one of the most common genres of stories that jocks told was the "I played while drunk/stoned," or the "I got drunk/stoned the night before the game" tale. Olmo, a big bruising guard who is now a hard-living, hard-drinking bachelor, told me a classic version of this tale before the homecoming game:

> Last night we really went out and hung one on. Me and Jaime and Arturo drank a six-pack apiece in a couple of hours. We were cruising around Daly City checking out the action. It was really dead. We didn't see nobody we knew except Arturo's cousin. We stopped at his place and drank some more and listened to some music. We stayed there till his old lady [mom] told us to go home. We got home pretty late, but before the sun come up, 'cause we're in training, ha ha.

[Conclusion]

. . . [T]he football ritual remains a powerful metaphor of American capitalist culture. In North Town, football is still a popular cultural practice deeply implicated in the reproduction of the local ruling class of white males, hence class, patriarchal, and racial forms of dominance. Local sports, especially football, are still central to the socialization of each new generation of youth and to the maintenance of the adolescent society's status system. In addition, this ritual is also central to the preservation of the community's adult status hierarchy. The local politics of the booster club, adult male peer groups, and Saturday morning coffee klatches ensnare coaches and turn a son's participation in the football ritual into an important symbolic reenactment of the father's social class and gender prominence. . . .

40 Medical Students' Contacts with the Living and the Dead

ALLEN C. SMITH III
SHERRYL KLEINMAN

Emotions are a taken-for-granted aspect of social life. We assume that the emotions we feel are inborn, that they are as natural as breathing. In one sense, this is true. Everyone feels anger, for example, as well as sadness and happiness. Sociologists, however, report that there is much more to our emotions than this. First, on a more obvious level, we learn from people around us how to express our feelings. There is nothing natural, for example, about football players patting one another's rears upon a successful play, or basketball players giving "high fives." These are learned ways to express emotions. So it is with males and females, children and adults, and so on: from tone of voice to facial expressions, some ways are deemed appropriate for one but not for the other. The second aspect is not so obvious: apparently people in different cultures experience somewhat different emotions. Some of the terms used in other cultures to describe feelings, for example, do not match the feelings we have. Although sociologists are researching this fundamental aspect of social life, we still know little about *the sociology of emotions* at this point.

In this selection, Smith and Kleinman examine social experiences that shape emotions. The setting is medical school, and the situation is contact with cadavers and patients. From these experiences, combined with the philosophical/academic orientation of today's medical schools, come a shaping of emotions so sweeping that it affects even medical practice itself.

ALL PROFESSIONALS DEVELOP a perspective different from, and sometimes at odds with, that of the public (Friedson 1970). "Professionals" are supposed to know more than their clients and to have personable, but not personal, relationships with them. Social distance between professional and client is expected (Kadushin 1962). . . . Because we associate authority in this society with an unemotional persona, affective neutrality reinforces professionals' power and keeps clients from challenging them. One element of professional socialization, then, is the development of appropriately controlled affect.

. . . Physicians ideally are encouraged to feel moderate sympathy toward patients, but excessive concern and all feelings based on the patient's or the physician's individuality are proscribed (Daniels 1960). Presumably, caring too much for the patient can interfere with delivering good service. Other feelings such as disgust or sexual attraction, considered natural in the personal sphere, violate fundamental medical ideals. Doctors are supposed to treat all patients alike (that is, well) regardless of personal attributes, and without emotions that might disrupt the clinical process or the doctor-patient relationship.

In this paper we examine another provocative issue—the physical intimacy inherent in medicine—and ask how medical students manage their inappropriate feelings as they make contact with the human body with all of their senses. We look closely at the situations that make them most uncomfortable: disassembling the dead human body (i.e., autopsy and dissection) and making "intimate" contact with living bodies (i.e., pelvic, rectal, and breast examinations). Even a seemingly routine physical exam calls for a physical intimacy that would evoke strong feelings in a personal context, feelings which are unacceptable in medicine.

The ideology of affective neutrality is strong in medicine; yet no courses in the medical curriculum deal directly with emotion management, specifically learning to change or eliminate inappropriate feelings. . . .

Methods

We studied students as they encountered the human body in clinical situations during the first three years of their training at a major medical school in the Southeast. . . . [We] observed for 35 hours in the gross anatomy laboratory, 34 hours in the physical diagnosis course (classroom, session on the pelvic examination, and practice with patients), and 168 hours in the five third-year clinical clerkships. We selected sites that included major body contact situations: dissection, practice sessions on physical examination skills, and services in the clerkships where contact with the breasts, genitals, and rectum is officially routine.

Over the same period we conducted open-ended, in-depth interviews with 16 first-year, 13 second-year, and 15 third-year students and with 18 others, including residents, attending physicians, nurses, spouses, and a counselor in the student health service. . . .

The Students' Problem

As they encounter the human body, students experience a variety of uncomfortable feelings including embarrassment, disgust, and arousal. Medical school, however, offers a barrier against these feelings by providing the anesthetic effect of long hours and academic pressure.

> You know the story. On call every third night, and stay in the hospital late most other evenings. I don't know how you're supposed to think when you're that tired, but you do, plod through the day insensitive to everything (Third-year male). . . .

Yet uncomfortable feelings break through. Throughout the program, students face provocative situations—some predictable, others surprising. They find parts of their training, particularly dissection and the autopsy, bizarre or immoral when seen from the perspective they had "for twenty-five years" before entering medical school.

> During the pelvis, we cut it across the waist. Big saws! The mad scientist! People wouldn't believe what we did in there. The cracking sound! That day was more than anxiety. We were really violating this person. . . . Drawn and quartered (First-year male).

> I did my autopsy ten days ago. That shook me off my feet. Nothing could have prepared me for it. The person was my age. . . . She just looked (pause) asleep. Not like the cadaver. Fluid, blood, smell. It smelled like a butcher shop.
>   And they handled it like a butcher shop. The technicians. Slice, move, pull, cut . . . all the organs, insides, pulled out in ten minutes (Second-year female).

Much of the students' discomfort is based on the fact that the bodies they have contact with are or were *people.* Suddenly students feel uncertain about the relationship of the person to the body, a relationship they had previously taken for granted.

> It felt tough when we had to turn the whole body over from time to time [during dissection]. It felt like real people (First-year female).

> Okay. Maybe he was a father. But the father part is gone. This is just the body. That sounds religious. Maybe it is. How else can I think about it? (First-year male)

When the person is somehow reconnected to the body, such as when data about the living patient who died are brought into the autopsy room, students feel less confident and more uneasy.

Students find contact with the sexual body particularly stressful. In the anatomy lab, in practice sessions with other students, and in examining patients, students find it difficult to feel neutral as contact approaches the sexual parts of the body.

> When you listen to the heart you have to work around the breast, and move it to

> listen to one spot. I tried to do it with minimum contact, without staring at her tit
> . . . breast . . . The different words (pause) shows I was feeling both things at once
> (Second-year male).

Though they are rarely aroused, students worry that they will be. They feel guilty, knowing that sexuality is proscribed in medicine, and they feel embarrassed. Most contact involves some feelings, but contact with the sexual body presents a bigger problem.

On occasion students feel unsure about the differences between the personal and the professional perspectives. Recalling the first day of "surface anatomy," when they are expected to remove their shirts in order to examine each other's backs before beginning dissection of the back, students remember an unspoken tension. The lab manual suggests that women wear bathing suits and tops, but few students read it in advance. Some of the few women who comply wear bras.

> I remember surface anatomy. That first day when they asked us to take our shirts
> off, including the girls. That was real uncomfortable. You know (pause) seeing
> some of the girls in bras. Some of them were wearing swimsuit tops. But (pause)
> and drawing on their chests. So I got a guy for a partner (First-year male).

> What's the difference between a bra and a bathing suit top? Don't know. But
> there is one! (First-year female)

When students are standing in the anatomy lab beside the cadavers, the difference between a bra and a bathing suit is surprisingly hard to describe. The differences are clear from a personal perspective, but in the technical objectivity of the laboratory, the details and meanings of the personal perspective seem elusive and irrational.

Students also feel disgust. They see feces, smell vomit, touch wounds, and hear bone saws, encountering many repulsive details with all of these senses.

> One patient was really gross! He had something that kept him standing, and
> coughing all the time. Coughing phlegm, and that really bothered me. Gross! Just
> something I don't like. Some smelled real bad. I didn't want to examine their axil-
> lae. Stinking armpits! It was just not something I wanted to do (Second-year fe-
> male).

When the ugliness is tied to living patients, the aesthetic problem is especially difficult. On opening the bowels of the cadaver, for example, students permit themselves some silent expressions of discomfort, but even a wince is unacceptable with repugnant living patients.

To make matters worse, students learn early on that they are not supposed to talk about their feelings with faculty members or other students. Feelings remain private. The silence encourages students to think about their problem as an individual matter, extraneous to the "real work" of medical school. They speak of "screwing up your courage," "getting control of yourself," "being tough enough," and "putting feelings inside." They worry that the faculty would consider them incompetent and unprofessional if they admitted their problem.

> I would be embarrassed to talk about it. You're supposed to be professional here. Like there's an unwritten rule about how to talk (First-year female). . . .

The "unwritten rule" is relaxed enough sometimes to permit discussion, but the privacy that surrounds these rare occasions suggests the degree to which the taboo exists. At times, students signal their uncomfortable feelings—rolling their eyes, turning away, and sweating—but such confirmation is limited. Exemplifying pluralistic ignorance, each student feels unrealistically inadequate in comparison with peers (yet another uncomfortable feeling). Believing that other students are handling the problem better than they are, each student manages his or her feelings privately, only vaguely aware that all students face the same problem. . . .

Emotion Management Strategies

How do students manage their uncomfortable and "inappropriate" feelings? The deafening silence surrounding the issue keeps them from defining the problem as shared, or from working out common solutions. They cannot develop strategies collectively, but their solutions are not individual. Rather, students use the *same* basic emotion management strategies because social norms, faculty models, curricular priorities, and official and unofficial expectations provide them with uniform guidelines and resources for managing their feelings.

TRANSFORMING THE CONTACT

Students feel uncomfortable because they are making physical contact with people in ways they would usually define as appropriate only in a personal context, or as inappropriate in any context. Their most common solution to this problem is cognitive (Hochschild 1979; Thoits 1985). Mentally they transform the body and their contact with it into something entirely different from the contacts they have in their personal lives. Students transform the person into a set of esoteric body parts and change their intimate contact with the body into a mechanical or analytic problem.

> I just told myself, "Okay, doc, you're here to find out what's wrong, and that includes the axillae [armpits]." And I detach a little, reduce the person for a moment . . . Focus real hard on the detail at hand, the fact, or the procedure or the question. Like with the cadaver. Focus on a vessel. Isolate down to whatever you're doing (Second-year female).

> Well, with the pelvic training (pause) I concentrated on the procedure, the sequence, and the motions . . . With the twenty-two year old, I concentrated on the order, sequence (pause), and on the details to check (Second-year male). . . .

Students also transform the moment of contact into a complex intellectual puzzle, the kind of challenge they faced successfully during previous years of schooling. They interpret details according to logical patterns and algorithms, and find answers as they master the rules.

> It helped to know that we were there for a training experience. My anxiety became the anxiety of learning enough. We saw a movie on traumas, like gunshots, burns, explosions. If I had just come off the street, I would have felt sick. But I focused on learning. Occupying my mind with learning and science (Second-year male).

> The patient is really like a math word problem. You break it down into little pieces and put them together. The facts you get from a history and physical, from the labs and chart. They fit together, once you begin to see how to do it . . . It's an intellectual challenge (Third-year female).

Defining contact as a part of scientific medicine makes the students feel safe. They are familiar with and confident about science, they feel supported by its cultural and curricular legitimacy, and they enjoy rewards for demonstrating their scientific know-how. In effect, science itself is an emotion management strategy. By competing for years for the highest grades, these students have learned to separate their feelings from the substance of their classes and to concentrate on the impersonal facts of the subject matter. In medical school they use these "educational skills" not only for academic success but also for emotion management.

The curriculum supports the students' efforts to focus on subpersonal facts and details. In twenty courses over the first two years, texts and teachers disassemble the body into systems and subsystems. Students are presented with an impossibly large number of anatomical and pathophysiological details which define the body as a collection of innumerable smaller objects in a complex system. Furthermore, faculty members reward students for recognizing and reciting the relevant facts and details and for reporting them in a succinct and unemotional fashion. Intellectualization is not merely acceptable; it is celebrated as evidence of superior performance in modern medicine. The curriculum equips the students with the substantive basis for their intellectual transformations of the body, and rewards them for using it.

The scientific, clinical language that the students learn also supports intellectualization. It is complex, esoteric, and devoid of personal meanings. "Palpating the abdomen" is less personal than "feeling the belly."

> When we were dissecting the pelvis, the wrong words kept coming to mind, and it was uncomfortable. I tried to be sure to use the right words, penis and testicles (pause) not cock and balls. Even just thinking. Would have been embarrassing to

make that mistake that day. School language, it made it into a science project (First-year female).

Further, the structure of the language, as in the standard format for the presentation of a case, helps the students to think and speak impersonally. Second-year students learn that there is a routine, acceptable way to summarize a patient: chief complaint, history of present illness, past medical history, family history, social history, review of systems, physical findings, list of problems, medical plan. In many situations they must reduce the sequence to a two- or three-minute summary. Faculty members praise the students for their ability to present the details quickly. Medical language labels and conveys clinical information, and it leads the students away from their emotions.

Transformation sometimes involves changing the body into a nonhuman object. Students think of the body as a machine or as an animal specimen, and recall earlier, comfortable experiences in working on that kind of object. The body is no longer provocative because it is no longer a body.

> After we had the skin off [the cadaver], it was pretty much like a car or something. It wasn't pleasant, but it wasn't human either (First-year female).

> [The pelvic exam] is pretty much like checking a broken toaster. It isn't a problem. I'm good at that kind of thing (Second-year male).

> You can't tell what's wrong without looking under the hood. It's different when I'm talking with a patient. But when I'm examining them it's like an automobile engine . . . There's a bad connotation with that, but it's literally what I mean (Third-year male). . . .

ACCENTUATING THE POSITIVE

As we hinted in the previous section, transforming body contact into an analytic event does not merely rid students of their uncomfortable feelings, producing neutrality. It often gives them opportunities to have *good* feelings about what they are doing. Their comfortable feelings include the excitement of practicing "real medicine," the satisfaction of learning, and the pride of living up to medical ideals.

Students identify much of their contact with the body as "real medicine," asserting that such contact separates medicine from other professions. As contact begins in dissection and continues through the third-year clinical clerkships, students feel excited about their progress. . . .

> This [dissection] is the part that is really medical school. Not like any other school. It feels like an initiation rite, something like when I joined a fraternity. We were really going to work on people (First-year male).

After years of anticipation, they are actually entering the profession; occasions of body contact mark their arrival and their progress. The students also feel a sense of privilege and power.

> This is another part that is unique to med school. The professor told us we are the only ones who can do this legally. It is special (pause) and uneasy (First-year female).

> I remember my second patient. An older guy . . . There I was, a second-year student who didn't know much of anything, and I could have done anything I wanted. He would have done whatever I told him (second-year male).

Eventually students see contact as their responsibility and their right, and forget the sense of privilege they felt at the beginning. Still, some excitement returns as they take on clinical responsibility in the third year. All of these feelings can displace the discomfort which also attends most contact. . . .

LAUGHING ABOUT IT

Students can find or create humor in the situations that provoke their discomfort. Humor is an acceptable way for people to acknowledge a problem and to relieve tension without having to confess weaknesses. In this case, joking also lets other students know that they are not alone with the problem. . . .

Where do students learn to joke in this way? The faculty, including the residents (who are the real teachers on the clinical teams), participate freely, teaching the students that humor is an acceptable way to talk about uncomfortable encounters in medicine.

> If I had to examine her I'd toss my cookies. I mean she is enormous. That's it! Put it in the chart! Breasts too large for examination! (Resident) (The team had just commented on a variety of disturbing behaviors that they observed with the patient.)

None of these comments is particularly funny out of context and without the gestures and tone of voice that faculty members use to embellish their words. Yet the humor is evident in person, akin to gallows humor, and thick with references to sexuality and aesthetic extremes (Fox 1979). Eager to please the faculty and to manage their emotions, students quickly adopt the faculty's humor. Joking about patients and procedures means sharing something special with the faculty, becoming a colleague. The idea implicit in the humor, that feelings are real despite the rule against discussing them, is combined with an important sense of "we-ness" that the students value.

Unlike the students' other strategies, joking occurs primarily when they are alone with other medical professionals. Jokes are acceptable in the hallways, over coffee, or in physicians' workrooms, but usually are unacceptable when outsiders might overhear. Joking is backstage behavior. Early in their training, students sometimes make jokes in public, perhaps to strengthen their identity as "medical student," but most humor is in-house, reserved for those who share the problem and have a sense of humor about it.

AVOIDING THE CONTACT

Students sometimes avoid the kinds of contact that give rise to unwanted emotions. They control the visual field during contact, and eliminate or abbreviate particular kinds of contact.

> We did make sure that it was covered. The parts we weren't working on. The head, the genitals. All of it really. It is important to keep them wrapped and moist, so they wouldn't get moldy. That made sense. But when the cloth slipped, someone made sure to cover it back up, even if just a little [pubic] hair showed (First-year female).

Keeping personal body parts covered in the lab and in examinations prevents mold, maintains a sterile field, and protects the patient's modesty. Covers also eliminate disturbing sites and protect students from their feelings. Such nonprofessional purposes are sometimes most important. Some students, for example, examine the breasts by reaching under the patient's gown, bypassing the visual examination emphasized in training. . . .

Conclusion

The emotion management strategies used by the students illustrate the culture of modern Western medicine. In relying on these strategies, the students reproduce that culture (Foucault 1973), creating a new generation of physicians who will support the biomedical model of medicine and the kind of doctor-patient relationship in which the patient is too frequently dehumanized. Students sometimes criticize their teachers for an apparent insensitivity to their patients, but they turn to desensitizing strategies themselves in their effort to control the emotions that medical situations provoke. These strategies exclude the patient's feelings, values, and social context, the important psychosocial aspects of medicine (Engel 1977; Gorlin and Zucker 1983). . . .

Our study suggests that the emotional socialization of professional training will influence the character of performance in the workplace and will have consequences for life outside the workplace. Medical students accept that they must change their perspective on the body in order to practice medicine, but they worry about the consequences. Often using the word "desensitization," they are concerned that medical training will dull their emotional responses too generally.

> Those feelings just get in the way. They don't fit, and I'm going to learn to get rid of them. Don't know how yet, and some of the possibilities are scary. What's left when you succeed? But what choice is there? (Second-year female).

It's kind of dehumanizing. We just block off the feelings, and I don't know what happens to them. This is pretty important to me. I'm working to keep a sense of myself through all this (Third-year male).

Quietly, because their concern is private and therefore uncertain, students ask questions we might all ask. Will we lose our sensitivity to those we serve? To others in our lives? To ourselves? Will we even know it is happening?

References

Daniels, M. 1960. "Affect and Its Control in the Medical Intern." *American Journal of Sociology* 55: 259–67.

Engel, G. 1977. "The Need for a New Medical Model: A Challenge for Biomedicine." *Science* 196 (4286): 129–36.

Foucault, M. 1973. *The Birth of the Clinic: An Archaeology of Medical Perception.* New York: Pantheon.

Fox, R. 1979. "The Human Condition of Health Professionals." Lecture delivered at the University of New Hampshire, November 19, 1979.

Friedson, E. *The Profession of Medicine.* New York: Dodd Mead, 1970.

Gorlin, R., and H. Zucker. 1983. "Physicians' Reactions to Patients: A Key to Teaching Humanistic Medicine." *New England Journal of Medicine* 308 (18): 1059–63.

Hochschild, A. 1979. "Emotion Work, Feeling Rules, and Social Structure." *American Journal of Sociology* 85 (3): 551–75.

Kadushin, C. 1962. "Social Distance between Client and Professional." *American Journal of Sociology* 67: 517–31.

Thoits, P. 1985. "Self-Labeling Processes in Mental Illness: The Role of Emotional Deviance." *American Journal of Sociology* 91: 221–49.

41 Police Accounts of Normal Force

JENNIFER HUNT

My personal contacts with the police have been infrequent and brief. Nevertheless, I have seen a policeman handcuff a rape suspect to a tree and then slap him in the face in front of a group of citizen-witnesses. I have heard another threaten the life of a suspect he was escorting near a stream, saying he wished the suspect would attempt to flee so he "could shoot her and watch her body float down the river." And in Mexico, after recovering my billfold and apprehending the two men who had picked my pocket, the secret police offered to hold the culprits while I beat them. They felt that I *ought* to beat them because, as they said, the men had caused me (and presumably them) so much trouble.

These events have convinced me that police violence is no random matter but is a regular part of the occupation. Why should that be? Is it because the police recruit certain personality types? As a sociologist, Hunt does not look for explanations lodged *within* people, such as "personality types." Rather, she examines the occupational culture, *external* conditions that affect people's orientations, in this instance how occupational norms affect recruits.

If you were a social reformer and you wanted to decrease police violence, where would you start? Keep in mind what Hunt found—the virtual absence of differences by gender, the distinction between formal and informal expectations, and the strong support for "normal" violence that is built into this occupation—and the lessons from the Zimbardo experiment in Part VI.

THE POLICE ARE REQUIRED to handle a variety of peacekeeping and law enforcement tasks including settling disputes, removing drunks from the street, aiding the sick, controlling crowds, and pursuing criminals. What unifies these diverse activities is the possibility that their resolution might require the use of force. Indeed, the capacity to use force stands at the core of the police mandate (Bittner, 1980). . . . The following research . . . explores how police themselves classify and evaluate acts of force as either legal, normal, or excessive. Legal force is that coercion necessary to subdue, control, and restrain a suspect in order to take him into custody. Although force not accountable in legal terms is technically labeled excessive by the courts and the public, the police perceive many forms of illegal force as normal. Normal force involves coercive acts that specific "cops" on specific occasions formulate as necessary, appropriate, reasonable, or understandable. Although not always legitimated or admired, normal force is depicted as a necessary or natural response of normal police to particular situational exigencies. . . . Brutality is viewed as illegal, illegitimate, and often immoral violence, but the police draw the lines in extremely different ways and at different points [from] either the court system or the public. . . .

The article is based on approximately eighteen months of participant observation in a major urban police department referred to as the Metro City P.D. I attended the police academy with male and female recruits and later rode with individual officers in one-person cars on evening and night shifts in high crime districts.[1] The female officers described in this research were among the first 100 women assigned to the ranks of uniformed patrol as a result of a discrimination suit filed by the Justice Department and a policewoman plaintiff.

Learning to Use Normal Force

The police phrase "it's not done on the street the way that it's taught at the academy" underscores the perceived contradiction between the formal world of the police academy and the informal world of the street. This contradiction permeates the police officer's construction of his world, particularly his view of the rational and moral use of force.

In the formal world of the police academy, the recruit learns to account for force by reference to legality. He or she is issued the regulation instruments and trained to use them to subdue, control, and restrain a suspect. If threatened with great bodily harm, the officer learns that he can justifiably use deadly force and fire his revolver. Yet the recruit is taught that he cannot use his baton, jack, or gun unnecessarily to torture, maim, or kill a suspect.

When recruits leave the formal world of the academy and are assigned to patrol a district, they are introduced to an informal world in which police recognize normal as well as legal and brutal force. Through observation and instruction, rookies gradually learn to apply force and account for its use in terms familiar to the street cop. First, rookies learn to adjust their arsenals to conform to street standards. They are encouraged to buy the more powerful weapons worn by veteran colleagues as these colleagues point out the inadequacy of a wooden baton or compare their convoy jacks to vibrators. They quickly discover that their department-issued equipment marks them as new recruits. At any rate, within a few weeks, most rookies have dispensed with the wooden baton and convoy jack and substituted . . . the more powerful plastic nightstick and flat-headed slapjack.[2]

Through experience and informal instruction, the rookie also learns the street use of these weapons. In school, for example, recruits are taught to avoid hitting a person on the head or neck because it could cause lethal damage. On the street, in contrast, police conclude that they must hit wherever it causes the most damage in order to incapacitate the suspect before they themselves are harmed. New officers also learn that they will earn the respect of their veteran co-workers not by observing legal niceties in using force, but by being "aggressive" and using whatever force is necessary in a given situation.

Peer approval helps neutralize the guilt and confusion that rookies often experience when they begin to use force to assert their authority. One female officer, for example, learned she was the object of a brutality suit while listening to the news on television. At first, she felt so mortified that she hesitated to go to work and face her peers. In fact, male colleagues greeted her with a standing ovation and commented, "You can use our urinal now." In their view, any aggressive police officer regularly using normal force might eventually face a brutality suit or civilian complaint. Such accusations confirm the officer's status as a "street cop" rather than an "inside man" who doesn't engage in "real police work."

Whereas male rookies are assumed to be competent dispensers of force unless proven otherwise, women are believed to be physically weak, naturally passive, and emotionally vulnerable.[3] Women officers are assumed to be reluctant to use physical force and are viewed as incompetent "street cops" until they prove otherwise. As a result, women rookies encounter special problems in learning to use normal force in the process of becoming recognized as "real street cops." It becomes crucial for women officers to create or exploit opportunities to display their physical abilities in order to overcome sexual bias and obtain full acceptance from co-workers. As a result, women rookies are encouraged informally to act more aggressively and to display more machismo than male rookies. . . .

For a street cop, it is often a graver error to use too little force and develop a "shaky" reputation than it is to use too much force and be told to calm down. Thus officers, particularly rookies, who do not back up their partners in appropriate ways or who hesitate to use force in circumstances where it is deemed necessary are informally instructed regarding their aberrant ways. If the problematic incident is relatively insignificant and his general reputation is good, a rookie who "freezes" one time is given a second chance before becoming generally known as an untrustworthy partner. However, such incidents become the subject of degrading gossip, gossip that pressures the officer either to use force as expected or risk isolation. Such talk also informs rookies about the general boundaries of legal and normal force.

For example, a female rookie was accused of "freezing" in an incident that came to be referred to as a "Mexican standoff." A pedestrian had complained that "something funny is going on in the drugstore." The officer walked into the pharmacy where she found an armed man committing a robbery. Although he turned his weapon on her when she entered the premises, she still pulled out her gun and pointed it at him. When he ordered her to drop it, claiming that his partner was behind her with a revolver at her head, she refused and told him to drop his.[4] He refused, and the stalemate continued until a sergeant entered the drugstore and ordered the suspect to drop his gun.

Initially, the female officer thought she had acted appropriately and even heroically. She soon discovered, however, that her hesitation to shoot had brought into question her competence with some of her fellow officers. Although many veterans claimed that "she had a lot a balls" to take her gun out at all when the suspect already had a gun on her, most contended "she shoulda shot him." Other policemen confirmed that she committed a "rookie mistake"; she had failed to notice a "lookout" standing outside the store and hence had been unprepared for an armed confrontation. Her sergeant and lieutenant, moreover, even insisted that she had acted in a cowardly manner, despite her reputation as a "gung-ho cop," and cited the incident as evidence of the general inadequacy of policewomen.

In the weeks that followed, this officer became increasingly depressed and angry. She was particularly outraged when she learned that she would not receive a commendation, although such awards were commonly made for "gun pinches" of this nature. Several months later, the officer vehemently expressed the wish that she had killed the suspect and vowed that next time she would "shoot first and ask questions later." The negative sanctions of supervisors and colleagues clearly encouraged her to adopt an attitude favorable to using force with less restraint in future situations. . . .

At the same time that male and female rookies are commended for using force under appropriate circumstances, they are reprimanded if their participation in force is viewed as excessive or inappropriate. In this way, rookies are instructed that although many acts of coercion are accepted and even demanded, not everything goes. They thereby learn to distinguish between normal and brutal force. . . .

Accounting for Normal Force

Police routinely normalize the use of force by two types of accounts: excuses and justifications. . . .

EXCUSES AND NORMAL FORCE

Excuses are accounts in which police deny full responsibility for an act but recognize its inappropriateness. Excuses therefore constitute socially approved vocabularies for relieving responsibility when conduct is questionable. Police most often excuse morally problematic force by referring to emotional or physiological states that are precipitated by some circumstances of routine patrol work. These circumstances include shootouts, violent fights, pursuits, and instances in which a police officer mistakenly comes close to killing an unarmed person.

Police work in these circumstances can generate intense excitement in which the officer experiences the "combat high" and "adrenaline rush" familiar to the combat soldier.[5] Foot and car pursuits not only bring on feelings of danger and excitement from the chase, but also a challenge to official authority. As one patrolman commented about a suspect: "Yeh, he got tuned up [beaten] . . . you always tune them up after a car chase." Another officer normalized the use of force after a pursuit in these terms:

> It's my feeling that violence inevitably occurs after a pursuit. . . . The adrenaline . . . and the insult involved when someone flees increases with every foot of the pursuit. I know the two or three times that I felt I lost control of myself . . . was when someone would run on me. The further I had to chase the guy the madder I got. . . . The funny thing is the reason for the pursuit could have been something as minor as a traffic violation or a kid you're chasing who just turned on a fire hydrant. It always ends in violence. You feel obligated to hit or kick the guy just for running.

Police officers also excuse force when it follows an experience of helplessness and confusion that has culminated in a temporary loss of emotional control. This emotional combination occurs most frequently when an officer comes to the brink of using lethal force, drawing a gun and perhaps firing, only to learn there were no "real" grounds for this action. The officer may then "snap out" and hit the suspect.[6] In one such incident, for example, two policemen picked up a complainant who positively identified a suspect as a man who just tried to shoot him. Just as the officers approached the suspect, he suddenly reached for his back pocket for what the officers assumed to be a gun. One officer was close enough to jump the suspect before he pulled his hand from his pocket. As it turned out, the suspect had no weapon, having dropped it several feet away. Although he was unarmed and under control, the suspect was punched and kicked out of anger and frustration by the officer who had almost shot him.

Note that in both these circumstances—pursuit and near-miss mistaken shootings—officers would concede that the ensuing force is inappropriate and unjustifiable when considered abstractly. But although abstractly wrong, the use of force on such occasions is presented as a normal, human reaction to an extreme situation. Although not every officer might react violently in such circumstances, it is understandable and expected that some will.

SITUATIONAL JUSTIFICATIONS

Officers also justify force as normal by reference to interactional situations in which an officer's authority is physically or symbolically threatened. [In contrast to excuses, which deny responsibility for the act but recognize that the act is blameworthy, justifications accept responsibility for the act but deny that the act is blameworthy.—Ed.] In such accounts, the use of force is justified instrumentally—as a means of regaining immediate control in a situation where that control has become tenuous. Here, the officer depicts his primary intent for using force as a need to reestablish immediate control in a problematic encounter, and only incidentally as hurting or punishing the offender.

Few officers will hesitate to assault a suspect who physically threatens or attacks them. In one case, an officer was punched in the face by a prisoner he had just apprehended for allegedly attempting to shoot a friend. The incident occurred in the stationhouse, and several policemen observed the exchange. Immediately, one officer hit the prisoner in the jaw and the rest immediately joined the brawl.

Violations of an officer's property such as his car or hat may signify a more symbolic assault on the officer's authority and self, thus justifying a forceful response to maintain control. Indeed, in the police view, almost any person who verbally challenges a police officer is appropriately subject to force. . . .

On rare occasions, women officers encounter special problems in these regards. Although most suspects view women in the same way as policemen, some seem less inclined to accord female officers *de facto* and symbolic control in street encounters, and on a few occasions seem determined to provoke direct confrontations with such officers, explicitly denying their formal authority and attempting none too subtly to sexualize the encounter. Women officers, then, might use force as a resource for rectifying such insults and for establishing control over such partially sexualized interactions. Consider the following woman officer's extended account providing such situational justifications for the use of force:

> . . . I'm sitting at Second Street, Second and Nassau, writing curfews up. And this silver Thunderbird . . . blows right by a stop sign where I'm sitting. And I look up and think to myself, "Now, do I want to get involved?" And I figure, it was really belligerent doing it right in front of me. So I take off after him, put my lights on and he immediately pulls over. So he jumps out of the car. I jump out of the car right away and I say, "I'm stopping you for that stop sign you just blew through. . . . Let me see your cards, please." Then he starts making these lip smacking noises at me everytime he begins to talk. He said, (smack) "The only way you're seeing my cards is if you lock me up and the only way you're gonna lock me up is if you chase me." And I said to him, "Well, look, I will satisfy you on one account. Now go to your car because I will lock you up. . . . And just sit in your car. I'll be right with you." He smacks his lips, turns around and goes to his car and he sits. And I call a wagon at Second and Nassau. They ask me what I have. I say, "I've got one to go." So as the wagon acknowledges, the car all of a sudden tears out of its spot. And I get on the air and say, "I'm in pursuit." And I give them a description of the car and the direction I'm going. . . . And all of a sudden he pulls over

about a block and a half after I started the pursuit. So I got on the air and I said, "I got him at Second and Washington." I jumped out of my car and as I jumped out he tears away again. Now I'm ready to die of embarrassment. I have to get back on the air and say no I don't have him. So I got on the air and said, "Look, he's playing games with me now. He took off again." I said, "I'm still heading South on Second Street." He gets down to Lexington. He pulls over again. Well, this time I pulled the police car in front of him. . . . I go over to the car and I hear him lock the doors. I pull out my gun and I put it right in his window. I say, "Unlock that door." Well, he looked at the gun. He nearly liked to shit himself. He unlocked the door. I holster my gun. I go to grab his arms to pull him out and all of a sudden I realize Anne's got him. So we keep pulling him out of the car. Throw him on the trunk of his car and kept pounding him back down on the trunk. She's punching his head. I'm kicking him. Then I take out my blackjack. I jack him across the shoulder. Then I go to jack him in the head and I jack Anne's fingers. . . . The next thing they know is we're throwing him bodily into the wagon. And they said, "Did you search him?" We go to the wagon, drag him out again. Now we're tearing through his pockets throwing everything on the ground. Pick him up bodily again, threw him in. . . . So I straightened it out with the sergeant. . . . I said, "What did you want me to do? Let any citizen on the street get stopped and pull away and that's the end of it?"

In this instance, a male suspect manages to convey a series of affronts to the officer's authority. These affronts become explicitly and insultingly sexual, turning the challenge from the claim that "no cop will stop me" to the more gender specific one, "no woman cop will stop me." Resistance ups the ante until the suspect backs down in the face of the officer's drawn revolver. The force to which the culprit was then subjected is normalized through all the accounts considered to this point—it is situationally justified as a means to reestablish and maintain immediate and symbolic control in a highly problematic encounter and it is excused as a natural, collective outburst following resolution of a dangerous, tension-filled incident. And finally, it is more implicitly justified as appropriate punishment, an account building upon standard police practices for abstract justification, to which I now turn.

ABSTRACT JUSTIFICATIONS

Police also justify the use of extreme force against certain categories of morally reprehensible persons. In this case, force is not presented as an instrumental means to regain control that has been symbolically or physically threatened. Instead, it is justified as an appropriate response to particularly heinous offenders. Categories of such offenders include: cop haters who have gained notoriety as persistent police antagonizers; cop killers or any person who has attempted seriously to harm a police officer (Westley, 1970:131); sexual deviants who prey on children and "moral women"; child abusers; and junkies and other "scum" who inhabit the street. The more morally reprehensible the act is judged, the more likely the police are to depict any violence directed toward its perpetrator as justifiable. Thus a man who exposes himself to children in a playground is less likely to experience police assault than one who rapes or sexually molests a child.

"Clean" criminals, such as high-level mafiosi, white-collar criminals, and professional burglars, are rarely subject to abstract force. Nor are perpetrators of violent and nonviolent street crimes who prey on adult males, prostitutes, and other categories of persons who belong on the street.[7] Similarly, the "psycho" or demented person is perceived as so mentally deranged that he is not responsible for his acts and hence does not merit abstract, punitive force (Van Maanen, 1978:233–34).

Police justify abstract force by invoking a higher moral purpose that legitimates the violation of commonly recognized standards. In one case, for example, a nun was raped by a seventeen-year-old male adolescent. When the police apprehended the suspect, he was severely beaten and his penis put in an electrical outlet to teach him a lesson. The story of the event was told to me by a police officer who, despite the fact that he rarely supported the use of extralegal force, depicted this treatment as legitimate. Indeed, when I asked if he would have participated had he been present, he responded, "I'm Catholic. I would have participated."

Excessive Force and Peer Responses

Although police routinely excuse and justify many incidents where they or their co-workers have used extreme force against a citizen or suspect, this does not mean that on any and every occasion the officer using such force is exonerated. Indeed, the concept of normal force is useful because it suggests that there are specific circumstances under which police officers will not condone the use of force by themselves or colleagues as reasonable and acceptable. Thus, officer-recognized conceptions of normal force are subject to restrictions of the following kinds:

1. Police recognize and honor some rough equation between the behavior of the suspect and the harmfulness of the force to which it is subject. There are limits, therefore, to the degree of force that is acceptable in particular circumstances. In the following incident, for example, an officer reflects on a situation in which a "symbolic assailant" (Skolnick, 1975:45) was mistakenly subject to more force than he "deserved" and almost killed:

> One time Bill Johnson and I . . . had a particularly rude drunk one day. He was really rude and spit on you and he did all this stuff and we even had to cuff him lying down on the hard stretcher, like you would do an epileptic. . . . So we were really mad. We said let's just give him one or two shots . . . slamming on the brakes and having him roll. But we didn't use our heads . . . we heard the stretcher go nnnnnBam and then nothing. We heard nothing and we realized we had put this man in with his head to the front so when we slammed on the brakes

his stretcher. . . . I guess it can roll four foot. Well, it was his head that had hit the front. . . . So, we went to Madison Street and parked. It's a really lonely area. And we unlocked the wagon and peeked in. We know he's in there. We were so scared and we look in and there's not a sound and we see blood coming in front of the wagon and think " . . . we killed this man. What am I gonna do? What am I gonna tell by family?" And to make a long story short, he was just knocked out. But boy was I scared. From then on we learned, feet first.

2. Similarly, even in cases where suspects are seen as deserving some violent punishment, this force should not be used randomly and without control. Thus, in the following incident, an officer who "snapped out" and began to beat a child abuser clearly regarded his partner's attempt to stop the beating as reasonable.

> . . . I knock on the door and a lady answers just completely hysterical. And I say, "Listen, I don't know what's going on in here," but then I hear this, just this screeching. You know. And I figure well I'm just going to find out what's going on so I just go past the lady and what's happening is that the husband had. . . . The kid was being potty trained and the way they were potty training this kid, this two-year-old boy, was that the boyfriend of this girl would pick up this kid and he would sit him down on top of the stove. It was their method of potty training. Well, first of all you think of your own kids. I mean afterwards you do. I mean I've never been this mad in my whole life. You see this little two-year-old boy seated on the top of the stove with rings around it being absolutely scalding hot. And he's saying "I'll teach you to go. . . . " It just triggered something. An uncontrollable. . . . It's just probably the most violent I ever got. Well you just grab that guy. You hit him ten, fifteen times . . . you don't know how many. You just get so mad. And I remember my partner eventually came in and grabbed me and said, "Don't worry about it. We got him. We got him." And we cuffed him and we took him down. Yeah that was bad.

Learning these sorts of restrictions on the use of normal force and these informal practices of peer control are important processes in the socialization of newcomers. This socialization proceeds both through ongoing observation and experience and, on occasion, through explicit instruction. For example, one veteran officer advised a rookie, "The only reason to go in on a pursuit is not to get the perpetrator but to pull the cop who gets there first offa the guy before he kills him."

Conclusion

The organization of police work reflects a poignant moral dilemma: For a variety of reasons, society mandates to the police the right to use force but provides little direction as to its proper use in specific, "real life" situations. Thus, the police, as officers of the law, must be prepared to use force under circumstances in which its rationale is often morally, legally, and practically ambiguous. This fact explains some otherwise puzzling aspects of police training and socialization.

The police academy provides a semblance of socialization for its recruits by teaching formal rules for using force. . . . [T]he full socialization of a police officer takes place outside the academy as the officer moves from its idealizations to the practicalities of the street. . . .

. . . [J]ustifications and excuses . . . conventionalize but do not reform situations that are inherently charged and morally ambiguous. In this way they simultaneously preserve the self-image of police as agents of the conventional order, provide ways in which individual officers can resolve their personal doubts as to the moral status of their action and those of their colleagues, and reinforce the solidarity of the police community.

*

Notes

1. Nonetheless masculine pronouns are generally used to refer to the police in this article, because the Metro P.D. remained dominated by men numerically, in style, and in tone. . . .

2. Some officers also substitute a large heavy duty flashlight for the nightstick. If used correctly, the flashlight can inflict more damage than the baton and is less likely to break when applied to the head or other parts of the body.

3. As the Metro City Police Commissioner commented in an interview: "In general, they [women] are physically weaker than males. . . . I believe they would be inclined to let their emotions all too frequently overrule their good judgment . . . there are periods in their life when they are psychologically unbalanced because of physical problems that are occurring within them."

4. The woman officer later explained that she did not obey the suspect's command because she saw no reflection of the partner in the suspect's glasses and therefore assumed he was lying.

5. The combat high is a state of controlled exhilaration in which the officer experiences a heightened awareness of the world around him. Officers report that perception, smell, and hearing seem acute; one seems to stand outside oneself, and the world appears extraordinarily vivid and clear. At the same time, officers insist that they are able to think rationally and instantly translate thoughts into action; when experienced, fear is not incapacitating but instead enhances the ability to act.

6. This police experience of fear and helplessness, leading to a violent outburst, may be analogized to a parent's reaction on seeing his child almost die in an accident. Imagine a scene in which a father is walking with his six-year-old son. Suddenly, the boy runs into the street to get a red ball on the pavement. The father watches a car slam on the brakes and miss the boy by two inches. He grabs his son and smacks him on the face before he takes him in his arms and holds him. . . .

7. The categories of persons who merit violence are not unique to the police. Prisoners, criminals, and hospital personnel appear to draw similar distinctions between morally unworthy persons; on the latter, see Sudnow (1967:105).

References

Bittner, E. (1980). *The Functions of the Police in Modern Society.* Cambridge, MA: Oelgeschlager, Gunn & Hain.

Hunt, J. (forthcoming). "The development of rapport through the negotiation of gender in field work among police." *Human Organization.*

Skolnick, J. (1975). *Justice Without Trial.* New York: John Wiley.

Sudnow, D. (1967). *Passing On: The Social Organization of Dying.* Englewood Cliffs, NJ: Prentice-Hall.

Van Maanen, J. (1978). "The asshole." In P. K. Manning and J. Van Maanen (eds.), *Policing: A View from the Street.* Santa Monica, CA: Goodyear.

Westley, W. A. (1970). *Violence and the Police: A Sociological Study of Law, Custom and Morality.* Cambridge, MA: MIT Press.

42 The My Lai Massacre

HERBERT KELMAN
V. LEE HAMILTON

War is a part of politics. When a nation's leaders are frustrated as other strategies for reaching international goals fail, war becomes a possibility. *War,* then, can be considered a technique—albeit a most violent one—to accomplish political objectives.

Nations vary in their willingness to go to war. Switzerland, for example, has vowed to never go to war, and for over 200 years has been at peace. The Swiss, however, do train their men to handle weapons in case another nation should attack them. The United States, in contrast, is very willing to invade other nations—in recent years Somalia, Haiti, Panama, Grenada, Desert Storm. To paraphrase the Allies' slogan for World War I, "to make the world safe for capitalism" seems to be the reason for these wars. Seldom is the matter put this crassly, of course, for the goal of controlling oil, although it sells well on Wall Street, doesn't go down well on Main Street—which provides the sons (and, increasingly, the daughters) to be sacrificed on the altar of profits.

While war can bring out the best in people—such as soldiers throwing themselves onto live grenades in order to save their buddies—it seems more likely to bring out the worst. *Dehumanization,* considering opponents as less than human and treating them as such, is one of the unfortunate consequences of prolonged wars. In this selection, Kelman and Hamilton analyze the case of dehumanization that received the most publicity in the war in Vietnam.

MARCH 16, 1968, was a busy day in U.S. HISTORY. Stateside, Robert F. Kennedy announced his presidential candidacy, challenging a sitting president from his own party—in part out of opposition to an undeclared and disastrous war. In Vietnam, the war continued. In many ways, March 16 may have been a typical day in that war. We will probably never know. But we do know that on that day a typical company went on a mission—which may or may not have been typical—to a village called Son (or Song) My. Most of what is remembered from that mission occurred in the subhamlet known to Americans as My Lai 4.

The My Lai massacre was investigated and charges were brought in 1969 and 1970. Trials and disciplinary actions lasted until 1971. Entire books have

447

been written about the army's year-long cover-up of the massacre (for example, Hersh, 1972), and the cover-up was a major focus of the army's own investigation of the incident. Our central concern here is the massacre itself—a crime of obedience—and public reactions to such crimes, rather than the lengths to which many went to deny the event. Therefore this account concentrates on one day: March 16, 1968.

Many verbal testimonials to the horrors that occurred at My Lai were available. More unusual was the fact that an army photographer, Ronald Haeberle, was assigned the task of documenting the anticipated military engagement at My Lai—and documented a massacre instead. Later, as the story of the massacre emerged, his photographs were widely distributed and seared the public conscience. What might have been dismissed as unreal or exaggerated was depicted in photographs of demonstrable authenticity. The dominant image appeared on the cover of *Life:* piles of bodies jumbled together in a ditch along a trail—the dead all apparently unarmed. All were Oriental, and all appeared to be children, women, or old men. Clearly there had been a mass execution, one whose image would not quickly fade.

So many bodies (over twenty in the cover photo alone) are hard to imagine as the handiwork of one killer. These were not. They were the product of what we call a crime of obedience. Crimes of obedience begin with orders. But orders are often vague and rarely survive with any clarity the transition from one authority down a chain of subordinates to the ultimate actors. The operation at Son My was no exception.

"Charlie" Company, Company C, under Lt. Col. Frank Barker's command, arrived in Vietnam in December of 1967. As the army's investigative unit, directed by Lt. Gen. William R. Peers, characterized the personnel, they "contained no significant deviation from the average" for the time. Seymour S. Hersh (1970) described the "average" more explicitly: "Most of the men in Charlie Company had volunteered for the draft; only a few had gone to college for even one year. Nearly half were black, with a few Mexican-Americans. Most were eighteen to twenty-two years old. The favorite reading matter of Charlie Company, like that of other line infantry units in Vietnam, was comic books" (p. 18). The action at My Lai, like that throughout Vietnam, was fought by a cross-section of those Americans who either believed in the war or lacked the social resources to avoid participating in it. Charlie Company was indeed average for that time, that place, and that war.

Two key figures in Charlie Company were more unusual. The company's commander, Capt. Ernest Medina, was an upwardly mobile Mexican-American who wanted to make the army his career, although he feared that he might never advance beyond captain because of his lack of formal education. His eagerness had earned him a nickname among his men: "Mad Dog Medina." One of his admirers was the platoon leader Second Lt. William L. Calley, Jr., an undistinguished, five-foot-three-inch junior-college dropout who had failed four of the seven courses in which he had enrolled his first year. Many viewed him as one of those "instant officers" made possible only by the army's then-desperate need for manpower. Whatever the cause, he was an insecure leader whose frequent claim was "I'm the boss." . . .

The Son My operation was planned by Lieutenant Colonel Barker and his staff as a search-and-destroy mission with the objective of rooting out the Forty-eighth Viet Cong Battalion from their base area of Son My village. Apparently no written orders were ever issued. Barker's superior, Col. Oran Henderson, arrived at the staging point the day before. Among the issues he reviewed with the assembled officers were some of the weaknesses of prior operations by their units, including their failure to be appropriately aggressive in pursuit of the enemy. Later briefings by Lieutenant Colonel Barker and his staff asserted that no one except Viet Cong was expected to be in the village after 7 A.M. on the following day. The "innocent" would all be at the market. Those present at the briefings gave conflicting accounts of Barker's exact orders, but he conveyed at least a strong suggestion that the Son My area was to be obliterated. As the army's inquiry reported: "While there is some conflict in the testimony as to whether LTC Barker ordered the destruction of houses, dwellings, livestock, and other foodstuffs in the Song My area, the preponderance of the evidence suggests that such destruction was implied, if not specifically directed, by his orders of 15 March" (Peers Report, in Goldstein et al., 1976, p. 94). . . .

Charlie Company's Captain Medina was briefed for the operation by Barker and his staff. He then transmitted the already vague orders to his own men. Charlie Company was spoiling for a fight, having been totally frustrated during its months in Vietnam—first by waiting for battles that never came, then by incompetent forays led by inexperienced commanders, and finally by mines and booby traps. In fact, the emotion-laden funeral of a sergeant killed by a booby trap was held on March 15, the day before My Lai. Captain Medina gave the orders for the next day's action at the close of that funeral. Many were in a mood for revenge. . . .

As March 16 dawned, much was expected of the operation by those who had set it into motion. Therefore a full complement of "brass" was present in helicopters overhead, including Barker, Colonel Henderson, and their superior, Major General Koster (who went on to become commandant of West Point before the story of My Lai broke). On the ground, the troops were to carry with them one reporter and one photographer to immortalize the anticipated battle.

The action for Company C began at 7:30 as their first wave of helicopters touched down near the subhamlet of My Lai. By 7:47 all of Company C was present and set to fight. But instead of the Viet Cong Forty-eighth Battalion, My Lai was filled with the old men, women, and children who were supposed to have gone to market. By this time, in their version of the war, and with whatever orders they thought they had heard, the men from Company C were nevertheless ready to find Viet Cong everywhere. By nightfall, the official tally was 128 VC killed and three weapons captured, although later unofficial body counts ran as high as 500. The operation at Son My was over. . . .

But what could have happened to leave American troops reporting a victory over Viet Cong when in fact they had killed hundreds of noncombatants? It is not hard to explain the report of victory; that is the essence of a cover-up. It is harder to understand how the killings came to be committed in the first place, making a cover-up necessary.

Mass Executions and the Defense of Superior Orders

Some of the atrocities on March 16, 1968, were evidently unofficial, spontaneous acts: rapes, tortures, killings. For example, Hersh (1970) describes Charlie Company's Second Platoon as entering "My Lai 4 with guns blazing" (p. 50); more graphically, Lieutenant "Brooks and his men in the second platoon to the north had begun to systematically ransack the hamlet and slaughter the people, kill the livestock, and destroy the crops. Men poured rifle and machine-gun fire into huts without knowing—or seemingly caring—who was inside" (pp. 49–50).

Some atrocities toward the end of the action were part of an almost casual "mopping-up," much of which was the responsibility of Lieutenant LaCross's Third Platoon of Charlie Company. The Peers Report states: "The entire 3rd Platoon then began moving into the western edge of My Lai (4), for the mop-up operation. . . . The squad . . . began to burn the houses in the southwestern portion of the hamlet" (Goldstein et al., 1976, p. 133). They became mingled with other platoons during a series of rapes and killings of survivors for which it was impossible to fix responsibility. Certainly to a Vietnamese, all GIs would by this point look alike: "Nineteen-year-old Nguyen Thi Ngoc Tuyet watched a baby trying to open her slain mother's blouse to nurse. A soldier shot the infant while it was struggling with the blouse, and then slashed it with his bayonet." Tuyet also said she saw another baby hacked to death by GIs wielding their bayonets. "Le Tong, a twenty-eight-year-old rice farmer, reported seeing one woman raped after GIs killed her children. Nguyen Khoa, a thirty-seven-year-old peasant, told of a thirteen-year-old girl who was raped before being killed. GIs then attacked Khoa's wife, tearing off her clothes. Before they could rape her, however, Khoa said, their six-year-old son, riddled with bullets, fell and saturated her with blood. The GIs left her alone" (Hersh, 1970, p. 72). All of Company C was implicated in a pattern of death and destruction throughout the hamlet, much of which seemingly lacked rhyme or reason.

But a substantial amount of the killing was *organized* and traceable to one authority: the First Platoon's Lt. William Calley. Calley was originally charged with 109 killings, almost all of them mass executions at the trail and other locations. He stood trial for 102 of these killings, was convicted of 22 in 1971, and at first received a life sentence. Though others—both superior and subordinate to Calley—were brought to trial, he was the only one convicted for the My Lai crimes. Thus, the only actions of My Lai for which *anyone* was ever convicted were mass executions, ordered and committed. We suspect that there are commonsense reasons why this one type of killing was singled out. In the midst of rapidly moving events with people running about, an execution of stationary targets is literally a still life that stands out and whose participants are clearly visible. It can be proven that specific people committed specific deeds. An execution, in contrast to the shooting of someone on the run, is also more likely to meet the legal definition of an act resulting from intent—with malice aforethought. Moreover, American military law specifically forbids the killing of unarmed civilians or military prisoners, as does the Geneva Convention between nations. Thus common sense, legal standards, and explicit doctrine all made such actions the likeliest target for prosecution. . . .

The day's quiet beginning has already been noted. Troops landed and swept unopposed into the village. The three weapons eventually reported as the haul from the operation were picked up from three apparent Viet Cong who fled the village when the troops arrived and were pursued and killed by helicopter gunships. Obviously the Viet Cong did frequent the area. But it appears that by about 8:00 A.M. no one who met the troops was aggressive, and no one was armed. By the laws of war Charlie Company had no argument with such people.

As they moved into the village, the soldiers began to gather its inhabitants together. Shortly after 8:00 A.M. Lieutenant Calley told Pfc. Paul Meadlo that "you know what to do with" a group of villagers Meadlo was guarding. Estimates of the numbers in the group ranged as high as eighty women, children, and old men, and Meadlo's own estimate under oath was thirty to fifty people. As Meadlo later testified, Calley returned after ten or fifteen minutes: "He [Calley] said, 'How come they're not dead?' I said, 'I didn't know we were supposed to kill them.' He said, 'I want them dead.' He backed off twenty or thirty feet and started shooting into the people—the Viet Cong—shooting automatic. He was beside me. He burned four or five magazines. I burned off a few, about three. I helped shoot 'em" (Hammer, 1971, p. 155). Meadlo himself and others testified that Meadlo cried as he fired; others reported him later to be sobbing and "all broke up." It would appear that to Lieutenant Calley's subordinates something was unusual, and stressful, in these orders. . . .

Among the helicopters flying reconnaissance above Son My was that of CWO Hugh Thompson. By 9:00 or soon after, Thompson had noticed some horrifying events from his perch. As he spotted wounded civilians, he sent down smoke markers so the soldiers on the ground could treat them. They killed them instead. He reported to headquarters, trying to persuade someone to stop what was going on. Barker, hearing the message, called down to Captain Medina. Medina, in turn, later claimed to have told Calley that it was "enough for today." But it was not yet enough.

At Calley's orders, his men began gathering the remaining villagers—roughly seventy-five individuals, mostly women and children—and herding them toward a drainage ditch. Accompanied by three or four enlisted men, Lieutenant Calley executed several batches of civilians who had been gathered into ditches. Some of the details of the process were entered into testimony in such accounts as Pfc. Dennis Conti's: "A lot of them, the people, were trying to get up and mostly they was just screaming and pretty bad shot up. . . . I seen a woman tried to get up. I seen Lieutenant Calley fire. He hit the side of her head and blew it off" (Hammer, 1971, p. 125).

Pfc. Gregory Olsen corroborated the general picture of the victims: "They were—the majority were women and children, some babies. I distinctly remember one middle-aged Vietnamese male dressed in white right at my feet as I crossed. None of the bodies were mangled in any way. There was blood. Some appeared to be dead, others followed me with their eyes as I walked across the ditch" (Goldstein et al., 1976, p. 502). . . .

It is noteworthy that during these executions more than one enlisted man avoided carrying out Calley's orders, and more than one, by sworn oath, directly refused to obey them. For example, Pfc. James Joseph Dursi testified, when asked if he fired when Lieutenant Calley ordered him to: "No. I just stood there. Meadlo turned to me after a couple of minutes and said 'Shoot! Why don't you shoot! Why don't you fire!' He was crying and yelling. I said, 'I can't! I won't!' And the people were screaming and crying and yelling. They kept firing for a couple of minutes, mostly automatic and semi-automatic" (Hammer, 1971, p. 143). . . .

Even those who obeyed Calley's orders showed great stress. For example, Meadlo eventually began to argue and cry directly in front of Calley. Pfc. Herbert Carter shot himself in the foot, possibly because he could no longer take what he was doing. We were not destined to hear a sworn version of the incident, since neither side at the Calley trial called him to testify.

The most unusual instance of resistance to authority came from the skies. CWO Hugh Thompson, who had protested the apparent carnage of civilians, was Calley's inferior in rank but was not in his line of command. He was also watching the ditch from his helicopter and noticed some people moving after the first round of slaughter—chiefly children who had been shielded by their mother's bodies. Landing to rescue the wounded, he also found some villagers hiding in a nearby bunker. Protecting the Vietnamese with his own body, Thompson ordered his men to train their guns on the Americans and to open fire if the Americans fired on the Vietnamese. He then radioed for additional rescue helicopters and stood between the Vietnamese and the Americans under Calley's command until the Vietnamese could be evacuated. He later returned to the ditch to unearth a child buried, unharmed, beneath layers of bodies. In October 1969, Thompson was awarded the Distinguished Flying Cross for heroism at My Lai, specifically (albeit inaccurately) for the rescue of children hiding in a bunker "between Viet Cong forces and advancing friendly forces" and for the rescue of a wounded child "caught in the intense crossfire" (Hersh, 1970, p. 119). Four months earlier, at the Pentagon, Thompson had identified Calley as having been at the ditch.

By about 10:00 A.M., the massacre was winding down. The remaining actions consisted largely of isolated rapes and killings, "clean-up" shootings of the wounded, and the destruction of the village by fire. We have already seen some examples of these more indiscriminate and possibly less premeditated acts. By the 11:00 A.M. lunch break, when the exhausted men of Company C were relaxing, two young girls wandered back from a hiding place only to be invited to share lunch. This surrealist touch illustrates the extent to which the soldiers' action had become dissociated from its meaning. An hour earlier, some of these men were making sure that not even a child would escape the executioner's bullet. But now the job was done and it was time for lunch—and in this new context it seemed only natural to ask the children who had managed to escape execution to join them. The massacre had ended. It remained only for the Viet Cong to reap the political rewards among the survivors in hiding.

The army command in the area knew that something had gone wrong. Direct commanders, including Lieutenant Colonel Barker, had firsthand reports, such as Thompson's complaints. Others had such odd bits of evidence as the claim of 128 Viet Cong dead with a booty of only three weapons. But the cover-up of My Lai began at once. The operation was reported as a victory over a stronghold of the Viet Cong Forty-eighth.

William Calley was not the only man tried for the event at My Lai. The actions of over thirty soldiers and civilians were scrutinized by investigators; over half of these had to face charges or disciplinary action of some sort. Targets of investigation included Captain Medina, who was tried, and various higher-ups, including General Koster. But Lieutenant Calley was the only person convicted, the only person to serve time.

The core of Lieutenant Calley's defense was superior orders. What this meant to him—in contrast to what it meant to the judge and jury—can be gleaned from his responses to a series of questions from his defense attorney, George Latimer, in which Calley sketched out his understanding of the laws of war and the actions that constitute doing one's duty within those laws:

LATIMER: Did you receive any training . . . which had to do with the obedience to orders?
CALLEY: Yes, sir.
LATIMER: . . . what were you informed [were] the principles involved in that field?
CALLEY: That all orders were to be assumed legal, that the soldier's job was to carry out any order given him to the best of his ability.
LATIMER: . . . what might occur if you disobeyed an order by a senior officer?
CALLEY: You could be court-martialed for refusing an order and refusing an order in the face of the enemy, you could be sent to death, sir.

> LATIMER: [I am asking] whether you were required in any way, shape or form to make a determination of the legality or illegality of an order?
>
> CALLEY: No, sir. I was never told that I had the choice, sir.
>
> LATIMER: If you had a doubt about the order, what were you supposed to do?
>
> CALLEY: . . . I was supposed to carry the order out and then come back and make my complaint (Hammer, 1971, pp. 240–41).

Lieutenant Calley steadfastly maintained that his actions within My Lai had constituted, in his mind, carrying out orders from Captain Medina. Both his own actions and the orders he gave to others (such as the instruction to Meadlo to "waste 'em") were entirely in response to superior orders. He denied any intent to kill individuals and any but the most passing awareness of distinctions among the individuals: "I was ordered to go in there and destroy the enemy. That was my job on that day. That was the mission I was given. I did not sit down and think in terms of men, women, and children. They were all classified the same, and that was the classification that we dealt with, just as enemy solders." When Latimer asked if in his own opinion Calley had acted "rightly and according to your understanding of your directions and orders," Calley replied, "I felt then and I still do that I acted as I was directed, and I carried out the orders that I was given, and I do not feel wrong in doing so, sir" (Hammer, 1971, p. 257).

His court-martial did not accept Calley's defense of superior orders and clearly did not share his interpretation of his duty. The jury evidently reasoned that, even if there had been orders to destroy everything in sight and to "waste the Vietnamese," any reasonable person would have realized that such orders were illegal and should have refused to carry them out. . . .

A jury of combat veterans proceeded to convict William Calley of the premeditated murder of no less than twenty-two human beings. (The army, realizing some unfortunate connotations in referring to the victims as "Oriental human beings," eventually referred to them as "human beings.") . . .

Lieutenant Calley was initially sentenced to life imprisonment. That sentence was reduced: first to twenty years, eventually to ten (the latter by Secretary of the Army Callaway in 1974). Calley served three years before being released on bond. The time was spent under house arrest in his apartment, where he was able to receive visits from his girlfriend. He was granted parole on September 16, 1975.

Sanctioned Massacres

The slaughter at My Lai is an instance of a class of violent acts that can be described as sanctioned massacres (Kelman, 1973): acts of indiscriminate, ruthless, and often systematic mass violence, carried out by military or paramilitary personnel while engaged in officially sanctioned campaigns, the victims of which are defenseless and unresisting civilians, including old men, women, and children. Sanctioned massacres have occurred throughout history. Within American history, My Lai had its precursors in the Philippine war around the turn of the century (Schirmer, 1971) and in the massacres of Native Americans. Elsewhere in the world, one recalls the Nazis' "final solution" for European Jews, the massacres and deportations of Armenians by Turks, the liquidation of the kulaks and the great purges in the Soviet Union, and more recently the massacres in Indonesia and Bangladesh, in Biafra and Burundi, in South Africa and Mozambique, in Cambodia and Afghanistan, in Syria and Lebanon. . . .

The occurrence of sanctioned massacres cannot be adequately explained by the existence of psychological forces—whether these be characterological dispositions to engage in murderous or profound hostility against the target— so powerful that they must find expression in violent acts unhampered by moral restraints. Instead, . . . it is more instructive to look not at the motives for violence but at the conditions under which the usual moral inhibitions against violence become weakened. Three social processes that tend to create such conditions can be identified: authorization, routinization, and dehumanization. Through authorization, the situation becomes so defined that the individual is absolved of the responsibility to make personal moral choices. Through routinization, the action becomes so organized that there is no opportunity for raising moral questions. Through dehumanization, the actors' attitudes toward the target and toward themselves become so structured that it is neither necessary nor possible for them to view the relationship in moral terms.

AUTHORIZATION

Sanctioned massacres by definition occur in the context of an authority situation, a situation in which, at least for many of the participants, the moral principles that generally govern human relationships do not apply. Thus, when acts of violence are explicitly ordered, implicitly encouraged, tacitly approved, or at least permitted by legitimate authorities, people's readiness to commit or condone them is enhanced. That such acts are authorized seems to carry automatic justification for them. Behaviorally, authorization obviates the necessity of making judgments or choices. Not only do normal moral principles become inoperative, but—particularly when the actions are explicitly ordered—a different kind of morality, linked to the duty to obey superior orders, tends to take over.

In an authority situation, individuals characteristically feel obligated to obey the orders of the authorities, whether or not these correspond with their personal preferences. They see themselves as having no choice as long as they accept the legitimacy of the orders and of the authorities who give them. . . . The basic structure of a situation of legitimate authority requires subordinates to respond in terms of their role obligations rather than their personal preferences; they can openly disobey only by challenging the legitimacy of the authority. . . .

An important corollary of the basic structure of the authority situation is that actors often do not see themselves as personally responsible for the consequences of their actions. Again, there are individual differences, depending on actors' capacity and readiness to evaluate the legitimacy of orders received. Insofar as they see themselves as having had no choice in their actions, however, they do not feel personally responsible for them. They were not personal agents, but merely extensions of the authority. Thus, when their actions caused harm to others, they can feel relatively free of guilt. A similar mechanism operates when a person engages in antisocial behavior that was not ordered by the authorities but was tacitly encouraged and approved by them—even if only by making it clear that such behavior will not be punished. In this situation, behavior that was formerly illegitimate is legitimized by the authorities' acquiescence.

In the My Lai massacre, it is likely that the structure of the authority situation contributed to the massive violence in both ways—that is, by conveying the message that acts of violence against Vietnamese villagers were *required,* as well as the message that such acts, even if not ordered, were *permitted* by the authorities in charge. The actions at My Lai represented, at least in some respects, responses to explicit or implicit orders. Lieutenant Calley indicated, by orders and by example, that he wanted large numbers of villagers killed. Whether Calley himself had been ordered by his superiors to "waste" the whole area, as he claimed, remains a matter of controversy. Even if we assume, however, that he was not explicitly ordered to wipe out the village, he had reason to believe that such actions were expected by his superior officers. Indeed, the very nature of the war conveyed this expectation. The principal means of military success was the "body count"—the number of enemy soldiers killed—and any Vietnamese killed by the U.S. military was commonly defined as a "Viet Cong." Thus, it was not totally bizarre for Calley to believe that what he was doing at My Lai was to increase his body count, as any good officer was expected to do.

Even to the extent that the actions at My Lai occurred spontaneously, without reference to superior orders, those committing them had reason to assume that such actions might be tacitly approved of by the military authorities. Not only had they failed to punish such acts in most cases, but the very strategies and tactics that the authorities consistently devised were based on the proposition that the civilian population of South Vietnam—whether "hostile" or "friendly"—was expendable. Such policies as search-and-destroy missions, the establishment of free-shooting zones, the use of antipersonnel weapons, the bombing of entire villages if they were suspected of harboring guerrillas, the forced migration of masses of the rural population, and the defoliation of vast forest areas helped legitimize acts of massive violence of the kind occurring at My Lai. . . .

ROUTINIZATION

Despite these forces, however, given the nature of the actions involved in sanctioned massacres, one might still expect moral scruples to intervene, but the likelihood of moral resistance is greatly reduced by transforming the action into routine, mechanical, highly programmed operations. Routinization fulfills two functions. First, it reduces the necessity of making decisions, thus minimizing the occasions in which moral questions may arise. Second, it makes it easier to avoid the implications of the action, since the actor focuses on the details of the job rather than on its meaning. The latter effect is more readily achieved among those who participate in sanctioned massacres from a distance—from their desks or even from the cockpits of their bombers.

Routinization operates both at the level of the individual actor and at the organizational level. Individual job performance is broken down into a series of discrete steps, most of them carried out in automatic, regularized fashion. It becomes easy to forget the nature of the product that emerges from the process. When Lieutenant Calley said of My Lai that it was "no great deal," he probably implied that it was all in a day's work. Organizationally, the task is divided among different offices, each of which has responsibility for a small portion of it. This arrangement diffuses responsibility and limits the amount and scope of decision-making that is necessary. There is no expectation that the moral implications will be considered at any of these points, nor is there any opportunity to do so. The organizational processes also help further legitimize the actions of each participant. By proceeding in routine fashion—processing papers, exchanging memos, diligently carrying out their assigned tasks—the different units mutually reinforce each other in the view that what is going on must be perfectly normal, correct, and legitimate. The shared illusion that they are engaged in a legitimate enterprise helps the participants assimilate their activities to other purposes, such as the efficiency of their performance, the productivity of their unit, or the cohesiveness of their group (see Janis, 1972).

Normalization of atrocities is more difficult to the extent that there are constant reminders of the true meaning of the enterprise. Bureaucratic inventiveness in the use of language helps to cover up such meaning. For example, the SS had a set of *Sprachregelungen,* or "language rules," to govern descriptions of their extermination program. The code names for killing and liquidation were "final solution," "evacuation," and "special treatment." The war in Indochina produced its own set of euphemisms, such as "protective reaction," "pacification," and "forced-draft urbanization and modernization." The use of euphemisms allows participants in sanctioned massacres to differentiate their actions from ordinary killing and destruction and thus to avoid confronting their true meaning.

DEHUMANIZATION

Authorization processes override standard moral considerations; routinization processes reduce the likelihood that such considerations will arise. Still, the inhibitions against murdering one's fellow human beings are generally so strong that the victims must also be stripped of their human status if they are to be subjected to systematic killing. Insofar as they are dehumanized, the usual principles of morality no longer apply to them.

Sanctioned massacres become possible to the extent that the victims are deprived in the perpetrators' eyes of the qualities essential to being perceived as fully human and included in the moral compact that governs human relationships. . . . Thus, when a group of people is defined entirely in terms of a category to which they belong, and when this category is excluded from the human family, moral restraints against killing them are more readily overcome.

Dehumanization of the enemy is a common phenomenon in any war situation. Sanctioned massacres, however, presuppose a more extreme degree of dehumanization, insofar as the killing is not in direct response to the target's threats or provocations. It is not what they have done that marks such victims for death but who they are—the category to which they happen to belong. They are the victims of policies that regard their systematic destruction as a desirable end or an acceptable means. Such extreme dehumanization becomes possible when the target group can readily be identified as a separate category of people who have historically been stigmatized and excluded by the victimizers; often the victims belong to a distinct racial, religious, ethnic, or political group regarded as inferior or sinister. The traditions, the habits, the images, and the vocabularies for dehumanizing such groups are already well established and can be drawn upon when the groups are selected for massacre. Labels help deprive the victims of identity and community, as in the epithet "gooks" that was commonly used to refer to Vietnamese and other Indochinese peoples.

The dynamics of the massacre process itself further increase the participants' tendency to dehumanize the victims. Those who participate as part of the bureaucratic apparatus increasingly come to see their victims as bodies to be counted and entered into reports, as faceless figures that will determine their productivity rates and promotions. Those who participate in the massacre directly—in the field, as it were—are reinforced in their perception of the victims as less than human by observing their very victimization. The only way they can justify what is being done to these people—both by others and by themselves—and the only way they can extract some degree of meaning out of the absurd events in which they find themselves participating (see Lifton, 1971, 1973) is by coming to believe that the victims are subhuman and deserve to be rooted out. And thus the process of dehumanization feeds on itself.

References

Goldstein, J., B. Marshall, and J. Schwartz, eds. 1976. *The My Lai Massacre and Its Cover-up: Beyond the Reach of Law?* (The Peers Report, with a supplement and introductory essay on the limits of law). New York: Free Press.

Hammer, R. 1971. *The Court-Martial of Lt. Calley*. New York: Coward, McCann, & Geoghegan.

Hersh, S. 1970. *My Lai 4: A Report on the Massacre and Its Aftermath*. New York: Vintage Books.

———. 1972. *Cover-up*. New York: Random House.

Janis, I. L. 1972. *Victims of Groupthink: A Psychological Study of Foreign-Policy Decisions and Fiascoes*. Boston: Houghton Mifflin.

Kelman, H. C. 1973. "Violence without Moral Restraint: Reflections on the Dehumanization of Victims and Victimizers." *Journal of Social Issues* 29 (4): 25–61.

Schirmer, D. B. 1971, April 24. "My Lai Was Not the First Time." *New Republic,* pp. 18–21.

IX Social Change

W HAT IMAGERY SHOULD WE USE? We are in a small, drift-
ing boat on a tumultuous sea of social change. Like a mighty wind, changing
events swirl around us, at times seeming to engulf us. Like a fire, change
threatens to devour us.

Regardless of the imagery, vast social change is a basic fact of contemporary life—and sometimes that change is threatening. Nothing seems to remain
the same. Familiar landmarks are torn down and replaced, seemingly
overnight, by a supermarket or another in an endless chain of fast-food outlets.
Farm fields and woods are paved over as they sprout malls and shopping centers. Crack moves into middle-class homes. Divorce rates soar while the
young, in confusion, postpone marriage. Clothing styles of the 1950s, cars of
the 1960s, furniture of the 1920s come back into fashion.

A universal compact disk with cinema-quality pictures destined to replace
videocassette recorders. C-cash for purchases on the Internet. A plane propelled by human muscle-power, and another that goes around the world without refueling. "Smart cards" to control access and security. Interactive television and "virtual reality." A wallet computer that functions as a credit/cash
card, a checkbook, a fax, and an e-mail communicator—and also dispenses
tickets for airlines and concerts. Long distance surgery, with patient and sur-
geon three thousand miles apart.

Although change is an essential part of today's society, it is anything but
new. Twenty-five hundred years ago, Heraclitus said, "Everything flows; nothing stands still." Six hundred years later, Marcus Aurelius Antoninus wrote,
"The universe is change." A more recent observer of the social scene put it this
way: "The only thing constant is the certainty of change."

While social change was indeed a part of past civilizations, there is an es-

461

sential difference between those changes and what we are experiencing today. Barring catastrophe in the form of human or natural disaster, change in ancient times was slow and orderly—sometimes so slow that even over generations the effects were barely perceptible. In all societies of the world, in fact, it was routinely the case that the father passed his occupation down to his son, who, in turn, passed it on to his son, and so on. Mothers, too, passed their occupation to their daughters. Thus the society that children lived in was practically identical to that into which their parents had been born. Although the players had changed, the basic social institutions, with their routine ways of handling things, remained the same over generations.

The contrast with our situation is stark. Most children today take it for granted that they are different from their parents—some even being amazed if they notice similarities with them. Adolescents routinely assume that their parents will not understand, for each represents a different world. With worlds so dissimilar, it is not uncommon for a grown child visiting his or her parents, following an absence of years or even months, to find that after "catching up"—about an hour or so—they have little or nothing left to talk about. Social change has sorted them into different worlds, their separate experiences imparting contrasting orientations to life.

"Adapt or die" may be the maxim under which living creatures exist. Only the organisms that adapt to changing circumstances survive, and humans are no exception. Confronted with challenge, humans adapt. They change their social institutions to match changing circumstances. The effects are highly visible as people modify their outward behaviors. But the consequences are hardly limited to the external, for they also penetrate people's inner life, changing their ideas, attitudes, and beliefs, their basic orientations to the world.

It is with discussions of this vital aspect of social life that we conclude this book. To provide a glimpse of how far we have come—which does not mean progress, only distance—we open this Part with a classic selection on small town life by Arthur J. Vidich and Joseph Bensman. Then, with Jerry Savells's article, we look at how one group, the Amish, resists social change. In the next selection, by James M. Jasper and Dorothy Nelkin, we examine the social movement that is having such an impact on our attitudes toward animals. Then George Ritzer confronts us with an analysis of the rationalization of society, pointing out how far reaching—and perhaps threatening—it is. We conclude with Arturo Madrid's reflection on changing racial-ethnic relations.

In conclusion, I would like to add that you, the reader, are the future. Certainly you cannot escape being shaped by your experiences of the vast changes occurring in society. For you to make better sense of your transforming experiences, however, I highly recommend the sociological imagination—the idea with which we began this book.

43 Small Town in Mass Society

ARTHUR J. VIDICH
JOSEPH BENSMAN

Although it makes us uncomfortable, we take for granted that our evening news will highlight the most recent kidnappings, bank robberies, holdups, carjackings, killings, stabbings, and drive-by shootings. So common are rapes, and still so shameful to their victims, that seldom are any but the most heinous brought to our attention. In the typical case that the media highlight, the victim was killed and the rape mentioned as a possibility. Dead, nude, and violated bodies of children incense us, but they, too, are now to be expected.

With our ideas of what we can expect formed by this background of "normal violence," some readers may assume that Vidich's and Bensman's analysis must be romanticized, an exaggerated imagery of the way things used to be. Granted what we face today, it certainly is difficult to believe that social life could ever have been as serene as that described here. Yet, prior to World War I, *most* Americans lived in small towns, with everyday life similar to those of the Springdalers. This selection is chosen to provide a background context for understanding how extensively society has changed.

"Just Plain Folks"

WHEN ONE BECOMES MORE intimately acquainted with the people of Springdale, and especially with the more verbal and prominent inhabitants, one finds that they like to think of themselves as "just plain folks." The editor of the paper, in urging people to attend public meetings or in reporting a social event, says, "all folks with an interest" should attend or "the folks who came certainly had a good time." Almost any chairman of a public gathering addresses his° audience as folks—"all right, folks, the meeting will get under way"—and the interviewer in his work frequently encounters the same expression— "the folks in this community," "the townfolk," "the country folk," "good folks," and "bad folks." Depending on context, the term carries with it a number of quite different connotations.

First and foremost, the term serves to distinguish Springdalers from urban dwellers, who are called "city people," an expression which by the tone in which it is used implies the less fortunate, those who are denied the wholesome virtues of rural life. City people are separated from nature and soil, from field and stream, and are caught up in the inexorable web of impersonality and loneliness, of which the public statement in Springdale is: "How can people stand to live in cities?" In an understandable and ultimate extension of this valuation one may occasionally hear references to the rural or country folk, in contrast to the villagers, the former being regarded by Springdalers as the "true folk."

The self-designation as "folk" includes everyone in the community; by its generality of reference it excludes neither the rich nor the poor, for everyone can share equally in the genuine qualities ascribed by the term. This is not to say that the community does not recognize scoundrels and wastrels in its own environment; quite the contrary, the scoundrel and allied types become all the more noticeable in the light of the dominant genuineness of rural life. It is rather to say that the standard of judgment by which character is assessed in Springdale includes no false or artificial values. To be one of the folks requires neither money, status, family background, learning, nor refined manners. It is, in short, a way of referring to the equalitarianism of rural life.

The term also includes a whole set of moral values: honesty, fair play, trustworthiness, good-neighborliness, helpfulness, sobriety, and clean living. To the Springdaler it suggests a wholesome family life, a man whose spoken word is as good as a written contract, a community of religious-minded people, and a place where "everybody knows everybody" and "where you can say hello to anybody." The background image of urban society and city people gives force and meaning to the preferred rural way of life.

Rural Virtues and City Life

The sense of community-mindedness and identification has its roots in a belief in the inherent difference between Springdale and all other places, particularly the nearby towns and big cities. For the Springdaler surrounding towns all carry stigmata which are not found in Springdale; the county seat is the locus of vice and corruption, the Finnish settlement is "red," University Town is snobbish and aloof, and Industrial Town is inhuman, slummy, and foreign. In the big city the individual is anonymously lost in a hostile and dog-eat-

*Again, in this classic article, the words "he," "him," and "his" follow the style of the time and are generic. You may wish to mentally replace these words with "they," "them," and "theirs."

dog environment. Being in the community gives one a distinct feeling of living in a protected and better place, so that in spite of occasional internal quarrels and the presence of some unwholesome characters, one frequently hears it said that "there's no place I'd rather live . . . there isn't a better place to raise a family . . . this is the best little town in the whole country." In the face of the outer world, Springdalers "stick up for their town."

The best example of community identification occurs when newspapers of neighboring towns choose to publicize negative aspects of Springdale life: making banner headlines over the dismissal of a school principal, publishing the names of youthful criminal offenders who come from good families. In such instances, irrespective of issue or factional position, anyone with an interest in the community comes to its defense: "We may have our troubles, but it's nothing we can't handle by ourselves—and quicker and better if they'd leave us alone." A challenge to the image of Springdale as a preferred place cuts deep and helps to re-create the sense of community when it is temporarily lost.

It is interesting that the belief in the superiority of local ways of living actually conditions the way of life. Springdalers *make an effort* to be friendly" and "*go out of their way* to help newcomers." The newspaper always emphasizes the positive side of life; it never reports local arrests, shotgun weddings, mortgage foreclosures, lawsuits, bitter exchanges in public meetings, suicides, or any other unpleasant happenings. By this constant focus on warm and human qualities in all public situations, the public character of the community takes on those qualities and, hence, it has a tone which is distinctly different from city life.

Relationships with nearby towns, in spite of the occasional voicing of hostility, also have a sympathetic and friendly competitive aspect. No one in Springdale would gloat over another town's misfortunes, such as a serious fire or the loss of an industry. Athletic rivalries have long histories and although there is a vocabulary of names and yells for "enemies," these simply stimulate competitiveness and arouse emotions for the night of the contest. No one takes victory or defeat seriously for more than a day or two and only in very rare instances is there a public incident when outsiders visit the town. "Nobody really wants trouble with other towns."

When one goes beyond neighboring communities, the Springdaler leaps from concrete images of people and places to a more generalized image of metropolitan life. His everyday experiences give him a feeling of remoteness from the major centers of industry, commerce, and politics. His images are apt to be as stereotyped as those that city people hold concerning the country. Any composite of these images would certainly include the following:

1. Cities breed corruption and have grown so big and impersonal that they are not able to solve the problems they create.
2. Cities are an unwholesome environment for children and families, and have had an unhealthy effect on family morals.

3. Urban politicians and labor leaders are corrupt and represent anti-democratic forces in American life.
4. Washington is a place overridden with bureaucrats and the sharp deal, fast-buck operator, both of whom live like parasites off hard-working country folk.
5. Industrial workers are highly paid for doing little work. Their leaders foment trouble and work against the good of the country.
6. Cities are hotbeds of un-American sentiment, harbor the reds, and are incapable of educating their youth to Christian values.
7. Big universities and city churches are centers of atheism and secularism and in spite of occasional exceptions have lost touch with the spiritual lesson taught by rural life.
8. Most of the problems of country life have their origin in the effects which urban life has on rural ways.

What is central, however, is the feeling of the Springdaler that these things do not basically affect him. While he realizes that machinery and factory products are essential to his standard of life and that taxation and agricultural policy are important, he feels that he is independent of other features of industrial and urban life, or, better, that he can choose and select only the best parts. The simple physical separation from the city and the open rural atmosphere make it possible to avoid the problems inherent in city life. Personal relations are face-to-face and social gatherings are intimate, church-going retains the quality of a family affair, the merchant is known as a person, and you can experience the "thrill of watching nature and the growth of your garden." Springdalers firmly believe in the virtues of rural living, strive to maintain them, and defend them against anyone who would criticize them.

"Neighbors Are Friends"

Almost all of rural life receives its justification on the basis of the direct and personal and human feelings that guide people's relations with each other. No one, not even a stranger, is a stranger to the circumambience of the community. It is as if the people in a deeply felt communion bring themselves together for the purposes of mutual self-help and protection. To this end the community is organized for friendliness and neighborliness, so much so that the term "friends" and "neighbors" almost stand as synonyms for "folk."

In its most typical form neighborliness occurs in time of personal and family crisis—birth, death, illness, fire, catastrophe. On such occasions friends and neighbors mobilize to support those in distress: collections of money are taken, meals are prepared by others, cards of condolence are sent. A man whose house or barn has burned may unexpectedly find an organized "bee" aiding in reconstruction. Practically all organizations have "sunshine" committees whose sole purpose is to send greeting cards. These practices are so widespread and ultimately may include so many people that an individual, unable to acknowledge all this friendliness personally, will utilize the newspaper's "card of thanks" column to express his public appreciation.

Borrowing and "lending back and forth" is perhaps the most widespread act of neighborliness. Farmers say they like to feel that "in a pinch" there is always someone whom they can count upon for help—to borrow tools, get advice, ask for labor. In spite of the advent of mechanized and self-sufficient farming and consequently the reduction of the need for mutual aid, the high public value placed on mutual help is not diminished. Though a farmer may want to be independent and wish to avoid getting involved in other people's problems and, in fact, may privately resent lending his machinery, it is quite difficult for him to refuse to assist his neighbor if asked. Even where technological advance has made inroads on the need for the practice, to support the public creed remains a necessity.

For housewives in a community where "stores don't carry everything" domestic trading and borrowing is still a reality; they exchange children's clothing and *do* borrow salt and sugar. In Springdale they say "you never have to be without . . . if you need something bad enough you can always get it; of course, sometimes people overdo it and that makes it bad for everybody, but after a while you find out who they are." The process of selectively eliminating the bad practitioners makes it possible to keep the operation of the practice on a high plane.

Neighborliness has its institutional supports and so is given a firm foundation. Ministers and church groups make it a practice to visit the sick in hospitals and homes and to remember them with cards and letters, and all other organizations—the Legion, Masons, Community Club, book clubs—designate special committees to insure that remembrance is extended to the bereaved and ill. The Legion and Community Club "help our own" with baskets of food and clothing at Christmas time and organize fund drives to assist those who are "burned out." The ideology of neighborliness is reflected in and reinforced by the organized life of the community.

To a great extent these arrangements between friends and neighbors have a reciprocal character: a man who helps others may himself expect to be helped later on. In a way the whole system takes on the character of insurance. Of course, some people are more conscious of their premium payments than others and keep a kind of mental bookkeeping on "what they owe and who owes them what," which is a perfectly permissible practice so long as one does not openly confront others with unbalanced accounts. In fact, the man who knows "exactly where he stands" with his friends and neighbors is better advised than the one who "forgets and can't keep track." The etiquette for getting and giving in Springdale is an art that requires sensitive adjustments to the moods, needs, and expectations of others. This ability to respond appropriately in given situations is the sign of the good neighbor. That this sensitivity is possessed by large numbers of people is attested to by the fact that friendliness and neighborliness contribute substantially to the community's dominant tone of personalness and warmth.

Of course, everyone does not participate equally or at the same level in being a good friend and neighbor. Deviations and exceptions are numerous. Neighborliness is often confined to geographical areas and to socially compatible groups. The wife of the lawyer is on neighborly terms with others like herself rather than with the wife of the carpenter. Farmers necessarily have less to do with people in the village and teachers are more apt to carry on friendly relations with each other. Those who are not willing to both give and take find themselves courteously eliminated from this aspect of local life. "People who are better off" simply by possessing sufficient resources do not find it necessary to call on friends and neighbors for help, though "everyone knows that if you went and asked them for something, they'd give it to you right away." Others have a more "independent turn of mind" and "will get by with what they have, no matter what, just to be free of mind"; the ideology of neighborliness is broad enough to include them "so long as they don't do anyone harm." The foreign elements, particularly the Poles, limit their everyday neighboring to their own group, but still by community definitions they are good neighbors because "you can always trust a Pole to deal square . . . if they owe you anything, they will always pay you back on time." Some folks are known as "just good people" who by choice "keep to themselves." By isolating themselves within the community they neither add nor detract from the neighborly quality of community life and so do not have an effect on the public character of the town.

The only group which does not fall within the purview of the conception of friend and neighbor is the 10 percent of the population that live "in shacks in the hills." The people who live in shacks "can't be trusted"; "they steal you blind"; "if you're friendly to them, they'll take advantage of you"; "if you lend them something you'll never see it again"; "they're bad . . . no good people . . . live like animals." Hence by appropriately extending the social definition to give it a broader base than mutual aid, all groups in the community, except the shack people, fulfill the image of good friend and neighbor. The self-conception then reinforces itself, serves as a model for achievement, and adds to the essential appearance of community warmth.

Springdalers affirm that on the whole most people in the community have good qualities. They are the qualities of "average folk" and "we like to think of ourselves as just a little above average." "Average people can get things done because nobody has any high-blown ideas and they can all work together to make the community a better place to live."

What is interesting about the usual definitions of good and bad people are the types that are excluded entirely. At this level those who go unrecognized, even in the negative statements, are the intellectuals, the bookish and the introverts. In a community that places a high premium on being demonstrably average, friendly, and open, the person who appears in public and "doesn't say much" is a difficult character to understand: "he's a good fellow, but you never know what he's thinking." "Book reading and studying all the time," while they have a place, "shouldn't be carried too far . . . you have to keep your feet on the ground, be practical." The intellectual is respected for his education, is admired for his verbal facility and sometimes can provide the right idea, but nevertheless he is suspect and "shouldn't be allowed to get into positions of responsibility." It is apparent that where stereotyped public definitions do not easily fit, nonconformity is still tolerated so long as it does not seriously interfere with the workings of the town.

In the community setting, the test case of the toleration and sympathy for nonconformity lies in attitudes toward cranks, psychotics, and "odd personalities": the ex-minister who writes poetry, the hermit who lives in the woods, the woman obsessed with the legal correctness of her husband's will, the spinster who screams at callers, the town moron, and the clinical catatonic. Needless to say, these represent only a small percentage of the population. The point is that Springdale is able to absorb, protect, and care for them; when in the infrequent instance they intrude on the public scene, they are treated with the same sympathy and kindness accorded a child. So long as nonconformity does not interfere with the normal functioning of the town, no price is exacted from the nonconformist. At the worst, the nonconforming types are surrounded by humor. They become local "characters" who add color and interest to the everyday life of the community; because they are odd and different, they are always available as a standard conversational piece. In this way the community demonstrates its kindness and "lives and lets live."

"We're All Equal"

With the exception of a few "old cranks" and "no goods," it is unthinkable for anyone to pass a person on the street without exchanging greetings. Customarily one stops for a moment of conversation to discuss the weather and make inquiries about health; even the newcomer finds others stopping to greet him. The pattern of everyone talking to everyone is especially characteristic when people congregate in groups. Meetings and social gatherings do not begin until greetings have been exchanged all around. The person who feels he is above associating with everyone, as is the case with some newcomers from the city, runs the risk of being regarded a snob, for the taint of snobbishness is most easily acquired by failing to be friendly to everyone.

It is the policy of the Community Club to be open to "everyone, whether dues are paid or not," and hardly a meeting passes without a repetition of this statement. Those who are the leaders of the community take pride in this organization specifically because it excludes no one, and this fact is emphasized time and again in public situations. Wherever they can, community leaders encourage broad participation in all spheres of public life: everyone is urged and invited to attend public meetings and everyone is urged to "vote not as a duty, but as a privilege." The equality at the ballot box of all men, each according to his own conscience, in a community where you know all the candidates personally, where votes can't be bought, and where you know the poll-keepers, is the hallmark of equality that underpins all other equality. "Here no man counts more than any other"; this is stated in every affirmation of rural political equality—"if you don't like the rascals, use your vote to kick them out."

The social force of the idea finds its most positive expression in a negative way. The ladies of the book clubs, the most exclusive and limited membership groups in springdale, find themselves in the ambiguous position of having to be apologetic for their exclusiveness. Because they are select in a community which devalues standoffishness, they are the only groups that are defensive in meeting the rest of the public. To the observer, they explain, "It's not that we want to be exclusive. It's just that sixteen is all you can manage in a book club. If anybody wants to be in a book club, she can start her own, like the Wednesday Group." By the same token they receive a large share of resentment; any number of vulgar expressions refer to this feminine section of the community.

The public ideology of equality has its economic correlates. One must not suppose that inequalities in income and wealth go unnoticed; rather, they are quite closely watched and known in Springdale. However, such differences, as in the image of the frontier community, are not publicly weighed and evaluated as the measure of the man.

In everyday social intercourse it is a social *faux pas* to act as if economic inequalities make a difference. The wealthiest people in town, though they have big homes, live quite simply without servants. The serviceman, the delivery boy, and the door-to-door canvasser knock at the front door and, though they may feel somewhat awkward on carpeted floors, are asked to enter even before stating their business. A man who flaunts his wealth, or demands deference because of it, is out of tune with a community whose "upper class" devalues conspicuous consumption and works at honest pursuits. "What makes the difference is not the wealth but the character behind it."

It is not a distortion to say that the good man is the working man and in the public estimation the fact of working transcends, indeed explains, economic differentials; work has its own social day of judgment and the judgment conferred is self-respect and respectability. Work, in the first instance, is the great social equalizer, and the purest form of work which serves as a yardstick for all other work is farm work. By this mechanism the "hard-working poor man" is superior to the "lazy rich man." The quotation marks are advised and indicate the hypotheticalness of the case because in common usage the two, work and wealth, go together. Where they don't it is because of misfortune, catastrophe, bad luck, or simply because the man is young and work has not yet had a chance to pay its dividends. But even wealth is the wrong word. Work is rather juxtaposed beside such terms as rich, solvent, well-off; wealth implies more economic differentiation than Springdalers like to think exists in their community. Thus, the measure of a man, for all public social purposes, is the diligence and perseverance with which he pursues his economic ends; the "steady worker," the "good worker," the "hard worker" in contrast to the "fly-by-night schemer," the "bandwagon jumper," and the "johnny-come-lately." For the Springdaler the test case is the vulgar social climber, the person who tries to "get in with the better people" by aping them in dress and possessions which only money can buy. In spite of the social and economic differences visible to the outside observer, the pervading appearance of the community is that of a social equality based on the humanness of rural life.

The Etiquette of Gossip

Like other small rural communities Springdale must face the classic problem of preserving individual privacy in the face of a public ideology which places a high valuation on positive expressions of equalitarianism and neighborliness. The impression of community warmheartedness which is given by the free exchange of public greetings and the easy way "everybody gets along with everybody else" has its counterpart in the absence of privacy implied by the factor of gossip. The observer who has been in the community for a length of time realizes that "everybody isn't really neighborly . . . that some people haven't talked to each other for years . . . that people whom you might think are friends hate each other . . . that there are people who are just naturally troublemakers . . . that he'd skin his own grandmother for a buck." However, such statements are never made in public situations. The intimate, the negative, and the private are spoken in interpersonal situations involving only two or three people. Gossip exists as a separate and hidden layer of community life.

That is why it is at first difficult for the observer to believe the often-repeated statement that "everybody knows everything about everybody else in Springdale," or, as stated otherwise, "in a small town you live in a glass house." It develops that the statements are true only to a degree: while one learns intimate and verifiable details of people's private lives, these never become the subject of open, public discussion.

In the private sphere—at what is commonly regarded as the level of gossip, either malicious or harmless—Springdalers tend to emphasize the negative and competitive qualities of life. One learns about domestic discords, sexual aberrations, family skeletons, ill-gained wealth, feuds, spite fences, black sheep, criminal records, and alcoholism. The major preoccupation, however, is reserved for "what he's worth" in the strictly monetary and material meaning of the expression:

"You'd think a man with his money would give more than $50 to the church."

"The reason he's got so much is because he never spends any, hasn't taken a vacation for thirty years, never contributes a cent to anything."

"There's a man who's got a fortune and you'd never guess it."

"What I couldn't do with his dough."

"The way they spend money, you'd think it was like picking leaves off a tree."

"Up to his neck in debt and he walks around like he had a million."

"Figure it out. He's working, his wife's working, they haven't got any kids, and they're collecting rent on two houses besides."

"He could be doing well if he stopped drinking."

"He may be taking in more than me, but then he's killing himself doing it."

"But, then, I haven't done so bad myself. There's the car, only four years left on the house, and two kids through school."

These and similar statements, however, serve the function of enabling a person to calculate his relative financial standing. They are encountered almost everywhere in private gossip, but remain unspoken and hidden in ordinary public situations.

What is interesting about gossip is that in Springdale it seldom hurts anyone. Because it occurs in small temporarily closed circles and concerns those who are not present, the subject of the gossip need never be aware of it. Moreover, the *mores* demand, or better still one should say that it is an iron law of community life, that one not confront the subject of gossip with what is said about him. For this reason, though everyone engages in the practice, no one *has* to learn what things are being said about him. In the rare instance where one hears about gossip about oneself, it comes as a distinct shock "to think that so-and-so could have said that about me."

In a way, then, it is true that everyone knows everything about everyone else but, because of the way the information is learned, it does not ordinarily affect the everyday interpersonal relations of people; in public view even enemies speak to each other. When the victim meets the gossiper, he does not see him as a gossip and the gossiper does not let the privately gained information affect his public gestures; both greet each other in a friendly and neighborly manner and, perhaps, talk about someone else. Because the people of the community have this consideration for other people's feelings ("we like to think of ourselves as considerate and kind, not out to hurt anybody . . . that's one of the main reasons you live in a small town"), relationships between people always give the impression of personalness and warmth.

The etiquette of gossip, which makes possible the public suppression of the negative and competitive aspects of life, has its counterpart in the etiquette of public conversation, which always emphasizes the positive. There are thus two channels of communication that serve quite different purposes. In public conversation one hears comments only on the good things about people—"a man who has always done good things for the town"; "a swell guy"; "she's always doing good things for people"; "a person who never asks anything in return." When failures occur, when the play "was a flop," as of course must happen from time to time, one senses what is almost a communal conspiracy against any further public mention of it. So too with the success of individuals—the man who after many years of diligence finally gets a good job, the person who completes a correspondence course, the local girl who gets a college degree, the local boy who makes good in the city, the man who finally succeeds in establishing himself in business, the winner of a contest, the high scorer, the person who has his name in a city newspaper—all such successes are given recognition in conventional conversation and in the press. At the public level all types of success are given public recognition while failure is treated with silence. It is because of the double and separate set of communication channels that negative gossip seldom colors the friendly ethos and the successful mood of the public life of the community.

44 Social Change Among the Amish

JERRY SAVELLS

With change in contemporary society so common, and so extensive, how is it possible to hold it back? Most of us are engulfed in social change so vast that it sweeps over us like a tide. Like it or not, we have little choice but to adapt. Isn't this the situation for everyone who lives in an industrialized society? Vast changes occur, and rapidly so, and our only choice seems to be how to adapt.

But not so for everybody. The Amish are an outstanding exception. This group of people, who broke from the Swiss-German Mennonite church in the late 1600s and settled in Pennsylvania around 1727, can now be found in about twenty states and Ontario, Canada. About 75 percent, however, live in just three states: Pennsylvania, Ohio, and Indiana. The Amish resist change. They maintain customs of dress, music, transportation, and morality from the 1600s and continue to reject "worldly ways." How do they manage to resist such pressure? That is the focus of Savells's article.

THE AUTHOR VISITED EIGHT Amish communities in six states from 1982 to 1986: Berne and Milroy, Indiana; Ethridge, Tennessee; Intercourse and Bird-in-Hand, Pennsylvania; Kalona, Iowa; Plain City, Ohio; and Montezuma, Georgia. Face-to-face interviews were conducted with a select number of the local Amish population and some of the non-Amish population who have frequent contact with the Amish, i.e., local merchants who sell to the Amish, craftpersons, farmers, mail carriers, drivers of the local milk trucks who travel to Amish farms almost daily, and others. A structured twelve-page questionnaire has been used to collect research data using a stratified random sample selected from the New American Almanac (1983) and the Ohio Amish Directory (1981). At this time, 130 questionnaires and/or personal interviews have been completed with selected Amish families. An additional fifty interviews have also been completed among so-called "conservative Mennonite" families for future comparisons.

Although the sample is small, it is encouraging since the Old Order Amish have spurned many efforts from the scientific community to investigate their lifestyle. This particular effort gave new meaning to the term "field research," since it represents approximately 6,500 miles of driving, spread over thirty months.

The Amish interviewees were polite and cordial, but they typically do not welcome outsiders intruding into their lives. They were both retiring and private in their demeanor, since they have not been socialized to desire interaction with strangers. Their lifestyle and religion promote voluntary isolation and this has been a major obstacle to anyone intent on collecting research data via personal interviews. Since the religious concerns of the Amish hold top priority, they would not engage intentionally in any activity that would have the potential of embarrassing members in the same church district.

Sociological Considerations

A brief visit to the public library will reinforce the observation that the Amish cherish many social values once widely embraced in our agrarian society of the Colonial period—values which are largely the antithesis of those that emerged in a modern urban, industrialized society. The Amish typically emphasize the importance of humility, modesty, strong obedience to God, and social conformity; they abhor pride, social snobbery, individualism, and winning through competition. Family bonds and their faith are indeed the cornerstones of the Amish lifestyle.

Unfortunately, what limited information is available to the lay public about the Old Order Amish is often sensationalized and distorted. Yet, there is a distinct feeling of "separateness" and "difference" with numerous references to their horse-and-buggy transportation, somewhat drab clothing, and their aloofness (or overt resistance) to those things considered "trendy" or fashionable.

The Amish are very ethnocentric with a strong sense of social solidarity. There is a consciousness-of-kind evident in their thinking and quick sanctions directed toward the non-believer or those displaying evidence of weakness in their faith. Indeed, some sociologists might argue that the Amish practice of insularity—with a limited tolerance of any deviation—is a major reason why they have survived as a model of the extended family of the past.

In his professional writing, journalist Alvin Toffler has pointed out the disastrous consequences of modern materialism, self-serving lifestyles, hedonistic behavior, the transience and rootlessness of this culture, and extreme emphasis upon competition, money, and careerism to determine one's self-worth. The latter suggest experiences both alien and repulsive to Amish tradition; they abhor the concept of personal achievement rather than seeking to express God's will, the modern habit of "powerbrokering" to gain social advantages, and mutual manipulation. . . . Social change is evident—but carefully controlled and monitored. They work to preserve traditions of the past, emphasize the importance of humility and divine guidance in controlling their own destiny, and maintain a strong posture of serving God rather than the interests of humanity.

An Operational Definition of Change

The Amish do not live within a social vacuum. They are surrounded by accelerating currents of social, political, and economic changes which directly influence their quality of life. One reasonably expects the Amish to be vulnerable to pressures toward modernization. For example, many have been asked to sell their land for commercial development at inflated prices. The changing economic climate in these eight communities and the frustration of competing in a money market where "megabucks" and agri-business threaten the small farmer are having a definite impact upon the Amish way of life.

Amish farmers and the future of their children are often adversely affected by soaring land prices, and the foreign trade imbalance can mean a restricted market for some of their farm exports. Furthermore, when the Amish farmer needs to borrow money for spring planting, the interest rate at the local bank can be especially painful for the small farmer with a limited cash flow.

The Amish are forced to compete in a "money market" where agribusiness and the profit motive often threaten some of their most cherished values. For example, our society promotes maximum efficiency, quality control through standardization, the accumulation of capital or wealth, competition among workers for career advancement, and the merits of mass production— basic trends essentially alien to the Amish pursuit of "devotedness, simplicity, and peace."

The Amish strongly advocate the "therapeutic value of real work." They believe that physical labor is good for mind, body, and soul in keeping with the biblical admonition of earning one's bread by the sweat of one's brow. Their work is labor-intensive, in contrast to the national marketplace dominated by the forces of technology and profit margins. Thus, the Amish do not view every new labor-saving device as desirable or progressive. . . .

Since life in any Amish community is ongoing, it is not possible or practical to totally isolate units of analysis, i.e., families, without the influence of outside variables. The Amish do not constitute an experimental group in a laboratory situation. Hence, one must be careful not to treat all indicators of social change as evidence of modernity. Some changes may be basically unique to one church district or community, and cannot be considered universal to all Amish. For example, the New Order Amish in both Kalona and Intercourse have accepted the practice of having closer contact with the outside world; some own cottage industries that cater to tourists and some have given their business cards to this researcher. In many Old Order communities this behavior would be unacceptable.

Pressures That Influence Modernization

The five major social institutions—family, religion, economics, education, and politics—were studied in this sample of Amish interviewees as an ethnographic method to identify and document patterns of modernity. Caution is both recommended and prudent to avoid the pitfalls of making global generalizations regarding the Amish lifestyle, since rules of behavior may vary among church districts or regions. The Amish define the behavioral expectations and boundaries of their communities through the *Ordnung,* the official rules of the Amish community. Any member found to have disobeyed the *Ordnung* would be subject to *Meidung,* or shunning. It is a measure of social and religious control still considered an acceptable practice by over eighty percent of the respondents in this study. This has the avowed purpose of encouraging the offender to seek forgiveness from God and other members of the church district as quickly as possible.

FAMILY

This institution is still greatly cherished by the Amish. It is not unusual to see three generations living together in either of the eight research sites. The average Amish family in this sample had seven children, but this researcher talked with some Amish families that had as many as thirteen children. Family size would appear to be more a reflection of age and economic security than sheer desire, since almost all Amish parents profess to want large families. Modern means of contraception are forbidden, unless medically prescribed to protect the health of the mother.

Several Amish parents were concerned that economic factors beyond their control represent a serious challenge to their children and may cause many of their youth to accept employment in occupations provided by outsiders. In Milroy, Indiana, several of the young married males commuted to Indianapolis with the assistance of a non-Amish driver to work as carpenters in the building industry—a situation that forces them to accommodate the expectations of a non-Amish employer. Being away from hearth and home was clearly not their first choice; it reduces the opportunities and time to share family activities. The subtle pressures of this experience can undermine cherished Amish values in the name of economic survival.

Amish parents prefer that their families remain self-supporting, since the daily sharing of work assignments tends to give prolonged contact between parent and child, with a "solidifying effect." The Amish still grow much of their food, provide for their own energy needs, and assume responsibility for their own well-being, rather than relying upon insurance companies, welfare programs, or Social Security to shield them from the hazards of life.

To help preserve this family-centered focus, Amish parents are careful to shield their children from the information explosion of our technological society—particularly as it is disseminated by the mass media and in the public schools. However, where outside employment is essential for survival, accommodation may become necessary through learning new skills or pursuing an advanced education.

The Amish family is still strongly patriarchal. The women's liberation movement has made very few incursions into any of these eight Amish communities. However, Amish women today are by no means totally subservient in a traditional sense. This researcher discovered that Amish women in some church districts can accept modest change without severe reprisals or shunning. For example, in Berne, it was a common practice for Amish women to use polyester cloth rather than 100 percent cotton for their family's clothing. Also, many of these clothes are now purchased, rather than handsewn. Some of the Amish wives in Berne used Mary Kay cosmetics, but only the creams, not the make-up. The latter is considered too "worldly."

RELIGION

The Amish in this sample show some gradual change in their religious practices. Over ten percent of the respondents had changed their religious preference from Old Order to New Order within the context of one generation. This change will definitely have a ripple effect for their children, grandchildren, and great-grandchildren. . . .

The Old Order Amish prohibit ownership of automobiles, telephones, and electricity in the home. However, farm tractors are now being used by the New Order Amish in some areas; in Kalona, tractors were acceptable if they had steel wheels, not rubber tires. The adoption of the latter would create too much mobility.

In both Plain City and Intercourse, diesel generators are now considered an acceptable innovation to supply the barn (not the house) with electricity. The Amish dairy farmer—like all other dairy farmers—must meet state health standards regarding proper refrigeration of milk which is sold commercially. Hence, it is very difficult to pinpoint where the Old Order Amish religious practices actually end and their lifestyle begins since the two are often "one and the same."

A few of the Amish in Berne are now beginning to use cameras, especially to photograph their children, a practice that would have brought immediate censure a few years ago. Even when this practice is known to other family members, it is regarded as a taboo topic for everyday conversation. Most of the Old Order Amish interviewed in Berne still believe that the Bible forbids taking "graven images" of persons.

ECONOMIC CHANGES

The economic security in some of the families interviewed appeared to be more fragile than that of previous generations. Wherever possible parents are still subdividing their farms so that their children will have the chance to enjoy the fruit of their labor in farming. However, with a shortage of affordable and available land for farming, the younger generation has found itself increasingly dependent upon ties with the non-Amish sector of the local economy. In Berne and Intercourse, some of the local Amish men work in craft-related industries, such as factories that manufacture furniture (mostly handcrafted), coal or wood burning stoves, and carriages. In Kolona some of the Amish girls work in a local cheese factory that purchases the bulk milk produced on Amish farms. The waitresses in some of the local restaurants are also members of the local Amish community.

This trend toward outside employment leaves the Amish especially vulnerable to forces of economic recession and a stagnant national economy. Since the Old Order Amish prohibit their members from pursuing an advanced education which would make them more competitive in the national job market, they are often underskilled in jobs that require moderate levels of technological sophistication.

The Amish are also forbidden to accept employment where joining a labor union is a condition of the workplace; thus, they have minimal job security in a formal sense. However, the Amish in this sample remained cheerful and optimistic that God would provide for their daily needs.

EDUCATION

As one moves from the environment of the Old Order Amish to the New Order Amish, one expects that the number of years of formal education might increase with each successive generation. There is a definite trend in that direction, since some of the New Order Amish want to develop marketable skills at a trade school or by taking correspondence courses. In Montezuma this researcher interviewed a young female from a New Order Amish family who is a registered nurse.

The Old Order Amish still maintain their own schools in most of the communities studied. In Berne the Old Order Amish can send their children to the eighth grade in an Amish school where funds for operating the school are provided by the parents of the children who attend, and an Amish teacher is provided, or they are permitted to send their children to a public school in Berne—only through the ninth grade.

Very few of the children in Old Order Amish families remain in school after reaching age sixteen—the age at which they can quit according to most state laws. In order to comply with legal requirements some Amish children voluntarily repeat the ninth grade—a sacrifice to the expectations of their Amish parents.

One Old Order Amish mother of several children indicated that she wanted her sons and daughters to consider going to college, preferably a Mennonite college, where they could receive training to become a member of a "noble" profession. Then they could serve the Amish community directly in professions such as teaching, and medical or veterinary practice.

This researcher found that most of the Amish adults were reasonably well informed about news events on a global scale. Some Amish families subscribe to both *The Budget,* an Amish-related newspaper, and a local or regional newspaper. Some have subscriptions to such mass circulation magazines as *Time, Newsweek, U.S. News and World Report, Reader's Digest, and National Geographic.* Most of the Amish adults do travel out-of-state to visit relatives and for recreation. In Montezuma, one respondent had recently returned from a trip to Australia.

POLITICS

The Old Order Amish in each of these eight communities do not permit their members to pursue or hold public office. To say that the Old Order Amish are politically uninvolved is not accurate. For example, they have petitioned the Congress of the United States to be exempt from payment of Social Security taxes since they do not allow their members to collect Social Security benefits. They have also sought a favorable hearing in the courts to have their children exempt from both mandatory attendance at public secondary schools and conscription into the military service.

The Old Order Amish in this sample showed an aloofness to affiliation with either major political party. Less than fifteen percent of the male interviewees had voted in either the 1980 or 1984 United States presidential election, when one of the most conservative candidates in recent history was representing the Republican Party. The Amish fear that politics with either party would certainly invite reprisals from the opposite party. Thus, it is in their best interest to remain neutral—a strong statement for the separation of church and state.

MODERNIZATION

This researcher found that the majority of the social changes that are occurring in these eight Amish communities are the result of very careful, selective, conscious deliberation, i.e., planned change. . . . One respondent added a word of caution regarding their non-use of so-called modern technology: "We do not feel that electricity, the telephone, and the automobile are evil in themselves; rather, our non-use helps us to keep from being drawn into the mainstream of the world."

Thomas Foster, a respected scholar of the Old Order Amish, has suggested that one of the most significant factors reinforcing Amish self-sufficiency is their reliance upon appropriate technologies that complement their lifestyle and religious beliefs, i.e., their sustained, practical use of human labor and power from wind, water, horses, wood, and the sun. These small-scale, labor-intensive technologies greatly reduce the need for large capital investments while keeping a lid on operating costs compared to their non-Amish peers. Foster maintains that in Ohio, for example, the Old Order Amish can earn profits on 75 to 150 acres of land at a time when Ohio's non-Amish farmers, who use diesel tractors and other costly equipment, have difficulty making a decent profit on acreage twice as large.

Social Change Among the Amish

Change has been regarded as neither evil nor good among the Amish. It can work for betterment, or it can create havoc. The Amish perceive that much of what is regarded as "modern" or "progress" by contemporary standards remains a source of temptation for their young, and potential conflict and disharmony for their communities if not kept at a proper distance. For example, the Amish do not believe electricity, telephones, and driving an automobile are inherently evil, but they realize that these so-called modern conveniences would alter the Amish lifestyle and that of future generations. The effects of this technology, e.g., high mobility with an automobile, would offer too much temptation and less concern for maintaining tradition.

Simply speaking, the Amish prefer not to become dependent upon these inventions, but prefer to maintain a quiet and simple life unfettered with the high-level complications of the modern world. Some outsiders feel the Amish have essentially avoided the acceptance of social change in order to maintain the pursuit of a Nirvana or heaven on earth. The Amish, on the other hand, rarely convey that they feel cheated by denying themselves in this life. . . .

Historians and sociologists have been aware that in other historical periods, religious ideology and practice have fueled powerful motivations for creating change—as seen in the kinship between the growth of Protestantism and industrialism in the Western World. Yet, the Amish have cited their religion as one of the most important reasons why they have essentially and successfully avoided much of the social change identified with the Industrial Revolution. Change is *not* welcome if it adversely affects their religious beliefs, their family stability, their nonresistant lifestyle, or if it creates too much conflict.

Where change has been accepted—and this can be measured figuratively more in inches than yards—it has ordinarily been seen as either an improvement of their ability to provide economically for their families or as reasonable for public safety and the public good. Two examples of the latter were the adoption in some states of batteries on horsedrawn transportation to provide flashing taillights at night as a safety precaution, and the adoption in some districts of diesel generators in their barns, primarily to cool and agitate milk in bulk tanks. To the Amish this is a preference, not a paradox. If it confuses outsiders, they do not feel a need to explain.

Although the vast majority of my sample had routine (daily or weekly) contact with outsiders, most felt that the average outsider did not understand their Amish lifestyle or values and the religious justification for the way they prefer to live. Thus, from an outsider's perspective, the Amish are resisting change simply to preserve tradition—but the Amish understand their actions to be "the will of God."

Summary and Conclusions

. . . Each generation experiences a certain amount of trial and error in finding norms and values that will best serve their unique needs. Tradition for the sake of tradition is hardly an answer to the complex problems facing the Amish. Although the Amish honor important traditions regarding their faith and their people, they also recognize that social and economic survival necessitates that some acceptance of change will be both normal and inevitable. As one Old Order Amish man remarked, "You cannot put a ship in the middle of the ocean and expect the deck to always stay dry."

Acculturation *is* occurring in the majority of Old Order Amish communities visited by this researcher, but it is neither rampant nor whimsical. Rather, social change has consistently been scrutinized carefully and accepted gradually—where the results could be monitored for any possible unwanted side effects. The Old Order Amish enclave is not so much a model of "paradise lost" as it is a model of "evasive innovation" to save and protect a small, but significant, religious minority who wish to be "in the world, but not of the world."

45 The Animal Rights Crusade

JAMES M. JASPER
DOROTHY NELKIN

People tend to assume that their values are good, right, and even moral. The more that we are committed to a value, the more its arbitrariness recedes from sight and the more that we assume its "rightness." An excellent example is attitudes toward animals. In tribal and agricultural societies, people viewed animals instrumentally; that is, they saw animals as instruments to help them accomplish tasks. A cow was to give milk and be eaten. A deer was to be hunted. A horse was for riding or to pull a plow. A dog was to pull a sleigh or to retrieve game. The assumption—considered good, right, and moral—was that animals should be used.

Such societies—and their ideas—are remote from our own life situation. Within the circumstances we face, we have developed a different set of attitudes about animals. For us, animals are to be appreciated. They are to be loved and cuddled, taken to vets for the best health care available. They are to be bathed and groomed—even their teeth should be brushed. Their feelings are sensitive and need to be protected: for the failures, we even train animal psychologists. Such assumptions, too, are presumed to belong to some fundamental morality of the universe, and we tend to see previous generations as misguided, even cruel and evil.

With attitudes toward animals still changing, coming generations may see ours as misguided, even bizarre. In the forefront of today's changing attitudes is the animal rights movement, the topic of this selection by Jasper and Nelkin.

CHANGES IN BELIEFS ABOUT ANIMALS extend back to the growth of towns and mercantile values in the midst of the aristocratic, agrarian societies of sixteenth- and seventeenth-century Europe. A new urban middle class appeared, and by the nineteenth century it had changed daily life in Western Europe. The "civilizing process" that discouraged the new bourgeoisie from spitting on the floor, wiping their noses on their sleeves, and eating with their hands, represented an increased concern for the feelings and sensibilities of others. . . .

As urbanization removed many people from their direct dependence on animals as a resource, except as a means of transportation, close experience with animals other than pets declined. The bourgeois wife in town had fewer chickens to feed or cows to milk, so that her appreciation of animals came from her pet dogs. By 1700, people were naming their pets, often with human names (especially in England); pets appeared regularly in paintings; and some even received legacies when their owners died. When pets died, they (unlike farm animals) were never eaten; often they were buried in style, with epitaphs written by their owners. As the family home and its members became privatized and idealized, so did the family pet.

This new attitude toward animals had a distinct basis in social class, as Robert Darnton's description in *The Great Cat Massacre* dramatically suggests. The massacre occurred in the 1730s at a Paris printing shop where the wife of the master printer was "impassioned" of several pet cats. They were fed at the table with the family, while the printer's apprentices ate table scraps—the cat food of the time—in the kitchen. In symbolic rebellion, the apprentices and workers captured sacksful of pet and stray cats, held a mock trial, and hanged them all. Torturing cats was an old European tradition: a favorite pastime at many holidays was to set cats on fire, largely to hear their terrible "caterwauling." The apprentices' action dramatized the conflict between the traditional view of animals and the emerging sensibility of the wealthy classes. The new moral sensitivity began in the rising middle classes, but quickly conquered much of the aristocracy, and eventually—although not widely until the twentieth century—the laboring classes. In each case, its apostles were mainly women, priests, and the occasional philosopher who articulated the changing beliefs.

Before the nineteenth century, only a few individuals had expressed a heightened moral sensitivity toward animals. Margaret Cavendish, Duchess of Newcastle, wrote extensively in the 1650s and 1660s about the human tendency to tyrannize other species. Considered highly eccentric by her peers, she criticized the hunting of song birds and claimed that "the groans of a dying beast strike my soul." In the eighteenth century, pastors and poets such as Alexander Pope, John Gay, and William Blake attacked cruelty to animals, reinterpreting the biblical acknowledgment of man's dominion over nature to mean thoughtful stewardship rather than ruthless exploitation. As the age of democratic revolutions ushered in new standards of respect and dignity for the rights of individuals, new attention was paid to the treatment of animals. In the often-quoted words of Jeremy Bentham in 1789, the question to ask about animals " . . . is not Can they *reason*? nor Can they *talk*? but, Can they *suffer*?" Here was a new criterion, one that placed humans and animals in the same circle rather than drawing a boundary between them. . . .

The nineteenth-century expansion of industry and cities in Britain and America accelerated the speed of bourgeois moral sensibilities, including sympathy for animals, across all social classes. The realities of nature had little bearing on the lives of those in cities, who were free to project onto nature a pleasant, pastoral image that overlooked its cruelties and dangers. They could forget the violent, precarious lives of animals in the wild and exaggerate their innocence and goodness. The romanticization of nature was largely a reaction to industrial society and the passing of rural life. . . .

Animal rights activists act as moral entrepreneurs, igniting and then building on moral outrage. They appeal to widespread beliefs about the similarities between humans and animals, the love of pets as part of the family, and anxieties about encroaching instrumentalism. And they use shocking images of common practices that violate deeply held sentiments about decency and justice to convert people to the cause.

Shocking visual images are perhaps their most powerful tool. Monkeys in restraining devices, furry raccoons in steel traps, kittens with their eyes sewn shut, and other images of constrained mammals appeal to anthropomorphic sympathies. People's worst fears of a science and a technology out of control seem justified by photographs of animals probed with scientific devices—rats with syringes down their throats, cats with electrodes planted on their heads. A bright patch of red blood on a black-and-white poster catches the eye. . . .

Most moral shocks inform the viewer about what others—scientific researchers, circus trainers, cosmetics companies—do to animals. Some, like New Age consumer efforts, try to shock viewers into thinking about their own actions—their own contribution to animal cruelty. Where did the hamburger in the neat styrofoam container come from? What was the original animal like? How did it live and how did it die? "Meat's no treat for those you eat!" What animal died to make your fur? "Are you wearing my mother on your back?" We are forced to think of animals, not as commodities, but as living beings with a point of view that we are invited to share.

Moral shocks are recruiting tools for protest movements, but the power of a shocking image is not by itself sufficient to build a movement. Membership generally requires time for activities, discretionary income to contribute, and a conviction that participants can make a difference. But shocks can be so persuasive that even people with no prior political experience become "converts." Moral crusades are often filled with recruits who have not been in other movements; the anti-abortion movement is one example. . . .

Moral truth requires missionary zeal. Those who believe they know the truth are often loud and shrill in their attacks. Fundamentalists hurl venomous labels at those who abuse animals. Scientists are "sadists," meat-eaters are "cannibals," factory farmers are "fascists," and furriers are "criminals." But even those who simply disagree with the fundamentalists become targets. At a public forum, Michael W. Fox of the Humane Society of the United States was asked whether there were any circumstances in which he would accept animal experimentation. He replied, "Just to ask that question indicates you are a speciesist and probably a sexist and a racist." Such labeling inevitably precludes further dialogue. . . .

The smug zeal of moral crusades is familiar. Seeing the moral world in black and white, many activists, especially those drawn into activism for the first time, are politically naïve and dismissive of majority sensibilities. In addition to saying that "A rat is a pig is a dog is a boy," PETA's [People for the Ethical Treatment of Animals] Ingrid Newkirk declared in a controversial statement, "Six million people died in concentration camps, but six billion broiler chickens will die this year in slaughterhouses." Others compare the plight of today's animals with that of African-American slaves before the Civil War. Those willing to grant moral rights to chickens easily make comparisons that offend mainstream tastes.

In the Gulf of St. Lawrence, the ice was said to have a red tinge after the seal hunt every March, when 100,000 seals were killed for their pelts. Most prized of all were the babies, which, for the first three weeks of life, have furry white coats. With their large eyes, they could bring out sentimental anthropomorphism in almost anyone. A Canadian film crew—expecting only to film seals in their natural habitat—caught part of the 1964 hunt, and the sight of baby seals being clubbed and spiked in the head caused outrage throughout the industrialized world and generated a major controversy, attracting the attention of both environmentalists and animal welfarists.

Brian Davies, then executive-secretary of the New Brunswick SPCA, merged his welfare perspective with the political arguments of environmentalists: "I discovered that an over-capitalized sealing industry was intent on killing the last seal pup in order to get a return on its equipment, and that those who profited from the seals gave not one thought to their suffering." Davis buttressed this critique of instrumentalism with an explicit anthropomorphic description: "Their hind flippers were like two hands crossed in prayer, and again, the five fingernails. I can well imagine why many biologists consider sea mammals the most advanced form of nonhuman life." Whether for anthropomorphic or other reasons, whales, dolphins, seals, and other sea mammals have aroused tremendous sympathies.

Davies later described the first baby seal he saw killed. "He was a little ball of white fur with big dark eyes and a plaintive cry . . . *he was only ten days old.* He went to meet, in a curious, friendly, and playful way, the first human he had ever seen and was . . . by the same human . . . clubbed on the head and butchered on the spot. He was skinned alive. I saw the heart in a body without a skin pumping frantically. From that very moment . . . ending the commercial whitecoat hunt was a cause that consumed me." As in a religious conversion, he knew his life would henceforth be devoted to what he called a "crusade against cruelty."

Those who believe that animals have absolute rights demand the elimination of all animal research. Condemning the instrumental rationality of science, they find it morally unacceptable to reduce animals to the status of raw materials, in pursuit of human benefit: "We don't consider animals to be a tool, the test tube with legs." Improving conditions is not enough, for as one poster puts it, "Lab animals never have a nice day."

Anti-vivisectionists insist that immoral methods can never be used to support even the most worthy goals. They support their impassioned argument by comparing laboratories to Nazi death camps: "For animal researchers, the ends justify the means. This argument has a familiar ring: Hitler used it when he allowed experiments to be done on Jews."

Farms have changed in recent decades. In 1964, British writer Ruth Harrison coined the term "Factory Farming" in her book *Animal Machines*. Describing the highly regimented conditions of slaughterhouses and the transport of animals by meat packing companies, she questioned the right of humans to place economic criteria over ethical considerations in the use of animals for food. Efficiency rules today's large farms. Chickens, which Americans consume at the rate of several billion a year, spend their lives in windowless buildings. They are subjected to intense light when they are young, because that stimulates rapid growth. They are kept in increasing darkness later in their seven-week lives, because this reduces their fighting with each other. Their beaks are cut off soon after they are born, so that they will do less damage to each other as they grow and fight. Each broiler chicken has about one half a square foot of space. Laying hens have the same space, but live longer, up to eighteen months, at which time they are sent to be slaughtered. Not just chickens, but pigs, veal calves, turkeys, and most other food animals are confined in small areas, often in darkness. Beef cattle spend their first six months in pastures, but then are shipped to cramped feedlots. These techniques have made American agriculture extremely efficient. . . .

Those who believe in the rights of animals as sentient beings support modest reforms, but only as a temporary measure, for their ultimate goal is to abolish altogether the production and consumption of meat. These groups have organized demonstrations and boycotts, picketed restaurants on Mother's Day, attacked turkey farms on Thanksgiving, and liberated restaurant lobsters. The ALF [Animal Liberation Front, a radical organization] has gone further, leaving butchers and slaughterhouses with broken windows and graffiti. Even remote ranches have had water systems broken, fences cut, and equipment damaged.

Both abolitionist and reformist organizations document the immorality of factory farming in brochures and magazines filled with gruesome photographs and ghoulish descriptions of cruelty in slaughterhouses and farms. These documents show contorted hens living their entire lives confined in wire cages so cramped that their toes grow around the wire. They describe the stressful conditions that cause pecking and cannibalism. Bulls are branded and castrated. Rabbits are "living machines" forced to produce eight to ten litters each year. Animals are crammed into trucks and shipped long distances to packing plants.

To highlight the immorality of industrial practices, the animal rights literature describes animals about to be killed for food or fun in human terms. Easily personified, veal calves are a favorite target of activists. Babies with large eyes, they are separated from their mothers ("yanked from their mothers' sides"), confined in stalls ("crated and tortured"), and kept anemic to produce lighter meat. Even lobsters are anthropomorphized: "They have a long childhood and an awkward adolescence . . . They flirt. Their pregnancies last nine months and they can live to be over one hundred years old." They also have feelings and scramble frantically to escape the pot, "much the way I suppose I would sound were I popped into a pot and boiled alive." . . .

Animal activists direct their moral outrage primarily against large corporations. Their rhetoric is couched in terms of *we* and *they,* two sides separated by a vast moral chasm. Fur and meat producers are depicted as villains, profiteering without regard to pain, and willing to place economic over moral value. Agribusiness thrives "on the backs of the least empowered groups in our social structure: farm workers, future generations, and, of course, farm animals." Animal activists exploit a long tradition of rhetoric against capitalism and the factory system to link animal rights with other social and political issues like exploitation and deprivation for profit.

A Trans-Species brochure describes "New MacDonald's Farm" as a full-scale factory in which animals are enslaved, becoming machines to produce meat. John Robbins—author of *Diet for a New America,* heir to the Baskin Robbins Ice Cream Company, and the president of Earthsave—eulogizes pigs in "The Joy and Tragedy of Pigs," noting their high IQs, superior problem-solving abilities, and "sophisticated and subtle relationships with their human companions." Having described the human qualities of pigs, Robbins naturally criticizes "pork production engineers," who treat pigs like "machines." He quotes a trade journal, *Hog Farm Management:* "Forget the pig is an animal. Treat him just like a machine in a factory. Schedule treatment like you would lubrication. Breeding season like the first step in an assembly line. And marketing like the delivery of finished goods." The critique of factory farms, in which machines dominate the production process with no regard for animals, follows Karl Marx's nineteenth-century attack on the treatment of human labor in factories. Factory life turns living beings—humans or animals—into cogs in a relentless machine.

The campaign against furs has had far greater impact—especially on the attitudes of consumers. A New York City lawyer tells a reporter that she feels "very conflicted" about owning a fur, as her own son tells her she is doing something immoral. A fashion agent has no desire to wear her mink coat, for "it's asking for trouble." A travel consultant says she is "a little nervous about walking down a street and being pelted with eggs or paint." A business executive says that when she bought her mink coat it did not occur to her to think about how animals are bred or killed. "Now I am aware of the brutality of trapping an animal, and I would not wear a trapped fur."

Environmentalists and animal protectionists had once attacked the fur industry primarily because of the cruelty involved in trapping wild animals. This view still dominated their discourse in 1979, when the Animal Welfare Institute published and widely distributed an exposé, *Facts on Furs,* that focused on leg-hold traps. But animal rightists equally condemn the ranching of fur animals, which now accounts for roughly 80 percent of furs sold. Although most ranched animals die from gas or lethal injection, critics claim that many foxes are still electrocuted by means of a clip on their lip and a probe in their anus. Such practices are seen as brutal and unwarranted, a blight on civilized society. . . .

Perhaps because protestors have had little success with ranchers, current anti-fur campaigns are aimed at those who wear furs more than at trappers, making department stores and fur salons the sites of protest. In 1987, Bob Barker, a popular television game show host, publicly refused to participate in a Miss U.S.A. pageant in which the women were to parade out in furs and remove them to reveal swim suits. One prize was to be a fur coat. The following year Barker attracted further media attention as the head of the Fur-Free Friday march in New York; he seemed to encourage demonstrators to spit on passersby wearing furs by saying that this tactic had been effective in changing public attitudes toward fur in Europe.

Demonstrators have picketed, spray-painted, and smashed the windows of fur stores, distributed the names and home addresses of furriers, harassed women by shouting or spitting on them, placed advertisements on subways and city buses, and sponsored fashion shows with the message "Real People Wear Fake Furs" and "Fake People Wear Real Furs." They have organized rock concerts, liberated beavers from fur farms, and held public memorial services for animals killed for furs. Graphic slogans provide effective moral shocks: "Somewhere There Are Animals Missing Their Paws," and "Wear the Bloody Side Out!" Like the anti-meat crusade, anti-fur films and photos dwell on the cruelty and pain inflicted on vulnerable and sensitive beings. A photograph of a rack of pelts is captioned: "A few moments ago, these were live, vulnerable beings capable of fear, happiness, hope, and pain." A sign on a New York City bus encourages empathy by portraying a trapped animal: "Get a Feel for Fur. Slam your hand in a car door." Some activists even oppose the wearing of wool, combining arguments based on pain (sheep may be nicked during shearing or may be cold once shorn) with rights talk (sheep should not be used for human ends).

Furriers launched a multimillion-dollar campaign against the animal protection movement. The movement has had even greater influence in European countries, where fur sales have drastically declined (fur sales have dropped 90 percent in the Netherlands, 75 percent in Britain and Switzerland since the early eighties), and Harrods, once boasting it sold every existing product, has abandoned its sale of fur coats. The industry defends itself as catering to consumer choice and protecting fundamental freedoms. A radio commercial by the fur industry asks the listener to imagine enjoying a steak dinner in a nice restaurant: "Suddenly there's a commotion. People are around your table jostling you. Shouting. Pointing at your steak and screaming that you are a killer." Ads in major newspapers proclaim, "Today fur. Tomorrow leather. Then wool. Then meat. . . ." The American Fur Industry/Fur Information Council of America ends with an appeal to American individualism: "The decision to wear fur is a personal one. We support the freedom of individuals to buy and wear fur. This freedom is not just a fur industry issue—it's everybody's issue." This defense of consumer choice as a fundamental freedom is as close to the high moral ground as the fur industry can come.

Furriers routinely label all animal activists as terrorists. Even the audience at a "Rock Against Fur" concert were "supporting terrorism." When Beauty Without Cruelty published ads with a list of celebrities under the caption "Say NO to furs—They did," the Fur Retailers Council wrote to each person listed. It implied they were being used by terrorist groups, and warned them to "review the enclosed material recently sent to police chiefs and sheriffs throughout the U.S. calling attention to violence and revenue-producing campaigns that often have very little relationship to animal care." The materials included lists of break-ins and animal thefts. Labeling the movement the "Animal Rights Protection Industry," the Council also provided information on the net worth of various organizations such as Greenpeace and the ASPCA (American Society for the Prevention of Cruelty to Animals). Both animal rightists and their opponents denounce each other as large, powerful, and ruthless.

Amidst the moral confusions of contemporary culture, animal rightists offer a clear position based on a set of compelling principles. They offer moral engagement and commitment in a secular society with few opportunities to sort out one's values, appealing especially to those who reject organized religion as a source of moral tenets. Animals are a perfect outlet for moral impulses, for—unlike people—they seem incapable of duplicity, infidelity, or betrayal. Like children, they are innocent victims unable to fight for their own interests. Thus, protecting animals sometimes inspires the shrill tone, the sense of urgency, and the single-minded obsession of a fundamentalist crusade. Its members become missionaries, defining the world in terms of the treatment of animals. They see the world as good or evil, and the villain—the person who exploits animals—becomes a model of malice. . . . Convinced of the truth of their moral mission, many animal rights activists feel justified in using radical tactics as well as revolutionary rhetoric to serve their cause of abolishing all animal exploitation. . . .

Animal rights is but one of many controversies that have grown out of a clash of basic moral values, of competing world views. Unlike conflicts based on interests, such controversies cannot be fully resolved. Yet, raising basic questions that reflect widespread social and political concerns, moral crusades can never be dismissed. To stubbornly defend current practices is to encourage further polarization. To denounce the movement as irrational, kooky, or terrorist is to miss the popular appeal of its moral intuitions and political beliefs. If a solution is possible in such rancorous conflict, it will require good faith from both sides to ensure the dialogue and compromise basic to a democratic conversation.

46 The McDonaldization of Society

GEORGE RITZER

A key term in sociology is *rationalization*. This term refers to choosing the most efficient means to accomplish tasks. In business it refers to the bottom line, calculating costs to produce the most gain. With rationalization, profit becomes king, while people, valued for what they bring to the bottom line, become expendable.

The rationalization of society, said Max Weber, the sociologist who first analyzed this process, is extremely significant, for it tends to ensnare us all. The traditional ways of doing things—which may be inefficient but which are also the source of huge satisfactions—are passing. In their place come bureaucracies with time and motion studies, cold analyses of every act, and a neglect of the people who make up the work setting. Weber didn't know how far reaching and accurate his analysis would prove. Rationalization threatens to engulf all of society, locking us all in what Weber called an iron cage of rationality. College administrators, for example, want to evaluate instructors not by how they challenge students to think or by how they open their minds to new perceptions, but, rather, by the sheer number of students they turn out each semester. Even traditional, routine, everyday aspects of family life are not impervious to this change, as becomes evident in Ritzer's analysis.

MCDONALD'S HAS SOUGHT to construct highly efficient systems, and *McDonaldization* implies the search for maximum efficiency in increasingly numerous and diverse social settings. *Efficiency* means the choice of the optimum means to a given end, but this definition requires some clarification. Although we use the term *optimum*, it is rare that the truly optimum means to an end is ever found. Rather, there is a search for a . . . far better means to an end than would be employed under ordinary circumstances. . . .

Wireless Keyboards and Self-Service Slurpees

The emphasis of McDonaldization on efficiency implies that contrasting, non-rational systems are less efficient, or even inefficient. The fast-food restaurant grew as a result of its greater efficiency in comparison to alternative methods of obtaining a meal. In the early 1950s, at the dawning of the era of the fast-food restaurant, the major alternative was the home-cooked meal made largely from ingredients previously purchased at various markets. . . .

But the home-cooked meal was, and still is, a relatively inefficient way of obtaining a meal. The restaurant has long been a more efficient alternative. But restaurants can be inefficient in that it may take several hours to go to the restaurant, consume a meal, and then return home. The desire for more efficient restaurants led to the rise of some of the ancestors of the fast-food restaurant—diners, cafeterias, and early drive-through or drive-in restaurants. The modern fast-food restaurant can be seen as being built on the latter models and as a further step in the direction of more efficient food consumption. . . .

Above all else, it was the efficiency of the McDonald brothers' operation that impressed Ray Kroc [the individual behind the franchising of McDonald's], as well as the enormous profit potential of such a system if it were applied in a large number of sites. Here is how Kroc described his initial reactions to the McDonald's system:

> I was fascinated by the simplicity and effectiveness of the system. . . . Each step in producing the limited menu was stripped down to its essence and accomplished with a minimum of effort. They sold hamburgers and cheeseburgers only. The burgers were . . . all fried the same way.

Kroc and his associates looked at each component of the hamburger in order to increase the efficiency with which it could be produced and served. For example, they started with only partially sliced buns that were attached to one another. However, it was found that buns could be used more efficiently if they were sliced all the way through and separated from one another. At first, the buns arrived in cardboard boxes and the griddle workers had to spend time opening the boxes, separating the buns, slicing them, and discarding the leftover paper and cardboard. In addition to separating and preslicing them, buns were made efficient to use by having them shipped in reusable boxes. Similar attention was devoted to the meat patty. For example, the paper between the patties had to have just the right amount of wax so that the patties would readily slide off the paper and onto the grill.

Kroc makes it clear that the goal of these kinds of refinements was greater efficiency:

> The purpose of all these refinements, and we never lost sight of it, was to make our griddle man's job easier to do quickly and well. And the other considerations of cost cutting, inventory control, and so forth were important to be sure, but they were secondary to the critical detail of what happened there at the smoking griddle. This was the vital passage of our *assembly-line,* and the product had to flow through it smoothly or the whole plant would falter. (Italics added.)

. . . Once diners enter the fast-food restaurant, the process continues to appear to be efficient. Parking lots are adjacent to the restaurant and parking spots are readily available. It's a short walk to the counter, and although there is sometimes a line, food is usually quickly ordered, obtained, and paid for. The highly limited menu makes the choice of a meal's components quite easy. This contrasts to the many choices available in many of the alternatives to the fast-food restaurant. With the food obtained, it is but a few steps to a table and the beginning of the "dining experience." The fare almost always involves an array of finger foods (for example, Chicken McNuggets and french fries) that can be popped into the diner's mouth with the result that the entire meal is ordinarily consumed in a few minutes. Because there is little inducement to linger, the diners generally gather the leftover paper, styrofoam, and plastic, discard them in a nearby trash receptacle, and are back in their car and on their way to the next (often McDonaldized) activity.

Not too many years ago, those in charge of fast-food restaurants discovered that there was a way—the drive-through window—to make this whole process far more efficient for both themselves and the consumer. Instead of the "laborious" and "inefficient" process of parking the car, walking to the counter, waiting in line, ordering, paying, carrying the food to the table, eating, and disposing of the remnants, the drive-through window offered diners the choice of driving to the window (perhaps waiting in a line of cars), ordering, paying, and driving off with the meal. It was even possible to engage in the highly efficient act of eating while driving, thereby eliminating the need to devote a separate time period to dining. The drive-through window is also efficient from the perspective of the fast-food restaurant. As more and more people use the drive-through window, fewer parking spaces, tables, and employees are needed. Further, consumers take their debris with them as they drive away, thereby eliminating the need for additional trash receptacles and employees to periodically empty those receptacles. . . .

"Home-Made" Fast Food and the StairMaster

Given the efficiency of the fast-food restaurant, the home kitchen has had to grow more efficient or it might have faced total extinction. Had the kitchen not grown more efficient, a comedian could have envisioned a time when the kitchen would have been replaced by a large, comfortable telephone lounge used for calling Domino's for pizza delivery. The key to the salvation of the kitchen was the development and widespread adoption of the microwave oven. The microwave is simply a far more efficient means than its major alternative, the convection oven, for preparing a meal. It is usually faster than the old oven and one can prepare a wider array of foods in it than the old-fashioned oven. Perhaps most importantly from the point of view of this chapter, it spawned the development of a number of microwavable foods (including soup, pizza, hamburgers, fried chicken, french fries, and popcorn) that permit the efficient preparation of the fare one usually finds in the fast-food restaurants. For example, one of the first microwavable foods produced by Hormel was an array of biscuit-based breakfast sandwiches "popularized in recent years by many of the fast-food chains," most notably McDonald's and its Egg McMuffin. Banquet rushed to market with microwavable chicken breast nuggets. In fact, many food companies now employ people who continually scout fast-food restaurants for new ideas for foods that can be marketed for the home. As one executive put it, "Instead of having a breakfast sandwich at McDonald's, you can pick one up from the freezer of your grocery store." As a result, one can now, in effect, enjoy fast food at home without venturing out to the fast-food restaurant. . . .

Another factor in the continued success of the fast-food restaurant is that it has many advantages over the "home-cooked" microwave dinner. For example, a trip to the fast-food restaurant offers people a dinner out rather than just another meal at home. For another, as Stan Luxenberg has pointed out in *Roadside Empires,* McDonald's offers more than an efficient meal, it offers fun—brightly lit, colorful, and attractive settings, garish packaging, special inducements to children, give-aways, contests—in short, it offers a kind of carnival-like atmosphere in which to buy and consume fast food. Thus, faced with the choice of an efficient meal at home or one in a fast-food restaurant, many people are still likely to choose the fast-food restaurant because it not only offers efficiency but a range of other rewards.

The microwave oven (as well as the range of products it spawned) is but one of many contributors to the increasing efficiency of home cooking. Among other obvious technological advances are the replacement of the hand beater by the electric beater; slicers, dicers, and even knives by the Cuisinart; and the presence of either stand-alone freezers or those that are an integral part of the refrigerator.

The large freezer has permitted a range of efficiencies, such as a few trips to the market for enormous purchases rather than many trips for small purchases. It has permitted the storage of a wide range of ingredients that can be readily extracted when needed for food preparation. It has allowed for the cooking of large portions which can then be divided up, frozen, and defrosted periodically for dinner. The widespread availability of the home freezer led to the expansion of the production of frozen foods of all types. The most notable frozen food from the point of view of efficiency is the "TV dinner." People can stock their freezers with an array of such dinners (for example, Chinese, Italian, and Mexican dinners as well as a wide variety of "American" cooking) and quite readily bring them out and pop them into the oven, sometimes even the microwave. . . .

The McDonaldization of food preparation and consumption has been extended to the booming diet industry. Diet books promising all sorts of efficient shortcuts to weight loss are often at the top of the best-seller lists. Losing weight is normally difficult and time-consuming, hence the lure of various diet books that promise to make weight loss easier and quicker, that is, more efficient.

For those on a diet, and many people are on more or less perpetual diets, the preparation of low-calorie food has been made more efficient. Instead of needing to cook diet foods from scratch, they may now purchase an array of prepared foods in frozen and/or microwavable form. For those who do not wish to go through the inefficient process of eating those diet meals, there are the diet shakes, like Slim•Fast, that can be mixed and consumed in a matter of seconds.

A fairly recent development is the growth of diet centers like Nutri/System and Jenny Craig. Nutri/System sells dieters, at substantial cost, prepackaged freeze-dried food. All the dieter need do is add water when it is time for the next meal. Freeze-dried foods are not only efficient for the dieter but also for Nutri/System, because they can be efficiently packaged, transported, and stored. Furthermore, the dieter's periodic visit to a Nutri/System center is efficiently organized. A counselor is allotted ten minutes with each client. During that brief time the counselor takes the client's weight, blood pressure, and measurements, asks routine questions, fills out a chart, and devotes some time to "problem-solving." If the session extends beyond the allotted ten minutes and other clients are waiting, the receptionist will buzz the counselor's room. Counselors learn their techniques at Nutri/System University where, after a week of training (no inefficient years of matriculation here), they earn certification and an NSU diploma.

There is a strong emphasis on efficiency in modern health clubs, including such chains as Holiday Spas. These clubs often offer, under one roof, virtually everything needed to lose weight and stay in shape, including a wide array of exercise machines, as well as a running track and a swimming pool. The exercise machines are highly specialized so that one may efficiently increase fitness in specific areas of the body. Thus, working out on running machines and the StairMaster—one kind of exercise machine—increases cardiovascular fitness, whereas using various weightlifting machines increases strength and muscularity in targeted areas of the body. Another efficiency associated with many of these machines is that one can do other things while exercising. Thus, many clubs have television sets throughout the gym allowing people to both watch television and exercise. The exerciser can also read, listen to music, or even listen to a book-on-tape while working out. The exercise machines also offer a high degree of calculability, with many of them registering miles run, level of difficulty, and calories burned. All of this in the kind of clean, sterile environment we have come to associate with McDonaldization.

"Selling Machines" and L. L. Bean

Shopping has also grown more efficient. The department store obviously is a more efficient place in which to shop than a series of specialty shops dispersed throughout the city or suburbs. The shopping mall increases efficiency by bringing a wide range of department stores and specialty shops under one roof. Kowinsky describes the mall as "an extremely efficient and effective selling machine." It is cost-efficient for retailers because it is the collection of shops and department stores ("mall synergy") that brings in throngs of people. And it is efficient for consumers because in one stop they can visit numerous shops, have lunch at a "food court" (likely populated by many fast-food chains), see a movie, have a drink, and go to an exercise or diet center.

The drive for shopping efficiency did not end with the malls. In recent years, there has been a great increase in catalogue sales (via L. L. Bean, Lands' End, and other mail-order companies), which enables people to shop while never leaving the comfort of their homes. Still more efficient, although it may require many hours in front of the tube, is home television shopping. A range of products is paraded in front of viewers who may simply phone each time a product catches their eye and conveniently charge their purchase to their credit card accounts. The latest advance in home shopping is the "scan-fone," an at-home phone machine that includes "a pen-sized bar-code scanner, a credit card magnetic-strip reader, and a key pad." The customer merely "scans items from a bar-coded catalogue and also scans delivery dates and payment methods. The orders are then electronically relayed to the various stores, businesses, and banks involved." Some mall operators fear that they will ultimately be put out of business because of the greater efficiency of shopping at home.

Video Rentals and Package Tours

With the advent of videotapes and video rental stores, many people no longer deem it efficient to drive to their local theater to see a movie. Movies can now be viewed, often more than one at a sitting, in one's own den. For those who wish even greater efficiency, viewers can buy one of the new televisions sets that enable viewers to see a movie while also watching a favorite television program on an inset on the television screen.

The largest video rental franchise in the United States is Blockbuster, which, predictably, "considers itself the McDonald's of the video business." Blockbuster has more than 2,000 outlets. . . . However, there may already be signs that Blockbuster is in danger of being replaced by even more efficient alternatives. One is pay-per-view movies offered by many cable companies.

Instead of trekking to the video store, all one need do is turn to the proper channel and phone the cable company. Another experimental alternative is an effort by GTE to deliver movies to one's home through fiber-optic cables. Just as the video store replaced many movie theaters, video stores themselves may soon be displaced by even more efficient alternatives.

. . . [T]ravel to exotic efficient locales has also grown more efficient. The best example of this is the package tour. Let us take, for example, a thirty-day tour of Europe. To make these efficient, only the major locales in Europe are visited. Within each of these locales, the tourist is directed toward the major sights. (In Paris, the tour would definitely stop at the Louvre, but perhaps not at the Rodin Museum.) Because the goal is to see as many of the major sights as possible in a short period of time, the emphasis is on the efficient transportation of people to, through, and from each of them. Buses hurtle to and through the city, allowing the tourist to glimpse the maximum number of sights in the time allowed. At particularly interesting or important sights, the bus may slow down or even stop to permit some picture-taking. At the most important locales, a brief stopover is planned; there the visitor can hurry through the site, take a few pictures, buy a souvenir, and then hop back on the bus to head to the next attraction.

There is no question that this is a highly efficient way of seeing the major tourist attractions of Europe. Indeed, the package tour can be seen as a vast people-moving mechanism that permits the efficient transport of people from one locale to another. If tourists attempted to see the major sights of Europe on their own, it would take more time to see the same things and the expense would be greater. There are, of course, costs associated with the package tour (for example, does the tourist ever really have time to experience Europe?), as there are with every other highly rational system, but we will reserve a discussion of them for later. . . .

Customized Textbooks, Books-on-Tape, "News McNuggets," and Drive-in Churches

Turning to the educational system, specifically the university, one manifestation of the pressure for greater efficiency is the machine-graded, multiple-choice examination. In a much earlier era, students were examined on a one-to-one basis by their professors. This may have been a very good way of finding out what students know, but it was (and is) highly labor intensive and inefficient. Later, the essay examination became very popular. While grading a set of essays was more efficient from the professor's perspective than giving individual oral examinations, it was still relatively inefficient and time-consuming. Enter the multiple-choice examination, the grading of which was a snap in comparison to giving oral tests or reading essays. In fact, the grading could be passed on to graduate assistants, an act that was very efficient for the professor. Now we have computer-graded examinations that maximize efficiency for both professors and graduate students.

The multiple-choice examinations still left the professor saddled with the inefficient task of composing the necessary sets of questions. Furthermore, at least some of the questions had to be changed each semester because new students were likely to gain possession of old exams. The solution: Textbook companies provided professors with books (free of charge) full of multiple-choice questions to go along with the textbooks required for use in large classes. Professors no longer had to make up their own questions; they could use those previously provided by the publisher. However, the professor still had to retype the questions or to have them retyped by the office staff. Recently, however, publishers have been kind enough to provide their sets of questions on computer disks. Now all the professor needs to do is select the desired questions and let the printer do the rest.* . . .

Publishers have provided other services to make teaching more efficient for those professors who adopt their textbooks. With the adoption of a textbook, a professor may receive many materials with which to fill class hours—lecture outlines, computer simulations, discussion questions, videotapes, movies, even ideas for guest lecturers and student projects. With luck, professors can use all of these devices and do little or nothing on their own for their classes. Needless to say, this is a highly efficient means of teaching from a professor's perspective, and it frees up valuable time for the much more valued activities (by professors, but not students) of writing and research. . . .

Another example of efficiency in publishing is the advent of books-on-tape. There is a number of companies that now rent or sell books recorded on audiotape. The availability of such tapes permits greater efficiency in "reading" books. Instead of doing nothing but reading, one can now engage in other activities (driving, walking, jogging, watching TV with the sound off) while listening to a book. Greater efficiency is also provided by many of these books-on-tape being available in abridged form so that they can be devoured far more quickly. Gone are the "wasted" hours listening to "insignificant" parts of novels. With liberal cutting, a book such as *War and Peace* can now be listened to in a sitting.

Most "serious," nontabloid newspapers (for example, *The New York Times* and *The Washington Post*) are relatively inefficient to read. This is especially true of stories that begin on page one and then carry over to one or more additional pages. Stories that carry over to additional pages are said to have "jumped," and many readers are resistant to "jumping" with the stories. *USA Today* eliminated this inefficient way of presenting and reading stories by starting and finishing most of them on the same page, in other words, by offering "News McNuggets." This was accomplished by ruthlessly editing stories so that narrative was dramatically reduced (and no words wasted), leaving a series of relatively bare facts. . . .

*Some publishers also offer a "call–in testing service." A professor can call a toll–free number, specify the desired questions, and the publisher ships the test to the professor—all free.——— Editor.

In the realm of religion, McDonaldization is manifest, among other places, in drive-in churches. Another is the widespread development of televised religious programs whereby people can get their religion in the comfort of their living rooms. A particularly noteworthy example of such religious rationalization occurred in 1985 when the Vatican announced that Catholics could receive indulgences through the Pope's annual Christmas benediction on TV or radio. ("Indulgences are a release by way of devotional practices from certain forms of punishment resulting from sin.") Before this development Catholics had to engage in the far less efficient activity of going to Rome for the Christmas benediction and manifesting the "proper intention and attitude" in order to receive their indulgences in person. . . .

[Destroying Relationships]

The fast-food restaurant offers its employees a dehumanizing setting within which to work. Few skills are required on the job. Said Burger King workers, "A moron could learn this job, it's so easy" and "Any trained monkey could do this job." Thus workers are asked to use only a minute proportion of all their skills and abilities. Employees are not only not using all of their skills, but they are also not being allowed to think and to be creative on the job. This leads to a high level of resentment, job dissatisfaction, alienation, absenteeism, and turnover among those who work in fast-food restaurants. In fact, the fast-food industry has the highest turnover rate—approximately 100 percent a year—of any industry in the United States. That means that the average worker lasts only about four months at a fast-food restaurant; the entire workforce of the fast-food industry turns over three times a year. . . .

The fast-food restaurant is also dehumanizing as far as the customer is concerned. Instead of a human dining experience, what is offered is eating on a sort of moving conveyor belt or assembly line. The diner is reduced to a kind of overwound automaton who is made to rush through the meal. Little gratification is derived from the dining experience or from the food itself. The best that can usually be said is that it is efficient and it is over quickly.

Some customers might even feel as if they are being fed like livestock in a highly rationalized manner. This point was made a number of years ago on television in a *Saturday Night Live* skit entitled "Trough and Brew," a take-off on a small fast-food chain called Burger and Brew. In the skit, some young executives learn that a new fast-food restaurant called Trough and Brew has opened and they decide to try it for lunch. They are next seen entering the restaurant and having bibs tied around their necks. After that, they discover a long trough, resembling a pig trough. The trough is filled with chili and is periodically refilled by a waiter scooping new supplies from a bucket. The customers bend over, stick their heads into the trough, and begin lapping up the chili as they move along the length of the trough making high-level business decisions. Every so often they come up for air and lap some beer from the communal "brew basin." After they have finished their "meal," they pay their bills, "by the head." Since their faces are smeared with chili, they are literally "hosed off" before they leave the restaurant. The young executives are last seen being herded out of the restaurant, which is being closed for a half-hour so that it can be "hosed down." *Saturday Night Live* was clearly pointing out, and ridiculing, the fact that fast-food restaurants tend to treat their customers like lower animals.

"Get Lost" and Wheel of Fortune

Another dehumanizing aspect of fast-food restaurants is that they minimize contact among human beings. Let us take, for example, the issue of how customers and employees relate. The nature of the fast-food restaurant turns these into fleeting relationships. Because the average employee stays only a few months, and even then only works on a part-time basis, the customer, even the regular customer, is rarely able to develop a long-term personal relationship with a counterperson. Gone are the days when one got to know well a waitress at a diner or the short-order cook at a local greasy spoon. Gone are the days when an employee knows who you are and knows what you are likely to order.

Not only are the relationships with a McDonald's employee fleeting (because the worker remains on the job only a short period of time), but each contact between worker and customer is of a very short duration. It takes little time at the counter to order, receive one's food, and pay for it. Both employees and customers are likely to feel rushed and to want to move on, customers to their dinner and employees to the next order. There is virtually no time for customer and counterperson to interact in such a context. This is even more true of the drive-through window, where thanks to the speedy service and the physical barriers, the server is but a dim and distant image.

The highly impersonal and anonymous relationship between customer and counterperson is heightened by the employees having been trained to interact in a staged and limited manner with customers. Thus, the customers may feel that they are dealing with automatons who have been taught to utter a few phrases rather than with fellow human beings. For their part, the customers are supposed to be, and often are, in a hurry, so they have little to say to the McDonald's employee. Indeed, it could be argued that one of the reasons for the success of fast-food restaurants is that they are in tune with our fast-paced and impersonal society. People in the modern world want to get on with their business without unnecessary personal relationships. The fast-food restaurant gives them precisely what they want.

Not only are the relationships between employee and customer limited greatly, but also other potential relationships. Because employees remain on the job for only a few months, satisfying personal relationships among employees are unlikely to develop. . . .

Relationships among customers are largely curtailed as well. Although some McDonald's ads would have us believe otherwise, gone are the days when people met in the diner or cafeteria for coffee, breakfast, lunch, or dinner and lingered to socialize with one another. Fast-food restaurants are clearly not conducive to such socializing. If nothing else, the chairs are designed to make people uncomfortable and interested in moving on to something else. The drive-through windows are a further step toward McDonaldization, by completely eliminating the possibility of interacting with other customers. . . .

Fast-food restaurants also tend to have negative effects on other human relationships. There is, for example, the effect on the so-called "family meal." The fast-food restaurant is not conducive to a long, leisurely, conversation-filled dinnertime. The family is unlikely to linger long over a meal at McDonald's. Furthermore, as the children grow into their teens, the nature of fast-food restaurants leads to separate meals as the teens go at one time with their friends, and the parents go at another time. Of course, the drive-through window only serves to reduce the possibility of a family meal. The family that gobbles its food while driving on to its next stop can hardly be seen as having what is called these days "quality time" with each other. Here is the way one journalist describes what is happening to the family meal:

> Do families who eat their suppers at the Colonel's, swinging on plastic seats, or however the restaurant is arranged, say grace before picking up a crispy brown chicken leg? Does dad ask junior what he did today as he remembers he forgot the piccalilli and trots through the crowds over to the counter to get some? Does mom find the atmosphere conducive to asking little Mildred about the problems she was having with third-conjugation French verbs, or would it matter since otherwise the family might have been at home chomping down precooked frozen food, warmed in the microwave oven, and watching *Hollywood Squares?*

There is much talk these days about the disintegration of the family, and the fast-food restaurants may well be a crucial contributor to that disintegration.

In fact, as implied above, dinners at home may now not be much different from meals at the fast-food restaurant. Families tended to stop having lunch together by the 1940s and breakfast altogether by the 1950s. Today, the family dinner is following the same route. Even when they eat dinner at home, the meal will probably not be what it once was. Following the fast-food model, people are growing more likely to "graze," "refuel," nibble on this, or snack on that, than they are to sit down to a formal meal. Also, because it is now deemed inefficient to do nothing but just eat, families are likely to watch television while they are eating, thereby efficiently combining two activities. However, the din, to say nothing of the lure, of dinnertime TV programs such as *Wheel of Fortune* is likely to make it difficult for family members to interact with one another.

A key technology in the destruction of the family meal is the microwave oven and the vast array of microwavable foods it helped generate. It is striking to learn that more than 70 percent of American households have a microwave oven. A recent *Wall Street Journal* poll indicated that Americans consider the microwave their favorite household product. In fact, the microwave in a McDonaldizing society is seen as an advance over the fast-food restaurant. Said one consumer researcher, "It has made even fast-food restaurants not seem fast because at home you don't have to wait in line." As a general rule, consumers are demanding meals that take no more than ten minutes to microwave, whereas in the past people were more often willing to spend about a half hour or even an hour cooking dinner. This emphasis on speed has, of course, brought with it poorer taste and lower quality, but people do not seem to mind this loss: "We're just not as critical of food as we used to be." . . .

Fast Food [and Homogenization]

Another dehumanizing effect of the fast-food restaurant is that it has contributed to homogenization around the country and, increasingly, throughout the world. Diversity, which many people crave, is being reduced or eliminated by the fast-food restaurant. This decline in diversity is manifest in the extension of the fast-food model to all sorts of ethnic foods. The settings are all modeled after McDonald's in one way or another and the food has been rationalized and compromised so that it is acceptable to the tastes of virtually all diners. One cannot find an authentically different meal in any of these ethnic fast-food chains.

The expansion of these franchises across the landscape of America means that one finds little difference among regions and among cities throughout the country. Tourists find more familiarity and predictability and less diversity as they travel around the nation, and this is increasingly true on a global scale. Apparently exotic settings are likely to be overrun with both American fast-food chains as well as indigenous varieties. The new and world's largest McDonald's and Kentucky Fried Chicken in Beijing are but two examples of this. . . . The spread of American and indigenous fast food throughout much of the world means that there is less and less diversity from one setting to another. The human craving for new and diverse experiences is being limited, if not progressively destroyed, by the national and international spread of fast-food restaurants. The craving for diversity is being supplanted by the desire for uniformity and predictability. . . .

Conclusion

Although I have emphasized the irresistibility of McDonaldization, my fondest hope is that I am wrong. Indeed, a major motivation is to alert readers to the dangers of McDonaldization and to motivate them to act to stem its tide. I hope that we are able to resist McDonaldization and can create instead a more reasonable, more human world.

McDonald's was recently sued by the famous French chef, Paul Bocuse, for using his picture on a poster without his permission. Enraged, Bocuse said: "How can I be seen promoting this tasteless, boneless food in which everything is soft." Nevertheless, Bocuse seemed to acknowledge the inevitability of McDonaldization: "There's a need for this kind of thing . . . and trying to get rid of it seems to me to be as futile as trying to get rid of the prostitutes in the Bois de Boulogne." Lo and behold, two weeks later, it was announced that the Paris police had cracked down on prostitution in the Bois de Boulogne. Said a police spokesman, "There are none left." Thus, just as chef Bocuse was wrong about the prostitutes, perhaps I was wrong about the irresistibility of McDonaldization. Yet, before we grow overly optimistic, it should be noted that "everyone knows that the prostitutes will be back as soon as the operation is over. In the spring, police predict, there will be even more than before." Similarly, it remains likely that no matter how intense the opposition, the future will bring with it more rather than less McDonaldization. . . . [F]aced with Max Weber's iron cage imagery of a future dominated by the polar night of icy darkness and hardness, the least the reader can do is to follow the words of the poet Dylan Thomas: "Do not go gentle into that good night. . . . Rage, rage against the dying of the light."

47 Being "The Other": Ethnic Identity in a Changing Society

ARTURO MADRID

The United States always has been a diverse society. During the Colonial period, there were English, French, British, Dutch, and Spanish settlers. They did not particularly like one another; lusting after one another's territory, finding customs of the others abrasive, they even went to war.

There was, of course, greater diversity in the Colonies than this, for there also were Native Americans and African Americans. Later came Asian Americans, and eventually people from just about everywhere on earth. The Anglos who controlled the social institutions—primarily politics, economics, and the military—thought of themselves as being the only "real" Americans. To the others, they denied citizenship. They found the others useful for labor, or considered them nuisances that had to be conquered and put on reservations in order for "the society" to progress.

Such attitudes still persist, but only as remnants. No longer are they presumed within the social institutions, as they once were, to be values that are correct, right, just, and moral. As our society undergoes further change in its racial-ethnic mix—one of the most significant changes taking place in the United States—ethnic-racial attitudes will change even farther. This selection by Madrid addresses some of these issues.

MY NAME IS ARTURO MADRID. I am a citizen of the United States, as are my parents and as were my grandparents and my great-grandparents. My ancestors' presence in what is now the United States antedates Plymouth Rock, even without taking into account any American Indian heritage I might have.

I do not, however, fit those mental sets that define America and Americans. My physical appearance, my speech patterns, my name, my profession (a professor of Spanish) create a text that confuses the reader. My normal experience is to be asked, "And where are *you* from?" My response depends on my mood. Passive-aggressive, I answer, "From here." Aggressive-passive, I ask, "Do you mean where I am originally from?" But ultimately my answer to those follow-up questions that will ask about origins will be that we have always been from here.

Overcoming my resentment I try to educate, knowing that nine times out of ten my words fall on inattentive ears. I have spent most of my adult life explaining who I am not. I am exotic, but—as Richard Rodriguez of *Hunger of Memory* fame so painfully found out—not exotic enough . . . not Peruvian, or Pakistani, or whatever. I am, however, very clearly the *other,* if only your everyday, garden-variety, domestic *other.* I will share with you another phenomenon that I have been a part of, that of being a missing person, and how I came late to that awareness. But I've always known that I was the *other,* even before I knew the vocabulary or understood the significance of otherness.

I grew up in an isolated and historically marginal part of the United States, a small mountain village in the state of New Mexico, the eldest child of parents native to that region, whose ancestors had always lived there. In those vast and empty spaces people who look like me, speak as I do, and have names like mine predominate. But the *americanos* lived among us: the descendants of those nineteenth-century immigrants who dispossessed us of our lands; missionaries who came to convert us and stayed to live among us; artists who became enchanted with our land and humanscape and went native; refugees from unhealthy climes, crowded spaces, unpleasant circumstances; and, of course, the inhabitants of Los Alamos, whose sociocultural distance from us was accentuated by the fact that they occupied a space removed from and proscribed to us. More importantly, however, they—*los americanos*—were omnipresent (and almost exclusively so) in newspapers, newsmagazines, books, on radio, in movies, and ultimately, on television.

Despite the operating myth of the day, school did not erase my otherness. It did try to deny it, and in doing so only accentuated it. To this day what takes place in schools is more socialization than education, but when I was in elementary school—and given where I was—socialization was everything. School was where one became an American, because there was a pervasive and systematic denial by the society that surrounded us that we were Americans. That denial was both explicit and implicit.

Quite beyond saluting the flag and pledging allegiance to it (a very intense and meaningful action, given that the United States was involved in a war and our brothers, cousins, uncles, and fathers were on the frontlines), becoming American was learning English, and its corollary: not speaking Spanish. Until very recently ours was a proscribed language, either *de jure*—by rule, by policy, by law—or *de facto*—by practice, implicitly if not explicitly, through social and political and economic pressure. I do not argue that learning English was not appropriate. On the contrary. Like it or not, and we had no basis to make any judgments on that matter, we were Americans by virtue of having been born Americans and English was the common language of Americans. And there was a myth, a pervasive myth, to the effect that if only we learned to speak English well—and particularly without an accent—we would be welcomed into the American fellowship.

Sam Hayakawa and the official English movement folks notwithstanding, the true text was not our speech, but rather our names and our appearance, for we would always have an accent, however perfect our pronunciation, however excellent our enunciation, however divine our diction. That accent would be heard in our pigmentation, our physiognomy, our names. We were, in short, the *other.*

Being the *other* involves contradictory phenomena. On the one hand being the *other* frequently means being invisible. Ralph Ellison wrote eloquently about that experience in his magisterial novel, *Invisible Man.* On the other hand, being the *other* sometimes involves sticking out like a sore thumb. What is she/he doing here?

For some of us being the *other* is only annoying; for others it is debilitating; for still others it is damning. Many try to flee otherness by taking on protective colorations that provide invisibility, whether of dress or speech or manner or name. Only a fortunate few succeed. For the majority of us otherness is permanently sealed by physical appearance. For the rest, otherness is betrayed by ways of being, speaking, or doing.

The first half of my life I spent downplaying the significance and consequences of otherness. The second half has seen me wrestling to understand its complex and deeply ingrained realities, striving to fathom why otherness denies us a voice or visibility or validity in American society and its institutions; struggling to make otherness familiar, reasonable, even normal to my fellow Americans.

I spoke earlier of another phenomenon that I am a part of: that of being a missing person. Growing up in northern New Mexico I had only a slight sense of us being missing persons. *Hispanos,* as we called (and call) ourselves in New Mexico, were very much a part of the fabric of the society, and there were *hispano* professionals everywhere about me: doctors, lawyers, schoolteachers, and administrators. My people owned businesses, ran organizations, and were both appointed and elected public officials.

My awareness of our absence from the larger institutional life of the society became sharper when I went off to college, but even then it was attenuated by the circumstances of history and geography. The demography of Albuquerque still strongly reflected its historical and cultural origins, despite the influx of Midwesterners and Easterners. Moreover, many of my classmates at the University of New Mexico were *hispanos,* and even some of my professors. I thought that would obtain at UCLA, where I began graduate studies in 1960. Los Angeles had a very large Mexican population and that population was visible even in and around Westwood and on the campus. Many of the groundskeepers and food-service personnel at UCLA were Mexican. But Mexican-American students were few and mostly invisible, and I do not recall seeing or knowing a single Mexican-American (or, for that matter, African-American, Asian, or American Indian) professional on the staff or faculty of that institution during the five years I was there. Needless to say, people like me were not present in any capacity at Dartmouth College, the site of my first teaching appointment, and of course were not even part of the institutional or individual mind-set. I knew then that we—a we that had come to encompass American Indians, Asian-Americans, African-Americans, Puerto Ricans, and women—were truly missing persons in American institutional life.

Over the past three decades the *de jure* and *de facto* types of segregation that have historically characterized American institutions have been under assault. As a consequence, minorities and women have become part of American institutional life. Although there are still many areas where we are not to be found, the missing persons phenomenon is not as pervasive as it once was. However, the presence of the *other,* particularly minorities, in institutions and in institutional life resembles what we call in Spanish a *flor de tierra* (a surface phenomenon): we are spare plants whose roots do not go deep, vulnerable to inclemencies of an economic, or political, or social, nature.

Our entrance into and our status in institutional life are not unlike a scenario set forth by my grandmother's pastor when she informed him that she and her family were leaving their mountain village to relocate to the Rio Grande Valley. When he asked her to promise that she would remain true to the faith and continue to involve herself in it, she asked why he thought she would do otherwise. "Doña Trinidad," he told her, "in the Valley there is no Spanish church." "But," she protested, "I read and speak English and would be able to worship there." The pastor responded, "It is possible that they will not admit you, and even if they do, they might not accept you. And that is why I want you to promise me that you are going to go to church. Because if they don't let you in through the front door, I want you to go in through the back door. And if you can't get in through the back door, go in the side door. And if you are unable to enter through the side door I want you to go in through the window. What is important is that you enter and stay."

Some of us entered institutional life through the front door; others through the back door; and still others through side doors. Many, if not most of us, came in through windows. Of those who entered through the front door, some never made it past the lobby; others were ushered into corners and niches. Those who entered through back and side doors inevitably have remained in back and side rooms. And those who entered through windows found enclosures built around them. For, despite the lip service given to the goal of the integration of minorities into institutional life, what has frequently occurred instead is ghettoization, marginalization, isolation.

Not only have the entry points been limited, but in addition the dynamics have been singularly conflictive. Gaining entry and its corollary, gaining space, have frequently come as a consequence of demands made on institutions and institutional officers. Rather than entering institutions more or less passively, minorities have of necessity entered them actively, even aggressively. Rather than waiting to receive, they have demanded. Institutional relations have thus been adversarial, infused with specific and generalized tensions.

The nature of the entrance and the nature of the space occupied have greatly influenced the view and attitude of the majority population within those institutions. All of us are put into the same box; that is, no matter what the individual reality, the assessment of the individual is inevitably conditioned by a perception that is held of the class. Whatever our history, whatever our record, whatever our validations, whatever our accomplishments, by and large we are perceived uni-dimensionally and dealt with accordingly. I remember an experience I had in this regard, atypical only in its explicitness. A few years ago I allowed myself to be persuaded to seek the presidency of a well-known state university. I was invited for an interview and presented myself before the selection committee, which included members of the board of trustees. The opening question of that brief but memorable interview was directed at me by a member of that august body. "Dr. Madrid," he asked, "why does a uni-dimensional person like you think he can be the president of a multi-dimensional institution like ours?"

Over the past four decades America's demography has undergone significant changes. Since 1965 the principal demographic growth we have experienced in the United States has been of peoples whose national origins are non-European. This population growth has occurred both through birth and through immigration. A few years ago discussion of the national birth rate had a scare dimension: the high—"inordinately high"—birth rate of the Hispanic population. The popular discourse was informed by words such as "breeding." Several years later, as a consequence of careful tracking by government agencies, we now know that what has happened is that the birth rate of the majority population has decreased. When viewed historically and comparatively, the minority populations (for the most part) have also had a decline in birth rate, but not one as great as that of the majority.

There are additional demographic changes that should give us something to think about. African Americans are now to be found in significant numbers in every major urban center in the nation. Hispanic Americans now number over [23] million people, and although they are a regionally concentrated (and highly urbanized) population, there is a Hispanic community in almost every major urban center of the United States. American Indians, heretofore a small and rural population, are increasingly more numerous and urban. The Asian-American population, which has historically consisted of small and concentrated communities of Chinese, Filipino, and Japanese Americans, has doubled over the past decade, its complexion changed by the addition of Cambodians, Koreans, Hmongs, Vietnamese, et al.

Prior to the Immigration Act of 1965, 69 percent of immigration was from Europe. By far the largest number of immigrants to the United States since 1965 has been from the Americas and from Asia: 34 percent are from Asia; another 34 percent are from Central and South America; 16 percent are from Europe; 10 percent are from the Caribbean; the remaining 6 percent are from other continents and Canada. As was the case with previous immigration waves, the current one consists principally of young people: 60 percent are between the ages of 16 and 44. Thus, for the next few decades, we will continue to see a growth in the percentage of non-European-origin Americans as compared to European Americans.

To sum up, we now live in one of the most demographically diverse nations in the world, and one that is increasingly more so.

During the same period, social and economic change seems to have accelerated. Who would have imagined at mid-century that the prototypical middle-class family (working husband, wife as homemaker, two children) would for all intents and purposes disappear? Who could have anticipated the rise in teenage pregnancies, children in poverty, drug use? Who among us understood the implications of an aging population?

We live in an age of continuous and intense change, a world in which what held true yesterday does not today, and certainly will not tomorrow. What change does, moreover, is bring about even more change. The only constant we have at this point in our national development is change. And change is threatening. The older we get the more likely we are to be anxious about change, and the greater our desire to maintain the status quo.

Evident in our public life is a fear of change, whether economic or moral. Some who fear change are responsive to the call of economic protectionism, others to the message of moral protectionism. . . . Much more serious, however, is the dark side of the populism which underlies this evergoing protectionism—the resentment of the *other*. An excellent and fascinating example of that aspect of populism is the cry for linguistic protectionism—for making English the official language of the United States. And who among us is unaware of the tensions that underlie immigration reform, of the underside of demographic protectionism?

. . . If you believe, as I do, that the well-being of a society is directly related to the degree and extent to which all of its citizens participate in its institutions, then you will have to agree that we have a challenge before us. In view of the extraordinary changes that are taking place in our society we need to take up the struggle again, irritating, grating, troublesome, unfashionable, unpleasant as it is. As educated and educator members of this society we have a special responsibility for ensuring that all American institutions, not just our elementary and secondary schools, our juvenile halls, or our jails, reflect the diversity of our society. Not to do so is to risk greater alienation on the part of a growing segment of our society; is to risk increased social tension in an already conflictive world; and, ultimately, is to risk the survival of a range of institutions that, for all their defects and deficiencies, provide us the opportunity and the freedom to improve our individual and collective lot.

Let me urge you to reflect on these two words—quality and diversity—and on the mental sets and behaviors that flow out of them. And let me urge you further to struggle against the notion that quality is finite in quantity, limited in its manifestations, or is restricted by considerations of class, gender, race, or national origin; or that quality manifests itself only in leaders and not in followers, in managers and not in workers, in breeders and not in drones; or that it has to be associated with verbal agility or elegance of personal style; or that it cannot be seeded, nurtured, or developed.

Because diversity—the *other*—is among us, it will define and determine our lives in ways that we still do not fully appreciate, whether the other is women (no longer bound by tradition, house, and family); or Asians, African Americans, Indians, and Hispanics (no longer invisible, regional, or marginal); or our newest immigrants (no longer distant, exotic, alien). Given the changing profile of America, will we come to terms with diversity in our personal and professional lives? Will we begin to recognize the diverse forms that quality can take? If so, we will thus initiate the process of making quality limitless in its manifestations, infinite in quantity, unrestricted with respect to its origins, and more importantly, virulently contagious.

I hope we will. And that we will further join together to expand—not to close—the circle.

Glossary

Account   One's version of an incident; often an excuse or justification for unexpected or inappropriate behavior. See *Excuse* and *Justification*.

Achieved status   A person's position or ranking achieved at least partly through personal efforts (such as becoming a college student) or failings (such as becoming a skid row alcoholic).

Aggregate   People grouped together for the purpose of social research because of characteristics they have in common. An example is U.S. females between the ages of 18 and 23 who wear contact lenses.

Alienation   Used in a couple of different meanings. The first is Weberian, a sense of separation, of not belonging, of being estranged. This meaning includes the idea that one has little control over the social world; may also include the feeling that one's world is meaningless. The second is Marxian, a sense of being separated from and not identifying with the product of one's labor.

Anomie   Normlessness; conflict between norms, weakened respect for norms, or absence of norms.

Anticipatory socialization   Learning the perspectives of a role before entering it. See *Role* and *Socialization*.

Ascribed status   A person's position or ranking assigned on the basis of arbitrary standards over which the individual has little or no control, such as age, race, or sex.

Authority   Power that is regarded as legitimate or proper by those over whom it is exercised.

Background expectancies   The taken-for-granted assumptions people have about the way the world is. See *Social construction of reality*.

Belief   An idea about some part of the natural or social world; a view of reality.

Body language   Giving and receiving messages through the movement or positioning of the body.

Bureaucracy   A form of organization characterized by multiple "layerings" of authority, usually depicted by a pyramid. Decisions flow downward, accountability for fulfilling orders goes upward, rules are explicit, emphasis is placed on written records, resources are directed toward efficiently reaching the goals of the organization, the "bottom line" is of utmost concern, and the personal is kept strictly separate from that which belongs to the organization. The reality does not necessarily match this *Ideal type*.

Case study   An in-depth investigation of a single event, experience, organization, or situation in order to better understand that case or to abstract principles of human behavior.

Charisma   Extraordinary personal qualities that attract followers. It varies from simply a "magnetic" personality to qualities so extraordinary that they are assumed to be supernatural.

Charismatic authority   Leadership exercised on the basis of charisma. See *Charisma* and *Traditional authority*.

Class   See *Social class*.

Class conflict   Karl Marx's term for the struggle between social classes; generally thought of as the struggle between the rich (and powerful) and the poor (and powerless), or those who own the means of economic production and those who do not.

Coding   Fitting data into classifications so they can be more easily analyzed.

Collective behavior   Relatively spontaneous, unstructured, and transitory ways of thinking, feeling, and acting that develop among a large number of people.

Community   Its primary meaning is that of people inhabiting the same geographical area who share common interests and feel a sense of "belonging." From this sense comes a derived meaning of people who share common interests and have a sense of "belonging" but who do not inhabit the same geographical area, such as in the phrase "a community of scholars."

Conflict theory   The theoretical view (or school) which emphasizes conflict as the inevitable outcome in society due to its various groups competing for limited resources. See *Functionalism* and *Symbolic interactionism*.

Conformity   Following social norms or expectations.

Conspicuous consumption   Thorstein Veblen's term for a change from an orientation toward saving in the Protestant ethic to showing off wealth by the elaborate consumption of goods.

Content analysis   The classification of the content of documents in order to identify its themes; such as presidential speeches, a series of medical novels, situation comedies, and so on.

Control group   The subjects in an experiment who are not exposed to the independent variable, as opposed to the experimental group who are subjected to this variable. See *Experiment*, *Experimental group*, *Independent variable*, and *Variable*.

Covert participant observation   See *Participant observation*.

Crime   An act prohibited by law.

Cultural diffusion   The process by which the characteristics of one culture are adopted by members of another culture.

Cultural relativity   The view that one cannot judge the characteristics of any culture to be morally superior to those of another. See its opposite, *Ethnocentrism*.

Culture   A way of life, or shared ways of doing things; includes nonmaterial culture (such as norms, beliefs, values, and language) and material culture (such as art, tools, weapons, and buildings). See *Ideal culture* and *Real culture*.

Culture lag (Cultural lag)   A term developed by William F. Ogburn to refer to the material culture changing more rapidly than the nonmaterial culture. Thought to be a primary factor in social change.

Culture of poverty   The distinctive culture said to exist among the poor of industrialized societies; its central features of defeatism, dependence, and a present time orientation are thought to trap people in poverty and to perpetuate it from one generation to the next.

Culture shock   The disorienting effect that immersion in a strange culture has on a visitor as he or she encounters markedly different norms, values, beliefs, customs, and other basic expectations of social life. One no longer is able to rely on the basics of one's socialization.

Data   The information scientists gather in their studies.

Definition of reality   A view of what the world or some part of the world is like. See *Social construction of reality*.

Dehumanization   The act or process of reducing people to objects that do not deserve the treatment given humans.

Demography   The study of the size, distribution, composition, and change in human populations.

Dependent variable   That which is being explained as the result of other factors; a variable or social phenomenon thought to be changed or influenced by another variable. See *Independent variable*.

Deviance   Violation of social norms or expectations.

Deviant   One who violates social norms or expectations. As used by sociologists, a neutrally descriptive rather than a negative term.

Deviant career   The main course of events during one's involvement in deviance; generally refers to those who are habitually, or at least for a period of time heavily, involved in some deviant activity.

Differential association   If a person associates with one group of people, he or she will learn one set of attitudes, ideas, and norms; associating with a different group teaches a different approach to life. Thus such differential association is highly significant in influencing people either to conform or to deviate.

Diffusion   The spread of an invention or discovery from one area or group to another.

Disclaimer   An excuse or justification for inappropriate behavior that is *about* to take place. Examples are: "Now don't get me wrong, but . . . ;" and "Let me play the devil's advocate for a minute."

Discrimination   The denial of rights, privileges, or opportunities to others on the basis of their group membership. See *Minority group*, *Racism*, and *Sexism*.

Division of labor   A concept developed by Emile Durkheim to refer to the work specializations in a society (the various ways in which work is divided, with some people specializing in financing or production, others in advertising or distribution, and so on).

Documents   In its narrow sense, written sources that provide data; in its extended sense, archival material of any sort, including photographs, movies, and so on.

Double standard   More stringent expectations being applied to one group than to another. *The* double standard refers to attitudes and ideas more favorable to males than to females—often to males being allowed more sexual freedom.

Downsizing   A fancy way of saying that to reduce costs a company is firing workers.

Downward social mobility   Movement from a higher to a lower social position. See *Social class*.

Dramaturgical analysis   Developed by Erving Goffman, this terms refers to viewing human interaction as theatrical performances. People are seen as actors, their clothing as costumes, what they do as parts they play, what they say as the delivery of lines, where they interact as a stage, and so on.

Dramaturgy   Refers to theatrical performances. The same as *Dramaturgical analysis*.

Ecology   The study of reciprocal relationships between organisms and their environment.

Education   One of the primary institutions of society whereby teaching of values, skills, and knowledge is transmitted from one generation to the next.

Ego   Commonly used as a term to refer to the self; technically, Freud's term for the conscious, rational part of an individual.

Endogamy   A cultural pattern of marrying *within* one's own social group. See *Exogamy*.

Ethnic cleansing   A recent term for killing people because of their ethnicity, with the goal of "cleaning out" an entire area for one's own ethnic group to inhabit.

Ethnic group A group of people with a sense of common ancestry, who generally share similar cultural traits and regard themselves as distinct from others.

Ethnic stratification Groups of people who are stratified on the basis of their ethnic group membership. See *Social stratification*.

Ethnocentrism Using the standards of one's own culture or subculture to evaluate the characteristics of other cultures or subcultures, generally from the point of view that one's own are superior. See its opposite, *Cultural relativity*.

Ethnography A report or study that details the major characteristics of the way of life of a group of people; can be of an entire preliterate tribe, an entire village, or a smaller group within a large society, such as a study of urban cabdrivers.

Ethnomethodology Developed by Harold Garfinkel, the term refers to the study of the worlds of reality that people construct, their taken-for-granted background assumptions, and the ways by which different people make sense out of their experiences.

Excuse An account of an event in which one acknowledges that an act is blameworthy, but denies responsibility for the act. See *Account* and *Justification*.

Exogamy A cultural pattern of marrying *outside* one's social group. See *Endogamy*.

Experiment A study in which the researcher manipulates one or more variables (independent variables) in order to measure the results on other variables (dependent variables). See *Variable*.

Experimental group The subjects in an experiment who are exposed to the independent variable, as opposed to the control group who do not experience this variable. See *Experiment*.

Extended family A family consisting of two or more generations (extended beyond the nuclear family), usually living together. See *Nuclear family*.

False consciousness A term developed by Karl Marx to refer to a person's understanding of his or her social class membership that does not square with objective facts; often used to refer to members of the working class identifying with capitalists.

Family People related by ancestry, marriage, or adoption who generally live together and form an economic unit, and whose adult members assume responsibility for the young. The form of the family varies remarkably from one culture to another.

Family of orientation The family into which one is born. See *Family* and *Family of procreation*.

Family of procreation The family created by marriage. See *Family* and *Family of orientation*.

Femininity Our behaviors and orientations as females. Assumed in sociology to be an expression not of biology but of cultural or social learning. See *Masculinity*.

Feral children Children who have been found in the wilderness, supposedly raised by animals. Not only do they possess no language, but they also exhibit few behaviors that we ordinarily associate with humans.

Field research   Another term for *Participant observation*.

Field study   Another term for *Participant observation*.

Field work   Another term for *Participant observation*.

Folk society   A term developed by Robert Redfield to refer to small, traditional societies in which there is little social change.

Folkways   Developed by William G. Sumner, this term refers to norms people are expected or encouraged to follow, but whose violation is not considered immoral; the ordinary rules, usages, conventions, and expectations of everyday life, such as, in U.S. society, the use of deodorant. See *Mores*.

Formal organization   A social group brought into existence to reach specific goals; often utilizes a bureaucratic mode of operation to achieve those objectives. See *Bureaucracy*.

Formal sanction   A social reward or punishment that is formally applied, often a part of ritual recognition for achievement (such as receiving a passing grade in school, or being promoted at work) or failure (such as receiving a failing grade in school, or being fired from one's job). See *Informal sanction* and *Sanction*.

Functionalism   The theoretical view (or school) that stresses how the parts of a society or social group are interrelated. Emphasis is placed on the contributions (functions) that one part makes for the adjustment or well-being of other parts. Each part, working properly, is seen as contributing to the stability of the whole. See *Symbolic interactionism* and *Conflict theory*.

Future shock   A term developed by Alvin Toffler to refer to the dizzying disorientation brought on by the rapid arrival of the future.

Gender   The social expectations attached to a person on account of that person's sex. Sex is biological, while gender is social. See *Femininity* and *Masculinity*.

Gender socialization   Learning one's gender. See *Gender*.

Generalize   To conclude that the research findings from a sample apply to a broader group.

Generalized other   The ideas we have of the expectations of a major reference group, or even of society in general.

Genocide   Killing an entire population, usually because of the group's biological and cultural traits.

Gentrification   The process by which the relatively affluent move to decaying urban neighborhoods, renovate buildings, and displace the poor.

Gestures   The movement and positioning of the body to communicate meaning. See *Body language*.

Heterosexuality   Sexual acts or feelings toward members of the opposite sex. See *Homosexuality*.

Hidden curriculum   The unwritten goals of schools, such as teaching obedience to authority and conformity to cultural norms.

Holocaust   The Nazi destruction, in death camps and by means of death squads, of Jews, gypsies, Slavs, homosexuals, the mentally retarded, and others considered threats to the purity of the so-called Aryan race.

Homosexuality   Sexual acts or feelings toward members of the same sex. See *Heterosexuality*.

Horizontal mobility   Movement from one social position to another that is approximately equivalent.

Human ecology   Study of the reciprocal relationships between people and their environment.

Hypothesis   A prediction about how two or more variables are related. See *Variable*.

Ideal culture   The way of life represented in people's values and norms, rather than by their actual practices. See *Real culture*.

Ideal type   Developed by Max Weber, this term refers to a model or description of something that is derived from examining a number of real cases and abstracting what appear to be the essential characteristics of those cases.

Identity formation   The process by which we develop a personal identity; our internalization of social expectations. The end result is that we come to think of ourselves in a certain way; that is, as we internalize people's reactions to us, we develop a "self."

Ideology   Statements or beliefs (especially of reasons and purposes) that justify a group's actions or interests; they buttress, uphold, or legitimate the existing social order.

Incest   Sexual intercourse with forbidden categories of kinfolk. See *Incest taboo*.

Incest taboo   The social prohibition against sexual intercourse with specific categories of kinfolk. See *Incest*.

Independent variable   That which is thought to affect or to cause change in some other factor; the variable thought to influence another variable. See *Dependent variable*.

Informal sanction   A social reward or punishment informally applied, often being a spontaneous gesture of approval or disapproval. Examples include staring, smiling, and gossip. See *Formal sanction* and *Sanction*.

Ingroup   The group to which an individual belongs, identifies, and feels loyalty. See *Outgroup*.

Institution   See *Social institution*.

Institutional(ized) racism   The use of social institutions to discriminate, exploit, or oppress a racial (or ethnic) group. See *Discrimination* and *Racism*.

Institutional(ized) sexism   The use of social institutions to discriminate, exploit, or oppress either males or females as a group. See *Discrimination* and *Sexism*.

Interaction   See *Social interaction*.

Interactional sociology   An emphasis on the study of social interaction. See *Participant observation, Qualitative sociology,* and *Structural sociology.*

Internalization   Experiences becoming part of one's "internal" consciousness.

Interview   Asking a respondent questions; can be face-to-face, by writing, or by some form of electronic communication such as by telephone or fax. See *Respondent.*

Interview bias   Effects that interviewers have on respondents that tilt answers in some direction.

Involuntary associations   Groups to which people belong, but about which they have little or no choice. Examples include grade school for youngsters and military service during periods of conscription. See *Voluntary associations.*

Justification   An account of an event in which one accepts responsibility for an act, while denying that the act is blameworthy. See *Account* and *Excuse.*

Kin   People who are related by birth, adoption, or marriage.

Kinfolk   See *Kin.*

Kinship   The network of people who are related to one another by birth, adoption, or marriage.

Labeling theory (or perspective)   The focus on the effects of labels (or terms) on people. This perspective stresses that acts are not inherently deviant (or criminal) but are such only because those acts have been so labeled (or defined). Deviants are those on whom the label of deviant has been successfully applied.

Life chances   The likelihood that an individual or group will benefit from their society's opportunities, goods and services, and other satisfactions in life.

Life course   The biological and social sequencing through which individuals pass; these cluster around birth, childhood, maturity, old age, and death.

Life expectancy   The average number of years a person can expect to live.

Life style   The general patterns that characterize an individual or group, including their clothing, manners, recreation, mating, and childrearing practices.

Looking-glass self   Charles Horton Cooley's term for the process by which people see themselves through the eyes of others. As people act, others react. In those reactions people see themselves reflected. Perceiving this, they interpret its meaning, which yields a particular self-image.

Masculinity   Our behaviors and orientations as males. Generally assumed in sociology to be an expression not of biology but of cultural or social learning. See *Femininity.*

Mass media   Forms of communication that reach a large audience, with no personal contact between the senders and receivers of the message. Examples are movies, radio, television, newspaper, magazines, plays, and books.

Master status (or trait)   A social role (or achieved or ascribed status) that cuts across most other social roles and provides a major basis for personal and public identity.

Material culture   See *Culture.*

Meanings   The significance that something has to someone. Also called symbols, mental constructs, ideas, and stereotypes. See *Qualitative sociology.*

Methodology (Methods)   The procedures scientists use to conduct their studies.

Military-industrial complex   The relationships between top leaders of the Pentagon and U.S. corporations by which they reciprocally support one another and thereby influence political decisions on their behalf.

Minority group   A group of people who are treated unequally because of their physical or cultural characteristics. See *Discrimination.*

Mores   (Pronounced MORE-rays) Developed by William G. Sumner, this term refers to norms whose violation is considered a moral transgression. Examples are the norms against murder and theft. See *Folkways.*

Negative sanction   Punishment for disapproved behavior. See *Sanction.*

Neutralization   Verbal techniques of deflecting social norms in order to avoid social disapproval; often called *Techniques of neutralization.* An example is saying, "The circumstances required it" or, "I didn't know what I was doing."

Nonmaterial culture   See *Culture.*

Nonverbal communication   Communication by the use of symbols other than language. Examples are *Body language* and traffic lights.

Norms   Rules concerning appropriate and inappropriate behavior by which people are judged and sanctions applied. See *Sanction.*

Nuclear family   A family consisting of a husband, wife, and their children. See *Extended family.*

Operational definition   The way in which a variable in a hypothesis is measured.

Organization   A social unit established for the purpose of attaining some agreed-upon goals.

Outgroup   A group to which an individual does not belong and with which he or she does not identify. See *Ingroup.*

Overt participant observation   See *Participant observation.*

Participant observation   A method of studying social groups in which the researcher participates in the group being studied. If the people being studied know the researcher is in their midst, this method is called *overt participant observation*; if they do not know they are being studied, it is called *covert participant observation.*

Peer group   Associates of similar social status who are usually close in age. Examples are one's playmates as a child and workmates as an adult.

Personal identity   Our ideas of who we are. Roughly equivalent to self concept. See *Public identity* and *Self*.

Personality   An individual's tendency over time to act (and think and feel) in ways similar to those he or she did in the past; the stable behavior patterns we come to expect of people.

Population   The target group to be studied.

Positive sanction   A reward for approved behavior. See *Sanction*.

Power   The ability to control others, even over their objections.

Power elite   C. Wright Mills's term to refer to a small group of people with interlocking interests who appear to make a nation's most important political decisions.

Prejudice   Attitudes, ideas, and feelings, often negative and about people one does not know. See *Discrimination* and *Ethnocentrism*.

Prestige   Favorable evaluation, respect, or social recognition.

Primary group   People whose relationship is intimate, face-to-face, expressive, and extended over time. Examples are one's family and close friends.

Prostitution   The exchange of sexual favors for some gain, usually economic.

Public identity   The ideas that others have of what we ought to be like. Roughly equivalent to the public social roles we play. See *Personal identity* and *Self*.

Qualitative sociology   Studies of social life in which the emphasis is on the *meanings* of people's experiences. The goal is to determine how people construct their worlds, develop their ideas and attitudes, communicate these with one another, and how their meanings affect their behavior, ideas about the self, and relationships to one another. See *Meanings* and *Quantitative sociology*.

Quantitative sociology   Studies of social life in which the emphasis is on precise measurement, or numbers. Sociologists with this orientation stress that proper measurement by the use of statistical techniques is necessary if one is to understand human behavior. See *Qualitative sociology*.

Questionnaire   An interview by means of a written form.

Race   A large number of people who share visible physical characteristics on the basis of which they regard themselves as a biological unit and are similarly regarded by others.

Racism   One racial or ethnic group dominating or exploiting another, generally based on seeing those they exploit as inferior. See *Discrimination* and *Ethnocentrism*.

Random sample   A sample in which everyone in the target population has the same chance of being included in the study.

Rapport   A feeling of trust and communication between people.

Rationalization (of society)   Weber's term for the process by which a society or other group adopts a bureaucratic orientation, with emphasis on efficiency, impersonal relations, and the bottom line.

Real culture   A people's actual way of life, as contrasted with the way of life expressed by their ideals. See *Ideal culture.*

Reference groups   The groups to which people refer when they evaluate themselves, their behavior, or actions they are considering.

Relative deprivation   Feeling deprived relative to what others have; the sense that the gap between the resources or rewards that one actually has and what others have is unjust.

Reliability   The extent to which studies produce consistent results.

Replication   The repetition of a study in order to test its findings.

Research methods   See *Methodology.*

Resocialization   Learning norms, values, and behaviors that contrast with one's previous experiences.

Respondent   A person who has been interviewed or who has filled out a questionnaire. (He or she has *responded* to the request for data.)

Rising expectations   A situation in which people who have accepted existing conditions in the past now feel they have a right to better conditions.

Rites of passage   Formal, customary rituals marking someone's transition from one social status to another. Examples include bar mitzvahs, confirmations, first communions, weddings, graduation ceremonies, and funerals. Also known as *rites de passage.*

Role   The part played by a person who occupies a particular status. See *Status.*

Role conflict   If a person finds himself or herself torn between conflicting demands of two or more roles, that person is said to be experiencing role conflict. Examples include a student wanting to date on the same night that he or she is supposed to study for a final examination.

Role taking   Figuratively putting yourself in the shoes of someone else and seeing how things look from that perspective.

Sample   The individuals intended to represent the population to be studied.

Sanction   A social reward for approved behavior, or punishment for disapproved behavior.

Secondary analysis   The analysis of data already collected by other researchers.

Secondary group   The more formal, impersonal, and transitory groups to which people belong, such as an introductory course in sociology.

Self   The sense of identity that individuals have of themselves as a distinct person;

this sense, idea, or conception is acquired through social interaction. See *Identity formation.*

Self-fulfilling prophecy   A false definition of a situation ("The bank is in trouble") that causes people to change their behavior ("People rush to the bank to withdraw their savings") and makes the originally false statement come true ("The bank is now in trouble as it does not have enough cash on hand to meet the unexpected demand for immediate withdrawals").

Sex role   The behaviors and characteristics that a male or female is expected to demonstrate, based on stereotypical cultural concepts of masculinity or femininity; assigned on the basis of one's sex organs.

Sex role socialization   Learning one's sex role. See *Sex role.*

Sexism   Males or females dominating or exploiting the other, with the exploitation generally based on seeing the other as inferior; usually used to refer to males dominating females. See *Discrimination* and *Ethnocentrism.*

Social change   Alteration in society, in its patterns of social structure, social institutions (or some small part of them), culture, and people's behavior.

Social class   A large number of people who have about the same amount of social power, based on different characteristics in different societies. In ours, some sociologists see the primary bases as the amount of one's income and education and the prestige of one's occupation. Other sociologists see the essential difference in terms of one's relationship to the means of production—whether one is a capitalist (owns the means of production) or a worker (works for capitalists).

Social class mobility   Changing one's social class, usually in relationship to that of one's parents. See *Social mobility.*

Social construction of reality   The process by which definitions of reality (views of what some part of the world is like) are socially created, objectified, internalized, and then taken for granted.

Social control   The techniques used to keep people in line or, if they step out, to bring them back into line. Examples include persuasion, coercion, ridicule, education, and punishment. See *Sanction.*

Social group   Any human group.

Social inequality   Another term for *Social stratification.*

Social institution   Standardized practices (clustered around a set of norms, values, beliefs, statuses, and roles) that develop around the attempt to meet a basic need of society. Examples include government and politics (for social order), education (for training in conformity and the transmission of skills and knowledge), and the military (for protection from external enemies and the implementation of foreign policy).

Social interaction   People acting in anticipation of the reactions of others; people influencing each other's feelings, attitudes, and actions.

Social mobility   Movement from one social position to another. See *Downward, Horizontal,* and *Upward social mobility.*

Social stratification   Large groups of people ranked in a hierarchy that gives them different access to the rewards their society has to offer.

Social structure   The ways in which the basic components of a group or society are related to one another.

Socialization   Refers to learning; the process of social interaction by which people learn the way of life of their society, or learn to play specific roles.

Society   A group of interacting individuals who share the same territory and participate in a common culture.

Sociobiology   The study of the biological bases of human behavior.

Sociology   The scientific study of human society and social behavior.

Status   One's position in a group or society, such as woman, mother, and plumber.

Stereotypes   A generalization (or idea) about people (or even animals and objects); a mental image that summarizes what is believed to be typical about these people.

Stigma   An indelible mark of social disgrace.

Stratification   See *Social stratification.*

Structural sociology   The emphasis is on the influence of social structure on human behavior, with a focus on social institutions and other group memberships. See *Aggregates, Qualitative sociology,* and *Social structure.*

Structured interview   An interview that uses closed-ended questions.

Subculture   A group that shares in the overall culture of a society but also has its own distinctive values, norms, beliefs, and life style. Examples include cabdrivers, singles, prostitutes, muggers, and physicians.

Subjective interpretation   See *Verstehen.*

Survey   The collection of data by having people answer a series of questions.

Symbol   Any act, object, or event that represents something, such as a traffic light, a gesture, or this definition. See *Symbolic interactionism.*

Symbolic interaction   People's interaction based on symbols. See *Symbolic interactionism.*

Symbolic interactionism   Developed by Herbert Blumer, this term refers to the school of thought (or theoretical perspective) that focuses on symbols as the basis of human behavior—the signs, gestures, and language by which people communicate with one another and change or refine their courses of action in anticipation of what others might do. See *Conflict theory* and *Functionalism.*

Techniques of neutralization   See *Neutralization*.

Technology   Tools or items used to accomplish tasks.

Theory   A statement that organizes a set of concepts in a meaningful way by explaining the relationship between them.

Total institution   Erving Goffman's term to refer to a place in which people are confined, cut off from the rest of society, and under the almost absolute control of the people in charge. Examples include prisons, the military, and convents.

Traditional authority   Authority that is legitimated by custom and practice. The explanation for something is, "We have always done it this way." See *Charismatic authority*.

Trust   The willingness to accept the definition someone offers of oneself or of a situation and to play a corresponding role based on that definition.

Unobtrusive measures   Techniques of observing people who do not know they are being studied.

Unstructured interview   An interview that uses open-ended questions.

Upward social mobility   Movement from a lower to a higher social position.

Validity   The extent to which an operational definition measures what it is intended to measure.

Value conflict   Disagreement over goals, ideals, policies, or other expressions of values.

Value judgment   A personal, subjective opinion based on one's own set of values.

Values   An idea about what is worthwhile.

Variable   Any condition or characteristic that varies from one situation or person or group to another. Examples include age, occupation, beliefs, and attitudes. See *Dependent variable*, *Experiment*, and *Independent variable*.

Verstehen   A term used by Max Weber to refer to the subjective interpretation of human behavior; that is, because we are members of a group or culture, we gain insight and understanding into what others are experiencing, allowing us to interpret those experiences. See *Qualitative sociology*.

Vertical social mobility   Movement to a higher or a lower social position.

Voluntary associations   Groups that people join voluntarily, often because they wish to promote some goal or to be with like-minded people. Examples include a church, a college class, and a bowling league. See *Involuntary associations*.

War   Armed confict between nations or politically distinct groups.

White-collar crime   Crimes committed by "respectable" persons of high status, frequently during the course of their occupation.

Appendix:
Correlation Chart

FORTY BASIC SOCIOLOGY TEXTS are listed alphabetically across the top of the correlation chart. The chapters of those texts are located in the column to the left of the boxes. The numbers *within* the boxes refer to the articles in *Down to Earth Sociology*.

Actually, in my own classroom I often do things just the opposite. I sometimes first build the course around the selections of *Down to Earth Sociology* and then supplement its readings with only a few chapters from the basic text. In this way, students are concentrating on *primary* sociological materials, rather than on secondary analyses. Moreover, I find that because of the inherent interest of most of these readings, as well as the engaging class activities that one can build around them (see the *Instructor's Manual* for suggestions), with this format students are very pleased with their introduction to sociology.

I have listed an article only once, which required very difficult choices as articles often fit well into more than a single chapter. The attempt, of course, has been to match the major emphasis of an article with the chapter's emphasis. In order to make certain that the articles in *Down to Earth Sociology* are distributed throughout a text's chapters, however, at times I have placed an article according to its secondary theme.

Because there are so many different ways of classifying these articles and each of us may see different ways of teaching them, you may prefer a different order than the one I have worked out. The *Instructor's Manual* contains a topical classification of articles that may be of value in this endeavor. Also, please note that texts listed as *Brief* may refer to books called Brief, Core, or Essentials.

The numbers within the boxes refer to selection numbers in **Down to Earth Sociology**.

The numbers directly below refer to chapters in the basic texts:

	Appelbaum & Chambliss, 2nd Edition, 1997	Brinkerhoff, White & Ortega, Brief, 3rd Edition, 1997	Brinkerhoff & White, 3rd Edition, 1997	Bryjak & Soroka, 3rd Edition, 1997	Calhoun, Light, & Keller, 7th Edition, 1997	Charon, 5th Edition, 1996	Curry, Jiobu, & Schwirian, 1st Edition, 1997	Doob, 5th Edition, 1997	Ferrante, 2nd Edition, 1995	Giddens, 2nd Edition, 1997
1	1–3	1–6	1–3	1–6	1–3	1–3	1–6	1–3	1–3	1–3
2	4–6	7–10	4–6	7–11	4–6	4–6	7, 9, 10, 43, 44, 46	4–6	20, 22, 30	4–6
3	7, 9, 10	11–14, 20, 21	7–10	16, 18–22, 41, 45	11, 16, 20	17, 20	12, 23–29	7–10	4–6	35, 46
4		16, 23–28, 41	31, 41	12–15	7, 9, 10	19	11, 16–18, 20	11, 16–18, 20, 21	7–10	7–10, 12–15
5	11–14, 17, 20, 29	18, 22, 29, 30, 33	21	29, 30	12–15, 41	18	8, 34, 35	12–14, 41	12, 15, 41	11, 17, 20
6	16	15, 31, 32, 34, 47	12–14	31–33, 47	23–28	7–11	22, 30, 31	23–28	11, 21	16, 23–28
7	23–28, 41	37	11, 20	34, 35	17, 18, 29, 30	21	32, 33, 47	22, 29, 30, 33, 35	35	29, 40
8	18, 30, 31	36, 38, 39	16, 23–28	23–28	31, 32, 47	22	13–15, 41	31, 32	16, 23–28, 42	34, 41
9	35	19, 35, 40, 42	18, 22, 29, 30	37		16, 23–28, 36	37	15, 34	17–19, 29, 33	18, 22, 30
10	32, 47	17, 43, 44	32, 47	36, 38–40	34	30–35, 42	36–39	47	31, 32, 47	31, 32, 47
11	15, 34	45	15, 34, 35	42	37	12–15, 29, 37–41, 47	38	37	34	44

12	46		43	36, 39	43-45	42	36, 38, 39	37	33, 42
13	33, 42	37	17	38	46	19, 21	19, 42	36, 39, 40	19
14	37	36, 39	44, 46	40		40	40	38	38
15	19, 21, 22	33		19, 21, 22, 46		45	43	43-46	37
16	36, 39	19		33, 42			44-46		21, 36, 39
17	38	38, 44		35					43
18	40	40		8					45
19				43, 44					
20	8, 43	17, 43		45					
21	44-46	45							
22		42, 46							
23									
24									

The numbers within the boxes refer to selection numbers in Down to Earth Sociology.

The numbers directly below refer to chapters in the basic texts:	Hebding and Glick, Brief, 5th Edition, 1996	Henslin, 3rd Edition, 1997	Henslin, Brief, 1st Edition, 1996	Hess, Markson, & Stein, 5th Edition, 1996	Johnson, 4th Edition, 1996	Jones, Gallagher, & McFalls, 1st Edition, 1995	Kammeyer, Ritzer, & Yetman, 7th Edition, 1997	Kendall, 1st Edition, 1996	Kornblum, 4th Edition, 1997	Landis, 9th Edition, 1995
1	1-6	1-3, 20, 22, 30	1-6	1-3	1-3	1-3	1-3	1-3	1-3	1-6
2	7, 9-11	7, 9, 10	7-10	4-6	7, 9, 10	26, 41	4-6	4-6	4-6	12-15, 41
3	12-14, 41	12-15, 39	12-14, 39-41	7, 9, 10	16, 19	4-6	7-10	7-10	7-10	7-11, 20
4	16, 19-21	11, 21, 29, 41, 44	11, 20, 21	16, 21	8	11, 20	11, 20, 21, 29	12-15, 40	35	16, 17
5	23-28	4-6	16-19	11-14, 20	30	16-18	12-16, 41	11, 16, 17, 20	12-14, 41	18, 22
6	33, 35	16	23-28	23-28	4-6	35	23-28	41	11, 20, 29	29-34, 45
7	15, 18, 22, 29-32, 34	46	29, 35		12-14	7-10		23-28	16, 23-28	21, 37
8	37	23-28	22, 30, 33	15	11, 17, 20, 29	23-25, 27, 28	18, 22, 30	18, 22, 29, 30	45	38
9	36, 38, 39, 40	35	31, 32, 47	18, 22, 29, 30	38-40	45	31, 32, 47	31-33, 47	17, 43, 44	19, 35, 42
10	42	18, 33	15, 34	34	43, 44	22, 30	34, 35	34	46	36, 39, 40
11	8, 17, 43	34	42, 46	31, 32, 47	23-28	37	37		22	43

	44-47	32, 47	37	37	18, 31, 33	31, 32, 47	36, 39	19, 35	18, 30	41, 46
12	44-47	32, 47	37	37	18, 31, 33	31, 32, 47	36, 39	19, 35	18, 30	41, 46
13			36, 38	19	32, 47	15, 34	19	42	31, 32, 47	45
14		19	43, 44	33, 42	15, 34, 35, 37	37	40	21, 37	15, 34	23-28
15		42	45	36	36	38	38	36, 38, 39		
16		37		38	22, 41, 42	19, 21, 33, 42	33, 42	43, 44	37	
17		31, 36		41	46	36, 39	17, 43	45, 46	38	
18		38		40	45	40	44-46		36, 39	
19		40		35, 44, 46		29			19, 21	
20		17, 43		8		43			33, 42	
21		45		17, 43		44, 46			40	
22		8		39						
23				45						
24										

The numbers within the boxes refer to selection numbers in **Down to Earth Sociology.**

The numbers directly below refer to chapters in the basic texts:

	Shepard, 6th Edition, 1997	Schaefer & Lamm, Brief, 2nd Edition, 1997	Schaefer & Lamm, 6th Edition, 1997	Russell, 2nd Edition, 1996	Popenoe, 10th Edition, 1995	Neuman, 1st Edition, 1995	Neubeck & Glasberg, 1st Edition, 1995	Macionis, Brief, 3rd Edition, 1996	Macionis, 6th Edition, 1997	Levin & Arluke, 1st Edition, 1997
	1–3	1–6	1–3	1–3	1–3	1	1–6	1–6	1–3	1–3
1	20, 22, 30	7–11	4–6	7–11, 20, 23, 29, 47	4–6	2, 3	35	7, 9, 10	4–6	4–6
2	4–6	12–14	7, 9–10		7, 9, 10	4–6	46, 20, 21	12	7, 9, 10	35
3	7–11	16–22	12–14		16	7–10	7–11	11, 20, 29	46	9–10
4	16	23–28	11, 20	35, 46	11	12–14, 29	12–15	16, 41	12, 41	11, 12, 20
5	12–14	29, 30, 36	16, 19	30	12–14	11, 20	18, 29, 30	23–28	11, 17, 20	16, 23–28
6	21, 41	31–33	23–28, 41	16, 22, 26, 36, 41, 42	18, 20–22	16, 23–28	17, 31, 32, 34, 47	18, 22, 30, 31, 33	16	7, 29
7	23–28	15, 34	18, 22, 30	12–15, 17, 18, 21, 24, 31–34	23–28, 41	21, 37	16, 23–28, 41	35	23–28	13–15, 41
8	18, 29, 31	37, 39	29, 35	19, 27, 28, 38–40, 44, 45	29, 35	19, 36, 38, 40	43–45	32, 47	22, 29	18, 30–31, 33
9	32, 47	36, 38	31, 32, 47	25, 37	30–33	22, 33, 35, 42	22, 33, 35, 42	13–15, 34	18, 30, 31, 33	16, 32, 47
10	15, 34, 35	41, 42	34	43	47	18, 30	19	19, 21, 42	35	46

12	42	32, 47	37–39	36, 39	17, 31, 32, 39, 47	40	4–b		40	42
13	19, 21, 22, 41	13–15, 34	36, 40	40	15, 34, 41	15, 34		37	43, 47	37
14	38, 44	21	17, 43	37	43	37		38		36, 39
15	37	19	8	38	44–46	36, 39		11, 33, 42		33, 42
16	34, 36, 39, 40	42	44, 46			38		36, 39		19
17	17, 43	37				42		40		38
18	45	38				19		17, 21, 43		40
19	8, 35, 46	36, 39				8		8		17, 43
20		40				17, 43		44, 45, 46		45
21		43				45				44, 46
22		8				44, 46				
23		45								
24		44								

The numbers within the boxes refer to selection numbers in **Down to Earth Sociology**.

The numbers directly below refer to chapters in the basic texts:

	Smelser, 5th Edition, 1995	Stark, 6th Edition, 1996	Thio, Brief, 3rd Edition, 1997	Thompson & Hickey, 2nd Edition, 1996	Thompson & Hickey, Brief, 1st Edition, 1996	Tischler, 5th Edition, 1996	Vander Zanden, Brief, 4th Edition, 1995	Yorburg, Brief, 1st Edition, 1995	Ward & Stone, 1st Edition, 1997	Willis, 1st Edition, 1997
1	1-6	1-3	1-6, 39	1-3	1-6	1-3	1-6	1-3	1-3	1,3
2	7-10	7-10	7-10	4-6	7, 9-11	4-6	7-11	4-6	4-6	4-6
3	22	4-6	12, 36, 41	7-11	12-14, 41	7-10	12-15	7, 10-16, 20, 41	10, 11, 20	41, 43-47
4	12, 40		11, 15, 20, 29	4-14	16, 17, 20-22	12-14	16-22	8, 29, 43-46	7-9	2, 7-11, 39
5	11, 20		16	16, 17	23-28	11, 16, 20	23-28	9, 21, 22	12-14	22, 31-38
6	42	11-15, 20	23-28	20-22, 41	18, 29, 30, 35	23-28	29, 30	8, 17, 18	16, 41	12-19, 21, 23
7	16, 23-28, 41	23-25	18, 22, 30	23-28	31, 32, 47	22, 29	31, 32, 34	23-28	23-28	20, 24-30, 40, 42
8	17, 21	16, 26-28, 41	31, 32	18, 29, 30, 33	15, 34	18, 30, 31	33, 35, 41, 42	31, 32, 34, 47	18, 22, 29, 30, 35	
9	18, 29, 30	29, 30	13, 14, 34	35	37	32, 47	37	37	31, 32, 47	
10	31, 32, 47	18, 22	37-39	31, 32, 47	36, 39	15, 34, 35	36, 38-40	19, 30, 35	15, 34	
11	13-15, 34	31, 32, 47		15, 34	38	37	43, 44	33, 42		

12	36	34	19, 21, 33, 35, 42		19, 33, 42	38	45–47	36, 39, 40	37
13	37	21, 37	40	37	40	36, 39		38	38
14	39	38	17, 43	36, 39	8, 43	19, 21, 33, 42			36, 39
15	38	33, 42	44–47	38	44–47	43			19
16	19, 35	19, 35, 36, 39, 40		42		17			40
17	33	44		19		40, 41			33, 42
18	43			40		45			43, 44
19	45	17, 43		43		44, 46			17, 21
20	44, 46	45, 46		44–46					45
21									46
22									
23									
24									

Name Index

Subject Index